Frommer's®

POSTCARDS FROM

Vancouver & Victoria 2003

Take a walk through the colorful Native American totem poles decorating Vancouver's Stanley Park. See chapter 6. © Wolfgang Kaehler Photography.

Nestled amid snowcapped mountains and lush forest, Vancouver offers big-city life in a wilderness setting. See chapter 6. © Wolfgang Kaehler Photography.

Watching the sun set over English Bay and False Creek while sipping a beer on a cafe patio is a great way to end the day. See chapter 9. © Catherine Karnow Photography.

Buy some fresh catch for dinner right off the docks at the Granville Island Public Market in Vancouver. See chapter 8.
© Bruce Forster/Getty Images.

Only 15 minutes from Vancouver, the narrow, shaky Capilano Bridge spans the canyon floor, shrouded in mist from a waterfall below. See chapter 6. © Andrea Pistolesi Photography.

One of North America's largest and best, the Vancouver Aquarium houses more than 8,000 marine species—including beluga whales—most in meticulously re-created settings. *See chapter 6.* © Peter Timmermans/Getty Images.

If you want to see orcas in the wild though, your best bet is a whale-watching tour from Victoria. *See chapter 13.* © Chris Huss/The Wildlife Collection.

Hints of Vancouver's turn-of-the-century boomtown days still linger within its post-modern landscape. See chapter 6 for architectural highlights. © Wolfgang Kaehler Photography.

At huge dim-sum palaces in Chinatown, carts of the little delicacies are rolled right to your table. Go with a large group and share. See chapter 5 for reviews of our favorite Chinatown restaurants. © Catherine Karnow Photography.

Stanley Park is North America's largest urban park. Rollerblade, bike, or jog its 5½-mile Seawall Walk and take in stunning views of the North Coast mountains and sandy beaches. See chapter 6. © Wolfgang Kaehler Photography.

Watch old pros pass down their Native American carving skills to a young generation of artisans in Victoria's Thunderbird Park. See chapter 14. © Tim Thompson Photography.

Situated along the Inner Harbour, the Empress Hotel is Victoria's most impressive landmark and makes a memorable introduction to the city. See chapter 13. © Robert Holmes Photography.

Victorian high tea is both a meal and a ritual—and nowhere is the experience as steeped in luxury and tradition as in the Empress Hotel. See chapter 12. © Dave Bartruff Photography.

One of the premier ski resorts in North America, the Whistler/Blackcomb complex boasts more vertical runs, more lifts, and more varied terrain than any other resort in North America . . . and if you want to get away from it all, British Columbia's wilderness is always within easy reach of the city at Garibaldi Park. See chapter 17.
Above, © Stefan Schulhof/Getty Images. *Below,* © Philip & Karen Smith/Getty Images.

A New Star-Rating System & Other Exciting News from Frommer's!

In our continuing effort to publish the savviest, most up-to-date, and most appealing travel guides available, we've added some great new features.

Frommer's guides now include a new **star-rating system.** Every hotel, restaurant, and attraction is rated from 0 to 3 stars to help you set priorities and organize your time.

We've also added **seven brand-new features** that point you to the great deals, in-the-know advice, and unique experiences that separate travelers from tourists. Throughout the guide, look for:

Finds	Special finds—those places only insiders know about
Fun Fact	Fun facts—details that make travelers more informed and their trips more fun
Kids	Best bets for kids—advice for the whole family
Moments	Special moments—those experiences that memories are made of
Overrated	Places or experiences not worth your time or money
Tips	Insider tips—some great ways to save time and money
Value	Great values—where to get the best deals

We've also added a **"What's New"** section in every guide—a timely crash course in what's hot and what's not in every destination we cover.

Here's what the critics say about Frommer's:

"Amazingly easy to use. Very portable, very complete."

—*Booklist*

"Detailed, accurate, and easy-to-read information for all price ranges."
—*Glamour Magazine*

"Hotel information is close to encyclopedic."
—*Des Moines Sunday Register*

"Frommer's Guides have a way of giving you a real feel for a place."
—*Knight Ridder Newspapers*

Other Great Guides for Your Trip:

Frommer's Canada
Frommer's Irreverent Guide to Vancouver
Frommer's British Columbia & the Canadian Rockies

Vancouver &
Victoria

2003

by Shawn Blore & Alexandra de Vries

Wiley Publishing, Inc.

Published by:

Wiley Publishing, Inc.

909 Third Ave.
New York, NY 10022

ISBN 0-7645-6697-0
ISSN 1045-9316

Editor: Lorraine Festa
Production Editor: Ian Skinnari
Cartographer: John Decamillis
Photo Editor: Richard Fox
Production by Wiley Indianapolis Composition Services

Front cover photo: Strolling through the Sunken Garden in Butchart Gardens in
Victoria.
Back cover photo: Vancouver skyline and harbor against a backdrop of mountains.

For information on our other products and services or to obtain technical support,
please contact our Customer Care Department within the U.S. at 800-762-2974,
outside the U.S. at 317-572-3993 or fax 317-572-4002.

Wiley also publishes its books in a variety of electronic formats. Some content that
appears in print may not be available in electronic formats.

Manufactured in the United States of America

5   4   3   2   1

Contents

List of Maps

About the Authors

A native of California and resident by turns of Ottawa, Amsterdam, Moscow, and (for nearly the past decade) Vancouver, **Shawn Blore** is a newspaper journalist, award-winning magazine writer, and author of the best-selling *Vancouver: Secrets of the City*. He is also a coauthor of *Frommer's Canada, Frommer's Brazil,* and *Frommer's Portable Rio de Janeiro*.

Alexandra de Vries took her first intercontinental flight at 6 weeks and developed a taste for travel early on. A resident by turns of Amsterdam and Rio de Janeiro, she now lives in Vancouver and reports on West Coast culture and places for Frommer's readers. She is also the co-author of Frommer's Brazil and Frommer's Portable Rio de Janeiro.

An Invitation to the Reader

In researching this book, we discovered many wonderful places—hotels, restaurants, shops, and more. We're sure you'll find others. Please tell us about them, so we can share the information with your fellow travelers in upcoming editions. If you were disappointed with a recommendation, we'd love to know that, too. Please write to:

Frommer's Vancouver & Victoria 2003
Wiley Publishing, Inc. • 909 Third Ave. • New York, NY 10022

An Additional Note

Please be advised that travel information is subject to change at any time—and this is especially true of prices. We therefore suggest that you write or call ahead for confirmation when making your travel plans. The authors, editors, and publisher cannot be held responsible for the experiences of readers while traveling. Your safety is important to us, however, so we encourage you to stay alert and be aware of your surroundings. Keep a close eye on cameras, purses, and wallets, all favorite targets of thieves and pickpockets.

New! Frommer's Star Ratings & Icons

Every hotel, restaurant, and attraction listing in this guide has been ranked for quality, value, service, amenities, and special features using a star-rating scale. In country, state, and regional guides, we also rate towns and regions to help you narrow down your choices and budget your time accordingly. Hotels and restaurants in the Very Expensive and Expensive categories are rated on a scale of one (highly recommended) to three stars (exceptional). Those in the Moderate and Inexpensive categories rate from zero (recommended) to two stars (very highly recommended). Attractions, towns, and regions are rated according to the following scale: zero stars (recommended), one star (highly recommended), two stars (very highly recommended), and three stars (must-see).

In addition to the rating system, we also use seven icons to highlight insider information, useful tips, special bargains, hidden gems, memorable experiences, kid-friendly venues, places to avoid, and other useful information:

(Finds   (Fun Fact   (Kids   (Moments   (Overrated   (Tips   (Value

The following abbreviations are used for credit cards:

| AE | American Express | DISC | Discover | V | Visa |
| DC | Diners Club | MC | MasterCard | | |

FROMMERS.COM

Now that you have the guidebook to a great trip, visit our website at **www.frommers.com** for travel information on nearly 2,500 destinations. With features updated regularly, we give you instant access to the most current trip-planning information available. At Frommers.com, you'll also find the best prices on airfares, accommodations, and car rentals—and you can even book travel online through our travel booking partners. At Frommers.com, you'll also find the following:

- Online updates to our most popular guidebooks
- Vacation sweepstakes and contest giveaways
- Newsletter highlighting the hottest travel trends
- Online travel message boards with featured travel discussions

What's New in Vancouver & Victoria

Though September 11 slowed travel across the globe, visits to Canada have been picking up as American travelers discover the safe and exotic land across the northern border. The low Canadian dollar only adds to the advantages of a Canadian holiday. Those exchanging U.S. dollars are getting their visit at a 40% to 50% discount as each US$ buys C$1.55. Occasionally the loonie dips even lower so keep an eye on those exchange rates. Border formalities have been stepped up, however, and even our friendly neighbors to the south have to submit to longer line-ups and increased scrutiny so plan accordingly. Make sure your travel documents are up to date and leave plenty of time to complete border formalities upon both arrival and departure, whether entering by land, air, or sea.

VANCOUVER Accommodations As one of the city's finest luxury hotels, the **Pan Pacific Hotel Vancouver** (300–999 Canada Place; © **800/ 937-1515** in the U.S. or 604/662-8111; www.panpacific.com) makes a fine place to lay your head any old day, particularly for those departing Vancouver on a cruise. The cruise ship terminal is connected to the Convention Center, which is connected to the Pan Pacific hotel so your room is only an easy elevator or escalator accessible stroll away from the ship. Ask about special cruise ship hotel packages in the shoulder season of May and September.

Hip and trendy **Yaletown** already had some of the city's best restaurants, happening nightspots, and upscale shopping. Now, this downtown neighborhood can finally add a hotel to its list of amenities. Opening in September 2002, **Opus Hotel** (322 Davie St; © **604/642-6787;** www.opushotel. com) offers boutique-style accommodation with attitude. Each of the 96 beautiful rooms has been styled according to one of five personalities, each of which has been given a name. Mike, for example, is a doctor from NYC who likes trendy minimalist stainless steel, while Susan is a Toronto fashion analyst who prefers her room decorated with bright colors and Armani-style accessories.

Dining Restaurateur Umberto Menghi is responsible for bringing some of the best Italian food to town. His il Giardino di Umberto Ristorante has been serving up fine dining for 26 years and is still a reference for classic Italian cuisine. His latest eatery, **Circolo** (1116 Mainland St.; © **604/ 687-1116;** www.umberto.com), located in Yaletown, offers the expected impeccable Italian dining but this restaurant's setting caters to this neighborhood's hip, young clientele; dining is a less formal, more late-night affair, and Menghi's Circolo melds together a restaurant, bar, and bistro under one roof, flanked outside with a wide green patio.

Good food and fabulous patios don't always go together—people will often put up with inferior food if the sunshine and views are good enough. However, the **Dockside Brewing**

Company (1253 Johnstone St., Granville Island; ℂ **604/685-7070**) doesn't compromise on either taste or views. Its revamped menu brings great pub food and casual dining on one of the city's best patios, tucked away in the Granville Island Hotel.

International food star Rob Feenie's Lumière has been a big hit ever since it first opened, but alas a scrumptious seven-course gourmet extravaganza is not something to treat oneself to every week. To fill the gap Feenie recently opened the less formal **Lumière Tasting Bar** (2551 W. Broadway; ℂ **604/739-8185;** www.lumiere.ca). All dishes can be ordered individually and cost only C$12 (US$7.75). Try one or two as an appetizer or light supper or share a handful with a friend for a more substantial meal. Even dropping in for a coffee and dessert is still a gourmet experience and popular with locals who can now enjoy Feenie's food without breaking the bank.

Nightlife   Cheers! The province of British Columbia finally approved new liquor laws in August 2002 making it possible for bars to stay open until 4am, while restaurant patrons can now order alcoholic beverages without having to order food. City zoning has also encouraged new night spots to open up around Granville Street and the new law allows them to stay open past their former 2am bedtime.

The new darling of the fashion industry trendsetters, **Ginger Sixty-Two** (1219 Granville St.; ℂ **604/688-5494**) serves up great martinis. The lounge is decorated in happening red, orange, and gold tones and has low couches strategically placed throughout the room for comfortable chilling. Almost directly across the street, **Crush** (180 Granville St.; ℂ **604/684-0355**) caters to a slightly younger crowd of 20-somethings who enjoy a good glass of wine or champagne cocktail while clubbing. The staff

sommelier is on hand to help you pick something appropriate from the wine list. The recently renovated **Heritage House Hotel** (455 Abbott St.; ℂ **604/685-7777**) brings a few upscale nightlife options to the grittier part of town close to Gastown. Hosting three separate bars and lounges, this historic site houses the Lotus Lounge, one of the hottest house music venues, the Milk Lounge with a mostly gay following (men on Fri and Ladies Only on Sat) and Honey, a comfortable lounge where a mixed crowd gathers for cocktails or beers.

VICTORIA   Accommodations

What were once known individually as the Gatsby Mansion Inn and Huntingdon Ramada Hotel have been revamped and re-christened as **Ramada Huntingdon Hotel & Suites at Belleville Park** (330 Quebec St.; ℂ **800/663-7557;** www.belle villepark.com). Right on Victoria's Inner Harbour, the new and improved BelleVille Park takes up the entire block, with an pleasant square and an outdoor cafe and patio connecting the hotel with the inn. Bed and breakfast aficionados will love the elegant Gatsby Mansion Inn with its original stained glass windows, hand-painted frescoes and period furniture. For modern conveniences check into the Huntingdon Ramada; the split level gallery rooms (lofts) on the third floor easily accommodate a family or group of four to six people.

SIDE TRIPS   It seems like Whistler never stops growing, but even with more than 2 million visitors a year there always seems to be room for more. The 2003 winter ski season is expected to last until June 8 with summer skiing continuing throughout June and July on Blackcomb's Horstman Glacier. In the next year keep an eye out for some new hotel development. Three new condo-style hotels and a shopping area will open up in Whistler Creek in the winter of

2003 and builders will soon break ground for the Four Seasons Hotel and London Mountain Lodge, slated to open in 2004. For up-to-date information and comprehensive travel planning assistance check out **www.mywhistler.com**.

Ucluelet, Tofino & Pacific Rim National Park The summer of 2002 saw the opening of a brand new resort on Tofino's Pacific Coast. **Long Beach Lodge** (Cox Bay, Tofino; ℂ 877/844-7873; www.longbeach lodgeresort.com) offers five-star luxury on the edge of Cox Bay. Guests can choose between ocean views and beachfront rooms but all 43 units come prepped for pampering. The resort's dining room makes the most of the spectacular scenery with large picture windows overlooking the rugged Pacific.

The Best of
Vancouver & Victoria

Vancouverites aren't much given to introspection—too much time spent outdoors—so it's perhaps a bit unfair to expect it of visitors. But if you really want to understand **Vancouver,** stand at the edge of the Inner Harbour (the Canada Place pavilion makes a good vantage point) and look up past the float-planes taking off over Stanley Park, around the container terminals, over the tony waterfront high-rises, and then up the steep green slopes of the North Shore mountains to the twin snowy peaks of the Lions. What you've seen—90% of it anyway—is the result of a collaboration, unique in history, between God and the Canadian Pacific Railway (CPR).

It was the Almighty—or Nature (depending on your point of view)—who raised the Coast Range and then sent a glacier slicing along its foot, simultaneously carving out a deep trench and piling up a tall moraine of rock and sand. When the ice retreated, water from the Pacific flowed in and the moraine became a peninsula, flanked on one side by a deep natural harbor and on the other by a river of glacial meltwater.

Some 10,000 years later, a CPR surveyor came by, took in the peninsula, the harbor, and the river, and decided he'd found the perfect spot for the railway's new Pacific terminus. He kept it quiet, as smart railwaymen tended to do, until the company had bought up most of the land around town. Then the railway moved in, set up shop, and the city of Vancouver was born.

Working indoors, Vancouverites have all fallen in love with the outside: mountain biking, windsurfing, kayaking, rock climbing, parasailing, snowboarding, skiing, and snowshoeing.

The rest of the world has taken notice of the blessed life people in these parts lead. *Outside* magazine voted it one of the 10 best cities in the world to live in. It's one of the 10 best to visit, according to *Condé Nast Traveler.* The World Council of Cities ranked it second only to Geneva for quality of life. Heady stuff, particularly for a spot that less than 20 years ago was routinely derided as the world's biggest mill town.

Eighty-some kilometers (50 miles) across the Strait of Georgia on Vancouver Island, **Victoria** had for years marketed itself quite successfully as a little bit of England on the North American continent. So successful was the sales job, Victorians soon began to believe it themselves. They began growing elaborate rose gardens, which flourished in the mild Pacific climate, and they cultivated a taste for afternoon tea with jam and scones.

For decades, this continued, until soon it was discovered that not many shared a taste for English cooking, so Victorian restaurants branched out into seafood, ethnic, and fusion. And lately, as visitors have shown more interest in exploring the natural world, Victoria has quietly added whale-watching and mountain-biking trips to its traditional London-style double-decker bus tours. The result, at the dawn of the new millennium, is that Victoria is the only city in the world where you can zoom out on a Zodiac in the morning to see a pod of killer whales, and make it back in time for a lovely afternoon tea.

1 Frommer's Favorite Vancouver Experiences

- **Watching the Fireworks Explode over English Bay:** Every August during the Celebration of Light, three international fireworks companies compete by launching their best displays over English Bay. As many as 500,000 spectators cram the beaches around English Bay, while those with boats sail out to watch from the water. See chapter 2.

- **Enjoying the F-F-F Festivals:** the Folk, the Fringe, and the Film, to be precise. The Folkfest brings folk and world-beat musicians to a waterfront stage in Jericho Park. The setting's gorgeous, the music's great, and the crowd is something else. Far more urban is the Fringe, a festival of new and original plays that takes place on artsy Granville Island. The plays are wonderfully inventive. Better yet, they're short and cheap so you can see a lot of them. In late September, the films of the world come to Vancouver. Serious filmies buy a pass and see all 500 flicks (or as many as they can before their eyeballs fall out). See chapter 2.

- **Exploring Chinatown:** Fishmongers call out their wares before a shop filled with crabs, eels, geoducks, and bullfrogs, while farther down the street elderly Chinese women haggle over produce as their husbands hunt for deer antler or dried sea horse at a traditional Chinese apothecary. And when you're tired of looking and listening, head inside to any one of a dozen restaurants to sample succulent Cantonese cooking. See chapters 5 and 7.

- **Strolling the Stanley Park Seawall:** Or jogging, running, blading, biking, skating, riding—whatever your favorite mode of transport is, use it, but by all means get out there. See chapter 6.

- **Visiting the Vancouver Aquarium:** It's a Jacques Cousteau special, live and right there in front of you. The Vancouver Aquarium does an extremely good job showing whole ecosystems. Fittingly enough, the aquarium has an excellent display on the Pacific Northwest, plus sea otters (cuter than they have any right to be), beluga whales, sea lions, and a Pacific white-sided dolphin. See chapter 6.

- **Kayaking on Indian Arm:** Vancouver is one of the few cities on the edge of a great wilderness, and one of the best ways to get there quickly is kayaking on the gorgeous Indian Arm. Rent a kayak or go with a company—they may even serve you a gourmet meal of barbecued salmon. See chapter 6.

- **Strolling the Beach:** It doesn't matter which beach, there's one for every taste. Wreck Beach below UBC is for nudists, Spanish Banks is for dog walkers, Jericho Beach is for volleyballers, Kitsilano Beach is for serious suntanning, and English Bay Beach is for serious people-watching. See chapter 6.

- **Picnicking at the Lighthouse:** Everyone has their favorite picnic spot—one of the beaches or up on the mountains. Ours is Lighthouse Park on the North Shore.

Southern British Columbia

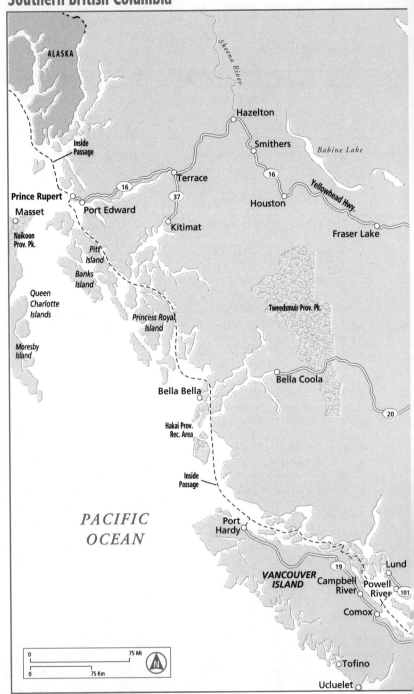

ALASKA

Skeena River

Hazelton

Inside Passage

Smithers

Babine Lake

Terrace   16

Prince Rupert

Masset

Port Edward   37

Kitimat

Houston

Yellowhead Hwy.

Fraser Lake

Naikoon Prov. Pk.

Pitt Island

Banks Island

Queen Charlotte Islands

Princess Royal Island

Tweedsmuir Prov. Pk.

Moresby Island

Bella Coola

Bella Bella

Hakai Prov. Rec. Area

20

Inside Passage

PACIFIC OCEAN

Port Hardy

VANCOUVER ISLAND   19   Campbell River   Powell River   Lund

101

Comox

0   75 Mi

0   75 Km

N

Tofino

Ucluelet

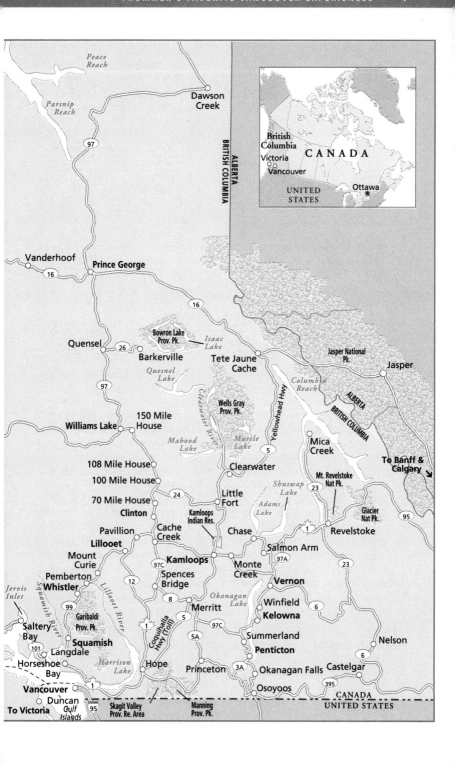

Not only do you get to look back over at Vancouver, but also, the walk down to the rocky waterline runs through a pristine, old-growth rainforest. See chapter 6.

- **Hiking the North Shore:** The forests of the North Shore are at the edge of a great wilderness and only 20 minutes from the city. Step into a world of muted light and soaring cathedral-like spaces beneath the tree canopy. Great North Shore trails include the very busy Grouse Grind, Cypress Falls Park, and the hike from Grouse back to Goat Mountain. (Whatever you do, go prepared. People die on those trails every year, cold and lost. A good local guidebook can give you more details on trails and tell you what you need to bring.) See chapter 6.

- **Exploring UBC's Museum of Anthropology:** The building—by native son Arthur Erickson—would be worth a visit in itself, but this is also one of the best places in the world to see and learn about West Coast Native art and culture. See chapter 6.

- **Visiting the Library:** We're serious. Vancouver's new main library building isn't so much a book depository as an urban gathering place. Outside, you'll find a permanent crowd of folks hanging out, playing music, or distributing political pamphlets. Inside is a huge glass atrium with little patio tables and several coffee bars, where folks sit and chat for hours. Sometimes they even go and look at books. See chapter 6.

- **Mountain Biking the Endowment Lands:** One of the best places to give this sport a try is on the trails running through the forest by the University of British Columbia. (The area is officially called Pacific Spirit Park, but everyone calls it the Endowment Lands.) On the east side of town, the trails on Burnaby Mountain are equally good, though steep enough to qualify as intermediate terrain. See chapter 6.

- **Having a Latte on Granville Island:** Down on False Creek, this former industrial site was long ago converted to an indoor public market and home for artists and artisans. Grab a latte at the public market and sit outside by the wharf and people- or boat-watch. See chapter 6.

- **Wandering the West End:** Encompassing the über-shopping strip known as Robson Street, as well as cafe-lined Denman and a forest of high-rise apartments, the West End is the urban heart of Vancouver. Enjoy the lush street trees, the range of architecture, and the neat little surprises on every side street. See chapter 7.

- **Watching the Sunset from a Waterside Patio:** Why else live in a city with such stunning views? Most establishments on False Creek, English Bay, and Coal Harbour have good waterside patios. For something different, head to the North Shore, where you don't get to see mountains, but you get fabulous city views. See chapter 9.

2 Frommer's Favorite Victoria Experiences

- **Savoring Afternoon Tea:** Yes, it's expensive and incredibly touristy, but it's also a complicated and ritual-laden art form. Besides, it's good. The Fairmont Empress and the Butchart Gardens dining rooms are both good. Not quite as formal but also worth a visit is Point Ellice house. See page 207.

- **Catching the Fireworks at Butchart Gardens:** The best fireworks have something of the best of flowers, just as the best flowers have all the fire of explosives. Saturday nights in the summertime at Butchart Gardens, you get both. See page 215.

- **Touring the Royal BC Museum:** One of the best small museums in the world, the Royal BC does exactly what a good regional museum should do—explain the region. It just does it so much better than most. See page 218.

- **Watching Orcas:** Of all the species of orcas (killer whales), those on the B.C. coast are the only ones that live in large and complicated extended families. This makes Victoria a particularly good spot to whale-watch because the orcas travel in large, easy-to-find pods. There's something magical about being out on the water and seeing a pod of 15 animals surface just a few hundred meters away. See chapter 13.

- **Touring by Miniferry:** Catch a Victoria Harbour Ferry and take a 45-minute tour around the harbor past the floating neighborhood of West Bay or up the gorge, where tidal waterfalls reverse direction with the changing tide. Moonlight tours depart every evening at sunset. See "Getting Around" in chapter 10 and "Organized Tours" in chapter 13.

- **Climbing Mount Douglas:** Actually, you don't even have to climb. Just drive up and walk around.

The whole of the Saanich Peninsula lies at your feet. See chapter 13.

- **Beachcombing:** This is the world's cheapest fun activity. Just find a beach, preferably a rocky one, and turn stuff over or poke through the tide pools and see what turns up. Of course, what you find depends on where you look. The best beaches are out along Highway 14, starting with East Sooke Regional Park, and moving out to French Beach, China Beach, Mystic Beach, and, the very best of all, Botanical Beach Provincial Park, some 60 km (37 miles) away by Port Renfrew. Remember to put the rocks back once you've had a peek. See chapter 13.

- **Strolling the Inner Harbour:** Watch the boats and aquatic wildlife come and go while walking along a paved pathway that winds past manicured flower gardens. The best stretch runs south from the Inner Harbour near the Government Buildings, past Undersea World, the Royal London Wax Museum, and the Seattle ferry dock. See chapter 14.

- **Biking the Dallas Road to Willows Bay:** Okay, we're view junkies, but where else can you find a bike path by an ocean with high mountain peaks for a backdrop? See chapter 14.

3 Frommer's Favorite Experiences Beyond Vancouver & Victoria

- **Skiing at Whistler and Blackcomb Resorts:** Why ski anywhere else? The best resorts in North America merged for a total of more than 200 runs on two adjoining mountains. Full-day lift passes are only about C$65 (US$42) for adults. See chapter 17.

- **Looking for Bald Eagles in Squamish:** The bald eagle is the national symbol of the United States, but in winter when the salmon are running, you can see more eagles in Squamish than just about anywhere else in the world. See chapter 6.

- **Watching for Whales and Storms in Pacific Rim National Park:** Few sights in nature match observing whales in the wild, except perhaps a winter storm on Vancouver Island's west coast. Here you can see both in abundance. See chapter 17.
- **Exploring B.C.'s Backcountry by Train or Horseback:** Exploring the B.C. backcountry—an incredibly beautiful land of alpine lakes, snowcapped peaks, grasslands, canyons, and high plateaus—could take the whole of a lifetime. But to get a taste of it, hop on board one of BC Rail's exploratory day trips. Those with time to see more can alight from the railcar and set off to explore on horseback. See chapter 17.

4 Two Trips of a Lifetime

British Columbia is really one of the most pristine, most spectacular, most naturally beautiful places on earth. What follows are two trips that can't be replicated anywhere else on the planet. More detailed descriptions are given in chapter 17.

- **Sailing the Great Bear Rain Forest:** There are next to no roads in this area of mountains, fjords, bays, channels, rivers, and inlets—the geography's too intense. Thanks to that isolation, this is also one of the last places in the world where grizzly bears are still found in large numbers, not to mention salmon, large trees, killer whales, otters, and porpoises. But to get there, you'll need a boat. And if you're going to take a boat, why not take a lovely 30m (100-foot) long, fully rigged sail boat?
- **Horse Trekking the Chilcotin Plateau:** The high plateau country of the B.C. interior has some of the most impressive scenery around. Soaring peaks rise above deep valleys, with mountain meadows alive with flowers that bloom for just a few weeks in high summer. Explore the territory on horseback and save your feet.

5 Best Vancouver Hotel Bets

For a complete description of these and other Vancouver accommodations, see chapter 4.

- **Best Historic Hotel: The Fairmont Hotel Vancouver,** 900 W. Georgia St. (© **800/866-5577** or 604/684-3131), was built by the Canadian Pacific Railway on the site of two previous hotels. It opened in 1929 as Vancouver's grandest hotel. The chateau-style exterior, the lobby, and even the rooms—now thoroughly restored—are built in a style and on a scale reminiscent of the great European railway hotels. See p. 58.
- **Best for Business Travelers: The Westin Grand,** 433 Robson St. (© **888/680-9393** or 604/602-1999) offers big work spaces, data ports, and lots of electrical plugs, plus—in the 40 Guest Office suites—speakerphones, cordless phones, and combo fax/laser printer/photocopiers. See p. 62.
- **Best for a Romantic Getaway:** At the **Beachside Bed & Breakfast,** 4208 Evergreen Ave., West Vancouver (© **800/563-3311** or 604/922-7773), you can stroll your own private beach, watch the passing seals and eagles, or soak in a beachside hot tub as the sun goes down over the city skyline. See p. 72.

- **Best Trendy Hotel:** Rooms decorated in funky apple greens and lemon yellows, a lobby of bold and bright colors and whimsically shaped glass chandeliers, and Pal the robotic dog who sniffs out newcomers by the check-in desk, make **Pacific Palisades Hotel,** 1277 Robson St. (© **800/663-1815** or 604/688-0461), the premier choice of trendy hotel aficionados. See p. 65.

- **Best for Families:** The **Rosedale on Robson Suite Hotel,** 838 Hamilton (at Robson St.), Vancouver (© **800/661-8870** or 604/689-8033), offers two-bedroom family suites that come furnished with bunk beds, decorated in either a sports or Barbie theme and equipped with a large toy chest and blackboard with crayons. On Saturday night the Rosedale staff put on a movie or craft night to take the little ones off their parents' hands for a while. Even the family dog or cat is welcome. See p. 63.

- **Best Architecture:** There's many a Vancouver hotel you wouldn't look at twice. But the graceful soaring tower of **Sheraton Vancouver Wall Centre Hotel,** 1088 Burrard St. (© **800/325-3535** or 604/331-1000), is truly an architectural gem. And if that doesn't grab ya, the top-quality amenities will. See p. 61.

- **Best Inexpensive Hotel:** With all the facilities of a convention center plus cheap comfortable rooms, **The University of British Columbia Conference Centre,** 5961 Student Union Blvd. (© **604/822-1000**), is the best inexpensive choice in the city. See p. 71.

- **Best B&B:** Built in 1905 by two Vancouver photographers, the **West End Guest House,** 1362

Haro St. (© **604/681-2889**), is filled with the artists' work as well as an impressive collection of Victorian antiques. Fresh-baked brownies or cookies accompany evening turndown service, and the staff is thoroughly professional. See p. 68.

- **Best Alternative Accommodation:** The **Rosellen Suites at Stanley Park,** 102–2030 Barclay St. (© **888/317-6648** or 604/689-4807), has spacious furnished apartments with fully equipped kitchens, dining areas, and living rooms for the same price as many standard hotel rooms. See p. 67.

- **Best Service:** What can we say? Consistently garnering four diamonds and five stars, the **Four Seasons Hotel,** 791 W. Georgia St. (© **800/332-3442** in the U.S. or 604/689-9333), just tries harder. See p. 58.

- **Best Location:** Everyone's definition of a great location is different, but the **Westin Bayshore Resort & Marina,** 1601 Bayshore Dr. (© **800/228-3000** or 604/682-3377), offers something for everyone: Steps from Stanley Park and Denman Street, the Westin boasts a waterfront location with access to the seawall only 10 blocks from downtown. And the view of the North Shore mountains is great. See p. 66.

- **Best Views:** So many Vancouver hotels have outstanding views that it's difficult to choose just one. Still, there's something special about the upper floors of the **Pan Pacific Hotel Vancouver,** 300–999 Canada Place (© **800/937-1515** in the U.S. or 604/662-8111). The harborside rooms have unimpeded views of Coal Harbour, Stanley Park, the Lions Gate Bridge, and the North Shore's mountains. See p. 60.

- **Best Health Club:** Stay at the **YWCA Hotel/Residence,** 733 Beatty St. (© **800/663-1424** or 604/895-5830), and you get free access to the best gym in town at the nearby co-ed YWCA Fitness Centre. For a more upscale gym there's the indoor/outdoor pool, fitness center, weight-and-exercise room, aerobics classes, whirlpool, and saunas at the **Four Seasons Hotel,** 791 W. Georgia St. (© **800/332-3442** in the U.S., or 604/689-9333). See p. 64 and 58.

- **Best Hotel Pool:** A toss-up between the large outdoor pool at the **Westin Bayshore Resort &**

Marina, 1601 Bayshore Dr. (© **800/228-3000** or 604/682-3377), and the **Pan Pacific Hotel's** lap pool and Jacuzzi, 300–999 Canada Place (© **800/937-1515** in the U.S. or 604/662-8111). Both offer unsurpassed views of the harbor and the mountains of the North Shore. See p. 66 and 60.

- **Best for Sports Fans:** The **Georgian Court Hotel,** 773 Beatty St. (© **800/663-1155** or 604/682-5555), is as close to the action as you can get with a bed in the room. B.C. Place Stadium is right across the street, and GM Place is just a few blocks away. See p. ###.

6 Best Victoria Hotel Bets

For a full description of these and other Victoria accommodations, see chapter 11.

- **Best Historic Hotel:** Architect Francis Rattenbury's masterpiece, **The Fairmont Empress,** 721 Government St. (© **800/866-5577** or 250/384-8111), has charmed princes (and their princesses), potentates, movie moguls, and the likes of you and me since 1908. See p. 187.

- **Best for Business Travelers:** With its central location, large desks and dataports, secretarial services, elegant lobby, small meeting rooms, dining rooms, and understated luxury at a reasonable price, **The Magnolia,** 623 Courtney St. (© **877/624-6654** or 250/381-0999), is Victoria's best spot for business. See p. 195.

- **Best Place to Pretend You Died and Went to Bel Air: The Aerie,** 600 Ebedora Lane, Malahat (© **250/743-7115**), a red-tiled mansion high atop Mount Malahat, features hand-carved king-size

beds, massive wood-burning fireplaces, chandeliered Jacuzzis, and faux marble finish by the gross ton. See p. 198.

- **Best Hotel Lobby:** The two-story plate glass demi-lune in the lobby of the **Delta Victoria Ocean Pointe Resort and Spa,** 45 Songhees Rd. (© **800/667-4677** or 250/360-2999), provides the best vantage in Victoria for watching the lights on the Legislature switch on. There are also comfy chairs and fireplaces to sit and get warm. See p. 187.

- **Best for Families:** The **Royal Scot Suite Hotel,** 425 Quebec St. (© **800/663-7515** or 250/388-5463), is a converted apartment building with spacious suites that'll make your family feel at home. They come with fully equipped kitchens, VCRs, and a video arcade and playroom in the basement. See p. 193.

- **Best B&B:** With rooms double the size of those in other B&Bs and every possible need taken care of, the friendly innkeepers at **The Haterleigh Heritage Inn,** 243 Kingston St. (✆ **250/384-9995**), do themselves proud. See p. 190.

- **Best Small Hotel:** The tastefully indulgent **Abigail's Hotel,** 906 McClure St. (✆ **800/561-6565** or 250/388-5363), has sumptuous sleeping chambers and warm, welcoming hosts. See p. 194.

- **Best Moderately Priced Hotel:** On the edge of the Inner Harbour, the **Admiral Inn,** 257 Belleville St. (✆ **888/823-6472** or ✆/fax 250/388-6267), provides friendly service, free bikes, and the most reasonably priced harbor view around. See p. 192.

- **Best Inexpensive Hotel:** While the rooms in the main hotel are just OK, the next-door suites and cottage operated by **The James Bay Inn,** 270 Government St. (✆ **800/836-2649** or 250/384-7151), are a veritable steal. See p. 194.

- **Most Romantic B&B:** The new Venetian and the Florentine rooms in **The Rosewood Victoria Inn,** 595 Michigan St. (✆ **800/335-3466** or **250/384-6644**), are the apogee of romantic luxury, the place to take a young bride or a long-time spouse. See p. 191.

- **Best Alternative Accommodation: The Boathouse,** 746 Sea Dr. (✆ **250/652-9370**), is a real (converted) boathouse, with a private dock and a rowing dinghy. Built in a secluded cove, the one-room cottage is a perfect spot for those seeking privacy. See p. 200.

- **Best Location:** Not only is **Swans Suite Hotel,** 506 Pandora Ave.

(✆ **800/668-7926** or 250/361-3310), in the heart of the old town and just a block from the harbor, it's also right above **Swans Pub,** one of the most pleasant restaurant/brewpubs in the entire city. See p. 197 and 255.

- **Best Spa:** The **Delta Victoria Ocean Pointe Resort and Spa,** 45 Songhees Rd. (✆ **800/667-4677** or 250/360-2999), houses the best spa in the Pacific Northwest. Complete skin and body treatments, aesthetics, and aromatherapy treatments pamper the body and spirit. The OPR also has the best hotel pool. See p. 187.

- **Best Fitness Center:** The fitness center at the **Hotel Grand Pacific,** 463 Belleville St. (✆ **800/228-5151** or 250/386-0450), offers aerobics classes, a 25m (27-yard) ozonated indoor pool, a separate kids' pool, and weight room; a sauna, whirlpool, and massage therapist help ease the pain from all that exercise. See p. 190.

- **Best Views:** With stunning panoramic harbor views in an elegant, Japanese-influenced decor, the **Laurel Point Inn,** 680 Montreal St. (✆ **800/663-7667** or 250/386-8721), is the place for view junkies. Outside of town, **The Aerie,** 600 Ebedora Lane, Malahat (✆ **250/743-7115**) offers private terraces with views across tree-clad mountains to a long blue coastal fjord. See p. 191 and 198.

- **Best Oceanside Inn:** In the little town of Sooke, just west of Victoria, the **Sooke Harbour House,** 1528 Whiffen Spit Rd. (✆ **250/642-3421**), offers quiet West Coast elegance and an exceptional restaurant. See p. 200.

7 Best Vancouver Dining Bets

For a full description of these and other Vancouver restaurants, see chapter 5.

- **Best Spot for a Romantic Dinner:** Dine at **il Giardino di Umberto Ristorante,** 1382 Hornby St. (© **604/669-2422**), in the summer and you can enjoy one of the loveliest courtyard patios in town, and even on the darkest of rainy winter nights the Tuscan villa–like dining room basks in the warm glow of the candlelight. See p. 81.
- **Best Spot for a Celebration:** Lumière, 2551 W. Broadway (© **604/739-8185**), is expensive but worth it to be pampered by chef Rob Feenie. See p. 90.
- **Best View:** On the top floor of the tallest building in Vancouver, towering 42 floors above the city, **Cloud 9,** 1400 Robson St. (© **604/662-8328**), has 360° views that go on forever. For a combination of truly top-notch food and a killer view, however, try **The Five Sails** in the Pan-Pacific Hotel, 999 Canada Place Way (© **604/891-2892**). See p. 79.
- **Best Wine List: Raincity Grill,** 1193 Denman St. (© **604/685-7337**), has a huge wine list that's focused on the Pacific Northwest and sold by the glass at a reasonable markup by a knowledgeable staff. Go on a tour of the region, glass by glass by glass. See p. 87.
- **Best Value:** Get gourmet-quality Indian cuisine in a West Broadway strip mall at **Sami's,** 986 W. Broadway (© **604/736-8330**). The well-known chef prepares amazing Indian cuisine with a hint of fusion; none of the main courses cost more than C$12 (US$8) or so. See p. 92.

- **Best for Kids: Romano's Macaroni Grill at the Mansion,** 1523 Davie St. (© **604/689-4334**), has a huge kids' menu, highchairs, and a great old mansion to explore—kids will love it. See p. 88.
- **Best Chinese Cuisine: Pink Pearl,** 1132 E. Hastings St. (© **604/253-4316**), has its fans, and not without reason, but the best Vancouver Chinese at the moment remains **Sun Sui Wah,** 3888 Main St. (© **604/872-8822**). It's definitely worth the trip. See p. 85 and 95.
- **Best French Cuisine:** From its early days, **Lumière,** 2551 W. Broadway (© **604/739-8185**), has been in the running for best restaurant in Vancouver. In 1999, 2000, and 2001 it won. You won't be disappointed. See p. 90.
- **Best Bistro:** The control-freak hostesses at **The SandBar,** 1535 Johnston St., Granville Island (© **604/669-9030**), are indeed an irritation, but the food is good; and the preening, posing, and people-watching opportunities are unmatched. See p. 93.
- **Best Service:** Owner John Bishop of the eponymous **Bishop's,** 2183 W. Fourth Ave. (© **604/738-2025**) makes every customer feel special. See p. 89.
- **Best Steak: Gotham Steakhouse and Cocktail Bar,** 615 Seymour St. (© **604/605-8282**), serves USDA prime, grilled to perfection. Need we say more? See p. 79.
- **Best Seafood:** The creativity of the chef, the quality of the ingredients, and the freshness of the seafood all combine to make **C,** 1600 Howe St. (© **604/681-1164**), the best seafood restaurant in Vancouver. See p. 78.

- **Best Tapas: La Bodega,** 1277 Howe St. (© **604/684-8815** or 604/684-8814), was serving tapas when chefs at all the new tapas upstarts were saving their nickels for a night at McDonald's. La Bodega still does it best. See p. 83.
- **Best West Coast Cuisine:** A full top-notch sushi bar plus inventive and ultra-fresh seafood dishes make the **Blue Water Café and Raw Bar,** 1095 Hamilton St., Yaletown (© **604/688-8078**), the place to try the best that the West has to offer. See p. 80.
- **Best Trendy Newcomer:** A room of sublimely understated elegance and a supremely talented kitchen are what makes foodies in the know flock to **Ouest,** 2881 Granville St. (© **604/738-8938**). See p. 91.
- **Best Italian:** A tough choice when there's so much top Italian in town, but the medal goes to **La Terrazza,** 1088 Cambie St. (© **604/899-4449**). See p. 82.
- **Best Japanese:** The most sublime of sushi is at **Tojo's Restaurant,** 202–777 W. Broadway (© **604/872-8050**). Just remember to take out an extra mortgage and practice your so-you're-a-movie-star-I-don't-care look. See p. 90.
- **Best Late-Night Dining:** Housed in a renovated heritage building, **The Brickhouse Bistro,** 730 Main St. (© **604/689-8645**), has plenty of character and great food. It's open well past midnight, when many of Vancouver's restaurants

have already gone to sleep. Nightcaps can be had downstairs in the bar. See p. 95.
- **Best Martinis:** At **Delilah's,** 1789 Comox St. (© **604/687-3424**), a two-page menu includes such lovelies as a Black Widow, a Boston Tea Partini, and the Edsel (soaked in lemon), all served in the wonderfully decadent lounge. See p. 86.
- **Best Outdoor Dining:** Situated right on the edge of Granville Island, the large patio at the **Dockside Brewing Company,** 1253 Johnston St., Granville Island (© **604/683-7373),** offers great views of False Creek. For unsurpassed ocean views reserve a table under the trees at **The Teahouse Restaurant** in Stanley Park, Ferguson Point (close to Third Beach; © **604/669-3281**). This patio also doubles as best sunset spot. See p. 92 and 87.
- **Best People-Watching:** In the heart of the Robson shopping area, **Joe Fortes Seafood and Chop House,** 777 Thurlow St. (© **604/669-1940**), is a favorite after-work gathering place for the young, rich, and beautiful—and those who wish to live as if they are. See p. 81.
- **Best Vegetarian: Annapurna,** 1812 W. Fourth Ave. (© **604/736-5959**). Fabulous, flavorful food; cozy little room; and the most reasonable wines in town. Who says you have to sacrifice when you're a veggie eater? See p. 93.

8 Best Victoria Dining Bets

For a full description of these and other Victoria restaurants, see chapter 12.

- **Best Spot for a Romantic Dinner: Camille's,** 45 Bastion Sq. (© **250/381-3433**), offers a quiet, intimate, candlelit room and a

wine list with a bottle or glass for every occasion. See p. 204.
- **Best Spot for a Business Lunch: The Marina Restaurant,** 1327 Beach Dr., Oak Bay (© **250/598-8555**), is casual but elegant, with white linens, sufficient space

between tables, comfortable seating, and an inspiring view. Plus there's ample parking—a rarity in Victoria. See p. 212.

- **Best Decor:** With better art than most museums, **Swans Brewpub,** 506 Pandora Ave. (in Swans Hotel; © 250/361-3310), wins out for best decor. See p. 255.
- **Best Bistro:** Great food, terrific wine list and a chance to stroll the ever-trendier neighborhood of Cook Street Village make **Cassis Bistro,** 253 Cook St. (© 250/384-1932), the top bistro choice. See p. 206.
- **Best View:** The chef at **The Aerie,** 600 Ebedora Lane, Malahat (© 250/743-7115), creates remarkable classic French dishes. You can savor a cassoulet of smoked duck and venison sausage with a vintage Château Margaux Pavilion Rouge while sitting atop a mountain looking out over a forest-clad fjord. See p. 211.
- **Best Fish and Chips: Barb's Place,** 310 Erie St. (© 250/384-6515), on Fisherman's Wharf, sells 'em freshly fried and wrapped in newspaper—just like they should. See p. 204.
- **Best Wine List:** Owner Sinclair Philip knows how to choose 'em and the **Sooke Harbour House,** 1528 Whiffen Spit Rd., Sooke (© 250/642-3421), has the awards—and more importantly the list—to prove it. See p. 211.
- **Best Value: Re-bar,** 50 Bastion Sq. (© 250/361-9223), offers large portions, terrific quality, and a funky laid-back atmosphere. See p. 210.
- **Best for Kids: Millos,** 716 Burdett Ave. (© 250/382-4422), treats youngsters to a night on the town, with a kids' menu, children-loving waiters, and exciting Greek dishes such as stuffed grape leaves and lemon soup. See p. 208.

- **Best Chinese Cuisine:** A billion and half people can't be wrong. Actually, all of China has yet to eat at **J&J Wonton Noodle House,** 1012 Fort St. (© 250/383-0680), but if they had, they'd love it. See p. 210.
- **Best French Cuisine:** At **The Aerie,** 600 Ebedora Lane, Malahat (© 250/743-7115), chef Christophe Letard's cooking is as unmistakably French as his accent. It's also quite wonderful. See p. 211.
- **Best Italian Cuisine:** All you have to do is ask around for Victoria's best Italian restaurant, and people will point you to **Il Terrazzo Ristorante,** 555 Johnson St., off Waddington Alley (© 250/361-0028). Excellent northern Italian cooking and points for the lovely patio. See p. 206.
- **Best West Coast:** True, there are Tuscan influences here, but the ingredients, preparation, and wine at **Café Brio,** 944 Fort St. (© 250/383-0009), all do credit to the West Coast surroundings. See p. 204.
- **Best Seafood Cuisine: Sooke Harbour House,** 1528 Whiffen Spit Rd. (© 250/642-3421), serves the best gifts from the sea and its own garden, like red sturgeon in a raspberry coulis, or seared scallops with sea asparagus. Dining here is always a culinary adventure, well worth the money and the trip. See p. 211.
- **Best Local Crowd: Pagliacci's,** 1011 Broad St. (© 250/386-1662). Noisy and crowded, this is the place to be seen while you devour a plate of spaghetti Bolognese or a piping-hot sausage and mushroom pizza. See p. 208.
- **Best Burgers and Beer: Six Mile Pub,** 494 Island Hwy., View Royal (© 250/478-3121), offers 10 house brews, juicy burgers

The Best Websites for Vancouver & Victoria

- **Entertainment info** (www.vancouvertoday.com): This site is a great place to turn to for current entertainment options in the Vancouver area.

- **Tourism BC** (www.hellobc.com): The official site of the provincial government tourism agency, this site provides good information on attractions, as well as higher-end accommodations.

- **Tourism Vancouver** (www.tourismvancouver.com): The official city tourism agency site provides a great overview of attractions, including an excellent calendar of events, plus a few last minute deals on accommodations.

- **Tourism Victoria** (www.tourismvictoria.com): Victoria's official tourism site functions much the same as Vancouver's, with up-to-date, comprehensive information about what to do and see around the city.

- **Whistler & Blackcomb Resorts** (www.whistler.net): This site offers a particularly helpful overview of activities and accommodations options available at North America's premier ski resort.

(even veggie burgers), and loads of British pub–style atmosphere. See p. 213.

- **Best Late-Night Dining:** At the great little **Süze Lounge and Restaurant,** 515 Yates St. (© 250/383-2829), you'll find lots of buzz till late at night, plus a young crowd that's there to see and be seen. See p. 208.

- **Best Outdoor Dining:** One of the prettiest spots on earth to dine, the **Deep Cove Chalet,** 11190 Chalet Rd., near Sidney (© 250/656-3541), also offers some very fine French cuisine. Located a 30-minute drive from Victoria, it's well worth the trip. See p. 212.

- **Best People-Watching:** You Süze, you don't lose (ugh!). There's lots

of eye-candy all night long at **Süze Lounge and Restaurant,** 515 Yates St. (© 250/383-2829). See p. 208.

- **Best Afternoon or High Tea:** If you're doing this high tea thing only once, you may as well do it right, and there's no better place than **The Fairmont Empress,** 721 Government St. (© 250/384-8111), Victoria's crown jewel of a hotel. See p. 207.

- **Best Fast Food: Sam's Deli,** 805 Government St. (© 250/382-8424), makes a great stop for a quick soup or sandwich. If you don't want to waste precious sightseeing time, order your food to go and head down to the waterfront. See p. 211.

2

Planning Your Trip to Vancouver & Victoria

Whether you're visiting Vancouver and Victoria for business or shopping, dining or dancing, beach walking or backwoods trekking, or all of the above, here are some tips to help you plan your trip.

1 Visitor Information & Entry Requirements

VISITOR INFORMATION

You can get Canadian tourism information at consulate offices in most major American cities. The provincial and municipal Canadian tourism boards are also great sources of travel information. Contact **Super Natural British Columbia–Tourism B.C.,** Box 9830 Stn. Prov. Government, Victoria, B.C. V8W 9W5 (© **800/ HELLO-BC** or 604/435-5622; www. hellobc.com; www.snbc-res.com for accommodation reservations), for information about travel and accommodations throughout the province.

    Tourism Vancouver's Tourist Info Centre, 200 Burrard St., Vancouver, B.C. V6C 3L6 (© **604/683-2000;** www.tourismvancouver.com), and **Tourism Victoria,** 812 Wharf St., Victoria (© **250/953-2033;** for hotel bookings only 800/663-3883 and 250/953-2022; www.tourismvictoria. com), can help you with everything from booking accommodations to making suggestions for what to see and do.

    If you're planning to spend time outside the cities, you may also wish to call or write the **Vancouver Coast and Mountains Tourism Region,** 250–1508 W. 2nd Ave., Vancouver, B.C. V6J 1H2 (© **604/739-9011;** www.coastandmountains.com). For

travel information on Vancouver Island and the Gulf Islands, see the **Tourism Association of Vancouver Island,** 203–335 Wesley St., Nanaimo, B.C. V9R 2T5 (© **250/ 754-3500;** www.islands.bc.ca).

    For cultural information, check out the website for *Vancouver Magazine* at www.vanmag.com.

ENTRY REQUIREMENTS

If you're driving from Seattle, you'll need to clear Customs at the Peace Arch crossing (open 24 hr.) in Blaine, Washington. You'll pass through **Canadian Customs** (© **800/461- 9999** or 204/983-3500) to enter Canada, and **U.S. Customs** (© **360/ 332-5771**) on your departure. Duty-free shops are located in Blaine at the last exit before the border going into Canada. On the Canadian side, the shops are a little more difficult to find. They're on the right, just after the speed limit drops to 35 kilometers per hour (22 mph).

    If you fly directly into Vancouver International Airport from another country, you'll go through Customs in the new International Terminal. Once you clear passport control, you and your luggage will go through Customs before you leave the terminal. (Even if you don't have anything to declare,

Customs officials randomly select a few passengers and search their luggage.)

DOCUMENTS FOR U.S. CITIZENS

Citizens or permanent U.S. residents don't require visas to enter Canada. American citizens need to show proof of citizenship and residence; a passport or birth certificate plus a driver's license is sufficient. Naturalized citizens should carry their naturalization certificates. However, with increased border security, it's best to err on the side of caution and bring your passport.

Permanent U.S. residents who are not U.S. citizens should carry their passports and Resident Alien Card (U.S. form I-151 or I-551). Foreign students and other noncitizen U.S. residents should carry their passports or a Temporary Resident Card (form 1688) or Employment Authorization Card (1688A or 1688B), a visitor's visa; I-94 Arrival-Departure Record, a current I-20 copy of IAP-66 indicating student status, proof of sufficient funds for a temporary stay, and evidence of return transportation. In either case, citizens of other countries traveling to Canada from the United States should check with the Canadian Consulate before departure to see if a visitor's visa is required.

If you're bringing children into Canada, you must have proof of legal guardianship. Lack of it can cause long delays at the border, because there have been cases of parents involved in custody cases abducting their children and attempting to flee to Canada (despite the fact that the Canadian and U.S. governments cooperate closely to resolve matters of this sort). If you're under 18 and not accompanied by a parent or guardian, you should bring a permission letter signed by your parent or legal guardian allowing you to travel to Canada.

DOCUMENTS FOR COMMONWEALTH CITIZENS

Citizens of Great Britain, Australia, and New Zealand don't require visas to enter Canada, but they do need to show proof of commonwealth citizenship (such as a passport), as well as evidence of funds sufficient for a temporary stay (credit cards work well here). Naturalized citizens should carry their naturalization certificates. Permanent residents of commonwealth nations should carry their passports and resident status cards. Foreign students and other residents should carry their passports or temporary resident cards or employment authorization cards, a visitor's visa, arrival-departure record, a current copy of student status, proof of sufficient funds for a temporary stay, and evidence of return transportation. Check with the Canadian Consulate before departure to see if you will also need a visitor's visa.

CUSTOMS REGULATIONS

Your personal baggage can include the following: boats, motors, snowmobiles, camping and sports equipment, appliances, TV sets, musical instruments, personal computers, cameras, and other items of a personal or household nature. If you are bringing excess luggage, be sure to carry a detailed inventory list that includes the acquisition date, serial number, and cost or replacement value of each item. It sounds tedious, but it can speed things up at the border. Customs will help you fill in the forms that allow you to temporarily bring in your effects. This list will also be used by U.S. Customs to check off what you bring out. You will be charged Customs duties for anything left in Canada.

Here are a few other things to keep in mind:

- If you bring more than US$10,000 in cash, you must file

a transaction report with U.S. Customs.

- Never joke about carrying explosives, drugs, or other contraband unless you want to have your bags and person searched in detail, plus face arrest for conspiracy. Remember, Canada is a foreign country. The officials don't have to let you in.

- Some prescription medicines may be considered contraband across the border. If you're bringing any, it's best to check with your doctor and bring a copy of your prescription, or contact the **Canadian Customs Office** (© **800/461-9999** or 204/983-3500).

- If you're over 18, you're allowed to bring in 40 ounces of liquor and wine or 24 12-ounce cans or bottles of beer and ale, and 50 cigars, 400 cigarettes, or 14 ounces of manufactured tobacco per person. Any excess is subject to duty.

- Gifts not exceeding C$60 (US$39) and not containing tobacco products, alcoholic beverages, or advertising material can be brought in duty-free. Meats, plants, and vegetables are subject to inspection on entry. There are restrictions, so contact the Canadian Consulate for more details if you want to bring produce into the country.

- If you plan to bring your dog or cat, you must provide proof of rabies inoculation during the preceding 36-month period. Other types of animals need special clearance and health certification. (Many birds, for instance, require 8 weeks in quarantine.)

- If you need more information concerning items you wish to bring in and out of the country, contact the **Canadian Customs Office** (© **800/461-9999** or 204/983-3500).

2 Money

CURRENCY

The Canadian currency system is decimal and resembles both British and U.S. denominations. Canadian monetary units are dollars and cents, with dollars coming in different colors, just like British currency. The standard denominations are C$5 (US$3.20), C$10 (US$6.50), C$20 (US$13), C$50 (US$33), and C$100 (US$65). The "loonie" (so named because of the loon on one side) is the C$1 (US65¢) coin that replaced the C$1 bill. A C$2 (US$1.30) coin, called the "toonie" because it's worth two loonies, has replaced the C$2 bill.

Banks and other financial institutions offer a standard rate of exchange based on the daily world monetary rate. Avoid C$100 bills when exchanging money, as many stores refuse to accept these bills. The best exchange rates can be had by withdrawing funds

from bank ATMs. Hotels will also gladly exchange your notes, but they usually give a slightly lower exchange rate. Almost all stores and restaurants accept American currency, and most will exchange amounts in excess of your dinner check or purchase. However, these establishments are allowed to set their own exchange percentages and generally offer the worst rates of all.

The exchange rate between Canadian and U.S. dollars should always be kept in mind. The figures charged in hotels and restaurants in Vancouver and Victoria are often incrementally higher than in comparable U.S. cities; the cost is typically about one-third less. Canada, at the moment, is a bargain.

TRAVELER'S CHECKS

Traveler's checks in Canadian funds are the safest way to carry money and

The Canadian Dollar & the U.S. Dollar

The prices cited in this guide are given in both Canadian and U.S. dollars, with all amounts over $10 rounded to the nearest dollar. Note that the Canadian dollar is worth almost 40% less than the U.S. dollar but buys nearly as much. As we go to press, C$1 is worth US65¢, which means that your C$100-a-night hotel room will cost only US$65 and your C$6 breakfast only US$3.90.

Here's a table of equivalents:

C$	US$	US$	C$
1	0.65	1	1.55
5	3.25	5	7.75
10	6.45	10	15.50
20	13.00	20	31.00
50	32.30	50	78.00
80	52.00	80	124.00
100	65.00	100	155.00

are universally accepted by banks (which may charge a small fee to cash them), larger stores, and hotels. If you are carrying American Express (© 604/669-2813) or Thomas Cook (© 604/641-1229) traveler's checks, you can cash them at the local offices of those companies free of charge.

ATM NETWORKS

The 24-hour PLUS and Cirrus ATM systems are widely available in both Vancouver and Victoria as well as throughout the smaller communities in British Columbia. The systems convert Canadian withdrawals to your account's currency within 24 hours, so don't panic if you call your bank and hear a one-to-one balance immediately after conducting a transaction. Cirrus network cards work at ATMs at the **Bank of Montreal** (© 604/665-2703), **CIBC** (© 800/465-2422), **Hong Kong Bank of Canada**

(© 604/641-1830), **Royal Bank** (© 800/769-2511), and **Toronto Dominion** (© 866/567-8888), and at all other ATMs that display the Cirrus logo. None of these ATM systems provides your current balance. You must know your four-digit PIN to access Canadian ATMs.

CREDIT & DEBIT CARDS

Major U.S. credit cards are widely accepted in British Columbia, especially American Express, MasterCard, and Visa. British debit cards like Barclay's Visa debit card are also accepted. Diners Club, Carte Blanche, Discover, JCB, and EnRoute are taken by some establishments, but not as many. The amount spent in Canadian dollars will automatically be converted by your issuing company to your currency when you're billed—generally at rates that are better than you'd receive for cash at a currency exchange.

3 When to Go

Tree experts say that a rainforest species like the Western Red Cedar needs at least 30 inches of precipitation a year. Vancouver gets about 47 inches a year, a cause for no small celebration among the local cedar population. Homo sapiens simply learn to adjust.

For example, most of that precipitation arrives in the wintertime, when, with a 30-minute drive to the mountains, you can trade the rain for snow. Skiing and snowboarding are popular and are practiced from mid-December until the mountain snowpack melts away in June. Except in Whistler, hotels in the winter are quiet and the restaurants are uncluttered. This is also the time when Vancouver's cultural scene is at its most active.

Around mid-February, the winds begin to slacken, the sun shines a bit more, and the blossoms on the cherry trees begin to poke their heads out, timid at first, but gaining more confidence with each day until, by the beginning of March, there's a riot of pink on every street. The sun comes out, and stays out. From then until the rains close in again in mid-October is prime visiting time for sun junkies. Of course, that's also when most other visitors arrive.

WEATHER

Both Vancouver and Victoria enjoy moderately warm, sunny summers and mild, rainy winters. Above the 49th parallel, you get more sun per summer day than you do down south. There are 16 hours of daylight in mid-June, which means more hours at the beach, shopping, or in the mountains than in other parts of North America. Only 10% of the annual rainfall occurs during the summer months. Victoria gets half as much rain as Vancouver, thanks to the sheltering Olympic Peninsula to the south and its own southeasterly position on huge Vancouver Island. The average annual rainfall in Vancouver is 46 inches; in Victoria, it's just 23 inches.

HOLIDAYS

The official British Columbian public holidays are as follows: New Year's Day (Jan 1); Good Friday, Easter, Easter Monday (Apr 18–21, 2003); Victoria Day (May 19, 2003); Canada Day (July 1); B.C. Day (Aug 4, 2003); Labour Day (Sept 1, 2003); Thanksgiving (Oct 13, 2003); Remembrance Day (Nov 11); Christmas (Dec 25); and Boxing Day (Dec 26).

Daily Mean Temperature & Total Precipitation for Vancouver, B.C.

	Jan	Feb	Mar	Apr	May	Jun	Jul	Aug	Sept	Oct	Nov	Dec
Temp (°F)	38.0	41.2	44.6	39.6	46.2	62.4	66.4	66.6	60.6	42.0	48.0	39.0
Temp (°C)	3.3	5.1	7.0	4.2	7.8	16.9	19.1	19.2	15.8	5.6	8.9	3.9
Prec. (in.)	5.9	4.9	4.3	3.0	2.4	1.8	1.4	1.5	2.5	4.5	6.7	7.0

VANCOUVER & VICTORIA CALENDAR OF EVENTS

Festivals held in Vancouver and Victoria draw millions of visitors each year. Things may seem a little quiet in the winter and early spring, but that's because most residents simply head for the ski slopes. Resorts such as **Whistler** and **Blackcomb** (© 604/932-2394) have events happening nearly every weekend. If no contact number or location is given for any of the events listed below, **Tourism Vancouver** (© 604/683-2000) should be able to provide further details.

VANCOUVER EVENTS

January

Polar Bear Swim, English Bay Beach. Thousands of hardy citizens show up in elaborate costumes to take a dip in the icy waters of English Bay. January 1.

Annual Bald Eagle Count, Brackendale. Bald eagles gather en masse every winter near Brackendale to feed on salmon. In January 1994, volunteers counted a world-record 3,700 eagles. The count starts at the

Brackendale Art Gallery (© 604/ 898-3333). First Sunday in January. Meet at 9am at the Art Gallery for a guided tour.

February

Chinese New Year, Chinatowns in Vancouver, Richmond, and Victoria. This is when the Chinese traditionally pay their debts and forgive old grievances to start the new lunar year with a clean slate. These Chinese communities launch a 2-week celebration, ringing in the new year with firecrackers, dancing dragon parades, and other festivities. Late January or early February (Feb 2 in 2003).

March

Vancouver Playhouse International Wine Festival (www. playhousewinefest.com), Vancouver. This is a major wine-tasting event featuring the latest international vintages. Each winery sets up a booth where you may try as many varieties as you like. Cheese and paté are laid out on strategically placed tables. Late March or early April (Mar 24–30 in 2003).

April

Baisakhi Day Parade, Vancouver. The Sikh Indian New Year is celebrated with a colorful parade around Ross Street near Marine Drive and ends with a vegetarian feast at the temple. Contact **Khalsa Diwan Gurudwara Temple** (© 604/324-2010) for more information. Mid-April.

Vancouver Sun Run, Vancouver. This is Canada's biggest 10K race, featuring over 40,000 runners, joggers, and walkers who race through 10 scenic kilometers (6.2 miles). The run downtown and finishes at B.C. Place Stadium. Call © 604/ 689-9441 for information or register online at www.sunrun.com. Late April.

May

Vancouver International Marathon, Vancouver. Runners from all over the world gather to compete in a run through the streets. For information, call © 604/872-2928. First Sunday in May (May 4, 2003).

New Play Festival, Vancouver. Emerging playwrights show off their latest works at Granville Island. Call © 604/685-6228 for more information. Mid-May.

Cloverdale Rodeo, Cloverdale, Surrey. Professional cowboys from all over North America compete in roping, bull and bronco riding, barrel racing, and many other events. There are pony rides for kids, great food, and a country-fair atmosphere. For information call © 604/ 576-9461. A long weekend in May (May 16–19, 2003).

International Children's Festival, Vancouver. Activities, plays, music, and crafts for children are featured at this annual event held in Vanier Park on False Creek. For information, call © 604/708-5655. Late May or early June (May 26–June 1, 2003).

June

SlugFest, Richmond Nature Park, 1185 Westminster Hwy (© 604/ 718-6188). Kids compete to find the biggest slug in the park. There are slug races as well as awards for the fastest, slowest, and ugliest slugs. Usually first weekend in June.

VanDusen Flower and Garden Show, Vancouver. Presented at the **VanDusen Botanical Garden,** 5251 Oak St., at 37th Street (© 604/878-9274), this is Vancouver's premier flora gala. Early June.

National Aboriginal Day Community Celebration, Vancouver. This event offers the public an opportunity to learn about Canada's

First Nations cultures. Many events take place at the **Vancouver Aboriginal Friendship Centre,** 1607 E. Hastings at Commercial Street Call (*C* **604/251-4844** for information. June 21.

Alcan Dragon Boat Festival, Vancouver. Traditional dragon-boat racing is a part of the city's cultural scene. Watch the races from False Creek's north shore, where more than 150 local and international teams compete. Four stages of music, dance, and Chinese acrobatics are presented at the **Plaza of Nations** (*C* **604/688-2382**). Third week in June.

DuMaurier International Jazz Festival, Vancouver. More than 800 international jazz and blues players perform at 25 venues ranging from the Orpheum Theatre to the Roundhouse. Many free performances. Call the **Jazz Hotline** (*C* **604/872-5200**) or visit www.jazzvancouver.com for more information. Late June/early July.

Bard on the Beach Shakespeare Festival, Vanier Park. The best backdrop for Shakespeare you will ever see! The Bard's plays are performed in a tent overlooking English Bay. Three different plays are shown every summer. Mid-June to late September, Tuesday through Sunday. Call the box office (*C* **604/739-0559** during the performance season or 604/737-0625 Oct–Apr) or check www.bardonthebeach.org.

Festival d'été francophone de Vancouver, various venues, includes street festival. A 4-day festival celebrating French music from around the world. Performers often include well-known Québec artists. Call (*C* **604/736-9806** for information. Mid-June.

July

Canada Day, Vancouver. Canada Place Pier (*C* **604/775-8687;** www.canadaplace.ca) hosts an all-day celebration that begins with the induction of new Canadian citizens. Music and dance are performed outdoors throughout the day. There's a 21-gun salute at noon, precision aerobatics teams perform overhead during the afternoon, and a nighttime fireworks display on the harbor tops off the festivities. Granville Island, Grouse Mountain, and other locations also host Canada Day events. July 1.

Steveston Salmon Festival, Steveston. A parade, salmon barbecue, special crafts exhibits, and other forms of entertainment take place in this heritage fishing village at the **Gulf of Georgia Cannery National Historic Site** (*C* **604/ 664-9009**). July 1.

Ecomarine Kayak Marathon, Vancouver. Competitors race sea kayaks in the Georgia Strait's open waters. The **Ecomarine Kayak Centre** (*C* **604/689-7575**), at Jericho Beach, hosts the race and can provide details. Mid-July.

Harrison Festival of the Arts (*C* **604/796-3664;** www.harrisonfestival.com) at Harrison Hot Springs, lower mainland. This arts festival in the Fraser River valley, just east of Vancouver, attracts an array of performing artists from around the world. Second week of July.

Dancing on the Edge, Vancouver. Canadian and international dance groups perform modern and classic works at the **Firehall Arts Centre** and other venues. Call (*C* **604/ 689-0691;** www.dancingontheedge. org) for more information. Early to mid-July.

Vancouver Folk Music Festival, Vancouver. International folk music is performed outdoors at Jericho Beach Park. Contact the **Vancouver Folk Music Society** at *©* **604/ 602-9798** for more information, or visit www.thefestival.bc.ca. Second or third weekend in July (July 18–20, 2003.)

Illuminares, Trout Lake Park. Evening lantern procession circling Trout Lake is a phantasmagoric experience. Drums, costumes, fire-breathing apparitions, and lots of elaborate handcrafted lanterns—floating lanterns, kids' lanterns, 10-foot-high four-person lanterns. Various performances start at dusk. For info call *©* **604/879-8611.** Third Saturday of July.

HSBC Power Smart Celebration of Light, Vancouver. Three international fireworks companies compete for a coveted title by launching their best displays accompanied by music over English Bay Beach. Don't miss the big finale on the fourth evening, which attracts as many as 500,000 spectators to the West End. (*Note:* Because of the crowds, the West End's streets and Kits Point are closed to vehicles each night.) Other prime viewing locations include Kitsilano Beach and Jericho Beach. End of July through first week in August.

Vancouver International Comedy Festival, Vancouver. Comedians from all over Canada and the United States perform at a variety of venues around town. Contact Ticketmaster for tickets at *©* **604/ 683-0883** or check www.comedyfest.com for more information. Last week of July, first week in August.

August

Powell Street Festival, Vancouver. An annual festival of Japanese culture includes music, dance, food, and more. Contact the Powell Street Festival Society (*©* **604/739-9388**) for more information. First weekend of August.

Festival Vancouver, Vancouver. The latest addition to the summer series, Festival Vancouver offers more than 50 extraordinary performances of music, including orchestral, choral, chamber, and world music plus opera and jazz. Call *©* **604/221-0080** or check www.festivalvancouver.bc.ca for more information. Early August.

Vancouver Pride Parade, Vancouver. Sponsored by the Vancouver Pride Society, this colorful gay- and lesbian-pride parade covers a route along Denman and Davie streets, beginning at noon. Celebrations at many local gay and lesbian nightclubs take place around town on the same weekend as it is a long weekend for locals (BC Day weekend). For more information, contact the Pride Society's website (*©* **604/687-0955;** www.vanpride.bc.ca). First Sunday in August.

Abbottsford International Air Show, Abbottsford. Barnstorming stuntmen and precision military pilots fly everything from Sopwith Camels to VTOLs and Stealth Bombers. This is one of the biggest air shows in the world. Call *©* **604/ 852-8511** or visit www.abbotsfordairshow.com for more information. Second weekend in August.

Harmony Arts Festival, West Vancouver. This event highlights the talent of North Shore artists, offering free exhibitions, demonstrations, studio tours, theater, concerts, markets, and workshops. Call *©* **604/ 925-7268** or visit www.harmonyarts.net for more information. First and second week of August.

Pacific National Exhibition, Vancouver. The year 2002 was supposed to be the final one for the 10th-largest North American country-style fair, as the city council has voted to convert the grounds to green space. However, the city's favorite fair has been granted a new lease on life and negotiations are under way to obtain a permanent stay at its current location. Offerings include one of North America's best all-wooden roller coasters, many other rides, big-name entertainment, and a demolition derby. Special events include livestock demonstrations, logger sports competitions, fashion shows, and a midway. Contact the Pacific National Exhibition (© **604/253-2311;** www.pne.bc.ca) for more details. Mid-August to Labour Day.

Wooden Boat Festival, Granville Island. This is a free event and a must for wooden-boat aficionados. Call © **604/688-9622.** Last weekend of August.

September

The Fringe—Vancouver's Theatre Festival, Vancouver. This is the best place to catch new theater. Centered around Granville Island and with venues around the Commercial Drive area (the Havana and the Cultch) and Yaletown's Roundhouse, the Fringe Festival features more than 500 innovative and original shows performed by over 100 groups from across Canada and around the world. All plays cost under C$12 (US$7.80). Call © **604/257-0350** or see www. vancouverfringe.com for more info. First and Second week of September.

The North Shore Heritage Weekend, North and West Vancouver A full weekend of walking and boat tours, craft and historic displays, a vintage-car exhibition, and afternoon teas at various locations on the North Shore, from Deep Cove to Horseshoe Bay. Call © **604/ 987-5618** for info. Third weekend in September.

Mid-Autumn Moon Festival, Dr. Sun Yat-sen Garden. This outdoor Chinese celebration includes a lantern festival, storytelling, music, and, of course, moon cakes. For more info call the Garden at © **604/662-3207.** Early to mid-September, according to the lunar cycle (15th day of the 8th month of the Chinese calendar).

October

Vancouver International Film Festival, Vancouver. This highly respected film festival features 250 new works, revivals, and retrospectives, representing filmmakers from 40 countries. Asian films are particularly well represented. Attendance reaches more than 140,000 viewers, not including the stars and celebrities who appear annually. Call © **604/685-0260** or visit www.viff. org for details. Late September and first 2 weeks of October.

Cranberry Harvest Festival, Richmond Nature Park, 1185 Westminster Hwy. (© **604/718-6188**). Cranberries are indigenous to British Columbia's bogs, and the Richmond Nature Park has one of the few remaining wild patches. The Saturday of Canada's Thanksgiving weekend, early October.

Vancouver International Writers and Readers Festival, Vancouver. Public readings conducted by Canadian and international authors as well as writers' workshops take place on Granville Island and at other locations in the lower mainland. Call © **604/681-6330** or try www.writersfest.bc.ca for details. Mid-October.

Parade of Lost Souls, Grandview Park. A bizarre and intriguing procession takes place around Commercial Drive to honor the dead and chase away bad luck. For more information, call ℭ **604/879-8611.** Last Saturday of October.

November

Remembrance Day. Celebrated throughout Canada, this day commemorates Canadian soldiers who gave their lives in war. Vintage military aircraft fly over Stanley Park and Canada Place, and, at noon, a 21-gun salute is fired from Deadman's Island. November 11.

Christmas Craft and Gift Market, Van Dusen Botanical Garden. Popular craft and gift market in a beautiful garden setting. For info, call ℭ **604/878-9274.** November and December.

December

Christmas Carol Ship Parade, Vancouver Harbour. Harbour cruise ships decorated with colorful Christmas lights sail around English Bay, while onboard guests sip cider and sing their way through the canon of Christmas carols. Throughout December.

Festival of Lights, Van Dusen Botanical Garden. Throughout December, the garden is transformed into a magical holiday land with seasonal displays and over 20,000 lights illuminating the garden. Call ℭ **604/878-9274** for info. December.

First Night, Vancouver. Vancouver closes its downtown streets for revelers in the city's New Year's Eve performing-arts festival and alcohol-free party. Events and venues change from year to year. Contact **Tourism Vancouver** at ℭ **604/683-2000** for more information. There's also a party in Victoria. December 31.

VICTORIA & SOUTHERN VANCOUVER ISLAND EVENTS

January

Annual Bald Eagle Count, Goldstream Provincial Park. When the salmon swim up Goldstream Provincial Park's spawning streams, the tourists aren't the only ones who come to watch. More than 3,000 bald eagles take up residence to feed on the salmon. The salmon run starts in October and the eagles arrive shortly thereafter. The eagle count usually takes place in mid- to late January when the numbers peak. Throughout December and January, the park offers educational programs, displays, and guest speakers. Call ℭ **250/478-9414** for exact dates and events.

Robert Burns's Birthday. Celebrating the birthday of the great Scottish poet, events around Victoria and Vancouver include Scottish dancing, piping, and feasts of haggis. Appropriate to the day, most events take place in Victoria's pubs. January 25.

February

Chinese New Year, Chinatown, Victoria. See "Vancouver Events," above. Late January or early February (Feb 2 in 2003).

Trumpeter Swan Festival, Comox Valley. A weeklong festival celebrates these magnificent white birds that gather in the Comox Valley. Check with the Vancouver Island tourist office (ℭ **250/754-3500**) for exact dates.

Flower Count, Victoria (ℭ **250/383-7191**). So many flowers bloom in Victoria and the surrounding area that the city holds an annual flower count. The third week in February is a great time to see the city as it comes alive in vibrant color.

March

Pacific Rim Whale Festival, Tofino, Ucluelet, and Pacific Rim National Park. Every spring, more than 20,000 gray whales migrate past this coastline, attracting visitors from all over the world to Vancouver Island's west coast beaches. In celebration of the gray whale, orca, humpback, and other whales in the area, the event features live crab races, storytelling, parades, art shows, Whales in the Park guided whale-spotting hikes, and whale-watching boat excursions. Call ☏ **250/726-4641** for more information. Mid-March to early April.

April

Annual Brant Wildlife Festival, Qualicum Beach (☏ **250/752-9171;** www.brantfestival.bc.ca). This is a 3-day celebration of the annual black brant migration to the area (20,000 birds). Guided walks through old-growth forest and salt- and freshwater marshes that are home to hundreds of bird species are a true feast for birders. Art, photography, and carving exhibitions as well as birding competitions highlight the event. Early to mid-April.

TerrifVic Dixieland Jazz Party, Victoria (☏ **250/953-2011**). The city hosts bands from the United States, Europe, and Latin America that perform swing, Dixieland, honky-tonk, fusion, and improv before dedicated audiences at venues all over Victoria. Mid-April.

May

Harbour Festival, Victoria. This 10-day festival takes place in the downtown district and features heritage walks, entertainment, music, and more. For information call ☏ **250/953-2033.** Last week of May.

Swiftsure Weekend. International sailing races make quite a spectacular sight on the waters around Victoria. For information call ☏ **250/953-2033.** End of May.

June

Jazz Fest International, Victoria (☏ **250/388-4423**). Jazz, swing, bebop, fusion, and improv artists from around the world perform at various venues around Victoria during this 10-day festival. Check www.vicjazz.bc.ca for the line-up. Last 10 days of June.

Folkfest, Victoria (☏ **250/388-4728**). This practically free (C$3/US$1.95 for the entire event) 8-day world-beat music festival presents daily performances from 11:30am to 11:30pm. Main venues are the Inner Harbour and Market Square in downtown Victoria. End of June or early July.

July

Canada Day, Victoria. The provincial capital celebrates this national holiday with events centered on the Inner Harbour, including music, food, and fireworks. Every city on Vancouver Island has similar festivities, though not as grand as those in Victoria itself. July 1.

Bathtub Race, Nanaimo. Competitors design and race what are perhaps the world's fastest motorized bathtubs. Contact the **Nanaimo Tourism Association** (☏ **800/663-7337**) for more information. End of July.

Victoria Shakespeare Festival, Victoria (☏ **250/360-0234**). Performances of the Bard's works take place around the Inner Harbour from the second week in July to the third week in August.

August

First Peoples Festival, Victoria (☏ **250/384-3211** or 250/953-3557). This free event highlights the culture and heritage of the Pacific Northwest First Nations peoples, featuring dances, performances, carving demonstrations, and heritage displays at the Royal British Columbia Museum. First weekend in August.

Canadian International Dragon Boat Festival, Victoria. Traditional dragon-boat races take place in the Inner Harbour, where 120 local and international teams compete. Mid-August.

September

Malahat Challenge (Vintage Car Rally), Nanaimo. Competitors race from Victoria to Nanaimo in an amazing array of classic chassis. An end-of-summer jazz festival occurs at the finish line in Nanaimo. For info, call the Nanaimo Tourism Association at © **800/663-7337.** Early September.

October

Royal Victorian Marathon, Victoria (© **250/658-0951,** www. royalvictoriamarathon.com). This annual race attracts runners from around the world (half-marathon course available too). The air is fresh, the temperature is usually just cool enough, and the course consists of gentle ups and downs. Early October (Canadian Thanksgiving weekend).

November

The Great Canadian Beer Festival, Victoria. Featuring samples from the province's best microbreweries, this event is held at the Victoria Conference Centre, 720 Douglas St. (© **250/952-0360**). Second week in November.

Remembrance Day. See "Vancouver Events," above. November 11.

December

Merrython Fun Run, Victoria (© **250/953-2033**). An annual event for nearly 20 years, this 10km (6¼-mile) race loops through downtown Victoria. Mid-December.

First Night. See "Vancouver Events," above. Call **Tourism Victoria** at © **250/953-2033** for more details. December 31.

4 Insurance & Safety

INSURANCE

American travelers should review their **health insurance** coverage for travel outside the United States. If you are not adequately covered, take advantage of one of the many health and accident plans that charge a daily rate for the term of your trip. They include the ones offered by Thomas Cook, the American Automobile Association (AAA), and Mutual of Omaha. Generally, plans cost about US$3 per day for up to 90 days. Canada has health care comparable in quality to that of the United States, but it is also comparably priced, and even for emergency services, insurance or other payment information will be required.

Auto insurance is compulsory in British Columbia. Basic coverage consists of "no-fault" accident and C$200,000 (US$130,000) third-party legal liability coverage. If you plan to drive in Canada, check with your insurance company to make sure that your policy meets this requirement. Always carry your insurance card, your vehicle registration, and your driver's license in case you have an accident. AAA also offers low-cost travel and auto insurance for its members. If you are a member and don't have adequate insurance, take advantage of this benefit.

Note: If you rent a car in British Columbia and plan to take it across the border into the U.S., make sure you let your rental agency know for insurance purposes.

Wallach & Company, 107 W. Federal St., P.O. Box 480, Middleburg, VA 20118 (© **800/237-6615;**

Tips **Just in Case . . .**

Even though southwestern British Columbia has never had a major shake, it is situated in an earthquake zone and has experienced many minor tremors. Check the exit and emergency information in your hotel's guest-services book. It will advise you where to go and how to exit after the tremors stop. The front pages of the Vancouver Yellow Pages also offer a quick course in emergency procedures. If you feel a tremor, get under a table or into a doorway.

---

www.wallach.com), offers a comprehensive travel policy that includes trip-cancellation coverage and emergency assistance in the event of illness, accident, or loss.

5 Tips for Travelers with Special Needs

FOR TRAVELERS WITH DISABILITIES

According to *We're Accessible,* a newsletter for travelers with disabilities, Vancouver is "the most accessible city in the world." There are more than 14,000 sidewalk wheelchair ramps, and motorized wheelchairs are a common sight in the downtown area. The stairs along Robson Square have built-in ramps, and most major attractions and venues have ramps or level walkways for easy access. Many Vancouver hotels have at least partial wheelchair accessibility, if not rooms built completely to suit. Most Sky-Train stations and the SeaBus are wheelchair accessible, and most bus routes are lift equipped. For more information about accessible public transportation, contact **Translink** (© **604/953-3333;** www.translink. bc.ca; or phone the department of accessible transit at 604/540-3400) and ask for its brochure, *Rider's Guide to Accessible Transit.*

Many downtown hotels are also equipping rooms with visual smoke alarms and other facilities for hearing-impaired guests. You'll also notice that downtown crosswalks have beeping alert signs to guide visually impaired pedestrians.

Victoria is, for the most part, similarly accessible. Nearly all Victoria hotels have rooms equipped to accommodate travelers with special needs, and downtown sidewalks are equipped with ramps, though very few intersections have beeping crosswalk signals for the visually impaired. The **Victoria Regional Transit System** (© **250/ 382-6161**) publishes the *Rider's Guide,* which includes complete information on which bus routes are equipped with lifts and/or low floors. The most notable spot in Victoria that isn't readily wheelchair accessible is the promenade along the water's edge in the Inner Harbour, which has only one rather challenging ramp near the Pacific Undersea Gardens.

FOR GAY & LESBIAN TRAVELERS

What San Francisco is to the United States, Vancouver is to Canada—the laid-back town on the coast with a large, thriving gay community. Much of the social activity centers in the West End—particularly Denman and Davie streets—where many gay singles and couples live. The best way to find out what's going on is to pick up a copy of the biweekly gay and lesbian tabloid, *Xtra! West,* which is available throughout the West End. To obtain a copy ahead of time, contact *Xtra! West,* 501–1033 Davie St., Vancouver, B.C. V6E 1M7 (© **604/684-9696**). Also check out the **Vancouver Pride Society** website (www.vanpride.bc.ca) for upcoming special events, including the annual Vancouver Pride Parade. Otherwise, here are some suggestions: Book a room at the West End Guest House or the Sylvia Hotel (see chapter 4, "Where to Stay in Vancouver") and head over to one of the numerous West End and downtown clubs such as the Odyssey (see chapter 9, "Vancouver After Dark"), or have coffee at Delaney's on Denman Street or at the Edge on Davie Street.

FOR SENIORS

Seniors often qualify for discounts at hotels and attractions and on public transit throughout Vancouver and Victoria. Make a habit of asking. You'll be pleasantly surprised at the number of discounts for which you're eligible. Discount transit passes for persons over 65 (with proof of age) may be purchased at shops in Vancouver and Victoria that display a FARE-DEALER SIGN (Safeway, 7-Eleven, and most newsstands). To locate a **Fare-Dealer vendor,** contact BC Transit (© **604/521-0400**). If you or your mate is over 50 and you are not already a member of the **AARP** (3200 E. Carson, Lakewood, CA 90712; © **800/424-3410;** www.aarp.org), consider joining. The AARP card is valuable for additional restaurant and travel bargains throughout North America.

FOR FAMILIES

Vancouver and Victoria are two of the most child-friendly, cosmopolitan cities around. Where else would you find a Kids Market that's filled with children's stores and is located next to a free water park that's equipped with water guns and changing rooms? In addition to the standard attractions and sights, you'll find a lot of adventurous, outdoor, and free stuff that both you and your kids will enjoy (see "Especially for Kids" in chapters 6 and 13). You can try entertaining restaurants that aren't cafeteria-style or fast-food establishments, but are decidedly kid-friendly. Some hotels even offer milk and cookies to kids for evening snacks, plus special menus and child-size terry robes.

FOR STUDENTS

This is definitely a student-oriented area. The University of British Columbia (UBC) in the Point Grey area, Burnaby's Simon Fraser University, and a number of smaller schools contribute to the enormous student population. Student travelers have a lot of free and inexpensive entertainment options, both day and night. The nightlife is active, centering around Yaletown, Granville Street, the West End, and Kitsilano. Pick up a copy of *The Georgia Straight* to find out what's happening. Many attractions and theaters offer discounts if you have your student ID with you. While many establishments will accept a school ID, the surest way to obtain student discounts is with an International Student Identity Card (ISIC), which is available to any full-time high-school or college student from the **Council on International Educational Exchange (CIEE),** 205 E. 42nd St., New York, NY 10017 (© **212/822-2700**), or from your local campus student society. The CIEE has offices in major U.S. cities. To find the location nearest you, call © **800/438-2643** or check the website www.ciee.org.

In Victoria, the University of Victoria (referred to locally as "U. Vic.") has a sprawling campus just east of downtown. The student population accounts for most, if not all, of Victoria's nightlife. Student discounts abound. Pick up a copy of Victoria's weekly paper, *Monday Magazine* (which comes out on Thurs), for current nightclub listings.

6 Getting to Vancouver

BY PLANE

THE MAJOR AIRLINES The Open Skies agreement between the United States and Canada has made flying to Vancouver easier than ever. Daily direct flights between major U.S. cities and Vancouver are offered by **Air Canada** (✆ 888/247-2262 or 800/661-3936), **United Airlines** (✆ 800/241-6522), **American Airlines** (✆ 800/433-7300), **Continental** (✆ 800/231-0856), and **Northwest Airlines** (✆ 800/447-4747). Direct flights on major carriers serve Phoenix, Dallas, New York, Houston, Minneapolis, Reno, San Francisco, and many other cities.

For domestic flights, travelers are left only a few options. Air Canada (✆ **888/247-2262**) operates flights to Vancouver and Victoria from all major Canadian cities, easily connecting with some of the regional airlines. The best and cheapest option for travelers in Western Canada is **Westjet** (✆ **888/WEST-JET** or 800/538-5696). Tickets can also be purchased online at www.westjet.com. Westjet operates regular flights from Vancouver and Victoria to Prince George, Kelowna, Edmonton, Calgary and further afield.

Non-U.S. and non-Canadian travelers can take advantage of the **Visit USA** air passes offered by **Continental** (✆ **800/231-0856**) and similar coupons from **Air Canada** (✆ **800/ 776-3000**). These tickets must be purchased outside North America in conjunction with an international fare. For roughly an additional US$439, you can get three flight coupons that allow you to fly anywhere on the continent (price varies seasonally). You can buy up to a maximum of nine coupons for US$769. Low-season discounts are also available.

NEW AIR TRAVEL SECURITY MEASURES

In the wake of the terrorist attacks of September 11, 2001, the airline industry began implementing sweeping security measures in airports. Expect a lengthy check-in process and extensive delays. Although regulations vary from airline to airline, you can expedite the process by taking the following steps:

- **Arrive early.** Arrive at the airport at least 2 hours before your scheduled flight.
- **Try not to drive your car to the airport.** Parking and curbside access to the terminal may be limited. Call ahead and check.
- **Don't count on curbside check-in.** Some airlines and airports have stopped curbside check-in altogether, whereas others offer it on a limited basis. For up-to-date information on specific regulations and implementations, check with the individual airline.
- **Be sure to carry plenty of documentation.** A government-issued photo ID (federal, state, or local) is now required. You may need to show this at various checkpoints. With an E-ticket, you may be required to have with you printed confirmation of purchase, and perhaps even the credit card with which you bought your ticket (see "All about E-Ticketing," below). This varies from airline to airline, so call ahead to make sure you have the proper documentation. And be sure that your ID is **up-to-date:** an expired driver's license, for example, may keep you from boarding the plane altogether.

Tips What You Can Carry On—And What You Can't

The Transportation Security Administration (TSA), the U.S. government agency that now handles all aspects of airport security, has devised new restrictions for carry-on baggage, not only to expedite the screening process but to prevent potential weapons from passing through airport security. Passengers are now limited to bringing just one carry-on bag and one personal item onto the aircraft (previous regulations allowed two carry-on bags and one personal item, like a briefcase or a purse). For more information, go to the TSA's website, www.tsa.gov. The agency has released an updated list of items passengers are not allowed to carry onto an aircraft:

Not permitted: knives and box cutters, corkscrews, straight razors, metal scissors, golf clubs, baseball bats, pool cues, hockey sticks, ski poles, ice picks.

Permitted: nail clippers, nail files, tweezers, eyelash curlers, safety razors (including disposable razors), syringes (with documented proof of medical need), walking canes and umbrellas (must be inspected first).

The airline you fly may have **additional restrictions** on items you can and cannot carry on board. Call ahead to avoid problems.

- **Know what you can carry on— and what you can't.** Travelers in the United States are now limited to one carry-on bag, plus one personal bag (such as a purse or a briefcase). The Transportation Security Administration (TSA) has also issued a list of newly restricted carry-on items; see the box "What You Can Carry On— and What You Can't."
- **Prepare to be searched.** Expect spot-checks. Electronic items, such as a laptop or cellphone, should be readied for additional screening. Limit the metal items you wear on your person.
- **It's no joke.** When a check-in agent asks if someone other than you packed your bag, don't decide that this is the time to be funny. The agents will not hesitate to call an alarm.
- **No ticket, no gate access.** Only ticketed passengers will be allowed beyond the screener checkpoints, except for those people with specific medical or parental needs.

FLYING FOR LESS: TIPS FOR GETTING THE BEST AIRFARE

Passengers within the same airplane cabin are rarely paying the same fare. Business travelers who need to purchase tickets at the last minute, change their itinerary at a moment's notice, or get home for the weekend pay the premium rate. Passengers who can book their ticket long in advance, who can stay over Saturday night, or who are willing to travel on a Tuesday, Wednesday, or Thursday after 7pm, will pay a fraction of the full fare. On many flights, even the shortest hops, the full fare is close to $1,000 or more, while a 7- or 14-day advance purchase ticket may cost less than half that amount. Here are a few other easy ways to save.

- Airlines periodically lower prices on their most popular routes.

Check the travel section of your Sunday newspaper for advertised discounts or call the airlines directly and ask if any **promotional rates** or special fares are available. You'll almost never see a sale during the peak summer vacation months of July and August, or during the Thanksgiving or Christmas seasons; but in periods of low-volume travel, you should pay no more than US$400 for a domestic cross-country flight. If your schedule is flexible, say so, and ask if you can secure a cheaper fare by staying an extra day, by flying midweek, or by flying at less-trafficked hours. If you already hold a ticket when a sale breaks, it may even pay to exchange your ticket, which usually incurs a US$100 to US$150 charge.

Note: The lowest-priced fares are often nonrefundable, require advance purchase of 1 to 3 weeks and a certain length of stay, and carry penalties for changing dates of travel.

- **Consolidators,** also known as bucket shops, are a good place to find low fares. Consolidators buy seats in bulk from the airlines and then sell them back to the public at prices usually below even the airlines' discounted rates. Their small ads usually run in Sunday newspaper travel sections. And before you pay, request a confirmation number from the consolidator and then call the airline to confirm your seat. Be aware that bucket shop tickets are usually nonrefundable or rigged with stiff cancellation penalties, often as high as 50% to 75% of the ticket price. Protect yourself by paying with a credit card rather than cash. Keep in mind that if there's an airline sale going on, or if it's high season, you can often get the same or better rates by contacting the airlines directly, so do some comparison shopping before you buy. Also check out the name of the airline; you may not want to fly on some obscure Third World airline, even if you're saving $10. And check whether you're flying on a charter or a scheduled airline; the latter is more expensive but more reliable. **Council Travel** (℃ **800/226-8624;** www.council travel.com) and **STA Travel** (℃ **800/781-4040;** www.sta travel.com) cater especially to young travelers, but their bargain-basement prices are available to people of all ages. **The TravelHub** (℃ **888/AIR-FARE;** www.travel hub.com) represents nearly 1,000 travel agencies, many of whom offer consolidator and discount fares. Other reliable consolidators include **1-800-FLY-CHEAP** (www.1800flycheap.com); **TFI Tours International** (℃ **800-745-8000** or 212/736-1140; www.lowestairprice.com), which serves as a clearinghouse for unused seats; or "rebators" such as **Travel Avenue** (℃ **800/333-3335;** www.travelavenue.com) and the **Smart Traveller** (℃ **800/448-3338** in the U.S. or 305/448-3338), which rebate part of their commissions to you.

- Search the **Internet** for cheap fares. Great last-minute deals are available through free weekly e-mail services provided directly by the airlines. See "Planning Your Trip Online," below, for more information.

- Look into courier **flights**—though they are usually not available on domestic flights. These companies hire couriers to hand-deliver packages or mail, and use your luggage allowance for themselves; in return, you get a deeply discounted ticket—for example, US$300 round-trip to Europe in winter. Flights often become available at the last minute, so check in often. **Halbart Express** has offices in New York (℃ **718-656-8189**), Los Angeles (℃ **310-417-9790**), and Miami (℃ **305-593-0260**). **Jupiter Air** (www.jupiter air.com) has offices in New York (℃ **718-656-6050**), Los Angeles

(℃ **310-670-5123**), and San Francisco (℃ **650-697-1773**).

- Join a travel club such as **Moment's Notice** (℃ **718/234-6295;** www.moments-notice. com) or **Sears Discount Travel Club** (℃ **800/433-9383,** or 800/255-1487 to join; www.trav-elersadvantage.com), which supply unsold tickets at discounted prices. You pay an annual membership fee to get the club's hot line number. Of course, you're limited to what's available, so you have to be flexible.

- Join frequent-flier clubs. It's best to accrue miles on one program, so you can rack up free flights and achieve elite status faster. But it makes sense to open as many accounts as possible, no matter how seldom you fly a particular airline. It's free, and you'll get the best choice of seats, faster response to phone inquiries, and prompter service if your luggage is stolen, your flight is canceled or delayed, or if you want to change your seat.

BY TRAIN

VIA Rail Canada, 1150 Station St., Vancouver (℃ **800/561-8630;** www. viarail.ca), connects with Amtrak at Winnipeg, Manitoba. From there, you travel on a spectacular route that runs between Calgary and Vancouver. Lake Louise's beautiful alpine scenery is just part of this enjoyable journey. **Amtrak** (℃ **800/872-7245;** www.amtrak. com) has regular service from Seattle and also has a direct route from San Diego to Vancouver. It stops at all major U.S. West Coast cities and takes a little under 2 days to complete the entire journey. Fares are US$190. Substantial seasonal discounts are available. Travelers can also purchase a 30-day North America **Railpass** for US$475 to US$675 at peak season. The pass can be used for rail connections to Vancouver.

> **Tips Cancelled Plans**
>
> If your flight is cancelled, don't book a new fare at the ticket counter. Find the nearest phone and call the airline directly to reschedule. You'll be relaxing while other passengers are still standing in line.

BC Rail, 1311 W. First St., North Vancouver (© 604/631-3500; www.bcrail.com), also connects Vancouver to Whistler and other cities in the province. The trip to Whistler is 2½ hours each way, and the fare includes breakfast or dinner. A one-way ticket costs C$49 (US$32) for adults, C$27 (US$18) seniors and children.

BY BUS

Greyhound Bus Lines (© 604/482-8747; www.greyhound.com) and **Pacific Coach Lines** (© 604/662-8074; www.pacificcoach.com) have their terminals at the Pacific Central Station, 1150 Station St. Greyhound Canada's **Canada Pass** offers 15 or 30 days of unlimited travel for C$399 to C$499 (US$259–US$324). Pacific Coach Lines provides service between Vancouver and Victoria. The cost is C$29 (US$19) one-way per adult and includes the ferry; daily departures are between 5:45am and 7:45pm. Pacific Coach Lines will also pick up passengers from most downtown hotels. Call © 604/662-8074 to reserve. **Quick Coach Lines** (© 604/940-4428) connects Vancouver to the Seattle–Tacoma International Airport. The bus leaves from Vancouver's Sandman Inn, 180 W. Georgia St., can pick up passengers from most major hotels and stops at the Vancouver International Airport. The 4½-hour ride costs C$44 (US$29) one-way or C$79 (US$51) round-trip.

BY CAR

You'll probably be driving into Vancouver along one of two routes. **U.S.**

Interstate 5 from Seattle becomes **Highway 99** when you cross the border at the Peace Arch. The 210km (130-mile) drive takes about 2½ hours. You'll drive through the cities of White Rock, Delta, and Richmond, pass under the Fraser River through the George Massey Tunnel, and cross the Oak Street Bridge. The highway ends there and becomes Oak Street, a very busy urban thoroughfare. Turn left onto 70th Avenue. (A small sign suspended above the left lane at the intersection of Oak St. and 70th Ave. reads CITY CENTRE.) Six blocks later, turn right onto Granville Street. This street heads directly into downtown Vancouver on the Granville Street Bridge.

Trans-Canada Highway 1 is a limited-access freeway running all the way to Vancouver's eastern boundary, where it crosses the Second Narrows bridge to North Vancouver. When traveling on Highway 1 from the east, exit at Cassiar Street and turn left at the first light onto Hastings Street (Hwy. 7A), which is adjacent to Exhibition Park. Follow Hastings Street 6.4km (4 miles) into downtown. When coming to Vancouver from Whistler or parts north, take Exit 13 (the sign says TAYLOR WAY, BRIDGE TO VANCOUVER) and cross the Lions Gate Bridge into Vancouver's West End.

BY SHIP & FERRY

The **Canada Place** cruise-ship terminal at the base of Burrard Street (© 604/665-9085) is a city landmark. Topped by five eye-catching white Teflon sails, Canada Place Pier juts out into the Burrard Inlet and is at the edge of the downtown financial district. **Princess Cruises, Holland America, Royal Caribbean, Crystal Cruises, Norwegian Cruise Lines, World Explorer Majesty Cruise Line,** and **Hanseatic, Seabourn,** and **Carnival** cruise lines dock at Canada Place and the nearby Ballantyne Pier to board passengers headed for Alaska via British Columbia's Inside Passage. They carry over 1,700,000 passengers annually on their nearly 350 Vancouver–Alaska cruises. Public-transit buses and taxis greet new arrivals, but you can also easily walk to many major hotels, including the Pan-Pacific, Waterfront Centre, and Hotel Vancouver. (If you're considering an Alaska cruise, late May and all of June generally offer the best weather, the most daylight, and the best sightseeing opportunities.)

BC Ferries (© 888/223-3779 or 250/386-3431; www.bcferries.bc.ca) has three Victoria–Vancouver routes. Its large ferries offer onboard facilities such as restaurants, snack bars, gift shops, business-center desks with modem connections, and indoor lounges. The one-way fare in peak season is C$9.50 (US$6.15) for adults, C$4.75 (US$3.10) for children 5 to 11, and C$35(US$23) per car. Children under 5 ride free. In the summer it is advisable to reserve a space when traveling with a vehicle, especially on long weekends and to and from the Gulf Islands. Call BC Ferries reservations at © **888/724-5223.**

The most direct route between the cities is the **Tsawwassen–Swartz Bay ferry,** which operates daily between 7am and 9pm. Ferries run every 2 hours. Check for extra sailings on holidays or peak travel season. The actual crossing takes 95 minutes. However, schedule an extra 2 hours for travel to and from both ferry terminals, including waiting time at the docks. Driving distance from Tsawwassen to Vancouver is about 12 miles. Take Highway 17 from Tsawwassen until it merges with Highway 99 just before the George Massey Tunnel; then follow the driving directions to Vancouver given in "By Car," above. If you prefer to travel by public transit, BC Transit has regular bus service to both terminals. From Swartz Bay, there's regular bus service to Victoria.

The **Mid-Island Express** operates between Tsawwassen and Duke Point, just south of Nanaimo. The 2-hour crossing runs eight times daily between 5:15am and 10:45pm.

The **Horseshoe Bay–Nanaimo ferry** has eight daily sailings, leaving Horseshoe Bay near West Vancouver and arriving 95 minutes later in Nanaimo. From there, passengers bound for Victoria board the E&N Railiner (see "By Train" under "Getting to Victoria," below) or drive south to Victoria via the Island Highway (Hwy. 1).

To reach Vancouver from Horseshoe Bay, take the Trans-Canada Highway (Highways 1 and 99) east and then take Exit 13 (Taylor Way) to the Lions Gate Bridge and downtown Vancouver's West End.

BY PACKAGE TOUR

Air Canada (© 888/247-2262) offers a number of fly/drive packages. And **SNV International,** 402–1045 Howe St., Vancouver (© **604/ 683-5101**), specializes in vacation packages to Vancouver and Victoria.

7 Getting to Victoria

BY PLANE

For more on air travel security and tips on getting reduced airfare, please see section 6, "Getting to Vancouver," above.

THE MAJOR AIRLINES Air Canada (© **888/247-2262** or

800/661-3936) and **Horizon Air** (© **800/547-9308**) offer direct connections from Seattle, Vancouver, Portland, Calgary, Edmonton, Saskatoon, Winnipeg, and Toronto. **Westjet's** regular flights connect to Kelowna, Prince George, Calgary, Edmonton, and other destinations (© **888/WEST-JET**; www.westjet. com).

Provincial commuter airlines, including floatplanes that land in Victoria's Inner Harbour and helicopters, service the city as well. They include **Air BC** (can be reached through Air Canada at © 888/247-2262); **Harbour Air Sea Planes** (© 604/688-1277); **Pacific Spirit Air** (also known as Tofino Air; © 800/665-2359), which serves Victoria in addition to the south and north Gulf Islands from Vancouver Airport and Tofino; **Kenmore Air** (© 800/543-9595); and **Helijet Airways** (© 250/382-6222 in Victoria, or 604/273-1414 in Vancouver).

BY TRAIN

Travelers on the **Horseshoe Bay–Nanaimo ferry** can board a train that winds down the Cowichan River Valley through Goldstream Provincial Park into Victoria. The VIA Rail's **E&N Railiner** leaves from Nanaimo at 3:37pm Monday through Saturday and arrives in Victoria at 6pm. On Sunday, it departs Nanaimo at 7:07pm and arrives in Victoria at 9:40pm. The Victoria **E&N Station,** 450 Pandora Ave. (© **800/561-8630** in Canada), is near the Johnson Street Bridge. The one-way fare from Nanaimo to Victoria is C$24 (US$16) for adults, C$22 (US$14) for seniors, youth and children C$12 to C$15 (US$7.80–US$9.75). Seven-day advance-purchase discounts and other specials are available. *Note:* This train service was slated to be cut; please check prior to planning your trip.

BY BUS

Pacific Coach Lines (© **800/661-1725** in Canada, or 604/662-8074; www.pacificcoach.com) operates bus service between Vancouver and Victoria. The 4-hour trip from the Vancouver bus terminal (Pacific Central Station, 1150 Terminal Ave.) to the Victoria Depot (710 Douglas St.) includes passage on the Tsawwassen–Swartz Bay ferry and costs C$29 (US$19) one-way per adult. Departures are daily between 5:45am and 7:45pm.

BY SHIP & FERRY

See "By Ship & Ferry" under "Getting to Vancouver," above, for information about BC Ferries service between Victoria and Vancouver.

BC Ferries also provides year-round service on 24 routes throughout the province, including the Gulf Islands and the Inside Passage. Most vessels have a restaurant, snack bar, gift shop, play area, game arcade, and executive center.

Three ferry services offer daily, year-round connections between Port Angeles, Bellingham, or Seattle, Washington, and Victoria. **Black Ball Transport** (© **250/386-2202** in Victoria, or 360/457-4491 in Port Angeles) operates between Port Angeles and Victoria. One-way fares are C$13 (US$8.45) for adults, C$48 (US$31) for a car and driver (rates are based on U.S.-dollar fare). *Note:* no credit cards or debit cards accepted. The crossing takes 1½ hours and there are four crossings per day in the summer (mid-June to Sept), and usually two sailings a day throughout the rest of the year (with a short two-week closure in Jan).

Clipper Navigation, 1000A Wharf St., Victoria (© **800/288-2535** in North America, or 250/382-8100 in Victoria), operates the *Victoria Clipper,* a high-speed catamaran that runs between Seattle and Victoria with some sailings stopping in the San Juan Islands. The *Victoria Clipper* is a passenger-only service; sailing time is approximately 3 hours with daily sailings. One-way adult fares are C$103 to C$117 (US$67–US$76), round-trip C$123 to C$195 (US$80–US$127).

June through October, Victoria San Juan Cruises' MV *Victoria Star* (© **800/443-4552** in North America, or 360/738-8099) departs the Fairhaven Terminal in Bellingham, Washington, at 9am and arrives in Victoria at noon. It departs Victoria at 5pm, arriving in Bellingham at 8pm.

One-way fares are C$77 (US$50) one-way or C$139 (US$90) round-trip for an adult and include a free salmon dinner on the return Victoria–Bellingham run. No meal is included with the trip from Bellingham to Victoria, but there is a snack bar with coffee service onboard.

Note: Remember to bring appropriate photo ID for the ferry services as all passengers go through Customs on international ferry trips.

BY PACKAGE TOUR
See "By Package Tour" under "Getting to Vancouver," above.

8 Planning Your Trip Online

With a mouse, a modem, and a certain do-it-yourself determination, Internet users can tap into the same travel-planning databases that were once accessible only to travel agents. Sites such as **Travelocity, Expedia,** and **Orbitz** allow consumers to comparison shop for airfares, book flights, learn of last-minute bargains, and reserve hotel rooms and rental cars.

But don't fire your travel agent just yet. Although online booking sites offer tips and hard data to help you bargain shop, they cannot endow you with the hard-earned experience that makes a seasoned, reliable travel agent an invaluable resource, even in the Internet age. And for consumers with a complex itinerary, a trusty travel agent is still the best way to arrange the most direct flights to and from the best airports.

Still, there's no denying the Internet's emergence as a powerful tool in researching and plotting travel time. The benefits of researching your trip online can be well worth the effort:

•**Last-minute specials,** known as "E-savers," such as weekend deals or Internet-only fares, are offered by airlines to fill empty seats. Most of these are announced on Tuesday or Wednesday and must be purchased online. They are only valid for travel that weekend, but some can be booked weeks or months in advance. Sign up for weekly e-mail alerts at airline websites (p. 41) or check mega-sites that compile comprehensive lists of E-savers, such as Smarter Living (www.smarterliving.com) or Web Flyer (www.webflyer.com).

• Some sites will send you **e-mail notification** when a cheap fare becomes available to your favorite destination. Some will also tell you when fares to a particular destination are lowest.

• The best of the travel planning sites are now **highly personalized;** they track your frequent-flier miles and store your seating and meal preferences, tentative itineraries, and credit-card information, letting you plan trips or check agendas quickly.

• All major airlines offer **incentives**—bonus frequent-flier miles, Internet-only discounts, sometimes even free cellphone rentals—when you purchase online or buy an E-ticket.

• Advances in mobile technology provide business travelers and

---

Frommers.com: The Complete Travel Resource

For an excellent travel-planning resource, we highly recommend **Frommers.com** (www.frommers.com). We're a little biased, of course, but we guarantee that you'll find the travel tips, reviews, monthly vacation giveaways, and online-booking capabilities thoroughly indispensable. Among the special features are our popular **Message Boards,** where Frommer's readers post queries and share advice (sometimes even our authors show up to answer questions); **Frommers.com Newsletter,** for the latest travel bargains and inside travel secrets; and Frommer's **Destinations Section,** where you'll get expert travel tips, hotel and dining recommendations, and advice on the sights to see for more than 2,500 destinations around the globe. When your research is done, the **Online Reservation System** (www.frommers.com/book_a_trip) takes you to Frommer's favorite sites for booking your vacation at affordable prices.

---

other frequent travelers with **the ability to check flight status, change plans, or get specific directions** from handheld computing devices, mobile phones, and pagers. Some sites will e-mail or page a passenger if a flight is delayed.

TRAVEL PLANNING & BOOKING SITES

The best travel planning and booking sites cast a wide net, offering domestic and international flights, hotel and rental-car bookings, plus news, destination information, and deals on cruises and vacation packages. Keep in mind that free (one-time) registration is often required for booking. Because several airlines are no longer willing to pay commissions on tickets sold by online travel agencies, be aware that these online agencies will either charge a $10 surcharge if you book a ticket on that carrier—or neglect to offer those air carriers' offerings.

The sites in this section are not intended to be a comprehensive list, but rather a discriminating selection to get you started. Recognition is given to sites based on their content value and ease of use and is not paid for—unlike some website rankings,

which are based on payment. *Remember:* This is a press-time snapshot of leading websites—some undoubtedly will have evolved or moved by the time you read this.

- **Travelocity** (www.travelocity.com or http://frommers.travelocity.com) and **Expedia** (www.expedia.com) are the most longstanding and reputable sites, each offering excellent selections and searches for complete vacation packages. Travelers search by destination and dates coupled with how much they are willing to spend.

- The latest buzz in the online travel world is about **Orbitz** (www.orbitz.com), a site launched by United, Delta, Northwest, American, and Continental airlines. It shows all possible fares for your desired trip, offering fares lower than those available through travel agents.

- **Qixo** (www.qixo.com) is another powerful search engine that allows you to search for flights and hotel rooms on 20 other travel-planning sites (such as Travelocity) at once. Qixo sorts results by price, after which you can book your travel directly through the site.

SMART E-SHOPPING

The savvy traveler is one armed with good information. Here are a few tips to help you navigate the Internet successfully and safely.

- **Know when sales start.** Last-minute deals may vanish in minutes. If you have a favorite booking site or airline, find out when last-minute deals are released to the public.
- **Shop around.** Compare results from different sites and airlines—and against a travel agent's best fare, if you can. If possible, try a range of times and alternate airports before you make a purchase.
- **Follow the rules of the trade.** Book in advance, and choose an off-peak time and date if possible. Some sites will tell you when fares to a particular destination tend to be cheapest.
- **Stay secure.** Book only through secure sites (some airline sites are not secure). Look for a key icon (Netscape) or a padlock (Internet Explorer) at the bottom of your Web browser before you enter credit card information or other personal data.
- **Avoid online auctions.** Sites that auction airline tickets and frequent-flier miles are the number-one perpetrators of Internet fraud, according to the National Consumers League.
- **Maintain a paper trail.** If you book an E-ticket, print out a confirmation, or write down your confirmation number, and keep it safe and accessible—or your trip could be a virtual one!

BY AIR: TRANSPORTATION SITES

Below are the websites for the major airlines operating throughout North America. These sites offer schedules and booking, and most of the airlines have E-saver alerts for weekend deals and late-breaking bargains.

- **Air Canada.** www.aircanada.com
- **America West.** www.americawest.com
- **American Airlines.** www.aa.com
- **Continental Airlines.** www.continental.com
- **Delta.** www.delta.com
- **Horizon Air.** www.horizonair.com
- **Northwest Airlines.** www.nwa.com
- **United Airlines.** www.ual.com
- **WestJet.** www.westjet.com

3

Getting to Know Vancouver

Losing yourself wandering around a fascinating new neighborhood is part of the joy of traveling. While that's certainly possible on a metaphorical level in Vancouver, getting physically lost is truly difficult—all you have to do to find your bearings is look up. The mountains are always in sight, and they're always north. If you're facing them, east is to your right, west is to your left, and the back of your head is pointing south. That one tip should keep you pointed in the right direction no matter where your exploration of the city takes you. The rest of this chapter offers more detailed information on how to find your way around town.

1 Orientation

ARRIVING

BY PLANE   **Vancouver International Airport** is 13km (8 miles) south of downtown Vancouver on uninhabited Sea Island, bordered on three sides by Richmond and the Fraser River delta. The International Terminal features an extensive collection of First Nations sculptures and paintings set amid grand expanses of glass under soaring ceilings. Turn around and look up just before you leave the International Terminal to catch a glimpse of Bill Reid's huge jade canoe sculpture, *The Spirit of Haida Gwaii.*

Tourist information kiosks on Level 2 of the Main and International arrival terminals (© **604/207-0953**) are open daily from 8am to 11pm. **Parking** is available at the airport for both loading passengers and long-term stays (© **604/207-7077** for all airport services inquiries). A **shuttle bus** links the Main and International terminals to the South Terminal, where smaller and private aircraft are docked.

The airport is easily accessible via three bridges. Travelers heading into Vancouver take the Arthur Laing Bridge, which leads directly to Granville Street, the most direct route to downtown.

There is an international departure surcharge of C$15 (US$9.75) per person for international air travelers outside of North America, C$10 (US$6.50) for passengers traveling within North America (including Hawaii and Mexico), and C$5 (US$3.25) for passengers on flights within British Columbia or the Yukon.

Leaving the Airport   The pale green **YVR Airporter** (© **604/946-8866**) provides **airport bus service** to downtown Vancouver's major hotels. It leaves from Level 2 of the Main Terminal every 15 minutes daily from 6:30am until midnight. The 30-minute ride to the downtown area whisks you through central Vancouver before taking the Granville Street Bridge into downtown Vancouver. The one-way fare is C$12 (US$7.80) for adults, C$8 (US$5.20) for seniors, and C$5 (US$3.25) for children. Bus service back to the airport leaves from selected downtown hotels every half-hour between 5:35am and 10:55pm. Scheduled pickups serve the Bus Station, Four Seasons, Hotel Vancouver,

Waterfront Centre Hotel, Georgian Court, Sutton Place, Landmark, and others. Ask the bus driver on the way in or ask your hotel concierge for the nearest pickup stop and time.

Getting to and from the airport with **public transit** is a pain. Buses are slow, and you have to transfer at least once to get downtown. Given that the YVR Airporter bus costs only C$12 (US$7.80), the hassle probably isn't worth the savings. If you insist, however, bus no. 424 will take you to the Airport Station. From there you take bus no. 98 that will take you into downtown Vancouver. BC Transit fares are C$2 (US$1.30) during off-peak hours and C$3 (US$1.95) during weekdays until 6:30pm. But transfers are free in any direction within a 90-minute period.

The average **taxi** fare from the airport to a downtown Vancouver hotel is approximately C$25 (US$16) plus tip. Because the meter charges for time when the cab is stuck in traffic and some hotels are closer to the airport than others, the fare can run up to C$40 (US$26). LimoJet Gold Express (© **604/ 273-1331**) offers flat-rate stretch-limousine service at C$34.25 (US$22) per trip to the airport (not per person) from any downtown location (other city destinations cost only a few dollars more), plus tip, and can easily accommodate six to eight people. The drivers accept all major credit cards.

Most major **car-rental firms** have airport counters and shuttles.

BY TRAIN & BUS   The main **Vancouver railway station** is at 1150 Station St., near Main Street and Terminal Avenue just south of Chinatown. You can reach downtown Vancouver from there by cab for about C$10 (US$6.50). There are plenty of taxis at the station entrance. One block from the station is the SkyTrain's Main Street Station (see section 2, "Getting Around"). Within minutes, you're downtown. The Granville and Waterfront stations are two and four stops away, respectively.

Greyhound Bus Lines and **Pacific Coach Lines** also have their terminals at the Pacific Central Station (1150 Station St.).

For information on arriving **by ferry**, see "Getting to Vancouver," in chapter 2.

VISITOR INFORMATION

TOURIST OFFICES & PUBLICATIONS   The **Vancouver Tourist Info Centre,** 200 Burrard St. (© **604/683-2000;** www.tourismvancouver.com), is your single best travel information source about Vancouver and the North Shore. If you've ever been to London, you'll be happy to know that Tourism Vancouver is similar to the British Tourist Authority. That means you can buy bus passes and pick up maps, brochures, and travel guides. The staff is outgoing and can be very helpful if you need directions or recommendations. If you have trouble finding accommodations, the office has catalogs of registered hotels and B&Bs; the staff will even make reservations for you. The Info Centre is open from May to Labour Day daily from 8am to 6pm; the rest of the year, it's open Monday through Friday from 8:30am to 5pm and Saturday from 9am to 5pm.

Tourism Richmond, George Massey Tunnel (© **604/271-8280**), has information about the Richmond and Delta areas, including the heritage fishing village of Steveston. It's open daily from 9am to 5:30pm in July and August and daily from 10am to 4pm September through June. The office is located north of the George Massey Tunnel and is easily accessible when driving in from Delta. If you plan to see more of this beautiful province, **Super Natural British Columbia** (© **800/663-6000** or 604/663-6000; www.hellobc.com) can help you.

Greater Vancouver

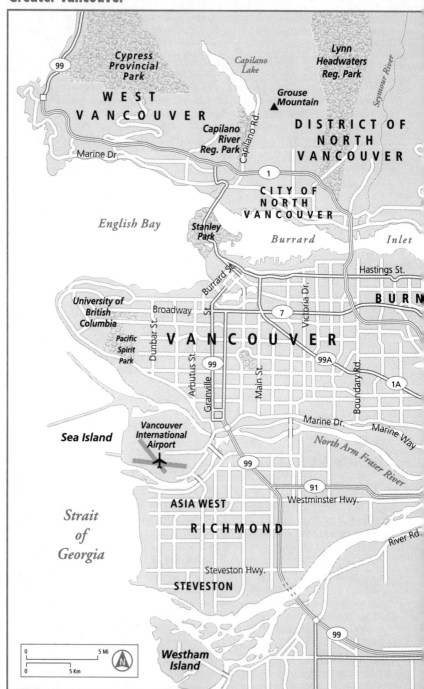

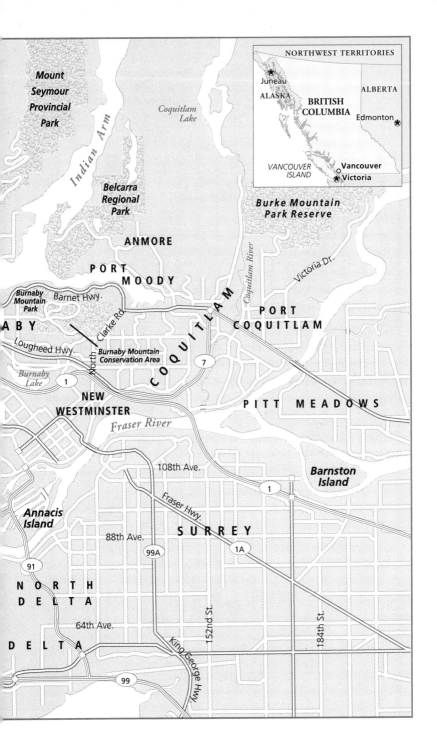

Mount
Seymour
Provincial
Park

Indian Arm

*Coquitlam
Lake*

Belcarra
Regional
Park

Burke Mountain
Park Reserve

ANMORE

Coquitlam River

Victoria Dr.

PORT
MOODY

Burnaby
Mountain
Park

Barnet Hwy.

PORT
COQUITLAM

Lougheed Hwy.

North Clarke Rd.

Burnaby Mountain
Conservation Area

7

*Burnaby
Lake*

1

ABY

NEW
WESTMINSTER

Fraser River

PITT MEADOWS

108th Ave.

Barnston
Island

1

Annacis
Island

Fraser Hwy.

SURREY

88th Ave.

99A

1A

91

NORTH
DELTA

152 St.

184th St.

64th Ave.

DELTA

King George Hwy.

99

Be sure to pick up a copy of the free weekly tabloid *The Georgia Straight* (℅ **604/730-7000**). It provides up-to-date schedules of concerts, lectures, art exhibits, plays, recitals, and other happenings. The *Straight* can be found all over the city in cafes, bookshops, and restaurants. Equally good—and with dollops more attitude—is the glossy city magazine *Vancouver* (℅ **604/877-7732**). "VanMag," as it's also known, is available on newsstands and on the Web at www.vanmag.com.

Two free monthly tabloids, *BC Parent* (℅ **604/221-0366**) and *West Coast Families* (℅ **604/689-1331**), are geared for families with young children, listing many kid-friendly current events. Gay and lesbian travelers will want to pick up a copy of *Xtra! West* (℅ **604/684-9696**), a free biweekly tabloid available in shops and restaurants throughout the West End.

CITY LAYOUT

With four different bodies of water lapping at its edges and mile after mile of shoreline, Vancouver's geography can seem a bit convoluted. That's part of the city's charm, of course, and visitors normally don't find it too hard to get their bearings. Think of the downtown peninsula as being like an upraised thumb on the mitten-shaped Vancouver mainland. Stanley Park, the West End, Yaletown, and Vancouver's business and financial center are located on the "thumb," which is bordered to the west by English Bay, to the north by Burrard Inlet, and to the south by False Creek. The mainland part of the city, the mitten, is mostly residential, with a sprinkling of businesses along main arterial streets. Both mainland and peninsula are covered by a simple rectilinear street pattern.

MAIN ARTERIES & STREETS

On the downtown peninsula, there are four key **east–west streets. Robson Street** starts at B.C. Place Stadium on Beatty Street, flows through the West End's more touristed shopping district, and ends at Stanley Park's Lost Lagoon on Lagoon Drive. **Georgia Street**—far more efficient for drivers than the pedestrian-oriented Robson—runs from the Georgia Viaduct on the eastern edge of downtown, through Vancouver's commercial core; it then carries on through Stanley Park and over the Lions Gate Bridge to the North Shore. Three blocks north of Georgia is **Hastings Street,** which begins in the West End, runs east through downtown, and then skirts Gastown's southern border as it runs eastward to the Trans-Canada Highway. **Davie Street** starts at Pacific Boulevard near the Cambie Street Bridge, travels through Yaletown into the West End's more residential shopping district, and ends at English Bay Beach.

Three **north–south downtown streets** will get you everywhere you want to go in and out of downtown. Two blocks east of Stanley Park is **Denman Street,** which runs from W. Georgia Street at Coal Harbour to Beach Avenue at English Bay Beach. This main West End thoroughfare is where locals dine out. It's also the shortest north–south route between the two ends of the Stanley Park Seawall.

Eight blocks east of Denman is **Burrard Street,** which starts near the Canada Place Pier and runs south through downtown, crosses the Burrard Street Bridge, and then forks. One branch, still **Burrard Street,** continues south and intersects W. Fourth Avenue and Broadway Avenue before ending at W. 16th Avenue on the borders of Shaughnessy. The other branch becomes **Cornwall Avenue,** which heads west through Kitsilano, changing its name to **Point Grey Road** and then **N.W. Marine Drive** before entering the University of British Columbia campus.

> ⌒ *Tips* **What's West**
>
> The thing to keep in mind, when figuring out what's where in Vancouver, is that this is a city where property is king, and the word "west" has such positive connotations that folks have always gone to great lengths to associate it with their particular patch of real estate. Thus we have the **West End** and the **West Side** and **West Vancouver,** which improbably enough is located immediately beside **North Vancouver.** It can be a bit confusing for newcomers, but fortunately each west has its own distinct character. The West End is a high-rise residential neighborhood located on the downtown peninsula. The West Side is one whole half of Vancouver, from Ontario Street west to the University of British Columbia. (The more working-class **East Side** covers the mainland portion of the city, from Ontario St. east to Boundary Rd.) Very tony West Vancouver is a city to itself on the far side of Burrard Inlet. Together with its more middle-class neighbor, North Vancouver, it forms an area called the **North Shore.**

Granville Street starts near the Waterfront Station on Burrard Inlet and runs the entire length of downtown, crosses the Granville Bridge to Vancouver's West Side, and carries on south across the breadth of the city before crossing the Arthur-Laing Bridge to Vancouver International Airport.

On the mainland portion of Vancouver, the city's east–west roads are successively numbered from First Avenue at the downtown bridges to 77th Avenue by the banks of the Fraser River. By far, the most important east–west route is **Broadway** (formerly Ninth Ave.), which starts a few blocks from the University of British Columbia (UBC) and extends across the length of the city to the border of neighboring Burnaby, where it becomes the **Lougheed Highway.** In Kitsilano, **W. Fourth Avenue** is also an important east–west shopping and commercial corridor. Intersecting with Broadway at various points are a number of important north–south commercial streets, each of which defines a particular neighborhood. The most significant of these streets are (from west to east) **Macdonald Street** in Kitsilano, **Granville Street, Cambie Street, Main Street,** and **Commercial Drive.**

FINDING AN ADDRESS   In many Vancouver addresses, the suite or room number precedes the building number. For instance, 100–1250 Robson St. is Suite 100 at 1250 Robson Street.

In downtown Vancouver, Chinatown's **Carrall Street** is the east–west axis from which streets are numbered and designated. Westward, numbers increase progressively to Stanley Park; eastward, numbers increase approaching Commercial Drive. For example, 400 W. Pender would be 4 blocks from Carrall Street heading toward downtown; 400 E. Pender would be 4 blocks on the opposite side of Carrall Street. Similarly, the low numbers on north–south streets start on the Canada Place Pier side and increase southward in increments of 100 per block (the 600 block of Thurlow Street is 2 blocks from the 800 block) toward False Creek and Granville Island.

Off the peninsula the system works the same, but **Ontario Street** is the east-west axis. Also, all east-west roads are avenues (for example, Fourth Ave.), while streets (for example, Main St.) run exclusively north–south.

STREET MAPS   The Travel Info Centres (see "Visitor Information," above) and most hotels can provide you with detailed downtown maps. A good all-around metropolitan area map is the Rand McNally Vancouver city map, which is available for C$3 (US$1.95) at the Vancouver Airport Tourism Centre kiosk. If you're an auto-club member, the Canadian Automobile Association (CAA) map is also good. It's not for sale, but is free to both AAA and CAA members and is available at AAA offices across North America. **International Travel Maps and Books,** 539 West Pender St. (© **604/687-3320**), has the city's most extensive selection of Vancouver and British Columbia maps and specialty guidebooks.

VANCOUVER'S NEIGHBORHOODS

Exploring Vancouver's fascinating and distinct neighborhoods is a key part of enjoying the city. For short profiles of the city's most interesting enclaves, see "Neighborhoods to Explore" in Chapter 6. For detailed walks through some of Vancouver's neighborhoods turn to Chapter 7 "Vancouver Strolls".

2 Getting Around

BY PUBLIC TRANSPORTATION

Translink (otherwise known as BC Transit; © **604/521-0400;** www.trans link.bc.ca) system includes electric buses, SeaBus catamaran ferries, and the magnetic-rail SkyTrain. It's an ecologically friendly, highly reliable, and inexpensive system that allows you to get everywhere, including the beaches and ski slopes. Regular service runs from 5am to 2am.

Schedules and routes are available at the Travel Info Centres, at many major hotels, online, and on buses. Pick up a copy of *Discover Vancouver on Transit* at one of the Travel Info Centres (see "Visitor Information" earlier in this chapter). This publication gives transit routes for many city neighborhoods, landmarks, and attractions, including numerous Victoria sites.

FARES   Fares are the same for the buses, SeaBus, and SkyTrain. One-way, all-zone fares are C$2 (US$1.30) after 6:30pm on weekdays and all day on weekends and holidays. At other times, a one-zone fare costs C$2 (US$1.30) and covers the entire city of Vancouver. A two-zone fare—C$3 (US$1.95)—is required to travel to nearby suburbs such as Richmond or North Vancouver, while a three-zone fare—C$4 (US$2.60)—is required for travel to the far-off edge city of Surrey. Free transfers are available on boarding and are good for travel in any direction and for the SkyTrain and SeaBus, but they do have a 90-minute expiration. **DayPasses,** which are good on all public transit, are C$8 (US$5.20) for adults and C$6 (US$3.90) for seniors, students, and children. They can be used for unlimited travel on weekdays or weekends and holidays. Tickets and passes are available at Travel Info Centres, both SeaBus terminals, convenience stores, drugstores, credit unions, and outlets displaying the "Fare-Dealer" symbol and can be bought in advance; most of these outlets also sell a transit map showing all routes for C$1.95 (US$1.25).

BY SKYTRAIN   The SkyTrain is a computerized, magnetic-rail train that services 20 stations along its 35-minute trip from downtown Vancouver east to Surrey through Burnaby and New Westminster. An extension, the Millennium line, was scheduled for completion at press time, in the fall of 2002. Not really of interest to most visitors, but those venturing off past Vancouver's Commercial Drive will find new stations at Broadway, Renfrew, and Rupert as well as new stations in New Westminster, towards Coquitlam.

BY SEABUS   The SS *Beaver* and SS *Otter* catamaran ferries annually take more than 700,000 passengers, cyclists, and wheelchair riders on a scenic 12-minute commute between downtown's Waterfront Station and North Vancouver's Lonsdale Quay. On weekdays, a SeaBus leaves each stop every 15 minutes from 6:15am to 6:30pm, then every 30 minutes until 1am. SeaBuses depart on Saturdays every half-hour from 6:30am to 12:30pm, then every 15 minutes until 7:15pm, then every-half hour until 1am. On Sundays and holidays, runs depart every half-hour from 8:30am to 11pm. Note that the crossing is a 2-zone fare on weekdays until 6:30pm.

BY BUS   Some key routes to keep in mind if you're touring the city by bus: **no. 5** (Robson St.), **no. 2** (Kitsilano Beach to downtown), **no. 50** (Granville Island), **no. 35** or **135** (to the Stanley Park bus loop), **no. 240** (North Vancouver), **no. 250** (West Vancouver–Horseshoe Bay), and buses **no. 4** and **10** (UBC to Exhibition Park via Granville St. downtown). In the summer, the **Vancouver Parks Board** operates a bus route through Stanley Park. Call ② **604/257-8400** for details on the free service or contact ② **604/953-3333** for general public transportation information.

BY TAXI

Cab fares start at C$2.30 (US$1.50) and increase at a rate of C$1.25 (US80¢) per kilometer, plus C30¢ (US20¢) per minute at stoplights or in stalled traffic. It's a little less than in most other major cities, but it still adds up. In the downtown area, you can expect to travel for less than C$10 (US$6.50) plus tip. The typical fare for the 13km (8-mile) drive from downtown to the airport is C$25 (US$16).

   Taxis are easy to find in front of major hotels, but flagging one can be tricky. Most drivers are usually on radio calls. But thanks to built-in satellite positioning systems, if you call for a taxi, it usually arrives faster than if you go out and hail one. Call for a pickup from **Black Top** (② **604/731-1111**), **Yellow Cab** (② **604/681-1111**), or **MacLure's** (② **604/731-9211**). **LimoJet** (② **604/273-1331**) offers flat-rate stretch limousine service to Vancouver Airport (see "By Plane" in section 1).

BY CAR

Vancouver has nowhere near the near-permanent gridlock of northwest cities such as Seattle, but the roads aren't exactly empty either. Fortunately, if you're just sightseeing around town or heading up to Whistler (a car is unnecessary in Whistler), public transit and cabs should see you through. However, if you're planning to visit the North Shore mountains or pursue other out-of-town activities, then by all means rent a car or bring your own. Gas is sold by the liter, averaging around C65¢ (US40¢) per liter. This may seem inexpensive until you consider that a gallon of gas costs about C$2.70 (US$1.75). Also, speeds and distances are posted in kilometers. The speed limit in the city is 50km per hour (30 mph); highway speed limits vary from 90km to 110km per hour (54–66 mph).

RENTALS   Rates vary widely depending on demand and style of car. If you're over 25 and have a major credit card, you can rent a vehicle from **Avis,** 757 Hornby St. (② **800/879-2847** or 604/606-2847); **Budget,** 501 W. Georgia St. (② **800/472-3325,** 800/527-0700, or 604/668-7000); **Enterprise,** 585 Smithe St. (② **800/736-8222** or 604/688-5500); **Hertz Canada,** 1128 Seymour St. (② **800/263-0600** or 604/688-2411); **National/Tilden,** 1130 W. Georgia St.

(© **800/387-4747** or 604/685-6111); or **Thrifty,** 1015 Burrard St. or 1400 Robson St. (© **800/847-4389** or 604/606-1666). These firms all have counters and shuttle service at the airport as well. To rent a recreational vehicle, contact Go West Campers, 1577 Lloyd Ave., North Vancouver (© **800/661-8813** or 604/987-5288; www.go-west.com).

PARKING   All major downtown hotels have guest parking; rates vary from free to C$25 (US$16) per day. There's public parking at **Robson Square** (enter at Smithe and Howe sts.), the **Pacific Centre** (Howe and Dunsmuir sts.), and **The Bay** department store (Richards near Dunsmuir St.). You'll also find larger **parking lots** at the intersections of Thurlow and Georgia, Thurlow and Alberni, and Robson and Seymour streets.

Metered **street parking** isn't impossible to come by, but it may take a trip or three around the block to find a spot. Rules are posted on the street and are strictly enforced. (Drivers are given about a 2-min. grace period before their cars are towed away when the 3pm no-parking rule goes into effect on many major thoroughfares.) Unmetered parking on side streets is often subject to neighborhood residency requirements. Check the signs. If you park in such an area without the appropriate sticker on your windshield, you'll get ticketed, then towed. If your car is towed away or you need a towing service and aren't a CAA or an AAA member, call **Unitow** (© **604/251-1255**) or **Busters** (© **604/685-8181**).

SPECIAL DRIVING RULES   Canadian driving rules are similar to those in the United States. Stopping for pedestrians is required even outside crosswalks. Seat belts are required. Children under 5 must be in child restraints. Motorcyclists must wear helmets. It's legal to turn right at a red light after coming to a full stop unless posted otherwise. Unlike in the United States, however, daytime headlights are mandatory. Though photo radar is no longer used in B.C. (the new government got elected partially on its pledge to eliminate the hated system), photo-monitored intersections are alive and well. If you run through a red light, you may get an expensive picture of your vacation from the police. Fines start at C$100 (US$65).

AUTO CLUB   Members of the American Automobile Association (AAA) can get assistance from the **Canadian Automobile Association (CAA),** 999 W. Broadway, Vancouver (© **604/268-5600,** or for road service 604/293-2222).

BY BIKE

There are plenty of places to rent a bike along Robson and Denman streets near Stanley Park. (For specifics, see "Outdoor Activities" in chapter 6.) Paved paths crisscross through parks and along beaches (see chapter 6), and new routes are constantly being added. Helmets are mandatory and riding on sidewalks is illegal except on designated bike paths.

You can take your bike on the SeaBus anytime at no extra charge. Bikes are not allowed in the George Massey Tunnel, but a tunnel shuttle operates four times daily from mid-May to September to transport you across the Fraser River. From May 1 to Victoria Day (the third weekend of May), the service operates on weekends only. All of the West Vancouver blue buses (including the bus to the Horseshoe Bay ferry terminal) can carry two bikes, first-come, first-served, and free of charge. In Vancouver, only a limited number of suburban routes allow bikes on the bus: bus no. 351 to White Rock, bus no. 601 to South Delta, bus no. 404 to the airport, and the 99 Express to UBC.

BY FERRY

Crossing False Creek to Vanier Park or Granville Island on one of the blue mini-ferries is cheap and fun. The **Aquabus** docks at the foot of Howe Street. It takes you either to Granville Island's public market or east along False Creek to Science World and Stamps Landing. The **Granville Island Ferry** docks at Sunset Beach below the Burrard Street Bridge and the Aquatic Centre. It goes to Granville Island and Vanier Park. Both companies' Granville Island ferries leave every 5 minutes from 7am to 10pm. Granville Island Ferry's boats to Vanier Park leave every 15 minutes from 10am to 8pm, as do the Aquabus ferries to Stamps Landing and Science World. One-way fares for both companies on all routes are $2.50 (US$1.60) for adults and C1.25 (US80¢) for seniors and children.

 FAST FACTS: Vancouver

American Express Find the office at 666 Burrard St. (© **604/669-2813**). It's open Monday through Friday from 8am to 5:30pm, Saturday from 10am to 4pm.

Area Codes The telephone area code for the lower mainland, including greater Vancouver and Whistler, is **604**. The area code for Vancouver Island, the Gulf Islands, and the interior of the province is **250**.

Business Hours Vancouver **banks** are open Monday through Thursday from 10am to 5pm and Friday from 10am to 6pm. Some banks, like Canadian Trust, are also open on Saturday. **Stores** are generally open Monday through Saturday from 10am to 6pm. Last call at the city's **restaurant bars** and **cocktail lounges** is 2am.

Child Care If you need cribs, car seats, play pens, or other baby accessories, **Cribs and Carriages** (© **604/988-2742**) delivers them right to your hotel.

Consulates The **U.S. Consulate** is at 1095 W. Pender St. (© **604/685-4311**). The **British Consulate** is at 800–1111 Melville St. (© **604/683-4421**). The **Australian Consulate** is at 1225–888 Dunsmuir St. (© **604/684-1177**). Check the Yellow Pages for other countries.

Currency Exchange Banks and ATMs have a better exchange rate than most foreign exchange bureaus (the latter charges transaction and service fees). See "Money," in chapter 2.

Dentist Most major hotels have a dentist on call. **Vancouver Centre Dental Clinic,** Vancouver Centre Mall, 11–650 W. Georgia St. (© **604/682-1601**), is another option. You must make an appointment. The clinic is open Monday through Wednesday 8:30am to 6pm, Thursday 8:30am to 7pm, Friday 9am to 6pm, and Saturday 9am to 4pm.

Doctor Hotels usually have a doctor on call. **Vancouver Medical Clinics,** Bentall Centre, 1055 Dunsmuir St. (© **604/683-8138**), is a drop-in clinic open Monday through Friday 8am to 4:45pm. Another drop-in medical center, **Carepoint Medical Centre,** 1175 Denman St. (© **604/681-5338**), is open daily from 9am to 9pm. See also "Emergencies," below.

Electricity As in the United States, electric current is 110 volts AC (60 cycles).

Emergencies Dial © **911** for fire, police, ambulance, and poison control.

Hospitals **St. Paul's Hospital,** 1081 Burrard St. (© **604/682-2344**), is the closest facility to downtown and the West End. West Side Vancouver hospitals include **Vancouver General Hospital Health and Sciences Centre,** 855 W. 12th Ave. (© **604/875-4111**), and **British Columbia's Children's Hospital,** 4480 Oak St. (© **604/875-2345**). In North Vancouver, there's **Lions Gate Hospital,** 231 E. 15th St. (© **604/988-3131**).

Hot Lines Emergency numbers include **Crisis Centre** (© 604/872-3311), **Rape Crisis Centre** (© 604/255-6344), **Rape Relief** (© 604/872-8212), **Poison Control Centre** (© 604/682-5050), **Crime Stoppers** (© 604/669-8477), **SPCA** animal emergency (© 604/879-7343), **Vancouver Police** (© 604/717-3535), **Fire** (© 604/665-6000), and **Ambulance** (© 604/872-5151). See also "Emergencies," above.

Internet Access Free Internet access is available at the Vancouver **public library** Central Branch, 350 W. Georgia St. (© **604/331-3600**). Just across the street, **Webster's Internet Cafe,** 340 Robson St. (© **604/915-9327**), charges for access but generally has a machine free. Or, for some late night surfing, try **Internet Coffee,** 1104 Davie St. (© **604/682-6668**).

Laundry & Dry Cleaning **Davie Laundromat,** 1061 Davie St. (© **604/682-2717**), offers self-service, drop-off service, and dry cleaning. **Laundry & Suntanning,** 781 Denman St. (© **604/689-9598**), doesn't have dry-cleaning services, but you can work on your tan while you wait.

Liquor Laws The legal drinking age in British Columbia is 19. Spirits are sold only in government liquor stores, but beer and wine can be purchased from specially licensed, privately owned stores and pubs. LCBC (Liquor Control of British Columbia) stores are open Monday through Saturday from 10am to 6pm, but some are open to 11pm.

Lost Property The **Vancouver Police** have a lost-property room (© **604/717-2726**), open 8:30am to 5pm Monday through Saturday. If you think you may have lost something on public transportation, call **Translink** (BC Transit) 8:30am to 5pm at © **604/682-7887**.

Luggage Storage & Lockers Most downtown hotels will gladly hold your luggage before or after your stay. Just ask at the front desk. Lockers are available at the main Vancouver railway station (which is also the main bus depot), **Pacific Central Station,** 1150 Station St., near Main Street and Terminal Avenue south of Chinatown (© **604/661-0328**), for C$2 (US$1.30) per day.

Mail Letters and postcards cost C65¢ (US40¢) to mail to the US and C$1.25 (US80¢) for overseas airmail service, C48¢ (US30¢) within Canada. You can buy stamps and mail parcels at the main post office (see "Post Office," below) or at any of the postal outlets inside drugstores and convenience stores. Look for a POSTAL SERVICES sign. You can mail items at the tall, red, rectangular mailboxes found every few blocks on the street.

Maps See "City Layout," earlier in this chapter.

Newspapers & Magazines The two local papers are the *Vancouver Sun* (www.vancouversun.com), published Monday through Saturday, and *The Province* (www.canada.com/vancouver/theprovince), published Sunday through Friday mornings. The free weekly entertainment paper, *The Georgia Straight,* comes out on Thursday. Other papers are the national *Globe and Mail* and the *National Post,* the *Chinese Oriental Star,* the Southeast Asian *Indo-Canadian Voice,* and the *Jewish Western Daily. Where Vancouver,* a shopping/tourist guide, can be found in your hotel room or at Tourism Vancouver. See "Visitor Information," earlier in this chapter, for more visitor-oriented publications.

Pharmacies **Shopper's Drug Mart,** 1125 Davie St. (✆ **604/685-6445**), is open 24 hours. Several Safeway supermarket pharmacies are open late; the one on Robson and Denman is open until midnight.

Police For emergencies, dial ✆ **911.** Otherwise, the **Vancouver City Police** can be reached at ✆ **604/717-3535.**

Post Office The **main post office** (✆ **800/267-1177**) is at West Georgia and Homer streets (349 W. Georgia St.). It's open Monday through Friday from 8am to 5:30pm.

Restrooms Hotel lobbies are your best bet for downtown facilities. The shopping centers like Pacific Centre and Sinclair Centre, as well as the large department stores like the Bay, also have restrooms.

Safety Overall, Vancouver is a safe city; violent-crime rates are quite low. However, property crimes and crimes of opportunity (such as items being stolen from unlocked cars) occur disturbingly frequently, particularly downtown. Vancouver's Downtown East Side, between Gastown and Chinatown, is a troubled neighborhood and should be avoided at night.

Taxes Hotel rooms are subject to a 10% tax. The **provincial sales tax (PST)** is 7% (excluding food, restaurant meals, and children's clothing). For specific questions, call the **B.C. Consumer Taxation Branch** (✆ **604/660-4500**).

Most goods and services are subject to a 7% **federal goods and services tax (GST).** Save your receipts. You can get a refund on short-stay accommodations and all shopping purchases. Each purchase must be greater than C$50 (US$33), and you must have a total of at least C$200 (US$130) to file a claim. (This refund doesn't apply to car rentals, parking, restaurant meals, room service, tobacco, or alcohol.) Hotels and the Info Centres can give you application forms, which you then mail to Revenue Canada on your return home. After processing, the government sends a check to your home address. For details on the GST, call ✆ **800/668-4748** in Canada or 902/432-5608 outside Canada, or visit www.ccra-adrc.gc.ca/visitors. PDF files of the refund forms are on the site for you to print out. If you want your refund right away, **Maple Leaf Tax Refund** (✆ **800/993-4313** or 604/893-8478) in the Hotel Vancouver, 900 W. Georgia St., will process your application and provide a refund on the spot, less an 18% processing fee. You have to bring your receipts, two pieces of ID (one of which shows your home address), your plane ticket, and the items you purchased to show to the processing agent. *Note:* if you arrived in Canada by car, Maple Leaf can only give you a refund on your accommodation bills. You can still get a refund on other items, but only by sending in forms by mail, and only if you have your receipts stamped by Canada Customs or a participating duty-free store when you drive out of the country.

Telephone Phones in British Columbia are identical to U.S. phones. The country code is the same as the U.S. code (**1**). Local calls normally cost C25¢ (US15¢). Many hotels charge up to C$1 (US65¢) per local call and much more for long-distance calls. You can save considerably by using your calling card. You can also buy prepaid phone cards in various denominations at grocery and convenience stores.

Time Zone Vancouver is in the Pacific time zone, as are Seattle and San Francisco. Daylight saving time applies April through October.

Tipping Tipping etiquette is the same as in the United States: 15% in restaurants, C$1 (US65¢) per bag for bellboys and porters, and C$1 (US65¢) per day for the hotel housekeeper. Taxi drivers get a sliding-scale tip—fares under C$4 (US$2.60) deserve a C$1 (US65¢) tip; for fares over C$5 (US$3.25), tip 15%.

Weather Call ✆ **604/664-9010** or 604/664-9032 for weather updates; dial ✆ **604/666-3655** for marine forecasts. Each local ski resort has its own snow report line. Whistler/Blackcomb's is ✆ **604/687-7507.** Cypress Ski area's is ✆ **604/419-7669.**

4

Where to Stay in Vancouver

The past few years have seen a lot of activity in the Vancouver hotel business. Lots of new rooms have opened up, some in the high end, and a lot more in the moderate-to-budget range. Other hotels have undergone extensive renovations, and good-natured competition has flourished among all the city's hostelries. So no matter what your budget, there's no reason to settle for second best. Most of the hotels are in the downtown area, or in the West End. Both neighborhoods are close to major sights and services. The West Side of Vancouver has a few hotels, plus many pleasant bed-and-breakfasts. Other good accommodations are found across Burrard Inlet on the North Shore.

There are only a few small areas to avoid when booking a room. Granville Street offers location without the price, but the area is a prime hangout for panhandling teenagers. Hotels on E. Hastings Street or E. Cordova Street are not worth the savings. These streets are in Vancouver's East Side skid row, which has some of Canada's highest property-crime rates.

Whichever area you choose, remember that quoted prices don't include the 10% **provincial accommodations tax** or the 7% **goods and services tax (GST).** Non-Canadian residents can get a GST rebate on short-stay accommodations by filling out the Tax Refund Application (see "Taxes" under "Fast Facts: Vancouver" in chapter 3).

RESERVATIONS Reservations are highly recommended June through September and during holidays. If you arrive without a reservation or have trouble finding a room, call **Super Natural British Columbia's Discover British Columbia** hot line at © **800/ 663-6000** or **Tourism Vancouver's** hot line at © **604/683-2000.** Specializing in last-minute bookings, either organization can make arrangements using its large daily listing of hotels, hostels, and B&Bs.

1 Downtown & Yaletown

All downtown hotels are within 5 to 10 minutes' walking distance of shops, restaurants, and attractions. Hotels in this area lean more toward luxurious than modest, a state of affairs reflected in their prices.

VERY EXPENSIVE

Delta Vancouver Suite Hotel ⭐   The Delta Vancouver Suite Hotel considers itself a Manhattan-style hotel. The spacious and bright lobby is decorated with black marble, cherry-colored wood, and stone white walls. The indoor atrium extends up to the third floor and connects to Simon Fraser University's conference space in the adjacent building. Suites are designed for business travelers, with a large workspace and amenities usually reserved for business-class rooms, including two phone lines, a speakerphone, and high speed Internet access. The layout of the rooms allows for a lot of natural light and, wherever possible, floor-to-ceiling windows. To upgrade from the standard

Downtown Vancouver Accommodations

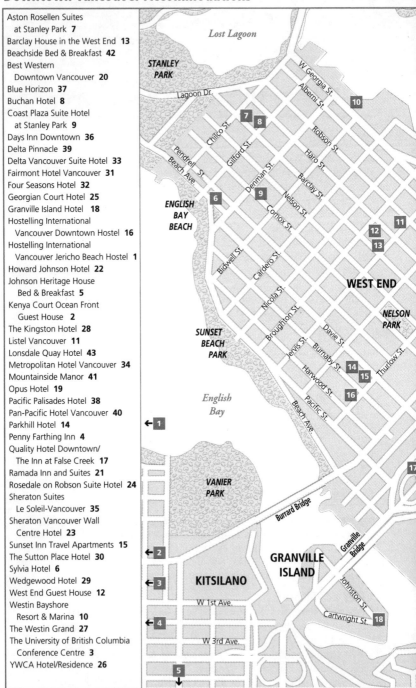

Aston Rosellen Suites
  at Stanley Park **7**
Barclay House in the West End **13**
Beachside Bed & Breakfast **42**
Best Western
  Downtown Vancouver **20**
Blue Horizon **37**
Buchan Hotel **8**
Coast Plaza Suite Hotel
  at Stanley Park **9**
Days Inn Downtown **36**
Delta Pinnacle **39**
Delta Vancouver Suite Hotel **33**
Fairmont Hotel Vancouver **31**
Four Seasons Hotel **32**
Georgian Court Hotel **25**
Granville Island Hotel **18**
Hostelling International
  Vancouver Downtown Hostel **16**
Hostelling International
  Vancouver Jericho Beach Hostel **1**
Howard Johnson Hotel **22**
Johnson Heritage House
  Bed & Breakfast **5**
Kenya Court Ocean Front
  Guest House **2**
The Kingston Hotel **28**
Listel Vancouver **11**
Lonsdale Quay Hotel **43**
Metropolitan Hotel Vancouver **34**
Mountainside Manor **41**
Opus Hotel **19**
Pacific Palisades Hotel **38**
Pan-Pacific Hotel Vancouver **40**
Parkhill Hotel **14**
Penny Farthing Inn **4**
Quality Hotel Downtown/
  The Inn at False Creek **17**
Ramada Inn and Suites **21**
Rosedale on Robson Suite Hotel **24**
Sheraton Suites
  Le Soleil-Vancouver **35**
Sheraton Vancouver Wall
  Centre Hotel **23**
Sunset Inn Travel Apartments **15**
The Sutton Place Hotel **30**
Sylvia Hotel **6**
Wedgewood Hotel **29**
West End Guest House **12**
Westin Bayshore
  Resort & Marina **10**
The Westin Grand **27**
The University of British Columbia
  Conference Centre **3**
YWCA Hotel/Residence **26**

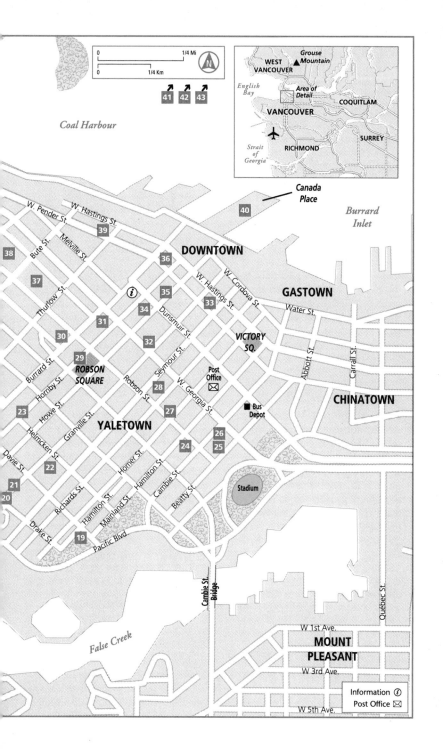

0 | 1/4 Mi
0 | 1/4 Km

41 42 43

Coal Harbour

Grouse
Mountain ▲
WEST
VANCOUVER

English
Bay

Area of
Detail

COQUITLAM

VANCOUVER

Strait
of
Georgia

RICHMOND

SURREY

Canada
Place

Burrard
Inlet

W. Pender St.

W. Hastings St.
39

DOWNTOWN
36

40

38

Bute St.
Melville St.

37

W. Cordova St.

GASTOWN

Thurlow St.

(i)

35

W. Hastings St.
33

Water St.

31

34

Dunsmuir St.

VICTORY
SQ.

Abbott St.

Carrall St.

30

32

Seymour St.

CHINATOWN

Burrard St.

29
ROBSON
SQUARE

Robson St.

28

Post
Office
✉

Hornby St.

27

W. Georgia St.

23

Howe St.

YALETOWN

■ Bus
Depot

Helmcken St.

Granville St.

26

Davie St.

24

25

22

Richards St.

Homer St.

Hamilton St.

Stadium

21

20

Hamilton St.

Mainland St.

Cambie St.

Drake St.

19

Beatty St.

Pacific Blvd.

False Creek

Cambie St.
Bridge

Québec St.

W 1st Ave.

MOUNT
PLEASANT

W 3rd Ave.

Information (i)
Post Office ✉

W 5th Ave.

Bed & Breakfast Registries

If you prefer to stay in a B&B, the following agencies specialize in matching guests with establishments that best suit their needs:

- **Born Free Bed & Breakfast of BC,** 4390 Frances St., Burnaby, B.C. V5C ZR3 (☎ **800/488-1941** or 604/298-8815; www.vancouverbandb.bc. ca).
- **Canada-West Accommodations Bed & Breakfast Registry,** P.O. Box 86607, North Vancouver, B.C. V7L 4L2 (☎ **800/561-3223** or 604/990-6730; www.b-b.com).
- **Town and Country Bed & Breakfast,** 2803 W. Fourth Ave. (P.O. Box 74542), Vancouver, B.C. V6K IK2 (☎/fax **604/731-5942**; www.town andcountrybedandbreakfast.com).

room to a full one-bedroom suite costs only an additional C$15 (US$9.70). The top three floors are reserved for Signature Club guests. The C$40 (US$26) premium upgrades you to a great view, down duvets, CD players, and access to the Signature Lounge with complimentary breakfast and afternoon cocktails.

550 W. Hastings St., Vancouver, B.C. V6B 1L6. ☎ **800/268-1133** or 604/689-8188. Fax 604/605-8881. www.deltahotels.com. 226 units. Oct 16–May C$195–C$270 (US$125–US$174) double. June–Oct 15 C$260–C$340 (US$167–US$219) double. Children under 18 stay free in parents' room. AE, DC, DISC, MC, V. Valet parking C$15 (US$9.70). **Amenities:** Restaurant; bar; indoor pool; health club; concierge; business center; 24-hr. room service; massage; babysitting; laundry service; dry cleaning; nonsmoking rooms; executive level rooms. *In room:* A/C, TV w/pay movies, dataport, minibar, coffeemaker, hair dryer, iron, safe.

The Fairmont Hotel Vancouver 🏵🏵   Thanks to a recent C$75-million renovation, the grande dame of Vancouver's hotels has been restored beyond her former glory. A landmark in the city since it first opened its doors in 1939, the hotel has been completely brought up to 21st century standards: the rooms are spacious, with a sitting area, modern lighting, and ample desks; the bathrooms gleam with marble floors and sinks. The decorations evoke an elegance of days gone by. The courtyard suites provide spacious accommodations with a large luxuriously furnished living room, separated from the bedroom with French glass doors. A state-of-the art spa features soothing day packages and a la carte treatments including body scrubs and wraps.

900 W. Georgia St., Vancouver, B.C. V6C 2W6. ☎ **800/866-5577** or 604/684-3131. Fax 604/662-1929. www. fairmont.com. 556 units. High season C$269–C$519 (US$174–US$335) double; C$449–C$599 (US$290–US$386) suite. Low season C$189–C$369 (US$122–US$238) double; C$369–C$449 (US$238–US$290) suite. Children under 18 stay free in parents' room. AE, DC, DISC, MC, V. Parking C$19 (US$12). Small pets accepted for a C$25 (US$16) charge. Wheelchair-accessible rooms and rooms for hearing-impaired guests available. **Amenities:** 2 restaurants (brasserie, grill); bar; indoor pool; health club; excellent spa; Jacuzzi; sauna; concierge; tour desk; car rental; business center; shopping arcade; salon; 24-hr. room service; massage; babysitting; laundry service; same-day dry cleaning; nonsmoking rooms; Entree Gold concierge level. *In room:* A/C, TV w/pay movies, dataport, minibar, coffeemaker, hair dryer, iron.

Four Seasons Hotel 🏵🏵 *(Kids*   It's a magic trick worthy of Doug Henning: In the heart of downtown, the 28-story Four Seasons just seems to disappear. Thanks to the camouflage by the Pacific Centre Mall and the surrounding office towers, most people walk right by without ever noticing its existence. But like any good magic trick, it's just illusion. Once inside there is nothing nondescript about the place; the elegant lobby opens up into a spacious garden terrace, the sunlight pouring in through skylights overhead. The guest rooms are tastefully appointed with French provincial furniture and marble bathrooms, while the high ceilings add a spacious feel. Higher floors provide glimpses of the mountains or the city. For a slightly larger room, reserve a deluxe corner room with wraparound floor-to-ceiling windows.

791 W. Georgia St., Vancouver, B.C. V6C 2T4. © **800/332-3442** in the U.S., or 604/689-9333. Fax 604/684-4555. www.fourseasons.com. 385 units. C$400–C$525 (US$258–US$339) double; C$445–C$475 (US$287–US$306) junior suite; C$375–C$570 (US$242–US$367) executive suite. Wheelchair-accessible units available. AE, DC, MC, V. Parking C$20 (US$13). Pets accepted. **Amenities:** 2 restaurants; bar; indoor and heated outdoor pool; outstanding exercise room; sauna; concierge; car rental; business center; shopping arcade; 24-hr. room service; massage; babysitting; laundry service; same-day dry cleaning; nonsmoking rooms. *In room:* A/C, TV/VCR, dataport (high speed and wireless Internet), minibar, hair dryer, iron, safe.

Georgian Court Hotel ★★ *(Finds* This modern, 14-story brick hotel is extremely well located—it's a block or two from B.C. Place Stadium, G.M. Place Stadium, the Queen Elizabeth Theatre, the Playhouse, and the Vancouver Public Library, making it ideal for sports fans, trade-show attendees, and culture vultures. The guest rooms are large and attractively decorated. And while the big-time celebs are usually whisked off to the glamorous top hotels, their entourages often stays at the Georgian Court, as it provides all the amenities and business-friendly extras such as three phones in every room, brightly lit desks, and complimentary high-speed Internet access without the heavy price tag.

773 Beatty St., Vancouver, B.C. V6B 2M4. © **800/663-1155** or 604/682-5555. Fax 604/682-8830. www. georgiancourt.com. 180 units. May 1–Oct 15 C$210–C$275 (US$135–US$177) double. Oct 16–Apr 30 C$125–C$215 (US$81–US$139) double. AE, DC, MC, V. Parking C$8 (US$5). **Amenities:** Restaurant (Swiss); bar; health club; Jacuzzi; sauna; concierge; business center; limited room service; babysitting; laundry service; dry cleaning; nonsmoking rooms. *In room:* A/C, TV, dataport, minibar, hair dryer, iron.

Le Soleil Hotel & Suites ★ Stepping into Le Soleil is like entering a European luxury hotel. The uniformed doorman welcomes you into a lobby decorated with crystal chandeliers, Italian marble, plush carpeting, and gilded, vaulted ceilings. The opulence of the hotel can get a bit overwhelming in the narrow guest hallways, but it comes off about right in the suites (all units except 10 doubles are suites). Interiors are furnished with maple-finished Biedermeier-style furniture. The sitting areas are comfortable; the sofas convert into beds. As you would expect, all the little touches are there—the fruit plate upon check-in, the turndown service with Godiva chocolates. Because the hotel is right downtown, nearly all suites feature skyline views. However, for the best views, not to mention ultimate luxury, the Penthouse suites will not disappoint. The Versace-inspired bedroom-and-den Penthouse has a Jacuzzi tub in the living room and 18-foot floor-to-ceiling windows.

567 Hornby St., Vancouver, B.C. V6C 2E8. © **877/632-3030** or 604/632-3000. Fax 604/632-3001. www.lesoleilhotel.com. 119 units. May 1–Oct 15 C$400 (US$258) double; C$430 (US$277) suite; C$1,500 (US$968) penthouse. Oct 16–Apr 30 C$300 (US$194) double; C$330 (US$213) suite; C$1,000 (US$645) penthouse. AE, DC, MC, V. Valet parking C$20 (US$13). Pets accepted. C$150 (US$97). **Amenities:** Restaurant (Italian); access to YWCA fitness facilities next door (C$11/US$7 per day); concierge; business center; 24-hr. room service; laundry service; same-dry cleaning; nonsmoking rooms. *In room:* A/C, TV w/pay movies, dataport, minibar, coffeemaker, hair dryer, iron, safe.

Metropolitan Hotel Vancouver ★★ The luxurious Metropolitan is centrally situated between the financial district and downtown shopping areas and caters to business travelers on weekdays. A very clever design in the feng shui tradition has rendered the tiny lobby quite elegant—it's furnished with overstuffed armchairs and dominated by a huge, hand-carved, gilded Chinese screen. Most units in the 18-story hotel have small balconies. All rooms have stately dark-wood furnishings, queen-size beds with Italian linens, marble bathrooms, fluffy bathrobes, and morning paper delivery.

645 Howe St., Vancouver, B.C. V6C 2Y9. ℂ **800/667-2300** or 604/687-1122. Fax 604/643-7267. www. metropolitan.com. 197 units. Nov–March C$209–C$299 (US$135–US$193) double. Apr–Oct C$229–C$385 (US$148–US$248) double. Children under 18 stay free in parents' room. Pets are accepted. AE, DC, MC, V. Underground valet parking C$23 (US$15) per day. **Amenities:** Restaurant (see Diva at the Met in chapter 5 for review); bar; indoor pool; squash courts; health club; concierge; business center; 24-hr. room service; in-room massage; babysitting; laundry service; same-day dry cleaning; nonsmoking rooms. *In room:* A/C, TV w/pay movies, dataport, iron, minibar, coffeemaker, hair dryer, safe.

Opus Hotel 🎭🎭 Are you a bit of a *Susan*—that's a Canadian fashionista who loves bright colors and Armani accessories? Or maybe you are more like *Mike*— a New Yorker with a penchant for sleek design and minimalist stainless steel? In the brand new Opus Hotel in Yaletown, each room is furnished according to one of five personalities, each with its own style, color, and flavor. From the outside, the seven-story brick building looks like any other Yaletown warehouse, but inside, designers have made liberal use of bold colors and interesting textures (fabric walls, mosaic covered pillars, colored marble floors) to create a unique boutique hotel. And nothing is missing in the guest rooms, either: Each room has a great bed (think firm mattress with top-quality linens), a CD player, lots of natural light (with huge windows that open), a large desk, spacious vanity, and a bathroom to die for. A number of the suites also come with a fireplace, wet bar, soaker tub for two, patio, and flat-screen TV. For the best views book one of the south facing rooms looking out towards False Creek.

322 Davie St., Vancouver, B.C. V6B 5Z6. ℂ **866/642-6787** or 604/642-6787. Fax 604/642-6780. www.opushotel.com. 96 units. Nov–Apr C$209–C$299 (US$134–US$193) double; suite C$325 (US$210). May–Oct C$289–C$379 (US$186–US$245) double; suite C$405 (US$261). Children 17 and under stay free in parents' room. Pets accepted. **Note:** Check website for updated rates for summer 2003 as well as special packages. AE, DC, MC, V. Valet parking C$20 (US$13). **Amenities:** Restaurant (French brasserie); bar; cardio room; concierge; 24-hr. room service; laundry service; dry cleaning; nonsmoking rooms. *In room:* A/C, TV w/pay movies, dataport, minibar, coffeemaker, hair dryer, iron, safe.

Pan Pacific Hotel Vancouver 🎭🎭 Since its completion in 1986, this 23-story luxury hotel atop the Vancouver Convention Centre has become perhaps the key landmark on the Vancouver waterfront; Canada Place, with its distinctive five white sails, and the cruise-ship terminal are at your door step. If you're taking an Alaskan cruise, this is the place to stay. Guests rooms begin on the ninth floor, above a huge glass atrium of a lobby that seems to invite the mountains and the harbor right in. Superior rooms face the city and offer a partial waterfront view. For the best views, book a deluxe room (for surcharge of about C$30/US$20), and you can wake to see the sun glinting on the mountains of the North Shore and the floatplanes drifting in with a morning tide of commuters from parts west and north. All rooms are very spacious, with a wide hallway entrance, large closet, and elegant maple furniture. Huge picture windows add to the brightness. Bathrooms are luxurious and particularly spacious. The hotel boasts an outstanding health club (C$15/US$10 daily fee), with classes, cardio room, universal gym, small inside track, and squash courts.

300–999 Canada Place, Vancouver, B.C. V6C 3B5. ℂ **800/937-1515** in the U.S., or 604/662-8111. Fax 604/685-8690. www.panpacific.com. 504 units. May–Oct C$490–C$590 (US$316–US$381) double. Nov–Apr C$390–C$450 (US$252–US$290) double. C$650–C$3,800 (US$419–US$2,452) suite year-round. AE, DC, DISC, MC, V. Parking C$21 (US$14). **Amenities:** 3 restaurants; bar; outdoor heated pool; squash courts; health club; spa; Jacuzzi; sauna; concierge; tour desk; car rental; business center; shopping arcade; 24-hr.

room service; massage; babysitting; laundry service; same-day dry cleaning; nonsmoking floors. *In room:* A/C, TV w/pay movies, dataport and high speed Internet, minibar, coffeemaker, hair dryer, iron, safe.

Sheraton Vancouver Wall Centre Hotel ★★★

The tallest—and at 735 rooms the largest—hotel in the city, the Wall Centre is hard to miss. Look for the towering two-tone oval spire, the result of a strange compromise between city hall—which wanted the tower to have clear glass—and the developer, who preferred his glass aviator-shades black. Completed in May 2001, the Wall Centre is development mogul Peter Wall's personal tribute to his favorite details in the world's finest accommodations. From the lobby's gold-leaf staircase, custom-designed furniture, and hand-blown glass chandeliers, to the half-dozen peepholes on each guest room door, the opulent decor would not look out of place in a modern-art gallery. All guest rooms—each with stunning floor-to-ceiling windows—are elegantly appointed with blond-wood furnishings, luxury bathrooms, heated floors, and king-size or double beds.

1088 Burrard St., Vancouver, B.C. V6Z 2R9. © 800/325-3535 or 604/331-1000. Fax 604/331-1000. www.sheratonvancouver.com. 733 units. Oct 23–May 14 C$129–C$249 (US$83–US$161) double; C$179–C$399 (US$115–US$257) suite. May 15–Oct 22 C$199–C$409 (US$128–US$264) double; C$249–C$549 (US$161–US$354) suite. Crystal Club upgrade C$25–C$40 (US$16–US$26). AE, DC, MC, V. Valet parking C$19 (US$12). **Amenities:** 2 restaurants (bistro, continental); 2 bars; indoor pool; state-of-the-art health club; spa; Jacuzzi; sauna; concierge; tour desk; car-rental desk; business center; salon; 24-hr. room service; babysitting; same-day laundry and dry cleaning; nonsmoking rooms; executive level rooms. *In room:* A/C, TV w/pay movies, high-speed Internet access, minibar, coffeemaker, hair dryer, iron, safe.

The Sutton Place Hotel ★★

Don't let the big pink hospital-like exterior fool you. Once you enter the lobby of this centrally located hotel, it's pure luxury. The grand lobby is elegantly decorated with beige marble, fresh flowers, chandeliers, and European artwork. All standard rooms are tastefully decorated in a classic European style. The one- or two-bedroom junior suites have a small parlor. In larger suites, double French doors separate the bedroom from the large sitting area.

Your four-legged friend can also receive grand treatment at the Sutton Place: For C$95 (US$61), you can purchase the VIP program, which comes with a gourmet dinner (T-bone or fresh tuna) and turndown service with doggie treats.

845 Burrard St., Vancouver, B.C. V6Z 2K6. © 800/961-7555 or 604/682-5511. Fax 604/682-5513. www.suttonplace.com. 397 units. Nov–Apr C$169–C$299 (US$109–$193) double; C$239–C$1,200 (US$154–US$774) suite. May–Oct C$239–C$450 (US$154–US$290) double; C$339–C$1,700 (US$219–US$1,097) suite. AE, DC, DISC, MC, V. Underground self- or valet parking C$17 (US$11). Bus: 22. **Amenities:** Restaurant (French); lounge (with bistro fare); indoor pool; health club; spa; Jacuzzi; sauna; complimentary bikes; children's program; concierge; business center; 24-hr. room service; laundry service; same-day dry-cleaning service; nonsmoking rooms. *In room:* A/C, TV w/pay movies, dataport and high-speed Internet, minibar, hair dryer, iron, safe.

Wedgewood Hotel ★★★

The only boutique hotel in downtown Vancouver, the Wedgewood offers elegant accommodations and fine amenities. A popular place with visiting movie stars (Goldie Hawn practically lived here while house-hunting in Vancouver), its staff truly know how to pamper their guests. All 89 units are spacious and have balconies; the best views are those facing the Vancouver Art Gallery and Law court, avoid the rooms that look out over the back of the hotel. Furnishings are in elegant blues and gold tones and the artwork in each room is original. Business travelers will appreciate the ample workspace, high-speed Internet access, and dual phone line. The one-bedroom suites are beautifully appointed and sleep four comfortably. To really stretch out, however, consider the penthouse suite on the 12th floor overlooking the Law Courts.

This large suite comes with a fireplace, a large patio, and a dream-come-true master bedroom with a heart-shaped bed. Good thing the hotel's fine Bacchus restaurant offers room service.

845 Hornby St., Vancouver, B.C. V6Z 1V1. ℂ **800/663-0666** or 604/689-7777. Fax 604/608-5349. www.wedgewoodhotel.com. 89 units. May–Sept C$220–C$380 (US$142–US$245) double; C$480 (US$310) suite C$680 (US$439) penthouse. Oct–Apr C$160–C$280 (US$103–US$181) double; C$380 (US$245) suite. Year round C$448–$700 (US$380–$450) penthouse. AE, DC, MC, V. Valet parking C$15 (US$10). **Amenities:** Restaurant (French); small weight room; sauna; concierge; business center; 24-hr. room service; laundry service; dry cleaning; nonsmoking rooms; executive rooms. *In room:* A/C, TV w/pay movies, VCR, dataport, minibar, coffeemaker, hair dryer, iron, safe.

The Westin Grand ✰✰✰   Just across from the public library, the Westin Grand offers high-end all-suite accommodations that are within easy walking distance of Yaletown, GM Place, and the Robson shopping area. The spacious suites are brightened by the natural light pouring in through the floor-to-ceiling windows—a nice foil to the somber mahogany furniture and earth-toned decor. Sitting rooms come with a kitchenette tucked away behind the blond-wood cabinet doors, and bedrooms have either queen or king beds. Business travelers can reserve the Westin's Guest Office, set up with a fax, printer, and in-room photocopier. Rooms for travelers with disabilities are available.

433 Robson St., Vancouver, B.C. V6B 6L9. ℂ **888/680-9393** or 604/602-1999. Fax 604/647-2502. www. westingrandvancouver.com. 207 suites. May–Sept C$189–C$429 (US$122–US$277) suite. Oct–Apr C$158–C$329 (US$102–US$212) suite. Up to 2 children under 17 stay free in parents' room. Additional person C$25 (US$16) extra. Pets accepted, C$50 (US$32) deposit. AE, DC, DISC, MC, V. Self-parking C$15 (US$10); valet parking C$19 (US$13). **Amenities:** Restaurant (West Coast); outdoor pool; excellent health club; Jacuzzi; sauna; children's program; concierge; business center; 24-hr. room service; in-room massage; babysitting; laundry service; same-day dry cleaning; nonsmoking rooms; executive rooms. *In room:* A/C, TV w/pay movies, dataport, kitchenette, minibar, coffeemaker, hair dryer, iron, safe.

MODERATE

Best Western Downtown Vancouver   The 12-story Best Western is just a 5-block walk from the theater area on Granville Street at the south end of downtown. All rooms are comfortable, and some rooms have harbor views. The corner rooms are a bit smaller than the rest, but they do have more light. This hotel is not overflowing with facilities, but the rooms are well furnished and the location is convenient. Accommodations with a full kitchen are available for an additional C$20 to C$25 (US$13–US$16).

718 Drake St. (at Granville St.), Vancouver, B.C. V6Z 2W6. ℂ **888/669-9888** or 604/669-9888. Fax 604/669-3440. www.bestwesterndowntown.com. 143 units; 32 with full kitchen. C$139–C$209 (US$90–US$135) double; C$280–C$350 (US$181–US$226) penthouse. Rates include deluxe continental breakfast. AE, DC, DISC, MC, V. Parking C$5 (US$3.25). **Amenities:** Restaurant; rooftop exercise room; Jacuzzi; sauna; game room; tour desk; shuttle service to downtown; babysitting; laundry service; nonsmoking rooms; corporate rooms. *In room:* A/C, TV/VCR, dataport, coffeemaker, hair dryer, iron, safe.

Days Inn Downtown   Situated in a heritage building dating back to 1910, Days Inn Downtown provides a central location for exploring Vancouver. The building is well maintained—all the rooms were refurbished in 1998, and the lobby underwent complete renovations in 1999. For travelers who don't need all the amenities of a large hotel, these rooms are comfortable and simply furnished. Ten of the rooms have showers only. Request a water view or consider a harbor-facing suite; rooms facing east stare directly at the concrete walls of the building next door.

921 W. Pender St., Vancouver, B.C. V6C 1M2. ℂ **800/329-7466** or 604/681-4335. Fax 604/681-7808. www. daysinnvancouver.com. 85 units (10 with shower only). May–Oct C$149–C$189 (US$96–US$122) double;

C$209 (US$135) suite. Nov–Apr C$105–C$125 (US$68–US$81) double; C$155 (US$100) suite. AE, DC, V. Valet parking C$10 (US$6.45). **Amenities:** Restaurant; bar; concierge; laundry service; same-day dry cleaning; nonsmoking rooms. *In room:* A/C, TV, dataport, fridge, coffeemaker, hair dryer, iron, safe.

Quality Hotel Downtown/The Inn at False Creek *(Kids)*   The Tex-Mex theme may seem out of place in Vancouver, but it works. The Inn at False Creek is a boutique hotel decorated with Mexican art, pottery, and rugs, in a kind of Santa Fe style. Room decor consists of dark green, terra-cotta, and earth tones, and brick for a touch of authenticity. The spacious suites are great for families— 15 have full kitchens, and a number of others have glassed-in balconies, which double as enclosed play areas (the hotel staff keeps a supply of board games and puzzles behind the front desk). Rooms on the back side are preferable because the hotel is situated beside the Granville Bridge on-ramp. The traffic noise is minimized in the front, however, by double-pane windows and black-out curtains. In the low season, the hotel's "City Passport" entitles guests to two-for-one discounts at numerous attractions, theaters, and restaurants.

1335 Howe St. (at Drake St.), Vancouver, B.C. V6Z 1R7. ⓒ 800/663-8474 or 604/682-0229. Fax 604/662-7566. www.qualityhotel.ca. 157 units. May–Sept. C$159 (US$103) double; C$189–C$209 (US$122–US$135) suite. Oct–Apr C$89 (US$57) double; C$109 (US$70) suite. AE, DC, DISC, MC, V. Parking C$8 (US$5) **Amenities:** Restaurant; bar; outdoor pool; access to nearby health club; Jacuzzi; sauna; concierge; tour desk; car rental; limited room service; babysitting; dry cleaning; nonsmoking rooms; executive-level rooms. *In room:* A/C, TV, dataport, coffeemaker, hairdryer, iron, safe, no phone.

Rosedale on Robson Suite Hotel *(★★)* *(Kids)*   Located directly across the street from Library Square, the Rosedale provides excellent value for the money, particularly when it comes to amenities. All rooms are one- or two-bedroom suites and feature separate living rooms with a pullout couch and full kitchenettes. Very family friendly, the Rosedale offers designated two-bedroom family suites: the kids' bedrooms are furnished with bunk beds and contain a large toy chest. On Saturday night, the Rosedale staff host a movie or craft night to take the little ones off their parents' hands for a while.

838 Hamilton (at Robson St.), Vancouver, B.C. V6B 6A2. ⓒ 800/661-8870 or 604/689-8033. Fax 604/689-4426. www.rosedaleonrobson.com. 275 units. May–Sept C$205–C$285 (US$132–US$184) suite. Oct–Apr C$125–C$185 (US$81–US$119) suite. Additional adult C$20 (US$13). Rates include continental breakfast. Pets accepted, C$10 (US$6.45) per day. AE, DC, DISC, MC, V. Parking C$8 (US$5). **Amenities:** Restaurant (NY deli); indoor lap pool; exercise room; Jacuzzi; sauna; steam room; concierge; children's programs; tour desk; car-rental desk; business center; limited room service; massage; babysitting; laundry service; dry cleaning; nonsmoking rooms; executive-level rooms. *In room:* A/C, TV w/pay movies, fax, dataport, kitchen, coffeemaker, hair dryer, iron.

INEXPENSIVE

Howard Johnson Hotel *(Finds)*   Yet another sign of south Granville's rapid gentrification, this formerly down-at-the-heels hotel was bought, gutted, renovated, and reopened in 1998 with an eye to the budget-conscious traveler. Hallways are decorated with photographs of Vancouver's early days, while the rooms themselves are comfortably if simply furnished. The suites have kitchenettes and sofa beds, convenient for families.

1176 Granville St., Vancouver, B.C. V6Z 1L8. ⓒ 888/654-6336 or 604/688-8701. Fax 604/688-8335. www.hojovancouver.com. May 1–Oct 15 C$129–C$149 (US$83–US$96) double; C$149–C$169 (US$96–US$109) suite. Oct 16–Apr 30 C$69–C$89 (US$45–US$57) double; C$99–C$119 (US$64–US$77) suite. Children under 17 stay free in parents' room. Rates include continental breakfast. AE, DC, MC, V. Parking C$8 (US$5). **Amenities:** Restaurant (Italian); bar; access to nearby health club; concierge; tour desk; laundry service; same-day dry cleaning; nonsmoking rooms. *In room:* A/C, TV w/pay movies, dataport, coffeemaker, hair dryer, iron, safe.

The Kingston Hotel (*Value*)   An affordable downtown hotel is a rarity for Vancouver; but if you can do without the frills, the Kingston offers a clean, comfortable place to sleep and a complimentary continental breakfast to start your day. Called a European-style hotel, it is indeed reminiscent of the small Parisian or Roman pensiones: no elevators, tiny rooms, and just 9 of the 55 rooms have private bathrooms and TVs. The rest have hand basins and the use of shared showers and toilets on each floor. Still, you will not find a cheaper option so close to all the downtown action.

757 Richards St., Vancouver, B.C. V6B 3A6. (C) 888/713-3304 or **604/684-9024.** Fax 604/684-9917. www. kingstonhotelvancouver.com. 55 units, 9 with private bathroom. C$58–C$115 (US$37–US$74) double. Extra person C$10 (US$6.45). Rates include continental breakfast. AE, MC, V. Parking C$10 (US$6.45) per day, ½ block away. **Amenities:** Sauna; coin-operated laundry; nonsmoking rooms. *In room:* TV (in units with private bathrooms).

Ramada Inn and Suites (*Finds*)   The Ramada was recently converted from a rooming house into a tourist hotel. The bright lobby and the guest rooms are all decorated in an Art Deco theme. The rooms are pleasant, with dark-wood furniture and small desks; everything is very new. Suites feature a sofa bed, kitchenette, and small dining area, making them very attractive for families. The location is convenient for exploring downtown and Yaletown, as well as hopping over to Granville Island or Kitsilano.

1221 Granville St., Vancouver, B.C. V6Z 1M6. (C) **888/835-0078** or 604/685-1111. Fax 604/685-0707. www. ramadavancouver.com. 116 units. May–Sept C$99–C$169 (US$64–US$109) double; Oct–Apr C$69–C$99 (US$45–US$64) double; suites C$20–C$40 (US$13–US$26) more than a standard room. AE, DC, DISC, MC, V. Valet parking C$10 (US$6.45). Pets accepted, C$20 (US$13) per night. **Amenities:** Restaurant (Irish); bar/lounge; laundry service; tour desk. *In room:* A/C, TV w/pay movies, dataport, kitchenette (in suites), coffeemaker, hair dryer.

YWCA Hotel/Residence (*ππ*) (*Value*)   Built in 1995, this attractive 12-story residence is next door to the Georgian Court Hotel. It's an excellent choice for travelers (male or female) as well as families with limited budgets. Bedrooms are simply furnished; some have TVs. There are quite a few reasonably priced restaurants nearby (but none in-house). Three communal kitchens are available for guests' use and all guest rooms have mini-fridges. (There are a number of small grocery stores nearby, as well as the Save-On Foods Supermarket a 10-min. walk west on Davie St.) There also are three TV lounges and free access to the best gym in town at the nearby co-ed YWCA Fitness Centre.

733 Beatty St., Vancouver, B.C. V6B 2M4. (C) **800/663-1424** or 604/895-5830. Fax 604/681-2550. www. ywcahotel.com. 155 units, 53 with private bathroom. C$54–C$86 (US$35–US$55) double with shared bathroom, C$74–C$132 (US$48–US$85) double with private bathroom. Additional person C$5 (US$3.20). Weekly, monthly, group, and off-season discounts available. AE, MC, V. Parking C$6 (US$4) per day. **Amenities:** Access to YWCA facility; coin-operated laundry; nonsmoking rooms. *In room:* A/C, TV in some rooms, dataport, fridge, hair dryer.

2 The West End

About a 10-minute walk from the downtown area, the West End's hotels are nestled amid the tree-lined residential streets bordering Stanley Park, within close proximity to Robson Street's many shops, restaurants, and attractions, as well as the surrounding beaches. Though there are fewer hotels here than downtown, the choices are more diverse.

EXPENSIVE

Delta Pinnacle (*ππ*)   Open since 2000, the Delta Pinnacle still hasn't lost its "new hotel" smell; everything gleams and glows and is in top-notch shape.

Located just between the West End and Coal Harbour, the hotel is close to Stanley Park, the waterfront, the cruise-ship terminal, and trendy Robson Street. All guest rooms have either two double beds or a king-size bed. Most bathrooms are large with a separate shower and tub combination and done up in beautiful marble. Oversize windows let in lots of light and the rooms above the 15th floor provide good city or mountain views. If you can, score one of the -19 rooms (2019, 2119, 2219 . . .); these oval-shaped units max out the window space and offer endless views, plus they're the largest rooms. The Signature rooms are worth the extra C$30 (US$19), but mostly for the access to the club lounge on the 25th floor with fantastic views of the mountains. Breakfast and hors d'oeuvres are served daily for Signature guests.

1128 West Hastings St., Vancouver B.C., V6E 4R5. © 800/268-1133 or 604/684-1128. Fax 604/298-1128. www.deltahotels.com. 434 units. June 1–Oct 14 C$219–C$329 (US$141–US$212) double. Oct 15–May 31 C$159–C$249 (US$103–US$161) double. Children 18 and under stay free in parents' room. AE, DC, MC, V. Self-parking C$16 (US$10) per day; valet parking C$21 (US$14) per day. Skytrain to Burrard Station. **Amenities:** Restaurant; bar; indoor lap pool; health club; Jacuzzi; sauna; concierge; business center; 24-hr. room service; laundry; same-day dry cleaning service; nonsmoking rooms; executive-level rooms. *In room:* A/C, TV/pay movies, dataport, minibar, coffeemaker, hair dryer, iron, safe.

Listel Vancouver ★★ *Finds*   This hotel has always had a killer location—right at the western end of the Robson Street shopping strip. Recently, the owners have been putting a lot of effort—and money—into making the interior match the address. Rooms now feature top-quality bedding and cherrywood furnishings, including cozy little window banquettes. Particularly noteworthy are the Gallery Rooms on the top two floors. Each of these rooms and suites is like a private gallery, hung with original artworks from the Buschlen Mowatt Gallery, one of the city's leading private art dealers. On a more practical note, these rooms feature upgraded amenities and better views. The upper-floor rooms facing Robson Street, with glimpses of the harbor and the mountains beyond, are worth the price. (The others face the alley and nearby apartment buildings.) Soundproof windows eliminate traffic noise, which can be pretty loud on summer weekends.

1300 Robson St., Vancouver, B.C. V6E 1C5. © 800/663-5491 or 604/684-8461. Fax 604/684-8326. www.listel-vancouver.com. 130 units. May–Sept C$260 (US$168) standard double; C$320 (US$206) gallery room double; C$600 (US$387) suite. Oct–Apr C$220 (US$142) standard double; C$260 (US$168) gallery room double; C$350 (US$226) suite. AE, DC, DISC, MC, V. Parking C$14 (US$9). **Amenities:** Restaurant; bar; exercise room; limited room service; same-day dry cleaning; nonsmoking rooms; concierge-level rooms. *In room:* A/C, TV, dataport, iron, minibar, coffeemaker, hair dryer.

Pacific Palisades Hotel ★★★ *Finds*   Walk into the Pacific Palisades lobby and you know right away that this is not just another standard-issue hotel. Bold and bright colors, whimsically shaped glass chandeliers, and a sleek metal fireplace give the hotel a contemporary modern look. Watch your step for Pal the robotic dog who likes to sniff out newcomers by the check-in desk.

Guest rooms are spread out over two towers, both of which have recently undergone extensive renovations; the revamped rooms are fabulous. All rooms have kitchenettes (everything but the stove) and are decorated in funky apple greens and lemon yellows with a splash of blue or red, an interesting counterpoint to the modern blond-wood furniture. The rooms are spacious with large wall-to-wall windows. Even bigger are the one-bedroom suites, which boast large living/dining rooms. All suites have balconies and can easily accommodate four adults. A couple of other perks that make this hotel a worthwhile choice are the complimentary afternoon wine tasting and the best minibar items in town (everyone's a sucker for animal crackers and licorice).

1277 Robson St., Vancouver, B.C. V6E 1C4. © **800/663-1815** or 604/688-0461. Fax 604/688-4374. www.pacificpalisadeshotel.com. 233 units. May 1–Oct 15 C$245 (US$158) double; C$275 (US$177) suite. Oct 16–Apr 30 C$185 (US$120) double; C$275 (US$177) suite. Full kitchens C$30 (US$19) extra. AE, DC, DISC, MC, V. Parking C$22 (US$14). **Amenities:** Restaurant (see Zin's in chapter 5 for review); bar; indoor lap pool; basketball court; excellent health club; spa services; Jacuzzi; sauna; bike rentals; concierge; tour desk; business center; 24-hr. room service; massage; babysitting; coin laundry and laundry service; same-day dry cleaning; nonsmoking rooms. *In room:* A/C, TV, dataport, kitchenette, minibar, fridge, coffeemaker, hair dryer, iron.

Westin Bayshore Resort & Marina ★★★ (Kids)   Thanks to a C$55-million renovation, this venerable resort hotel looks better than ever. The lobby has been completely redesigned to show off the surrounding park and mountains; achieving much the same thing are two new restaurants and a coffee bar, with two outdoor decks overlooking the harbor. Perched on the water's edge overlooking Stanley Park's eastern entrance, the Bayshore is still just a short stroll along the seawall from the Canada Place Pier and downtown, and the neighborhood just keeps getting better. Rooms in the original 1961 building have been completely refurbished with classic-looking decor and modern gadgets such as high-speed Internet, two phone lines, and comfortable lighting. In the newer tower, the rooms are spacious and bright; all come with balconies and large windows. Both towers offer unobstructed views of the harbor's dazzling array of sailboats, luxury yachts, and floatplanes. This family-friendly hotel provides children with their own welcome package upon check-in and organizes Super Saturdays, a behind-the-scenes tour of the hotel's operations and movie night for the young ones, giving the parents the night off.

1601 Bayshore Dr., Vancouver, B.C. V6G 2V4. © **800/228-3000** or 604/682-3377. Fax 604/687-3102. www. westinbayshore.com. 510 units. Mid-Apr to Oct C$289 (US$186) double; C$450–C$700 (US$290–US$452) suite. Nov to mid-Apr C$195 (US$126) double; C$370–C$420 (US$239–US$271) suite. Children under 19 stay free in parents' room. AE, DC, MC, V. Self-parking C$18 (US$12); valet parking C$19 (US$12). **Amenities:** 2 restaurants; bar; indoor and magnificent outdoor pool with mountain view; health club; Jacuzzi; sauna; watersports rental; children's programs; concierge; tour desk; car rental; business center; shopping arcade; 24-hr. room service; massage; babysitting; laundry service; same-day dry cleaning; nonsmoking rooms. *In room:* A/C, TV w/pay movies, dataport, minibar, coffeemaker, hair dryer, iron.

MODERATE

Barclay House in the West End ★★ (Finds)   The Barclay House, located on one of the West End's quiet maple-lined streets just a block from the historic Barclay Square, opened as a bed-and-breakfast in 1999. Built in 1904 by a local developer, this beautiful house can be a destination on its own. The elegant parlors and dining rooms are perfect for lounging on a rainy afternoon or sipping a glass of complimentary sherry before venturing out for dinner in the trendy West End. On a summer day, the front porch with its comfortable chairs makes for a cozy place to read. All rooms are beautifully furnished in Victorian style; a number of the pieces are family heirlooms. Modern conveniences such as CD players, TV/VCRs, and luxurious bathrooms blend in perfectly. The Penthouse offers skylights, a fireplace, and romantic claw-foot tub; the South Room contains a queen-size brass bed and an elegant sitting room.

1351 Barclay St., Vancouver, B.C. V6E 1H6. © **800/971-1351** or 604/605-1351. Fax 604/605-1382. www. barclayhouse.com. 5 units. C$145–C$225 (US$93–US$145) double. MC, V. Free parking. **Amenities:** Access to nearby fitness center; massage; concierge; nonsmoking rooms. *In room:* TV/VCR w/pay movies, extensive video library, fridge, hair dryer, iron.

Blue Horizon ★ (Finds)   This unmistakable, blue-tiled, 1960s high-rise on Robson Street capitalizes on one of Vancouver's best assets—the view. The small lobby features a tall glass sculpture entitled *Water and Air*, and the theme has been carried throughout the restaurant and lounge on the ground floor. Upstairs, the rooms are spacious—every room is a corner room, which maximizes light and window space. In 2000 the hotel renovated all its guest rooms, giving them a clean, contemporary look. The best views are on the 15th floor and higher. All feature sizable sitting areas, and, of course, balconies.

1225 Robson St., Vancouver, B.C. V6E 1C5. ℂ **800/663-1333** or 604/688-1411. Fax 604/688-4461. www. bluehorizonhotel.com. 214 units. C$89–C$199 (US$57–US$128) double; C$127-C$279 (US$82–US$180) suite. Children under 16 stay free in parents' room. Extra person C$15 (US$10). AE, DC, MC, V. Self-parking C$9 (US$6). **Amenities:** Restaurant; indoor pool; exercise room; Jacuzzi; sauna; concierge; tour desk; babysitting; same-day dry cleaning; nonsmoking rooms. *In room:* A/C, TV w/pay movies, dataport, iron, minibar, fridge, coffeemaker, hair dryer, safe.

Coast Plaza Suite Hotel at Stanley Park

Built originally as an apartment building, this 35-story hotel above the Denman Place Mall attracts a wide variety of guests, from business travelers and bus tours to film and TV actors. They come for the large rooms, affordable one- or two-bedroom suites, and amazing views of English Bay. Undoubtedly the best room, the two-bedroom corner suite is bigger than most people's West End apartments and boasts a spectacular view of the ocean. Don't even think of booking these during the Fireworks (see HSBC Power Smart Celebration of Light, p. 25), unless it's for 2008 maybe? The one-bedroom suites and standard rooms are still very spacious, all with floor-to-ceiling windows and a balcony; about half the units have full kitchens. Furnishings are plain and comfortable, if a little dated, but the hotel is working on an upgrade.

1763 Comox St., Vancouver, B.C. V6G 1P6. ℂ **800/663-1144** or 604/688-7711. Fax 604/688-5934. www. coasthotels.com. 267 units. C$129–C$199 (US$83–US$128) double; C$155–C$290 (US$100–US$187) suite. AE, DC, DISC, MC, V. Parking C$8 (US$5.20). Pets accepted. **Amenities:** 2 restaurants; bar; indoor pool; access to Denman Fitness Centre in mall below; Jacuzzi; sauna; concierge; tour desk; downtown shuttle service; business center; shopping arcade; 24-hr. room service; babysitting; coin laundry; same-day dry cleaning; nonsmoking rooms. *In room:* A/C, TV, dataport, iron, minibar, fridge, coffeemaker, hair dryer.

Parkhill Hotel *(Value*

A favorite among Asian tourists, the 24-story Parkhill offers an affordable alternative for those wishing to stay in the West End. Located in the heart of Davie Street, its guests are within walking distance of dozens of restaurants, nightlife, shopping, and the beach. Not particularly luxurious, this hotel offers comfortable and spotless accommodations. Formerly an apartment building, the studios have been converted into hotel rooms, resulting in very spacious units with lots of closet space; all have balconies. Except for the corner suites, which feature a king-size bed and pullout couch, all rooms are identical; you just pay more according to the view. For the best views reserve a deluxe room (20th–23rd floors) facing north or west, catching both the mountains and English Bay. Located on floors 14 through 19 are Superior rooms with still excellent views; standard units are on floors 4 through 13.

1160 Davie St., Vancouver, B.C. V6E 1N1. ℂ **800/663-1525** or 604/685-1311. Fax 604/681-0208. www. parkhillhotel.com. 192 units. May 16–Sept 30 C$185–C$220 (US$119–US$142) double. Oct 1–May 15 C$109–C$139 (US$70–US$90) double. AE, DC, MC, V. Parking C$10 (US$6.45). **Amenities:** 2 restaurants; bar; heated outdoor pool; small exercise room; concierge; tour desk; business center; limited room service; laundry service; same-day dry cleaning; nonsmoking rooms. *In room:* A/C, TV, dataport, coffeemaker, hair dryer, iron.

The Rosellen Suites at Stanley Park *(★★ (Kids*

Staying at the Rosellen is like having your own apartment in the West End. Stanley Park and the seawall are within a few blocks and busy Denman Street with its many restaurants and shops is just three blocks east. Converted into a hotel to meet the demand for rooms during the 1986 Expo, the Rosellen has remained a favorite among travelers, with a high rate of repeat guests.

The hotel offers a no-frills stay; the lobby is only open during office hours, and guests receive their own key. The largest apartment—1,150 square feet—is known as the director's suite, with two bedrooms, a large dining room, a spacious kitchen, and more storage room than you know what to do with. The remaining apartments are certainly smaller than this mammoth one, but none of them really skimp on size. The one-bedroom suites sleep four comfortably, and all units come with fully equipped kitchens, making them a great option for families.

100–2030 Barclay St., Vancouver, B.C. V6G 1L5. **☎** **888/317-6648** or 604/689-4807. Fax 604/684-3327. www.rosellensuites.com. 31 units. June–Sept C$175(US$113) 1-bedroom apt; C$200–C$280 (US$129–US$181) 2-bedroom apt; C$375 (US$242) penthouse. Oct–May C$110(US$71) 1-bedroom apt; C$140–C$200 (US$90–US$129) 2-bedroom apt; C$300 (US$194) penthouse. Minimum 3-night stay. Rates include up to 4 people in a 1-bedroom apt and 6 in a 2-bedroom apt. Cots and cribs free. AE, DC, DISC, MC, V. Limited parking C$5 (US$3.25); reserve when booking room. Pets accepted, C$15 (US$9.70) per day. **Amenities:** Access to nearby health club and tennis courts; coin laundry; nonsmoking rooms. *In room:* TV, dataport, modern kitchen, coffeemaker, hair dryer, iron.

Sunset Inn Travel Apartments *(Value)*   Just on the edge of the residential West End neighborhood, the Sunset Inn offers spacious accommodations for a very reasonable price. Units are either studios or one-bedroom apartments and come with fully equipped kitchens. Like many other hotels in this part of town, the Sunset Inn started its life as an apartment building, which means that the rooms are much bigger than your average hotel room. All have balconies, but the views are nothing special in this part of town. For those traveling with children, the one-bedroom suites have a separate bedroom and a pullout couch (two in the larger one-bedrooms) in the living room. The furnishings currently are a bit dated with eighties-style black-and-chrome dining sets and such, but the hotel is in the process of updating and renovating the rooms. If style matters, request a refurnished unit when making your reservation.

1111 Burnaby St., Vancouver, B.C. V6E 1P4. **☎** **800/786-1997** or 604/688-2474. Fax 604/669-3340. www.sunsetinn.com. 50 units. C$88–C$168 (US$57–US$108) studio; C$98–C$188 (US$63–US$121) 1-bedroom suite. Weekly rates and other off-season discounts available. AE, DC, MC, V. Free parking. **Amenities:** Exercise room; coin laundry; nonsmoking rooms. *In room:* TV, kitchen, coffeemaker.

West End Guest House *★★ (Finds)*   A beautiful heritage home built in 1906, the West End Guest House is a fine example of what the neighborhood looked like up until the early '50s, before the concrete towers and condos replaced the original Edwardian homes. Decorated with beautiful early-20th-century antiques and an amazing collection of vintage photographs of Vancouver, this is a wonderful respite from the hustle and bustle of the West End. The seven guest rooms are beautifully furnished and offer the ultimate in bed-time luxury: feather mattresses, down duvets, and your very own resident stuffed animal. Particularly indulgent is the Grand Queen Suite, an attic-level bedroom with skylights, brass bed, fireplace, sitting area, and claw-foot bathtub. Owner Evan Penner pampers his guests with a scrumptious breakfast and serves iced tea and sherry in the afternoon. Throughout the day, guests have access to the porch kitchen stocked with home-baked munchies and refreshments. If you ask nicely, Penner will even crank up the gramophone.

1362 Haro St., Vancouver, B.C. V6E 1G2. **☎** **604/681-2889.** Fax 604/688-8812. www.westendguesthouse.com. 7 units. C$145–C$250 (US$94–US$161) double. Rates include full breakfast. AE, DISC, MC, V. Free valet parking. **Amenities:** Complimentary bikes; concierge; business center; laundry service; nonsmoking facility. *In room:* TV/VCR, dataport, hair dryer.

INEXPENSIVE

Buchan Hotel   Built in 1926, this charming three-story building is tucked away on a quiet tree-lined residential street in the West End. It's less than 2 blocks from Stanley Park and Denman Street and 10 minutes by foot from the business district. The standard rooms are quite plain; be prepared for cramped quarters and tiny bathrooms, half of which are shared, yet still nice and clean. The best rooms in the house are the executive rooms. These front-corner rooms are nicely furnished, and the bathrooms are spotless. There are only four of them, so book in advance. The hotel also offers in-house bike and ski storage.

1906 Haro St., Vancouver, B.C. V6G 1H7. (C) **800/668-6654** or 604/685-5354. Fax 604/685-5367. www. buchanhotel.com. 60 units, 30 with private bathroom. C$45–C$75 (US$29–US$48) double with shared bath, C$70–C$95 (US$45–US$61) double with private bath; C$110–C$135 (US$71–US$87) executive room. Children 2 and under stay free in parents' room. Weekly rates and off-season discounts available. AE, DC, MC, V. Street parking available. **Amenities:** Reading lounge; activities desk; nonsmoking rooms; coin laundry. *In room:* TV, iron and hairdryer available upon request, no phone.

Hostelling International Vancouver Downtown Hostel   Located in a converted nunnery, this new and modern curfew-free hostel is an extremely convenient base of operations from which to explore downtown. The beach is a few blocks south; downtown is a 10-minute walk north. Most beds are in quad dorms, with a limited number of doubles and triples available. Except for two rooms with a private bathroom, all bathroom facilities are shared. Rooms and facilities are accessible for travelers with disabilities. There are common cooking facilities, as well as a rooftop patio and game room. The hostel is extremely busy in the summertime, so book ahead. Many organized activities such as ski packages and tours can be booked at the hostel. There's free shuttle service to the bus/train station and Jericho Beach.

1114 Burnaby St. (at Thurlow St.), Vancouver, B.C. V6E 1P1. (C) **888/203-4302** or 604/684-4565. Fax 604/684-4540. www.hihostels.ca. 68 rooms (44 4-person shared rooms, 24 double or triple private rooms). Beds C$20 (US$13) IYHA members, C$24 (US$15) nonmembers; doubles C$55 (US$35) members, C$64 (US$41) nonmembers; triples C$70 (US$45) members, C$86 (US$55) nonmembers. Annual adult membership C$35 (US$23). MC, V. Limited free parking. **Amenities:** Bike rental; activities desk; game room; coin laundry. *In room:* No phone.

Sylvia Hotel   Built in 1912 when the West End was relatively unpopulated, the Sylvia is on the shores of English Bay just a few blocks from Stanley Park. One of Vancouver's oldest hotels, the gray-stone, ivy-wreathed exterior is grand, and the lobby sets up high expectations with its beautiful stain-glass windows, marble staircase, red carpets, and overstuffed chairs. Alas, the elegance does not carry over to the rooms, which are rather plainly furnished with slightly mismatched furniture. The best rooms are located on the higher floors facing English Bay; views of the water get better in the winter when the tall trees lining the beach lose their leaves. The suites have fully equipped kitchens and are large enough for families. Sixteen rooms in the 12-year-old low-rise annex have individual heating but offer less atmosphere.

1154 Gilford St., Vancouver, B.C. V6G 2P6. (C) **604/681-9321.** Fax 604/682-3551. www.sylviahotel.com. 118 units. Apr–Sept C$75–C$135 (US$48–US$87) double. Oct–Mar C$75–C$100 (US$48–US$65) double. Children under 18 stay free in parents' room. AE, DC, MC, V. Parking C$7 (US$4.50). **Amenities:** Restaurant; bar; concierge; limited room service; dry cleaning; nonsmoking rooms. *In room:* TV, dataport, hair dryer.

3 The West Side

Right across False Creek from downtown and the West End is Vancouver's West Side. If your agenda includes a Granville Island shopping spree, exploration of the island's numerous artists' studios and galleries, or strolls through the sunken garden at Queen Elizabeth Park; or if you require close proximity to the airport without staying in an "airport hotel," you'll find both cozy B&Bs and hotels that will meet your needs.

EXPENSIVE

Granville Island Hotel ★★ (Finds) One of the city's best kept hotel secrets is the Granville Island Hotel. Not only can you stroll, jog, or blade to this hotel but how about kayaking or sailing in? Tucked away on the edge of Granville Island, the hotel offers a unique waterfront setting in the heart of some of the city's most interesting galleries and theaters, and just a short stroll from the cornucopia that is the Granville Island food market. A recent expansion has brought the number of rooms to 85. The transition between the original wing and the new addition is practically seamless and all rooms are spacious with large bathrooms and soaker tubs. Most rooms also have a microwave (or you can request one from housekeeping) to warm up any goodies you bring back from the market. Thanks to large windows, the rooms are extremely bright and take advantage of the fabulous views of False Creek. The very best views, however, are to be had in one of the Penthouse suites, located in the new wing. These units are humongous, celebrity-worthy suites with private deck, dining room with fireplace and sitting area, large bedroom, and raised Jacuzzi tub. Ultimately affordable at C$450 (US$290) in high season and C$350 (US$226) the rest of the year, advance booking is required.

1253 Johnston St., Vancouver, B.C. V6H 3R9. ⓒ **800/663-1840** or 604/683-7373. Fax 604/683-3061. www. granvilleislandhotel.com. 85 units. C$160–C$230 (US$103–US$148) double; C$190–C$260 (US$123–US$168) 1-bedroom suite; C$350–C$450 (US$226–US$290) penthouse suite. Off-season discounts available. AE, DC, DISC, MC, V. Parking C$6 (US$3.90). Pets accepted. **Amenities:** Restaurant; brew pub; access to nearby health club and tennis courts; small exercise room; Jacuzzi; bike rental; concierge; tour desk; car-rental desk; business center; limited room service; massage; babysitting; laundry; same-day dry cleaning; nonsmoking rooms. *In room:* A/C, TV w/pay movies, fax, dataport, minibar, coffeemaker, hair dryer, iron.

MODERATE

Kenya Court Ocean Front Guest House ★ (Finds) Every room in this three-story architectural landmark at Kitsilano Beach has an unobstructed waterfront view of Vanier Park, English Bay, downtown Vancouver, and the Coast Mountains. It's an ideal launching pad for strolls around Granville Island, Vanier Park, the Maritime Museum, the Vancouver Museum, and other Kitsilano sights. Each guest suite—with a living room, bathroom, separate bedroom, and full kitchen—is a large converted apartment that's been tastefully furnished. A full breakfast is served in the rooftop glass solarium.

2230 Cornwall Ave., Vancouver, B.C. V6K 1B5. ⓒ **604/738-7085.** H&dwilliams@telus.net. 4 units. C$135–C$165 (US$87–US$106) double. Extra person C$50 (US$32). No credit cards. Garage or street parking. **Amenities:** Nonsmoking facility; outdoor pool; tennis; jogging trails nearby. *In room:* TV, fax, kitchenette, fridge, coffeemaker, hair dryer, iron.

INEXPENSIVE

Hostelling International Vancouver Jericho Beach Hostel Located in a former military barracks, this hostel is surrounded by an expansive lawn adjacent to Jericho Beach. Individuals, families with children over age 5, and groups are welcome. The 10 private rooms can accommodate up to six people. These particular accommodations go fast; so if you want one, call far in advance. The dormitory-style arrangements are well maintained and supervised. Linens are provided. Basic, inexpensive food is served in the cafe April through October.

During the rest of the year, food is available at the front desk. You have the option of cooking for yourself year-round in the hostel's kitchen. The hostel's program director operates tours and activities.

1515 Discovery St., Vancouver, B.C. V6R 4K5. © 888/203-4303 or 604/224-3208. Fax 604/224-4852. www. hihostels.ca. 286 beds in 14 dorms; 10 private family rooms. No private bathrooms. C$18 (US$12) IYHA members, C$22 (US$14) nonmembers dorm rooms; C$50–C$75 (US$32–US$48) members, C$60–C$90 (US$39–US$58) nonmembers family rooms. Annual adult membership C$37 (US$24). MC, V. Parking C$3 (US$1.95). Children under 5 not allowed. **Amenities:** Cafe; bike rental; activities desk; coin laundry; nonsmoking rooms.

Johnson Heritage House Bed & Breakfast ★★ (Finds) Innkeeper Ron Johnson is a collector. His antique phonographs, coffee grinders, wooden giraffes, hobby horses, Indonesian stone sculpture, and countless other objects are on charming display in various nooks and crannies of this old Craftsman home in Vancouver's quiet Kerrisdale neighborhood (a 15-min. drive from the Vancouver airport and about a 10-min. drive to downtown). The Garden room downstairs is quiet and self-contained, with big bright windows overlooking a garden brimming with raspberries and blueberries. Upstairs, the small but cozy Sunshine room (shower only) offers a balcony with a view of the back garden, while the larger Mountain View room offers an excellent view of the Lions and the other peaks of the North Shore. And though the private bathroom for the Mountain View is across the hall, it comes with a giant two-person claw-foot tub. Best of all is the Carousel room. It's large and bright, with a big four-poster brass bed, a slate fireplace, and a generously sized bathroom. A full breakfast is served in the spacious dining room that looks out onto the tree-shaded garden.

2278 W. 34th Ave., Vancouver, B.C. V6M 1G6. © 604/266-4175. Fax 604/266-4175. www.johnsons-inn-vancouver.com. 4 units, 1 with shower only. C$125–C$180 (US$81–US$116) double. Rates include full breakfast. No credit cards. Free parking. **Amenities:** Non-smoking facility; Internet access. *In room:* TV/VCR, dataport with high-speed Internet access, hair dryer, iron.

Penny Farthing Inn Built in 1912, this landmark house on a quiet residential street is filled with antiques and stained glass. There's a common room with a fireplace; in the backyard, an English-country-style garden is filled with trees and fragrant flowers. All the guest rooms are decorated with lovely pine furniture. On the top floor, Abigail's Suite is bright and self-contained with nice views from both front and back. Bettina's Room features a fireplace and a small balcony. Sophie's Room, though smaller, has a nice porch with two wicker chairs. Lucinda's Room—with a private bathroom across the hall—offers the best value of the four. Coffee and a selection of teas and hot chocolate are always on hand for guests. Fix a cuppa and watch the resident cats at play while you relax.

2855 W. Sixth Ave., Vancouver, B.C. V6K 1X2. © 866/739-9002 or 604/739-9002. Fax 604/739-9004. www.pennyfarthinginn.com. 4 units. May–Oct C$120 (US$77) double; C$175 (US$113) suite. Nov–Apr C$100 (US$64) double; C$150 (US$96) suite. Rates include full breakfast. No credit cards. Street parking. **Amenities:** Free use of bikes; business center; Internet access; nonsmoking rooms. *In room:* TV/VCR and CD player (in suites only), dataport, fridge, coffeemaker, hair dryer.

The University of British Columbia Conference Centre ★★ (Value) The University of British Columbia is in a pretty forested setting on the tip of Point Grey—a convenient location if you plan to spend a lot of time either in Kitsilano or at the university itself. It's also not bad if you have a car, but otherwise, it's a good half-hour bus ride from downtown. Although these are student dorms most of the year, rooms are usually available—but don't expect luxury. The 17-story Walter Gage Residence offers new and comfortable accommodations; many are located on the upper floors with sweeping views of the city and ocean.

One- and six-bedroom suites here come equipped with private bathrooms, kitchenettes, TVs, and phones. Each studio suite has a twin bed; each one-bedroom suite features a queen bed; the six-bedroom Tower suites—a particularly good deal for families—each feature one double bed and five twin beds. Located next door, the year-round Gage Court suites have two twin beds in one bedroom and a queen-size Murphy bed in the sitting room.

5961 Student Union Blvd., Vancouver, B.C. V6T 2C9. ✆ 604/822-1000. Fax 604/822-1001. www.ubc accommodation.com. About 1,900 units. Gage Towers and Pacific Spirit Hostel units only available May 10–Aug 26. Gage Towers: C$37–C$59 (US$24–US$38) standard or premium single with shared bathroom; C$89–C$209 (US$57–US$135) studio, 1-, or 6-bedroom suites. Pacific Spirit Hostel: C$24 (US$16) single; C$48 (US$31) double; C$59 (US$38) studio suite with private bathroom. Located adjacent to the Gage Residence, the 47 West Coast Suites are available year-round: May–Sept C$129–C$139 (US$83–US$90) suite; Oct–Apr C$119–C$129 (US$77–US$83) suite. AE, MC, V. Free parking May–Aug 26 at Gage Towers; other areas C$5 (US$3.25) per day. Bus: 4, 10, or 99. **Amenities** (nearby on campus): Restaurant; cafeteria; pub; public golf course; Olympic-size swimming pool; tennis courts; weight room; sauna for C$5 (US$3.35) per person; video arcade; laundry; all rooms nonsmoking. *In room:* A/C, TV, hair dryer.

4 The North Shore (North Vancouver & West Vancouver)

The North Shore cities of North and West Vancouver are pleasant and lush and much less hurried than Vancouver. Staying here also offers easy access to the North Shore mountains and its attractions, including hiking trails, the Capilano Suspension Bridge, and the ski slopes on Mount Seymour, Grouse Mountain, and Cypress Bowl. Staying here is also often cheaper than in Vancouver. The disadvantage is that if you want to take your car into Vancouver, there are only two bridges, and during rush hours they're painfully slow. The SeaBus, however, is not only quick, but fairly scenic.

EXPENSIVE

Lonsdale Quay Hotel ⭐ Directly across the Burrard Inlet from the Canada Place Pier, the Lonsdale Quay Hotel is at the water's edge above the Lonsdale Quay Market at the SeaBus terminal. An escalator rises from the midst of the market's food, crafts, and souvenir stalls to the front desk on the third floor. The rooms are simply furnished and tastefully decorated, without the grandeur or luxurious touches of comparably priced downtown hotels. Nevertheless, the hotel has unique and fabulous harbor and city views, is only 15 minutes by bus or car from Grouse Mountain Ski Resort and Capilano Regional Park, and provides easy access to the BC Rail and ferry terminals.

123 Carrie Cates Court, North Vancouver, B.C. V6M 3K7. ✆ 800/836-6111 or 604/986-6111. Fax 604/986-8782. www.lonsdalequayhotel.com. 83 units. High season C$125–C$225 (US$81–US$145) double or twin; C$350 (US$226) suite. Low season C$90–C$165 (US$58–US$106) double or twin; C$250 (US$161) suite. Extra person C$25 (US$16). Senior discount available. AE, DC, DISC, MC, V. Parking C$7 (US$4.50); free on weekends and holidays. SeaBus: Lonsdale Quay. **Amenities:** 2 restaurants; small exercise room; spa; bike rental; children's play area; concierge; tour desk; shopping arcade; limited room service; massage; babysitting; laundry service; same-day dry cleaning; nonsmoking hotel; executive-level rooms. *In room:* A/C, TV, dataport, minibar, coffeemaker, hair dryer, iron.

MODERATE

Beachside Bed & Breakfast ⭐⭐ *(Finds)* Vancouver is blessed by geography, and this B&B takes full advantage; it sits on its own private little beach on the shores of English Bay, with a sweeping view of Stanley Park, the Lion's Gate Bridge, and the tall skyline of downtown Vancouver. The upstairs common area of this split-level house features wall-to-ceiling windows and binoculars for gazing at the seals and bald eagles and (on rare occasions) killer whales that swim by. There's also a fireplace, VCR and videos, and lots of good books should the ocean view lose its appeal. Downstairs are two beachfront rooms featuring floor-to-ceiling windows. The Seaside room features a jetted tub for two in a somewhat small but private bathroom, while the Oceanfront room has a huge private Jacuzzi big enough for six. Located out back, the smallest and least expensive of the rooms—Diane's Room—features a small patio but lacks an ocean view.

4208 Evergreen Ave., West Vancouver, B.C. V7V 1H1. 📞 800/563-3311 or 604/922-7773. www.beach.bc.ca. 3 units. C$150–C$300 (US$97–US$194) double. Extra person C$30 (US$19). Rates include breakfast tray. MC, V. Free parking, movies. Bus: 250, 251, 252, or 253. **Amenities:** Beachside Jacuzzi; nonsmoking hotel. *In room:* TV/VCR, fridge, microwave, coffeemaker, hair dryer, iron.

INEXPENSIVE

Mountainside Manor   This is the closest house to the ski slopes and hiking trails of Grouse Mountain and the glorious nature of the North Shore. But though it sits high above the city on the edge of the forest, the Manor is anything but rustic. Indeed, it's an ultramodern home with a contemporary, even avant-garde feel. The upstairs City Room features a four-poster bed and a view of the Vancouver skyline, while the Panorama Room—the largest of the rooms—has a queen-size bed, a Jacuzzi, and views of the mountains, the city, English Bay, and Vancouver Island. Downstairs you'll find a common room with a fireplace, but even better is the backyard hot tub with a view of the soaring North Shore peaks.

5909 Nancy Greene Way, North Vancouver, B.C. V7R 4W6. 📞 **800/967-1319** or 604/990-9772. Fax 604/985-8470. www.mtnsideaccom.com May–Oct C$110–C$145 (US$71–US$94) double. Nov–Apr C$95–C$135 (US$61–US$87) double. Rates include full breakfast. Off-season discounts available. MC, V. Free parking. *In room:* TV, coffeemaker, hair dryer, iron, no phone.

5

Where to Dine in Vancouver

Two thousand restaurants? Five thousand? Hard to say really, but Vancouverites do dine out more than residents of any other Canadian city. Outstanding meals are available in all price ranges and in many different cuisines, from Caribbean to Mongolian and Japanese. Even better, over the past few years Vancouverites have come to expect top quality, and yet they absolutely refuse to pay the kind of top dollar restaurant-goers pay in New York or San Francisco. For discerning diners from elsewhere, Vancouver is a steal.

The cuisine buzzword here is West Coast. Justifiable pride in local produce, game, and seafood is combined with innovation and creativity. More restaurants are shifting to seasonal, even monthly, menus, giving their chefs greater freedom. The trend to tapas remains alive and well. By contrast, *fusion*—the promiscuous mixing of spices and ingredients from around the globe—is dying out, replaced by a new culinary rectitude.

Once less than palatable, British Columbian wines have improved to the point that local vintners are now winning international acclaim. The big wine-producing areas are in the Okanagan Valley (in southern British Columbia's dry interior) or else on southern Vancouver Island. (If you have a few extra days, either area is definitely worth a visit.) Fortunately, these wines have received far less publicity than they deserve, so some great bargains can still be had.

There's no provincial tax on restaurant meals in British Columbia, but venues add the 7% federal goods and services tax (GST). Restaurant hours vary. Lunch is typically served from noon to 1 or 2pm; Vancouverites begin dining around 6:30pm, later in summer. Reservations are recommended at most restaurants and are essential at popular places.

1 Restaurants by Cuisine

AMERICAN
Sophie's Cosmic Café (West Side, $, p. 94)
The Tomahawk Restaurant ★ (North Shore, $, p. 97)

BISTRO
The Brickhouse Bistro ★★ (East Side, $$, p. 95)
Bukowski's (East Side, $$, p. 95)

CANADIAN
Rooster's Quarters (The West End, $, p. 89)

CARIBBEAN
The Reef ★★ (East Side, $$, p. 96)

CASUAL
Bin 941 Tapas Parlour (Downtown/Yaletown, $$, p. 82)
Bukowski's (East Side, $$, p. 95)
Cactus Club Café (The West End, $$, p. 91)
Café Zen (West Side, $$, p. 92)

The Cat's Meow (West Side, $$, p. 91)

Dockside Brewing Company ⚘ (West Side, $$, p. 92)

The Locus Café (East Side, $$, p. 96)

Mark's Fiasco (West Side, $$, p. 92)

The SandBar ⚘⚘ (West Side, $$, p. 93)

Zin's ⚘ (The West End, $$, p. 88)

CHINESE/DIM SUM

Park Lock Seafood Restaurant (Gastown/Chinatown, $$, p. 84)

Pink Pearl ⚘ (Gastown/Chinatown, $$, p. 85)

Shao Lin Noodle Restaurant (West Side, $, p. 94)

Sun Sui Wah ⚘⚘ (East Side, $$$, p. 95)

COFFEE

Caffé Artigiano ⚘ (The West End, $, p. 98)

Epicurean Delicatessen Caffé (Kitsilano, $, p. 99)

CONTINENTAL

Delilah's ⚘⚘ (The West End, $$$, p. 86)

DESSERTS

Death by Chocolate ⚘ (many locations, $, p. 98)

FAMILY STYLE

Romano's Macaroni Grill at the Mansion ⚘⚘ (The West End, $$, p. 88)

Sophie's Cosmic Café (West Side, $, p. 94)

Rooster's Quarters (The West End, $, p. 89)

The Tomahawk Restaurant ⚘ (North Shore, $, p. 97)

FISH & CHIPS

Olympia Oyster & Fish Co. Ltd. (Downtown/Yaletown, $, p. 83)

FRENCH

Lumière ⚘⚘⚘ (West Side, $$$$, p. 90)

Lumière Tasting Bar ⚘⚘⚘ (West Side, $$$$, p. 90)

Ouest ⚘⚘ (West Side, $$$, p. 91)

The Smoking Dog ⚘ (West Side, $$$, p. 91)

GREEK

Stephos (The West End, $, p. 89)

INDIAN

Annapurna ⚘⚘ (West Side, $, p. 93)

Sami's ⚘⚘ (West Side, $$, p. 92)

Vij's ⚘ (West Side, $$, p. 93)

ITALIAN

Amarcord ⚘⚘ (Downtown/Yaletown, $$$, p. 80)

Cin Cin ⚘⚘ (The West End, $$$, p. 85)

Circolo ⚘ (Downtown/Yaletown, $$$, p. 80)

il Giardino di Umberto Ristorante ⚘⚘⚘ (Downtown/Yaletown, $$$, p. 81)

Gusto ⚘⚘⚘ (The North Shore, $$$, p. 97)

La Terrazza ⚘⚘ (Downtown/Yaletown, $$$, p. 82)

Romano's Macaroni Grill at the Mansion ⚘⚘ (The West End, $$, p. 88)

JAPANESE

Gyoza King (The West End, $, p. 89)

Tanpopo (The West End, $$, p. 88)

Tojo's Restaurant ⚘⚘ (West Side, $$$$, p. 90)

PIZZA

Incendio ⚘ (Gastown/Chinatown, $, p. 85)

SEAFOOD

Blue Water Café and Raw Bar ⚘⚘⚘ (Downtown/Yaletown, $$$, p. 80)

Downtown Vancouver Dining

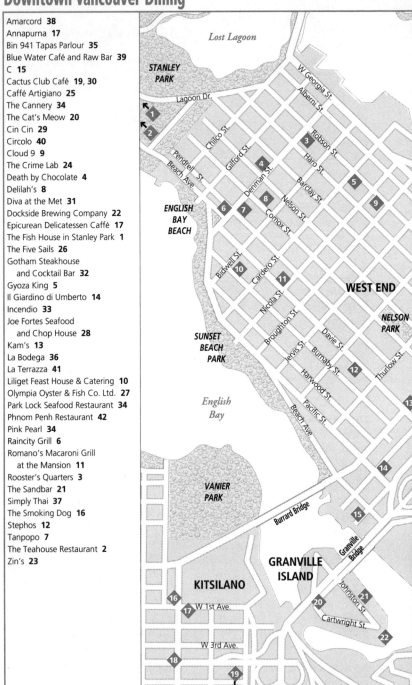

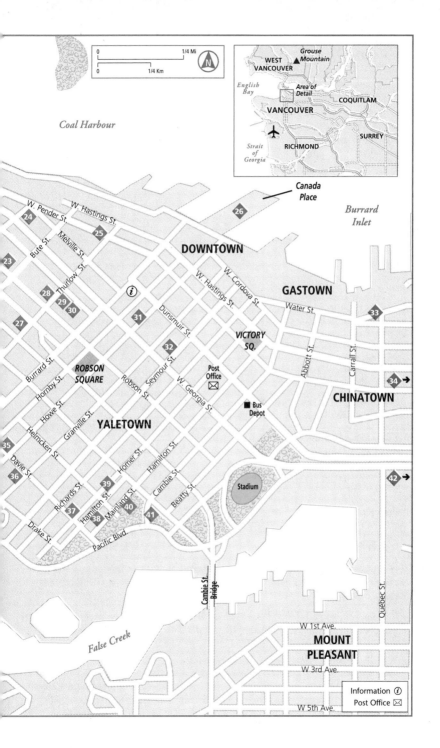

C ✸✸✸ (Downtown/Yaletown, $$$$, p. 78)

The Cannery ✸ (Gastown/China-town, $$$, p. 83)

The Fish House in Stanley Park ✸ (The West End, $$$, p. 86)

Joe Fortes Seafood and Chop House ✸✸ (Downtown/Yale-town, $$$, p. 81)

The Salmon House on the Hill ✸ (North Shore, $$$, p. 97)

Sun Sui Wah ✸✸ (East Side, $$$, p. 95)

SINGAPORIAN

Kam's (The West End, $$, p. 87)

STEAK

Gotham Steakhouse and Cocktail Bar ✸✸ (Downtown/Yaletown, $$$$, p. 79)

Mark's Fiasco (West Side, $$, p. 92)

TAPAS

Bin 941 Tapas Parlour (Down-town/Yaletown, $$, p. 82)

La Bodega ✸✸ (Downtown/ Yaletown, $$, p. 83)

TEX-MEX/SOUTHWESTERN

Cactus Club Café (The West End, $$, p. 91)

The Locus Café (East Side, $$, p. 96)

THAI

Simply Thai ✸ (Downtown/ Yaletown, $$, p. 83)

VEGETARIAN

Annapurna ✸✸ (West Side, $, p. 93)

The Naam Restaurant ✸ (West Side, $, p. 94)

VIETNAMESE

Phnom Penh Restaurant (Gas-town/Chinatown, $, p. 85)

WEST COAST (PACIFIC NORTHWEST)

The Beach House at Dundarave Pier ✸✸ (North Shore, $$$, p. 96)

Bishop's ✸✸ (West Side, $$$$, p. 89)

Bukowski's (East Side, $$, p. 95)

C ✸✸✸ (Downtown/Yaletown, $$$$, p. 78)

Cloud 9 ✸✸ (Downtown/Yale-town, $$$$, p. 79)

The Crime Lab ✸ (Downtown/Yaletown, $$, p. 82)

Diva at the Met ✸✸ (Down-town/Yaletown, $$$$, p. 79)

The Five Sails ✸✸ (Downtown/Yaletown, $$$$, p. 79)

Liliget Feast House & Catering ✸ (The West End, $$$, p. 86)

Raincity Grill ✸✸ (The West End, $$$, p. 87)

The Salmon House on the Hill ✸ (North Shore, $$$, p. 97)

The Teahouse Restaurant ✸ (The West End, $$$, p. 87)

2 Downtown & Yaletown

VERY EXPENSIVE

C ✸✸✸ SEAFOOD/WEST COAST It's become almost habit to quietly backhand the conspicuous consumption of the '80s generation—what's forgotten is just how well they consumed. C brings it all back, in a room done up in brilliant shades of Miami white, with the decor itself providing a little postindustrial commentary. Look for pale-green bread baskets made from cut sheets of heavy-gauge rubber, footrests upholstered with truck-tire retreads, and faux vinyl siding in the restrooms. Beyond the decor, however, C re-creates the '80s through the sheer indulgent quality with which they serve fish. C's taster box—a kind of small wooden high-rise of appetizers—includes salmon gravlax cured in Saskatoon berry tea, artichoke carpaccio, abalone tempura, and grilled garlic squid. A variety of seafood main courses are available, but for the ultimate dining experience, let chef Robert Clark show off (he's dying to), and order the seven-course sampling menu. Savor the exquisite cuisine as you watch the sun go down over the marina.

1600 Howe St. ℂ **604/681-1164**. www.crestaurant.com. Reservations recommended. Main courses C$21–C$32 (US$14–US$21). AE, DC, MC, V. Dinner daily 5:30–11pm; lunch Mon–Fri 11:30am–2:30pm and Sun 11am–2:30pm. Valet parking C$7 (US$4.55). Bus: 1 or 2.

Cloud 9 ★★ *(Moments* WEST COAST   Want the city laid out at your feet and delivered to your table? Take the elevator to the Landmark Hotel's 42nd floor. The view may be of English Bay, Stanley Park with the North Shore Mountains, or the towers of downtown. Yes, it's a revolving restaurant, but hang on just a minute before you think "tourist trap" and dive for the escape hatch. The restaurant has been working hard on improving the menu, and the new chef offers cuisine that almost equals the superlative views. Seafood plays an important role here, but other high points include steak, lamb, chicken, and a few Asian dishes. The prices are slightly higher than in comparable restaurants, but consider that a fair premium for the million-dollar view.

If you decide not to stay for supper, the lounge has excellent—and reasonably priced—martinis. On weekends there's a small cover.

1400 Robson St. ℂ **604/662-8328**. Reservations recommended. Lunch main courses C$8–C$12 (US$5.20–US$7.80); dinner main courses C$20–C$40 (US$13–US$26); brunch C$23 (US$15). AE, DC, MC, V. Daily 6:30–10:30am, 11:30am–2pm, 5–11pm; Sun brunch 11:30am–2:30pm. Bus: 5.

Diva at the Met ★★ WEST COAST   Since opening a few years ago next to the newly revamped Metropolitan Hotel, Diva at the Met and its chef Michael Noble have made walking off with city restaurant awards a bit of a habit. Noble himself has represented Canada at the Bocuse d'Or competition in France. His dishes extol the virtues of fresh seasonal ingredients and a light approach to spices and seasonings. Starters include house-smoked salmon with Québec foie gras. For the main course, try halibut cheeks with black-olive tapenade. Diva's tasting menu is also very popular, and its weekend brunch is among the best in town.

645 Howe St. ℂ **604/602-7788**. www.metropolitan.com. Reservations recommended. Dinner main courses C$26–C$44 (US$17–US$28); lunch C$12–C$23 (US$7.80–US$15). AE, DC, DISC, MC, V. Daily 6:30am–1am. Bus: 4 or 7.

The Five Sails ★★ WEST COAST   The Five Sails's view of Coal Harbour, the Lions Gate Bridge, and the Coast Mountains is as spectacular as the food. For a number of years the Five Sails served up its own interpretation of West Coast or Pacific Northwest cuisine, but a recent makeover and new chef have turned the ship around and set a course for France. Look for appetizers that combine pasta with seafood, like the Dungeness crab ravioli served with a basil flan and tomato emulsion. As a hotel restaurant, Five Sails does cover the bases with chicken, steak, and vegetarian dishes; for something more French, try the Marseille bouillabaisse, thick with seafood, or the grilled halibut with sautéed morel mushrooms, shallot confit, and finished with a rich veal jus. The Five Sails's fine wine selection highlights a different B.C. winery every month.

999 Canada Place Way, in the Pan-Pacific Hotel. ℂ **604/891-2892**. Reservations recommended. Main courses C$25–C$38 (US$16–US$25); tasting menu C$55–C$65 (US$35–US$42). AE, DC, MC, V. Daily 6–10pm. SkyTrain: Waterfront.

Gotham Steakhouse and Cocktail Bar ★★ STEAK   Since Gotham first opened its doors, a number of high-profile restaurants have brought home the beef—but nobody does it like Gotham. The room is of ambitious proportions—a 40-foot high timber ceiling divided down the middle with a cocktail bar on one side, a dining room on the other, and a patio with fireplace balancing things out. Furnishings are aggressively masculine. The wine list is encyclopedic. And then there's the food: The deep-fried calamari appetizer was a light and tasty revelation. Jumbo shrimp were sumo-sized. And the steaks are incredible: a porterhouse cut the size of a catcher's mitt, a petit filet mignon as tall as half a bread loaf. The meat just melts away on your tongue. Better to pass on the forgettable veggie side dishes entirely and spend the money on another glass of French merlot. The service is impeccable.

615 Seymour St. ⓒ **604/605-8282.** Fax 604/605-8285. www.gothamsteakhouse.com. Reservations recommended. Main courses C$27–C$49 (US$17–US$2). AE, DC, MC, V. Dinner daily 5–11pm (cocktail bar somewhat later). Bus: 4 or 7.

EXPENSIVE

Amarcord ⭐⭐ NORTHERN ITALIAN   Traditional Northern Italian cuisine doesn't get much respect these days, but that's just what Amarcord does, and so well that it's worth swearing off mango-corn chutney sauté and rediscovering the joys of freshly made pasta or risotto teamed with a lovingly prepared sauce. Think gnocchi with Italian sausage, fresh tomato and basil, or linguini with mussels, scallops, and tiger prawns. Wines hail from Tuscany and California. The atmosphere is formal without being fussy—a place you could bring your 9-year-old. Service is knowledgeable and very friendly.

104–1168 Hamilton St. ⓒ **604/681-6500.** Reservations recommended. Main courses C$14–C$20 (US$9.10–US$13). AE, DC, MC, V. Mon–Fri 11:30am–2pm; daily 5:30–10pm. Closed on holidays. Bus: 2.

Blue Water Café and Raw Bar ⭐⭐⭐ SEAFOOD   If you had to describe the Blue Water Café in one word it would be *fresh,* as in fresh seafood and a fresh concept. The raw bar, presided over by Masanori (Max) Katsuno, serves sushi, oysters, sashimi, and a range of Asian-inspired seafood dishes. We started off with "sushi" rolls of scallops and thinly sliced cucumbers wrapped in smoked salmon. For the main courses we gladly put ourselves in the hands of James Walt who works his magic in the large open kitchen. A lightly seared yellow fin tuna in a citrus-pepper crust came served on a bed of yellow beans, seasoned with herb- and basil-infused oil. When in season, order the diver-caught sea scallops, plainly grilled and served with sautéed zucchini, pancetta, and arugula in a maple-chive dressing. Since opening in the fall of 2000, the Blue Water has become one of Vancouver's hottest restaurants, a place to see and be seen. Reservations are recommended on weekends, but it is just as much fun to wait at the bar, watching the sushi maestro at work while you try one of the frozen vodkas or house martinis made with "squeezed-to-order" fruit juice.

1095 Hamilton St., Yaletown. ⓒ604/688-8078. www.bluewatercafe.net. Reservations recommended. Main courses C$17–C$30 (US$11–US$19). AE, DC, MC, V. Daily 11am–1am (light menu 3–5pm and 11pm–1am). Bus: 2.

Circolo ⭐ ITALIAN   The newest addition to a restaurant empire that already includes more formal Italian establishments in Whistler and Gastown (Umberto al Porto Borgo), as well as the 26-year-old original il Giardino di Umberto Ristorante on Hornby St., Circolo represents Umberto Menghi's move into the rough-and-tumble restaurant competition of trendy Yaletown, where the clientele is younger and prettier, dining options abound, and dinner is a less formal, more late night affair. Menghi's strategy with Circolo is to meld together a restaurant, bar, and bistro under one roof, and flank it outside with a wide green patio. Decor is a bit over the top, with lots of gold gilt and limitless little cherubim flitting here and there over the banquettes. The cuisine—a mix of traditional northern Italian and local seafood—is excellent, and remarkably reasonably priced. The antipasto platter comes heaped with scallops, prawns, prosciutto, tuna, and grilled peppers. Mains include a lovely, delicate veal served in port wine jus and accompanied by crunchy grilled veggies, as well as a melt-on-your tongue entree of ahi tuna. The wine is divided evenly between B.C., Italy, and California, and if mark-ups on some of the bottles are a tad high, Umberto makes up for it with a large selection of wines by the glass. Indeed, if you're not in the mood for a full meal, the bar at Circolo is a great place to have a glass and snack while you watch the pretty people preen (Thurs–Sat accompanied by music from a baby grand piano). On warm weather days Circolo's patio is one of the city's finest.

1116 Mainland St. © 604/687-1116. Fax 604/669-9723. www.umberto.com/circolo.htm. Reservations required. Main courses C$16–C$33 (US$10–US$21). AE, DC, MC, V. Mon–Sat 5pm–1am. Bus: 2.

Il Giardino di Umberto Ristorante ★★★ ITALIAN Twenty-six years ago,
restaurant magnate Umberto Menghi started humbly with this small restaurant tucked away in a yellow heritage house at the bottom of Hornby Street. His empire now includes Umberto al Porto Borgo Antico on Water Street, Circolo in Yaletown (see above), and two locations in Whistler (Trattoria and Il Caminetto), but Il Giardino still serves up the best Italian fare in town. A larger restaurant now adjoins the original house, opening up into a spacious and bright dining room that recreates the ambience of an Italian villa. The menu leans heavily to Tuscan favorites emphasizing pasta and game. Entrees include classics such as osso buco with saffron risotto and squash tortellini with portobello mushrooms in truffle oil. A daily list of specials makes the most of seasonal fresh ingredients, often offering outstanding seafood dishes. We tasted the plumpest mussels steamed in a rich garlic-and-white-wine broth, followed by a delicious halibut topped with artichoke and grilled vegetables. Desserts go creatively beyond tiramisu: try the mandarin orange/blood orange panna cotta or lemon mascarpone gelato with hazelnut pound cake. Like all of Umberto's establishments, the wine list is comprehensive and well chosen, with many excellent bottles reasonably priced at under C$40 (US$26). After sampling the cuisine, more than a few devoted foodies have run off to enroll in Umberto's Tuscan cooking school, set in one of the hill towns of Tuscany.

1382 Hornby St. © 604/669-2422. Fax 604/669-9723. www.umberto.com. Reservations required. Main courses C$14–C$33 (US$9.10–US$21). AE, DC, MC, V. Mon–Fri noon–2:30pm; Mon–Sat 6–11pm. Bus: 1 or 22.

Joe Fortes Seafood and Chop House ★★ SEAFOOD Named after the
burly Caribbean seaman and popular local hero who became English Bay's first lifeguard, Joe Fortes has been known for years as the place where the young and tanned would meet for mutual schmoozing and raw oysters. A little older and more sun-savvy crowd—now much diluted with tourists—still brings a buzz to the large casual dining room. For a sit-down dinner, guests have the choice of two levels of indoor dining or a table on the fabulous rooftop patio, weather permitting. The kitchen serves up good seafood at affordable prices. We really enjoyed the chef's choice of more unusual seafood items such as the pan-fried skate. Also on offer were marlin, ling cod, mahimahi, snapper, and sable wish as

well as the more standard choices of salmon, halibut, and tuna. Each selection arrives simply grilled or sautéed and is served with freshly grilled vegetables. Indecisive types can order a trio of fish, sampling the various catches of the day. Heavy on the white, the wine list is gargantuan and includes some outrageously expensive C$1,000 (US$645) bottles, but luckily for those of us who have seen their mutual funds take a nose dive there is plenty in the C$30 (US$19) range.

777 Thurlow St. (at Robson). ℭ **604/669-1940.** www.joefortes.ca. Reservations recommended. Main courses C$17–C$37 (US$11–US$24). AE, DC, DISC, MC, V. Daily 11am–10:30pm. Bus: 5.

La Terrazza ✹✹ ITALIAN   Located on the edge of Yaletown, La Terrazza's sleek, modern exterior contrasts sharply with the warm bustling dining room inside. Two of the three owners hail from Italy, and the kitchen is in the capable hands of Neapolitan chef Gennaro Iorio. No fusion or complicated culinary acrobatics here; on the contrary, many dishes stand out for their simplicity. The menu changes with the seasons, and a new tasting menu with matching wines highlights a different culinary region of Italy every month. One of the more intriguing appetizers is the bocconcini cheese, wrapped in prosciutto and radicchio, grilled and drizzled with strawberry vinaigrette. Main courses include various pasta dishes, but following the chef's recommendation, we tried the roasted guinea hen and duck breast with Frangelico brandy; both were outstanding (though the duck breast was the hands-down favorite). The wine list is extensive, offering selections from all over the world. Save room for dessert, particularly the white cheesecake baked in phyllo pastry topped with sour cherries and fruit coulis.

1088 Cambie St. ℭ **604/899-4449.** www.laterrazza.ca. Reservations recommended. Main courses C$16–C$30 (US$10–US$19). AE, DC, MC, V. Mon–Thurs 5–11pm; Fri–Sat 5pm–midnight; Sun 5–10pm. Bus: 2.

MODERATE

Bin 941 Tapas Parlour TAPAS/CASUAL   Still booming five years on, Bin 941 is the latest in trendy tapas dining. True, the music's too loud and the room's too small, but the food that alights on the bar or ever so tiny tables is quite delicious, and, like all tapas, fun to eat. Look especially for local seafood offerings like scallops and tiger prawns in bonito butter sauce. Sharing is unavoidable in this sliver of a bistro, so come prepared for socializing. So successful was the original model that a second Bin, dubbed Bin 942, has opened up at 1521 West Broadway (ℭ **604/ 673-1246**). And thanks to the "loose" liquor laws, both Bins are now open until 2am.

941 Davie St. ℭ **604/683-1246.** www.bin941.com. Reservations not accepted. All plates are C$11 (US$7.15). MC, V. Daily 5pm–2am. Bus: 4, 5, or 8.

The Crime Lab ✹ WEST COAST   Illuminated by the cheap glow of neon and with menus covered by lurid jacket drawings of 1930s pulp fiction, the Crime Lab is an eternity of fun. The martini list is inspired by figures from Vancouver's underworld. Tables are tight in this stiletto-thin establishment, but for a group of 8 to 12, it's tough to beat the triangular table set at the point of the Lab's long blade. Like most Vancouver restaurants, the menu covers all possibilities, but seafood is the specialty. Appetizers are superb—crab cakes with mango ginger aioli; mussels steamed with a salsa of scallions, cilantro, and vinegar; or Earl Bay oysters with a vinaigrette of sake ginger and cucumber. Main courses such as seafood paella are proof of the kitchen's abilities. The wine list sticks close to home, and service is friendly and knowledgeable.

1280 W. Pender St. ℂ **604/732-7463.** Reservations accepted. Main courses C$15–C$19 (US$9.75–US$12). AE, DC, MC, V. Mon–Sat 5pm–2am; Sun 5pm–midnight. Bus: 135.

La Bodega ★★ *(Value)* TAPAS   On a cold and rainy winter evening there is no better retreat than this warm, dark Spanish bar. Grab one of the tables or sneak into a little romantic corner and order some soul-warming Mediterranean comfort food. Expect authentic Spanish tapas—garlic prawns, ceviche, marinated mushrooms, pan-fried squid, and good black olives. Specials on the blackboard regularly include *conejo* (rabbit with tomatoes and peppers), quail, and B.C. scallops. All of it comes with lots of crusty bread for soaking up the wonderful garlicky goo. La Bodega has a good selection of Portuguese and Spanish wines and the best sangria in town.

1277 Howe St. ℂ 604/684-8815. Reservations accepted. Tapas C$3.95–C$7.95 (US$2.55–US$5.10); main courses C$11–C$18 (US$7.15–US$12). AE, DC, MC, V. Mon–Fri 4:30–midnight; Sat 5pm–midnight; Sun 5–11pm. Bus: 4 or 7.

Simply Thai ★ THAI   Finally, an authentic Thai restaurant in the trendy heart of Yaletown. The small restaurant, decorated in light wood, terra-cotta tiles, and pale yellow brighten up even the most dreary winter evenings. Watch chef and owner Siriwan in the open kitchen as he cooks up a combination of northern and southern Thai dishes, always using the freshest ingredients. The appetizers are perfect finger foods: *gai satay* features succulent pieces of grilled chicken breast marinated in coconut milk and spices and covered in a peanut sauce, while the weird but delicious *cho muang* consists of violet colored dumplings stuffed with minced chicken. Main courses run the gamut of Thai cuisine: noodle dishes and coconut curries with beef, chicken, or pork, as well as a good number of vegetarian options. Don't miss the *tom kha gai*, a deceptively simple-looking coconut soup with chicken, mushrooms, and lemon grass. Siriwan creates a richly fragrant broth that balances the delicate flavors of the lemon grass and other spices with the thick coconut milk. There is no better remedy for those winter blahs.

1211 Hamilton St. ℂ **604/642-0123.** Reservations recommended on weekends. Main courses C$9–C$17 (US$5.80–US$11). AE, DC, MC, V. Daily 11:30am–3pm; Sun–Wed 5pm–10pm; Thurs–Sat 5pm–midnight. Bus: 2.

INEXPENSIVE

Olympia Oyster & Fish Co. Ltd. *(Finds)* FISH & CHIPS   This little hole in the wall, just off Vancouver's trendiest shopping street, serves up the city's best fish and chips. On any given day you'll find West End residents, German tourists, and well-heeled shoppers toting their "daily catch" from Mexx or Banana Republic vying for counter space. There are only a few tables and a window-seat counter, plus three sidewalk tables (weather permitting), but the fish is always fresh and flaky and can be grilled if you prefer. Choose from sole, halibut, or cod, which may be combined with oysters or prawns too. If you want to take home smoked salmon, the staff will wrap it up or ship it if you prefer.

820 Thurlow St. ℂ **604/685-0716.** Main courses C$6–C$10 (US$3.90–US$6.50). AE, MC, V. Mon–Fri 10am–8pm; Sat 10am–7pm; Sun 11am–7pm. Bus: 5.

3 Gastown & Chinatown

EXPENSIVE

The Cannery ★ SEAFOOD   At least some of the pleasure of eating at The Cannery comes from simply finding the place. Hop over the railway tracks and

Moments Dinner on the Starlight Express

BC Rail's Pacific Starlight Dinner Train departs from the North Vancouver train terminal, transporting passengers past West Vancouver's waterfront mansions, along Howe Sound's scenic shoreline, past Porteau Cove, and back. The elegant restored coaches recall a time when rail travel was as much about going as it was about getting somewhere. The cars are appointed with inlaid wood, brass, and all the other touches you'd expect in a first-class dining car from rail travel's golden age.

Seating in the salon (C$84/US$54 per person, excluding taxes, tips, and alcohol) is slightly less expensive than seating in the glass-domed observation car (C$100/US$65 per person), but the spectacular 360° view of the sun setting over Howe Sound and the surrounding mountains is worth every cent. Bring your camera. Even more than the views, the fine service and excellent West Coast cuisine make either choice worthwhile. Recent entree selections have included roasted British Columbia salmon, stuffed breast of guinea fowl, filet of beef tenderloin, and beef Wellington. For dessert, the white-chocolate soup is fast becoming the signature dish.

The train operates every Wednesday through Sunday evening from May 1 to November 1, departing from the BC Rail Station, 1311 W. First St., North Vancouver, at 6:15pm and returning at 9:45pm. The dress code calls for "fine dining attire" but recommends that women don't wear high heels. For information or reservations, contact BC Rail Passenger Services (© **800/363-3733** or 604/984-5246; www.bcrail.com/starlight/).

thread your way past container terminals and fish-packing plants until you're sure you're lost, and then with a last turn the road opens onto a brightly lit parking lot and there it is—a great ex-warehouse of a building hanging out over the waters of Burrard Inlet. The building itself—its beam-laded warehouse interior, loaded with old nets and seafaring memorabilia—is another hefty portion of The Cannery's charm. As for the view, it's simply stunning, one of the best in Vancouver. You'll find good, solid, traditional seafood here, often alder-grilled, with ever-changing specials to complement the salmon and halibut basics. Chefs Frederic Couton and Jacques Wan have been getting more inventive of late, but when an institution is 31 years old and still going strong, no one's ever *too* keen to rock the boat. The wine list is stellar, and the desserts are wonderfully inventive.

2205 Commissioner St., near Victoria Dr. © **604/254-9606.** www.canneryseafood.com. Reservations recommended. Main courses C$17–C$27 (US$11–US$17). AE, DC, DISC, MC, V. Mon–Fri 11:30am–2:30pm; Mon–Sat 5:30–10:30pm; Sun 5:30–9:30pm. Closed Dec 24–26. Bus: 7 to Victoria Dr. From downtown, head east on Hastings St., turn left on Victoria Dr. (2 blocks past Commercial Dr.), then right on Commissioner St.

MODERATE

Park Lock Seafood Restaurant *Kids* CHINESE/DIM SUM   If you've never done dim sum, this traditional dining room in the very heart of Chinatown is the place to give it a try. From 8am to 3pm daily, waitresses wheel little carts loaded with Chinese delicacies past white-linen-covered tables. When you see something you like, you grab it. The final bill is based upon how many little dishes are left on your table. Dishes include spring rolls, *hargow* and *shumai* (steamed shrimp, beef, or pork dumplings), prawns wrapped in fresh white noodles, small steamed buns, sticky rice cooked in banana leaves, curried squid, and lots more. Parties of four or more are best—that way you get to try each other's food.

544 Main St. (at E. Pender St., on the 2nd floor). (C) **604/688-1581.** Reservations recommended. Main courses C$10–C$35 (US$6.45–US$23); dim sum dishes C$2.50–C$3.25 (US$1.60–US$2.10). AE, MC, V. Daily 8am–3pm; Tues–Sun 5–10pm. Bus: 19 or 22.

Pink Pearl *Finds Kids* CHINESE/DIM SUM   After 20 years in the business, this is still Vancouver's best spot for dim sum. The sheer volume and bustle are astonishing. Dozens of waiters parade a cavalcade of little trolleys stacked high with baskets and steamers and bowls filled with dumplings, spring rolls, shrimp balls, chicken feet, and even more obscure and delightful offerings. At the tables, extended families of Chinese banter, joke, and feast. Towers of empty plates and bowls pile up in the middle, a tribute to the appetites of hungry brunchers, as well as the growing bill; fortunately, dim sum is still a steal, perhaps the best and most fun way to sample Cantonese cooking.

1132 E. Hastings St. (C) **604/253-4316.** www.pinkpearl.com. Main courses C$12–C$35 (US$7.75–US$23); dim sum C$2.95–C$6 (US$1.90–US$3.90). AE, DC, MC, V. Daily 9am–10pm. Bus: 10.

INEXPENSIVE

Incendio *Finds* PIZZA   If you're looking for something casual and local that won't be full of other people reading downtown maps, this little Gastown hideaway is sublime. The 22 pizza combinations are served on fresh, crispy crusts baked in an old wood-fired oven. Pastas are homemade, and you're encouraged to mix and match—try the mussels with spinach fettuccine, capers, and tomatoes in lime butter. The wine list is decent; the beer list is inspired. And now, there's a patio. Sunday night features all-you-can-eat pizza for C$8 (US$5.20). Much to the delight of Kitsilano residents a second location with a slightly larger menu has opened up next to the Fifth Avenue movie theatre at 2118 Burrard ((C) **604/736-2220**).

103 Columbia St. (C) **604/688-8694.** Main courses C$8–C$12 (US$5.20–US$7.75). AE, MC, V. Mon–Thurs 11:30am–3pm and 5–10pm; Fri 11:30am–3pm and 5–11pm; Sat 5–11pm; Sun 4:30–10pm. Closed Dec 23–Jan 3. Bus: 1 or 8.

Phnom Penh Restaurant VIETNAMESE   This family-run restaurant serves a mixture of Vietnamese and slightly spicier Cambodian cuisine. Phnom Penh is a perennial contender for, and occasional winner of, *Vancouver Magazine*'s award for the city's best Asian restaurant. The walls are adorned with artistic renderings of ancient Cambodia's capital, Angkor. Khmer dolls are suspended in glass cases, and the subdued lighting is a welcome departure from the harsh glare often found in inexpensive Chinatown restaurants. Try the outstanding hot-and-sour soup, loaded with prawns and lemon grass. The deep-fried garlic squid served with rice is also delicious. For dessert, the fruit-and-rice pudding is an exotic treat.

244 E. Georgia St., near Main St. (C) **604/682-5777.** Dishes C$5.15–C$14 (US$3.30–US$9.10). AE, MC. Wed–Mon 10am–9pm. Bus: 8 or 19.

4 The West End

EXPENSIVE

Cin Cin *** MODERN ITALIAN   Cin Cin is known almost as well for its patrons as for the food it serves. Celebrities, models, politicians, and tourists all frequent this second-story, villa-style bistro. But don't expect much attitude; the casual dining room surrounds an open kitchen, which is built around a huge alderwood-fired oven. The heated terrace overlooking Robson Street is an equally pleasant dining and people-watching spot. Dishes range from elegant pastas and pizzas—capellini alla pomodoro, penne puttanesca, and pizza Margherita—to more substantial dishes such as rosemary-marinated rack of lamb, sea bass crusted with porcini mushrooms, and smoked chicken breast. The award-winning wine list is extensive, as is the selection of wines by the glass.

1154 Robson St. ⓒ **604/688-7338**. www.cincin.net. Reservations recommended. Main courses C$16–C$32 (US$10–US$21). AE, DC, MC, V. Mon–Fri 11:30am–2:30pm; daily 5–11pm. Bus: 5 or 22.

Delilah's 🎔🎔 CONTINENTAL   Walk down the steps from the Denman Place Mall and you've entered Delilah's French bordello of a room—red velvet chaise longues, little private corner rooms, cherubim cavorting on the ceiling, and wall-mounted lamps with glass shades. First order of business is a martini—Delilah's forte, and the fuel firing the laughter and conversation all around. The two-page martini list comes with everything from the basic Boston Tea Partini (Citron vodka and iced tea in a glass with sugared rim and lemon wedge) to the ultimate in Southern excess, the Miranda (pineapple, vodka, and fresh floating fruit). The staff are brisk and helpful and run to the Miranda side—flamboyant, friendly, and over the top. The menu is seafood heavy, which Delilah's does well, sticking to freshness and simple sauces such as the seared jumbo scallops with saffron risotto or grilled swordfish with a sun-dried cherry-cranberry compote. The chef gets in a bit over his head with land-based fare, so go with the flow and order something from the sea.

1789 Comox St. ⓒ **604/687-3424**. Reservations accepted for parties of 6 or more. Fixed-price menu C$24 (two courses)–C$33.50 (four courses) (US$15–US$22). AE, DC, MC, V. Daily 5:30pm–midnight. Bus: 5 to Denman St.

The Fish House in Stanley Park 🎔 SEAFOOD   Reminiscent of a more genteel era, this white-clapboard clubhouse is surrounded by public tennis courts, bowling greens, and ancient cedar trees. Three rooms decorated in hunter green with dark wood and whitewashed accents reinforce the clubhouse atmosphere. The menu includes such innovative dishes as pan-seared Alaskan scallops with sweet chili glaze, lemon grass–crusted prawn satay, and a smoked-salmon sampler. The oyster bar has at least a half-dozen fresh varieties daily. The desserts are sumptuous. The restaurant/bar draws a mix of golfers, strollers, and local execs.

8901 Stanley Park Dr. ⓒ **877/681-7275** or 604/681-7275. www.fishhousestanleypark.com. Reservations recommended. Main courses C$17–C$30 (US$11–US$19). AE, DC, DISC, MC, V. Mon–Sat 11:30am–10pm; Sun 11am–10pm. Closed Dec 24–26. Bus: 1, 35, or 135.

Liliget Feast House & Catering 🎔 *Finds* WEST COAST   The nondescript entrance gives no hint to the unique restaurant located downstairs from an East Indian restaurant. The dining room is filled with natural cedar columns rising from the water-worn stone floor; the tables are sunken into stone platforms around a central cedar-and-stone walkway. Recorded song-stories about potlatch ceremonies play in the background. The food is traditional West Coast First Nations fare. Appetizers include grilled oysters, clam fritters, grilled prawns, breaded and fried smelt, salmon or venison soup, and bannock (delicious fried bread). Entrees like sweet alder-smoked salmon, lightly smoked duck breast, and grilled marinated venison steak are sumptuous. Local side dishes include fiddleheads, sea asparagus, and wild rice. Available in various sizes, the "Potlatch

Platters" are an ideal way to sample a bit of everything. For people curious about modern First Nations culture, this is one experience that shouldn't be missed.

1724 Davie St. ℂ **604/681-7044.** www.liliget.com. Reservations recommended. Main courses C$17–C$30 (US$11–US$19). Spring–fall daily 5–10pm; winter Wed–Sun 5–10pm. AE, DC, MC, V. Bus: 5.

Raincity Grill ⭐⭐ WEST COAST   Raincity's room is long and low and hugs the shoreline, the better to let the evening sun pour in. With the location—by English Bay Beach—and the spacious patio, you wonder if the owner didn't have to kill for the spot. Then you realize he's paying off the view with volume—they do pack 'em in at Raincity, making dinner more of a social occasion than you may have wished for. Ah, but the view. And the food. Raincity's forte is local ingredients, West Coast style. That means appetizers of barbecued quail with a sage and goat-cheese polenta, crispy jumbo spot prawns, or a salad of smoked steelhead. Entrees include grilled Fraser Valley free-range chicken and fresh-caught spring salmon. And then there's the award-winning wine list. It's huge and, in keeping with the restaurant's theme, it sticks pretty close to home. Better yet, most varieties are available by the glass.

1193 Denman St. ℂ **604/685-7337.** www.raincitygrill.com. Reservations recommended. Main courses C$21–C$29 (US$14–US$19). AE, DC, MC, V. Daily 5–10:30pm; Sat–Sun 10:30am–2:30pm. Bus: 1 or 5.

The Teahouse Restaurant ⭐ WEST COAST   The best approach to the Teahouse, perched on Ferguson Point in Stanley Park overlooking English Bay, is on foot along the seawall from English Bay (about a 30-minute walk from the Bay). Choose a sunny day, and arrive an hour before sunset so you can take in the magnificent views as you climb up the steps to the restaurant and get settled in with a glass of champagne. There are no bad seats but true sunset hounds may wish to reserve a window seat in the conservatory. If you can tear yourself away long enough to look at the menu you'll notice fresh local ingredients with an Asian twist. Appetizers include wok-fried squid with Thai chilies and oyster sauce and barbecue duck rolls with plum dipping sauce. Main courses lean heavily towards seafood, including B.C. salmon, seared scallops, and potato-crusted sea bass. The dishes are well done and beautifully presented, a fine companion to the spectacular setting. But even after the sun fades, the lights cast a magical glow on the trees and garden.

Ferguson Point, Stanley Park. ℂ **604/669-3281.** www.vancouverdine.com. Reservations recommended. Main courses C$19–C$29 (US$12–US$19). AE, DC, MC, V. Mon–Sat 11:30am–2:30pm; Sun 10:30am–2:30pm; dinner daily 5–10pm. Afternoon tea Mon–Sat 2:30–4:30pm.

MODERATE

Kam's SINGAPORIAN   Vancouver's downtown overflows with excellent Japanese fare, and cheap Chinese is a dime a dozen, but good, affordable Southeast Asian can be hard to come by. Thankfully, Kam's cooks up generous portions of tasty Singaporean cuisine. Relentless traders that they are, Singaporeans incorporated many flavors and dishes from surrounding nations, so Kam's varied menu includes such dishes as Indonesian-style *gado gado* (vegetable salad doused in peanut sauce) and *nasi goreng* (fried rice), Malaysian chicken sate, and numerous Thai curry dishes. A unique Singaporean dish that's perfect for warming up on rainy day is the spicy *laksa*, a rich broth with coconut milk, juicy chicken and prawns, and rice noodles. All dishes lean towards the spicy but can certainly be tamed upon request. Keep in mind that the portions are large; we recently dined with a group of six and were plenty stuffed sharing three appetizers and four main courses.

1043 Davie St. ☎ **604/669-3389.** Main courses C$8.50–C$13 (US$5.50–US$8.40). AE, MC, V. Mon–Fri 11am–2:40pm; Sat–Sun noon–2:40pm; daily 5–10pm. Bus: 5.

Romano's Macaroni Grill at the Mansion ★★ Kids FAMILY STYLE/ITAL-IAN

Housed in a huge stone mansion built in the early 20th century by sugar baron B. T. Rogers, Romano's is fun and casual. Wood paneling, stained-glass windows, and chandeliers surround tables covered with red-and-white checked tablecloths. The menu is Southern Italian, and the pastas are definitely favorites. This isn't high-concept Italian; the food is simple, understandable, and consistently good. You're charged for the house wine based on how much you pour from the bottle. Your kids will love the children's menu—which features lasagna and meat loaf as well as tasty pizzas—and the permissive staff that bursts into opera at the slightest provocation.

1523 Davie St. ☎ **604/689-4334.** Reservations recommended. Main courses C$8–C$16 (US$5.20–US$10); children's courses C$4.95–C$6 (US$3.20–US$3.90). AE, DC, MC, V. Mon–Thurs noon–10pm; Fri–Sat noon–11pm; Sun 11am–10pm. Bus: 5.

Tanpopo JAPANESE

Occupying the second floor of a corner building on Denman Street, Tanpopo has a partial view of English Bay, a large patio, and a huge menu of hot and cold Japanese dishes. But the line of people waiting 30 minutes or more every night for a table are here for the all-you-can-eat sushi. The unlimited fare includes the standards—makis, tuna and salmon sashimi, California and B.C. rolls—as well as cooked items such as tonkatsu, tempura, chicken kara-age, and broiled oysters. There are a couple of secrets to getting seated. You might try to call ahead, but they take only an arbitrary percentage of reservations for dinner each day. Otherwise, you can ask to sit at the sushi bar.

1122 Denman St. ☎ **604/681-7777.** Reservations recommended for groups. Main courses C$7–C$19 (US$4.50–US$12). AE, DC, MC, V. Daily Sun–Thurs 11:30am–10pm; Fri–Sat 11:30am–11pm. Bus: 5.

Zin's ★ CASUAL

Located on Vancouver's Robson-street fashion heartland, Zin's made quite a splash when it opened, if only for its interior: an ultra-modern combination of black floors and purple, orange, and red walls and furnishings, the hard edges tempered by gauze curtains and lots of flickering candles in funky holders. The other reason behind the Zin's buzz was its creation of a new concept: taste tripping. Zin's takes you on a food trip around the globe, dish by dish. Unlike fusion, where flavors from all over the world arrived together on one plate, with taste tripping, the global dishes arrive chastely one after the other. Zin's chef may start you off with a grilled *naan* bread and mint tomato chutney or maybe a pure and unadulterated spicy Thai soup. For the main course you could go for a French goat cheese fondue (served with baguettes for dipping) or a Malaysian *laksa* seafood stew in coconut broth. Still not tired of traveling? Try the rich and creamy vegetable risotto, served with mesclun greens, a Parmesan crisp, and a pesto vinaigrette. For your safety and dining comfort, Zin's chef maintains the integrity of each cuisine and the quality of each dish throughout the culinary voyage. Every month the chef also pauses at a specific destination, offering a number of specials representative of the local cuisine. For casual dining the wine list is one of the best, with nearly 50 wines by the glass and the best selection of Zinfandels in town.

1277 Robson St. ☎ **604/408-1700.** www.zin-restaurant.com. Main courses C$11–C$17 (US$7.10–US$11). AE, DC, MC, V. Mon–Wed 7am–midnight; Thurs–Sat 7am–1am; Sun 8am–11pm.

INEXPENSIVE

Gyoza King JAPANESE   Gyoza King features an entire menu of *gyoza*—succulent Japanese dumplings filled with prawns, pork, vegetables, and other combinations—as well as Japanese noodles and staples like *katsu-don* (pork cutlet over rice) and *o-den* (a rich, hearty soup). This is the gathering spot for hordes of young Japanese visitors looking for cheap eats that still approximate home cooking. Seating is divided among Western-style tables, the bar (where you can watch the chef in action), and the Japanese-style low table, which is reserved for larger groups if the restaurant is busy. The staff is very courteous and happy to explain the dishes.

1508 Robson St. (C) **604/669-8278.** Main courses C$6–C$13 (US$3.90–US$8.40). AE, MC, V. Sat–Sun 11:30am–3pm; Mon–Sat 5:30pm–2am; Sun 5:30pm–midnight. Bus: 5.

Rooster's Quarters *(Kids* CANADIAN/FAMILY-STYLE   Rooster's Quarters offers the antidote to diet food. Succulent baby back ribs are served in a sweet-and-tangy maple barbecue sauce, and the Québec-style barbecued chicken is crisp on the outside, tender and juicy on the inside. If those don't hit the spot, try the *poutine,* a Québec dish of french fries covered with melted curd cheese and brown gravy. The atmosphere is as casual as the menu, making Rooster's a great place to bring the kids. True, it can get a little crowded, but just pick out a table and seat yourself if there is no line. That's what the regulars do.

836 Denman St. (C) **604/689-8023.** Dishes C$8–C$16 (US$5.20–US$10). AE, MC, V. Daily 11am–11pm. Bus: 5.

Stephos *(Value* GREEK   A fixture on the Davie St. dining scene, Stephos has been packing them in since Zorba was a boy. The cuisine is simple Greek fare at its finest and cheapest. Customers line up outside for a seat amid Greek travel posters, potted ivy, and whitewashed walls (the average wait is about 10–15 min., but it could be as long as 30 min.). Once you're inside, the staff will never rush you out the door. Order some pita and dip (hummus, spicy eggplant, or garlic spread) while you peruse the menu. An interesting appetizer is the *avgolemono* soup, a delicately flavored chicken broth with egg and lemon, accompanied by a plate of piping hot pita bread. When choosing a main course, keep in mind that portions are huge. The roasted lamb, lamb chops, fried calamari, and a variety of souvlaki are served with rice, roast potatoes, and Greek salad. The beef, lamb, or chicken pita come in slightly smaller portions served with fries and *tzatziki* (garlic sauce).

1124 Davie St. (C) **604/683-2555.** Reservations accepted for parties of 5 or more. Main courses C$4.25–C$10 (US$2.75–US$6.45). AE, MC, V. Daily 11:30am–11:30pm. Bus: 5.

5 The West Side

VERY EXPENSIVE

Bishop's *★★★* PACIFIC NORTHWEST   Whether you arrive on foot or by limousine (there are guests in both categories), owner John Bishop will greet you at the door and lead you to a table in his elegant dining room hung with fine paintings and wood sculpture from the Pacific Northwest. Like the art work, all ingredients are top-quality and locally grown, not to mention organic. Everything is seasonal, and the menu changes weekly, but at any given time Bishop's will have a small collection of the best Pacific Northwest dishes available—anywhere. Appetizers might include grilled spot prawns with fennel and blood orange, or Salt Spring Island goat cheese coated with toasted hazelnuts in a rasp-berry vinaigrette. Entrees could include roasted rack of suckling pig, or roasted wild spring salmon with rhubarb compote. The wine selection isn't huge—there simply isn't the space—but it's exceptionally well chosen with vintages from along the Pacific Coast. If you plan on splurging one night, this is one of the best places to do it.

2183 W. Fourth Ave. ⓒ 604/738-2025. www.bishopsonline.com. Reservations required. Main courses C$28–C$36 (US$18–US$23). AE, DC, MC, V. Mon–Sat 5:30–11pm; Sun 5:30–10pm. Closed Jan 1–15. Bus: 4 or 7.

Lumière ★★★ FRENCH   The success of this French dining experiment in the heart of Kitsilano has turned chef Rob Feenie into a hot commodity. He now regularly jets off to New York to teach folks back east how to do it right. And how's that? Preparation and presentation are immaculately French, while ingre-dients are resolutely local, which makes for interesting surprises—fresh local gin-ger with the veal, or raspberries in the foie gras. Lumière's tasting menus are a series of 8 or 10 delightful plates that change with the season, perfectly matched to a local wine (not included in the fixed price) and gorgeously presented. Din-ers simply choose one of the four tasting menus (one menu is vegetarian) and then sit back and let the pilots in Lumière's kitchen take them on a culinary journey they won't forget. If you can afford it, it's a voyage you shouldn't miss.

2551 W. Broadway. ⓒ 604/739-8185. Reservations recommended. Tasting menu (8 courses) C$60–C$100 (US$39–US$65). AE, DC, MC, V. Tues–Sun 5:30–9:30pm. Bus: 9 or 10.

Lumière Tasting Bar ★★★ FRENCH   The darling of foodies across the continent, Rob Feenie is not one to sit still. After the success of Lumière (see above) he recently opened up Lumière Tasting Bar, where patrons may sample just a few dishes instead of committing to the full seven-course meal. He serves these tasty little confections for C$12 (US$7.75) a plate, which is a steal con-sidering Feenie hasn't compromised on quality or taste. On a recent visit we sampled seared sablefish with a sauté of potatoes and leeks and an ahi tuna with a cucumber salad and chili-lime dressing. The confit of lamb shoulder was fall-off-the-bone tender and was accompanied by a tasty ratatouille. Also outstand-ing were the short ribs served in a mushroom broth with *shimeji* (Japanese mushrooms). Vegetarians will find fewer options than in the restaurant, but fish and meat lovers will find plenty to rave about.

2551 W. Broadway. ⓒ 604/739-8185. www.lumiere.ca. Reservations not accepted. All dishes C$12 (US$7.75). AE, DC, MC, V. Tues–Sun 5:30–11pm. Bus: 9 or 10.

Tojo's Restaurant ★★ JAPANESE   I had never met Hideki Tojo, or even tried his cooking, until one afternoon at Vancouver's first-ever sumo wrestling demonstration, a diminutive man on the tatami mat next to me lifted up a bento box and proffered a tray of delicate sushi rolls. As two thunderous giants eyed each other in the ring, I picked out a piece with fresh salmon and popped it in my mouth. Incredible. A thousand pounds of screaming human flesh were smashing each other in the ring, but my attention was entirely captured by the exquisite flavors exploding in my mouth. Back in Tojo's modest sushi bar, the ever-changing menu offers such specialties as sea urchin on the half shell, her-ring roe, lobster claws, tuna, crab, and asparagus. I'd like to say I've since become a regular, but at the prices Tojo charges for his creations, regulars are either film stars or fully mortgaged for the next seven generations. Still, it's a wonderful splurge.

202–777 W. Broadway. ℭ **604/872-8050.** Reservations recommended. Full dinners C$23–C$100 (US$15–US$65). AE, DC, MC, V. Mon–Sat 5–10:30pm. Closed Christmas week. Bus: 9.

EXPENSIVE

Ouest ★★ FRENCH   The word out West is *contemporary.* The decor of this west-side eatery is a showcase of what Modern looks like at the start of the new millennium: crisp, clean, and (unlike stripped down '70s functionalism) unafraid to make use of the finest materials in pursuit of an understated elegance. The contemporary French cuisine follows a similar philosophy: Top-quality ingredients are judiciously paired with only enough seasoning or sauce to express their natural flavors. Call it the less-is-more approach to French cuisine. Starters to look for include the parfait of foie gras and chicken livers with Okanagan apple jelly, or the fricassee of escargot and wild mushrooms. Mains to remember include corn-fed chicken with morels and wild rice or pan-fried halibut with mushroom crust and baby leeks. Perhaps the best option, however, is to put yourself in the chef's capable hands and choose the seven-course menu gourmand (C$89/US$57). The selection of wines by the glass is disappointingly limited here, but there is a good selection of half-bottles. The service is excellent.

2881 Granville St. ℭ **604/738-8938.** www.ouestrestaurant.com. Reservations recommended. Main courses C$28–C$37 (US$19–US$24). AE, DC, MC, V. Daily 5:30pm–11pm. Bus: 8.

The Smoking Dog ★ FRENCH   To date, the little Kitsilano neighborhood of Yorkville Mews has remained a local secret, perhaps because the few tourists who do venture into this delightful one-block stretch are immediately confronted with a confusing variety of choices. Should one stop at one of the three cafes, the tapas bar, the sushi spot, the vegan cafe, or this traditional Parisian bistro, complete with patio umbrellas, obsequious waiters dressed in black, and a friendly bear of an owner who greets everyone at the door? Food-wise, the Dog is undoubtedly the best (and priciest) of the lot, featuring New York pepper steak, grilled halibut with Pernod sauce, and scallops with beurre blanc. If the weather allows, grab a spot on the heated patio and enjoy the bustling street life.

1889 W. First Ave. ℭ **604/732-8811.** Reservations accepted. Main courses C$22–C$30 (US$14–US$19). AE, DC, MC, V. Mon–Fri 11:30am–3pm; Mon–Sat 5:30–10:30pm. Bus: 2 or 22.

MODERATE

Cactus Club Café (Value) TEX MEX/SOUTHWESTERN/CASUAL   So it's not fine dining. That's not why you're here. The crowd is young, the room is fun, the beer is cold, and the waitresses invariably beautiful. Dinner almost always starts at the bar, 'cause there's always a line and they don't take reservations. Hang out, have a beer and some calamari, hot wings, or potato skins. When you finally reach your table, the food is consistently good—sizzling fajitas, six variations of Caesar salad, slow-cooked Jamaican-style jerk chicken, and succulent barbecued ribs.

1530 Broadway at Granville ℭ **604/687-3278.** (also 1136 Robson St. and other locations.) Main courses C$6–C$19 (US$3.90–US$12). AE, MC, V. Daily 11am–midnight (later in the summer). Bus: 9 or 10.

The Cat's Meow CASUAL   Locals may be unfamiliar with the Cat's Meow, but tell them it's where Isadora's used to be and their eyes light up. The long-running cooperative restaurant was missed when it finally closed. Fortunately, the Cat's Meow has done a good job filling the delightful room and patio by providing tasty, affordable sandwiches, burgers, pizzas, and pastas. Appetizers such as crab cakes and salmon canapés perfectly match a beer on a sunny day. The back patio overlooks a water-play area, where kids can frolic in the sprinklers and fountains. Later in the evening kids and parents give way to a younger crowd.

1540 Old Bridge St., Granville Island. ✆ 604/647-2287. www.thecatsmeow.ca. Main courses C$8–C$19 (US$5.20–US$12). AE, MC, V. Mon–Wed 9:30am–midnight; Thurs–Sat 9:30am–1am; Sun 9:30am–11pm. Bus: 50.

Café Zen CASUAL   Sandal-clad traffic from next-door Kits Beach has turned the stretch of Yew Street between Cornwall and Second avenues into something of a casual dining mecca. There are numerous pasta options, a couple of pubs, and several neighborhood restaurants, one of the more popular of which is Café Zen. A great breakfast and lunch spot anytime of the week, on weekends this little cafe develops positively un-Zen like bustle. By 10am the dining room is packed and waiting guests spill out the doorway and up the long steep sidewalk. What's the attraction? A huge brunch menu, fast and efficient service, reasonable prices, and the best Eggs Benny in town.

1631 Yew St. (at York). ✆ 604/731-4018. Main courses C$6–C$12 (US$3.90–US$7.75). MC, V. Daily 7am–5pm. Bus: 2, 4, 7, or 22.

Dockside Brewing Company ✿ *Finds* CASUAL   One of the city's best patios is tucked away on the far side of Granville Island, inside the Granville Island Hotel. Overlooking False Creek's bustling seawall and Marina, the Dockside Brewing Company offers the perfect urban retreat and on less than patio-perfect days, the restaurant offers terrific views, too. The on-site microbrewery produces an excellent selection of seasonal beers (order the six-beer sampler to determine your favorite) and the recently revamped kitchen serves up tasty Asian-inspired food. Perfect as a snack or appetizer are the tiger prawns or chili squid, lightly grilled and generously sprinkled with garlic, ginger and lemon grass. Main courses include pizzas, made from scratch and baked in the wood-burning oven and affordable pastas; for a kick try the penne Calabrese with Italian sausage, red peppers, and spicy tomato sauce. Other menu highlights include seafood entrees such as Cajun-spiced snapper with mango salsa, herb crusted halibut with lemon beurre blanc, and alder-grilled salmon; all are served with a generous helping of rice pilaf and seasonal grilled vegetables. The wine list showcases a number of fine Okanagan wines at very reasonable prices. The lunch menu also includes a selection of sandwiches, burgers, and wraps.

1253 Johnstone St., Granville Island. ✆ 604/685-7070. Reservations recommended for large groups. Main courses C$12–C$24 (US$7.75–US$15). AE, DC, MC, V. Daily 11:30am–10pm (bar stays open later). Bus: 50 or Aquabus.

Mark's Fiasco *(Kids)* STEAK/CASUAL   Mark's is the casual pub of choice for the Kitsilano jock-boy crowd, with a brass bar, 15 microbrews on tap, and at least four channels of sports on strategically placed TVs. On the restaurant side, Mark's offers a well-rounded menu of pastas, pizzas, seafood, and meat dishes. Appetizers include steamed mussels, fried calamari, and a delicious baked spinach dip. With a burger and fries starting at C$7 (US$4.50), crayons on every paper-covered table, and a congenial staff, Mark's is also kid-friendly.

2468 Bayswater St. (at W. Broadway). ✆ 604/734-1325. www.markjamesgroup.com. Reservations recommended. Main courses C$7–C$19 (US$4.50–US$12). AE, MC, V. Daily 11:45am–11pm (bar stays open later). Bus: 9.

Sami's ✿✿ *Finds* INDIAN   Always in the running for best Indian food in Vancouver, Sami's is still going strong. For a short time there was a second, downtown location, but that restaurant left the warm nest of chef Sami Lalji and went off in its own direction. This means that those wanting to try the original fabulous East-meets-West South Asian cooking will have to make the trip out to a strip mall off West Broadway again. But the food is worth the journey, offering inventive and delicious dishes—try the Mumbai-blackened New York steak set atop spiked mashers with blueberry coriander jus—that won't put a large hole in your wallet. Service is efficient and knowledgeable. No reservations accepted; expect a line.

986 W. Broadway. ℂ **604/736-8330**. Reservations not accepted. Main courses C$12 (US$7.75). DC, MC, V. Mon–Sat 11:30am–2:30pm; daily 5–11pm. Bus: 9.

The SandBar ✪✪ CASUAL   Fridays and Saturdays the bar and patio become refuges for the dolled up and decked out as 20-something singles, rebounding baby boomers, and long-toothed cougars all head out on the prowl. Those who are not ready to tear into the pickup scene can actually sink their teeth into a number of fairly decent tapas, perfect for sharing with a couple of friends. The mussels and clams come wonderfully steamed, positively demanding that one sop up the juices with some warm bits of bread. Shrimp and pork pot stickers or dumplings provide the Asian component of a menu that spans the globe. Mexican-inspired fishcakes are served with a pineapple salsa, while fish taquitos come with a chipotle dip sauce. The menu also offers a number of main courses, including cedar-planked grilled salmon and a daily pasta special that in season may feature fresh B.C. scallops in a light tomato sauce. In summer the patio on the third floor is fabulous for lazing about in the warm sunshine, while come fall or winter it's a good spot to cuddle up beneath a heat lamp in the big leather chair. Be nice to your greeter, and she may show you the way.

1535 Johnston St., Granville Island. ℂ **604/669-9030**. www.mysandbar.com. Reservations not accepted for patio. Tapas C$5.75–C$12 (US$3.70–US$7.80); main courses C$10–C$20 (US$6.45–US$13). AE, MC, V. Daily 11am–midnight; kitchen may close at 10:30pm. Bus: 50 to Granville Island.

Vij's ✪ INDIAN   Vij doesn't take reservations, but then he really doesn't have to: There's a line outside his door every single night. Patrons huddled under Vij's violet neon sign are treated to complimentary tea and *papadums*. For a few dollars more, an Indian Pale Ale (IPA) can be rustled up to help soothe the wait. Inside, the decor is as warm and subtle as the seasonings, which are all roasted and ground by hand, then used with studied delicacy. The menu changes monthly, though some of the more popular entrees remain constants. Recent offerings included coconut curried chicken and saffron rice and marinated pork medallions with garlic-yogurt curry and *naan* (flat bread). Vegetarian selections abound, including curried vegetable rice pilaf with cilantro cream sauce and Indian lentils with naan and *raita* (yogurt-mint sauce). The wine and beer list is short but carefully selected. And for teetotalers, Vij has developed a souped-up version of the traditional Indian chai, the chaiuccino.

1480 W. 11th Ave. ℂ **604/736-6664**. Fax 604/736-3701. Reservations not accepted. Main courses C$14–C$24 (US$9.10–US$15). AE, DC, MC, V. Daily 5:30–10pm, later if busy. Closed Dec 24–Jan 8. Bus: 8 or 10.

INEXPENSIVE

Annapurna ✪✪ *Value* INDIAN/VEGETARIAN   Annapurna gets my vote as Vancouver's best vegetarian restaurant, and it's up there in the running for best Indian as well. A Kitsilano favorite, the restaurant's small dining room is hung with dozens of rice-paper lamps in whites, yellows, oranges, and reds that, when combined with the mirrors, bask the room in a soft, warm glow. The menu is all vegetarian, but with the amazing combinations of Indian spices, herbs, and local vegetables, the dishes are rich and satisfying. Appetizers include samosas, pakoras, and lentil dumplings soaked in tangy yogurt with chutney. A variety of breads, such as paratha, naans, and chapatis, are served piping hot. Entrees such as *aloo-ghobi* (potato curry with cauliflower, onions, and cilantro) or *navrattan korma* (seasonal vegetables simmered in poppy-seed paste, flavored with saffron, aniseed, and sliced almonds) can be prepared from mild to screaming hot. The wine list is small but very reasonably priced. With food, wine, and atmosphere this good, Annapurna lets you feel like you're splurging when you're not.

1812 W. Fourth Ave. ☎ **604/736-5959.** Main courses C$10–C$11 (US$6.45–US$7.10). AE, MC, V. Daily 11:30am–10pm. Bus: 4 or 7.

The Naam Restaurant ⭐ *Kids* VEGETARIAN

Back in the sixties, when Kitsilano was Canada's hippie haven, the Naam was tie-dye central. Things have changed a tad since then, but Vancouver's oldest vegetarian and natural-food restaurant retains a pleasant granola feel. The decor is simple, earnest, and welcoming: well-worn wooden tables and chairs, plants, an assortment of local art, and a fabulous garden patio. The brazenly healthy fare ranges from all-vegetarian burgers, enchiladas, and burritos to tofu teriyaki, Thai noodles, and a variety of pita pizzas. The sesame spice fries are a Vancouver institution. And though the Naam is not quite vegan, they do cater to the anti-egg-and-cheese crowd with specialties like the macrobiotic Dragon Bowl of brown rice, tofu, peanut sauce, sprouts, and steamed vegetables. As with all Naam dishes, quality is excellent. The only real trick is to arrive well before you're actually hungry. Serving staff will invariably disappear on an extended search for personal fulfillment at some point during your meal.

2724 W. Fourth Ave. ☎ **604/738-7151.** www.thenaam.com. Reservations accepted on weekdays only. Main courses C$4.95–C$10 (US$3.20–US$6.50). AE, MC, V. Daily 24 hr. Live music every night 7–10pm. Bus: 4 or 22.

Shao Lin Noodle Restaurant *Kids* CHINESE/DIM SUM

Ever wonder how fresh your noodles really are? At Shao Lin you can watch the noodle chef make them right before your eyes. Unique for Vancouver, Shao Lin is one of the few places where, behind a glass enclosure, each order of noodles is made from scratch. The chefs mix, knead, toss, stretch, and compress the dough until it almost magically gives way to thin strands. After a quick boil, the noodles are added to the dish of your choice. Two or three dishes make a satisfying meal for two; choose from a wide variety of meat and vegetable dishes. Want more entertainment at your table? Order the special tea and watch the server pour it from a 3-foot-long pot originally designed to allow male servants to maintain a polite distance from an 18th-century Chinese empress. Watch the server's steady hand as he aims the spout of boiling water in the center of your tiny cup—just don't make any sudden movements.

548 W. Broadway. ☎ **604/873-1816.** Main courses C$5–C$10 (US$3.25–US$6.50). No credit cards. Mon–Fri 11am–3pm; Sat–Sun 11:30am–3:30pm; daily 5–9:30pm. Bus: 9.

Sophie's Cosmic Café *Kids* FAMILY-STYLE/AMERICAN

Sophie's is readily identifiable by the giant silver knife and fork bolted to the storefront. Inside, every available space has been crammed with toys and knickknacks from the 1950s and 1960s, creating an experience much akin to having lunch inside a McDonald's Happy Meal. For that very reason, children are inordinately fond of

Sophie's. Crayons and coloring paper are always on hand. The menu is simple: pastas, burgers and fries, great milkshakes, and a few classic Mexican dishes. The slightly spicy breakfast menu is hugely popular with Kitsilano locals, lines can stretch to half an hour or more on post-hangover Sunday mornings.

2095 W. Fourth Ave. © **604/732-6810.** Main courses C$4.85–C$17 (US$3.15–US$11). MC, V. Daily 8am–9:30pm. Bus: 4 or 7.

6 The East Side

Many of these "east side" restaurants are on Main Street, which is on the border-lands between upscale west and working-class east. Main thus has some funky urban authenticity to go with its ever-increasing trendiness.

EXPENSIVE

Sun Sui Wah ★★ *Kids* CHINESE/DIM SUM/SEAFOOD   One of the most elegant and sophisticated Chinese restaurants in town, the award-winning Sun Sui Wah is well known for its seafood. Fresh and varied, the catch of the day can include fresh crab, rock cod, geoduck, scallops, abalone, oyster, prawns, and more. Pick your own from the tank or order from the menu if you'd rather not meet your food eye-to-eye before it's cooked. The staff is quite helpful for those unfamiliar with the cuisine. Dim sum is a treat, with the emphasis on seafood. Just point and choose. For land lovers and vegetarians, there are plenty of other choices, though they are missing out on one of the best seafood feasts in town.

3888 Main St. © **604/872-8822.** www.sunsuiwah.com. Also in Richmond: 102 Alderbridge Place, 4940 No. 3 Rd. (© 604/273-8208). Reservations accepted. Main courses C$11–C$50 (US$7.15–US$32). AE, DC, MC, V. Daily 10:30am–3pm and 5–10:30pm. Bus: 3.

MODERATE

The Brickhouse Bistro ★★ *Value* BISTRO   There were once two partners who opened a bar in a slightly seedy part of town. It ought to do well, they reasoned, for there are many with money here, who have recently bought condos and have nowhere to drink. And do well it did. Encouraged, the partners refurbished the room above their successful bar, and opened a bistro—a casual, funky place, all bricks and wood beams. They hired a chef capable of cooking simple but superior food, dishes like New Zealand rib eye in Madeira jus or specials of fresh fish. To lure customers, the partners kept prices very low. A selection of B.C. wines was also available, at two-thirds the price charged by other bistros. Word of the cuisine and ambience has spread far and wide, so that dinner on a weekend a pleasant social affair. But the Brickhouse is still a tasty steal.

730 Main St. © **604/689-8645.** Reservations accepted. Main courses C$10–C$16 (US$6.50–US$10). MC, V. Tues–Thurs 6pm–midnight; Fri–Sat 6pm–1am. Bus: 3.

Bukowski's BISTRO/WEST COAST/CASUAL   The last and booziest of the American Beat poets gets what he always wanted, a bistro named in his honor. So what if he never made it to Vancouver, much less the Bohemian-and-becoming-more-so strip on Commercial Drive. The cuisine is not Polish, but instead a fusion-y kind of comfort food perfectly suited to casual dining. Think beef satay, charbroiled chicken on focaccia bread, catfish with black-bean salsa, or steak with peppercorn garlic jus. And beer. Or any one of several wines featured on a daily blackboard. Even more attractive than the food is the friendly, buzzing atmosphere and a clientele slightly too rich to really be artists, but hip enough to dress the part. Service is wonderfully unhurried. Dawdle for hours if you will, reading the snippets of Sylvia Plath inscribed on your table.

1447 Commercial Dr. ⓒ **604/253-4770.** Reservations accepted. Main courses C$8–C$15 (US$5.20–US$9.75). MC, V. Mon–Thurs 5pm–1am; Fri–Sat noon–1am; Sun noon–midnight. Live Jazz Mon–Thurs. Bus: 20.

The Locus Café CASUAL/TEX-MEX/SOUTHWESTERN   Even if you arrive on your lonesome, you'll have plenty of friends soon enough—the Locus is a cheek-by-jowl kind of place, filled with a friendly, funky crowd of artsy Mount Pleasant types. A big bar dominates the room, overhung with "swamp-gothic" lacquer trees and surrounded by a tier of stools with booths and tiny tables farther out. Cuisine originated in the American Southwest but picked up an edge somewhere along the way, demonstrated in the roasted half-chicken with a cumin-coriander crust and sambuca citrus demi-glace. Keep an eye out for fish specials, such as grilled tomba tuna with a grapefruit and mango glaze. The pan-seared calamari makes a perfect appetizer. Bowen Island brewery provides the beer, so quality's high. Your only real problem is catching the eye of the hyper-busy bartender.

4121 Main St. ⓒ **604/708-4121.** Reservations recommended. Main courses C$9–C$15 (US$5.85–US$9.75). MC, V. Mon–Sat 11am–1:30am; Sun 11am–midnight. Bus: 3.

The Reef ★★ *Value* CARIBBEAN   The "JERK" in the phone number refers neither to the Steve Martin film nor to the guy two cubicles down from you at the office, but rather to a spicy marinade: bay leaves, scotch bonnets, allspice, garlic, soya, green onions, vinegar, and cloves. The result is piquant, scrumptious chicken. The Reef serves up a number of jerk dishes, including their signature quarter jerk chicken breast. Other dishes are equally delightful, including a tropical salad of fresh mango, red onions, and tomatoes; shrimp with coconut milk and lime juice; grilled blue marlin; and Trenton spiced ribs. Choose a glass of wine from the thoughtfully selected list, and you have gourmet dining in a great room—cleverly decorated with chicken wire, bamboo, and original mixed media artwork—at a bargain price. Afternoons, the tiny patio is drenched in sunlight, while in the evenings a DJ spins the sounds of the Islands.

4172 Main St. ⓒ **604/874-JERK.** www.thereefrestaurant.com. Reservations accepted. Main courses C$9–C$15 (US$5.85–US$9.75). AE, DC, MC, V. Mon–Fri 11am–midnight; Sat 10am–1am; Sun 10am–midnight. Bus: 3.

7 The North Shore
EXPENSIVE

The Beach House at Dundarave Pier ★★ WEST COAST   Set on a dramatic waterfront location, the House offers a panoramic view of English Bay. Those on the heated patio also get sunshine, but they miss out on the rich interior of this restored 1912 teahouse. The food is consistently good—innovative, but not so experimental that it leaves the staid West Van burghers gasping for breath. Appetizers include soft-shell crab with salt-and-fire jelly; grilled scallops with baby spinach, crispy onions, and red-pepper cream; and grilled portobello mushroom with Okanagan Valley goat cheese. Entrees have included garlic-crusted rack of lamb with honey balsamic glaze and baked striped sea bass with basil mousse and rock prawns. The wine list is award winning.

150 25th St., West Vancouver. ⓒ **604/922-1414.** www.beachhousewestvan.com. Reservations recommended. Main courses C$12–C$16 (US$7.80–US$10) lunch, C$17–C$29 (US$11–US$19) dinner. AE, DC, MC, V. Mon–Sat 11am–3pm; Sun brunch 10:30am–3pm; Sun–Thurs 5–10pm; Fri–Sat 5–11pm. Light appetizers served 3–5pm. Bus: 255 to Ambleside Pier.

Gusto ★★★ ITALIAN   West Vancouverites have always had numerous fine dining options, but for folks in more working-class North Vancouver (to the east of the Lion's Gate Bridge) times were always tougher. That is until the father-and-son Corsis team opened Gusto just steps from the Lonsdale Quay SeaBus Terminal. The Corsis family has done a fabulous job in creating a comfortable and pleasant dining room: it's bathed in warm earth tones and a rustic decor. However they truly outdid themselves with the menu, focusing on the cuisine from their native Central Italy. To start, order a glass of Italian bubbly and try the bocconcini wrapped in prosciutto and drizzled with cherry vinaigrette or the grilled calamari in a tomato coulis. Signature main courses include pistachio-crusted sea bass; duck breast with chanterelles and butternut squash confit; and the outstanding spaghetti quattro, a spicy concoction of minced chicken, black beans, garlic, and chili. Stuffed pastas are made from scratch; the mushroom agnolotti with truffle and cream sauce melts in your mouth. The wine list leans heavily to Bella Italia offering a good selection of reasonably priced Chianti and other table wines. There are also a number of limited editions merlots, cabernets, and zinfandels. Finally, save space at the end for the *pera cotta,* a port-poached pear served with pistachio gelato.

1 Lonsdale Ave., North Vancouver. ✆ 604/924-4444. www.quattrorestaurants.com. Reservations recommended. Dinner main courses C$16–C$32 (US$10 –US$21); lunch C$9–C$17 (US$5.80–US$11) AE, DC, MC, V. Mon–Sat 11am–3pm; Sun brunch 10:30am–3pm; Sun–Thurs 5–10pm; Fri–Sat 5–11pm. Seabus to Lonsdale Quay.

The Salmon House on the Hill ★ WEST COAST/SEAFOOD   High above West Vancouver, the Salmon House offers a spectacular view of the city and Burrard Inlet. The rough-hewn cedar walls are adorned with a growing collection of indigenous West Coast art. Chef Dan Atkinson's menu reflects his extensive research into local ingredients and First Nations cuisine. An alderwood-fired grill dominates the kitchen, lending a delicious flavor to many of the dishes. To start, we recommend the Salmon House Sampler, featuring smoked and candied salmon, accompanied by fresh salsas, chutneys, and relishes. Entrees include a Japanese-style sesame-crusted tuna in a mustard and wasabi sauce, and a rum-and-maple-syrup–marinated salmon topped with a vanilla bean and pineapple salsa. Desserts bear little resemblance to early First Nations cuisine: mocha torte with pecan-toffee crust, blueberry tiramisu. The wine list earned an award of excellence from *Wine Spectator.*

2229 Folkstone Way, West Vancouver. ✆ 604/926-3212. www.salmonhouse.com. Reservations recommended for dinner. Lunch main courses C$11.25–C$15 (US$7.25–US$9.70); dinner main courses C$18–C$30 (US$12–US$19). AE, DC, MC, V. Mon–Sat 11:30am–2:30pm; Sun brunch 11am–2:30pm; Sun–Thurs 5–10pm; Fri–Sat 5–10:30pm. Bus: 251 to Queens St.

INEXPENSIVE

The Tomahawk Restaurant ★ *Finds* FAMILY STYLE/AMERICAN   Just a typical American-style diner, but with one critical difference that makes it worth a visit. The Tomahawk is wall-to-wall and roof-beam tall with Native knick-knacks and gewgaws and some truly first-class First Nations art. It all started back in the 1930s when proprietor Chick Chamberlain began accepting carvings from Burrard Band Natives in lieu of payment. Over the years the collection just kept growing. So how's the food? Good, in a burgers-and-fries kind of way. Portions are large, burgers are tasty, and milkshakes come so thick the spoon stands up straight like a totem pole.

1550 Philip Ave., North Vancouver. ℂ **604/988-2612.** Reservations not accepted. Main courses C$4.25–C$17 (US$2.75–US$11). AE, DC, MC, V. Sun–Thurs 8am–9pm; Fri–Sat 8am–10pm. Bus: 239 to Philip Ave.

8 Coffee, Sweets, and Ice Cream

Caffè Artigiano *(Finds)* When a friend of a friend told me Caffè Artigiano's lattes were *absolutely* the best in town, I shrugged them off as just another Vancouver coffee snob talking up their daily java the way some discuss fine wine. Later, however, when I found myself walking by the small shop on the corner of West Pender, I thought I'd give it a try to see what all the hoopla was about. Watching owners Vince or Sammy at work, one discovers instantly that this is no ordinary joe. The trick is to start with the perfect beans, brew the coffee to an exact temperature, give the steamed milk the respect it deserves, and pour it out ever so slowly forming a perfect leaf shaped pattern in your handmade ceramic cup. This is latte making elevated to an art form. And the taste! With a nose of finest Arabia, an elegant body of deepest ebony, this coffee dances flittingly across your tongue leaving barest hints of subtle mocha and a soupçon of flavor from the Eastern African hills.

1101 West Pender St. ℂ **604/685-5333.** www.caffeartigiano.com. Sweets and sandwiches under C$7 (US$4.55). Mon–Fri 7am–7pm. Closed Sat–Sun. Bus: 22 to Burrard and West Pender.

Death by Chocolate If your idea of heaven includes rich desserts, then Death by Chocolate is the place to get dispatched. The large menu comes with photographs, but beware: Objects on the page may appear smaller than they are; sharing is encouraged. Some of the tested favorites include: Simply Irresistible, chocolate pudding with fudge center, covered in chocolate sauce; and Devil in Disguise, mocha fudge ice cream in Kahlúa chocolate sauce. Guilt-prone types can salve their consciences with more wholesome, fruitier desserts. Hell-bent

 Caffeine Nation

"I've never seen so much coffee in all my life. The whole town is on a caffeine jag," said Bette Midler, when she performed in Vancouver.

Though the population had been softened up to the idea by a generation of Italian immigrants, the recent fine-coffee explosion started first in our sister city to the south. There are now more than 60 of the Seattle-based **Starbucks** shops in the city, as well as Blenz, Roastmasters, and other chain cafes. The Starbucks franchises facing each other on Robson and Thurlow are famed for the movie stars who drop in and the regular crowd of bikers who sit sipping lattes on their hogs. The city's best java joint—fittingly enough—is **Vancouver's Best Coffee,** 2959 W. Fourth Ave. (ℂ **604/739-2136**), on a slightly funky section of West Fourth Avenue at Bayswater.

Nearly as good and far more politically correct is **Joe's Cafe,** 1150 Commercial Dr. (ℂ **604/255-1046**), in the heart of the immigrant- and activist-laden Commercial Drive area. Lesbian activists, Marxist intellectuals, Guatemalan immigrants, and little old Portuguese men all sit and sip their cappuccinos together peacefully.

ultra-chocoholics, on the other hand, should order up a Multitude of Sins: chocolate cake, chocolate mousse, chocolate crepes stuffed with fruit, chocolate sauce, and, well, you get the idea.

Various locations, including 1001 Denman St. © **604/899-CHOC,** and 1598 W. Broadway, © **604/730-CHOC.** www.deathbychocolate.ca. C$4.95–C$11 (US$3.22–US$7.15). AE, MC, V. Generally open until midnight; hr. vary at each location.

Epicurean Delicatessen Caffè *(Finds*   A real Italian *caffè* in Kitsilano, the Epicurean brews a mean espresso. Locals and visitors flock to this tiny neighborhood deli, packing the sidewalk spots on nice days or the cozy small tables inside when the weather turns gray. Italian sweets, biscotti, and sorbet go well with any of the coffees, but for a savory treat have a peek at the glass display case in the back. Freshly made antipasti, cold cuts, salads, pannini sandwiches and risotto are just some of the delectables available for lunch or takeout. The menu changes regularly, as the owners try out new recipes. Let them know if you have a favorite, and you may find it in store next time.

1898 West First Ave. © **604/731-5370.** Fax 604/731-5369. Everything under C$9 (US$5.85). Daily 8am–9pm. Bus: 22 to Cornwall and Cypress.

La Casa Gelato *(Finds*   No self-respecting ice-cream fiend could possibly pass up a visit to La Casa Gelato. Trust us, it's worth the trek out to this obscure industrial area near Commercial Drive, where ice-cream lovers gather for a taste of one or more of the 198 flavors in store. Of course you don't get that many flavors by simply serving up chocolate, vanilla, and strawberry. How about garlic, lavender, durian-fruit, basil, or hot chili ice cream? We love the pear with gorgonzola sorbet. You're entitled to at least several samples before committing to one or two flavors so go ahead and be adventurous.

1033 Venables St. © **604251-3211.** Fax 604/251-3922. Everything under C$6 (US$3.90). Daily 10am–11pm. Bus: 10 to Commercial and Venables.

6

Exploring Vancouver

A city perched on the edge of a great wilderness, Vancouver offers unmatched opportunities for exploring the outdoors. Paradoxically, within the city limits Vancouver is intensely urban. There are sidewalk cafes to match those in Paris and shopping streets that rival London's. The forest of downtown residential high-rises looks somewhat like New York, while the buzz and movement of Chinatown reminds you of San Francisco or Canton. Comparisons with other places soon begin to pall, however, as you come to realize that Vancouver is entirely its own creation: a self-confident, sparklingly beautiful city, like no place else on earth.

SIGHTSEEING SUGGESTIONS

If You Have 1 Day

See the sights while you eat your eggs. The breakfast spot with the best view is the **Cafe Pacifica** (*(C)* **604/895-2480**) in the lobby of the Pan-Pacific Hotel, where you can watch the morning rush of floatplanes dropping in. After breakfast, walk or ride or in-line skate the **Stanley Park Seawall** (★). While in Stanley Park, say hi to the sea otters in the **Vancouver Aquarium.** By now it's definitely lunchtime, so come back to the West End and have lunch at one of the sidewalk cafes on **Denman.** Then wander through the **West End** (there's a good walking tour in chapter 7); maybe stop by the Vancouver Art Gallery or the public library. Wherever you wander, try to finish up around sunset at the foot of Denman Street on **English Bay Beach** (★). Have supper at one of the nearby restaurants specializing in West Coast cuisine. Then head up to **Robson Street** and watch the evening parade of beautiful people.

If You Have 2 Days

On day 2, grab a coffee and a croissant and head down to **Chinatown.** Explore the area for a bit—it's often most active in the early hours— then go for dim sum. Afterwards, drive or take the bus out to the **Museum of Anthropology** on the campus of UBC. The masks and carvings are worth the trip. While out at UBC, walk down the steep trail to **Wreck Beach** (bear in mind there are nudists at the bottom), or come back and explore the urban waterfront at **Granville Island.** Have dinner in **Kitsilano** or across False Creek in **Yaletown**. Then go barhopping, or find a brew pub and try some of the local ales.

If You Have 3 Days

On day 3, get active—go **kayaking** on Indian Arm, **mountain biking** through the Endowment Lands, **hiking** through Cypress Falls park, or take the **tram** up to Grouse Mountain. Take a picnic lunch along (if you've come by SeaBus, then Lonsdale Quay is a good spot for supplies) and eat outside.

Lighthouse Park in West Vancouver is a particularly good picnic area. Come suppertime, eat at one of the North Shore restaurants with a view of the city—the **Salmon House,** the **Beach House,** or the **Grouse Nest** up on Grouse Mountain.

If You Have 4 Days or More
On days 4 and 5, the thoroughly urban can retreat to the city and spend the next 2 days exploring neighborhoods like **Kitsilano,** the **Punjabi market,** and **Commercial Drive,** and touring your way through Vancouver's **art gallery,** maritime **museum,** and **public library.** For **outdoors lovers,** make like a Nike ad, and just do it. Go to Whistler and go skiing. Head to Squamish and see the bald eagles. Hike up to Joffre Lake and touch the glacier. Do a horse trek in the high country, or take your bike. Sail up into grizzly country. Kayak Clayoquot Sound.

1 The Top Attractions
DOWNTOWN & THE WEST END

Vancouver Aquarium Marine Science Centre ✸✸✸   One of North America's largest and best, the Vancouver Aquarium houses more than 8,000 marine species, most in meticulously re-created environments.

In the icy-blue Arctic Canada exhibit, you can see beluga whales whistling and blowing water at unwary onlookers. Human-sized freshwater fish inhabit the Amazon Rain Forest gallery, while overhead, an hourly rainstorm is unleashed in an atrium that houses three-toed sloths, brilliant blue and green poison tree frogs, and piranhas. Regal angelfish glide through a re-creation of Indonesia's Bunaken National Park coral reef, and blacktip reef sharks menacingly scour the Tropical Gallery's waters. (Call for the shark and sea otter feeding times.) The Pacific Canada exhibit is dedicated to sea life indigenous to B.C. waters, including the Pacific salmon and the giant Pacific octopus.

On the Marine Mammal Deck, there are sea otters, Steller sea lions, beluga whales, and a Pacific white-sided dolphin. During regularly scheduled shows, the aquarium staff explain marine mammal behavior while working with these impressive creatures.

Stanley Park. (🕐 604/659-FISH. www.vanaqua.org. Admission C$14.95 (US$9.65) adults; C$12 (US$7.80) seniors, students, and youths 13–18; C$9 (US$5.85) children 4–12; free for children under 4. Late June–Labour Day daily 9:30am–7pm; Labour Day–late June daily 10am–5:30pm. Bus: 135; "Around the Park" shuttle bus June–Sept only. Parking C$5 (US$3.25) summer, C$3 (US$1.95) winter.

Vancouver Art Gallery ✸✸   Designed as a courthouse by British Columbia's leading early-20th-century architect Francis Rattenbury (the architect of Victoria's Empress hotel and the Parliament buildings), and renovated into an art gallery by British Columbia's leading late-20th-century architect Arthur Erickson (see the "Arthur Erickson" box, later in this chapter), the VAG is an excellent stop for anyone who wants to see what sets Canadian and West Coast art apart from the rest of the world. There is an impressive collection of paintings by B.C. native Emily Carr, as well as examples of a unique Canadian art style created during the 1920s by members of the "Group of Seven," who included Vancouver painter Fred Varley. On the contemporary side, the VAG hosts rotating exhibits of sculpture, graphics, photography, and video art, some from B.C. artists, many from around the world. Geared to younger audiences, the Annex Gallery offers rotating presentations of visually exciting educational exhibits.

Downtown Vancouver Attractions

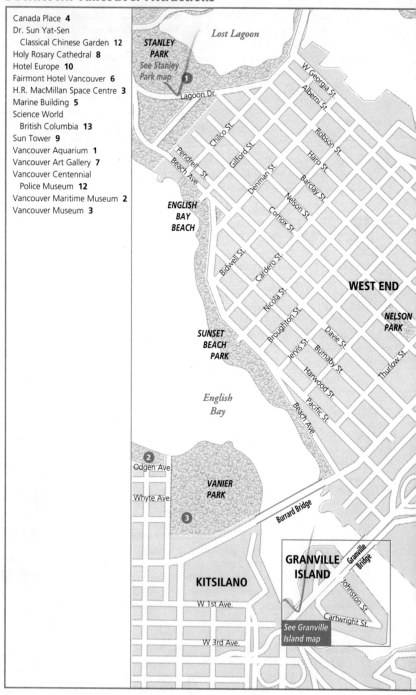

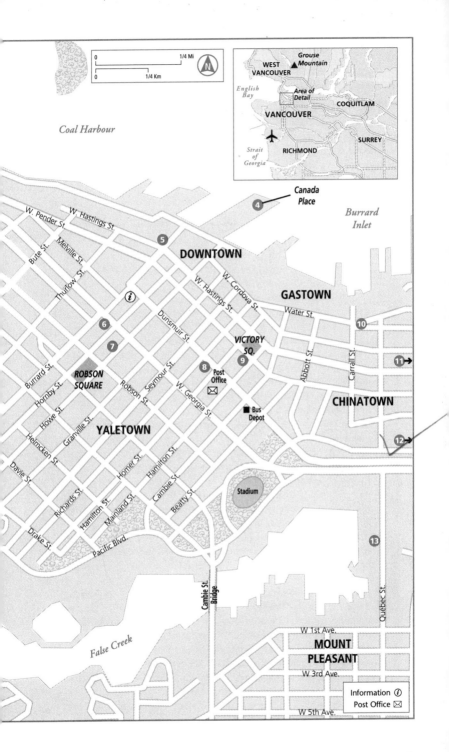

Coal Harbour

Burrard Inlet

Canada Place ④

DOWNTOWN

⑤

GASTOWN

W. Pender St.
W. Hastings St.

Bute St.
Melville St.
Thurlow St.

W. Cordova St.

W. Hastings St.

Water St.

ⓘ

Dunsmuir St.

⑥

⑩

⑦

VICTORY SQ.

Abbott St.
Carrall St.

ROBSON SQUARE

⑧ Post Office ⊠

⑨

⑪→

Burrard St.

Robson St.

Seymour St.

Hornby St.

W. Georgia St.

CHINATOWN

Howe St.

YALETOWN

■ Bus Depot

⑫→

Helmcken St.

Granville St.

Richards St.

Homer St.

Hamilton St.

Cambie St.

Davie St.

Stadium

Hamilton St.

Mainland St.

Beatty St.

⑬

Drake St.

Pacific Blvd.

Québec St.

Cambie St. Bridge

W 1st Ave.

MOUNT PLEASANT

False Creek

W 3rd Ave.

| Information ⓘ |
| Post Office ⊠ |

W 5th Ave.

0   1/4 Mi
0   1/4 Km

WEST VANCOUVER
▲ Grouse Mountain

English Bay

Area of Detail

COQUITLAM

VANCOUVER

SURREY

Strait of Georgia

✈

RICHMOND

750 Hornby St. ℂ **604/662-4719** or 604/662-4700. www.vanartgallery.bc.ca. Admission C$11 (US$7.15) adults, C$8 (US$5.20) seniors, C$6.50 (US$4.20) students and youths, C$30 (US$19) family, free for children 12 and under. Thurs 5–9pm by donation. Mon–Wed and Fri–Sun 10am–5:30pm; Thurs 10am–9pm. Closed Mon–Tues in fall and winter. SkyTrain: Granville. Bus: 3.

THE WEST SIDE

Granville Island ★★★ *Kids* Almost a city within a city, Granville Island has so much to offer that even a day may not be enough to experience it all—but you can certainly give it a good shot. Browse for crafts, pick up some fresh seafood, enjoy a great dinner, watch some Shakespeare in the park or attend the

---

 Granville's Greatest Hits

Even though the bustling Public Market makes a fine destination in itself, Granville Island offers so much more. To really get a feel for this neighborhood, stroll along the side streets and explore the alleys and lanes away from the main entrance.

Some must-see or -do attractions:

- RailSpur Alley's 12 artist studios are perfect for browsing; stop in at the **Al'Arte Silk** to see some of the beautifully hand-painted wearable silk art (RailSpur Alley 1369) or pause at the excellent **Kharma Café** for a latte and pastry (RailSpur Alley 1363; ℂ **604/647-1363**).
- Art exhibits at the **Emily Carr Institute** (1399 Johnston St.; ℂ **604/844-3800**) showcase the works of the institute's grads and students. You may be looking at the next Andy Warhol. Open daily 9am to 6pm; admission is free.
- In the summer check the **Performance Works** (ℂ **604/687-3020**) schedule for any free outdoor Shakespeare presentations or see what's playing at the **Arts Club Theatre** (ℂ **604/687-1644**) or **Waterfront Theatre** (ℂ **604/685-1731**).
- Paddle off into the sunset by renting a kayak from one of the marinas on the west side of the island. Beginners can take lessons or head out on a guided tour. **Ecomarine Ocean Kayak Centre** (ℂ **604/689-7575**) has everything to get you started. A three-hour kayak lesson for C$55 (US$36) teaches you the basic strokes. Or, explore the waters around Stanley Park with a guide (C$89/US$57). Experienced paddlers may rent equipment (C$48/US$31 per day for a single kayak).
- Granville Islands is one big playground. On a rainy day tuck into the Kids Only Market (daily 10am–6pm) to check out toys, kites, clothes, art supplies and an indoor play area or visit the **Granville Island Museum** (ℂ **604/683-1939**) to admire its collection of model boats and trains. The museum is open daily from 10am to 5:30pm; admission is C$3.50–C$6.50(US$2.25–US$4.20), free for children four and under. On warm summer days the Waterpark is the place to be (free of charge) and any day of the year kids never get tired of chasing sea gulls on the dock. Open daily (weather permitting) from 10am to 6pm, late May until Labour Day.

Granville Island

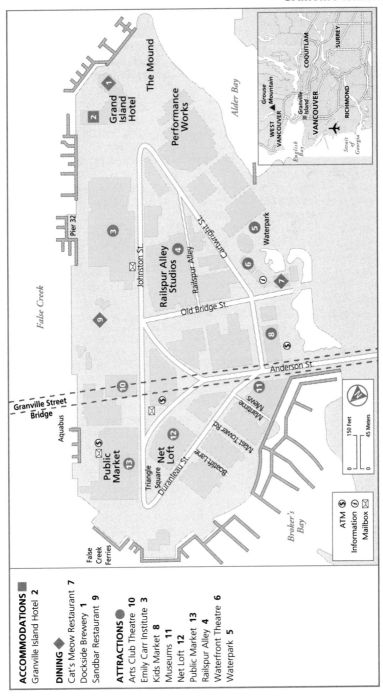

The Mound

Grand Island Hotel

Performance Works

Alder Bay

Pier 32

False Creek

Johnston St.

Railspur Alley Studios

Cartwright St.

Railspur Alley

Waterpark

Old Bridge St.

Anderson St.

Granville Street Bridge

Aquabus

False Creek Ferries

Public Market

Triangle Square

Net Loft

Mast Tower Rd.

Maritime Mews

Bodhitt Lane

Duranleau St.

Broker's Bay

ATM Ⓢ
Information ⓘ
Mailbox ⊠

0 ──── 150 Feet
0 ──── 45 Meters

GROUSE MOUNTAIN
COQUITLAM
SURREY
WEST VANCOUVER
VANCOUVER
RICHMOND
Granville Island
English Bay
Strait of Georgia

ACCOMMODATIONS ■
Granville Island Hotel **2**

DINING ◆
Cat's Meow Restaurant **7**
Dockside Brewery **1**
Sandbar Restaurant **9**

ATTRACTIONS ●
Arts Club Theatre **10**
Emily Carr Institute **3**
Kids Market **8**
Museums **11**
Net Loft **12**
Public Market **13**
Railspur Alley **4**
Waterfront Theatre **6**
Waterpark **5**

Tips More Time to Explore

If you can't bear to leave the island, consider staying at the Granville Island Hotel (page 70). One of the best-kept secrets in town, this hotel is reasonably priced, has a fabulous waterfront location, and located steps from all the Island has to offer.

---

latest theater performance, rent a yacht, stroll along the waterfront, or simply run through the sprinkler on a hot summer day; it's all there and more!

Once a declining industrial site, Granville Island started its transformation in the late seventies when the government encouraged new people-friendly developments. Maintaining its original industrial look, the former warehouses and factories now house galleries, artist studios, restaurants, and theaters; the cement plant on the waterfront is the only industrial tenant left. Access to Granville Island is by Aquabus from the West End, Yaletown, or Kitsilano or across the bridge at Anderson Street (access from W. 2nd Ave.). Three-hour parking is free but avoid driving on weekends and holidays; you will spend more time in your car than in the galleries. Check the website (www.granville-island.net) for upcoming events and festivals or stop by the information center, behind the Kids Market.

Located on the south shore of False Creek, under the Granville Street Bridge. The market is open daily 9am–6pm. For studio and gallery hours and other information about Granville Island, contact the information center at ℂ 604/666-5784.

H.R. MacMillan Space Centre *(Kids*   Housed in the same building as the Vancouver Museum, the space center and observatory has hands-on displays and exhibits that will delight budding astronomy buffs and their parents (or older space buffs and their children). Displays are highly interactive: In the Cosmic Courtyard you can try your hand at designing a spacecraft or maneuvering a lunar robot. Or, punch a button and a get a punchy video explanation of the Apollo 17 manned-satellite engine that stands before you. Most exciting of all perhaps is the Virtual Voyages Simulator, which takes you on a voyage to Mars or a collision course with an oncoming comet. In the GroundStation Canada Theatre, there are video presentations about Canada's contributions to the space program and about space in general. The StarTheatre shows movies—many of them for children—on an overhead dome. And on selected nights, you can shoot the moon through a half-meter telescope for C$10 (US$6.50) per camera (ℂ 604/736-2655).

1100 Chestnut St., in Vanier Park. ℂ 604/738-STAR. www.hrmacmillanspacecentre.com. Admission C$12.75 (US$8.20) adults, C$9.75 (US$6.30) seniors and youths 11–18, C$8.75 (US$5.65) children 5–10, C$5.25 (US$3.40) children under 5, C$40 (US$26) families (up to 5, maximum 2 adults). Additional Virtual Voyages experiences C$5.25 (US$3.40) each. Open Tues–Sun 10am–5pm. Closed Dec 25. Bus: 22.

Museum of Anthropology *(★★★*   This isn't just any old museum. In 1976, architect Arthur Erickson (see the "Arthur Erickson" box, later in this chapter) re-created a classic Native post-and-beam structure out of modern concrete and glass to house one of the world's finest collections of West Coast Native art.

Enter through doors that resemble a huge, carved, bent-cedar box. Artifacts from potlatch ceremonies flank the ramp leading to the Great Hall's collection of totem poles. Haida artist Bill Reid's touchable cedar bear and sea wolf sculptures sit at the Cross Roads, where source books rest on a reading-height display wall. Reid's masterpiece, *The Raven and the First Men,* is worth the price of admission all by itself. The huge carving in glowing yellow cedar depicts a Haida creation myth, in which Raven—the trickster—coaxes humanity out into the world from its birthplace in a clamshell. Some of Reid's fabulous creations in gold and silver are also on display. Intriguingly, curators have recently begun salting contemporary Native artworks in among the old masterpieces—a sign that West Coast artistic traditions are alive and well.

The Masterpiece Gallery's argillite sculptures, beaded jewelry, and hand-carved ceremonial masks lead the way to the Visible Storage Galleries, where more than 15,000 artifacts are arranged by culture. You can open the glass-topped drawers to view small treasures and stroll past larger pieces housed in tall glass cases. (You can also read more detailed information about the items in conveniently placed reference catalogs.)

Also at the museum is the somewhat incongruous Koerner Ceramics Gallery, a collection of European ceramics that—while interesting—is really only there because old man Koerner had the money to endow the wing to hold his collection.

Don't forget to take a walk around the grounds behind the museum. Overlooking Point Grey are two longhouses built according to the Haida tribal style, resting on the traditional north–south axis. Ten hand-carved totem poles stand in attendance along with contemporary carvings on the longhouse facades.

6393 NW Marine Dr. ☎ **604/822-3825.** www.moa.ubc.ca. Admission C$7 (US$4.55) adults, C$5 (US$3.25) seniors, C$4 (US$2.60) students and children 6–18, C$20 (US$13) families, free for children under 6. Free Tues after 5pm. Late May to early Sept Wed–Mon 10am–5pm, Tues 10am–9pm; early Sept to late May Wed–Sun 11am–5pm, Tues 11am–9pm. Closed Dec 25–26. Bus: 4, 10, or 99 (10-min. walk from UBC bus loop)

Science World British Columbia ☆ (*Kids*)   Science World is impossible to miss. It's in the big blinking geodesic dome on the eastern end of False Creek. Inside, it's a hands-on scientific discovery center where you and your kids can light up a plasma ball, walk through a 1,700-square-foot maze, walk through the interior of a camera, create a cyclone, watch a zucchini explode as it's charged with 80,000 volts, stand inside a beaver lodge, play in wrist-deep magnetic liquids, create music with a giant synthesizer, and watch mind-blowing three-dimensional slide and laser shows as well as other optical effects. In the OMNIMAX Theatre—a huge projecting screen equipped with Surround-Sound—you can take a death-defying flight through the Grand Canyon and perform other spine-tingling feats. Science World also hosts many spectacular

---

360 Degrees of Vancouver

The most popular (and most touristed) spot from which to view Vancouver's skyline is high atop the space needle observation deck at the **Lookout!, Harbour Centre Tower,** 555 W. Hastings St. (☎ **604/689-0421**). It's a great place for first-time visitors who want a panorama of the city. The glass-encased Skylift whisks you up 166m (553 ft.) to the rooftop deck in less than a minute. The 360° view is remarkable. (Yes, that is Mt. Baker looming above the southeastern horizon.) Skylift admission is C$10 (US$6.50) for adults, C$9 (US$5.85) for seniors, C$7 (US$4.55) for students and youth, C$2 (US$1.30) children 6 and under and C$28 (US$18) for families. It's open daily in summer from 8:30am to 10:30pm and in winter from 9am to 9pm.

traveling exhibitions, such as "Backyard Monsters," which features giant robotic bugs.

1455 Quebec St. ✆ 604/443-7443. www.scienceworld.bc.ca. Admission C$12.75 (US$8.25) adults; C$8.50 (US$5.50) seniors, students, and children; free for children under 4. Family pass, including 2 adults and 4 children C$39.75 (US$26). Combination tickets available for OMNIMAX film. Mon–Fri 10am–5pm; Sat–Sun and holidays 10am–6pm. SkyTrain: Main Street–Science World.

Vancouver Maritime Museum *(Kids)*   This museum houses the 1920s Royal Canadian Mounted Police Arctic patrol vessel *St. Roch.* That may not sound like much, but from the time Chris Columbus proved that the continent directly west of Europe was not Cathay, every European explorer's overriding quest was to find the Northwest Passage, the seagoing shortcut to the riches of the east. This little ship is the one that finally did it. The boat has been preserved in a large atrium, with most of its original stores and equipment still onboard. Tours of the *St. Roch* are particularly popular with children—they get to clamber around the boat poking and prodding stuff.

The other half of the museum holds intricate ship models (a few too many of these, unless you're a serious model buff), antique wood and brass fittings, maps, prints, and a number of permanent exhibits, including "Pirates!"—a treasure chest of an exhibit filled with pirate lore, artifacts, and a miniature ship where kids can dress up and play pirate for the day. Also kid-oriented is the Children's Maritime Discovery Centre, which houses computers, a wall of drawers filled with ship models and artifacts, and observation telescopes aimed at the ships moored in English Bay. Here kids can dress up in more naval costumes.

If the weather is pleasant, be sure to walk across the expansive front lawn at the edge of False Creek to Heritage Harbour, where the museum keeps a collection of beautiful vintage boats. It's also where you can catch the miniferry to Granville Island or the West End.

1905 Ogden Ave., in Vanier Park. ✆ 604/257-8300. www.vmm.bc.ca. Admission C$8 (US$5.20) adults, C$5.50 (US$3.55) seniors and students, C$18 (US$12) families, free for children under 6. Daily 10am–5pm. Closed Mon Labour Day to Victoria Day (early Oct to late May). Bus: 22, then walk 4 blocks north on Cypress St. Boat: False Creek Ferries dock at Heritage Harbour.

Vancouver Museum   Established in 1894, the Vancouver Museum is dedicated to amassing evidence of the city's history, from its days as a Native settlement and European outpost to the city's early-20th-century maturation into a modern urban center. The exhibits allow visitors to walk through the steerage deck of a 19th-century passenger ship, peek into a Hudson's Bay Company frontier trading post, or take a seat in an 1880s Canadian Pacific Railway passenger car. Re-creations of Victorian and Edwardian rooms show how early Vancouverites decorated their homes. Rotating exhibits include a display of the museum's collection of neon signage from Vancouver's former glory days as the West Coast's glitziest neon-sign-filled metropolis during the 1940s and 1950s.

1100 Chestnut St. ✆ 604/736-4431. www.vanmuseum.bc.ca. Admission C$8 (US$5.20) adults, C$5.50 (US$3.55) youths. Group rates available. Fri–Wed 10am–5pm; Thurs 10am–9pm. Closed Mon Sept–June. Bus: 22, then walk 3 blocks south on Cornwall Ave. Boat: Granville Island Ferry to Heritage Harbour.

VanDusen Botanical Gardens *(★)*   In contrast to the flower fetish displayed by Victoria's famous garden, Vancouver's biggest botanical garden concentrates on whole ecosystems. From trees hundreds of feet high down to the little lichens on the smallest of damp stones, the gardeners at VanDusen attempt to re-create the plant life of an enormous number of different environments. Depending on which trail you take you may find yourself wandering through the Southern

Hemisphere section, the Sino-Himalayan garden, or the northern California garden where giant sequoias reach for the sky. Other parts of the garden highlight individual families; in the maple ghetto, for example, you can marvel at a good two dozen different maples, from the standard eastern sugar maple to the delicate Japanese cut-leaf variety. And should all this tree gazing finally pall, head for the farthest corner of the garden where there lurks a devilishly difficult Elizabethan garden maze.

5251 Oak St. (at W. 37th Ave.) ℭ 604/878-9274. www.vandusengarden.org. Admission C$7 (US$4.55) adults, C$5 (US$3.25) seniors and youth 13–18, C$3.50 (US$2.25) children 6–12, C$16 (US$10) families, free for children under 6. Off-season discounts. Open daily 10am–dusk. Bus: 17.

GASTOWN & CHINATOWN

Dr. Sun Yat-sen Classical Chinese Garden ✪   This small reproduction of
a Classical Chinese Scholar's garden truly is a remarkable place, but to get the full effect you have to take the guided tour. Untrained eyes (like ours) will insist on seeing only gaggles of tourists wandering round a pretty pond surrounded by bamboo and funny shaped rocks. The engaging guides, however, can explain that the garden is based on the yin-yang principle, or the idea of harmony through dynamic opposition. To foster opposition (and thus harmony) in the garden, Chinese designers constantly place contrasting elements in juxtaposition: Soft moving water flows across solid stone; smooth swaying bamboo grows around gnarled immovable rocks; dark pebbles are placed next to light pebbles in the floor. Moving with the guide, you discover the yin-yang principle applies to larger elements in a more complex fashion as well.

578 Carrall St. ℭ 604/689-7133. www.vancouverchinesegarden.com. C$7.50 (US$4.85) adults, C$6 (US$3.90) seniors, C$5 (US$3.25) children and students, children under 5 free; family pass costs C$18 (US$12). Free guided tour included. Daily May 1–June 14 10am–6pm; June 15–Aug 31 9:30am–7pm; Sept 1–Sept 30 10am–6pm; Oct 1–Apr 30 10am–4:30pm. Bus: 19 or 22.

Vancouver Centennial Police Museum   A bizarre, macabre, and utterly delightful little place, the Police Museum is dedicated to memorializing some of the best crimes and crime-stoppers in the city's short but colorful history. Housed in the old Vancouver Coroner's Court—where actor Errol Flynn was autopsied after dropping dead in the arms of a 17-year-old girl—the museum features photos, text, and vintage equipment from files and evidence rooms of Vancouver's finest. The confiscated illegal-weapons display looks like the props department for the film *Road Warrior.* There's also a morgue with bits and pieces of damaged body parts on the wall, a simulated autopsy room, a forensics lab, and a police radio room. On the lighter side, the museum also houses an immense collection of matchbox-sized toy police cars from around the world.

240 E. Cordova St. ℭ 604/665-3346. www.city.vancouver.bc.ca/police/museum. Admission C$6 (US$3.90) adults, C$4 (US$2.60) students and seniors, free for children 6 and under. Year-round Mon–Fri 9am–3pm; May 1–Aug 31 also Sat 10am–3pm. Bus: 4 or 7.

NORTH VANCOUVER & WEST VANCOUVER

Capilano Suspension Bridge & Park *(Overrated*   Vancouver's first and oldest tourist trap (built in 1889), this attraction still works—mostly because there's still something inherently thrilling about standing on a narrow, shaky walkway, 69m (230 ft.) above the canyon floor, held up by nothing but a pair of tiny cables. Set in a beautiful 8-hectare (20-acre) park about 15 minutes from the city, the suspension bridge itself is a 135m (450-ft.) long cedar-plank and steel-cable footbridge, which sways gently above the Capilano River. You can nervously cross above kayakers and salmon shooting the rapids far below.

In addition to the bridge, there's a **carving centre** where Native carvers demonstrate their skill; an exhibit describing the region's natural history; guides in period costume who recount Vancouver's frontier days; a pair of restaurants; and—surprise—a gift shop. It's all quite well done, but the fact remains that you're paying a substantial entrance fee to walk across a bridge. It's particularly strange when you realize that nearby there's the Lynn Canyon suspension bridge, which is almost as high, even prettier, set in a far larger forest, almost completely untouristed, and absolutely free. (See the box "The *Other* Suspension Bridge," below.)

3735 Capilano Rd., North Vancouver. ℂ 604/985-7474. www.capbridge.com. Admission C$13.95 (US$9) adults, C$10.75 (US$7) seniors, C$8 (US$5.20) students, C$3.75 (US$2.40) children 6–12, free for children under 6. Winter discounts available. May–Sept daily 8:30am–dusk; Oct–Apr daily 9am–5pm. Closed Dec 25. Bus: 246 from downtown Vancouver, 236 from Lonsdale Quay SeaBus terminal.

Grouse Mountain Resort ★★   Once a small local ski hill, Grouse has been slowly developing itself into a year-round mountain recreation park, offering impressive views and instantaneous access to the North Shore mountains. Located only a 20-minute drive from downtown, the SkyRide gondola transports

---

(Finds   The *Other* Suspension Bridge

Lynn Canyon Park, in North Vancouver between Grouse Mountain and Mount Seymour Provincial Park on Lynn Valley Road, offers a cheaper and possibly more impressive alternative to the Capilano Suspension Bridge. True, the **Lynn Canyon Suspension Bridge** ★★ is both shorter and a little lower that the Capilano bridge (see "The Top Attractions," above), but the waterfall and swirling whirlpools in the canyon below add both beauty and a certain fear-inducing fascination, more than enough to make up for the loss of altitude. Plus, it's free.

The park in which the bridge is located is a gorgeous 247-hectare (617-acre) rainforest of cedar and Douglas fir, laced throughout with walking trails. It's also home to an **Ecology Centre,** 3663 Park Rd. (ℂ 604/981-3103), which presents natural history films, tours, and displays that explain the local ecology. Staff members lead frequent walking tours. The center is open daily from 10am to 5pm.

Six kilometers (4 miles) up Lynn Valley Road is the **Lynn Headwaters Regional Park** (ℂ 604/985-1690 for trail conditions), one of the best places close to the city to taste the breathtaking nature of the Northwest. Until the mid-1980s, this was an inaccessible wilderness and bear habitat. The park and the bears are now managed by the Greater Vancouver Regional Parks Department, B.C. Parks, 1610 Mt. Seymour Rd., North Vancouver, B.C. V7G 2R0 (ℂ 604/924-2200; www.gov.bc.ca/wlap or www.gov.bc.ca/srm), and there are 12 marked trails of various levels of difficulty. Some meander by the riverbank, others climb steeply up to various North Shore peaks, and one leads to a series of cascading waterfalls. To get there, take the SeaBus to Lonsdale Quay, then transfer to bus no. 229; or take the Trans-Canada Highway to the Lynn Valley Road exit (about a 20-min. drive from downtown).

you to the mountain's 1,110m (3,700-ft.) summit in about 10 minutes. (Hikers and cardio-fitness fiends can take a near vertical trail called the Grouse Grind. The best of them can do it in 28 min.) At the top, there's a bar, restaurant, large-screen theater, ski and snowboard area, hiking and snowshoeing trails, skating pond, children's snow park, interpretive forest trails, logger sports show, helicopter tours, mountain bike trails, and a Native feast house. Some of these activities are offered free with your SkyRide ticket, but most aren't. Still, the view is one of the best around: the city and the entire lower mainland, from far up the Fraser Valley east across the Gulf of Georgia to Vancouver Island. The Himwus Feast House has gotten good reviews for its Native food and dance.

6400 Nancy Greene Way, North Vancouver. ⓒ 604/984-0661. www.grousemountain.com. SkyRide C$21.95 (US$14) adults, C$19.95 (US$12.90) seniors, C$12.95 (US$8.35) youths, C$7.95 (US$5.15) children 6–12, free for children under 6. SkyRide free with advance Observatory Restaurant reservation. Daily 9am–10pm. SeaBus: Lonsdale Quay, then transfer to bus no. 236.

2 Architectural Highlights

Vancouver was leveled by fire in 1886 (the same year it was incorporated as a city), so most of its architecture is less than a century old. The city had a reputation as a boomtown from the start, attracting a number of famous architects who were eager to practice their art in new and less developed surroundings. The results range from the slightly absurd to the truly impressive. Serious architecture buffs should pick up a copy of *Exploring Vancouver: The Essential Architectural Guide,* by authors Kalman, Phillips, and Ward.

HISTORIC BUILDINGS & MONUMENTS

Vancouver's oldest surviving edifice is the **Hastings Sawmill Store Museum,** 1575 Alma St., Jericho Beach (ⓒ **604/734-1212**). Housed in an 1865 heritage structure that served as the city's first general store, it was moved here by barge in 1930 from its original Gastown location. Inside, you'll find Victorian period clothing, furnishings, hardware, toiletries, woven Native basketry, and historical photographs. Admission is by donation. The museum is open from mid-June to mid-September, Tuesday through Sunday from 11am to 4pm, and on weekends from mid-September to mid-June from 1 to 4pm. Take bus no. 4 or 7 to Alma Street.

The triangular **Hotel Europe,** 43 Powell St., was an architectural wonder when it opened in 1912. Designed by local architects Parr and Fee, the luxury hotel proudly stood as Vancouver's first steel-reinforced concrete structure and fireproof hotel—a concept so foreign that contractors had to be imported from Cincinnati. The design was an intentional imitation of New York's Flatiron Building (erected in 1903), and the lobby became famous for its marble and brass detailing. Subsequent renovations had stripped the building of only a few of its interesting features. Unfortunately, when Gastown fell into decline during and after the Great Depression, so did the hotel. The main entrance was blocked off to expand the lobby's beer parlor, and the original entrance balcony lamps were stolen. Recent renovations have saved the hotel and other historic buildings surrounding Maple Tree Square from the wrecking ball (see "Walking Tour 2," in chapter 7). The hotel appeared in *Legends of the Fall,* among other movies.

Topped by a patina-green copper cupola and mansard windows, the **Sun Tower,** 100 W. Pender St. at Beatty Street, stands amid a somewhat desolate landscape that is slowly being redeveloped. Designed by W. T. Whiteway and erected in 1911, the 17-story hexagonal structure is crowned by a 3-story beaux arts copper roof. The heritage building was constructed by Vancouver mayor L. D. Taylor, who ran his *Vancouver World* newspaper enterprise here from 1912 until 1915. The *Vancouver Sun* took over the building in 1937 and stayed until 1963.

At the outbreak of World War II, Point Grey residents watched artillery carriages rumble through the streets toward the headlands, followed by more weighty ordnance as the Point Grey Battery—complete with concrete gun emplacements and officers' quarters—was erected on the cliffs on the end of Point Grey. The installation was closed 9 years later and abandoned during the 1960s. In the 1970s, however, the site was reclaimed for the **UBC Museum of Anthropology.** In a particularly elegant touch, architect Arthur Erickson turned the foundation of a death-dealing gun emplacement into the pedestal for his friend Bill Reid's master carving, *The Raven and the First Men,* which depicts the origins of life.

The Art Deco **Marine Building,** 355 Burrard St. at Thurlow Street, was the British Empire's tallest structure when it opened in 1930. Designed by McCarter and Nairne, the building was meant to emulate a rocky promontory rising from the sea. Its facade is detailed with terra-cotta, brass, stone, and marble bas-reliefs depicting the local aquatic environment. Its best features are in the lobby near the elevators. The vaulted ceiling is lit by sconces shaped like ships' prows, the center of the stone floor is inlaid with a giant zodiac, and the ornate brass elevator doors open to reveal even more ornate wood inlay inside.

John S. Archibald and John Schofield designed the Canadian Pacific Railway's **Fairmont Hotel Vancouver** (p. 58). Replacing a smaller hotel on the same site, the dignified French Renaissance structure took 10 years to complete. When it finally opened in 1929, it dominated Vancouver's skyline. Topped by a green-patina copper roof decorated with intricately carved stone gargoyles and a statue of the Roman god Hermes, the grand hotel's exterior walls are made of Haddington Island stone—the same stone used in Victoria's Parliament buildings. Sweeping marble staircases and a grand Edwardian lobby elegantly grace the interior.

Built in the shape of a ship with five soaring Teflon sails, **Canada Place Pier** is to Vancouver what the Opera House is to Sydney, Australia—a focal point on the downtown waterfront. Built in time for Expo '86, the pier houses Vancouver's largest convention center, a hotel, the Alaska cruise ship terminal, restaurants, and the CN IMAX Theatre.

Another Expo '86 structure is the giant sparkling silver sphere at the east end of False Creek—**Science World British Columbia.** Originally erected as the Expo Centre, it's been expanded and renovated to house a wealth of entertaining and educational permanent and traveling exhibits for children and adults (see "The Top Attractions," earlier in this chapter).

The **Vancouver Museum** (p. 108) sits on a promontory near the Burrard Street Bridge. A little over a century ago, Vanier Park was the site of a Native village inhabited by the Coast Salish tribe. During World War II it became a military defense base, and in the 1960s it was dedicated as a park. The museum's roof resembles the unique cone-shaped, woven-cedar-bark hat worn by Coast Salish men. The crab-shaped metal fountain standing in front of the museum is possibly Vancouver's most photographed object.

Resembling the Roman Coliseum with its multiple tiers of arches (architect Moshe Safdie denies there was any intentional similarity), **Library Square** ✪ on Robson Street contains voluminous rooms of books, a coffee shop and small

---

Fun Fact **Arthur Erickson**

Vancouver's best-known architect, Arthur Erickson is a puzzling contradiction. A firm believer in listening to what the landscape has to say, Erickson often turns a deaf ear to the needs of those who inhabit his buildings. Combine these features with exceptional eloquence, a driven personality, and flamboyant charm, and you get a lot of buildings, all of which look good on paper—and some that also work in real life. As this is his native town, Vancouver is blessed with a great deal of Erickson's work. Those with an interest can check out the **Museum of Anthropology** (1973), 6993 NW Marine Dr., UBC; the **Provincial Law Courts** (1973), 800 Smithe St.; **Simon Fraser University** (1963), Burnaby Mountain, Burnaby; the **MacMillan Bloedel Building** (1969), 1075 W. Georgia St.; and the **Khalsa Diwan Society Sikh Temple** (1970), 8000 Ross St.

---

restaurant, a day-care center, and a seven-story reading atrium where visitors can comfortably take in the view. Many do. In fact, the atrium and the square outside have become two of Vancouver's favorite public gathering spots.

Behind sheltered walls in the heart of Chinatown lies the **Dr. Sun Yat-sen Classical Garden** (p. 109), a painstakingly exact Ming Dynasty private courtyard garden.

CHURCHES & TEMPLES

Despite its reputation as one of North America's more secular cities, Vancouver has a wide variety of churches, synagogues, temples, and other houses of worship that serve its growing and ethnically diverse population. Vancouver has more than 60 Catholic churches as well as dozens of Protestant churches; Orthodox, Conservative, Reform, and Hasidic Jewish temples; and Sikh, Buddhist, and Islamic temples.

Holy Rosary Cathedral, 646 Richards St. (© **604/682-6774**), is a Gothic Revival–style Roman Catholic cathedral built in 1899 to 1900. On Sunday mornings, the carillon bells call the congregation to worship.

Colorful late-morning Sikh wedding ceremonies frequently take place at the Arthur Erickson–designed **Khalsa Diwan Gurudwara Temple,** 8000 Ross St. (© **604/324-2010**). You are welcome to observe a ceremony if you call for permission in advance.

The Byzantine iconography and architecture of **St. George's Greek Orthodox Cathedral,** 4500 Arbutus Street, at W. 31st Avenue (© **604/266-7148**), constructed in 1930, are as classic as the Sunday services, which are conducted in Greek.

Golden porcelain roof tiles sweep upward to two glittering flying dragons high atop the International Buddhist Society's **Kuan-Yin Buddhist Temple,** 9160 Steveston Hwy., Richmond (© **604/274-2822**). After ascending the bleached granite stairway, you are greeted by two marble lions as you enter the burnt-red doorway of the Main Gracious Hall. Inside, a treasury of Chinese sculpture, woodwork, painting, and embroidery is on display. The center courtyard contains a ceramic mural of the goddess Kuan-Yin resting in a bamboo grove and a magnificent bonsai collection. Visitors are welcome to participate in prayers on Saturday at 9am and in other religious and cultural events.

On your way to this beautiful temple, check out the **Buddha Supplies Centre,** 4185 Main St. (© **604/873-8169**), where you can pick up incense or joss sticks and tiny paper replicas of earthly belongings like CD players, Mercedes vehicles, and cellular phones (they're burned to send the deceased off with ample luxuries).

COLLEGES & UNIVERSITIES

During the academic year, more than 32,000 students attend the **University of British Columbia (UBC),** one of Canada's largest universities. Many UBC attractions are open to the public, including the **Museum of Anthropology** (p. 106); the **UBC Botanical Garden** and **Nitobe Memorial Garden** (see "Parks & Gardens," below); **TRIUMF (Tri-University Meson Facility),** 4004 Wesbrook Mall (© **604/222-1047**), where the world's largest subatomic cyclotron is housed; the **M. Y. Williams Geological Museum,** Geological Sciences Centre, Stores Road, Gate 6 (© **604/822-2449**); and the **UBC Astronomical Observatory** and the **UBC Geophysical Observatory,** Main Mall, Gate 1 (© **604/822-6186**), open for public viewing every clear Saturday, starting one hour after sunset. For campus tours, call © **604/822-8687.**

You can also use the university's sports facilities, including the **Aquatic Centre, Thunderbird Winter Sports Centre,** and nearby **tennis courts.** Miles of trails wind through the **Pacific Spirit Park** and **Point Grey beaches,** overlooking the Strait of Georgia and English Bay (see "Outdoor Activities," later in this chapter).

The **Belkin Art Gallery** (© **604/822-2759**), **Frederic Wood Theatre** (© **604/822-2678**), and **UBC School of Music** (© **604/822-5574**) are venues that present student and professional work (see chapter 9 for details on the latter two). Also worth checking out is the **Chan Centre for the Performing Arts** (© **604/822-9197**). For more information, contact the **Public Affairs Office,** 6251 Cecil Green Park Rd., © **604/822-3131**). To get to UBC, take bus no. 4 or 10, or the 99 B-Line.

Sitting atop 360m (1,200-ft.) Burnaby Mountain, the **Simon Fraser University** campus has an expansive view of metropolitan Vancouver. Architect Arthur Erickson won immediate acclaim for his stunning design when the school opened in 1965. Though it has since won mixed reviews from the students, the SFU campus was for many years known and loved by *X-Files* fans as none other than FBI headquarters.

The **Museum of Archaeology and Ethnology** (© **604/291-3325**) exhibits historic Native works created by Inuit, Kwakiutl, and other provincial aboriginal bands, while contemporary work is shown at the **University Art Gallery** (© **604/291-4266**). Admission to both is free. For more information about points of interest at Simon Fraser University, call © **604/291-3210** or campus tours at © **604/291-3397.** Take bus no. 135, 144, or 145 to the campus.

3 Neighborhoods to Explore

The best way to get to know a city is to explore its different neighborhoods. Here's a quick guide on where to go and what to look for. For more in-depth explorations, turn to the neighborhood walking tours in chapter 7.

THE WEST END

This was Vancouver's first upscale neighborhood, settled in the 1890s by the city's budding class of merchant princes. By the 1930s, most of these formerly grand Edwardian homes had become rooming houses, and in the late '50s, as the baby boomers left home, the Edwardians came down and high-rise apartments went up. The resulting neighborhood owes more to Manhattan than to the sprawling cities of the west. All the necessities of life are contained within the West End's border: great cafes, good nightclubs, many and varied bookshops, and some of the best restaurants in the city. That's part of what makes it such a sought-after address, but it's also the little things, like the street trees, the mix of high-rise condos and old Edwardians, and the way that, in the midst of such an urban setting, you now and again stumble on a view of the ocean or the mountains.

GASTOWN

The oldest section of Vancouver, Gastown's charm shines through the souvenir shops and panhandlers. For one thing, it's the only section of the city that has the feel of an old Victorian town—the buildings stand shoulder to shoulder and cobblestones line the streets. The current Gastown was built from scratch just a few months after an 1886 fire wiped out the entire city. (There are photographs of proper-looking men in black coats selling real estate out of tents on the still-smoking ashes.) Also, rents in Gastown have stayed low so it's still the place to look for a new and experimental art gallery, or a young fashion designer setting up shop on a little back street, or even (until a few months ago) a "Legalize Marijuana" campaigner selling grow lights and cannabis seeds out of a storefront cafe.

Alcohol has always been a big part of Gastown's history. The neighborhood is named for a saloonkeeper—Gassy Jack Deighton—who, according to local legend, talked the local mill hands into building a saloon as Vancouver's first structure in return for all the whisky they could drink. Nowadays, Gastown is still liberally endowed with pubs and clubs—it's one of two or three areas where Vancouverites congregate when the sun goes down.

CHINATOWN

Chinatown's a kick, mostly because there's little that's overtly touristy about it. For the thousands of Cantonese-speaking Canadians who live in the surrounding neighborhoods, it's simply the place they go to shop. And for many others who have moved to more outlying neighborhoods, it's still one of the best places to come and eat. One of North America's more populous Chinatowns, the area was settled about the same time as the rest of Vancouver, by migrant laborers brought in to build the Canadian Pacific Railway. Many white settlers resented the Chinese labor, and periodically race riots broke out. At one point Vancouver's Chinatown was surrounded with Belfast-like security walls. By the '40s and '50s, however, the area was mostly threatened with neglect. In the '70s, there was a serious plan to tear the whole neighborhood down and put in a freeway. A huge protest stopped that, and now the area's future seems secure. For visitors, the fun is to simply wander, look, and taste.

YALETOWN

Vancouver's former warehouse district, Yaletown has long since been converted to an area of apartment lofts, nightclubs, restaurants, high-end furniture shops, and a fledgling multimedia biz. For visitors, it features some interesting cafes and patios, some high-end shops, and a kind of gritty urban feel that you won't find elsewhere in Vancouver.

FALSE CREEK NORTH (CONCORDE PACIFIC)

Stretching along Pacific Boulevard on the north shore of False Creek, Concorde's 30-odd high-rise towers are bright and shiny and brand spanking new. Perhaps a bit too new—like a pair of sneakers that need to lose a little gloss before they'll really be comfortable. The area's worth visiting, though, if only to admire one of the largest—and so far, most successful—urban redevelopment projects on the continent.

GRANVILLE ISLAND

Part crafts fair, part farmers market, part artist's workshop, part mall, and part heavy industrial site, Granville Island seems to have it all. Some 20 years ago the federal government decided to try its hand at a bit of urban renewal, so they took this piece of industrial waterfront and redeveloped it into . . . well, it's hard to describe. But everything you could name is there: theaters, pubs, restaurants, artists' studios, bookstores, crafts shops, an art school, a hotel, a cement plant, and lots and lots of people. One of the most enjoyable ways to experience the Granville Island atmosphere is to head down to the Granville Island Public Market, grab a latte (and perhaps a piece of cake or pie to boot), then wander outside to enjoy the view of the boats, the buskers, and the children endlessly chasing flocks of squawking seagulls.

KITSILANO

Hard to believe, but in the '60s Kitsilano was a neighborhood that had fallen on hard times. Nobody respectable wanted to live there—the 1920s homes had all been converted to cheap rooming houses—so the hippies moved in. The neighborhood became Canada's Haight-Ashbury, with coffeehouses, head shops, and lots of incense and long hair. Once the boom generation stopped raging against the machine, they realized that Kitsilano—right next to the beach, but not quite downtown—was a groovy place to live and a darn fine place to own property. Real estate began an upward trend that has never stopped, and Kits became thoroughly yuppified. Nowadays, it's a fun place to wander. There are great bookstores and trendy furniture and housewares shops, lots of consignment clothing stores, snowboard shops, coffee everywhere, and lots of places to eat. Indeed, every third storefront is a restaurant. The best parts of Kitsilano are the stretch of W. Fourth Avenue between Burrard and Balsam streets, and W. Broadway between Macdonald and Alma streets.

SHAUGHNESSY

Shaughnessy's a terrible place to wander around, but it's a great place to drive. Designed in the 1920s as an enclave for Vancouver's budding elite, this is Vancouver's Westmount or Nob Hill. (Distances within the neighborhood are a little too great for a comfortable stroll.) Thanks to the stranglehold Shaughnessy exerts on local politics—every second mayor hails from this neighborhood—traffic flow is carefully diverted away from the area, and it takes a little bit of driving around to find your way in. It's an effort worth making, however, if only to see the stately homes and monstrous mansions, many of which are now featured in film shoots. To find the neighborhood, look on the map for the area of curvy and convoluted streets between Cypress and Oak streets and 12th and 32nd avenues. The center of opulence is the Crescent, an elliptical street to the southwest of Granville and 16th Avenue.

RICHMOND

Twenty years ago Richmond was mostly farmland, with a bit of sleepy suburb. Now it's Asia West, an agglomeration of shopping malls geared to the new—read: rich, educated, and successful—Chinese immigrant. The residential areas of the city are not worth visiting (unless tract homes are your thing), but malls like the Aberdeen Mall or the Yao Han Centre are something else. It's like getting into your car in Vancouver and getting out in Singapore.

STEVESTON

Steveston, located at the southwest corner of Richmond by the mouth of the Fraser River, once existed for nothing but salmon. Fishermen set out from its port to catch the migrating sockeye, and returned there, to have the catch cleaned and canned. Huge processing plants covered its waterfront, where thousands of workers gutted millions of fish. Much of that history is reprised in the **Gulf of Georgia Cannery National Historic Site,** near the wharf at Bayview Street and Fourth Avenue (© **604/664-9009**). Since the fishery was automated long ago, Steveston's waterfront has been fixed up into a pleasant place to stroll. There are public fish sales, charter trips up the river or out to the Fraser delta, and, above all, a pleasant, laid-back, small-town atmosphere.

COMMERCIAL DRIVE

Known as "The Drive" to Vancouverites, it's the 12-block section from Venables Street to E. Sixth Avenue. The Drive has a counterculture feel to it. There are posters for Cuba Libre! rallies, and bits of graffiti reading "Smash Capitalism!" But The Drive also has an immigrant feel to it. The first wave of Italians left cafes such as **Calabria,** 1745 Commercial Dr. (© **604/253-7017**) and **Caffe Amici,** 1344 Commercial Dr. (© **604/255-2611**). More recent waves of Portuguese, Hondurans, and Guatemalans have also left their mark. And lately, lesbians and vegans and artists have moved in—the kind of trendy moneyed folks who love to live in this kind of milieu. Shops and restaurants reflect the mix. Think Italian cafe next to the Marxist bookstore across from the vegan deli selling yeast-free Tuscan bread.

PUNJABI MARKET

India imported. Most of the businesses on this 4-block stretch of Main Street, from 48th up to 52nd avenues, are run by and cater to Indo-Canadians, primarily Punjabis. The area is best seen during business hours, when the fragrant scent of spices wafts out from food stalls, while the sound of Hindi pop songs blares from hidden speakers. Young brides hunt through sari shops or seek out suitable material in discount textile outlets. **Memsaab Boutique,** 6647 Main St. (© **604/322-0250**), and **Frontier Cloth House,** 6695 Main St. (© **604/325-4424**), specialize in richly colored silk saris, shawls, fabrics, and costume jewelry. A good place to eat is **Nirvana,** 2313 Main St. (© **604/872-8779**), which offers a medley of Indian favorites.

DOWNTOWN

Most of Vancouver's commercial and office space lives in the sort of square patch starting at Nelson Street and heading north to the harbor, with Homer Street and Burrard Street forming the east and west boundaries respectively. Many of the city's best hotels are also found in this area, clustering especially near the water's edge. The most interesting avenues for visitors are Georgia and Granville streets. Georgia Street—in addition to being the prime address for class A commercial property—is where you'll find the Vancouver Art Gallery, the Coliseum-shaped Vancouver Public Library, and the Pacific Centre regional shopping mall. Vancouver's recently revived great white way, Granville Street is the home of bars and clubs and theaters and pubs and restaurants (along with one or two remaining porn shops to add that touch of seedy authenticity).

4 Vancouver's Plazas & Parks

OUTDOOR PLAZAS

Unlike many a city, Vancouver's great urban gathering places stand not at the center but on the periphery; the two **seawalls,** one at one end of Denman street by **English Bay,** the other at the other end of Denman by **Coal Harbour,** are the West Coast equivalent of an Italian piazza, the places where Vancouverites go to stroll and be seen. On warm sunny days, they're packed.

Designed by architect Arthur Erickson to be Vancouver's central plaza, **Robson Square**—between Hornby and Howe streets from Robson to Smithe streets—has never really worked. Though beautifully executed with shrubbery, cherry trees, sculptures, and a triple-tiered waterfall, the square suffers from a basic design flaw: It's sunk one story below street grade, and folks don't seem to like that. Just opposite Robson square, however, the steps of the **Art Gallery** are a great people place, filled with loungers, political agitators, and old men playing chess.

Just down the street a little **Library Square**—at the corner of Robson and Homer streets—is immensely popular with locals, and has been since it was built just 4 years back. People sit on the Coliseum-like steps, bask in the sunshine, read, harangue passersby with half thought-out political ideas, and generally seem to enjoy themselves.

PARKS & GARDENS

Park and garden lovers are in heaven in Vancouver. You can encounter raccoon families in the West End, go downhill or cross-country skiing in West Vancouver, spot bald eagles and peregrine falcons in Richmond, or observe tai chi masters in Chinatown. You can wander a Japanese garden and with the same ticket see one of the largest living botany collections on the West Coast up on the UBC campus. For general information about Vancouver's parks, call © **604/257-8400.**

Stanley Park ⭐ is a 400-hectare (1,000-acre) rainforest near the busy West End. It is named after the same Lord Stanley whose name is synonymous with professional hockey success—the Stanley Cup. The park is filled with towering western red cedar trees, walking trails, manicured lawns, flower gardens, and placid lagoons, such as Lost Lagoon, which used to flow away at low tide before the construction of the road leading to the Lions Gate Bridge. It's surrounded by water except for a small portion of its eastern edge that connects it to the West End. Stanley Park houses the Vancouver Aquarium, a petting zoo, three restaurants and a handful of snack bars, cricket greens, a swimming pool, a miniature railway, and a water park. It also boasts abundant wildlife, including beavers, coyotes, bald eagles, raccoons, trumpeter swans, brant geese, ducks, and skunks, as well as pristine natural settings and amazing marine views. This is where Vancouverites go to run, skate, bike, walk, or just sit. As North America's largest urban park, it is 20% larger than New York's Central Park (which is only 354 hectares/886 acres) and considerably safer. Take bus no. 23, 35, or 135 to the Stanley Park loop at the base of West Georgia Street.

In Chinatown, the **Dr. Sun Yat-sen Classical Garden** (p. 109) is a small, tranquil oasis in the heart of the city. On the West Side, **Queen Elizabeth Park**—at Cambie Street and West 33rd Avenue—sits atop a 150m (500 ft.) high extinct volcano and is the highest urban vantage point south of downtown, offering panoramic views in all directions. It's Vancouver's most popular location for wedding-photo sessions, with well-manicured gardens and a profusion of

Booked seat 6A, open return.

Rented red 4-wheel drive.

Reserved cabin, no running water.

Discovered space.

With over 700 airlines, 50,000 hotels, 50 rental car companies and 5,000 cruise and vacation packages, you can create the perfect getaway for you. Choose the car, the room, even the ground you walk on.

Travelocity.com
A Sabre Company
Go Virtually Anywhere.

Stanley Park

Ferguson Point **16**
Fish House Restaurant **19**
Girl in a Wet Suit statue **9**
Hollow Tree/Geographic Tree **14**
Hummingbird Trail/Malkin Bowl **3**
Japanese Monument **5**
Mallard Trail/Brockton Oval **7**
Nature Center **1**
Prospect Point **12**
Ravine Trail/ Beaver Lake **11**
Second Beach **18**
Siwash Rock **13**
Teahouse Restaurant **17**
Third Beach **15**
Totem Poles **8**
Vancouver Aquarium **6**
Vancouver Children's Zoo/
Variety Kids Farmyard **4**
Vancouver Rowing Club **2**
Variety Kids Water Park **10**

Pedestrian/Cycle Route
Cycle Route
Cycle/Roller Route
Seawall Pedestrian Walk
Railway

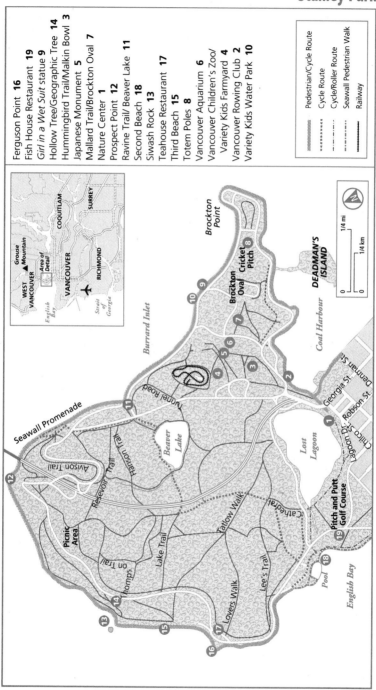

colorful flora. There are areas for lawn bowling, tennis, pitch-and-putt golf, and picnicking. The **Bloedel Conservatory** (© 604/257-8570) stands next to the park's huge sunken garden, an amazing reclamation of an abandoned rock quarry. A 42m (140-ft.) high domed structure, the conservatory houses a tropical rainforest with more than 100 plant species as well as free-flying tropical birds. Admission to the conservatory is C$3.95 (US$2.55) for adults and C$2.95 (US$1.90) for seniors and children. Take bus no. 15 to reach the park.

VanDusen Botanical Gardens (p. 108) is nearby. This 22-hectare (55-acre) formal garden features rolling lawns, lakes, an Elizabethan hedge maze, and marble sculptures.

Serious plant lovers will love the University of British Columbia. The prime attraction on the campus is the 28-hectare (70-acre) **UBC Botanical Garden,** 6804 S.W. Marine Dr., Gate 8 (© 604/822-4208), which boasts over 10,000 species of trees, shrubs, and flowers grouped into a B.C. Native garden, a physic (or medicinal) garden, a food garden, and several others. There's also an excellent plant and seed store. Nearby is the **Nitobe Memorial Garden,** 6565 NW Marine Dr., Gate 4 (© 604/822-6038), an exquisitely beautiful traditional Japanese garden. From early March to mid-October, both gardens are open daily from 10am to 6pm. Admission to the Botanical Garden is C$4.75 (US$3.10) for adults; C$2 (US$1.30) for seniors, students and youth; children under 6 are admitted free. Admission for Nitobe Memorial Garden is C$2.75 (US$1.75) for adults and C$1.75 (US$1.15) for seniors, students, and children 6 and older. A dual pass for both gardens is C$6 (US$3.85) for adults only. Free guided tours are offered at both gardens on Mondays and Wednesdays at 1pm, but pre-booking is essential. (If no one books the tour, guides don't show up). From October 5 to March 6, the Botanical Garden is open daily during daylight hours, while the Nitobe Memorial Garden is open Monday through Friday from approximately 10am to 2:30pm. Both gardens are free in the off-season period.

Out near UBC, **Pacific Spirit Park** (usually called the Endowment Lands) comprises 754 hectares (1,885 acres) of temperate rainforest, marshes, and beaches and includes nearly 35km (22 miles) of trails suitable for hiking, riding, mountain biking, and beachcombing. Across the Lions Gate Bridge, there are six provincial parks that delight outdoor enthusiasts year-round. Good in winter or for those averse to heavy climbing is the publicly maintained **Capilano River Regional Park,** 4500 Capilano Rd. (© 604/666-1790), surrounding the Capilano Suspension Bridge & Park (p. 109). Hikers can follow a gentle trail by the river for 7km (4½ miles) down the well-maintained **Capilano trails** to the Burrard Inlet and the Lions Gate Bridge, or about a mile upstream to **Cleveland Dam,** which serves as the launching point for white-water kayakers and canoeists.

The **Capilano Salmon Hatchery,** on Capilano Road (© 604/666-1790), is on the river's east bank about a half a kilometer (¼ mile) below the Cleveland Dam. Approximately 2 million Coho and Chinook salmon are hatched annually in glass-fronted tanks connected to the river by a series of channels. You can observe the hatching fry (baby fish) before they depart for open waters, as well as the mature salmon that return to the Capilano River to spawn. Admission is free, and the hatchery is open daily from 8am to 7pm (until 4pm in the winter). Drive across the Lions Gate Bridge and follow the signs to North Vancouver and the Capilano Suspension Bridge. Or take the SeaBus to Lonsdale Quay and transfer to bus no. 236; the trip takes less than 45 minutes.

Eight kilometers (5 miles) west of the Lions Gate Bridge on Marine Drive West, West Vancouver, is **Lighthouse Park** ⚓. This 74-hectare (185-acre) rugged-terrainforest has 13km (8 miles) of groomed trails and—because it has never been clear-cut—some of the largest and oldest trees in the Vancouver area. One of the paths leads to the 18m (60-ft.) **Point Atkinson Lighthouse,** on a rocky bluff overlooking the Strait of Georgia and a fabulous view of Vancouver. It's an easy trip on bus no. 250. For information about other West Vancouver parks, call © **604/925-7200** weekdays.

Driving up-up-up the mountain from **Lighthouse Park** will eventually get you to the top of **Cypress Provincial Park.** Stop halfway at the scenic viewpoint for a sweeping vista of the Vancouver skyline, the harbor, the Gulf Islands, and Washington State's Mount Baker, which looms above the eastern horizon. The park is 12km (7½ miles) north of Cypress Bowl Road and the Highway 99 junction in West Vancouver. Cypress Provincial Park has an intricate network of trails maintained for hiking during the summer and autumn and for downhill and cross-country skiing during the winter.

Rising 1,430m (4,767 ft.) above Indian Arm, **Mount Seymour Provincial Park,** 1700 Mt. Seymour Rd., North Vancouver (© **604/986-2261**), offers another view of the area's Coast Mountains range. The road to this park roams through stands of Douglas fir, red cedar, and hemlock. Higher than Grouse Mountain, Mount Seymour has a spectacular view of Washington State's Mount Baker on clear days. It has challenging hiking trails that go straight to the summit, where you can see Indian Arm, Vancouver's bustling commercial port, the city skyline, the Strait of Georgia, and Vancouver Island. The trails are open all summer for hiking; during the winter, the paths are maintained for skiing, snowboarding, and snowshoeing. Mount Seymour is open daily from 7am to 10pm.

The Fraser River delta is south of Vancouver. Thousands of migratory birds following the Pacific flyway rest and feed in this area, especially at the 340-hectare (850-acre) **George C. Reifel Bird Sanctuary,** 5191 Robertson Rd., Westham Island (© **604/946-6980**), which was created by a former bootlegger and wetland-bird lover. Many other waterfowl species have made this a permanent habitat. More than 263 species have been spotted, including a Temminck's stint, a spotted redshank, bald eagles, Siberian (trumpeter) swans, peregrine falcons, blue herons, owls, and coots. The **Snow Goose Festival,** celebrating the annual arrival of the huge, snowy white flocks, is held here during the first weekend of November. The snow geese stay in the area until mid-December. (High tide, when the birds are less concealed by the marsh grasses, is the best time to visit.) An observation tower, 3km (2 miles) of paths, free birdseed, and picnic tables make this wetland reserve an ideal outing spot from October to April, when the birds are wintering in abundance. The sanctuary is wheelchair accessible and open daily from 9am to 4pm. Admission is C$4 (US$2.60) for adults and C$2 (US$1.30) for seniors and children.

The **Richmond Nature Park,** 1185 Westminster Hwy. (© **604/718-6188**), was established to preserve the Lulu Island wetlands bog. It features a Nature House with educational displays and a boardwalk-encircled duck pond. On Sunday afternoons, knowledgeable guides give free tours and acquaint visitors with this unique environment. Admission is by donation.

5 Especially for Kids

Pick up copies of the free monthly newspapers *BC Parent,* 4479 W. 10th Ave., Vancouver, B.C. V6R 4P2 (© **604/221-0366**); and *West Coast Families,* 8–1551 Johnston St., Vancouver, B.C. V6H 3R9 (© **604/689-1331**). *West*

Coast Families' centerfold, "Fun in the City," and event calendar list everything currently going on, including **CN IMAX** (see chapter 9) shows at Canada Place Pier, **OMNIMAX** (© **604/443-7443**), shows at Science World British Columbia, and free children's programs. Both publications are available at Granville Island's Kids Market and at neighborhood community centers throughout the city.

Stanley Park offers a number of attractions for children. Stanley Park's Children's Farm (© **604/257-8530**) has peacocks, rabbits, calves, donkeys, and Shetland ponies (see "Parks & Gardens," above). Next to the petting zoo is Stanley Park's Miniature Railway (© **604/257-8531**). The diminutive steam locomotive with passenger cars runs on a circuit through the woods, carrying nearly as many passengers annually as all of the Alaska-bound cruise ships combined. Special events include a Ghost and Goblins ride in October, and during the winter holidays, the railway is strung with festive lights. The zoo and railway are open daily May through September (11am–4pm), plus Christmas week and on weekends October through March. Admission for the petting zoo is C$4(US$2.60) for adults, seniors and students pay C$3(US$1.95), and kids ages 2 to 12 pay C$2 (US$1.30). Summer admission for the railway is C$3 (US$1.95) for adults, C$2.25 (US$1.45) for youth and seniors, C$1.50 (US$1) for kids; rates vary for some of the events.

Also in Stanley Park, the **Vancouver Aquarium Marine Science Centre** ℛ (p. 101) has sea otters, sea lions, whales, and numerous other marine creatures, as well as many exhibits geared towards children. Across Burrard Inlet on the North Shore, **Maplewood Farm,** 405 Seymour River Place, North Vancouver (© **604/929-5610**), has more than 200 barnyard animals (cows, horses, ponies, pigs, sheep, donkeys, ducks, chickens, and more) living on its 2-hectare (5-acre) farm, which is open daily year-round. A few working farms once operated in the area but were put out of business by competition from the huge agricultural concerns in Fraser River valley. The parks department rescued this one and converted it into an attraction. The ticket booth (a former breeding kennel) sells birdseed for feeding the ducks and other fowl, as well as guidebooks. The farm also offers pony rides. Special events include the summertime Sheep Fair, the mid-September Farm Fair, 101 Pumpkins Day in late October, and the Country Christmas weekend. The farm is open Tuesday through Sunday from 10am to 4pm, and on designated holiday Mondays during the same hours. Admission is C$3.20 (US$2.05) for adults, C$1.65 (US$1.10) for seniors and children. Take bus no. 210 and transfer to the no. 211 or 212.

Forty-five minutes east of the city, the **Greater Vancouver Zoo,** 5048–264th St., Aldergrove (© **604/856-6825**), is a lush 48-hectare (120-acre) farm filled with lions, tigers, jaguars, ostriches, elephants, buffalo, elk, antelope, zebras, giraffes, a rhino, hippos, and camels. In all, 124 species roam free or in spacious paddocks on the grounds. Located 48km (30 miles) from Vancouver, the wildlife reserve also has food service and a playground. It's open daily from 9am until dusk. Admission is C$12 (US$7.80) for adults, C$9 (US$5.85) for seniors and children 3 to 15, and free for children under 3 with an adult.

Right in town, **Science World British Columbia** (p. 107) is a hands-on kids' museum where budding scientists can get their hands into everything. At the **Vancouver Maritime Museum** (p. 108), kids can dress up like a pirate or a naval captain for a day, or board the RCMP ice-breaker *St. Roch* (p. 108).

The **Burnaby Village Museum,** 6501 Deer Lake Ave., Burnaby (© **604/293-6501**), is a 3.5-hectare (9-acre) re-creation of the Victorian era. You can walk along boardwalk streets among costumed townspeople, watch a blacksmith pound horseshoes, shop in a general store, ride a vintage carousel, peek into an authentic one-room schoolhouse, and visit a vintage ice-cream parlor that's been at the same location since the turn of the 20th century. At Christmastime the whole village is aglow in Christmas lights and Victorian decorations. Admission is C$7.50 (US$4.80) for adults; C$5.55 (US$3.60) for seniors, travelers with disabilities, students and youths 13 to 18; C$4.65 (US$3) for children 6 to 12; and free for children under 6. It's open daily from 11am to 4:30pm. From the Metrotown Skystation take bus no. 110 to Deer Lake.

The **Fort Langley National Historic Site,** 23433 Mavis Ave., Fort Langley (© **604/513-4777**), is the birthplace of British Columbia. In 1827, the Hudson's Bay Company established this settlement to supply its provincial posts. Costumed craftspeople demonstrate blacksmithing, coppering, and woodworking skills, bringing this landmark back to life. It's open daily from 10am to 5pm March through October, and weekdays only 10am to 5pm from November through February. Admission is C$4 (US$2.60) for adults, C$3 (US$1.95) for seniors, C$2 (US$1.30) for children 6 to 16, and free for children under 6; a family pass is C$10 (US$6.50). Take the SkyTrain to Surrey Central Station; transfer to bus no. 501.

Note: The main street of Fort Langley Village, Glover Road, is packed with antiques shops, cafes, and a bookstore. Only a 2-minute stroll from the historic site, it makes a fine lunch destination.

At **Granville Island's Water Park and Adventure Playground,** 1496 Cartwright St., kids can really let loose with movable water guns and sprinklers. They can also have fun on the water slides or in the wading pool. The facilities are open during the summer daily (weather permitting) from 10am to 6pm. Admission is free; changing facilities are nearby at the False Creek Community Centre (© **604/257-8195**).

Open during summer, **Splashdown Park,** 4799 Nu Lelum Way, Tsawwassen (© **604/943-2251**), is a 3-minute drive from the Tsawwassen ferry terminal, just south of Vancouver. With 13 enormous water slides, a giant hot tub, a pool, a picnic area, inner tubes, and volleyball and basketball courts, it's a great escape for kids of all ages. During summer it's open daily from 10am to 8pm, weather permitting; call ahead for exact hours. Admission is C$19.95 (US$12.90) for anyone over 48 inches tall, C$13.95 (US$9) for anyone under 48 inches tall, and C$11.95 (US$7.70) for people entering the park but not going on the water slides; a family pass (two adults and two children) costs C$69.95 (US$45).

Rainy days are no problem at the **Playdium at Metrotown,** 4700 Kingsway, Burnaby (© **604/433-7529;** www.playdium.com), where a huge variety of electronic diversions awaits kids and adults. It's open Sunday through Thursday from 11am to 11pm, Friday and Saturday from 11am to 2am. Cost depends on the number of games you play. On Sundays from 4pm to midnight you can purchase 3 hours of playtime for C$22 (US$14), and on Fridays between 8pm and 2am, 4 hours of unlimited games comes to C$25 (US$16).

For a more traditional family experience, go to **Playland Family Fun Park,** Exhibition Park, East Hastings and Cassiar streets (© **604/255-5161**). Admission for unlimited rides is C$23 (US$15) for those 4 feet and taller, and C$10 (US$6.50) for those under 4 feet tall for limited rides. Admission for an adult with a paying child under 12 is C$10 (US$6.50). Relive your childhood at this amusement park by riding on the ornate carousel and wooden roller coaster and playing miniature golf. There's also a Nintendo Pavilion, Electric City Arcade, and petting zoo. The park is open weekends and holidays from late April to mid-June and Labour Day to the end of September from 11am to 7pm; mid-June to Labour Day daily from 11am to 9pm. Take bus no. 14 or 16.

The prospect of walking high above the rushing waters is the main draw at the **Capilano Suspension Bridge & Park** (p. 109) and the **Lynn Canyon Suspension Bridge** (see the box "The *Other* Suspension Bridge," earlier in this chapter). In winter, **Mount Seymour Provincial Park** (see "Skiing & Snowboarding," below) and **Grouse Mountain Resort** (see "The Top Attractions," earlier in this chapter) offer ski programs for kids and adults.

Granville Island's **Kids Market,** 1496 Cartwright St. (© **604/689-8447**), is open daily from 10am to 6pm. Playrooms and 28 shops filled with toys, books, records, clothes, and food are all child-oriented. Kids will also love taking the Aquabus or Granville Island Ferry (see "By Ferry," in chapter 3) to get there.

Only a 45-minute drive north of Vancouver, the **B.C. Museum of Mining,** Highway 99, Britannia Beach (© **800/896-4044**), is impossible to miss. Located at the head of Howe Sound, it's marked by a 235-ton truck parked in front. It offers guided tours of the old copper mine, live demonstrations of mining techniques, and includes an underground mine tour and even a gold-panning area where anyone can try straining gravel for the precious metal. It's open daily from 9am to 4:30pm; call ahead for tour schedule. The museum is closed from Thanksgiving (early Oct) until early May. Admission is C$12.95 (US$8.35) for adults and C$10.95 (US$7.10) for students, youth and seniors; free for children under 5; family rate C$45 (US$29).

6 Organized Tours

If you don't have the time to arrange your own sightseeing tour, let the experts take you around Vancouver. They will escort you in a bus, trolley, double-decker bus, seaplane, helicopter, boat, ferry, taxi, vintage car, or horse-driven carriage.

BUS TOURS

Gray Line of Vancouver, 255 E. First Ave. (© **604/879-3363;** www.grayline.ca/vancouver), offers a wide array of tour options. The "Deluxe Grand City Tour" is a 3½-hour excursion through Stanley Park, Gastown, Chinatown, Canada Place, Queen Elizabeth Park, Robson Street, Shaughnessy, and English Bay Beach. Offered year-round, it costs C$40 (US$26) for adults and C$31 (US$20) for children. Departing at 9:15am and 2pm, the bus picks you up from downtown hotels approximately 30 minutes before departure. The daily "Mountains and Sea Tour" takes you up to Grouse Mountain and the Capilano Suspension Bridge. Departing daily at 2pm, it costs C$72 (US$46) for adults and C$49 (US$32) for children, including admission and the SkyTram. Other offerings include day, overnight, and multinight package tours of Vancouver, Victoria, and Whistler, plus helicopter tours and dinner cruises.

Vancouver Trolley Company, 4012 Myrtle St., Burnaby (© **604/451-5581;** www.vancouvertrolley.com), operates gas-powered trolleys along a route through Downtown, Chinatown, the West End, and Stanley Park. Between 9am and 6pm in summer (4:30pm in winter), passengers can get on and off at any of the 23 stops, explore, and catch another scheduled trolley. Onboard, drivers provide detailed tour commentary. Tickets are C$25 (US$16) for adults and C$12 (US$7.75) for children 4 to 12.

West Coast City and Nature Sightseeing, 4012 Myrtle St., Burnaby (© **604/451-1600;** www.vancouversightseeing.com), offers a variety of minicoach tours, including Grouse Mountain/Capilano Suspension Bridge for C$74 (US$48) for adults, C$70 (US$45) for seniors and students, and C$47 (US$30) for children; and Whistler/Shannon Falls for C$73 (US$47) for adults, C$70 (US$45) seniors and students, and C$40 (US$26) for children; as well as Vancouver City/Capilano Suspension Bridge: C$55 (US$35) for adults, C$52 (US$34) for seniors and students, and C$33 (US$21) for children. Children under 4 go free. Upon request, the staff also offers customized tours such as a Native Culture Tour, garden tour, bear habitat tour on Mount Seymour, or a visit to the city's art galleries. Minicoaches pick up passengers from downtown hotels, cruise ships, the airport, and the bus/railway station; phone for departure times. Charters and private tours are also available.

RAIL TOURS

On the **Pacific Starlight Dinner Train** (p. 84), a gourmet meal is served in the dome or salon car onboard a vintage locomotive as it travels from North Vancouver to Porteau Cove along the edge of Howe Sound. It costs C$89.95 (US$57.50) for adults and C$69.95 (US$45) per child for the salon car. For the dome car the cost is C$112.95 (US$73), with no discount for children. Prices include taxes, gratuities, and meals. The dinner train runs from May to late September, Friday through Sunday; in October, weekends only. Additional Wednesday and Thursday departures are available in the summer; call 𝕮 **800/363-3733** for days of operation. Trains depart the BC Rail Station, on 1311 West First St., North Vancouver, at 6:15pm and return to the station at 10pm.

BOAT TOURS

Harbour Cruises, Harbour Ferries, no. 1, north foot of Denman Street (𝕮 **604/688-7246;** www.boatcruises.com), will take you on a 3-hour Sunset Dinner Cruise, including a catered gourmet meal and onboard entertainment; cost for adults, seniors, and students is C$65 (US$41); for children 2 to 11, C$55 (US$35). The cruise leaves at 7pm May through October. The 4-hour Indian Arm Luncheon Cruise includes a salmon lunch, with departure at 11am. Cost for adults, seniors and children is C$50 (US$32).

The company also conducts a 75-minute narrated Harbour Tour aboard the **MPV *Constitution,*** an authentic 19th-century stern-wheeler with a smokestack. Tours depart at 11:30am, 1pm, and 2:30pm daily from mid-May to mid-September, once a day at 2pm in April and October. Fares are C$18 (US$12) for adults, C$15 (US$9.75) for seniors and youths (12–17), C$6 (US$3.90) for children 5 to 11, and free for children under 5. **Paddlewheeler River Adventures,** New Westminster Quay, New Westminster (𝕮 **604/525-4465;** www.vancouverpaddlewheeler.com), operates Fraser River tours from New Westminster aboard the 19th-century vessel *SS Native.* The company offers a 3-hour entertainment cruise Wednesday through Saturday evenings with live music, departing at 7pm. Ticket price is C$20 (US$13); food and beverages can be purchased on board. More interesting but alas not regularly scheduled are the lunch cruises and day trips up to historic Fort Langley. Please check the website or contact the office for upcoming special events. Experience one of the world's largest commercial ports on **Burrard Water Taxi,** 2255 Commissioner St. (𝕮 **604/293-1160**). There are no scheduled tour times, so call ahead to book. The guides offer a fascinating insider's view of the busy harbor. The water taxis are available for tours at a rate of C$145 (US$94) per hour for 12 people. When the boats aren't escorting visitors around the harbor, they're shuttling the captains and crews of the freighters anchored in the Burrard Inlet to and from their vessels.

AIR TOURS

Baxter Aviation, Barbary Coast Marina, P.O. Box 1110, Nanaimo, B.C. V9R 6E7 (© **800/661-5599** or 604/683-6525; www.baxterair.com), operates 11 daily floatplane flights from downtown Vancouver. The 30-minute "Vancouver Scenic" tour flies over Stanley Park and the Coast Mountains; the 5-hour "Whistler Mountain Resort" tour includes a 3-hour stopover. Fares range from C$76 (US$49) per person for 30 minutes to C$359 (US$233) per person for 5 hours, with a variety of midrange tours in between. Other packages offer flights to Victoria, Johnstone Strait, glacial lakes, and prime fly-fishing and whale-watching spots.

Harbour Air (© **604/688-1277;** www.harbour-air.com) is on Coal Harbour just steps west of the Canada Place Pier. Look for the seaplanes arriving and departing. Thirty-minute seaplane flights over downtown Vancouver, Stanley Park, and the North Shore are C$85 (US$55) per person, C$70 (US$45) if your party includes four or more people. Many longer tours to alpine lakes and glaciers and nearby islands, as well as regularly scheduled flights to Victoria, Nanaimo, and Prince Rupert, are also available.

Helijet Charters, 5911 D Airport Rd. S., Richmond (© **800/987-4354** or 604/270-1484; www.helijet.com), offers a variety of daily tours that depart from the Vancouver Harbour Heliport near Canada Place Pier. The "West Coast Spectacular" is a 20-minute tour of the city, Stanley Park, and North Shore mountains for C$140 (US$90) per person. For a bird's-eye view of the city, the 30-minute "Greater Vancouver Scenic Tour" costs C$195 (US$126) per person, and the "North Shore Discovery" tour lasts 45 minutes and costs C$275 (US$177) per person; these prices are per person with a minimum of three people. Tours that depart from the Grouse Mountain summit take 10 to 15 minutes and cost C$75 to C$110 (US$48–US$71) per person. The "Fly, Dine, and Drive" package takes you by helicopter from downtown Vancouver to the top of Grouse Mountain for dinner, returning to the city by limousine; it costs C$275 (US$177) per person for a party of two. Custom mountaintop heli-picnics, heli-golfing packages, and special trips can also be arranged.

SPECIALTY TOURS

Early Motion Tours, 1–1380 Thurlow St. (© **604/687-5088**), offers private sightseeing tours around Vancouver aboard a restored 1930 Model A Ford Phaeton convertible that holds up to four passengers plus the driver. Reservations are required. Limousine rates apply: C$100 (US$65) per hour for up to four people, and include a souvenir Polaroid of you in the car. There is a 1-hour minimum. The office is open daily from 7:30am to 8pm.

AAA Horse & Carriage Ltd., Stanley Park (© **604/681-5115;** www.stanleyparktours.com), carries on a century-old tradition of horse-drawn carriage rides through Stanley Park. Tours depart every 30 minutes between mid-March and October from the lower aquarium parking lot on Park Drive across from the Vancouver Rowing Club near the Georgia Street park entrance. Tours last an hour and cover portions of the park that even most locals have never seen. Rates are C$18.65 (US$12) for adults, C$17 (US$11) for seniors and students, C$11.20 (US$7.25) for children 3 to 12, and children under 3 go free; a family rate is available for $55.95 (US$36) and includes two adults or seniors and two children or students.

Yes, the truth is out there and so are the *X-Files* fans. Even though the series has ended, die-hards can still depart on **the X Tour** (℃ **604/609-2770;** www. x-tour.com) for guided tours of *X-Files* shooting locations around Vancouver, along with other sights guaranteed to delight the true believer. Costs are from C$25 (US$16) per adult for a 1-hour walking tour to C$149 (US$96) per person (minimum of two) for a 3-hour limo tour.

WALKING TOURS

Walkabout Historic Vancouver (℃ **604/720-0006;** www.walkabouthistoric vancouver.com) offers 2-hour walking tours through Vancouver historic sites, complete with guides dressed as 19th-century schoolmarms. Tours depart daily at 9am, noon, and 3pm February through November, and by request during other months. The cost is C$18 (US$11.60) per person. Walking tours of Chinatown are available from the **Chinese Cultural Centre** (℃ **604/687-7993**) for C$5 (US$3.25) adults, C$4 (US$2.90) seniors, and C$3 (US$1.95) students and children. July through September, tours depart daily at 11am and 1:30pm; during other times, please phone ahead to book a tour. During the summer months the **Architectural Institute of BC** (℃ **604/638-8588,** ext. 306; www.aibc.bc.ca/public/arch_tours/arch-tours-set.html) offers a number of free architectural walking tours of downtown Vancouver neighborhoods. The 2-hour tours run Wednesday through Sunday and depart from different locations in the city. Call for details and to book. The Vancouver Tourism Info Centre at 200 Burrard St. (see also chapter 3) has a number of brochures on self-guided tours throughout the city.

7 Outdoor Activities

Just about every imaginable sport has a world-class outlet within the Vancouver city limits. Downhill and cross-country skiing, snowshoeing, sea kayaking, flyfishing, hiking, paragliding, and mountain biking are just a few of the options. Activities that can be practiced close by include rock climbing, river rafting, and heli-skiing. If you don't find your favorite sport listed here, take a look at chapter 17, "Side Trips: The Best of British Columbia."

An excellent resource for outdoor enthusiasts is **Mountain Equipment Co-op,** 130 W. Broadway (℃ **604/872-7858**). The MEC's retail store has a knowledgeable staff, and the Co-op also publishes an annual mail-order catalogue.

BEACHES

Only 10% of Vancouver's annual rainfall occurs during June, July, and August; 60 days of summer sunshine is not uncommon. In addition to being a great place for viewing sunsets, **English Bay Beach** ⚑, at the end of Davie Street off Denman Street and Beach Avenue, has an interesting history. It was Joe Fortes's front yard for more than 35 years. Fortes was a legendary Caribbean-born lifeguard and bartender who made English Bay Beach his home. The bathhouse dates to the turn of the 20th century, and a huge playground slide is mounted on a raft just off the beach every summer.

South of English Bay Beach, near the Burrard Street Bridge and the Vancouver Aquatic Centre, is **Sunset Beach.** Running along False Creek, it's actually a picturesque strip of sandy beaches filled with hulking sections of driftwood that serve as windbreaks and provide a little privacy for sunbathers and picnickers. There's a snack bar, a soccer field, and a long, gently sloping grassy hill for people who prefer lawn to sand.

On **Stanley Park's** western rim, **Second Beach** is a quick stroll north from English Bay Beach. A playground, a snack bar, and an immense heated freshwater pool—C$4.15 (US$2.70) for adults, C$2.90 (US$1.87) for seniors, C$3.10 (US$2) for youths 13 to 18, and C$2.10 (US$1.35) for children 6 to 12—make this a convenient spot for families. Farther along the seawall lies secluded **Third Beach,** which is due north of Stanley Park Drive. Locals tote along grills and coolers to this spot, a popular place for summer-evening barbecues and sunset watching. The hollow tree, Geographic Tree, and Siwash Rock are neighboring points of interest.

Kitsilano Beach , along Arbutus Drive near Ogden Street, is affectionately called Kits Beach. It's an easy walk from the Maritime Museum and the False Creek ferry dock. A heated saltwater swimming pool is open throughout the summer. Admission is the same as for Second Beach Pool, above. The summertime amateur theater, **Kitsilano Showboat,** attracts a local crowd looking for evening fun.

Farther west on the other side of Pioneer Park is **Jericho Beach** (Alma St. off Point Grey Rd.). This is another local after-work and weekend social spot. **Locarno Beach,** off Discovery Street and NW Marine Drive, and **Spanish Banks,** NW Marine Drive, wrap around the northern point of the UBC campus and University Hill. (Be forewarned that beachside restrooms and concessions on the promontory end abruptly at Locarno Beach.) Below UBC's Museum of Anthropology is **Point Grey Beach,** a restored harbor defense site. The next beach is **Wreck Beach**—Canada's largest nude beach. You get down to Wreck Beach by taking the very steep Trail 6 on the UBC campus near Gate 6 down to the water's edge. Extremely popular with locals, Wreck Beach is also the city's most pristine and least-developed sandy stretch. The Wreck Beach Preservation Society maintains it. It's bordered on three sides by towering trees.

At the northern foot of the Lions Gate Bridge, **Ambleside Park** is a popular North Shore spot. The quarter-mile beach faces the Burrard Inlet.

BICYCLING & MOUNTAIN BIKING

The most popular cycling path in the city runs along the **Seawall** around the perimeter of Stanley Park. Offering stunning views of the city, the Burrard Inlet, and English Bay, this pathway is extremely popular with cyclists, in-line skaters, and pedestrians alike. Other marked cycle lanes traverse the rest of the city, among them the cross-town **Off-Broadway** route, the **Adanac** route, and the **Ontario Street** route. Runners and cyclists have separate lanes on developed park and beach paths. Some West End hotels offer guests bike storage and rentals. One of the city's most scenic cycle paths has been extended and now runs all the way from Canada Place Pier to Pacific Spirit Park. It connects Canada Place, Stanley Park and the Seawall Promenade, English Bay and Sunset beaches, and Granville Island to Vanier Park, Kitsilano and Jericho beaches, and Pacific Spirit Park. Cycling maps are available at most bicycle retailers and rental outlets.

Local mountain bikers love the cross-country ski trails on **Hollyburn Mountain** in Cypress Provincial Park. The Secret Trail Society started building trails 4 years ago along **Grouse Mountain's** backside, and they are now considered some of the lower mainland's best. Mount Seymour's very steep **Good Samaritan Trail** connects to the Baden-Powell Trail and the Bridle Path near Mount Seymour Road. The route is recommended only for world-class mountain bikers— the types who pour Gatorade on their Wheaties. Closer to downtown, both **Pacific Spirit Park** and **Burnaby Mountain** offer excellent beginner and intermediate off-road trails.

Hourly rentals run around C$3.75 (US$2.40) for a one-speed "Cruiser" to C$10 (US$6.45) for a top-of-the-line mountain bike; C$15 to C$40 (US$9.70–US$26) for a day, helmets and locks included. Bikes and child trail-ers are available by the hour or day at **Spokes Bicycle Rentals & Espresso Bar,** 1798 W. Georgia St. (© **604/688-5141**). **Alley Cat Rentals,** 1779 Robson St., in the alley (© **604/684-5117**), is a popular shop that rents city or mountain bikes, child trailers, child seats, locks, helmets, and in-line skates (protective gear included). **Bayshore Bicycle and Rollerblade Rentals,** 745 Denman St. (© **604/688-2453**), rents 21-speed mountain bikes, bike carriers, tandems, city bikes, in-line skates, and kids' bikes.

BOATING

You can rent 15- to 17-foot power boats for as little as a few hours or up to several weeks at **Stanley Park Boat Rentals Ltd.,** Coal Harbour Marina (© **604/682-6257**). **Granville Island Boat Rentals, Ltd.,** 1696 Duranleau St., Granville Island (© **604/682-6287**), offers hourly, daily, and weekly rentals of 15- to 19-foot speedboats. **Jerry's Boat Rentals,** Granville Island (© **604/644-3256**), is just steps away and offers similar deals. Rates on all the above begin at around C$30 (US$19) per hour and C$150 (US$97) per day for a 17-foot sport boat that holds four. **Delta Charters,** 3500 Cessna Dr., Richmond (© **800/661-7762** or 604/273-4211; www.deltacharters.com), has weekly and monthly rates for 32- to 58-foot powered boat craft. Prices begin around C$1,600 (US$1,032) per week for a boat that sleeps four (which isn't a bad deal when you consider that you won't need a hotel room).

CANOEING & KAYAKING

Both placid, urban False Creek and the incredibly beautiful 30km (19-mile) North Vancouver fjord known as Indian Arm have launching points that can be reached by car or bus. Rentals range from C$15 (US$9.70) per hour to C$50 (US$32) per day for single kayaks and about C$50 (US$32) per day for canoe rentals. Customized tours range from C$70 to C$110 (US$45–US$71) per person.

Ecomarine Ocean Kayak Centre, 1668 Duranleau St., Granville Island (© **888/425-2925** or 604/689-7575; www.ecomarine.com), has 2-hour, daily, and weekly kayak rentals, as well as courses and organized tours. The company also has an office at the **Jericho Sailing Centre,** 1300 Discovery St., at Jericho Beach (© **604/222-3565**). In North Vancouver, **Deep Cove Canoe and Kayak Rentals** (at the foot of Gallant St.), Deep Cove (© **604/929-2268;** www.deep covekayak.com), is an easy starting point for anyone planning an Indian Arm run. It offers hourly and daily rentals of canoes and kayaks as well as lessons and customized tours.

Lotus Land Tours, 2005–1251 Cardero St. (© **800/528-3531** or 604/684-4922; www.lotuslandtours.com), runs guided kayak tours on Indian Arm. Tours come complete with transportation to and from Vancouver, a barbecue salmon lunch, and incredible scenery. Operator Peter Loppe uses very wide stable kayaks, perfect for first-time paddlers. One-day tours cost C$145 (US$94) for adults, C$99 (US$64) for children.

ECOTOURS

Lotus Land Tours, 2005–1251 Cardero St. (© **800/528-3531** or 604/684-4922), runs guided kayak tours on Indian Arm (see "Canoeing & Kayaking," above). From late November to the end of January, this small local company also offers unique float trips on down the Squamish River to see the large concentration of bald eagles up close. **Rockwood Adventures,** 1330 Fulton Ave. (© **604/926-7705**); www.rockwoodadventures.com), has guided walks of the North Shore rainforest, complete with a trained naturalist and a gourmet lunch. Tours cover Capilano Canyon, or Lighthouse Park, and start at C$70 (US$45) for a half-day, including snack and drink, or C$130 (US$84) for a full-day trip to Bowen Island, including transportation, guide, and lunch. Seniors and children's discounts available.

FISHING

Five species of salmon, rainbow and Dolly Varden trout, steelhead, and even sturgeon abound in the local waters. To fish, you need a nonresident saltwater or freshwater license. Tackle shops sell licenses, have information on current restrictions, and often carry the *BC Tidal Waters Sport Fishing Guide* and *BC Sport Fishing Regulations Synopsis for Non-tidal Waters.* Independent anglers should also pick up a copy of the *BC Fishing Directory and Atlas.* The *Vancouver Sun* prints a daily **fishing report** in the B section that details which fish are in season and where they can be found.

   Hanson's Fishing Outfitters, 102–580 Hornby St. (© **604/684-8988;** www.hansons-outfitters.com), and **Granville Island Boat Rentals,** 1696 Duranleau St. (© **604/682-6287**), are outstanding outfitters. Licenses for freshwater fishing are C$15 (US$9.70) for 1 day or C$30 (US$19) for 8 days for non BC-residents. Saltwater fishing licenses cost C$8 (US$5.20) for 1 day, C$20 (US$13) for 3 days, and C$35 (US$23) for 5 days. For more details on fishing around the province check **www.fisheries.gov.bc.ca. Bonnie Lee Fishing Charters Ltd.,** on the dock at the entrance to Granville Island (mailing address: 744 W. King Edward Ave., Vancouver, B.C. V5Z 2C8; © **604/290-7447**), is another reputable outfitter and also sells fishing licenses.

   You can pick up equipment at **Hanson's Fishing Outfitters** (see above) or **Ruddick's Fly Shop,** 1654 Duranleau St. (© **604/985-5650**). If you go to Granville Island, be sure to stop by the **Granville Island Sport Fishing Museum,** 1502 Duranleau (© **604/683-1939**).

   Fly-fishing in national and provincial parks requires special permits, which you can get at any park site for a nominal fee. Permits are valid at all Canadian parks.

GOLF

This is a year-round Vancouver sport. With five public 18-hole courses and half a dozen pitch-and-putt courses in the city and dozens more nearby, no golfer is far from his or her love. The public **University Golf Club,** 5185 University Blvd. (© **604/224-1818**), is a great 6,560-yard, par-71 course with a clubhouse, pro shop, locker rooms, bar and grill, and sports lounge. Or call **A-1 Last Minute Golf Hotline** (© **800/684-6344** or 604/878-1833) for substantial discounts and short-notice tee times at more than 30 Vancouver-area courses. There's no membership fee. A number of excellent public golf courses, maintained by the **Vancouver Board of Parks and Recreation** (© **604/257-8400;** www.city.vancouver.bc.ca/parks), can be found throughout the city. **Langara Golf Course,** 6706 Alberta St., around 49th and Cambie Street (© **604/713-1816**), built in 1926 and recently renovated and redesigned, is one of the most popular golf courses in the province. Greens fees top out at C$45 (US$29) for an adult, with discounts for youth, seniors, and weekday tee times. To reserve phone © **604/280-1818** up to 5 days in advance or call the city at © **604/257-8400** during office hours for more information.

Leading private clubs are situated on the North Shore and in Vancouver. Check with your club at home to see if you have reciprocal visiting memberships with one of the following: **Capilano Golf and Country Club,** 420 Southborough Dr., West Vancouver (✆ **604/922-9331**); **Marine Drive Golf Club,** W. 57th Avenue and S.W. Marine Drive (✆ **604/261-8111**); **Seymour Golf and Country Club,** 3723 Mt. Seymour Pkwy., North Vancouver (✆ **604/929-2611**); **Point Grey Golf and Country Club,** 3350 SW Marine Dr. (✆ **604/261-3108**); and **Shaughnessy Golf and Country Club,** 4300 SW Marine Dr. (✆ **604/266-4141**). Greens fees range from C$42 to C$72 (US$27–US$46).

HIKING

Great trails for hikers of all levels run through Vancouver's dramatic environs. Good trail maps are available from the **Greater Vancouver Regional Parks District** (✆ **604/432-6350**) and from **International Travel Maps and Books,** 539 Pender St. (✆ **604/687-3320**), which also stocks guidebooks and topographical maps. Or pick up a local trail guide at any bookstore.

Just a few yards from the entrance to Grouse Mountain Resort is one entry to the world-famous **Baden-Powell Trail,** a 42km (26-mile) span of thick forest, rocky bluffs, and snow-fed streams racing through ravines. It starts at Cates Park on the Dollarton Highway and stretches west to Horseshoe Bay. Even if you only want to cover the stretch from Grouse Mountain to Mount Seymour, start early and be ready for some steep ascents. The timer guide at the trail head marker has been annotated by hikers who've found it takes longer to do the loop than is indicated. Give yourself a full day for this hike.

If you're looking for a challenge without the time commitment, hike the aptly named **Grouse Grind** from the bottom of Grouse Mountain to the top; then buy a one-way ticket down on the Grouse Mountain SkyRide gondola. The one-way fare (down) is C$5 (US$3.20) per person.

If you're looking for a bit more scenery with a bit less effort, take the Grouse Mountain SkyRide up to the **Grouse chalet** and start your hike at an altitude of 1,100m (3,700 ft.). The trail north to Goat Mountain is well marked and should take approximately 6 hours round-trip, though you may want to build in some extra time to linger on the top of Goat and take in the spectacular 360° views of Vancouver, Vancouver Island, and the snow-capped peaks of the Coast Mountains.

Lynn Canyon Park, Lynn Headwaters Regional Park, Capilano River Regional Park, Mount Seymour Provincial Park, Pacific Spirit Park, and **Cypress Provincial Park** (see "The Top Attractions" and "Parks & Gardens," above) have good, easy to challenging trails that wind up through stands of Douglas fir and cedar and contain a few serious switchbacks. Pay attention to the trail warnings posted at the parks; some have bear habitats. And always remember to sign in with the park service at the start of your chosen trail. Golden Ears, in Golden Ears Provincial Park, and The Lions, in West Vancouver, are for seriously fit hikers.

ICE-SKATING

Robson Square has free skating on a covered ice rink directly under Robson Street between Howe and Hornby streets. It's open from November to early April. Rentals are available in the adjacent concourse. The **West End Community Centre,** 870 Denman St. (✆ **604/257-8333**), also rents skates at its enclosed rink, which is open October through March. The enormous Burnaby 8 Rinks **Ice Sports Centre,** 6501 Sprott, Burnaby (✆ **604/291-0626**), is the Vancouver

Canucks' official practice facility. It has eight rinks, is open year-round, and offers lessons and rentals. Call ahead to check hours for public skating.

IN-LINE SKATING

You'll find locals rolling along beach paths, streets, park paths, and promenades. If you didn't bring a pair of blades, try **Bayshore Bicycle and Rollerblade Rentals,** 745 Denman St. (© **604/688-2453**). Rentals generally run C$8 (US$5) per hour or C$19 (US$12) for 8 hours.

JOGGING

You'll find fellow runners traversing the **Stanley Park Seawall** ⚐, **Lost Lagoon,** and **Beaver Lake.** If you're a dawn or dusk runner, take note that this is one of the world's safer city parks. However, if you're alone, don't tempt fate—stick to open and lighted areas. Other prime areas in the city are Kitsilano Beach, Jericho Beach, and Spanish Banks for nice flat running along the ocean, or take the seawall all around False Creek. If you feel like doing a little racing, competitions take place throughout the year; ask for information at any runners' outfitters, such as **Forerunners,** 3504 W. Fourth Ave. (© **604/732-4535**), or **Running Room,** 679 Denman St. (corner of Georgia; © **604/684-9771**). Check **www.racehead quarters.com** for running events around Vancouver and British Columbia.

PARAGLIDING

Summertime paragliding may be the ultimate flying experience. Most of the areas in British Columbia where it's offered are outside Vancouver: **Whistler Paragliding,** in Whistler (© **604/938-8830**), offers an introductory tandem flight at C$140 (US$90) or 3-day course for C$285 (US$184) where you will learn ground handling, complete short hops, and fly with an instructor. In North Vancouver, **First Flight Paragliding School** (© **604/988-1111**) offers tandem flights in summer only from the peak of Grouse Mountain, at C$150 (US$97) for 2 hours. The actual flight takes approximately 20 minutes.

SAILING

Navigating sailboats in the unfamiliar surrounding straits is unsound unless you enroll in a local sailing course before attempting it. Knowing the tides, currents, and channels is essential. Multiday instruction packages sometimes include guided Gulf Island cruises.

If all you want is to get out for a day, you can charter a 3-hour yacht cruise with one of the following outfitters. **Cooper Boating Centre,** 1620 Duranleau St. (© **604/687-4110;** www.cooperboating.com), offers cruises, boat rentals, and sail-instruction packages on 20- to 43-foot boats. Boat rentals start at C$69 (US$45) for a half-day rental in the off season and go as high as C$600 (US$387) for a full-day rental in the peak season, depending on the size of the boat.

SKIING & SNOWBOARDING

Top-notch skiing lies outside the city at the **Whistler** and **Blackcomb Resorts,** 11km (70 miles) north of Vancouver (see chapter 17). However, if you have only a day or two in Vancouver, you don't even have to leave the city to get in a few runs. It seldom snows in the city's downtown and central areas, but Vancouverites can ski before work and after dinner at the three ski resorts in the North Shore mountains.

Grouse Mountain Resort, 6400 Nancy Greene Way, North Vancouver (© **604/984-0661;** snow report 604/986-6262; www.grousemountain.com), is about 3km (2 miles) from the Lions Gate Bridge, overlooking the Burrard Inlet and Vancouver's skyline (see "The Top Attractions," earlier in this chapter). Four chairs, two beginner tows, and two T-bars take you to 24 alpine runs. The resort has night skiing, special events, instruction, and a spectacular view, as well as a 90m (300-ft.) half pipe for snowboarders. Though the area is small, all skill levels are covered, with two beginner trails, three blue trails, and five black-diamond runs, including Coffin and Inferno, which follow the east slopes down from 1,230m to 750m (4,100–2,500 ft.). Rental packages and a full range of facilities are available. Lift tickets good for all-day skiing are C$35 (US$23) for adults, C$19 (US$12) for seniors, C$25 (US$16) for youths, and C$15 (US$10) for children 6 through 12; children under 6 go free.

   Mount Seymour Provincial Park, 1700 Mt. Seymour Rd., North Vancouver (© **604/986-2261;** snow report 604/986-3999; www.mountseymour.com), has the area's highest base elevation; it's accessible via four chairs and a tow. Lift tickets are C$29 (US$19) all day for adults, C$19 (US$12) for seniors, C$24 (US$15) for youths 12 to 19, C$14 (US$9) for children 6 to 11. Nighttime skiing is C$19 (US$12) for adults, C$17 (US$11) for seniors and youths 12 to 19, and C$9 (US$5.85) for children 6 to 11. In addition to day and night skiing, the facility offers snowboarding, snowshoeing, and tobogganing along its 22 runs. There are 26km (16 miles) of cross-country trails. The resort specializes in teaching first-timers. Camps for children and teenagers, and adult clinics, are available throughout the winter.

   Mount Seymour has one of Western Canada's largest equipment rental shops, which will keep your measurements on file for return visits. Shuttle service is available during ski season from various locations on the North Shore, including the Lonsdale Quay SeaBus. For more information call © **604/986-2261.**

   Cypress Bowl, 1610 Mt. Seymour Rd. (© **604/926-5612;** snow report 604/ 419-7669; http://cypressmountain.com/default.html), has the area's longest vertical drop (525m/1,750 ft.), challenging ski and snowboard runs, and 16km (10 miles) of track-set cross-country ski trails (including 5km/3 miles set aside for night skiing). Full-day lift tickets are C$42 (US$27) for adults, with reduced rates for youths, seniors, and children. Cross-country full-day passes are C$15 (US$9.75) for adults, with reduced rates for youths, seniors, and children. Snowshoe trail tickets are available for C$6 (US$3.85). Discounts for half-day, nighttime, and multiday tickets are available. Cypress also offers excellent one-day and five-day lesson packages for skiing or riding as well as an intro class to cross country skiing (classic and skate).

   Cypress Mountain Sports, 510 and 518 Park Royal S., West Vancouver (© **604/878-9229**), offers shuttle service to and from the ski area. Round-trip tickets are C$9 (US$5.85). Cypress Mountain Sports stocks a complete selection of downhill, cross-country (including backcountry, skating, racing, and touring), and snowboarding equipment and accessories. The rental and repair department, staffed by avid skiers, offers a broad selection of equipment. Rental and repair prices are quite reasonable. The store also offers guided hikes in summer and snowshoe treks in winter.

SWIMMING & WATER SPORTS

Vancouver's midsummer saltwater temperature rarely exceeds 65°F (18°C). Some swimmers opt for fresh- and saltwater pools at city beaches (see "Beaches," earlier in this chapter). Others take to the water at public aquatic centers.

   The **Vancouver Aquatic Centre,** 1050 Beach Ave. at the foot of Thurlow Street (© **604/665-3424**), has a heated, 50m Olympic pool, saunas, whirlpools, weight rooms, diving tanks, locker rooms, showers, child care, and a tot pool. Adult admission is C$4 (US$2.60). The new, coed **YWCA Fitness Centre,** 535 Hornby St. (© **604/895-5777**), in the heart of downtown, has a 6-lane, 25m ozonated (much milder than chlorinated) pool, steam room, whirlpool, conditioning gym, and aerobic studios. A day pass is C$12 (US$7.75) for adults. UBC's **Aquatic Centre** (call © **604/822-4522** for the pool schedule), located next door to the Student Union Building and the bus loop, has designated hours when facilities are open for public use. Adult admission is C$4 (US$2.60), C$3 (US$1.95) for youths and students, and C$2.25 (US$1.45) for seniors.

TENNIS

The city maintains 180 outdoor hard courts that have a 1-hour limit and accommodate patrons on a first-come, first-served basis from 8am until dusk. Local courtesy dictates that if people are waiting, you surrender the court on the hour. (Heavy usage times are evenings and weekends.) With the exception of the Beach Avenue courts, which charge a nominal fee, all city courts are free.

Stanley Park has 4 courts near Lost Lagoon and 17 courts near the Beach Avenue entrance, next to the Fish House Restaurant. **Queen Elizabeth Park's** 18 courts service the central Vancouver area, and **Kitsilano Beach Park's** ⚡ 10 courts service the beach area between Vanier Park and the UBC campus.

You can play at night at the **Langara Campus** of Vancouver Community College, on West 49th Avenue between Main and Cambie streets. The **UBC Coast Club,** on Thunderbird Boulevard (© **604/822-2505**), has 10 outdoor and 4 indoor courts. Indoor courts are C$12 (US$7.80) per hour, plus C$3 (US$1.95) per person; outdoor courts are C$3 (US$1.95) per person.

Bayshore Bicycle and Rollerblade Rentals, 745 Denman St. (© **604/688-2453**), rents tennis rackets for C$10 (US$6) per day.

WHITE-WATER RAFTING

Located just a 2½-hour drive from Vancouver on the wild Nahatlatch river, **Reo Rafting** (© **800/736-7238** or 604/461-7238; www.reorafting.com) offers some of the best guided white-water trips in the province, at a very reasonable price. One-day packages—including breakfast, lunch, all your gear, and 4 to 5 hours on the river—start at C$110 (US$71). Multiday trips and group packages are also available. Whistler also offers excellent rafting on the Green River; see chapter 17 for information.

WILDLIFE WATCHING

Vancouver is an internationally famous stop for naturalists, ecotourists, and thousands of migratory birds; so bring your cameras, binoculars, and spotting books! Orcas, salmon, bald eagles, herons, beavers, and numerous rare, indigenous marine and waterfowl species live in the metropolitan area.

During the winter, thousands of bald eagles line the banks of the **Squamish, Cheakamus,** and **Mamquam** rivers to feed on spawning salmon. The official January 1994 eagle count in Brackendale (a small community near Squamish) recorded 3,700—the largest number ever seen in North America. To get there by car, take the scenic **Sea-to-Sky Highway** (Hwy. 99) from downtown Vancouver to Squamish and Brackendale; the trip takes about 60 minutes. The route winds along the craggy tree-lined coast of Howe Sound through the town of Britannia Beach and past two beautiful natural monuments: Shannon Falls and the continent's tallest monolithic rock face, the Stawamus Chief. Alternatively, you can take a **Greyhound** bus, Pacific Central Station, 1150 Station St., Vancouver

(© **604/482-8747;** www.greyhound.ca; trip time: 1¼ hr.). Contact **Squamish & Howe Sound Visitor Info Centre** (© **604/892-9244;** www.squamish chamber.bc.ca) for more information.

The annual summer salmon runs attract more than bald eagles. Tourists also flock to coastal streams and rivers to watch the waters turn red with leaping coho and sockeye. The salmon are plentiful at the **Capilano Salmon Hatchery** (see "Parks & Gardens," earlier in this chapter), **Goldstream Provincial Park** (see chapter 13, "Exploring Victoria"), and numerous other fresh waters.

Along the Fraser River delta, more than 250 bird species migrate to or perennially inhabit the **George C. Reifel Sanctuary's** wetland reserve. Nearby, **Richmond Nature Park** has educational displays for young and first-time birders plus a boardwalk-encircled duck pond (see "Parks & Gardens," earlier in this chapter).

Stanley Park and **Pacific Spirit Park** are both home to heron rookeries. You can see these large birds nesting just outside the Vancouver Aquarium. Ravens, dozens of species of waterfowl, raccoons, skunks, beavers, and even coyotes are also full-time residents.

WINDSURFING

Windsurfing is not allowed at the mouth of False Creek near Granville Island, but you can bring a board to **Jericho** and **English Bay beaches** ✪ or rent one there. Equipment sales, rentals (including wet suits), and instruction can be found at **Windsure Windsurfing School,** 1300 Discovery St., at Jericho Beach (© **604/224-0615**). Rentals start at C$17 (US$11) per hour, wetsuit rental extra.

8 Spectator Sports

Spectators and participants will find plenty of activities in Vancouver. You can get schedule information on all major events at Tourism Vancouver's **Travel Info Centre,** 200 Burrard St. (© **604/683-2000**). You can also get information and purchase tickets from Ticketmaster at the **Vancouver Ticket Centre,** 1304 Hornby St. (© **604/280-3311**), which has 40 outlets in the greater Vancouver area. (Like every other Ticketmaster, they do charge a fee.) Popular events, Canucks games, and the Vancouver Indy can sell out weeks or months in advance, so it's a good idea to book ahead.

AUTO RACING

In late July, the CART Indy Series mounts its biggest annual event, the **Molson Indy,** 750 Pacific Blvd. (© **604/684-4639** for information, 604/280-4639 for tickets). General admission starts at C$15 (US$9.75), depending on the race day. A 3-day general admission ticket costs C$55 (US$35). The race roars through Vancouver's streets around B.C. Place Stadium and the north and south shores of False Creek, attracting more than 350,000 spectators.

FOOTBALL

The Canadian Football League's **B.C. Lions** (© **604/930-5466;** www.bclions.com) play their home and Grey Cup championship games (in good seasons) in the 60,000-seat **B.C. Place Stadium,** 777 Pacific Blvd. S. (at Beatty and Robson sts.). Canadian football differs from its American cousin: It's a three-down offense game on a field that's 10 yards longer and wider. Some of the plays you see will have NFL fans leaping out of their seats in surprise. Tickets run C$20 to C$60 (US$13–US$39).

HOCKEY

The National Hockey League's **Vancouver Canucks** play at **General Motors Place** (otherwise known as the Garage), 800 Griffith's Way (© **604/899-4600;** event hot line 604/899-7444; www.canucks.com). Tickets are C$26 to C$95 (US$17–US$62).

HORSE RACING

Thoroughbreds run at **Hastings Park Racecourse,** Exhibition Park, East Hastings and Cassiar streets (© **604/254-1631;** www.hastingspark.com), from mid-April to October. Post time varies, please call ahead or check the website for the latest schedule. There is a decent restaurant, so you can make a full evening or afternoon of dining and racing. Place a wager or two.

RUNNING

The **Sun Run** in April and the **Vancouver International Marathon** in May attract many runners from around the world and even more spectators. Contact the **Vancouver International Marathon Society,** 1601 Bayshore Dr., in the Westin Bayshore Hotel (© **604/872-2928**), or the **Vancouver Sun Run,** 655 Burrard St. (© **604/689-9441**), for information.

SOCCER

The American Professional Soccer League's **Vancouver Whitecaps** (© **604/ 899-9283**) play at Swangard Stadium (© **604/435-7121,** www.whitecaps soccer.com) in Burnaby. Admission is normally C$14 to C$22 (US$9–US$14).

7

Vancouver Strolls

Down below's Stanley Park. On the side of the trees there's a beach. You can't see it [points over to left]. Steveston's over there. [points to left] Coast Guard station. There's the Yacht Club, and beyond it, the docks. Then over on the other side of the inlet, there's Grouse Mountain. It's about 4,000 feet high. There's a restaurant on top of it. Nice restaurant.

—from the screenplay for *Playback*, by Raymond Chandler

Chandler's detective Philip Marlowe was one of Hollywood's most enduringly popular creations, but studio executives so hated his set-in-Vancouver screenplay that it never made it into celluloid. Too bad. Chandler's geography in the above excerpt was a bit off, but there's no doubt he had the right idea. The best way to get to know Vancouver is to wear out some of the ol' shoe leather, to get out and snoop around a little. The tours below provide some clues on where to begin.

WALKING TOUR 1   DOWNTOWN & THE WEST END

Start	**The Hotel Vancouver.**
Finish	**Cathedral Place.**
Time	**2 to 3 hours, not including museum, shopping, and eating stops.**
Best Times	**Daytime, particularly during the week when the Law Courts building is open.**
Worst Times	**Too late in the evening when the shops and offices have closed.**

An appropriate place to begin this tour is:

❶ The Hotel Vancouver

At 900 W. Georgia St. (© **604/684-3131**), the hotel is owned by the Canadian Pacific Railway (CPR), just as the city itself was for many, many years. In return for agreeing in 1885 to make Vancouver its western terminus, the CPR was given 2,400 hectares (6,000 acres) of prime downtown real estate—nearly the whole of downtown. The Hotel Vancouver is built in the CPR's signature château style, complete with verdigris-green copper roof. It's worth stepping inside for a moment to experience the Gatsbyesque ambience of the lobby.

Leaving by the Burrard Street exit, turn left. When you reach the corner, turn right, cross Burrard Street, and you're on:

❷ Robson Street

The shops on this corner get more foot traffic than any other in Canada. Things were different back in the '50s, when so many German delis and restaurants opened up that for a time the street was nicknamed "Robsonstrasse." Beginning in the 1980s, these older stores were replaced with high-end clothiers and new restaurants and gift shops with signs in Japanese. Whether you're into shopping or not, Robson Street is still a great place to walk and people-watch, listening to the babble of Cantonese, Croatian,

Japanese, and other tongues that surrounds you.

Two blocks farther down Robson at Bute Street, turn left and walk 1 block south through a minipark to Barclay Street and you're in:

③ The West End

Beginning in about 1959, this down-at-its-heels neighborhood of once-grand Edwardian houses was transformed by the advent of the concrete high-rise. By 1970, most of the Edwardians had been replaced by towers, and the West End had become one of the densest—and simultaneously one of the most livable—inner cities on the continent. The minipark at Bute and Barclay is one of the things that makes the neighborhood so successful: Traffic is kept to a minimum on West End streets, so that residents—though they live in the city center—can enjoy a neighborhood almost as quiet as that of a small town.

Turn right and walk west down Barclay Street and you'll see some of the other elements that make the West End such a sought-after enclave: the gardens and street trees and the range and variety of buildings—including even a few surviving Edwardians, like the Arts and Crafts house at 1351 Barclay, or the set of two houses at the corner of Barclay and Nicola streets, otherwise known as:

④ Barclay Square

This beautifully preserved bit of 19th-century Vancouver consists of Barclay Manor, built in the Queen Anne style in 1890, and Roedde House, a rare domestic design by British Columbia's leading 19th-century institutional architect Francis Rattenbury. Roedde House (1415 Barclay St.; © **604/684-7040**) is now a museum, open for guided tours Tuesday through Friday at 2pm; C$4 (US$2.60) admission. Every third Sunday, tea is served in the parlor from 2 to 4pm for C$5 (US$3.25) per person.

Turn left and walk south down Nicola Street for 1 block—past Fire Station No. 6, then turn right and go west on Nelson 1 block, then left again onto Cardero Street, passing by the tiny Cardero Grocery at 1078 Cardero St. All the grocery needs of the West End were once supplied by little corner stores like this one. Turn right and walk 2 blocks west on Comox Street to reach Denman Street, the perfect place to:

TAKE A BREAK
If Robson Street is the place Vancouverites go for hyperactive shopping sprees, Denman is where they go to sit back, sip a latte, and watch their fellow citizens stroll past. The **Bread Garden**, 1040 Denman St. (© **604/685-2996**), is a fine spot for coffee and baked goods, particularly if you can nab a table on their outdoor terrace. One block down on the west side of the street, **Delany's on Denman**, 1105 Denman St. (© **604/662-3344**), is a favorite man-watching spot for members of the West End's sizable gay community. Straight people are more than welcome too, of course, and the pies and cakes at this little cafe are to die for. Two blocks farther downhill and you're at:

⑤ English Bay Beach

The place to be when the sun is setting, or on one of those crystal-clear days when the mountains of Vancouver Island can be seen looming in the distance—or any day at all really, so long as the sun is shining. Every January 1, shivering Vancouverites in fancy costumes surround the bathhouse at the very foot of Denman Street (entrance at beach level) to take part in the annual Polar Bear Swim.

Walk southeastward a little bit on Beach Avenue and you come to a tiny green space with a band shell known as:

⑥ Alexandra Park

Back around the turn of the 20th century, a big Bahamian immigrant named Joe Fortes used to make his home in a cottage near this spot, that is, when he wasn't down on the beach teaching local kids to swim. In recognition of his many years of free service,

Walking Tour 1: Downtown & the West End

0   1/4 mi
0   1/4 km

"Take a Break" stop

Coal Harbour

Lost Lagoon Dr.

Chilco St.

Gilford St.

Denman St.

Pender St.

Georgia St.

Melville St.

Hastings St.

Bidwell St.

Barclay St.

Haro St.

Robson St.

Nelson St.

Pender St.

finish here

start here

Comox St.

Cardero St.

Nicola St.

Broughton St.

Jervis St.

Bute St.

Thurlow St.

Davie St.

Burnaby St.

Harwood St.

Pacific St.

Beach Ave.

Burrard St.

Hornby St.

Howe St.

Granville St.

Seymour St.

Richards St.

Homer St.

Nelson St.

Granville Mall

Sunset Beach Park

Vanier Park

Pacific Blvd.

Granville St. Bridge

Cambie St. Bridge

Granville Island

False Creek

False Creek Park

WEST VANCOUVER

Grouse Mountain

English Bay

Area of Detail

VANCOUVER

RICHMOND

1 Fairmont Hotel Vancouver
2 Robson Street
3 The West End
4 Barclay Square
5 English Bay Beach
6 Alexandra Park
7 The Gabriola
8 Pendrell St.
9 Mole Hill
10 BC Hydro Building
11 Provincial Law Courts
12 Robson Square
13 Vancouver Art Gallery
14 Canadian Craft Museum

the city finally appointed Fortes its first lifeguard. Later, a marble water fountain was erected in his memory by the Beach Avenue entrance to the park.

On the far side of the park, head up Bidwell Street 1 block to Davie Street, cross the street, turn right, walk 2 blocks farther on Davie Street, and on your left at no. 1531 you'll see:

⑦ The Gabriola

This was the finest mansion in the West End when it was built in 1900 for sugar magnate B. T. Rogers. Its name comes from the rough sandstone cladding, quarried on Gabriola Island in the Strait of Georgia. Unfortunately for Rogers, the Shaughnessy neighborhood soon opened up across False Creek, and the West End just wasn't a place a millionaire could afford to be seen anymore. By 1925 the mansion had been sold off and subdivided into apartments. Since 1975 it's been a restaurant of one sort or another—currently the Macaroni Grill. The wrought-iron tables in the garden are particularly fine spots to sit out on summer days.

Cut through the garden, then turn left on Nicola Street and walk up through the Nicola Street minipark, then turn right on:

8 Pendrell Street

A few interesting bits of architecture reside on this street. At the corner of Broughton Street is the Thomas Fee house (1119 Broughton St.), where one of the city's leading turn-of-the-20th-century developer-architects made his home. Note how the modern addition has been blended with the old Edwardian structure. Farther along, at the southeast corner of Pendrell and Jervis streets, is St. Paul's Episcopal Church, a 1905 Gothic Revival church built entirely of wood, an act of faith that has so far been rewarded. One block farther along at 1254 Pendrell is the Pendrellis—a piece of architecture so unbelievably awful, one gets a perverse delight just looking at it. Built as a seniors home at the height of the '70s craze for concrete, the multistory tower is one great concrete block, with nary a window in sight.

At Bute Street, turn left and walk 1 block north to Comox Street, and you're at:

9 Mole Hill

These 11 preserved Edwardian homes provide a rare view of what the West End would have looked like in, say, 1925. That they exist at all is more or less a fluke. The city bought the buildings in the 1970s but continued renting them out, thinking one day to tear them down for a park. By the 1990s, however, heritage had become all important. The residents of the houses waged a sophisticated political campaign, renaming the area Mole Hill and bringing in nationally known architectural experts to plead the case for preservation. The city soon gave in.

Cut across the park to Nelson Street and continue down Nelson Street past Thurlow Street to 970 Burrard St., where stands:

10 The BC Hydro Building

Built in 1958 by architect Ned Pratt, it was one of the first modernist structures erected in Canada, and has since become a beloved Vancouver landmark, thanks in no small part to its elegant shape and the attention to detail at every scale. Note how the windows, the doors, even the tiles in the lobby and forecourt echo the six-sided lozenge shape of the original structure. In the mid-90s, the building was converted to condominiums and rechristened The Electra.

From here, continue on Nelson Street, crossing Burrard Street and Hornby Street to:

11 The Provincial Law Courts

Internationally recognized architect Arthur Erickson (see the box on p. 113) has had an undeniable impact on his native city of Vancouver. His 1973 Law Courts complex covers three full city blocks, including the Erickson-renovated Vancouver Art Gallery at its north end. Linking the two is Robson Square, which Erickson—and everyone else—envisioned as the city's main civic plaza. As with so many Erickson designs, this one has elements of brilliance—the boldness of the vision itself, the cathedral-like space of the courthouse atrium—but, alas, was marred by Erickson's fetish for raw concrete and by his unconscious disdain for the mere human beings forced to make use of his creations.

As an example of the latter, note the unmarked concrete stairway—the one that looks like a parking garage exit—at the corner of Nelson and Hornby streets. Unpromising as it seems, this is actually the entranceway to a very pleasant elevated pedestrian concourse, and one of three possible pathways we can take. The second and best route—available only during business hours—is to enter the courthouse and walk through the glorious glass-covered atrium. This is a truly inspired space, so it's worth timing your visit to when the doors are open. The fallback route, should the courthouse be locked and the stairway impossible to find, is to turn left and proceed down Hornby Street between the double row of street trees, cross over Smithe Street, and carry on to about halfway down the block, then cut right into the courtyard by the Motor Vehicle office (look for the giant orange paper clip sculpture).

Whichever way you go, 2 blocks north of this point you'll end up at:

⑫ Robson Square

Though it's best if you come down the zigzagging steps from the Law Courts concourse (hidden behind the waterfalls are the offices of the Crown Attorney—the Canadian equivalent of a district attorney), Robson Square is still somewhat underwhelming. Its basic problem is that it's sunk 6m (20 ft.) below street grade, and psychologically, most folks have an aversion to basements and cellars. So although there's a pleasant cafe in the square and an outdoor ice rink in the wintertime, Robson square lacks the throngs of people that should attend a real civic plaza. On the other hand, the steps of the old courthouse on the far side of Robson are a great gathering place, the perfect spot to see jugglers and buskers, pick up a game of outdoor speed chess, or listen to an activist haranguing the world at large about the topic du jour.

To the left of the steps (and directly across from Robson Square) at 750 Hornby St. is the:

⑬ Vancouver Art Gallery

Designed as a courthouse by Francis Rattenbury, and renovated into an art gallery by Arthur Erickson, the Vancouver Art Gallery (p. 101) is home to a tremendous collection of works by West Coast painter Emily Carr, as well as rotating exhibits ranging from Native masks to the video installations of Stan Douglas. Film buffs may remember the entrance steps and inside lobby from the movie *The Accused.*

To continue, go round the gallery by the left-hand side and proceed down Hornby Street. Note the fountain on the Art Gallery's front lawn. It was installed by a very unpopular provincial government as a way—according to some—of forever blocking protesters from gathering on the gallery lawn. Cross Georgia Street and have a glance inside the Hong Kong Bank building (885 W. Georgia St.) at the massive pendulum designed by artist Alan Storey. The lobby doubles as an art gallery and frequently features interesting exhibits.

Cross to the west side of Hornby, and carry on about halfway down the block, then turn to your left and walk up the short flight of stairs to a small outdoor courtyard. On the north side at 639 Hornby St. is the:

⑭ Cathedral Place

Often overlooked by Vancouverites, just a few steps away from busy Georgia Street, sits the peaceful and quiet Cathedral Place. The courtyard has the feel of a formal French garden and makes a great lunch spot. However, before you rest your tired legs, take a quick look at the building across the courtyard (at 639 Hornby St.). It housed the Canadian Craft Museum until budget cuts forced its doors shut in 2002. This is the quintessential postmodern structure, with small Art Deco parts melded onto a basically Gothic edifice. Some of the panels on its front were salvaged from the Georgia Medical-Dental building, a much loved skyscraper that used to stand on this site.

WALKING TOUR 2   GASTOWN & CHINATOWN

Start	**Canada Place.**
Finish	**Maple Tree Square.**
Time	**2 to 4 hours, not including shopping, eating, and sightseeing stops.**

| **Best Times** | Any day during business hours, but Chinatown is particularly active in the mornings. If you arrive before noon, you can indulge in dim sum at many of the restaurants. |
| **Worst Times** | Chinatown's dead after 6pm, except on weekends in the summer, when they close a few streets to traffic and hold a traditional Asian Night market from 6:30 to 11pm. |

Chinatown and Gastown are two of Vancouver's most fascinating neighborhoods. Gastown has history and great old-fashioned architecture. Chinatown has all that plus the buzz of modern-day Cantonese commerce. One small travel advisory, however: The two neighborhoods border on Vancouver's Downtown Eastside—otherwise known as skid road—an area of taverns and cheap rooming hotels that is troubled by alcoholism and drug use. While there is very little actual danger for outsiders, there is a good chance of stumbling across a scary looking down-and-outer here and there, particularly around Pigeon Park at the corner of Carrall and Hastings streets. The tour route has been designed to avoid these areas.

Begin the tour at:

① 999 Canada Place

With its five tall Teflon sails and bowsprit jutting out into Burrard Inlet, Canada Place is supposed to look like a great sailing ship. Some folks see it, some don't. Inside it's a hotel, cruise ship terminal, and convention center. Around the outside there's a promenade with plaques at regular intervals explaining the sights or providing historical tidbits.

To follow the promenade, start by the fountain with the flags of Canada's provinces and territories just above it and head north out along the walkway. (***Note:*** An ongoing expansion of the cruise ship may block your access to the end of the pier. If so, proceed directly to stop 2.) At the far end of the pier—the prow—a pair of bronze lions point up and out toward a pair of peaks on the North Shore also called the Lions (supposedly for their resemblance to the Landseer Lions in Trafalgar Square, but mostly because the local morality squad wanted to eliminate forever the name given the peaks by the rough-minded early settlers—Sheila's Paps). Turn and look back over the railway tracks. The line of low-rise

older buildings just beyond the railway tracks is Gastown.

To continue the tour, walk back toward shore along the promenade, drop down the steps, turn left, and curve along the sidewalk until you pass the Aqua Riva restaurant. Then turn left and go up the steps and walk along an elevated pathway until you see a large wooden abstract sculpture. You're now at 200 Granville St. in:

② Granville Square

Had some forward-looking politicians and developers had their way, all of Gastown and Chinatown would have been replaced by towers and plazas like the one you see here at 200 Granville. The plans had been drawn up and the bulldozers were set to move around 1970 when a coalition of hippies, heritage lovers, and Chinatown merchants took to the barricades in revolt. This building was the only one ever built, and the plan was abandoned soon afterwards.

At the east side of the plaza is a set of stairs leading down to 601 W. Cordova St. at:

③ Waterfront Station

Though this beaux arts edifice was converted to the SeaBus terminal in the 1970s (SkyTrain was added in 1986), this building still shows its

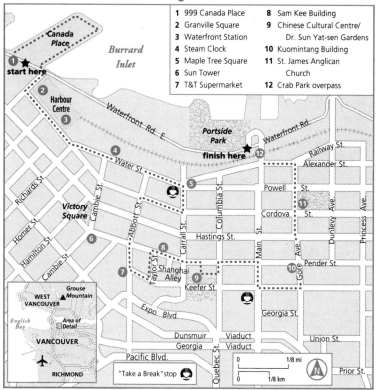

1 999 Canada Place
2 Granville Square
3 Waterfront Station
4 Steam Clock
5 Maple Tree Square
6 Sun Tower
7 T&T Supermarket
8 Sam Kee Building
9 Chinese Cultural Centre/
   Dr. Sun Yat-sen Gardens
10 Kuomintang Building
11 St. James Anglican
   Church
12 Crab Park overpass

origins as the CPR's Vancouver passenger-rail terminal. Look up high on the walls and you can see oil paintings depicting scenes you might see as you take the train across Canada—much easier then than now. On the main floor there's a Starbucks and some tourist shops.

Leave by the front doors, turn left, and wander east onto the cobblestones of Water Street, Gastown's main thoroughfare. **The Landing,** at 375 Water St., is home to some high-end retail stores and offices, including the office of the **BC Film Commission** (© **604/660-2732**), where you can pick up a list of the film and TV productions being shot in the city. There's also a truly fine brew pub on the basement floor called **Steamworks**

(© **604/689-2739**). Like most of Gastown's buildings, the Landing was built in the boom years between the Great Fire of 1886 and World War I. Klondike gold fueled much of the construction. As you walk along, note the **Magasin Building** at 322 Water St. Each of the column capitals bears the bronze head of a Gastown notable, among them Ray Saunders, the man who designed the:

④ Steam Clock

A quirky kind of timepiece, the Steam Clock gives a breathy rendition of the Westminster Chimes every 15 minutes. It draws its power from the city's underground steam-heat system. A plaque on the base of the clock explains the mechanics of it all.

Carry on down, past Hills Indian Crafts (165 Water St.), where Bill Clinton picked up a little bear statuette as a gift for you-know-who. Cross to the south side of the street at Abbot Street and continue on Water Street until you come to the Gaoler's Mews building (12 Water St.). Duck in through the passageway and:

TAKE A BREAK
The name **Gaoler's Mews** refers to Vancouver's very first jail, which was built on this site. When that burned to the ground in the 1886 fire, the jail was replaced by a fire hall. The current structure was built as a parking garage but was renovated in the 1970s into a remarkably pleasant complex joined to a common courtyard/atrium. **The Black Cat Coffee** has fine coffee, while the **Paprika Cottage Restaurant** offers more substantial fare. For excellent beer and superior food, however, try the **Irish Heather**, 217 Carrall St. (© 604/688-9779), accessible either via its back solarium—facing onto the mews—or by going out through the far passageway onto Carrall Street. You have to come this way eventually in order to reach:

⑤ Maple Tree Square

A historic spot, Maple Tree Square is where Vancouver first began. The statue by the maple tree (not the original one, but a replacement tree planted in more or less the same spot) is of Gassy Jack Deighton, a riverboat captain and innkeeper who erected Vancouver's first significant structure—a saloon—in 1867. Deighton got the nickname Gassy thanks to his propensity for jawing on at length (gassing, as it was known) about whatever topic happened to spring to mind. In 1870, when the town was officially incorporated as Granville, it was home to exactly six businesses: a hotel, two stores, and three saloons. Most folks called it Gastown, after Jack.

Just a half block south of the statue is a little laneway with the rather

foreboding name of Blood Alley. So far as I can ascertain, nothing too nefarious ever happened here; the name appears to have been invented to appeal to tourists. Strangely, however, there's nothing much to see in this sanguine spot.

Continue south on Carrall Street to W. Cordova, turn right and walk 1 block west until you reach Abbot Street. Turn left and walk 2 blocks south down Abbot, crossing W. Hastings Street and stopping at W. Pender Street, where you get a great view of the:

⑥ Sun Tower

At 500 Beatty St., it was the tallest building in the British Empire when it was built in 1911 to house the publishing empire of one Louis D. Taylor, publisher of *Vancouver World*. Not only was the building big, it was also slightly scandalous, thanks to the nine half-nude caryatids who gracefully support the cornice halfway up the building. Unfortunately, the girls couldn't bear the debt load with quite the same aplomb; three years later Louis D. was forced to sell.

Cross Pender Street and continue on Abbot Street, rounding the curve of the building on your right-hand side until you come to the entrance of 179 Keefer Place at:

⑦ T&T Supermarket

So you've seen supermarkets? Unless your hometown is Hong Kong or Singapore, you haven't seen one like this. Just have a gander at the seafood display inside the doors: king crab, scallops, three different kinds of oysters, lobster, geoduck, all alive, some pinching mad. Farther in is a host of wondrous products for sale, including strange Asian fruits like rambutan, lychee, and the pungent durian. Browse at will, maybe pick up something you don't recognize, and have an impromptu picnic in nearby Andy Livingstone Park.

Outside, walk 1 block east on Keefer Street to Taylor Street. The park is to your right, but to continue the tour turn left. Walk 1 block back up to Pender Street, then turn right and walk 1 more block. You're in Chinatown, an area distinguished architecturally by tall narrow buildings with recessed balconies, commercially by a profusion of vegetable and apothecary shops, and culturally by the sheer exuberance of immigrant life.

First stop, at 8 W. Pender St., is the:

⑧ Sam Kee Building

The world's thinnest office building—4 feet 11 inches deep—was Sam Kee's way of thumbing his nose at both the city and his greedy next-door neighbor. In 1912, the city expropriated most of Kee's land in order to widen Pender Street, but refused to compensate him for the tiny leftover strip. Kee's neighbor, meanwhile, hoped to pick up the leftover sliver dirt cheap. The building was Kee's response. Huge bay windows helped maximize the available space, as did the extension of the basement well out underneath the sidewalk (note the glass blocks in the pavement). The building is now home to Jack Chow insurance.

Just behind the Sam Kee Building is the forlorn-looking **Shanghai Alley,** which just 40 years ago was jam-packed with stores, restaurants, a pawnshop, a theater, rooming houses, and a public bath. More interesting is the **Chinese Freemason's building,** just across the street at 1 W. Pender. The building could be a metaphor for the Chinese experience in Canada. On predominantly Anglo Carrall Street, the building is the picture of Victorian conformity. On the Pender Street side, on the other hand, the structure is exuberantly Chinese.

One block farther east on Pender Street is the:

⑨ Chinese Cultural Centre/Dr. Sun Yat-sen Gardens

A modern building with an impressive traditional gate, the cultural center provides services and programs for the neighborhood's thousands of Chinese-speaking residents. Through the smaller inner gate, the Dr. Sun Yat-sen Classical Chinese Garden (p. 109) is well worth a visit. The only full-size classical Chinese garden outside China, it was modeled after a Ming Period (1368–1644) scholar's retreat in the Chinese city of Suzhou.

Exit the gardens by the gate on the right-hand (east) side, then turn left and you'll find the **Chinese Cultural Centre Museum and Archives** at 555 Columbia St. From here, go back up to Pender and turn right and continue going east, peeking in here and there to explore apothecaries like **Vitality Enterprises** at 126 E. Pender. At Main Street, turn right and walk south 1 block to Keefer Street and:

TAKE A BREAK
Though it's Canada's largest Chinese restaurant, **Floata Seafood Restaurant,** 400–180 Keefer St. (📞 **604/602-0368**), isn't easy to find. In classic Hong Kong restaurant style, it's on the third floor of a bright red shopping plaza/parking garage. Time your arrival for midmorning dim sum (a kind of moving Chinese smorgasbord).

To continue the tour, keep strolling east on Keefer Street. You'll pass grill shops displaying roasted ducks and bakeries like the **Garden Bakery and Tea House,** 249 E. Pender St. (📞 **604/682-1608**), where the display counters are filled with freshly made *bao* (buns filled with sweetened pork or black beans). The **New Chong Lung Seafood and Meat Market** at the corner of Gore and Keefer streets is also worth a look. The market stocks geoduck, salmon, and that local favorite, bullfrog. All (except the frogs) are available for shipping anywhere in the world.

Turn left and walk 1 block north up Gore to 296 E. Pender St. to find the:

⑩ Kuomintang Building
Though often a mystery to outsiders, politics was and remains an important part of life in Chinatown. Vancouver was long a stronghold of the Chinese Nationalist Party or Kuomintang (KMT). The party's founder, Dr. Sun Yat-sen, stayed in Vancouver for a time raising funds. In 1920, the party erected this building to serve as its Western Canadian headquarters. When the rival Chinese Communist party emerged victorious from the Chinese civil war in 1949, KMT leader Chiang Kai-shek retreated to Taiwan. Note the Taiwanese flags on the roof.

Carry on down Gore 2 more blocks and you come to 303 E. Cordova St., where stands:

⑪ St. James Anglican Church
Architect Adrian Gilbert Scott had designed a cathedral in Cairo before getting this commission, and it shows. Step inside to experience a hushed and beautiful gloom. One block east on Pender, the **Vancouver Police Museum** in the former Coroner's

Court (240 E. Cordova) is well worth a visit. Among other displays, the museum has the autopsy pictures of Errol Flynn, who died in Vancouver in 1959 in the arms of his 17-year-old personal assistant.

Back on Gore Street, walk north, passing by Sunrise market (cheapest veggies in town) to Alexander Street. Turn left and walk 1 block west on Alexander to the:

⑫ Crab Park overpass
City Hall calls it Portside Park, and that's how it appears on the map, but to everyone else it's Crab Park. It was created after long and vigorous lobbying by eastside activists, who reasoned that poor downtown residents had as much right to beach access as anyone else. The park itself is pleasant enough, though perhaps not worth the trouble of walking all the way up and over the overpass. What is worthwhile, however, is walking halfway up to where two stone Chinese lions stand guard. From here, you can look back at Canada Place—where the tour started—or at the container port and fish plant to your right.

To bring the tour to an end, return back to Alexander Street and walk 2 blocks west back to Maple Tree Square (stop 5).

	KITSILANO, GRANVILLE ISLAND
WALKING TOUR 3	& YALETOWN

Start	The Caper's Building, 2285 W. Fourth Ave. (at Vine), in Kitsilano (accessible via bus no. 4 and no. 7).
Finish	Vancouver Public Library Central Branch at Homer and Georgia streets.
Time	2 to 4 hours, not including shopping, eating, and sightseeing stops.
Best Times	Any day during business hours.
Worst Times	After 6pm, when Granville Island's shops have closed.

This tour takes you through three of Vancouver's most interesting neighborhoods: the former hippie enclave of Kitsilano, the industrial park turned public market called Granville Island, and the funky former warehouse district of Yaletown. The tour also includes a stroll along the beach.

Walking Tour 3: Kitsilano, Granville Island & Yaletown

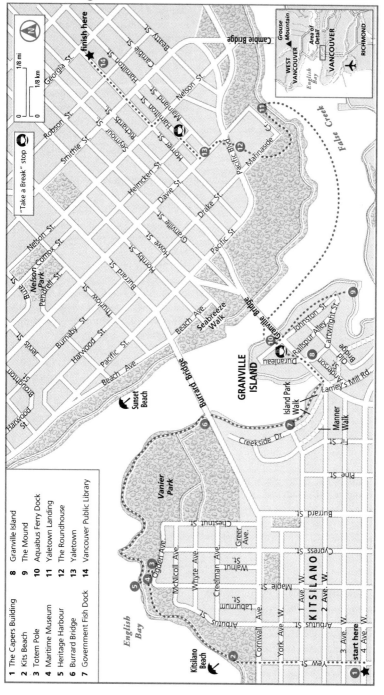

1 The Capers Building
2 Kits Beach
3 Totem Pole
4 Maritime Museum
5 Heritage Harbour
6 Burrard Bridge
7 Government Fish Dock

8 Granville Island
9 The Mound
10 Aquabus Ferry Dock
11 Yaletown Landing
12 The Roundhouse
13 Yaletown
14 Vancouver Public Library

"Take a Break" stop

finish here

start here

KITSILANO

GRANVILLE ISLAND

English Bay

Kitsilano Beach

Vanier Park

Sunset Beach

Nelson Park

Pendrell Park

False Creek

Grouse Mountain

Area of Detail

WEST VANCOUVER

VANCOUVER

RICHMOND

English Bay

0 1/8 mi
0 1/8 km

We begin at 2285 W. Fourth Ave. at:

❶ The Capers Building

Back in the 1960s, Kitsilano was Canada's hippie-central, a Haight-Ashbury-like enclave of head shops, communes, and coffeehouses. At one point in the early 1970s, Vancouver's oh-so-square mayor, Tom Campbell, proposed rounding up all the tie-dyed long-hairs and shipping them off to a central detention center. Fortunately, that was never done, and as the years passed the hippies' waistlines and wallets got thicker, run-down communes and boarding houses were renovated or replaced with new apartments and condos, and the shops came to reflect Kitsilano's new affluence, though still with a touch of counterculture.

The retail/office/apartment building at 2285 W. Fourth Ave. was built according to an innovative energy-efficient design and now serves as the home of the environmentally focused **David Suzuki Foundation;** an excellent bookstore called **Duthie's;** and **Capers,** an organic supermarket. The small outdoor patio is a great place to grab a coffee and people-watch. Farther east on Fourth Avenue there are several good retro-clothing shops, a travel bookstore, a number of furniture and interiors boutiques, several bakeries, and numerous other spots in which to grab a bite.

To continue the tour from here, walk north (downhill) 4 blocks on Yew Street and cross north over Point Grey Road, which leads you onto:

❷ Kits Beach

Vancouver is blessed with beaches. They stretch almost unbroken from here to the University of British Columbia, 10km (6 miles) west on the tip of the Point Grey peninsula, and each has its own distinct personality. Below UBC, Wreck Beach is a semi-wild strand for nudists and nature lovers. Beaches in between cater to dogs, picnicking families, and lone hikers. Kits Beach is the home of the spandex and testosterone set. The action on the volleyball courts is fast and furious. For the less than physically perfect, the logs lined up on the beach make it a fine place to lay out a blanket and laze the day away. Small children can often be found playing on the nearby swings, while older kids favor the lifeguarded swimming area or the world's largest outdoor saltwater swimming pool. On a clear day, the views of the mountains are tremendous.

Walk down the beach and around the corner on the paved pathway to the:

❸ Totem Pole

Carved by the exceptional Kwakiutl carver Mungo Martin (who also did many of the poles displayed in the Museum of Anthropology and in Stanley Park), the 10 figures on this 30m (100-ft.) tall pole each represent an ancestor of the 10 Kwakiutl clans. An identical pole was presented to Queen Elizabeth in 1958 to mark B.C.'s centenary. It now stands in Windsor Great Park.

Turn north (toward the mountains) and walk down the steps to the:

❹ Maritime Museum

Ever since it was realized that Columbus had found a new continent instead of Cathay, every European explorer's overriding quest was to find the Northwest Passage, the seagoing shortcut to the riches of the East. The little ship housed inside the Maritime Museum, 1905 Ogden Ave. (© **604/ 257-8300**) is the one that finally did it. Tours of the RCMP vessel, the *St. Roch,* are available at regular intervals through the day (see "The Top Attractions," in chapter 6). Out back of the museum, the junk on the lawn by the north side all comes from various ships wrecked on the B.C. coast.

Proceed down the crushed-stone pathway to:

❺ Heritage Harbour

Many older wooden boats find shelter here, including the seiner BCP45 shown on the back of the old Canadian $5 bill. Those interested in a shortcut can pick up a ferry (**False Creek Ferries,** ✆ **604/684-7781**) at this point and float down to Granville Island (stop 8). On weekdays and off-season the ferries run less frequently. Hours and fares are posted on the sign at the end of the dock.

Walkers should proceed east (toward the city) along the shoreline. To your right stands artist Chung Hung's massive twisted iron sculpture, *Gate to the Northwest Passage.* Just beyond that, the conical building is the **Vancouver Museum,** 1100 Chestnut St. (✆ **604/736-4431**) and **H.R MacMillan Space Centre** (✆ **604/738-STAR**). The low building next to that is the **Vancouver Archives,** 1150 Chestnut (✆ **604/736-8561**), home to some truly fascinating panoramic photographs of Vancouver back in the early days.

Carry on along the pathway around the point, passing the Coast Guard station on your right, and you're walking underneath the:

❻ Burrard Bridge

In 1927, the city fathers commissioned noted urban planner Harland Bartholomew to provide some guidance on how to expand their rather raw seaport city. One of Bartholomew's first injunctions: Build beautiful bridges! The Burrard Bridge is the result, an elegant steel span with two castles guarding the approaches at either end. Motorists often wonder what's inside the now inaccessible rooms atop the decorated castle keeps. The answer: not much. Maintenance bric-a-brac mostly, together with the remains of an elevator that was never installed.

Cross beneath the bridge and continue along the pedestrian path. You'll have to go up the steps to walk above the fenced-off docks (or go around the back for wheelchair access) before coming down on the other side at the:

❼ Government Fish Dock

Want to buy fresh from the boat? This is the place to do it. Find fresh salmon in season (summer and early fall), prawns, scallops, and other shellfish much of the rest of the year. Sales take place every day in high season and on weekend mornings the rest of the year. Hours and availability, of course, depend on the catch.

From here, amble on down the seaside walkway past the gaggle of Canada geese (in the spring there are usually also downy Canada goslings) to:

❽ Granville Island

Okay, so it's not really an island. But it is a fascinating collection of shops and restaurants, theaters, a hotel, artists' workshops, housing, and still-functioning heavy industry—one of the few successful examples of 1970s urban renewal. The **Granville Island Information Centre,** 1592 Johnston St. (✆ **604/666-5784**), near the Public Market, has excellent free maps, but they're not really necessary—the place is so compact, the best thing to do is simply wander and explore.

To continue the tour, bear left down Duranleau Street. Shops in this section specialize in marine tours of all kinds, which makes it a good place to look for a fishing charter or kayak tours. The **Net Loft** building on the far side of the street is a great spot for pottery, glasswork, paper products, and ladies' hats, both classic and funky. It's also home to **Blackberry Books,** 1663 Duranleau (✆ **604/685-6188**). Just past the Net Loft is **Triangle Square,** an open space where street buskers often perform. Cut through the square, cross the street, and:

TAKE A BREAK
You name it, so long as it's edible, the **Granville Island Public Market** probably has it, from chocolate to fresh salmon to fresh bread to marinated mushrooms to strawberries picked this morning out in the Fraser Valley. Those with an immediate hunger gravitate to the far side of the market, where **A La Mode** (© 604/685-8335) sells lattes and rhubarb-strawberry pie that will have you trading in your mother for whoever does their baking. The most fun way to feed yourself, however, is to roam the market stalls for picnic supplies—artichoke hearts, Danish cheese, cold smoked salmon, Indian candy, pepper paté, fresh baked bread—then head outside for an alfresco feast at one of the tables on the dock overlooking False Creek. The views are great, the fresh air invigorating, and, if you've brought small children along, it's the perfect place to play that endlessly fascinating (to kids) game of Catch the Seagull.

When your hunger pangs have eased, continue east on the water's edge—note the Aquabus ferry dock, to which we'll be returning later—and follow the path around the Arts Club pub, underneath the Granville Street Bridge, and then to your right, away from the water, and go through what is, perhaps, the perfect little outdoor courtyard. You emerge on the far side next to a carving shed where First Nations artists can be seen working on a canoe or totem pole. Turn right and proceed down Johnston Street. This is the more industrial section of the island, and gravel and cement trucks are not uncommon. About halfway down the street is **Emily Carr College,** a high-caliber school of photography and art. Student projects are often on display in the lobby gallery. At the far end of Johnston Street is the **Dockside Brewpub,** 1253 Johnston St. (© 604/685-7070), a pub blessed with good beer and a geographically advantaged patio (it's on the edge of False Creek).

Alternatively, just to the right, you can climb the low circular hill known as:

⑨ The Mound
Gaze out over False Creek. The blinking geodesic dome at the far end of the creek is **Science World** (p. 107). In the same direction but closer is a small marina and restaurant complex, situated on Leg-in-Boot Square. The name refers to an incident late in the 19th century when a human leg, boot and all, washed up on what was then a highly industrial shoreline. Police posted the leg up in a public place for a week or so in hopes that someone would come forward to identify it (or maybe claim it?), but no one ever did.

Descend from The Mound and retrace your steps (or wind your way back through some of the side streets) to the:

⑩ Aquabus Ferry Dock
From here Aquabus harbor ferries (© 604/689-5858) arrive and depart to a variety of places including Leg-in-Boot Square and Science World down the Creek. Our destination is on the far side of False Creek at the:

⑪ Yaletown Landing (at the foot of Davie Street)
The small forest of high-rises ringing the north shore of False Creek are the creation of one company—Concorde Pacific, owned by Hong Kong billionaire Li Ka Shing. Formerly a railway switching yard, the area was transformed for the Expo '86 World's Fair. When the fair came to an end, the provincial government sold the land to Li Ka Shing for a song on the understanding he would build condominiums. And did he ever. The towers have been rising at the rate of three or four a year ever since.

At the landing site, note the large art piece, *Street Light,* designed by Bernie Miller and Alan Tregebov and installed in 1997. The large panels, each of which depicts a seminal event in False Creek's history, have been arranged so that on the anniversary of that event the sun will shine directly through the panel, casting a shadowed image on the street.

From here, turn to the left and walk along the waterfront to David Lam Park, turn right, and follow the path to:

⑫ The Roundhouse

The Roundhouse is so named because that's exactly what this brick and timber frame building was, back when this land was the CPR's switching yard. The structure has since been converted into a community center. It's worth ducking inside, whether to experience this wonderful space, make use of the public restrooms, or have a look at the locomotive that pulled the first passenger train ever to chug into Vancouver, way back in 1887.

Leave the Roundhouse by the front entrance on Pacific Boulevard, then cross the street and walk up Davie Street 1 block to Mainland Street. You're now in:

⑬ Yaletown

Vancouver's former warehouse district, Yaletown was originally where roughneck miners from Yale (up the Fraser Valley) came to drink and brawl. The city considered leveling the area in the 1970s until someone noticed that the former loading docks would make fine terraces and the low brick buildings themselves could be renovated into offices and condos. Though it's taken 20 years for the neighborhood to really catch on, the result is a funky upscale district of furniture shops, restaurants, multimedia companies, and "New York–style" lofts. Note the metal canopies over the loading docks on many buildings— they used to keep shipping goods dry, now they do the same for tourists and latte-sipping Web programmers. Turn right and walk up Mainland to Helmcken Street and:

From here, continue on Mainland or Hamilton 1 block up to Nelson Street, then turn

left and go up 2 blocks to Homer Street. Turn right and walk up 3 blocks to the:

TAKE A BREAK
Helmcken Street between Mainland and Hamilton streets has something for every taste. For coffee and pastry lovers there's a **Bread Garden** at Hamilton and Helmcken. Heartier appetites can grab pub grub at **Milestones** on the opposite corner. For those who prefer their barley and yeast in liquid form, there's the **Yaletown Brewing Company** at 1111 Mainland St. Remember, if it's raining at 11:30am on a Thursday, all pints of brewed-on-the-premises beer are C$3.75 (US$2.40) for the rest of the day.

⑭ Vancouver Public Library

Designed by noted architect Moshe Safdie to look like the ruin of a Roman coliseum, the library (350 W. Georgia St.; ✆ **604/331-3600**) was enormously controversial when it first went up. Architectural critics pooh-poohed it as derivative and ignorant of West Coast architectural traditions. But when the public got a look at the building, it was love at first sight. The steps out front have become a popular public gathering place, the lofty atrium inside a favored hangout spot and "study-date" locale for visiting language-school students and teens with protective parents. Go and have a look for yourself. Grab a coffee. Browse the books. Enjoy.

From here, a short walk west along Georgia Street will take you to the Granville Street bus mall, where there are public buses running to any and all destinations.

8

Vancouver Shopping

Blessed with a climate that seems semitropical in comparison to the rest of Canada, Vancouverites never really developed a taste for indoor malls. Instead, most residents shop on the street—parking the car or, better yet, leaving it at home—and browse from one window to the next, on the lookout for something new. Below are a few thoughts on where to start exploring.

1 The Shopping Scene

Outside of malls, stores in Vancouver generally open Monday through Saturday from 9am to 6pm. A few exceptions: Stores on Robson Street stay open later (usually until 9pm), while stores in Kitsilano open later (around 10am). On Sundays most stores are open 11am to 6pm, but a few remain closed all day. Malls such as the Pacific Centre are open from 9am to 7pm Monday through Wednesday, 9am to 9pm Thursday through Saturday, and 10am to 6pm on Sunday. Come Christmas shopping season, stores extend their hours from 9am to 9pm 7 days a week.

ROBSON STREET   It's been said that the corner of Robson and Burrard gets more foot traffic than any other corner in Canada. Urban myth? Who knows. Anyway, it's a busy, colorful parade of humanity, many from Asia (hence the sushi bars and shops with Japanese signs), most with money. Look for high-end fashions, with a focus on clothes for the younger set.

SOUTH GRANVILLE   The 10-block stretch of Granville Street—from Sixth Avenue up to 16th Avenue—is where Vancouver's old-money enclave of Shaughnessy comes to shop. Classic and expensive men's and women's clothiers and housewares and furniture boutiques predominate. This area is also the heart of Vancouver's gallery row.

WATER STREET   Though a little too heavy on the knickknack shops, Water Street and Gastown are by no means just a tacky tourist enclave. Look for antique and cutting-edge furniture, galleries of First Nations art, and funky basement retro shops.

MAIN STREET   Antiques, and lots of 'em. From about 19th up to 27th, Main Street is chockablock with antiques shops. Rather than outbid each other, the stores have evolved so that each covers a particular niche, from Art Deco to country kitchen to fine Second Empire. It's a fun place to browse, and if your eyes start to glaze over at the thought of yet another divan, the area also has cafes, bookshops, and clothing stores.

GRANVILLE ISLAND   A rehabilitated industrial site beneath the Granville Street Bridge, the Public Market is paradoxically one of the best places to pick up salmon and other seafood. It's also a great place to browse for crafts and gifts. Particularly interesting is Kids Market, a kind of mini-mall for children, complete with a Lilliputian entranceway, toy, crafts, and book stores, and play areas and services for the not-yet-10 demographic.

ASIA WEST   If you've never been to Hong Kong, or are just itching to get back, this new commercial area on Richmond's No. 3 Road between Capstan and Alderbridge roads is the place to shop. Stores in four new malls—the Yaohan Centre, President Plaza, Aberdeen Centre, and Parker Place—cater to Vancouver's newly arrived Asian community by bringing in goods direct from Asia. If the prices seem a bit high, a simple inquiry is often enough to bring them plummeting down as much as 80%.

PUNJABI MARKET   India imported. The 4 blocks of Main Street on either side of 49th Avenue contain the whole of the subcontinent, shrunk down to a manageable parcel. Look for fragrant spice stalls and sari shops and textile outlets selling luxurious fabrics—at bargain-basement prices.

2 Shopping A to Z

ANTIQUES

Bakers Dozen Antiques   This charming shop specializes in antique toys, model ships and boats, folk art, and unusual 19th- and early-20th-century furniture. 3520 Main St. ☎ 604/879-3348.

Mihrab *(Finds)*   Part museum, part subcontinental yard sale, Mihrab specializes in one-of-a-kind Indian antiques for the house and garden. Think intricately carved teak archways or tiny jewel-like door pulls, all selected by partners Lou Johnson and Kerry Lane on frequent trips to the subcontinent. 2229 Granville St. ☎ 604/879-6105. www.mihrabantiques.com.

Uno Langmann Limited   Catering to upscale shoppers, Uno Langmann specializes in European and North American paintings, furniture, silver, and objets d'art from the 18th through early 20th centuries. Open Tuesday through Saturday 10am to 5pm. 2117 Granville St. ☎ 604/736-8825. www.langmann.com.

Vancouver Antique Centre   Housed in a heritage commercial building, this maze contains 14 separate shops on two levels, specializing in everything from china, glass, and jewelry to military objects, sports, toys, retro; '50s and '60s collectibles; home furnishings; and watches. There are even more shops in the neighboring buildings. Open Monday through Saturday 11am to 5:30pm. 422 Richards St. ☎ 604/669-7444.

BOOKS

Blackberry Books   Books about art, architecture, and fine cuisine are the specialties of this Granville Island store, which also has a wide variety of more general categories. New titles are displayed with staff reviews posted beside them. 1663 Duranleau St. ☎ 604/685-4113 or 604/685-6188. www.bbooks.ca.

Chapters   Chapters seems to have won folks over with the sheer quality of its book-buying experience—stores are pleasant and well planned, with little nooks and comfy benches; coffee is often available on the ground floor. And though it pains a local booster like myself to say it, Chapters' book selection is—gasp—every bit as good as homegrown favorite Duthie's. 788 Robson St. ☎ 604/682-4066. www.chapters.ca. Also at 2505 Granville St. (☎ 604/731-7822).

Duthie Books 4th Ave.   Since 1957, this locally owned chain has been synonymous with good books in Vancouver. Though its recent financial troubles and retrenchment have left Duthie's with just one store, it remains a particularly good place to find local authors, in addition to an excellent inventory of Canadian and international titles. The staff is knowledgeable, and the shop offers custom services such as special, by-mail, and out-of-print ordering. 2239 W. Fourth Ave., Kitsilano. ✆ 604/732-5344. www.duthiebooks.com.

Granville Book Company   Located in the heart of Vancouver's entertainment district, this bookstore has a great selection and staff with a true love for books. Generous open hours make this a great spot for browsing after dinner or before a movie. Open daily 9am to midnight. 850 Granville St. ✆ 877/838-BOOK or 604/687-2213. www.granvillebooks.com.

International Travel Maps and Books *Finds*   Best selection of travel books, maps, charts, and globes in town. The selection of special-interest British Columbia guides is impressive, with topics ranging from backcountry skiing and minimum-impact hiking to off-road four-wheeling. This is the hiker's best source for detailed topographic charts of the entire province. One of the city's secret bargains is the bin of free, outdated provincial maps near the door that often includes maps of the parks around Whistler (outside Vancouver, the province changes slowly enough that they're still accurate). 539 West Pender St. ✆ 604/687-3320. Also at 530 W. Broadway (✆ 604/879-3621). www.itmb.com.

Kidsbooks *Kids*   The largest and most interesting selection of children's literature in the city also has an amazing collection of puppets and regular readings. 3083 W. Broadway. ✆ 604/738-5335. Also 3040 Edgemont Blvd., North Vancouver (✆ 604/986-6190).

Little Sister's Book & Art Emporium   What makes one book literature and another pornography? To see for yourself, come down and browse this West End bookstore's large selection of lesbian, gay, bisexual, and transgender books, videos, and magazines, as well as its huge adult novelties department. Open daily 9am to 11pm. 1238 Davie St. ✆ 604/669-1753. www.lsisters.com.

CAMERA

Dunne & Rundle foto source   Dunne & Rundle is conveniently located downtown and can handle repairs for most major brands and sells parts, accessories, and film. 891 Granville St. ✆ 604/681-9254. www.dunneandrundle.com.

CHINA, SILVER & CRYSTAL

You can find a great array of sophisticated international china and crystal in the downtown stores. On Granville Island you can observe potters, silversmiths, and glassblowers as they work their magic.

Gallery of BC Ceramics   This Granville Island gallery loft is owned and operated by the Potters Guild of British Columbia. It presents a lively, juried collection of sculptural and functional ceramic works by close to 100 B.C. potters. The gallery also carries a full range of books for ceramics enthusiasts. Closed on Mondays in January and February. Gallery hours change seasonally, so phone ahead to confirm hours of operation. 1359 Cartwright St. ✆ 604/669-5645. www.bc potters.com.

Martha Sturdy Originals *Finds*   Local designer Martha Sturdy—once best known for her collectible, usable, handblown glassware trimmed in gold leaf—is now creating a critically acclaimed line of cast-resin housewares, as well as limited-edition couches and chairs. Expensive, but, if you've got the dough, well worth it. 3039 Granville St. ✆ 604/737-0037. www.marthasturdy.com.

CHINESE GOODS

T&T Supermarket *Finds*   Racks and racks of goods you won't find at home (unless your home is China), but the real entertainment is the seafood bins and the produce section, where strange and ungainly comestibles lurk: fire-dragon fruit, lily root, and enoki mushrooms. 181 Keefer St. © **604/899-8836.**

Ten Ren Tea & Ginseng Co.   Whether you prefer the pungent aroma of Chinese black or the exotic fragrance of chrysanthemum, jasmine, or ginger flower, you must try the numerous varieties of drinking and medicinal teas in this Chinatown shop. It also carries Korean, American, and Siberian ginseng for a lot less than you might pay elsewhere. 550 Main St. © **604/684-1566.**

Tung Fong Hung Foods Co. *Finds*   If you've never been to a Chinese herbalist, this is the one to try: jars, bins, and boxes full of such things as dried sea horse, thinly sliced deer antler, and bird's nest. It's lots of fun to explore and potentially good for what ails you. Chinese remedies can have side effects, however, so before ingesting anything unfamiliar, it's usually wise to consult the on-site herbalist. 536 Main St. © **604/688-0883.**

CIGARS & TOBACCO

Just remember: if they're Cuban, you'll have to light up on this side of the border.

La Casa del Habano Directly across from Planet Hollywood on Robson Street, Casa del Habano has Vancouver's largest walk-in humidor. Cigars range in price from a few dollars to over a hundred. 980 Robson St. © **604/609-0511.** www.lacasa delhabanocanada.com.

Vancouver Cigar Company   The selection here is reputed to be the city's most extensive, featuring brands such as Cohiba, Monte Cristo, Macanudo, Hoyo De Monterrey, Romeo y Julieta, Partagas, Ashton, and A. Fuente. The shop also carries a complete line of accessories. 1093 Hamilton St. © **604/685-0445.** www.vancouvercigar.com.

DEPARTMENT STORES

The Bay (Hudson's Bay Company)   From the establishment of its early trading posts during the 1670s to its modern coast-to-coast chain, the Bay has built its reputation on quality goods. You can still buy a Hudson's Bay woolen "point" blanket (the colorful stripes originally represented how many beaver pelts each blanket was worth in trade), but you'll also find Tommy Hilfiger, Polo, DKNY, and more. 674 Granville St. © **604/681-6211.** www.hbc.com.

Hills of Kerrisdale *Value*   This neighborhood department store in central Vancouver is a city landmark. Carrying full lines of quality men's, women's, and children's clothes, as well as furnishings and sporting goods, it's a destination for locals because the prices are often lower than those in the downtown core. 2125 W. 41st Ave. © **604/266-9177.**

DISCOUNT SHOPPING

The strip of West Fourth Avenue between Cypress and Yew streets has recently emerged as consignment-clothing central. New shops open regularly.

In-Again Clothing *Value*   Good variety of seasonal consignment clothing. The selection keeps up with fashion trends. Don't miss the collection of purses, scarves, and belts. 1962 W. Fourth Ave. © **604/738-2782.**

Second Suit for Men & Women *Value*   This resale- and sample-clothing store has the best in men's and women's fashions, including Hugo Boss, Armani, Donna Karan, Nautica, Calvin Klein, and Alfred Sung. The inventory changes rapidly. 2036 W. Fourth Ave. ℂ 604/732-0338.

FASHIONS
FOR CHILDREN

Isola Bella *Kids*   This store imports an exclusive collection of rather expensive, high-fashion newborn and children's clothing from designers like Babar, Babymini, Milou, Petit Bateau, and Paul Smith. 5692 Yew St. ℂ 604/266-8808.

Please Mum *Kids*   This Kitsilano store sells attractive Canadian-made toddler's and children's cotton clothing. 2951 W. Broadway. & 604/732-4574. www.please mum.com.

FOR MEN & WOMEN

Vancouver has the Pacific Northwest's best collection of clothes from Paris, London, Milan, and Rome, in addition to a great assortment of locally made, cutting-edge fashions. International designer outlets include **Chanel Boutique,** 900 W. Hastings St. (ℂ 604/682-0522); **Salvatore Ferragamo,** 918 Robson St. (ℂ 604/669-4495); **Gianni Versace Boutique,** 757 W. Hastings St. (ℂ 604/683-1131); **Polo/Ralph Lauren,** the Landing, 375 Water St. (ℂ 604/682-7656); and **Plaza Escada,** Sinclair Centre, 757 W. Hastings St. (ℂ 604/688-8558).

It seems that almost every week a new designer boutique opens in Yaletown, Kitsilano, or Kerrisdale.

Christine and Company *Finds*   More than 20 years ago, Christine Morton started out selling delicate, antique, lacy sleepwear along with a few of her own lingerie creations. She then expanded to silky blouses and heirloom-quality trousseau lingerie. And she's now regarded as the city's hottest bridal-wear designer. 201–657 Marine Dr., West Vancouver. ℂ 604/922-0350. www.christine vancouver.com.

Dorothy Grant *Finds*   Designed to look like a Pacific Northwest longhouse, this shop is where First Nations designer Dorothy Grant exhibits her unique designs as well as her husband's (acclaimed artist Robert Davidson) collection of exquisitely detailed Haida motifs, which she appliqués on coats, leather vests, jackets, caps, and accessories. The clothes are gorgeous and collectible. She also carries contemporary Haida art and jewelry. Check the website for some samples of the collection. Open Monday through Friday 10am to 5:30pm or by appointment. 1656 W. 75th St. (corner of Granville St., near Vancouver's International Airport). ℂ 604/681-0201. www.dorothygrant.com.

Dream 311   Big-name designs can be found anywhere, but this little shop is one of the few places to show early collections—clothing and jewelry—of local designers. 311 W. Cordova. ℂ 604/683-7326.

Leone   Shop where the stars shop. Versace, Donna Karan, Byblos, Armani, and fabulous Italian and French accessories are sold in this very elegant building; valet parking provided and private after-hours shopping by appointment for VIPs. Sinclair Centre, 757 W. Hastings St. ℂ 604/683-1133. www.leone.ca.

Roots Canada   Proudly Canadian, this chain features sturdy casual clothing. You'll find leather jackets, leather bags, footwear, outerwear, and athletic wear for the whole family. 1001 Robson (corner of Burrard). ℂ 604/683-4305. www.roots.ca.

Swimco Located near Kitsilano Beach, this store caters to swimmers and sun-bathers. You will find a large variety of bikinis and bathing suits in the latest prints and colors for men, women, and children. 2166 W. Fourth Ave. © **604/732-7946. www.swimco.com.**

Venus & Mars *Finds* Add some drama to your life. This Gastown boutique features Vancouver designer Sanné Lambert's work, specializing in one-of-a-kind handmade gowns and velvet robes. Some plus sizes available. 315 Cambie St. © **604/687-1908. www.venusandmars.nu.**

Zonda Nellis Design Ltd. *Finds* Rich colors and intricate patterns highlight this Vancouver designer's imaginative hand-woven separates, pleated silks, sweaters, vests, and soft knits. Nellis has also introduced a new line of hand-painted silks and sumptuous, sheer hand-painted velvet eveningwear. 2203 Granville St. © **604/736-5668, www.zondanellis.com.**

VINTAGE CLOTHING

Deluxe Junk Co. The name fits—there's tons of junk. Amid the polyester jackets and worn-out dress shirts, however, are some truly great finds. Some real bargains have been known to pop up. 310 W. Cordova St. © **604/685-4871. www.deluxe junk.com.**

Legends Retro-Fashion Specializing in unique retro clothing, Legends is well known among vintage purists for its cache of one-of-a-kind pieces. Most of the clothes, such as evening dresses, shoes, kid gloves, and other accessories, are in immaculate condition. 4366 Main St. © **604/875-0621.**

Tapestry Vintage Clothing Consignment shop with an interesting collection of vintage women's clothing. Open Wednesday through Sunday noon to 6pm. 321 Cambie St., Gastown. © **604/687-1719.**

True Value Vintage Clothing This underground shop has a collection of funky fashions from the 1930s through the 1990s, including tons of fake furs, leather jackets, denim, soccer jerseys, vintage bathing suits, formal wear, smoking jackets, sweaters, and accessories. 710 Robson St. © **604/685-5403.**

FIRST NATIONS ART

You'll find First Nations art all over the city. You don't have to purchase a pricey antique to acquire original Coast Salish or Haida work. As the experts at the **Museum of Anthropology** explain, if an item is crafted by any of the indigenous Pacific Northwest artisans, it's a real First Nations piece of art. The culture is ancient yet still very much alive. Pick up a copy of ***Publication No. 10: A Guide to Buying Contemporary Northwest Coast Art*** by Karen Duffel (available at the Museum of Anthropology), which details how to identify and care for these beautifully carved, worked, and woven pieces.

Even if you're not in the market, go gallery-hopping to see works by Haida artists **Bill Reid** (the province's best-known Native artist) and **Richard Davidson,** and by Kwakwaka'wakw artist and photographer **David Neel.**

Coastal Peoples Fine Arts Gallery This Yaletown boutique offers an extensive collection of fine First Nations jewelry. The motifs—bear, salmon, whale, raven, and others—are drawn from local myths and translated into 14-karat or 18-karat gold and sterling-silver creations. Inuit sculptures and items made of glass or wood are also worth a look. Custom orders can be filled quickly and shipped worldwide. 1024 Mainland St. © **604/685-9298. www.coastalpeoples.com.**

Images for a Canadian Heritage   This store and the Inuit Gallery of Vancouver (see below) are government-licensed First Nations art galleries, featuring traditional and contemporary works such as Native designs on glass totems and copper plates. With a museum-worthy collection, this shop deserves a visit whether you're buying or not. 164 Water St. ☎ **604/685-7046.** www.imagesfor canada.com.

Inuit Gallery of Vancouver   Home to one of Canada's foremost collections of Inuit and First Nations art. Prices are for serious buyers, but it's worth a visit. 206–220 Water St. ☎ **604/688-7323.**

Leona Lattimer Gallery *(Finds)*   This beautiful gallery presents museum-quality displays of Pacific Northwest First Nations art, including ceremonial masks, totem poles, limited-edition silk-screen prints, argillite sculptures, and expensive gold and silver jewelry. Prices start at a few dollars for an original print and escalate quickly to the three-digit mark for most items. 1590 W. Second Ave. ☎ **604/732-4556.** www.leonalattimer.com.

Marion Scott Gallery   For more than 20 years, this gallery has been well regarded for its Inuit (Eskimo) and First Nations art collections. 481 Howe St. ☎ **604/685-1934.** www.marionscottgallery.com.

FIRST NATIONS CRAFTS

Bold, traditional, and innovative geometric designs; intricate carvings; strong primary colors; and rich wood tones are just a few of the elements you'll find in First Nations crafts.

Hill's Native Art   In a re-creation of a trading post interior, this shop sells moccasins, ceremonial masks, Cowichan sweaters, wood sculptures, totem poles (priced up to C$35,000/US$22,581), silk-screen prints, soapstone sculptures, and gold, silver, and argillite jewelry. 165 Water St. ☎ **604/685-4249.** www.hills nativeart.com.

Khot-La-Cha Salish Handicrafts *(Finds)*   Hand-tanned moose-hide crafts, wood carvings, Cowichan sweaters, porcupine-quill jewelry, and bone, silver, gold, and turquoise accessories are just a few of the selections at this Coast Salish crafts shop. Open Monday through Saturday 10am to 5pm. 270 Whonoak St., North Vancouver. ☎ **604/987-3339.** Turn South on Capilano Rd. (off Marine Dr.) and turn first left (Whonoak is parallel to Capilano Rd).

Museum of Anthropology   Works by contemporary First Nations artisans as well as books about the culture and publications on identifying and caring for Pacific Northwest crafts. University of British Columbia, 6393 NW Marine Dr. ☎ **604/ 822-5087.**

FOOD

You'll find **salmon** everywhere in Vancouver. Many shops package whole, fresh salmon with ice packs for visitors to take home. Shops also carry delectable smoked salmon in travel-safe, vacuum-packed containers. Some offer decorative cedar gift boxes; most offer overnight air transport. Try other salmon treats such as salmon jerky and Indian candy (chunks of marinated smoked salmon), which are available at public markets such as **Lonsdale Quay Market** and **Granville Island Public Market.**

And even though salmon is the most popular item to buy in Vancouver, coffee flows like water—as does Belgian chocolate.

Chocolate Arts *(Finds* The works at this West Fourth Avenue chocolatier are made with exquisite craftsmanship. Seasonal treats include pumpkin truffles around Halloween or eggnog truffles for Christmas. They even make chocolate toolboxes filled with tiny chocolate tools. Look for the all-chocolate diorama in the window—it changes every month or so. Native masks of thick dark chocolate make great gifts. 2037 W. Fourth Ave. © 604/739-0475.

The Lobsterman Live lobsters, Dungeness crabs, oysters, mussels, clams, geoducks, and scallops are just a few of the varieties of seafood swimming in the saltwater tanks at this Granville Island fish store. The staff steams the food fresh on the spot, free. Salmon and other seafood can also be packed for air travel. 1807 Mast Tower Rd. © **604/687-4531.** www.lobsterman.com.

Murchie's Tea & Coffee This Vancouver institution has been the city's main tea and coffee purveyor for more than a century. You'll find everything from Jamaican Blue Mountain and Kona coffees to Lapsang Souchong and Kemun teas. The knowledgeable staff will help you decide which flavors and blends fit your taste. There's also a fine selection of bone china and crystal serving ware as well as coffeemakers and teapots. 970 Robson St. © **604/669-0783.** www.murchies.com.

Salmon Village For those wanting to pick up some salmon to take home, Salmon Village has a good selection from which to choose. Smoked Salmon or jerky are vacuum sealed for travel, and fresh salmon can be packed in an icebox or (for a price) shipped to you anywhere on the planet. 779 Thurlow St. © **604/ 685-3378.** www.salmonvillage.com.

South China Seas Trading Company The South Seas have always been a source of intrigue. This shop re-creates a bit of that wonder, with a remarkable collection of rare spices and hard-to-find sauces. Look for fresh kaffir lime leaves, Thai basil, young ginger, sweet Thai chili sauce, and occasional exotic produce like mangosteens and rambutans. Pick up recipes and ideas from the knowledgeable staff. Granville Island Public Market. © **604/681-5402.**

GALLERIES

On the first Thursday of every month, many galleries host free openings from 5 to 8pm. Check the *Georgia Straight* or *Vancouver Magazine* for listings or **www.art-bc.com** for more details on Vancouver's art scene.

Buschlen Mowatt The city's leading "establishment" gallery. Look for paintings, sculptures, and prints from well-known Canadian and international artists. 111–1445 W. Georgia St. © **604/682-1234.** www.buschlenmowatt.com.

Diane Farris Gallery Contemporary painting and sculpture, from up-and-coming artists and those who already have arrived. 1590 W. Seventh Ave. © **604/ 737-2629.** www.dianefarrisgallery.com.

Monte Clark Gallery *(Value* This cutting-edge gallery—in the otherwise slightly staid confines of south Granville's gallery row—is one of the best spots to look for that rising superstar without the rising prices. 2339 Granville St. © **604/ 730-5000.** www.monteclarkgallery.com .

GIFTS & SOUVENIRS

Buddha Supply Centre *(Finds* Want money to burn? At Chinese funerals people burn joss—paper replicas of earthly belongings—to help make the afterlife for the deceased more comfortable. This shop has more than 500 combustible products to choose from, including $1-million notes (drawn on the bank of hell), luxury penthouse condos, and that all-important cellphone. 4158 Main St. © 604/873-8169.

Escents Beautifully displayed, the large collection of soaps, bath oils, shampoos, and other body products here come in a variety of scents, such as the fresh ginger-citrus twist or the relaxing lavender sea. Locally produced and made with minimal packaging, the all-natural environmentally friendly products come in convenient sizes and prices. 1172 Robson St. © 604/682-0041. www.escentsaroma therapy.com.

The Ocean Floor If you want to bring home a few gifts from the sea, then select from this Granville Island shop's collection of seashells, ship models, lamps, chimes, coral, shell jewelry, stained glass, and marine brass. 1522 Duranleau St., Granville Island © 604/681-5014.

JEWELRY

Costen Catbalue *Finds* One-of-a-kind pieces in platinum and gold are made on the premises by a team of four goldsmiths and artists Mary Ann Buis and Andrew Costen. The two artists' styles complement each other; Buis favors contemporary and clean lines, and Costen's designs tend towards a more ornate Renaissance style. 1832 West 1st Ave. © 604/734-3259.

Forge & Form Master Granville Island metal designers Dietje Hagedoorn and Jürgen Schönheit specialize in customized gold and silver jewelry. Renowned for their gold and silver bow ties, they also create unique pieces like "tension set" rings, which hold a stone in place without a setting. Their studio is located just past the False Creek Community Centre. 1334 Cartwright St. © 604/684-6298.

Karl Stittgen and Goldsmiths *Finds* Stittgen's gold pins, pendants, rings, and other accessories demonstrate his eye for clean, crisp design and fine craftsmanship. Each work is a miniature architectural wonder. 2203 Granville St. © 604/737-0029.

The Raven and the Bear If you've never seen West Coast Native jewelry, it's worth making a trip. Deeply inscribed with stylized creatures from Northwest mythology, these rings, bangles, and earrings are unforgettable. (See also "First Nations Art," above.) 1528 Duranleau St. © 604/669-3990.

MALLS & SHOPPING CENTERS

Pacific Centre Mall This 3-block complex contains 200 shops and services, including Godiva, Benetton, Crabtree & Evelyn, and Eddie Bauer. 700 W. Georgia St. © 604/688-7236.

Park Royal Shopping Centre Park Royal consists of two malls that face each other on Marine Drive, just west of the Lions Gate Bridge. GAP, Coast Mountain Sports, Cypress Mountain Sports, Future Shop, Marks & Spencer, Disney, Eaton's, the Bay, Eddie Bauer, and a public market are just a few of the 250 stores in the center. Cinemas, bowling lanes, a golf driving range, community and special events, and a food court are next door. 2002 Park Royal S., West Vancouver. © 604/925-9576. www.shopparkroyal.com.

Sinclair Centre The Sinclair Centre incorporates four Vancouver landmarks: the Post Office (1910), Winch Building (1911), Customs Examining Warehouse (1913), and Federal Building (1937). Now restored, they house elite shops like Armani and Leone, as well as smaller boutiques, art galleries, and a food court. 757 W. Hastings St. ℂ 604/659-1009. www.sinclaircentre.com.

Vancouver Centre   The Bay, restaurants, a food fair, and more than 115 specialty stores connect underground to the adjoining Pacific Centre Mall (see above). 650 W. Georgia St. ℂ 604/688-5658.

MARKETS

There are **green markets** scattered throughout the city. There's also a huge **flea market** in an old warehouse by the railway tracks, with as great a mix of stuff as you could possibly imagine.

Chinatown Night Market *(Value)*   Across Asia, prime shopping time comes only after the sun has gone down and the temperature has dropped to something bearable. Friday and Saturday nights May through September, merchants in Chinatown bring the tradition to Canada by closing two separate blocks to traffic and covering them with booths, tables, and food stalls offering all manner of things, useful and otherwise. Come down, grab a juicy satay skewer, sip the juice from a freshly cracked coconut, and see what's up. 200 Keefer St. and 200 E. Pender St. Phone the Vancouver Tourism Info Centre at ℂ 604/683-2000.

Granville Island Public Market *(Finds)*   This 50,000-square-foot public market features produce, meats, fish, wines, cheeses, arts and crafts, and lots of fast-food counters offering a little of everything. The market is open daily 9am to 6pm. From mid-June to September, the Farmers' Truck Market operates here Thursday from 9am to 6pm. 1669 Johnston St. ℂ 604/666-6477. www.granville island.com.

Lonsdale Quay Market *(Kids)*   Located at the SeaBus terminal, this public market is filled with produce, meats, fish, specialty fashions, gift shops, food counters, coffee bars, a hotel, and Kids' Alley (a section dedicated to children's shops and a play area). The upper floor houses a variety of fashion stores, bookstores, and gift shops. 123 Carrie Cates Court, North Vancouver. ℂ 604/985-6261. www. lonsdalequay.com.

New Westminster Quay Public Market   A smaller version of Granville Island, it is located 25 minutes away by SkyTrain from downtown Vancouver. The market has a variety of gift shops, specialty stores, a food court, a delicatessen, and produce stands. Once finished browsing the market, make sure to have a gander at the neighboring Fraser River. A walkway extends along the river and allows great views of the waterfront, the busy boat traffic, and the occasional seal or sea lion. 810 Quayside, New Westminster. ℂ 604/520-3881.

Vancouver Flea Market *(Value)*   Near the train/bus terminal, Vancouver's largest flea market boasts more than 350 stalls. Admittedly, most are stocked with cheap T-shirts, linens, used tools, and such, but it's still possible to discover some real finds. Go early or the savvy shoppers will have already cleaned out the real gems. Open weekends and holidays 9am to 5pm. 703 Terminal Ave. ℂ 604/ 685-0666. Admission C60¢ (US40¢), free for children under 12.

MUSIC

The Magic Flute   Located in the heart of Kitsilano's Fourth Avenue shopping area, the Magic Flute carries a large selection of classical music, including recordings of local choirs and orchestras. The collection also includes jazz, world music, and soundtracks. Listening stations allow you to "browse" before you buy. 2203 W. Fourth Ave. ℂ 604/736-2727. www.magicflute.com.

Virgin Megastore With over 150,000 titles housed in a three-story, 42,000-square-foot space, it's Canada's largest music and entertainment store. 788 Burrard St. at Robson St. ℂ 604/669-2289. www.virginmega.com.

Zulu Records *Finds* A few blocks east of the Magic Flute, Zulu Records specializes in alternative music, local and import, new and used. You will also find a good selection of vinyl and magazines. The staff is happy to make recommendations and bring you up to speed on what's hot in the local music scene. 1972 W. Fourth Ave. ℂ 604/738-3232. www.zulurecords.com.

SHOES

David Gordon This may be Vancouver's oldest Western boot, hat, and accessories store, but it's far from stodgy. Boots include an extensive selection of Tony Lama, Boulet, Durango, HH Brown, and Dan Post. You'll also find Vans, Doc Martens, and a lineup of other funky footwear that attracts skateboarders and club kids. 822 Granville St. ℂ 604/685-3784.

John Fluevog Boots & Shoes Ltd. This native Vancouverite has a growing international cult following of designers and models clamoring for his under-C$200 (US$129) urban and funky creations. You'll find outrageous platforms and clogs, Angelic Sole work boots, and a few bizarre experiments for the daring footwear fetishist. 837 Granville St. ℂ 604/688-2828. www.fluevog.com.

SPECIALTY

Lush Although it has the look of an old-fashioned deli store with big wheels of cheese, slabs of sweets, chocolate bars, dips, and sauces, take a bite and you'd be washing your mouth with soap—literally. All these beautiful, mouthwatering displays are indeed soaps, shampoos, skin treatments, massage oils, and bath bombs. Made from all natural ingredients, these deceptively real looking treats are the perfect pampering gift. 1025 Robson St. ℂ 604/687-5874. www.lushcanada.com.

The Market Kitchen Store Everything you'd like to have on your kitchen counters or in your kitchen drawers—gourmet kitchen accessories, baking utensils, and gadgets. Anyone need a citrus zester? 2–1666 Johnston (Net Loft, Granville Island). ℂ 604/681-7399.

Spy-Central *Finds* A haven for spies, paranoids, and the just plain snoopy, Spy-Central offers cellphone scanners, miniature cameras, and night-vision gear. Clumsy shoppers take note: If you break it, they know your credit-card number. 788 Beatty St. ℂ 604/642-0324.

Three Dog Bakery Beagle Bagels, Scottie Biscotti, or Gracie's Rollovers. Canines will have a hard time deciding on a favorite treat from this gone-to-the-dogs bakery. The store also has leashes, collars, greeting cards, and other dog paraphernalia. 2186 W. Fourth Ave. ℂ 604/737-3647. www.threedog.com.

SPORTING GOODS

A 2-block area near the Mountain Equipment Co-op (see below) has now become Outdoor Central, with at least a half-dozen stores such as **Altus Mountain Gear** (137 W. Broadway; ℂ 604/876-25255); **Great Outdoors Equipment** (222 W. Broadway; ℂ 604/872-8872); and **AJ Brooks** (147 W. Broadway; ℂ 604/874-1117). Just a block north on 8th Ave., you'll find **Taiga** (380 W. 8th Ave.; ℂ 604/875-8388) for inexpensive fleece and other quality outdoor gear.

Boardhead Central Not a shop, but a phenomenon. In the past few years, the corner of Fourth Avenue and Burrard Street has become the spot for high-quality snow/skate/surf board gear and the spot to see top-level boarders and their groupies hanging out. **Pacific Boarder:** 1793 W. Fourth Ave. ((✆ **604/734-7245**). **Thriller:** 1710 W. Fourth Ave. ((✆ 604/736-5651). **West Beach**: 1766 W. Fourth Ave. ((✆ 604/731-6449); sometimes hosts pro-skate demos on the half-pipe at the back of the store.

Comor Sports   "Go play outside" is Comor's motto, and they certainly have the goods to get you out there having fun. Pick up some skateboard garb, swimwear, or hiking shoes to enjoy the sunshine. Need in-line skates? The staff can assist you in choosing from the overwhelmingly large collection of wheels. Winter fiends can load up on warm fleece, skis, and boards, as well as other snow toys. 1090 W. Georgia St. (✆ **604/899-2111**. www.comorsports.com.

Mountain Equipment Co-op   A true West Coast institution and an outdoors lover's dream come true, this block-long store houses the best selection of top-quality outdoor gear: rain gear, clothing, hiking shoes, climbing gear, backpacks, sleeping bags, tents, and more. Memorize the MEC label; you're sure to see it later—at the beach, the bar, the concert hall. 130 W. Broadway. (✆ **604/ 872-7858**. www.mec.ca.

TOYS

The Games People *Kids*   The Games People carries a huge selection of board games, strategy games, role-playing games, puzzles, models, toys, hobby materials, and other amusements. It's difficult to walk past this store, whether you're an adult or a kid. 157 Water St. (✆ **604/685-5825**.

Kids Market *Kids*   Probably the only mall in North America dedicated to kids, the Kids Market on Granville Island features a Lilliputian entranceway, toy and craft and book stores, play areas, and services for the younger set, including even a "fun hairdresser." 1496 Cartwright St. (on Granville Island). (✆ **604/689-8447**. www.kids market.ca.

Kites on Clouds *Kids*   This little Gastown shop has every type of kite. Prices range from C$10 to C$20 (US$6.50–US$13) for nylon or Mylar dragon kites to just under C$200 (US$129) for more elaborate ghost clippers and nylon hang-glider kites. The Courtyard, 131 Water St. (✆ **604/669-5677**.

WINE

British Columbia's **wines** are worth buying by the case, especially rich, honey-thick ice wines, such as Jackson-Triggs gold-medal-winning 1994 Johannesburg Riesling Ice wine, and bold reds, such as the Quail's Gate 1994 Limited Release Pinot Noir. Five years of restructuring, reblending, and careful tending by French and German master vintners have won the province's vineyards world recognition.

When buying B.C. wine, look for the VQA (Vintner Quality Alliance) seal on the label; it's a guarantee that all grapes used are grown in British Columbia and meet European standards for growing and processing.

Summerhill, Cedar Creek, Mission Hill, and **Okanagan Vineyards** are just a few of the more than 50 local estates producing hearty cabernet sauvignons, honey-rich ice wines, and oaky merlots. These wines can be found at any government-owned **LCB** liquor store, such as the one at 1716 Robson St. ((✆ **604/ 660-4576**) and at some privately owned wine stores.

Marquis Wine Cellars   The owner and staff of this West End wine shop are dedicated to educating their patrons about wines. They conduct evening wine tastings, featuring selections from their special purchases. They also publish monthly newsletters. In addition to carrying a full range of British Columbian wines, the shop also has a large international selection. 1034 Davie St. © **604/684-0445** or 604/685-2246. www.marquis-wines.com.

The Okanagan Estate Wine Cellar   This department store annex, located in the Vancouver Centre mall concourse's Market Square, offers a great selection of British Columbian wines by bottle and case. The Bay, 674 Granville St. © **604/681-6211.**

9

Vancouver After Dark

Vancouver is a fly-by-the-seat-of-the-pants kind of town. There's so much to see and do—and the outdoors always beckons—that Vancouverites wait till the day or the hour before a show to plunk their cash down on the barrel. It drives promoters crazy. Vancouver is blessed with entertainment options, from cutting-edge theater companies to a well-respected opera and symphony to folk and jazz festivals that draw people from up and down the coast. And then there are the bars and pubs and clubs and cafes—lots of them—for every taste, budget, and fetish; you just have to get out there and see.

For an overview of Vancouver's nightlife, pick up a copy of the weekly tabloid, the *Georgia Straight.* Or get a copy of *Xtra! West,* the free gay and lesbian biweekly tabloid, available in shops and restaurants throughout the West End. The Thursday edition of the *Vancouver Sun* contains the weekly entertainment section **Queue.** The monthly *Vancouver Magazine* is filled with listings and strong views about what's really hot in the city. Check out their website, www.van mag.com.

The **Vancouver Cultural Alliance Arts Hotline,** 100–938 Howe St. (© **604/684-2787** or 604/681-3535; www.allianceforarts.com), is a great information source for all performing arts, literary events, and art films, including where and how to get tickets. The office is open Monday through Friday from 9am to 5pm.

Ticketmaster (Vancouver Ticket Centre), 1304 Hornby St. (© **604/ 280-3311;** www.ticketmaster.ca), has 40 outlets in the Vancouver area.

1 The Performing Arts

Three major theaters in Vancouver regularly host touring performances. The **Orpheum Theatre,** 801 Granville St. (© **604/665-3050;** www.city.vancouver. bc.ca/theatres/orpheum/orpheum.html), is an elegant 1927 theater that originally hosted the Chicago-based Orpheum vaudeville circuit. The theater also hosts pop, rock, and variety shows. The **Queen Elizabeth Complex,** 600 Hamilton St., between Georgia and Dunsmuir streets (© **604/665-3050;** www. city.vancouver.bc.ca), comprises the Queen Elizabeth Theatre and the Vancouver Playhouse. It hosts major national and touring musical and theater productions. It's also home to the Vancouver Opera and Ballet British Columbia. The 670-seat Vancouver Playhouse presents chamber-music performances and recitals. Located in a converted turn-of-the-20th-century church, the **Vancouver East Cultural Centre** (the "Cultch" to locals), 1895 Venables St. (© **604/ 251-1363;** www.vecc.bc.ca), coordinates an impressive program that includes avant-garde theater productions, performances by international musical groups, festivals and cultural events, children's programs, and art exhibitions.

On the campus of UBC, the **Chan Centre for the Performing Arts,** 6265 Crescent Rd. (© **604/822-2697;** www.chancentre.com), showcases the work of

---

Finds **Art on the Edge**

For more original performance fare, don't miss **The Fringe—Vancouver's Theatre Festival** (✆ **604/257-0350;** www.vancouverfringe.com). Centered on Granville Island, the Fringe Festival features more than 500 innovative and original shows each September, all costing under C$12 (US$7.80).

---

the UBC music and acting students and also hosts a winter concert series. Designed by local architectural luminary, Bing Thom, the Chan Centre's crystal-clear acoustics are the best in town.

THEATER

Theater isn't only an indoor pastime here. There is an annual summertime Shakespeare series, **Bard on the Beach,** in Vanier Park (✆ **604/737-0625**). You can also bring a picnic dinner to Stanley Park and watch **Theatre Under the Stars** (see below), which features popular musicals and light comedies.

Arts Club Theatre Company   The 425-seat Granville Island Mainstage presents major dramas, comedies, and musicals, with post-performance entertainment in the Backstage Lounge. The Arts Club Revue Stage is an intimate, cabaret-style showcase for small productions, improvisation nights, and musical revues such as *The Cripple of Inishmaan* and *The Threepenny Opera.* The smaller Art Deco Stanley Theatre has recently undergone a glorious renovation and now plays host to longer running plays and musicals, such as *The Mousetrap* and *My Fair Lady.* The box office is open 9am to 7pm. Granville Island Stage, 1585 Johnston St., and The Stanley Theatre, 2750 Granville St. ✆ **604/687-1644.** www.artsclub.com. Tickets C$13–C$45 (US$8.45–US$29). Senior, student, and group discounts available.

The Centre in Vancouver for Performing Arts   Originally built as the Ford Centre in 1996, this theatre was hailed as Vancouver's newest prime entertainment venue but the final call came soon when its owner went bankrupt. The good-as-new, hardly used theater sat empty until the spring of 2002. The new owners, four brothers from Hong Kong who now reside in Colorado, have given the venue a new life and are once again bringing big productions to town. Check the calendar or contact Ticketmaster for an updated schedule. 777 Homer St. ✆ **604/602-0616.** www.centreinvancouver.com. Tickets C$25–C$70 (US$16–US$46). Tickets available through Ticketmaster only; call ✆ 604/280-3311.

Firehall Arts Centre   Housed in Vancouver's Firehouse No. 1, the Centre has for 20 years been home to the cutting-edge Firehall Theatre Company. Expect original and experimental plays, such as last year's hit *Filthy Rich* by George F. Walker and Kudelka's *Janus/Janis.* Dance events, arts festivals, and concerts are also staged here. The box office is open Monday through Friday 9:30am to 5pm and for one hour before the show begins. 280 E. Cordova St. ✆ **604/689-0926.** www.firehall.org. Tickets C$8–C$18 (US$5.20–US$12). Senior and student discounts available.

Frederic Wood Theatre *(Value)*   Forget that "student production" thing you've got in your head. Students at UBC are actors in training, and their productions are extremely high-caliber. For the price, they're a steal. Their presentations range from classic dramatic works to Broadway musicals to new plays by Canadian playwrights. The box office is open Monday through Friday 10:30am to 3pm. All shows start at 7:30pm. There are no performances during the summer.

Gate 4, University of British Columbia. ℂ **604/822-2678**. www.theatre.ubc.ca. Tickets C$16 (US$10) adults, C$10 (US$6.50) students and seniors.

Theatre Under the Stars   From mid-July to mid-August, old-time favorite musicals like *Annie Get Your Gun, Joseph and the Amazing Technicolour Dream Coat, West Side Story, South Pacific,* and *Grease* are performed outdoors by a mixed cast of amateur and professional actors. Bring a blanket (it gets cold once the sun sets) and a picnic dinner for a relaxing evening of summer entertainment. The box office is open Monday through Saturday 10am to 5pm and 7 to 8pm. Malkin Bowl, Stanley Park. ℂ **604/257-0366** or 604/687-0174. www.tuts.bc.ca. Tickets C$23 (US$15) adults, C$17 (US$11) seniors and youth, C$10 (US$6.50) children 6–10.

Vancouver Playhouse   Well into its third decade, the company at the Vancouver Playhouse presents a program of six plays each season, usually a mix of the internationally known, nationally recognized, and locally promising. The box office opens 30 minutes before show time. You can also buy tickets over the phone through **Ticketmaster** at ℂ **604/280-4444**. 600 Hamilton, between Georgia and Hamilton sts. in the Queen Elizabeth complex. ℂ **604/665-3050**. www.city.vancouver. bc.ca/theatres. Tickets usually C$8–C$16 (US$5.20–US$10). Senior and student discounts available.

OPERA
Vancouver Opera   In a kind of willful flirtation with death, the Vancouver Opera Company alternates between obscure or new (and Canadian!) works and older, more popular perennials, often sung by international stars such as Placido Domingo and Bryn Terfel. The formula seems to work, as the company is over 35 years old and still packing 'em in. The season runs October through May, with performances normally in the Queen Elizabeth Theatre. In 2003, look for Strauss' *Elektra* (Mar 22–29) and crowd-pleaser La Boheme by Puccini (May 3-12). The fall performances had not been announced as of press time. The box office is open Monday through Friday 9am to 4pm. 500–845 Cambie St. ℂ **604/ 683-0222**. www.vanopera.bc.ca. Tickets usually C$36–C$96 (US$23–US$62).

CLASSICAL MUSIC
Fans of chamber music, baroque fugues, Russian romantic symphonies, and popular show tunes will find world-class concert performances in Vancouver.

University of British Columbia School of Music   September through November and during January and March, UBC presents eight faculty and guest-artist concerts. They feature piano, piano and violin, opera, or quartets, plus occasional performances by acts like the Count Basie Orchestra. If the concert is in the Chan Centre, go. There are few halls in the world with such beautiful acoustics. Recital Hall, Gate 4, 6361 Memorial Rd. ℂ **604/822-5574**. www.music.ubc.ca. Tickets purchased at the door C$4–C$24 (US$2.60–US$15) adults, C$4–C$14 (US$2.60–US$9.10) seniors and students. Many concerts are free. The Wed noon hr. series costs C$4 (US$2.60).

Vancouver Bach Choir   Vancouver's international, award-winning amateur choir, a 150-voice ensemble, presents five major concerts a year at the Orpheum Theatre. Specializing in symphonic choral music, the Choir's sing-along performance of Handel's *Messiah* during the Christmas season is a favorite. 805–235 Keith Rd., West Vancouver. ℂ **604/921-8012**. www.vancouverbachchoir.com. Tickets C$20–C$35 (US$13–US$23) depending on the performance. Tickets available through Ticketmaster at ℂ 604/ 280-4444.

Vancouver Cantata Singers   This semiprofessional, 40-person choir specializes in early music. The company performs works by Bach, Brahms, Monteverdi,

Stravinsky, and Handel, as well as Eastern European choral music. The season normally includes three programs: in October, December, and March at various locations. 5115 Keith Rd., West Vancouver. © 604/921-8588. www.cantata.org. Tickets C$20 (US$13) adults, C$16 (US$10) seniors and students. Tickets at Ticketmaster (© 604/280-4444) or at the door.

Vancouver Chamber Choir Western Canada's only professional choral ensemble presents an annual concert series at the Orpheum Theatre, the Chan Centre, and Ryerson United Church. Under conductor John Washburn, the choir has gained an international reputation. 1254 W. Seventh Ave. © 604/738-6822. www.vancouverchamberchoir.com. Tickets C$15–C$35 (US$9.75–US$23) adults, C$13–C$25 (US$8.45–US$16) seniors and students. Tickets through Ticketmaster at © 604/280-4444.

Vancouver New Music This company presents seven annual concerts, featuring the works of contemporary and avant-garde composers as well as mixed-media performances that combine dance and film. Performances take place at the Vancouver East Cultural Centre between September and June. The society also hosts an annual new-music festival, the next one taking place in the last week of October 2003. 837 Davie St. © 604/663-0861. www.newmusic.org. Tickets C$20–C$35 (US$13–US$23) adults, C$16 (US$10) students.

Vancouver Symphony At its home in the Orpheum Theatre during the fall, winter, and spring, Vancouver's active orchestra presents the "Masterworks" series of great classical works; "Casual Classics," featuring light classics from a single area or composer and a casually dressed orchestra; "Tea & Trumpets," highlighting modern classics and ethnic works, hosted by the CBC's Otto Lowy; "Symphony Pops," selections of popular and show tunes; and "Kid's Koncerts," a series geared toward school-age children. The traveling summer concert series takes the orchestra from White Rock and Cloverdale on the U.S. border to the tops of Whistler and Blackcomb Mountains. The box office is open Monday through Friday 1 to 5pm. On the day of the performance the box office is open from 6pm until show time.601 Smithe St. © 604/876-3434 for ticket information. www.vancouversymphony.ca. Tickets C$22–C$60 (US$14–US$39) adults. Senior and student discounts available.

DANCE

The recently opened **Scotiabank Dance Centre** provides a new focus point for the Vancouver dance community. Renovated by Arthur Erickson, the former bank building now offers studio and rehearsal space to more than 30 dance companies and is open to the general public for events, workshops, and classes. 677 Davie St. For more information, call © 604/606-6400 or check www.vkool. com/dancentre.

For fans of modern and original dance, the time to be here is early July, when the **Dancing on the Edge Festival** (© 604/689-0691; www.dancingonthe edge.org) presents 60 to 80 envelope-pushing original pieces over a 10-day period. For more information about other festivals and dance companies around the city, call the **Dance Centre** at © 604/606-6400.

Ballet British Columbia Just over 16 years old, this company strives to present innovative works, such as those by choreographers John Cranko and William Forsythe, along with more traditional fare, including productions by visiting companies, such as the American Ballet Theatre, the Royal Winnipeg Ballet, and the Moscow Classical Ballet. Performances are usually at the Queen

Elizabeth Theatre, at 600 Hamilton St. 1101 W. Broadway. ℂ **604/732-5003**. www. balletbc.com. Tickets C$23–C$47 (US$15–US$30) adults. Senior and student discounts available.

2 Laughter & Music

COMEDY CLUBS

Vancouver TheatreSports League   Part comedy, part theater, and partly a take-no-prisoner's test of an actor's ability to think extemporaneously, Theatre-Sports involves actors taking suggestions from the audience and spinning them into short skits or full plays, often with hilarious results. Since moving to the Arts Club Stage, Vancouver's TheatreSports leaguers have had to reign in their normally raunchy instincts for the more family-friendly audience—except, that is, for Friday and Saturday at 11:45pm, when the Red-Hot Improv show takes the audience into the R-rated realm. New Revue Stage, Granville Island. ℂ **604/687-1644**. www.vtsl.com. Shows Wed–Thurs 7:30pm, Fri–Sat 8, 10, and 11:45pm. Weekends C$15 (US$9.75) adults, C$12(US$7.80) seniors and students; weeknights C$13 (US$8.45) adults, C$9.75 (US$6.30) seniors and students.

Yuk Yuk's Komedy Kabaret   A constantly changing lineup of leading Canadian and American stand-up comics play at Yuk Yuk's. Amateurs take the stage for Tuesday night open mike. In the 200-seat theater, it's hard to get a bad seat. Plaza of Nations, 750 Pacific Blvd. ℂ **604/687-5233**. www.yukyuks.com. Shows Tues–Thurs 9pm, Fri–Sat 9 and 11pm. Cover C$5–C$10 (US$3.25–US$6.50).

STRICTLY LIVE

Besides the listings below, every June the **Vancouver International Jazz Festival** (ℂ **604/872-5200;** www.jazzvancouver.com) takes over many venues and outdoor locations around town. The festival includes a number of free concerts. The **Vancouver Folk Festival** (ℂ **800/986-8363** or 604/602-9798; www.the-festival.bc.ca) takes place outdoors in July on the beach at Jericho Park. The **Coastal Jazz and Blues Society,** the organizer of the Jazz Festival, 316 W. Sixth Ave. (ℂ **604/872-5200;** www.jazzvancouver.com), has information on current and upcoming events throughout the year.

The Commodore Ballroom   Every town should have one, but sadly very few do: a huge old-time dance hall, complete with a suspended hardwood dance floor that bounces gently up and down beneath your nimble or less-than-nimble toes. And though the room and floor date back to the jazz age, the lineup nowadays includes many of the best modern bands coming through town. Sightlines are excellent. Indeed, the Commodore is one of the best places we know to catch a midsize band—and thanks to a recent renovation, the room looks better than ever. 868 Granville St. ℂ **604/739-7469**. www.commodoreballroom.com. Tickets C$5–C$50 (US$3.25–US$32).

The Roxy   Live bands play every day of the week in this casual club, which also features show-off bartenders with Tom Cruise *Cocktail*-style moves. The house bands Joe's Garage and Dr. Strangelove keep the Roxy packed, and on weekends the lines are long. Theme parties (often with vacation giveaways), Extreme Karaoke, Canadian content, '80's only, and other events add to the entertainment. 932 Granville St. ℂ **604/684-7699**. www.roxyvan.com. Cover C$4–C$8 (US$2.60–US$5.20).

The WISE Club *(Finds*   Folk, folk, and more folk. In the far-off reaches of East Vancouver (okay, Commercial Dr. area), the WISE Club was unplugged long before MTV ever thought of reaching for the power cord. Bands are local and international, and the room's a lot of fun—like a church basement or community center—with alcohol. 1882 Adanac St. © 604/254-5858. Cover depends on show; C$15 (US$9.75) for most bands.

Yale Hotel   This century-old tavern on the far south end of Granville is Vancouver's one and only home of the blues. Visiting heavyweights have included Koko Taylor, Stevie Ray Vaughan, Junior Wells, and Jeff Healey. The pictures in the entryway are a who's who of the blues. When outside talent's not available, the Yale makes do with what's homegrown, including Long John Baldry and local bluesman Jim Byrne. There are shows Monday through Saturday at 9:30pm. On Saturday and Sunday, there is an open-stage blues jam from 3 to 7pm.1300 Granville St. © 604/681-9253. www.theyale.ca. Cover Thurs–Sat C$3–C$15 (US$1.95–US$9.75).

ALMOST LIVE

Over the past few years, DJs have slowly replaced bands on the local music scene. Bars that exclusively book live music are nearly nonexistent; many places feature DJs only, and a few offer a mix.

Dine and Dance   For an old-fashioned night of dinner and dancing, try the Pan Pacific's Dine and Dance event. Every Saturday the Café Pacificat features an excellent seafood dinner buffet and tunes from the golden era of Big Band. The floor to ceiling windows provide a spectacular backdrop of ocean and mountains to the dance floor as couples spin and jive to the music, a great way to work up an appetite for seconds at the dessert buffet. Bands start playing at 8:30 pm. 300–999 Canada Place. © 604/662-8111. Seafood buffet C$45 (US$29) per person, 6:30–11:30pm..

Hot Jazz Society *(Finds*   Playing everything from Dixieland to swing, Latin to progressive, this club caters to fans of both jazz and dance. The dance floor is packed no matter who's playing. On Tuesday nights the Wow Big Band plays swing tunes, and on Thursday nights dance lessons are included in the price of admission. Call for the weekly calendar. 2120 Main St. © 604/873-4131. Cover C$4–C$12 (US$2.60–US$7.80) for special acts; otherwise no cover.

The Purple Onion   Some clubs DJ to survive, some have bands; the Onion serves up both, all for the same cover. The Club room is a dance floor pure and simple. At the moment, an '80s dance party is alternating nights with house. Monday is Underground Brit night, with the DJ spinning the tunes of Radiohead and Bowie. Down the hall and round a left turn is the Lounge, where the house band squeals out funky danceable jazz for a slightly older crowd three nights a week. During the Jazz Festival, this place hops. 15 Water St. © 604/602-9442. www.purpleonion.com. Cover C$5–C$8 (US$3.25–US$5.20).

3 Bars, Pubs & Other Watering Holes

Though things are finally improving, when it comes to liquor regulations, our city is still a bizarre and Byzantine place. For historical and political reasons too difficult to get into, bars and pubs are still seen by officialdom as a Bad Thing, so new pub licenses are next to impossible to come by. What are available are restaurant licenses and, as Vancouverites love a drink as much as anyone, there are many restaurants that look suspiciously like pubs. For years, patrons in a restaurant could only drink if they were eating or—here's the Kafkaesque kicker—had the intention of eating. That regulation was just recently taken off the books, but there are still lots of rules about liquor and food sales ratios and other such bureaucratic bunk. So, if a waitress in a place that looks for all the world like a pub asks if you'll be eating, take the appetizer menu, smile, and say "Yes." Occasionally, after a few pints you'll be asked to buy some fries or wings or even a large chocolate chip cookie in order to satisfy the letter of the law. Take it in stride, or take off for a new pub (er, restaurant); just please, don't take offense—remember, it's our bureaucrats, not us.

Generally bars are open until 2am every day but Sunday, when they close at midnight.

BARS MASQUERADING AS RESTAURANTS

The Alibi Room   Higher-end, trendy restaurant/bar brought to you at least in part by *X-Files* Gillian Anderson, the Alibi Room offers upstairs diners modern cuisine and a chance to flip through shelves full of old film scripts. Monthly script readings provide a venue for ever-hopeful wannabe screenwriters (last Sun of the month, call for details). Downstairs there's a DJ and dance floor. Located on the eastern edge of Gastown. 157 Alexander St. ⓒ **604/623-3383**. www.alibiroom.com.

The Atlantic Trap and Gill   Regulars in this sea shanty of a pub know the words to every song sung by the Irish and East Coast bands that appear onstage most every night. Guinness and Keith's are the brews of choice, and don't worry too much about ordering food. As the song goes: *"I'se the bye that orders the pint, I'se the bye that drinks her, keep your menus up in sight, and the government's none the wiser."* Or something like that. 612 Davie St. ⓒ **604/806-6393**.

Cellar Restaurant and Jazz Club   Jazz has a loose definition on the West Coast. In this dark downstairs Kitsilano boîte, the live sounds stretch to include funk, fusion, jazz, and occasionally even hip hop. Local jazz aficionados swear by this place and almost begged us not to list their favorite hangout for fear of crowds. 3611 W. Broadway. ⓒ **604/738-1959**. www.cellarjazz.com. Cover C$3–C$15 (US$1.95–US$9.75)

DV8   Even skate rats and snowboarders have to alight sometime, and this little Davie Street eatery is where the tribe comes to quaff pints and swap a brand of shoptalk incomprehensible to anyone born before Reagan took office. Bask in their youth. Enjoy the beer. DJs and live music weekly. Also check out the gallery space for monthly changing exhibits of innovative artwork. 515 Davie St. ⓒ **604/682-4388**. www.dv8lounge.com.

The Jupiter Cafe *(Finds*)   Located just off busy Davie Street in the West End, the Jupiter Cafe combines a post-apocalyptic industrial look with lounge chic. Black ceilings, exposed pipes, and roof struts mix surprisingly well with chandeliers, velvet curtains, and plush chairs. More important, the Jupiter is open late (till 4am some nights). True, it can be a challenge to flag down your waiter, but that gives you more time to scope out the crowd: gay and straight, funky and preppy, casual and dressed to kill. A huge outdoor patio provides a pleasant refuge from the street, but on colder nights it's the exclusive domain of die-hard smokers. The menu—burgers, pastas, and pizzas—is largely decorative. 1216 Bute St. ⓒ **604/609-6665**.

Monsoon Restaurant   What this slim little bistro in the otherwise sleepy section of Main and Broadway does really well is beer and fusion-induced tapas, accompanied by a buzzing atmosphere generated by interesting and sometimes beautiful people. Kitchen open until 11pm on weekdays, later on weekends. 2526 Main St. © **604/879-4001.**

Naked *(Finds* Naked is located up a marble staircase on the top floor of a former bank building downtown. The room is something out of Arabian Nights; rich warm light from candles and lanterns diffuses through billowing swaths of fabric hanging around low divans, couches, and foot-high tables. It's the perfect place to meet friends for cocktails—early or late—and share some food, served up in the kitchen of the downstairs Ballantynes Restaurant. DJs spin acid and/or jazz and other down-tempo grooves, without drowning out all conversation. Open Fri andSat from 9pm until around 3am. 432 Richards St. © **604/609-2700.**

Urban Well The tanned and taut from nearby Kits Beach drop into the Well as the sun goes down, and often don't emerge until the next day. Monday and Tuesday there's comedy; not too long ago Robin Williams dropped by and told a few jokes. DJs keep things groovy the rest of the week. Regulars line up on the patio counter to people-watch, while inside there's a tiny dance floor for demonstrating once again that you can get down in beach sandals. 1516 Yew St. © **604/ 737-7770.** www.urbanwell.com.

The Whip Gallery Restaurant The Whip's the one place in the city where the wall art and the clientele match. The folks sipping and munching look like they could—and probably did—produce the art hanging on the walls. Young and angry isn't the look here. Whip customers have some success under their belts and are mellowing into their 40s and 50s. Jazz combos sometimes set up in the corner. 209 E. Sixth Ave. © **604/874-4687.**

ACTUAL BARS

The Arts Club Backstage Lounge The Arts Club Lounge has a fabulous location under the bridge by the water on the edge of False Creek. The crowd is a mix of tourists and art school students from neighboring Emily Carr College. Friday and Saturday, there's a live band in the evenings. Most other times, if the sun's out, the waterfront patio is packed. 1585 Johnston St., Granville Island. © **604/ 687-1354.**

The Brickhouse Bar *(Finds* Anthropologists and urban planners often speak of Gentrifiers—that tribe of mostly younger humanity who move into a down-at-heels neighborhood and by their presence and earning ability transform "gritty" into "funky," and then as the even-more-upscale yuppies arrive, into just plain freaking expensive. Main Street is still in the funky stage, and an evening at the Brickhouse is your chance to watch the tribe at play. The warm and bustling bar has pool tables, comfy couches, and wall-length tropical tanks. The tapas menu from the upstairs bistro is superb. 730 Main St. © **604/689-8645.**

The Irish Heather A bright, pleasant Irish pub in the dark heart of Gastown, the Heather boasts numerous nooks and crannies, some of the best beer in town, and a menu that does a lot with the traditional Emerald Isle spud. The clientele is from all over the map, including artsy types from the local gallery scene, urban pioneers from the new Gastown condos, and kids from Kitsilano looking for some safe but authentic grunge. 217 Carrall St. © **604/688-9779.**

The Lennox Pub Part of the renewal of Granville Street, this new pub fills a big void in the neighborhood; it's a comfortable spot for a drink without having to deal with lines or ordering food. The beer list is extensive, containing such hard-to-find favorites as Belgian Kriek, Hoegaarden, and Leffe. There is a great selection of single-malt scotches, too. The pub has a turn-of-the-20th-century feel with lots of brass, wood paneling, and a long bar. The menu covers all the pub-food basics. 800 Granville St. ✆ **604/408-0881.**

SPORTS BARS

The Shark Club Bar and Grill   The city's premier sports bar, the Shark Club—in the Sandman Inn—features lots of wood and brass, TVs everywhere, and on weekend evenings, lots of young and beautiful women who don't look terribly interested in sports. Despite this—or because of it—weekend patrons often score. 180 W. Georgia St. ✆ **604/687-4275.** C$4–C$6 (US$2.60–US$3.90) on Fri and Sat.

BARS WITH VIEWS

If you're in Vancouver, odds are you're here for the views. Everybody else is. The entire population could go make more money living in a dull flat place like Toronto, but we stay because we're addicted to the scenery. As long as that's your raison d'être, you may as well do it in style at one of the places below.

Cardero's Marine Pub   On the water at the foot of Cardero Street, this Coal Harbour pub and restaurant offers an unmatched view of Stanley Park, the harbor, and the North Shore. Overhead heaters take away the chill when nights grow longer. 1583 Coal Harbour Quay. ✆ **604/669-7666.**

Cloud Nine   View junkies will think they're in heaven. As this sleek hotel-top lounge rotates 6° a minute, your vantage point circles from volcanic Mount Baker to the Fraser estuary to English Bay around Stanley Park to the towers of downtown, the harbor, and East Vancouver. And who knew paradise served such good martinis? 1400 Robson St. (42nd floor of the Empire Landmark Hotel). ✆ **604/662-8328.** Cover C$5 (US$3.25) Thurs–Sat.

The Dockside Brewing Company   Located in the Granville Island Hotel, this watering hole offers an unmatched view of False Creek and great brews to boot. The food's also pretty good. Atmosphere is laid-back hip, but don't arrive too late; shortly after the sun goes down the mostly 30-something patrons remember that now they have homes to go to. 1253 Johnson St. ✆ **604/685-7070.**

The Flying Beaver Bar *Finds*   A West Coast tradition: Beaver and Cessna pilots pull up to the floating docks and step ashore to down a few in the float-plane pub. Located beneath the flyway of Vancouver International, the Beaver offers nonflyers great views of incoming jets, along with mountains, bush planes, river craft, and truly fine beer. 4760 Inglis Rd., Richmond. ✆ **604/273-0278.**

LOUNGES

Bacchus Lounge   Step into Bacchus and bask in the low light cast by the fireplace and tealights, its Turneresque wall paintings, and the irony-free evocation of piano bars of yore. Lounge has (or had) staged a hip, self-aware second coming, but for Bacchus it's still and forever the days of Ike and Mamie's first White House term. The piano man in the corner pounds out Neil Diamond, and the crowd of boomers and their children hum along. In the Wedgewood Hotel, 845 Hornby St. ✆ **604/608-5319.** www.wedgewoodhotel.com.

Gerard Lounge   Upscale taken to the edge of hyperbole, the Gerard faithfully re-creates the atmosphere of an English club, including not just the rustic oil paintings and dead animals on the walls, but also the lesser sons of the local (Hollywood) nobility having a bit of a rip with the native girls. The Gerard is also known for its exotic cocktails and Tuesday Chocoholic's Buffet. 845 Burrard St. © 604/682-5511. www.suttonplace.com.

Ginger Sixty-Two. The once trendy, then slummy, and now yuppifying Granville Street has recently seen some great new places open. Ginger Sixty Two is one of the most successful newcomers. A mix of lounge, restaurant, and club, it's the new darling of the fashion industry trendsetters who love to be spotted here. The room is funky warehouse-chic-meets-adult-rec-room, decorated in happening red, orange, and gold tones. Comfy crash pads are strategically placed throughout the room and plenty of pillows help prop up those less-than-young in the joints. 1219 Granville St. © 604/688-5494.

Gotham Cocktail Bar   A clear case of the law of unintended consequences: The lounge adjoining this new steak house was designed for a male clientele— thick leather benches and a room-long mural of sensuous women in Jazz Age clothes. Men certainly did show up—well-off suits in their 30s and 40s particularly—but they were soon a tiny minority midst the great gaggles of women, all seemingly sharing Ally McBeal's age, romantic aspirations, and hem length. 615 Seymour St. © 604/605-8282.

BREW PUBS

Sailor Hägar's Brew Pub   Best brews on offer on the North Shore and only a short uphill stroll from the Seabus terminal. The room itself is nothing to write home about—just a popular local pub, with students, firemen, and off-duty search and rescue personnel munching nachos, savoring Sailor Hägar's brews, and playing billiards. 235 W. First St., North Vancouver. © 604/984-3087.

Steamworks Pub & Brewery   Winding your way from room to room in this Gastown brewery is almost as much fun as drinking. Upstairs, by the doors, it's a London city pub where stockbrokers ogle every new female entrant. Farther in by the staircase, it's a refined old-world club, with wood paneling, leather chairs, and great glass windows overlooking the harbor. Down in the basement it's a Bavarian drinking hall—long lines of benches, set up parallel to the enormous copper kettles, support large groups of people intent on sucking back the brew in depth and at length. Fortunately, the beer's good. Choose from a dozen in-house beers. 375 Water St. © 604/689-2739. www.steamworks.com.

Yaletown Brewing Company   Remember, if it's raining at 11:30am on a Thursday, all pints of brewed-on-the-premises beer are C$3.75 (US$2.40) for the rest of the day. The excellent beer is complemented by an extremely cozy room, a great summertime patio, and a good appetizer menu. Resist the urge to stay for supper, however. Snacks are the true forte. Sunday, all pizzas are half-price. 1111 Mainland St. © 604/681-2739.

4 Dance Clubs

Generally clubs are open until 2am every day but Sunday, when they close at midnight.

Au Bar   An address is unnecessary for Au Bar; the long Seymour Street corral of those not-quite-beautiful-enough for expedited entry immediately gives it away. Inside, this newest of downtown bars is packed with beautiful people milling from bar to dance floor to bar (there are two) and back again. Observing them is like watching a nature documentary on the Discovery Channel. 674 Seymour St. © 604/648-2227. Cover C$5–C$8 (US$3.25–US$5.20).

Crush   Wine snobs will feel right at home at the Crush Champagne Lounge; unique for a dance club, this venue has a professional sommelier on staff to help you make your wine selection. The drink list also includes a large selection of sexy champagne cocktails and bubbly by the glass. The lounge has a small dance floor and the music is mellow R&B, soul, classic lounge, and jazz. Now it may just be the fancy drinks, but this crowd likes to dress up for the occasion; no fleece or Goretex in sight. 1180 Granville St. ℂ **604/684-0355.** Cover C$5 (US$3.25).

Luv-a-fair   Where the pale-skinned go to sweat: '80s early in the week, then Brit pop, alt-rock, house, and industrial mayhem as they head toward the weekend. Girls dance on the catwalk; approachable guys shake their stuff on the floorboards. The pool table and Foosball are behind the chain-link fence in the upstairs mezzanine. 1275 Seymour St. ℂ **604/685-3288.** Cover C$3–C$6 (US$1.95– US$3.90).

The Palladium Club   Dancing is the order of the evening at this industrial space with a dance floor the size of Texas and a ceiling soaring up so high you can hardly make out the duct work. Monday, young 20-somethings dive into the '80s; Tuesday, Wednesday, and Saturday it's house; and Sunday night the Goths come out to play. For the boogie-less, there's pool. 1036 Richards St. ℂ **604/ 687-6794.** Cover varies, up to C$10 (US$6.50).

The Plaza Cabaret   This former movie theater makes a great night club with its high ceilings and spacious dance floor. Lineups start early at this popular club. Wednesday night is Salsa Jam, with free salsa lessons available at 9pm for those who want some help with the moves; Thursday is Breakfast Club '80s night, the bad music that just won't go away. 881 Granville St. ℂ **604/646-0064.** Cover C$6–C$8 (US$3.90–US$5.20).

The Rage   Tune in to radio station Z95 on the weekends after 8pm, and you'll hear exactly what's going on in this airplane hangar of a dance club: Five bars and speaker stacks loud enough to liquefy your brain make this the weekend house party to beat. Plaza of Nations, 750 Pacific Blvd. ℂ **604/685-5585.** Cover Fri C$6 (US$3.90), Sat C$7 (US$4.55).

Richards on Richards   Dick's on Dicks has been packing 'em in longer than you'd care to know. What's the attraction? For years, the club was a notorious pickup spot. Things have mellowed a touch since then, but as the line of limos out front on busy nights attests, Dick's is still hot. Inside there are two floors, four bars, a laser light system, and lots of DJ'ed dance tunes and concerts. Live music acts have included the likes of Junior Wells, James Brown, and, just recently, 2 Live Crew and Jack Soul. 1036 Richards St. ℂ **604/687-6794.** www.richards onrichards.com. Cover Fri–Sat C$8 (US$5.20) for the club; concerts C$10–C$30 (US$6.45–US$20).

Sonar   Loud bass. Flashing lights. The endlessly thrumming rhythms of house. It's a combination that really works best with the aid of psychogenic substances with four-letter initials. Of course, the Sonar crowd of ravers-on-holiday already know that. 66 Water St. ℂ **604/683-6695.** www.sonar.bc.ca. Cover varies, C$5–C$10 (US$3.25–US$6.50) and up to C$20 (US$12.90) for special events.

Voda Nightclub   Voda has quickly made a name for itself, attracting folks young, old, and in-between, with the only real common denominator being cash. Intriguing interior boasts a mix of waterfalls, rocks, and raw concrete—like a beautiful piece of 1950s Modernism. The small dance floor basks in the warm light from the hundreds of candles everywhere. Monday night is old-fashioned

R&B and funk, Tuesday's reserved for bands playing Latin or reggae, Thursday nights are martini elegant and a mix of DJs and bands fill out the rest of the week. In the Westin Grand Hotel, 783 Homer St. ☎ **604/684-3003.** Cover C$5 (US$3.25).

5 Gay & Lesbian Bars

The near complete lack of persecution in laid-back Vancouver has had a curious effect on the city's gay scene—it's so attitude-free it's often hard to tell apart from the straight dance world, male go-go dancers and naked men in showers notwithstanding. Many clubs feature theme nights and dance parties, drag shows are ever popular, and every year in early August, as Gay Pride nears, the scene goes into overdrive. The **Gay Lesbian Transgendered Bisexual Community Centre,** 2–1170 Bute St. (☎ **604/684-5307;** www.lgtbcentrevancouver. com), has information on the current hot spots, but it's probably easier just to pick up a free copy of *Xtra West!,* available in most downtown cafes.

The Dufferin Pub   Buff at the Duff is a city institution; other drag shows might be raunchier, but none have quite the style. Shows are Monday through Thursday. Friday and Sunday the go-go boys strut their stuff (and yes, they do take it all off). The rest of the time—and before, during, and after many of the shows—the DJs keep you grooving. 900 Seymour St. ☎ **604/683-4251.** www.dufferin hotel.com.

The Fountain Head Pub   Where do you go when you've run rings round the bathhouse and the disco ball no longer beckons? Reflecting the graying and— gasp!—mellowing of Vancouver's boomer-age gay crowd, the hottest new hang-out for homos is, well, a pub, the Fountain Head, located in the heart of the city's gay ghetto on Davie Street. Open a little over a year, the Fountain Head offers excellent microbrewed draught, good pub munchies, and a pleasant humming atmosphere till the morning's wee hours. Limited cruising has been known to happen, but more often customers come with friends and have things other than intimacy in mind. Indeed, most of the bragging at the 'Head involves the size of people's portfolios. 1025 Davie St. ☎ **604/687-2222.**

Global Beat   Billed as a "restaurant lounge," this casual pub next door to the Odyssey has a relaxed atmosphere. There's no heavy cruising, but there are billiards tables, a great pub menu, inexpensive food and drinks, and the occasional surprised cruise ship passenger. 1249 Howe St. ☎ **604/689-2444.**

Heritage House Hotel   This aging beauty of a downtown hotel plays host to three separate bars and lounges with a largely gay clientele. Downstairs, the Lotus Lounge is one of the hottest house music venues in town, particularly on Straight Up Fridays when the all female DJ team spins sexy funky house. On Saturdays clubbers gather for the deep underground house also referred to as Westcoast house. On the main floor, the Milk Lounge has a popular gay following, men flock to Friday's Cream night and on Saturdays it's Ladies Only. The third venue also on the main floor is Honey, a comfortable lounge where a mixed crowd gathers for cocktails or beers. On most nights the DJs keep the music on a mellow, conversational level. However, on Saturdays decibels go up significantly when the Queen Bee review, a New York–style cabaret drag show fills the house. 455 Abbott St. ☎ **604/685-7777.** Cover Milk and Lotus C$5–C$12 (US$3.25–US$7.80) some nights, Honey only on Sat C$7 (US$4.55).

Numbers Cabaret   A multilevel dance club and bar, Numbers has been around for 20 years and hasn't changed a bit. Extroverts hog the dance floor while admirers look on from the bar above. On the second floor, carpets, wood paneling, pool tables, darts, and a lower volume of music give it a neighborhood pub feel. 1042 Davie St. © 604/685-4077. Cover Fri–Sat C$3 (US$1.95).

The Odyssey If this is what lay over the rainbow, I don't think anyone ever told Dorothy. Odyssey is the hottest and hippest gay/mixed dance bar in town (alley entrance is for men; women go in by the front door). The medium-size dance space is packed. Up above, a mirrored catwalk is reserved for those who can keep the beat. Shows vary depending on the night. Monday it's Sissy Boy, Saturday it's Fallen Angel go-go dancers, and Sunday it's the Feather Boa drag show. And on Thursday, it's "Shower Power"—yes, that is a pair of naked men in the shower above the dance floor. No, you're not in Kansas anymore. 1251 Howe St. © 604/689-5256. www.theodysseynightclub.com. Cover C$3–C$5 (US$1.95–US$3.25). Wed no cover.

6 Other Diversions

CINEMA
Thanks to the number of resident moviemakers (both studio and independent), Vancouver is becoming quite a film town. First-run theaters show the same Hollywood fare seen everywhere in the world (on Tues at a discount rate), but for those with something more adventurous in mind, there are lots of options.

Attendance at the **Vancouver International Film Festival** (© 604/685-0260; www.viff.org) reaches over 100,000, not including the stars and celebrities who regularly drop in. At this highly respected October event, over 250 new works are shown, representing filmmakers from 40 countries. Asian films are particularly well represented.

ART HOUSE & REPERTORY THEATERS
Since 1972, the **Pacific Cinematheque,** 1131 Howe St. (© 604/688-FILM (3456); www.cinematheque.bc.ca), has featured classic and contemporary films from around the world. Screenings are organized into themes, such as "Jean Luc Godard's Early Efforts," film noir, or the "Hong Kong Action Flick: A Retrospective." Schedules are available in hipper cafes, record shops, and video stores around town. Admission is C$7 (US$4.55) for adults, C$5 (US$3.25) for seniors and students; double features cost C$1 (US65¢) extra. Annual membership, required to purchase tickets, is C$5 (US$3.25).

The alternative theater, the **Blinding Light!,** 36 Powell St. (© 604/878-3366; www.blindinglight.com), is the Vancouver venue for all that is offbeat and experimental in film. Screenings to date have included new Vancouver shorts, bring-your-own-movie nights, experimental animation, and found-in-the-attic home movies and industrial films from the '50s and '60s. Admission is C$5 (US$3.25), with a C$3 (US$1.95) annual membership fee. There's also a yearly Vancouver Underground Film Festival.

SPECIALTY THEATERS
At the **CN IMAX,** Canada Place (© 604/682-IMAX), a gargantuan screen features large-format flicks about large and none-too-bright denizens of the animal kingdom (sharks, wolves, elephants, X-treme athletes). A similar large screen at the **Alcan Omnimax,** Science World (© 604/443-7440), features flicks about empty, wide-open spaces: Antarctica, Alaska, Arkansas, and the like.

Way off in the strip-mall lands of farthest Kingsway stands the **Raja,** 3215 Kingsway (© 604/436-1545), a modest single-screen movie house dedicated to bringing in the best flicks from Bombay, the world's moviemaking capital. For those unfamiliar with the Indian masala genre, expect raw violence mixed with big production numbers—think *Mary Poppins* does *Die Hard.* Sometimes there are English subtitles, though strictly speaking they're not necessary. If Kingsway is too far off, there's another Raja on 639 Commercial Dr. (© **604/253-0402**).

CASINOS

Well, it's not Vegas, and there's no alcohol and no floor shows, but on the other hand, you haven't really lived till you've sat down for some serious gambling with a room full of Far Eastern big shots trying to re-create the huge night they had in Happy Valley or Macau. Betting limits are in force, so you can't lose too much, and half of the proceeds go to charity, so it's all for a good cause.

To try your hand at pai gow poker, blackjack, roulette, sic bo, or mini bac, check out the **Gateway Casino,** 611 Main St. (3rd floor), in the heart of Chinatown (© **604/688-9412**). Open from 10am to 4am daily, the maximum bet is C$500 (US$325). Another place to let it ride is the **Great Canadian Casino Downtown,** 1133 W. Hastings St. (© **604/682-8415**), open daily from noon to 2am. For blackjack, roulette, pai gow poker, and mini-baccarat you can also try the **Royal Diamond Casino,** 750 Pacific Blvd., in the Plaza of Nations (© **604/899-1061;** www.rdc.com). Here you can play high roller from noon to 4am daily.

10

Getting to Know Victoria

I was in the Bengal Lounge, sinking in a leather fantasy of an armchair, when I first began to understand something of Victoria. Sipping on a cold drink, looking smugly at the pukka fans wafting back and forth on the ceiling and the light from the roaring fire ricocheting off the glass eyeballs of the Bengal tiger mounted above the mantelpiece, I found it easy for a moment to imagine I was Somerset Maugham—or better still, Stamford Raffles—that the year was 1845, and that The Fairmont Empress was a grand colonial hotel, an outpost of Empire on the edge of a barbarous wasteland.

. . . Except that the drink I was sipping was a fluorescent blue martini, the music wafting from an unseen sound system was 1960s jazz, and the coats piled up on a nearby armchair were made not of wool or oilskin but of Gore-Tex and fleece. These small tokens of reality aside, however, it was a seductive and compelling vision.

I asked my drinking companion—the editor of the local alternative paper—just who first came up with Victoria's "little patch of Empire" shtick.

"For a while at the turn of the century people here actually bought into it," he said. "They'd come out from England and, whatever their politics back home, here they'd morph into super-patriots, singing 'God Save the Queen' at the drop of a hat."

World War I largely put an end to that, he continued, but then in the 1920s, Victoria was hit by another shock—the population began to drop as business shifted over to Vancouver. Local merchants panicked. And it was then that San Francisco–born George Warren of the Victoria Publicity Bureau put forward his proposal: Sell the Olde England angle.

Warren had never been to England and had no idea what it looked like. But to him, Victoria seemed English. To the city's merchants, Warren's scheme seemed like just the thing. And so it was. For three-plus generations it served the city well. While other places were leveling their downtowns in the name of progress, Victoria nurtured and preserved its heritage buildings, adding gardens and lavish city parks. Soon enough it possessed that rarest of commodities for a North American city, a gorgeous, walkable 19th-century city center.

True, the "this is Sussex" paradigm meant ignoring some details. Whales sometimes swam into the Inner Harbour. Snowcapped mountain peaks loomed just across the water from Ross Bay. Trees in the surrounding forests towered far higher than Big Ben.

Only in the past half decade, in fact, has Victoria finally begun to make use of its stunning physical surroundings. Whale-watching is now a major industry. Kayak tours are becoming ever more popular. Mountain bikes have taken to competing for road space with the bright-red double-decker buses. Still, ecotourism is in its infancy. Many of the tours and expeditions on offer have never been done before. Guides regard the territory with the same fresh eye as visitors.

But if making peace with where you are has made for better business, it has also brought its share of challenges, at least one of them existential. If Victoria is no longer a little bit o' Blimey, just what exactly is it? The best answer, surprisingly enough, comes from another journalist, the poet of the Empire himself, Rudyard Kipling.

"To realize Victoria," Kipling wrote after visiting the city around 1908, "you must take all that the eye admires most in Bournemouth, Torquay, the Isle of Wight, the Happy Valley at Hong Kong, the Doon, Sorrento and Camps Bay; add reminisces of the Thousand Islands, and arrange the whole round the Bay of Naples, with some Himalayas in the background. Real estate agents recommend it as a little piece of England—the Island on which it stands is about the size of Great Britain—but no England is set in any such seas or so fairly charged with the mystery of the large ocean beyond. The high, still twilights along the beaches are out of the old East, just under the curve of the world."

1 Orientation

Victoria is on the southeastern tip of Vancouver Island, across the Strait of Juan de Fuca from Washington State's snowcapped Olympic peninsula. It's 72km (45 miles) south of the 49th Parallel, the border between most of Canada and the contiguous United States.

Once you've arrived, head for the Inner Harbour. Lovingly restored vintage sailboats are berthed side by side with modern watercraft in the snug harbor, right in the heart of the city. A waterfront causeway runs along it in front of The Fairmont Empress hotel, one of Victoria's most picturesque spots. Just a few blocks away are the Royal British Columbia Museum, Undersea World, the Crystal Gardens, Thunderbird Park's totem poles, downtown and Old Town's shopping streets and restaurants, and Beacon Hill Park.

ARRIVING

BY PLANE   The **Victoria International Airport** is near the Sidney ferry terminal, 26km (16 miles) north of Victoria off the Patricia Bay Highway (Highway 17). For airport information, call ✆ **250/953-7500.** Highway 17 heads south to Victoria, becoming Douglas Street as you enter downtown.

The **airport bus service,** operated by AKAL Airport (✆ **250/386-2525**), makes the trip into town in about half an hour. Buses leave every 30 minutes daily from 4:30am to midnight; the fare is C$13 (US$8.45) one-way or C$23 (US$15) round-trip. Drop-offs are made at most hotels, and pickups can be arranged as well. A limited number of hotel courtesy buses also serve the airport. A cab ride into downtown Victoria costs about C$40 (US$26) plus tip. **Empress Cabs** and **Blue Bird Cabs** (see "Getting Around," below) make airport runs.

Several **car-rental firms** have desks at the airport. Though all accept people without reservations, during peak travel times they may sell out a few days in advance. They include **Avis** (✆ **250/656-6033**), **Hertz** (✆ **250/656-2312**), and **National** (✆ **250/656-2541**).

BY TRAIN, BUS & FERRY   VIA Rail trains arrive at Victoria's **E&N Station,** 450 Pandora Ave., near the Johnson Street Bridge (✆ **800/561-8630** in Canada).

The **Victoria Bus Depot** is at 700 Douglas St., behind The Fairmont Empress hotel. **Pacific Coach Lines** (✆ **250/385-4411**) offers daily service to and from Vancouver. **Laidlaw Coach Lines** (© 250/385-4411) has daily scheduled runs to Nanaimo, Port Alberni, Campbell River, and Port Hardy.

For information on arriving by **ferry,** see "Getting to Victoria," in chapter 2.

VISITOR INFORMATION
TOURIST OFFICES & MAGAZINES   On the Inner Harbour's wharf, across from The Fairmont Empress hotel, is the **Tourism Victoria Visitor Info Centre,** 812 Wharf St. (© **250/953-2033;** www.tourismvictoria.com). You can get there on bus no. 1, 27, or 28 to Douglas and Courtney streets. If you didn't reserve a room before you arrived, you can go to this office or call its **reservations hot line** (© **800/663-3883** or 250/953-2033) for last-minute bookings at hotels, inns, and B&Bs. The staff will help you locate discounts. The center is open daily: September 1 to June 15 9am to 5pm and June 16 to August 31 8:30am to 7:30pm.

If you want to explore the rest of 456km (285-mile) long Vancouver Island, contact the **Tourism Association of Vancouver Island,** Suite 203, 335 Wesley St., Nanaimo, B.C. V9R 2T5 (© **250/754-3500;** www.islands.bc.ca).

For details on the after-dark scene, pick up a copy of *Monday* magazine (© **250/382-6188;** www.mondaymag.com/monday/), available free in cafes and record shops around the city. *Monday* not only is an excellent guide to Victoria's nightlife but also has driven at least one mayor from office with its award-winning muckraking journalism. The online version has detailed entertainment listings.

WEBSITES   See "The Best Websites for Vancouver & Victoria," in chapter 1.

CITY LAYOUT
Victoria was born at the edge of the Inner Harbour in the 1840s and grew outward from there. The areas of most interest to visitors, including the **downtown** and **Old Town,** lie along the eastern edge of the **Inner Harbour.** (North of the Johnson Street Bridge is the **Upper Harbour,** which is almost entirely industrial.) A little farther east, the **Ross Bay** and **Oak Bay** residential areas around Dallas Road and Beach Drive reach the beaches along the open waters of the Strait of Juan de Fuca.

Victoria's central landmark is **The Fairmont Empress** hotel on Government Street, right across from the Inner Harbour wharf. If you turn your back to the hotel, the downtown and Old Town are on your right, while the provincial **Legislative Buildings** and the **Royal BC Museum** are on your immediate left. Next to them is the dock for the **Seattle–Port Angeles ferries** and beyond that the residential community of **James Bay.**

MAIN ARTERIES & STREETS   Three main **north–south arteries** intersect just about every destination you may want to reach in Victoria.

Government Street goes through Victoria's main downtown shopping-and-dining district. Wharf Street, edging the harbor, merges with Government Street at The Fairmont Empress hotel. **Douglas Street,** running parallel to Government Street, is the main business thoroughfare as well as the road to Nanaimo and the rest of the island. It's also Trans-Canada Highway 1. The "Mile 0" marker sits at the corner of Douglas and Dallas Road. Also running parallel to Government and Douglas streets is **Blanshard Street** (Hwy. 17), the route to the Saanich Peninsula, including the Sidney–Vancouver ferry terminal, and Butchart Gardens.

Important **east–west streets** include the following: **Johnson Street** lies at the northern end of downtown and the Old Town, where the small E&N Station sits opposite Swans Hotel at the corner of Wharf Street. The Johnson Street Bridge is the demarcation line between the Upper Harbour and the Inner Harbour. **Belleville Street** is the Inner Harbour's southern edge. The Legislative Buildings and the ferry terminal are here. Belleville Street loops around westward toward Victoria Harbour before heading south, becoming Dallas Road. **Dallas Road** follows the water's edge past residential areas and beaches before it winds northward up to Oak Bay.

FINDING AN ADDRESS   Victoria addresses are written like those in Vancouver: The suite or room number precedes the building number. For instance, 100–1250 Government St. refers to suite 100 at 1250 Government St.

Victoria's streets are numbered from the city's southwest corner and increase in increments of 100 per block as you go north and east. (1000 Douglas St., for example, is 2 blocks north of 800 Douglas St.). Fort Street starts its 500 block at Wharf Street.

STREET MAPS   Detailed street maps are available free at the **Tourism Victoria Visitor Info Centre** (see "Visitor Information," above). The best map of the surrounding area is the *B.C. Provincial Parks* map of Vancouver Island, also available at the Info Centre.

NEIGHBORHOODS IN BRIEF

Downtown & Old Town These areas have been the city's social and commercial focal points since the mid-1800s, when settlers first arrived by ship. This is also the area of the city most popular with visitors, filled with shops, museums, heritage buildings, and lots of restaurants. The area reflects its fascinating Barbary Coast–style history, which includes rum smuggling, opium manufacturing, gold prospecting, whaling, fur trading, and shipping.

The two neighborhoods are usually listed together because it's difficult to say where one leaves off and the other begins. The Old Town consists of the pre-1900 commercial sections of the city that grew up around the original Fort Victoria at View and Government streets. Roughly speaking, it extends from Fort Street north to Pandora and from Wharf Street east to Douglas. Downtown is everything outside of that, from the Inner Harbour to Quadra Street in the east and from Belleville Street in the south up to Herald Street at the northern edge of downtown.

Chinatown Victoria's Chinatown is tiny—2 square blocks—but venerable. In fact, it's the oldest Chinese community in North America. Its many interesting historic sites include Fan Tan Alley, Canada's narrowest commercial street, where legal opium manufacturing took place in the hidden courtyard buildings flanking the 1.2m (4-ft.) wide way. (If you saw the movie *Bird on a Wire,* you may remember Mel Gibson riding through Fan Tan Alley in a great motorcycle chase scene.)

James Bay, Ross Bay & Oak Bay When Victoria was a busy port and trading post, the local aristocracy—merchant princes and their merchant princess daughters, for the most part—would retire to homes in these neighborhoods to escape the hustle-bustle in the city center below. Today they remain beautiful residential communities. Houses perch on hills overlooking the straits or nestle amid lushly landscaped gardens. Golf courses, marinas, and

a few cozy inns edge the waters, where you can stroll the beaches or go for a dip if you don't mind a slight chill.

2 Getting Around

Strolling along the Inner Harbour's pedestrian walkways and streets is very pleasant. The terrain is predominantly flat, and, with few exceptions, Victoria's points of interest are accessible in less than 30 minutes on foot.

BY PUBLIC TRANSPORTATION

BY BUS   The **Victoria Regional Transit System (BC Transit),** 520 Gorge Rd. (℃ **250/382-6161;** www.bctransit.com), operates 40 bus routes through greater Victoria as well as the nearby towns of Sooke and Sidney. You can take the bus to Butchart Gardens and the Vancouver ferry terminal at Sidney. Regular service on the main routes runs daily 6am to just past midnight.

Schedules and routes are available at the Tourism Victoria Visitor Info Centre (see "Visitor Information," above), where you can pick up a copy of the *Victoria Rider's Guide* or *Discover Vancouver on Transit: Including Victoria.* Popular Victoria bus routes include **no. 2** (Oak Bay), **no. 5** (downtown, James Bay, Beacon Hill Park), **no. 14** (Victoria Art Gallery, Craigdarroch Castle, University of Victoria), **no. 61** (Sooke), **no. 70** (Sidney, Swartz Bay), and **no. 75** (Butchart Gardens).

Fares are calculated on a per-zone basis. One-way single-zone fares are C$1.75 (US$1.15) for adults and C$1.10 (US75¢) for seniors and children 5 to 13; two zones cost C$2.50 (US$1.65) and C$1.75 (US$1.15), respectively. Transfers are good for travel in one direction only, with no stopovers. A **Day-Pass,** C$5.50 (US$3.60) for adults and C$4 (US$2.60) for seniors and children 5 to 13, covers unlimited travel throughout the day. You can buy passes at the Tourism Victoria Visitor Info Centre (see "Visitor Information," above), convenience stores, and ticket outlets throughout Victoria displaying the "Fare-Dealer" symbol.

BY FERRY   Crossing the Inner, Upper, and Victoria Harbours by one of the blue 12-passenger **Victoria Harbour Ferries** (℃ **250/708-0201**) is cheap and fun. Identical to Vancouver's False Creek Ferries, these boats have big windows all the way around and look like they're straight out of a cartoon. Fortunately, the harbor is smooth sailing. May through September, the ferries to The Fairmont Empress hotel, Coast Harbourside Hotel, and Ocean Pointe Resort hotel run about every 15 minutes daily 9am to 9pm. In March, April, and October, ferry service runs daily 11am to 5pm. November through February, the ferries run only on sunny weekends 11am to 5pm. The cost per hop is C$3 (US$1.95) for adults and C$1.50 (US$1) for children.

Instead of just taking the ferry for a short hop across, try the 45-minute **Harbour tour** for C$12 (US$7.80) adults and C$6 (US$3.90) children, or the

---

The Ferry Ballet

Starting at 9:45am every Sunday during summer, the ferries gather in front of The Fairmont Empress to perform a **ferry "ballet"**—it looks much like the hippo dance in Disney's *Fantasia.*

50-minute **Gorge tour** for C$14 (US$9.10) adults, C$7 (US$4.55) children, and C$12 (US$7.80) seniors.

BY CAR

If you're planning out-of-town activities, you can rent a car in town or bring your own. If you have a city-bound agenda, make sure your hotel has parking. Keep a few things in mind: Traffic is heavy and parking is scarce. Gas is sold by the liter, averaging around C70¢ (US45¢). That may seem inexpensive until you consider that a gallon of gas costs about C$2.80 (US$1.85). In addition, speeds and distances are posted in kilometers. You can easily explore the downtown area by foot.

RENTALS   Car-rental agencies in Victoria include the following: **Avis,** 1001 Douglas St. (✆ **800/879-2847** or 250/386-8468; bus no. 5 to Broughton St.); **Budget,** 757 Douglas St. (✆ **800/268-8900** or 250/953-5300); **Hertz,** 655 Douglas St., in the Queen Victoria Inn (✆ **800/263-0600** or 250/360-2822); and **National,** 767 Douglas St. (✆ **800/227-7368** or 250/386-1312). These three can be reached on the no. 5 bus to the Convention Centre. Rates run about C$32 to C$48 (US$21–US$31) per day for a compact to midsize vehicle.

PARKING   Metered **street parking** is hard to come by in the downtown area, and rules are strictly enforced. Unmetered parking on side streets is rare. All major downtown hotels have guest parking, with rates from free to C$20 (US$13) per day. There are parking lots at **View Street** between Douglas and Blanshard streets, **Johnson Street** off Blanshard Street, **Yates Street** north of Bastion Square, and **the Bay** on Fisgard at Blanshard Street.

DRIVING RULES   Canadian driving rules are similar to regulations in the United States. Seat belts must be worn, children under 5 must be in child restraints, and motorcyclists must wear helmets. It's legal to turn right on a red light after you've come to a full stop. Unlike the U.S., daytime headlights are mandatory. Some of the best places on Vancouver Island can be reached only via gravel logging roads, on which logging trucks have absolute right-of-way. If you're on a logging road and see a logging truck coming from either direction, pull over to the side of the road and stop to let it pass.

AUTO CLUB   Members of the **American Automobile Association (AAA)** can get emergency assistance from the **British Columbia Automobile Association (BCAA)** (✆ **800/222-4357**).

BY BIKE

Biking is the easiest way to get around the downtown and beach areas. There are bike lanes throughout the city and paved paths along parks and beaches. Helmets are mandatory, and riding on sidewalks is illegal, except where bike paths are indicated. You can rent bikes starting at C$6 (US$3.90) per hour and C$20 (US$13) per day (lock and helmet included) from **Cycle BC,** 747 Douglas St. (✆ **250/380-3453**).

BY TAXI

Within the downtown area, you can expect to travel for less than C$6 (US$3.90), plus tip. It's best to call for a cab; drivers don't always stop on city streets for flag-downs, especially when it's raining. Call for a pickup from **Empress Cabs** (✆ **250/381-2222**) or **Blue Bird Cabs** (✆ **250/382-4235**).

 *FAST FACTS:* **Victoria**

American Express The office is at 1213 Douglas St. (☎ **250/385-8731**) and is open Monday through Friday 8:30am to 5pm and Saturday 10am to 4pm. Get there on bus no. 5 to Yates Street.

Area Code The telephone area code for all of Vancouver Island, including Victoria and most of British Columbia, is **250.** For the greater Vancouver area, including Squamish and Whistler, it's **604.**

Business Hours Victoria **banks** are open Monday through Thursday 10am to 3pm and Friday 10am to 6pm. **Stores** are generally open Monday through Saturday 10am to 6pm. Some establishments are open later, as well as on Sundays, in summer. Last call at the city's **bars** and **cocktail lounges** is 2am.

Consulates See "Fast Facts: Vancouver" in chapter 3.

Currency Exchange The best exchange rates in town can be found at banks and by using ATMs. **Royal Bank,** 1079 Douglas St. at Fort Street, is in the heart of downtown. Take bus no. 5 to Fort Street.

Dentist Most major hotels have a dentist on call. **Cresta Dental Centre,** 3170 Tillicum Rd., at Burnside Street in the Tillicum Mall (☎ **250/384-7711;** bus no. 10), is open Monday through Friday 8am to 9pm, Saturday 9am to 5pm, and Sunday 11am to 5pm.

Doctor Hotels usually have doctors on call. The **Tillicum Mall Medical Clinic,** 3170 Tillicum at Burnside Street (☎ **250/381-8112;** bus no. 10 to Tillicum Mall), accepts walk-in patients daily 9am to 9pm.

Electricity The same 110 volts AC (60 cycles) as in the United States.

Emergencies Dial ☎ **911** for fire, police, ambulance, and poison control.

Hospitals Local hospitals include the **Royal Jubilee Hospital,** 1900 Fort St. (☎ **250/370-8000;** emergency 250/370-8212) and the **Victoria General Hospital,** 1 Hospital Way (☎ **250/727-4212;** emergency 250/727-4181). You can get to both hospitals on bus no. 14.

Hot Lines Emergency numbers include: **Royal Canadian Mounted Police** (☎ 250/380-6261), **Emotional Crisis Centre** (☎ 250/386-6323), **Sexual Assault Centre** (☎ 250/383-3232), **Poison Control Centre** (☎ 800/567-8911), **Help Line for Children** (dial ☎ 0 and ask for Zenith 1234).

Internet Access Try the Cafecentral @Cyberstation, 1113 Blanshard St. (☎ **250/386-4657**). Most hotels also have Internet stations as does the Victoria Public Library; see below.

Library The **Greater Victoria Public Library** (☎ **250/382-7241;** bus no. 5 to Broughton St.) is at 735 Broughton St., near the corner of Fort and Douglas streets.

Luggage Storage/Lockers Most hotels will store bags for guests who are about to check in or who have just checked out. Otherwise, coin lockers for C$1 (US65¢) are available outside the bus station (behind The Fairmont Empress hotel). Take bus no. 5 to the Convention Centre.

Newspapers The morning *Times Colonist* comes out daily. The weekly entertainment paper *Monday* magazine comes out, strangely enough, on Thursday.

Pharmacies **Shopper's Drug Mart,** 1222 Douglas St. (© **250/381-4321;** bus no. 5 to View St.), is open Monday through Friday 7am to 8pm, Saturday 9am to 7pm, and Sunday 9am to 6pm. **McGill and Orme,** 649 Fort St., at the corner of Broad Street (© **250/384-1195;** bus no. 5 to Fort St.), is open Monday through Saturday 9am to 6pm, and Sunday noon to 4pm.

Police Dial © **911.** The **Victoria City Police** can also be reached by calling © **250/995-7654.**

Post Office The **main post office** is at 714 Yates St. (© **250/953-1352**), bus no. 5 to Yates Street. There are also postal outlets in **Shopper's Drug Mart** (see "Pharmacies," above) and in other stores displaying the CANADA POST postal outlet sign. Supermarkets and many souvenir and gift shops also sell stamps.

Safety Crime rates are quite low in Victoria, but transients panhandle throughout the downtown and Old Town areas. The most common crimes are property crimes, which are usually preventable with a few extra common-sense precautions.

Weather Call © **250/656-3978** for weather updates.

11

Where to Stay in Victoria

Victoria has been welcoming visitors for well-nigh 100 years, so it knows how to do it with style. You'll find a wide choice of fine accommodations in all price ranges, most in the Old Town or around the Inner Harbour. All are in or within easy walking distance of the downtown core. A half-hour drive east or west takes you to Sooke and Malahat—wonderful hideaways offering more peace and solitude.

Remember that reservations are absolutely essential in Victoria May through September. If you arrive without a reservation and have trouble finding a room, **Tourism Victoria** (② **800/663-3883** or 250/382-1131) can make reservations for you at hotels, inns, and B&Bs. It deals only with establishments that pay a fee to list with them; fortunately most do.

Quoted prices don't include the 10% provincial accommodations tax or the 7% goods-and-services tax (GST). Non-Canadians can get a GST rebate on short-stay accommodations by filling out the Tax Refund Application (see "Taxes" under "Fast Facts: Vancouver" in chapter 3).

1 The Inner Harbour & Nearby

VERY EXPENSIVE

Delta Victoria Ocean Pointe Resort and Spa ★★ On the Inner Harbour's north shore, the luxurious modern "OPR" (as the staff call it) offers commanding views of downtown, the legislature, and The Fairmont Empress. Other great pluses are the things you expect in a top property—fancy giveaway stuff in the bathrooms, fluffy robes, and large beds with fine linen. In a city with a fetish for floral prints, the OPR's decor is refreshingly modern—polished woods and solid muted colors and not a lot of bric-a-brac. The rooms facing the Outer Harbour have fabulously large floor-to-ceiling bay windows. However, the prime view rooms face the Inner Harbour, looking out over Victoria's spectacular waterfront. In the grand lobby, that floor-to-ceiling theme is repeated with windows two stories tall, facing downtown. The Spa is one of the best in Victoria and accommodation/spa packages are available; check the website for specials.

45 Songhees Rd., Victoria, B.C. V9A 6T3. ② **800/268-1133** or 250/360-2999. Fax 250/360-1041. www.delta hotels.com. 250 units. Apr 16–May 31 C$322–C$574 (US$209–US$370) double. June 1–Oct 11 C$448–C$736 (US$289–US$475) double. Oct 12–Dec 31 C$340–C$448 (US$219–US$289) double. Jan 1–Apr 15 C$295–C$403 (US$190–US$260) double. Promotional rates available all seasons. Children under 17 stay free in parents' room. Wheelchair-accessible units available. AE, DC, MC, V. Underground valet parking C$12 (US$7.75). Bus: 24 to Colville. Pets under 30 lb. accepted. **Amenities:** 2 restaurants; bar; indoor pool; 2 lighted tennis courts; health club; spa; Jacuzzi; sauna; watersports rental; bike rental; concierge; 24-hr. business center; shopping arcade; 24-hr. room service; in-room massage; babysitting; same-day dry cleaning; non-smoking rooms; executive level rooms. *In room:* A/C, TV/VCR w/pay movies, fax, dataport, minibar, coffeemaker, hair dryer, iron, safe.

The Fairmont Empress ★★ Francis Rattenbury's 1908 harborside creation is such a joy to look at, The Fairmont Empress should probably charge for the view. When you see it, you'll know immediately that you absolutely *have* to stay there. However, here's one thing you should know before throwing down the credit card: With 90 different configurations, not all rooms are created equal. Some of the deluxe rooms and all the Entree Gold rooms are a dream (or a Merchant/Ivory set), with large beds, wide windows, high ceilings, and abundant natural light. The Entree Gold rooms also include private check-in, a concierge, breakfast in the private lounge, and extras like CD players and TVs in the bathrooms. Many of the other rooms—despite a C$4 million renovation (US$2.6 million) in 1996—are built to the "cozy" standards of 1908. And the fact that they come with down duvets, ceiling fans, and minibars doesn't make them any bigger. If you can afford an Entree Gold or a deluxe room—go for it. If you can't, it may be better to admire The Fairmont Empress from afar or confine your relationship to afternoon visits.

721 Government St., Victoria, B.C. V8W 1W5. (**C**) **800/441-1414** or 250/384-8111. Fax 250/381-4334. www. fairmont.com. 476 units. June–Sept C$209–C$479 (US$135–US$309 double). Oct–May C$159–C$279 (US$103–US$180) double. Year-round C$425–C$1,500 (US$274–US$968) suite. Wheelchair-accessible units available. AE, DC, DISC, MC, V. Underground valet parking C$19 (US$12). Bus: 5. Small pets allowed for C$25 (US$16). **Amenities:** 2 restaurants; bar; afternoon tea; indoor pool; health club; Jacuzzi; sauna; concierge; car rental; business center; shopping arcade; 24-hr. room service; in-room massage; babysitting; laundry service; same-day dry cleaning service; nonsmoking rooms; executive level rooms. *In room:* TV w/pay movies, dataport, minibar, hair dryer, iron.

EXPENSIVE

Andersen House Bed & Breakfast ★★   The art and furnishings in Andersen House are drawn from the whole of the old British Empire and a good section of the modern world beyond. The 1891 house has the high ceilings, stained-glass windows, and ornate fireplaces typical of the Queen Anne style, but the art and decorations are far more eclectic: hand-knotted Persian rugs, raku sculptures, large cubist-inspired oils, and carved-wood African masks. Each room has a unique style: The sun-drenched Casablanca room on the top floor, for example, boasts Persian rugs, a four-poster queen bed, and a lovely boxed window seat. All rooms have private entrances and come with books and CD players and CDs; all feature soaker tubs or two-person Jacuzzis. The Andersens have also recently opened Baybreeze Manor ((**C**) **250/721-3930;** www.bay breezemanor.com), a restored 1885 farmhouse that's a 15-minute drive from

---

 The Best Bed & Breakfast Registries

If you prefer to stay at a B&B other than those listed in this chapter, the following agencies specialize in matching guests to the B&Bs that best suit their needs (see chapter 4 for more information):

- **Born Free Bed & Breakfast of BC,** 4390 Frances St., Burnaby, B.C. V5C 2R3 ((**C**) **800/488-1941** in the U.S., or 604/298-8815; www.vancouver bandb.bc.ca).
- **Canada-West Accommodations Bed & Breakfast Registry,** P.O. Box 86607, North Vancouver, B.C. V7L 4L2 ((**C**) **800/561-3223** or 604/990-6730; www.b-b.com).
- **Town and Country Bed & Breakfast,** P.O. Box 74542, 2803 W. Fourth Ave., Vancouver, B.C. V6K IK2 ((**C**) and fax **604/731-5942;** www.town andcountrybedandbreakfast.com.)

Victoria Accommodations

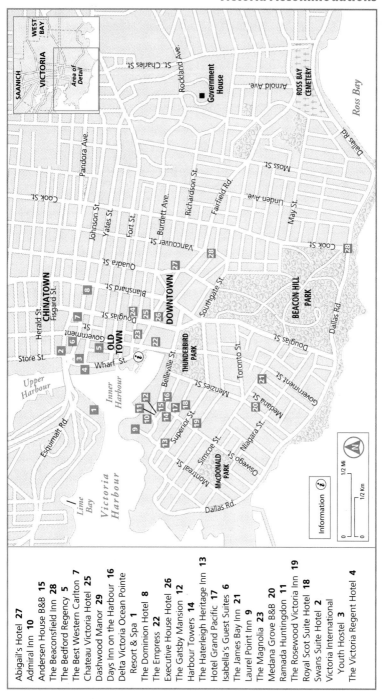

Abigail's Hotel **27**
Admiral Inn **10**
Andersen House B&B **15**
The Beaconsfield Inn **28**
The Bedford Regency **5**
The Best Western Carlton **7**
Chateau Victoria Hotel **25**
Dashwood Manor **29**
Days Inn on the Harbour **16**
Delta Victoria Ocean Pointe
  Resort & Spa **1**
The Dominion Hotel **8**
The Empress **22**
Executive House Hotel **26**
The Gatsby Mansion **12**
Harbour Towers **14**
The Haterleigh Heritage Inn **13**
Hotel Grand Pacific **17**
Isabella's Guest Suites **6**
The James Bay Inn **21**
Laurel Point Inn **9**
The Magnolia **23**
Medana Grove B&B **20**
Ramada Huntingdon **11**
The Rosewood Victoria Inn **19**
Royal Scot Suite Hotel **18**
Swans Suite Hotel **2**
Victoria International
  Youth Hostel **3**
The Victoria Regent Hotel **4**

downtown. The two farmhouse units feature hardwood floors, fireplaces, queen beds, and Jacuzzi tubs, as well as free bicycle, canoe, and kayak usage and easy access to Cadboro Beach.

301 Kingston St., Victoria, B.C. V8V 1V5. ☎ **250/388-4565.** Fax 250/721-3938. www.andersenhouse.com. 4 units, 2 manor units. June–Sept C$195–C$275 (US$126–US$177) double (up to 40% discount Oct–May); C$250 (US$161) manor unit. Off-season C$115–C$195 (US$74–US$126) manor unit. Rates include breakfast. MC, V. Some free off-street parking. Bus: 30 to Superior and Oswego sts. Children under 12 not accepted. **Amenities:** Jacuzzi; nonsmoking rooms. *In room:* TV/VCR, coffeemaker, hair dryer, iron.

Harbour Towers ⋆   Though there are a few standard rooms in this 12-story tower by the Inner Harbour, the one- and two-bedroom suites are a better value, with fully equipped kitchens containing two-burner stoves, microwaves, and small refrigerators. Thanks to a recent renovation, the last of the 1970s decor is gone, replaced by contemporary furnishings with teal and burgundy accents. All units feature floor-to-ceiling windows opening onto private balconies. You can guarantee a harbor view by paying an extra C$15 (US$9.70). For C$40 (US$26) extra, the 11th-floor "Royal Treatment" suites add a continental breakfast, a newspaper, upgraded amenities, free local calls, robes, and unobstructed views. The 12th-floor deluxe penthouse suites have fireplaces and stereo systems.

345 Quebec St., Victoria, B.C. V8V 1W4. ☎ **800/663-5896** or 250/385-2405. Fax 250/480-6593, www. harbourtowers.com. 195 units. Apr 16–May 31 C$220 (US$142) double; C$290–C$520 (US$187–US$400) suite. June 1–Oct 13 C$260 (US$167) double; C$370–C$620 (US$239–US$400) suite. Oct 14–Apr15 C$180 (US$115) double; C$230–C$500 (US$148–US$323) suite. Promotional rates available. Children 16 and under stay free in parents' room. Extra adult C$15 (US$9.70). Pets are welcome, C$15 (US$9.70) per day. AE, DC, MC, V. Underground parking C$2 (US$1.30). Bus: 30 or 31 to Superior and Oswego Sts. **Amenities:** Restaurant; bar; indoor pool; completely renovated health club; spa; Jacuzzi; sauna; children's center; business center; 24-hr. room service; babysitting; laundry service; same-day dry cleaning; nonsmoking rooms. *In room:* TV w/pay movies, dataport, minibar, coffeemaker, hair dryer, iron.

The Haterleigh Heritage Inn ⋆⋆⋆   Haterleigh owner and innkeeper Paul Kelly is a font of information, on Victoria in general and on this lovingly restored 1901 home in particular. With his wife, Elizabeth, he runs this exceptional B&B that captures the essence of Victoria's romance with a combination of antique furniture, stunning stained-glass windows, and attentive personal service. The spacious rooms boast high arched ceilings, large windows, sitting areas, and enormous bathrooms, some with hand-painted tiles and Jacuzzi tubs. On the top floor, the new and somewhat cozy Angel's Reach room features a big four-poster bed. The second-floor Secret Garden room has a small balcony with stunning views of the Olympic mountain range. The Day Dreams room downstairs is the dedicated honeymoon suite, but truth be told, all the suites make for wonderful romantic weekends. The bathrooms come with terrycloth robes, candles, and plastic champagne flutes. A full gourmet breakfast is served family-style at 8:30am sharp. Paul likes it that way because it gives guests a chance to meet and chat. There's complimentary sherry in the drawing room each evening.

243 Kingston St., Victoria, B.C. V8V 1V5. ☎ **250/384-9995.** Fax 250/384-1935. www.haterleigh.com. 7 units. C$225–C$344 (US$145–US$222) double. Rates include full breakfast. MC, V. Free parking. Bus: 30 to Superior and Montreal sts. **Amenities:** Jacuzzi; nonsmoking rooms. *In-room:* hair dryer.

Hotel Grand Pacific ⋆⋆   Formerly known as the Clarion, this hotel morphed into the Grand Pacific after gobbling up a small hotel in front that was blocking its access to Victoria's bustling Inner Harbour. That hotel was demolished and the Grand Pacific expanded into the vacuum, filling the space with a beautiful oceanfront lobby fronted by a large plaza with patio seating that encourages guests to take in the view. Rooms and suites were also upgraded as part of the expansion. Standard rooms in the new wing face the mountains and Ogden Point or, for a bit more money, the Inner Harbour and The Fairmont Empress hotel. Beautifully appointed with comfortable furniture, the standard rooms are nonetheless a tad on the small side. All have balconies. Suites provide the best views, overlooking the harbor and The Fairmont Empress hotel. The executive suites, which are spacious and bright and feature a large separate bedroom, are more pleasant than the junior suites, which lack bedroom windows.

463 Belleville St., Victoria, B.C. V8V 1X3. © 800/663-7550 or 250/386-0450. Fax 250/380-4473. www. hotelgrandpacific.com. 304 units. Oct–April C$99–C$299 (US$65–US$195) double; C$189–C$439 (US$123–US$286) 1-bedroom suite. May–Sept C$139–C$329 (US$91–US$214) double; C$319–C$469 (US$208–US$305) 1-bedroom suite. Off-season and weekend discounts vary, even within high season. Extra person C$30 (US$19). Pets are welcome, C$60 (US$39) per visit. AE, DC, DISC, MC, V. Self parking free; valet parking C$7 (US$4.50). Bus: 30 to Superior and Oswego sts. **Amenities:** 2 restaurants; bar; indoor lap pool; squash courts; superior health club; spa; Jacuzzi; concierge; tour desk; car rental; business center; 24-hr. room service; massage; babysitting; laundry service; same-day dry cleaning; nonsmoking rooms. *In room:* A/C, TV w/pay movies, dataport, minibar, coffeemaker, hair dryer, iron, safe.

Laurel Point Inn ★★   Strolling through the lobby of the Laurel Point Inn is like entering an early James Bond movie. The original owners were deeply enamored of Japan, so the lobby and hotel design reflect Japanese artistic principals: elegant simplicity, blond-wood surfaces, and the subtle integration of light, water, and stone. As for the James Bond part, that comes from the aura of 1970s cool. That sense of Eastern suave is heightened as you pass the little gurgling fountains on your way to the elevator; in your room you'll find a crisp cotton kimono laid out—something to slip into before stepping onto the private terrace, with a panoramic view of the harbor and the hills. The hotel, occupying most of a promontory jutting out into the Inner Harbour, consists of a new south wing and the original north wing. Rooms in the north wing are better than many in town, but as Moneypenny might say, "Not really up to your standard, are they, James?" The south wing is where you want to be: All the rooms here are suites, featuring blond wood with black marble accents, shoji-style sliding doors, Asian artworks, and deep tubs and floor-to-ceiling glassed-in showers in the bathrooms.

680 Montreal St., Victoria, B.C. V8V 1Z8. © 800/663-7667 or 250/386-8721. Fax 250/386-9547. www. laurelpoint.com. 200 units. Oct 16–April C$124 (US$80) double; C$179 (US$115) studio suite; C$224 (US$145) 1-bedroom suite. May–Oct 15 C$229–C$249 (US$148–US$161) double; C$279–C$299 (US$180–US$193) studio suite; C$329–C$349 (US$212–US$225) 1-bedroom suite. Seasonal discounts available. Children under 12 stay free in parents' room. Additional person C$15 (US$9.70). Wheelchair-accessible units available. AE, DC, DISC, MC, V. Free valet parking. Bus: 30 to Montreal and Superior sts. Pets accepted for C$25 (US$17). **Amenities:** Restaurant (West coast cuisine); bar; indoor pool; complimentary access to YMCA facilities; Jacuzzi; sauna; concierge; business center; 24-hr. room service; massage; babysitting; same-day dry cleaning; nonsmoking hotel. *In room:* A/C, TV w/pay movies, dataport, coffeemaker, hair dryer, iron.

The Rosewood Victoria Inn ★★★   Though now with a new name and owner, what used to be the Holland House Inn still provides all the amenities and comfort of a modern B&B in a classy and romantic setting. All rooms (10 in the original building, 7 in the adjacent coach house connected to the inn via an atrium) are tastefully decorated, each done in a unique style. Some have wood-burning or gas fireplaces, others balconies, large tubs, or Jacuzzis; a number have canopied beds and vaulted ceilings. Two of the newest rooms, the Venetian and the Florentine, are gorgeous; both decorated in pale greens and beige, these rooms provide the ultimate in luxury with elegant sitting areas, a gas fireplace, and fine linens. Soak in the Venetian's romantic two-person hot tub or relax in the Florentine's private garden patio. After a scrumptious breakfast served in the conservatory, step outside and you're a block behind the Legislature and Royal BC Museum and just a 5-minute walk to the Inner Harbour.

595 Michigan St., Victoria, B.C. V8V 1S7. ✆ **800/335-3466** or 250/384-6644. Fax 250/384-6117. www.rose woodvictoria.com. 17 units. June–Sept C$145–C$295 (US$94–US$190) double. Oct–May C$100–C$250 (US$65–US$161) double. Extra person C$35 (US$23). Rates include full breakfast. Wheelchair-accessible unit available. AE, MC, V. Free parking. Bus: 5 to Superior and Government sts. Children under 10 not accepted. *In room:* TV, coffeemaker, hair dryer.

MODERATE

Admiral Inn ★★ *Value*   The family-operated Admiral is in an attractive three-story building on the Inner Harbour, near the Washington-bound ferry terminal and close to restaurants and shopping. The combination of comfortable rooms and reasonable rates attracts young couples, families, seniors, and other travelers in search of a harbor view at a price that doesn't break the bank. The rooms are pleasant and comfortably furnished, with balconies or terraces. The suites come with full kitchens. Some units can sleep up to six (on two double beds and a double sofa bed). The owners provide sightseeing advice as well as extras like free bicycles and an Internet terminal in the lobby.

257 Belleville St., Victoria, B.C. V8V 1X3. ✆ **888/823-6472.** ✆ and fax 250/388-6267. www.admiral.bc.ca. 29 units. June–Sept C$147–C$175 (US$95–US$113) double; C$226 (US$146) 1-bedroom suite with view. Oct–June 15 C$87–C$115 (US$56–US$74) double; C$126–C$166 (US$81–US$107) 1-bedroom suite with view. Extra person C$10 (US$6.45). Children under 12 stay free in parents' room. Rates include continental breakfast. Senior, weekly, and off-season discounts available. AE, DC, MC, V. Free parking. Bus: 5 to Belleville and Government sts. Pets welcome. **Amenities:** Bike rental; tour desk; business center; coin laundry; dry cleaning; car rental desk; nonsmoking rooms. *In room:* A/C, TV, kitchenette or kitchen, coffeemaker, hair dryer, iron.

Days Inn on the Harbour   This newly refurbished hotel is across from the MV *Coho* ferry terminal on the edge of the Inner Harbour. It has subtle nautical decor: In the lobby is a scale model of the HMS *Royal Sovereign,* a 17th-century English vessel. The restaurant and lounge are named for the HMS *Swiftsure,* one of the last of the tall ships that served in the Pacific. Half the rooms face the Inner Harbour; the other half has views of the nearby residential area. View rooms cost a little more, but the vista is worth it. The rooms come with queen, king, or two double beds (the most expensive) and are outfitted with comfortable modern furnishings and step-up bathtubs. Eighteen rooms are equipped with kitchenettes.

427 Belleville St., Victoria, B.C. V8V 1X3. ✆ and fax **250/386-3451.** www.daysinnvictoria.com. 71 units. May–June C$125–C$165 (US$81–US$106) double. July–Sept C$173–C$203 (US$111–US$131) double. Oct–Apr C$95–C$125 (US$61–US$81) double. Units with kitchenette C$10 (US$6.45) extra. Children under 12 stay free in parents' room. Off-season discounts available. Pets welcome at C$10 (US$6.45) per day. AE, DC, MC, V. Free parking. Bus: 5 to Belleville and Government sts. **Amenities:** Restaurant; bar; seasonal heated outdoor pool; year-round Jacuzzi; tour desk; laundry service; nonsmoking floors. *In room:* TV, some units with kitchens, coffeemaker, hair dryer, safe.

The Gatsby Mansion   Built in 1897, this white clapboard Victorian across from the Seattle–Port Angeles ferry has been faithfully restored to resemble a period museum, from the foyer, with its hand-painted ceramic-tiled fireplace and rich wood paneling, to the stained-glass windows and velvet tapestries throughout the inn. The atmosphere is that of a slightly dashing 1920s seaside resort, with frescoed ceilings supporting crystal chandeliers. The rooms feature down duvets, fine linen, and lots of Victorian antiques. Some rooms have views of the Inner Harbour, while others have private parlors.

309 Belleville St., Victoria, B.C. V8V 1X2. ✆ **800/563-9656** or 250/388-9191. Fax 250/920-5651. www. bellevillepark.com. 20 units. C$139–C$319 (US$90–US$206) double. Rates include full breakfast.

Off-season discounts available. AE, DC, MC, V. Free parking. Bus: 30 or 31 to Belleville and Government sts. **Amenities:** Restaurant; Jacuzzi; sauna; bike rental; limited room service; massage; laundry service; non-smoking rooms. *In room:* TV w/pay movies, coffeemaker, hair dryer.

Medana Grove Bed & Breakfast   Just a few blocks from the Inner Harbour, this charming 1908 James Bay district home is tucked away on a quiet residential street. You can't miss it, just look for the traditional red English call box (telephone booth) on the front lawn. The front parlor and dining room on the main floor of this small bed-and-breakfast are beautifully restored with lovely stained-glass windows, a fireplace, antique furniture, and hardwood floors. The three guest rooms are more plainly furnished but provide comfortable accommodations. The smallest bedroom, with a queen-size bed, is located on the ground floor, across from the parlor. The other two rooms are on the second floor, up a narrow staircase. The one overlooking the front of the house accommodates three people with one double and one single bed. The quietest room in the house, with a king-size bed, looks out toward the garden. Friendly hosts Garry and Noreen Hunt are happy to help you plan your stay in Victoria. Smoking and pets aren't permitted.

162 Medana St., Victoria, B.C. V8V 2H5. © **800/269-1188** or 250/389-0437. Fax 250/389-0425. www.victoriabnb.com. 3 units. Mid-May to mid-Sept C$110–C$135 (US$71–US$87) double. Rates include gourmet breakfast. Off-season discounts available; call for rates. MC, V. Street parking. Bus: 11 to Simcoe at Menzies.

Ramada Huntingdon Hotel & Suites at Belleville Park *(Kids)*   Though the new Extended Play name makes for quite a mouthful, the recently remixed Ramada Huntingdon is certainly worth a spin. Set within a stone's throw of the Victoria Inner Harbour, the Parliament Buildings, and The Fairmont Empress Hotel, the Ramada and the adjacent Gatsby Mansion Inn (owned by the same company) are set on a beautifully landscaped block (the self-declared Belleville Park) with a lovely courtyard, cafes, and artist studios. When it was built in 1981 the 116-room Ramada came with heavy faux British manor accents. Fortunately this let's-pretend-we're-British fetish is fading somewhat in Victoria and the only country manor traces still to be found are in the wall decorations (lots of horse and hunting scenes) and floral patterns on walls and fabric. Otherwise, the three-story Ramada is a pleasant low-key hotel with a number of excellent rooms, particularly for those traveling with children. Even the standard rooms feel spacious, and all rooms come equipped with fridges. The prime rooms, however, are the gallery rooms or lofts on the third floor. These split levels suites come with a full kitchen and sitting room with TV and pullout double bed on the ground floor and a master bedroom (and second TV) upstairs; all sleep four comfortably, some even accommodate six. Those wanting to escape colder climates can book special rates in the rainy but mild Victoria winter season.

330 Quebec St., Victoria, B.C. V8V 1W3. © **800/663-7557** or 250/381-3456. Fax 250/382-7666. www.bellevillepark.com. 116 units. May–Sept C$149 (US$98) double; C$169–C$259 (US$111–US$170) suite. Oct–Apr C$89–C$159 (US$58–US$105) double; C$109–C$179 (US$72–US$118) suite. AE, DC, MC, V. Parking C$5 (US$3.30) **Amenities:** Restaurant (international); bar; Jacuzzi; sauna; limited room service; laundry; dry cleaning; mostly nonsmoking rooms; executive-level rooms. *In room:* A/C (3rd-floor gallery suites only), TV, dataport, fridge, coffeemaker, hair dryer, iron.

Royal Scot Suite Hotel *(★★ Kids)*   A block from the Inner Harbour, the Royal Scot provides excellent value, particularly if you opt for a studio or bedroom. It was constructed as an apartment building, so the rooms are spacious (okay, huge). Each studio suite has a divider separating the bedroom from the living room, dining area, and kitchen. One-bedroom suites have separate bedrooms with king, queen, or twin beds. All suites have lots of closet space, fully equipped kitchens, complimentary refreshments, and sofa beds in the living rooms. The decor runs to pastels, pinks, and florals (this is Victoria, after all). In summer, the Royal Scot fills up with families. Kids make heavy use of the game room and video arcade, which (thankfully) is tucked away out of earshot of other guests. In winter, the hotel is favored by retirees from the prairie provinces escaping subzero weather.

425 Quebec St., Victoria, B.C. V8V 1W7. ② **800/663-7515** or 250/388-5463. Fax 250/388-5452. www. royalscot.com. 176 units. June–Sept C$139 (US$90) double; C$149–C$329 (US$96–US$212) suite. Oct–May C$119 (US$77) double; C$119–C$259 (US$77–US$167) suite. Weekly, monthly, and off-season rates available. AE, DC, MC, V. Free parking. Bus: 5 to Belleville and Government sts. **Amenities:** Restaurant; indoor pool; exercise room; Jacuzzi; sauna; game room; tour desk; shuttle service to downtown; limited room service; laundry service; nonsmoking rooms. *In room:* TV, kitchen, coffeemaker, hair dryer, iron.

INEXPENSIVE

The James Bay Inn ★★ *Value*   The Inner Harbour/James Bay area isn't especially blessed with cheap digs, but this Edwardian manor on the edge of Beacon Hill Park is one of the few. Built in 1907, it still offers one of the best accommodation deals in downtown. The standard rooms located in the main building of this four-story walk-up are somewhat small and very simply furnished, but management has begun serious renovations, including new beds and TVs in the rooms. The real bargains, however, are the next-door suites and cottage. The four suites are located in a renovated heritage property. The two studios are a tad on the small side but come with a separate full-size kitchen. The generously sized one-bedroom suites also feature a full kitchen, a bedroom with queen bed, and a separate living-room area with TV and pullout couch. Furnishings and decorations are elegant and modern, blissfully free of florals and bric-a-brac. Want to bring your friends? Reserve the cottage, a fully furnished two-bedroom house cater-corner to the James Bay Inn. With space for eight people and a peak-season price of C$275 (US$177), it's a steal.

270 Government St., Victoria, B.C. V8V 2V2. ② **800/836-2649** or 250/384-7151. Fax 250/385-2311. www. jamesbayinn.bc.ca. 45 units. May–June C$80–C$119 (US$52–US$77) double. July–Sept C$107–C$189 (US$69–US$122) double. Oct–Apr C$57–C$99 (US$37–US$64) double. Cottage May–Sept C$149–C$225 (US$96–US$145) double; Oct–Apr C$129 (US$83) double. Extra person C$10 (US$6.45), up to 8 people. AE, MC, V. Free limited parking. Bus: 5 or 30 to Niagara St. **Amenities:** Restaurant; bar; tour desk; nonsmoking rooms. *In room:* TV, dataport, hair dryer, iron.

2 Downtown & Old Town

EXPENSIVE

Abigail's Hotel ★★★   The most serious existential problem you'll face here is determining at exactly what point you slipped from semi-sensuous luxury into full decadent indulgence. It could be when you first entered your room and saw the fresh flowers in crystal vases or came across the marble fireplace with wood in place. More likely, it's when you slipped into the double Jacuzzi in your marble bathroom or nestled into your four-poster canopied bed. In a Tudor mansion just east of downtown, Abigail's began life in the 1920s as a luxury apartment house before being converted to a boutique hotel and then being taken over in the mid-1990s by Daniel Behune and his German-born wife, Frauke. Not all rooms come with all the frills, but pampering is always an objective. In the original building, some of the 16 rooms are bright and sunny and beautifully furnished, with pedestal sinks and goose-down comforters. Others boast soaker tubs and double-sided fireplaces, so you can relax in the tub by the light of the fire. The six Celebration Suites in the Coach House addition are the apogee of indulgence. Abigail's chef prepares a multicourse gourmet breakfast that may include lemon-pecan muffins, French toast with chocolate and raspberries, and eggs with champagne-and-chive sauce, served in the sunny breakfast room.

906 McClure St., Victoria, B.C. V8V 3E7. ⓒ **800/561-6565** or 250/388-5363. Fax 250/388-7787. www. abigailshotel.com. 23 units. C$219–C$389 (US$141–US$251) double. Rates include full breakfast. Winter discounts up to 50%. AE, MC, V. Free parking. Bus: 1 to Cook and McClure sts. Children under 10 not accepted. **Amenities:** Concierge; tour desk; dry cleaning; nonsmoking rooms. *In-room:* dataport, hair dryer, iron.

The Beaconsfield Inn 🏠🏠 Built in 1905 by Victoria's leading domestic architect, Samuel McClure, this elegantly restored Edwardian mansion is located just a few blocks from Beacon Hill park and the Inner Harbour. Commissioned by local industrial baron R.P. Rithet as a wedding gift for his daughter Gertrude, it seems only fitting that it survives today as a charming retreat favored by newlyweds and other incurable romantics. The lovely inn boasts fir paneling, mahogany floors, antique English furnishings, and delicate stained glass. The nine guest rooms are lavishly decorated and filled with fresh flowers from the garden. Some suites also have fireplaces or skylights and French doors that open onto the garden. For couples who want to get away from it all, book the cozy Beaconsfield Suite. Located on the third floor, this attic room has a four-poster canopy bed, an elegant sitting area in front of the wood-burning fireplace, a jetted tub, and a window seat. Or try the Emily Carr suite for the ultimate indulgence, featuring a Jacuzzi tub within sight of the fireplace and a chandelier above the two-person shower. A gourmet breakfast is served in the sunroom or the dining room, and afternoon tea is served in the library. Children, pets, and smoking aren't permitted.

998 Humboldt St., Victoria, B.C. V8V 2Z8. ⓒ **888/884-4044** or 250/384-4044. Fax 250/384-4052. www. islandnet.com/beaconsfield. 9 units. May 16–June 19 C$169–C$299 (US$109–US$193) double. June 20–Sept 18 C$219–C$359 (US$141–US$232) double. Sept 19–Oct 16 C$169–C$299 (US$109–US$193) double. Oct 17–May 15 C$129–C$229 (US$83–US$148) double. Full breakfast, afternoon tea, and sherry hour included. MC, V. Free parking. Bus: 1 or 2 to Humboldt and Quadra sts. Children not permitted. **Amenities:** Access to nearby health club; Jacuzzi; massage; concierge; dry cleaning; nonsmoking hotel. *In room:* Hair dryer, no phone.

The Magnolia 🏠🏠 A new boutique hotel in the center of Victoria, the Magnolia offers a taste of luxury at a reasonable price. The tiny lobby, with a fireplace, a chandelier, and overstuffed chairs, immediately conveys a sense of quality. The room decor manages to be classic without feeling frumpy, from the two-poster beds with high-quality linen and down duvets to the bathrooms with walk-in showers and deep tubs. The windows extend floor to ceiling, providing excellent harbor views from some rooms. The needs of business travelers are also kept in mind: work desks are well lit and large enough to spread your work out. Two phone lines run to every room, and the phone itself is cordless. The top-floor Diamond Suite features a sitting room with fireplace. The hotel also boasts a microbrewery and a full day spa—not necessarily to be enjoyed in that order.

623 Courtney St., Victoria, B.C. V8W 1B8. ⓒ **877/624-6654** or 250/381-0999. Fax 250/381-0988. www. magnoliahotel.com. 66 units. June 1–Oct 15 C$269–C$329 (US$174–US$212) double; C$499(US$323) suite. Oct 16–Apr 15 C$169–C$219 (US$109–US$141) double; C$289(US$186) suite. Apr 16–May 31 C$209–C$229 (US$135–US$148) double; C$309 (US$199) suite. Rates include continental breakfast. AE, DC, MC, V. Valet parking C$10 (US$6.45). Pets are welcome for a C$60 (US$39) charge. Bus: 5 to Courtney St. **Amenities:** Restaurant; bar; access to nearby health club; spa; concierge; salon; limited room service; massage; laundry service; same-day dry cleaning; executive rooms. *In room:* A/C, TV w/pay movies, dataport, minibar, fridge, coffeemaker, hair dryer, iron.

The Victoria Regent Hotel ★ *Value*   There's something vaguely seedy about the Regent's exterior. It could be the wedding-cake architecture. Or it could be that the hotel's foundation, jutting out onto the Inner Harbour, has the air of a deserted underground parking garage, late at night. Anyway, the impression doesn't carry over to the rooms and suites, which are large and comfortable, if a little dated when it comes to furnishings. The views on the harbor side are good. The beds in the suites are either king or queen, and all come with pullout couches in the sitting room. All the suites have full kitchens, which makes the Regent popular with visiting snowbirds in winter.

1234 Wharf St., Victoria, B.C. V8W 3H9. © 800/663-7472 or 250/386-2211. Fax 250/386-2622. www. victoriaregent.com. 48 units. May–June C$169–C$199 (US$109–US$128) double; C$229–C$459 (US$148–US$296) suite. July–Oct 17 C$199 (US$128) double; C$259–C$459 (US$167–US$296) suite. Oct 18–Apr 30 C$129(US$83) double; C$189–C$369 (US$122–US$238) suite. Rates include continental breakfast. Additional person C$20 (US$12.90). Children under 16 stay free in parents' room. Wheelchair-accessible units available. AE, DC, DISC, MC, V. Free underground parking. Bus: 6, 24, or 25 from the Johnson St. Bridge to the hotel on Wharf St. **Amenities:** Restaurant; access to nearby health club; concierge; tour desk; business center; limited room service; babysitting; laundry service; same-day dry cleaning; nonsmoking rooms; executive level rooms. *In room:* TV/VCR, dataport, minibar, coffeemaker, hair dryer, iron.

MODERATE

The Best Western Carlton *Kids*   In the heart of Victoria's shopping and entertainment district, the Best Western is ideally located for those who like to step right into the hustle and bustle of downtown. All rooms are comfortably furnished. Almost half the units come with a fully equipped kitchen, and even the standard rooms are quite spacious. Perfect for families traveling together, the junior suites boast two double beds, a sitting area with a pullout couch, a dining room table, and full kitchen. One-bedroom suites are also available; a number of these are wheelchair accessible. The Best Western prides itself on being a child-friendly hotel, and young guests are greeted with a goody bag, treats and toys, and a special room service delivery of milk and cookies.

642 Johnson St., Victoria, B.C. V8W 1M6. © 800/663-7241 or 250/388-5513. Fax 250/388-5343. www. bestwesterncarlton.com. 103 units. AE, MC, V. Oct–Apr C$89–C$129 (US$57–US$83) double; C$109–C$149 (US$70–US$96) junior or 1-bedroom suite. May–Sept C$159–C$209 (US$103–US$135) double; C$179–C$229 (US$116–US$148) junior or 1-bedroom suite. Children 17 and under stay free in parents' room. Extra person C$20 (US$13). Free parking Oct–April; C$8 (US$5.20) per day May–Sept. Bus: 5 to Douglas and Johnson sts. Pets C$10 (US$6.45) per day. **Amenities:** Restaurant; exercise room; children's programs; concierge; tour desk; salon; limited room service; laundry service and coin laundry; nonsmoking rooms. *In room:* A/C, TV w/pay movies, coffeemaker, hair dryer, iron.

Chateau Victoria Hotel *Value*   This 18-story hotel was built in 1975 on the site of the "parrot lady's" house: Victoria Jane Wilson lived in a big white manor on the hill behind The Fairmont Empress. When she died in 1949, she left her house and fortune to Louis, her talking parrot, with explicit instructions that the bird remain in the house for as long as he lived. His caretaker passed on in 1966, and the estate's lawyers talked Louis into moving to a retirement home so the house could be demolished to make way for an apartment tower (Louis lasted until 1985). Because this was the original idea, the hotel's rooms and one-bedroom suites are spacious; many suites have kitchenettes, and all have private balconies. The decor was a bit dowdy—1970s colonial furniture, but the hotel is in the process of renovating its rooms. The standard ones have just seen a complete overhaul with new furniture, lighting, and drapes; and many of the bathroom fixtures have already been replaced. Don't think luxury, but value for your money.

740 Burdett Ave., Victoria, B.C. V8W 1B2. © 800/663-5891 or 250/382-4221. Fax 250/380-1950. www. chateauvictoria.com. 177 units. May–Sept C$147–C$260 (US$95–US$168) double. Oct–Apr C$126–C$180

(US$81–US$116) double. . Children under 18 stay free in adults' room. AE, DC, DISC, MC, V. Free parking. Bus: 2 to Burdett Ave. **Amenities:** Rooftop restaurant; bar; indoor pool; exercise room; Jacuzzi; concierge; business center; limited room service; babysitting; laundry service; same-day dry cleaning; nonsmoking rooms. *In room:* TV w/pay movies, dataport, coffeemaker, hair dryer, iron.

Executive House Hotel *Kids*   You can't miss the Executive House, a concrete high-rise looming above The Fairmont Empress on Old Town's east side; the 1960s-style architecture is unmistakably New World. Step inside, however, and you'll find an ambience evoking 1880s London. If the transition—or the thought of staying in a 13-story British club—isn't too much for you, this place is really rather nice. A lot of thought went into designing the rooms, which are of better-than-average size. Some suites come with a queen bed in the bedroom and a fold-out sofa, so parents can put the kids to bed and relax on the sofa bed. Other suites have a double bed in the living room and bedroom, so business associates traveling together can economize. The furnishings are a bit fussy, but hey, it's 1880. Each penthouse-level suite has a Jacuzzi in its own little atrium, a fireplace, a garden terrace with a panoramic view, a dining table, and a fully equipped kitchen.

777 Douglas St., Victoria, B.C. V8W 2B5. (C) **800/663-7001** or 250/388-5111. Fax 250/385-1323. http://executivehouse.com. 179 units. C$179(US$115) double; C$199–C$295 (US$128–US$190) suite; C$295–C$895 (US$190–US$577) penthouse rooms and suites. Extra person or pets C$15 (US$10). 10%–50% seasonal discount, depending on availability. Children under 16 stay free in parents' room. AE, DC, DISC, MC, V. Parking C$2.15 (US$1.40) per night. Bus: 2 to the Convention Center. Pets accepted for C$15 (US$10) per night. **Amenities:** 2 restaurants (steak and seafood, continental); 3 bars; exercise room; fully equipped spa; concierge; car-rental desk; limited room service; babysitting; same-day laundry service; same-day dry cleaning; nonsmoking rooms; executive level rooms; car rental desk. *In room:* TV w/pay movies, dataport, fridge, coffeemaker, hair dryer, iron, safe.

Isabella's Guest Suites ★ *Finds*   The owners of Willy's bakery have two suites located above the shop that are available year-round for tourists looking for affordable accommodation in the heart of the city. What can one expect from a cheap downtown room over a bakery? A lot! Actually, you will be blown away by these gorgeous apartments. The one overlooking the front is a large, elegantly furnished studio with a bed/sitting room that opens into a dining room and full kitchen. Bright colors and cheerful accents, upscale rustic furniture, high ceilings, large windows, and plenty of space make this a great home base for exploring Victoria. The second unit, a one-bedroom suite, overlooks the alley and patio of Il Terrazzo restaurant. The living room is painted in bright red, which goes surprisingly well with the wood floors and funky furniture, whereas the bedroom with a king-size bed is done in softer tones. Do we need to add that the bathroom has a lovely claw-foot tub, breakfast is included and served at the bakery, parking is free, and you have your own front door? Not bad at all for a cool C$150 (US$97) a night.

537 Johnson St., Victoria, B.C. V8W 1M2. (C) **250/381-8414.** Fax 250/381-8415. www.isabellasbb.com/willies. 2 units. May–Sept C$150 (US$97) double. Oct–April C$130 (US$84) double. Breakfast included. Free parking. Bus: 5. *In room:* TV, full kitchen, iron, hair dryer.

Swans Suite Hotel ★★ *Kids*   This heritage building was abandoned for years until 1988, when Victoria renaissance man (entrepreneur, art collector, and eccentric bon vivant) Michael Williams turned it into a hotel, restaurant, brew pub, and nightclub all in one. Just by the Johnson Street Bridge, it's one of Old Town's best-loved buildings. Like any great inn, Swans is small, friendly, and charming. The suites are large, with the quirky layouts you'd expect in a heritage renovation. Many are split-level, featuring open lofts and huge exposed beams.

All come with fully equipped kitchens, dining areas, living rooms, and queen-size beds. The two-bedroom suites have the space and "Upstairs, Downstairs" feel of little town houses; they're great for families, accommodating up to six comfortably. Swans also works for business travelers—it's one of the few hotels in town with dual dataports. The original Pacific Northwest artwork is a little disappointing—high-quality stuff, but not nearly up to the avant-garde level Williams set for himself with the pieces hung in the bar and restaurant. Williams, alas, passed on in 2001, leaving most of his substantial holding—Swans included—to the University of Victoria. There is no smoking in the hotel.

506 Pandora Ave., Victoria, B.C. V8W 1N6. ✆ **800/668-7926** or 250/361-3310. Fax 250/361-3491. www.swanshotel.com. 30 suites. July–Sept C$159–C$179 (US$103–US$115) studio or 1-bedroom suite, C$249 (US$161) 2-bedroom suite (based on 4 people); Oct–June C$99–C$145 (US$64–US$94) studio or 1-bedroom suite, C$179–C$205 (US$115–US$132) 2-bedroom suite (based on 4 people). Additional person C$20 (US$13) extra. Children under 12 stay free in parents' room. AE, DC, DISC, MC, V. Parking C$8 (US$6). Bus: 23 or 24 to Pandora Ave. **Amenities:** Restaurant (bistro); brew pub; limited room service; laundry service; same-day dry cleaning; nonsmoking hotel. *In room:* TV, dataport, kitchen, coffeemaker, hair dryer, iron.

INEXPENSIVE

The Dominion Hotel *Value*   Victoria's oldest hotel, the Dominion opened in 1876 and recently underwent a C$7-million (US$4.5-million) restoration. It's a lovely family-oriented heritage property decorated throughout the public areas with rich woods, marble floors, brass trim, and red velvet upholstery on antique chairs. The rooms have more modern appointments but maintain the flavor of times past, with ceiling fans and brass lamps. There are dozens of types of rooms. The deluxe rooms, occupying the four corners of each floor, are spacious and comfortable.

759 Yates St., Victoria, B.C. V8W 1L6. ✆ **800/663-6101** or 250/384-4136. Fax 250/382-6416. www.dominion-hotel.com. 101 units. May 1–Oct 15 C$129–C$149 (US$83–US$96) double. Oct 16–Apr 30 $65–C$85 (US$42–US$55) double. Children under 16 stay free in parents' room. AE, MC, V. Parking C$5–C$10 (US$3.25–US$6.45) Bus: 10, 11, or 14 to Yates St. **Amenities:** 3 restaurants; access to nearby health club (YMCA); limited room service; babysitting; laundry service; dry-cleaning service; nonsmoking rooms. *In room:* TV, coffeemaker, hair dryer.

Victoria International Youth Hostel   The location is perfect—right in the heart of Old Town. In addition, this hostel has all the usual accouterments, including two kitchens (stocked with utensils), a dining room, a TV lounge with VCR, a game room, a common room, a library, laundry facilities, an indoor bicycle lockup, 24-hour security, and hot showers. The dorms are on the large side (16 to a room), showers are shared and segregated by gender, and a couple of family rooms are available (one of which has a private toilet). There's an extensive ride board, and the collection of outfitter and tour information rivals that of the tourism office. The front door is locked at 2:30am, but you can make arrangements to get in later.

516 Yates St., Victoria, B.C. V8W 1K8. ✆ **250/385-4511**. Fax 250/385-3232. www.hihostels.ca. 104 beds. International Youth Hostel members C$17 (US$11), nonmembers C$20 (US$13). Wheelchair-accessible unit available. MC, V. Parking on street. Bus: 70 from Swartz Bay ferry terminal. **Amenities:** Game room; tour desk; laundry facilities.

3 Outside the Central Area

EXPENSIVE

The Aerie ★★   On a forested mountain slope by a fjord about half an hour from town, this Mediterranean-inspired villa was designed, built, and decorated by Maria Schuster, an Austrian hotelier with extravagant tastes and no shortage of self-confidence. The initial result was perhaps a tad too over the top, so in recent years Schuster has been quietly stripping away some of the leopard skin and white leather furnishings. In its current configuration, the Aerie, a member of the prestigious Relais & Châteaux, is no longer overwhelming, just spectacular. In particular, the view over Finlayson Inlet—seen from your room, the indoor pool, the outdoor whirlpool, or the dining room—is quite simply stunning. Inside, the Aerie offers six room configurations: All include big comfortable beds with top-quality linen, and all but the standard rooms include a soaker tub for two. As you move into the master and residence suites you get private decks and fireplaces. Dining is an integral part of the experience, and the Aerie restaurant (p. 211) is among the best in all Victoria.

600 Ebedora Lane (P.O. Box 108), Malahat, B.C. V0R 2L0. © 800/518-1933 or 250/743-7115. Fax 250/743-4766. www.aerie.bc.ca. 24 units. Apr 6–May 17 C$225–C$295 (US$145–US$190) double; C$345–C$455 (US$223–US$294) suite. May 18–Oct 31 C$285–C$325 (US$184–US$210) double; C$375–C$495 (US$242–US$319) suite. Nov 1–Apr 5 C$185–C$230 (US$119–US$148) double; C$285–C$350 (US$184–US$226) suite. Rates include 7am breakfast hamper at your door and full breakfast later. Accommodation and dinner packages available. AE, DC, MC, V. Free parking. Take Hwy. 1 North, turn left at the Spectacle Lake turnoff; take the first right and follow the winding driveway up. **Amenities:** Restaurant; bar; indoor pool; indoor and outdoor hot tubs; tennis courts; small weight room; full spa; concierge; tour desk; 24-hr. room service; massage; laundry; dry cleaning; all nonsmoking rooms. *In room:* A/C, TV, dataport, minibar, coffeemaker, hair dryer, iron.

Dashwood Manor *(Overrated)*   This 1912 mock-Tudor manor does indeed have a good location: on the edge of Beacon Hill Park, just across Dallas Road from the beach and the Strait of Juan de Fuca. Inside, however, it's all a bit of a disappointment. True, the rooms are large and bright and the furniture and appointments are all authentically antique. Perhaps too antique. There's something stuffy in the state of Dashwood—as if the Edwardian era had been shellacked in place lo these past nine decades. The plumbing is certainly authentically British; where one might expect (given the prices) deep soaker tubs and Jacuzzis, there is instead (with one exception) naught but your standard bed-sitter shower-tub combo. Kitchens come well stocked for do-it-yourself breakfast. Complimentary sherry, port, and wine are laid out in the lobby in the evenings.

1 Cook St., Victoria, B.C. V8V 3W6. © **800/667-5517** or 250/385-5517. Fax 250/383-1760. www.dashwoodmanor.com. 14 suites. Apr–Oct C$165–C$285 (US$106–US$184) suite. Nov–Mar C$75–C$125 (US$48–US$81) suite. Apr–May and Oct C$80–C$285 (US$52–US$184) suite. Extra person C$45 (US$29). AE, DC, MC, V. Free parking. Bus: 5 to Dallas Rd. and Cook St. **Amenities:** Nonsmoking rooms. *In room:* TV, kitchen, fridge, coffeemaker, hair dryer, iron.

Oak Bay Beach Hotel and Marine Resort *(★) (Finds)*   A grand Tudor mansion built during the glory days of Victoria's "ye-olde-Englande" shtick, the Oak Bay also just happens to sit perched on the edge of Haro Strait overlooking the San Juan Islands. For decades the hotel's owners made much of the former, showcasing Edwardian and Victorian antiques in the rooms and fireplace-dominated lobby. Rooms are still very British. Priced according to size and view, they come decorated with antique British furnishings and offer bay windows and private balconies overlooking the waterfront. The second-floor fireplace suites are the best choice. In the past few years, however, as more people have come to recognize Victoria for the outdoors town it is, the Oak Bay has finally begun to make good use of its oceanside location. Outdoor adventure trips—many on the sea—are now an integral part of the Oak Bay experience. Among these are moonlight kayaking trips, guided hiking or mushroom hunting trips to nearby Chatham and Discovery Islands, whale-watching trips, and guided cycling trips to the wineries or cheese dairies of the nearby Cowichan Valley.

1175 Beach Dr., Victoria, B.C. V8S 2N2. ✆ **800/668-7758** or 250/598-4556. Fax 250/598-6180. www.oak baybeachhotel.com. 50 units. C$225–C$340 (US$145–US$219) double; C$340–C$450 (US$219–US$290) suite. Off-season discounts. Individual packages available through "Build your own package" system. AE, DC, MC, V. Free parking. Bus: 2 to Newport and Margate sts. **Amenities:** Restaurant; pub; evening hot chocolate and cookies; extensive outdoor packages including guided hikes, kayak trips, bike trips, and whale-watching; free bicycles; tour desk; complimentary shuttle service; concierge; laundry; nonsmoking rooms. *In room:* A/C, TV, coffeemaker, hair dryer, iron.

Sooke Harbour House ★★★ This little (but expanding) inn/restaurant, at the end of a sand spit about 30km (19 miles) west of Victoria, has earned an international reputation (voted 2nd-best Country Inn *in the world* by *Gourmet Magazine* in 2000) thanks to the care lavished on the guests and rooms by owners Frederique and Sinclair Philip. Frederique looks after the rooms, sumptuously furnishing and decorating each according to a particular Northwest theme. The Herb Garden room, looking out over a garden of fragrant herbs and edible flowers, is done in pale shades of mint and parsley. The large split-level Thunderbird room is a veritable celebration of First Nations culture, with books, carvings, totems, and masks, including one of a huge Thunderbird. Thanks to some clever architecture, all the rooms are awash in natural light and have fabulous ocean views. In addition, all boast wood-burning fireplaces and sitting areas, all but one have sun decks, and most have Jacuzzis or soaker tubs. The other half of the Harbour House's reputation comes from the outstanding cooking of Sinclair Philip (p. 212).

1528 Whiffen Spit Rd., Sooke, B.C. V0S 1N0. ✆ **800-889-9688** or 250/642-3421. Fax 250/642-6988. www. sookeharbourhouse.com. 28 units. May–June and Oct C$280–C$490 (US$180–US$316) double. July–Sept C$299–C$555 (US$193–US$358) double. Nov–Apr C$230–C$355 (US$148–US$229) Mon–Fri double; C$255–C$455 (US$165–US$294) weekend double. Rates include full breakfast and picnic lunch (no picnic lunch weekdays Nov–April). MC, V. Free parking. Pets accepted, C$20 (US$13) per day. Take the Island Hwy. (Hwy. 1) to the Sooke/Colwood turnoff (junction Hwy. 14). Follow Hwy. 14 to Sooke. About 1.6km (1 mile) past the town's only traffic light, turn left onto Whiffen Spit Rd. **Amenities:** Restaurant; golf course; access to nearby health club; spa; limited room service; massage; babysitting; laundry service; nonsmoking rooms. *In room:* Dataport, fridge, coffeemaker, hair dryer, iron.

MODERATE

The Boathouse ★★ *(Finds* It's a short row (or a 25-min. walk) to Butchart Gardens from this secluded red cottage in Brentwood Bay, a converted boathouse set on pilings over Saanich Inlet. The only passersby you're likely to encounter are seals, bald eagles, otters, herons, and raccoons, plus the occasional floatplane flying in. The cottage is at the end of a very long flight of stairs behind the owner's home. Inside are a new queen bed, a dining table, a kitchen area with a small refrigerator and toaster oven, an electric heater, and a reading alcove with a stunning view all the way up Finlayson Arm. Toilet and shower facilities are in a separate bathhouse, 17 steps back uphill. All the makings for a delicious continental breakfast are provided in the evening, plus free coffee and newspaper delivery. Just below the boathouse is a floating dock—which doubles as a great sun deck—moored to which is a small dinghy reserved for the exclusive use of guests. There can perhaps be nothing more stylish than pulling up to the Butchart Gardens dock in your own private watercraft.

746 Sea Dr., RR 1, Victoria, B.C. VM8 1B1. ✆ **250/652-9370.** http://members.shaw.ca/boathouse. 1 unit. C$175 (US$113) double. Rate includes continental breakfast. AE, MC, V. Free parking. Closed mid-Oct to Apr 1. Bus: 75 to Wallace Dr. and Benvenuto Ave. No children. *In room:* Fridge, coffeemaker, hair dryer, iron.

INEXPENSIVE

Point-No-Point Resort ★ *Finds*   Away from it all in your own little cabin, you'll have 40 acres of wilderness around you and a wide rugged beach in front of you, with nothing to do but laze away the day in your hot tub. Or walk the beach. Or the forest. Or look at an eagle. Or three. That's Point-No-Point. Since 1950 this oceanfront resort has been welcoming guests, first to a pair of tiny cabins, now to 24 units. Cabins vary depending on when they were built. All have fireplaces, full kitchens, and bathrooms; newer ones have hot tubs on their private decks. Food isn't included in the price, so come prepared. Lunch and afternoon tea are available daily at the small but sunny central dining room. Dinner is served Wednesday through Sunday. The dining-room tables are conveniently equipped with binoculars, so you won't miss a bald eagle as you eat.

1505 West Coast Hwy. (Hwy. 14), Sooke, B.C. V0S 1N0. © **250/646-2020.** Fax 250/646-2294. www.point nopointresort.com. 25 units. C$125–C$220 (US$81–US$142) cabin. AE, MC, V. Free parking. Pets accepted, C$10 (US$6.45) per night. No public transit. **Amenities:** Jacuzzi. *In room:* Kitchen, no phone.

University of Victoria Housing, Food, and Conference Services *Value* One of the best deals going is found at the University of Victoria, when classes aren't in session and summer visitors are welcomed. All rooms have single or twin beds and basic furnishings, and there are bathrooms, pay phones, and TV lounges on every floor. Linens, towels, and soap are provided. The suites are an extremely good value—each has four bedrooms, a kitchen, a living room, and 1½ bathrooms. The disadvantage, of course, is that the U. Vic. campus is a painfully long way from everywhere—the city center is about a half-hour drive away. For C$5 (US$3.25) extra per day, however, you can make use of the many on-campus athletic facilities. Each of the 28 buildings has a coin laundry.

P.O. Box 1700, Sinclair at Finerty Rd., Victoria, B.C. V8W 2Y2. © **250/721-8395.** Fax 250/721-8930. www. hfcs.uvic.ca/uvichfcs.htm. 898 units. MC, V. May–Aug C$38 (US$25) single; C$50 (US$33) twin; C$146 (US$94) suite. Discounts available for longer stays. Rates include full breakfast and taxes; suite rates include taxes. Parking C$5 (US$3.25). Closed Sept–Apr. Bus: 4 or 14 to University of Victoria. **Amenities:** Indoor pool; access to athletic facilities; coin laundry; nonsmoking rooms.

12

Where to Dine in Victoria

Though early Victoria settlers were intent on re-creating a little patch of the Old Country on their wild western island, the one thing they were never tempted to import was British cooking. Thankfully. Instead, following the Canadian norm, each little immigrant group imported its own cuisine, so that now Victoria is a cornucopia of culinary styles from around the world. With over 700 restaurants in the area, there's something for every taste and wallet. (The one aspect of English cuisine Victoria did import was the quaint but delicious custom of afternoon tea. American visitors in particular should give it a try—you'll never go back to lukewarm water with a tea bag on the side.)

Note that the touristy restaurants along Wharf Street serve up mediocre food for folks they know they'll never have to see again. The canny visitor knows to head inland (even a block is enough) where the proportion of tourists to locals drops sharply and the quality jumps by leaps and bounds.

Most restaurants close at 10pm, especially on weekdays. Reservations are strongly recommended for prime sunset seating during summer. There's no provincial tax on restaurant meals in British Columbia, just the 7% federal goods and services tax (GST).

1 Restaurants by Cuisine

BAKERY
  Q V Bakery & Café (Downtown,
    $, p. 210)

BISTRO
  Cassis Bistro ★★ (Downtown,
    $$$, p. 206)
  Süze Restaurant ★★ (Downtown,
    $$, p. 208)

CHINESE
  Don Mee Restaurant ★
    (Downtown, $, p. 210)
  J&J Wonton Noodle House ★★
    (Downtown, $, p. 210)

CONTINENTAL
  The Marina Restaurant ★★
    (Greater Victoria, $$$, p. 212)

DELI
  Sam's Deli ★★ (Downtown, $,
    p. 211)

FISH & CHIPS
  Barb's Place ★★ (Inner Harbour,
    $, p. 204)

FRENCH
  The Aerie ★★ (Greater Victoria,
    $$$$, p. 211)
  Deep Cove Chalet ★★ (Greater
    Victoria, $$$, p. 212)

GREEK
  Millos ★★ (Downtown, $$,
    p. 208)

INDIAN
  Da Tandoor (Downtown, $$,
    p. 206)

ITALIAN
  Café Brio ★★ (Downtown, $$$,
    p. 204)
  Il Terrazzo Ristorante ★★
    (Downtown, $$$, p. 206)

Pagliacci's ★★ (Downtown, $$, p. 208)

Zambri's ★★★ (Downtown, $$, p. 209)

PASTA

Herald Street Caffe ★ (Downtown, $$, p. 207)

PUB GRUB

Six Mile Pub ★★ (Greater Victoria, $, p. 213)

SEAFOOD

The Blue Crab Bar and Grill ★★ (Inner Harbour, $$$, p. 203)

Pescatore's Fish House (Inner Harbour, $$, p. 203)

THAI

Siam Thai Restaurant (Downtown, $, p. 211)

VEGETARIAN

Green Cuisine (Downtown, $, p. 210)

Re-bar ★★ (Downtown, $, p. 210)

WEST COAST (PACIFIC NORTHWEST)

Café Brio ★★ (Downtown, $$$, p. 204)

Camille's ★★ (Downtown, $$$, p. 204)

Herald Street Caffe ★ (Downtown, $$, p. 205)

Sooke Harbour House ★★★ (Greater Victoria, $$$$, p. 211)

The Victorian Restaurant ★ (Inner Harbour, $$$, p. 203)

2 The Inner Harbour

EXPENSIVE

The Blue Crab Bar and Grill ★★ SEAFOOD   Victoria's best seafood spot, the Blue Crab combines fresh ingredients, inventive recipes, and beautiful presentation. It also has a killer view—floatplanes slip in and out while you're dining, little ferries chug across the harbor, and the sun sets slowly over the Sooke Hills. What's on the daily specials board is entirely dependent on what came in on the boats or floatplanes that day—salmon, spotted prawns, and crab (in season) are strong possibilities. Occasionally, little Salt Spring Island lambs are on offer. The chef is particularly fond of unusual combinations, such as sea bass with taro root, grapefruit, and blood orange or house-smoked chicken sausage in portobello-mushroom broth. The service is deft, smart, and obliging.

146 Kingston St., in the Coast Hotel. ✆ **250/480-1999.** Reservations recommended. Main courses C$20–C$30 (US$13–US$19). AE, DC, MC, V. Daily 6:30am–10:30pm (dinner from 5pm). Bus: 30 to Erie St.

The Victorian Restaurant ★ WEST COAST   One of the only good bets when it comes to waterfront dining in Victoria is this elegant restaurant in the Ocean Pointe Resort. The views are tremendous, and in recent years the food has begun to win some recognition, including awards from *Wine Spectator* and *Western Living* magazines. In culinary terms, the chef takes few risks, sticking to fresh ingredients with a slight emphasis on seafood but enough lamb, steak, and veggie dishes to cover all the bases. The service is polished, and the wine list one of the better ones in town.

45 Songhees Rd., in the Ocean Pointe Resort. ✆ **250/360-2999.** www.oprhotel.com. Reservations recommended. Main courses C$14–C$29 (US$9.10–US$19). AE, MC, V. Daily 5:30–9:30pm. Bus: 24 to Colville.

MODERATE

Pescatore's Fish House SEAFOOD   For a town surrounded by an ocean literally teeming with fish, Victoria is surprisingly lacking in good seafood restaurants. Fortunately there's Pescatore's for those with no such hang-ups. The food in this Italian-influenced restaurant floats somewhere between good and very good. The grand ceilings and striking wall paintings by local artist Luis Merino set the ambience, and the well-stocked oyster bar will grab your attention. Get past that and you're faced with the lunch specials, including prawns, crab cakes, and lushly creamy seafood bisques. Come suppertime, the menu expands to include scallops, trout, and salmon. There are also burgers and New York strip loin.

614 Humboldt St., across from The Fairmont Empress. © 250/385-4512. www.pescatores.com. Reservations recommended. Main courses C$15–C$26 (US$9.75–US$17). AE, DC, MC, V. Mon–Sat 11am to around 11pm; Sun 5–10pm.

INEXPENSIVE

Barb's Place ★★ *(Kids)* FISH & CHIPS   The best "chippie" in town, Barb serves lightly breaded halibut and hand-hewn chips served in folded-newspaper pouches from a floating restaurant at Fisherman's Wharf. There are picnic tables to sit on and boats, seagulls, and lots of other eye candy to amuse the kids. Barb's is a favorite among locals.

310 Erie St. © **250/384-6515.** Reservations not accepted. Menu items C$2.25–C$9 (US$1.50–US$5.85). MC, V. Daily 10am–sunset.

3 Downtown & Old Town

EXPENSIVE

Café Brio ★★ WEST COAST/ITALIAN   Still Victoria's most exciting restaurant after 5 years, Café Brio is a collaboration between restaurateurs Sylvia Marcolini and Greg Hays (who together created the Herald Street Caffe and the revamped Marina) and chef Jeff Keenliside. The result is a Tuscan-influenced cuisine that strongly reflects the seasons, fresh local produce, and Brio's location on the edge of the Pacific. Appetizers may include potato-crusted Alaskan scallops with heirloom tomatoes, purple basil, and crème fraîche, while entrees may feature seared ahi tuna with mushroom pave and pinot-noir sauce, venison, duck, and free-range chicken. Vegetarians will enjoy the tasting menu (C$27/US$17) that includes three dishes created with fresh seasonal ingredients such as the heirloom tomato and fava bean bruschetta or the crispy eggplant, zucchini, and portobello mushroom served on braised greens. The wine list is excellent, with an impressive selection of B.C. and international reds and whites. The service is deft and knowledgeable and the kitchen stays open as long as guests keep ordering.

944 Fort St. © 250/383-0009. Reservations recommended. Main courses C$16–C$29 (US$10–US$19). AE, MC, V. Mon–Fri 11:45am–2pm; daily 5:30pm–closing.

Camille's ★★ WEST COAST   The most romantic of Victoria's restaurants, Camille's is seductively tucked away in a two-room enclave beneath the old Law Chambers. The decor contrasts blinding white linen with century-old exposed brick, stained-glass lamps, antique books, and old wine bottles. Chef and owner David Mincey uses only the freshest local ingredients; he was one of the founders of a Vancouver Island farm cooperative, which brings local farmers together with local restaurants. The ever-changing menu displays Mincey's love for cheeky invention: Think duck confit with little mandarin slices on a bed of baby greens or fresh sockeye salmon served with fresh local raspberries. A delicate roasted rack of lamb is also a perennial specialty. The reasonable and extensive wine list comes

Victoria Dining

Barb's Place **20**
The Blue Crab Bar and Grill **19**
Café Brio **12**
Camille's **9**
Cassis Bistro **21**
Da Tandoor **13**
Don Mee Restaurant **2**
Green Cuisine **4**
Herald Street Caffe **1**
Il Terrazzo Ristorante **5**
J&J Wonton Noodle House **15**
Millos **18**
Pagliacci's **11**
Pescatore's Fish House **17**
Q V Bakery & Café **3**
Re-bar **8**
Sam's Deli **16**
Siam Thai Restaurant **10**
Süze Lounge & Restaurant **7**
The Victorian Restaurant **6**
Zambri's **14**

with liner notes that are amusing and informative. On Sundays, wine tastings introduce you to the best cellar selections.

45 Bastion Sq. ⓒ 250/381-3433. www.camillesrestaurant.com. Reservations recommended. Main courses C$16–C$24 (US$10–US$15). AE, MC, V. Daily 5:30–10pm.

Cassis Bistro ✿✿ BISTRO   If you've got the time, the pretty neighborhood of Cook Street Village is worth a stroll, but if you've only come for the food, this cozy candlelit bistro is exactly the right place. Chef and owner John Hall describes the menu as eclectic Italian, which means dishes from the whole boot plus borrowings here and there from Asia and France. Far-flung as the cuisine may be, ingredients are resolutely local; Hall works with an extensive network of local farmers and growers who provide him with the region's best products. Recent highlights on this ever-changing menu have included ling cod filet, lightly seared and served with Japanese *shimeji* mushrooms; smoked tuna ravioli in a miso jus; and a braised Gulf Island halibut on a bed of spinach and finely sliced pancetta in a rich game stock. Being partial to duck, we were won over by the Fraser Valley duck breast served on a bed of warm goat cheese crouton. Pickled bing cherries added just that exquisite hint of sweetness to the tender duck breast. And if you thought Hall was passionate about food, just get him going on the topic of wine.

253 Cook St. ⓒ 250/384-1932. Reservations recommended. Main courses C$23–C$27 (US$15–US$18). MC, V. Tues–Sat 5:30–9:30pm.

Il Terrazzo Ristorante ✿✿ ITALIAN   This quirky, charming spot in a converted heritage building off Waddington Alley is always a top contender for Victoria's best Italian restaurant. The food hails from northern Italy—think wood-oven-roasted meats and pizzas as well as homemade pastas. But there's also an emphasis on fresh produce and local seafood, with appetizers such as thinly sliced smoked tuna over fresh arugula with horseradish dressing and potato pancakes and entrees like linguine with prawns, mussels, clams, calamari, and tomatoes in a white wine/saffron broth. The atmosphere is bustling and upbeat, with the exposed brick walls, wood beams, and intriguing nooks and crannies offering extra spice. And not surprisingly, given the name, Il Terrazzo indulges those who love patio dining—the courtyard not only is romantically furnished with flowers, marble tables, and wrought-iron chairs, but also has warming heaters for when nights grow colder. That, a good Chianti, and a piping hot *pizzetta* are enough to keep even the fiercest chill at bay.

555 Johnson St., off Waddington Alley. ⓒ 250/361-0028. www.ilterrazzo.com. Reservations recommended. Main courses C$15–C$31 (US$9.75–US$20). AE, MC, V. Mon–Sat 11:30am–3:30pm (Oct–Apr no lunch on Sat); daily 5–10pm. Bus: 5.

MODERATE

Da Tandoor *Finds* INDIAN   The best of Victoria's several Indian restaurants, Da Tandoor hides itself behind an unprepossessing facade on the outer edge of Fort Street's antiques row. The cuisine, however, is well worth the 10-minute walk from downtown. Tandoori chicken, seafood, and lamb are the house specialties; but the extensive menu also includes masalas, vindaloos, goshts, and vegetarian dishes, as well as classic appetizers like vegetable and meat samosas, pakoras, and papadums. If you get inspired to try it at home, the restaurant sells a wide variety of spices and chutneys.

1010 Fort St. ⓒ 250/384-6333. Reservations recommended. Main courses C$9–C$21 (US$5.90–US$14). MC, V. Mon–Fri 5–10pm; Sat–Sun 5–10:30pm.

Moments **Taking Afternoon Tea**

Okay, so it's expensive and touristy. Go anyway. Far from a simple beverage, afternoon tea is both a meal and a ritual. The pot is warmed; the water poured over the tea leaves is boiling hot. The sweet and subtle flavor will almost certainly put you off the warm-water-and-tea-bag thing for life.

Any number of places in Victoria serve afternoon tea (some also refer to it as high tea—both come with sandwiches and berries and tarts, but high tea usually includes some more substantial savory fare such as a pasty [meat-and-vegetable filled turnover]). Still, though the caloric intake at a top-quality tea can be substantial, it's really all about the ritual. For that reason you don't want to go to any old teahouse, but a place where you could be sipping with the Marquess of Pomp and the Lord of Circumstance. Note that in summer, afternoon tea becomes highly popular. Consider booking at least a week ahead, if not longer.

If you want the experience, you may as well do it right and go for the best. **The Fairmont Empress** ✪, 721 Government St. (© 250/384-8111; bus no. 5 to the Convention Centre), serves tea in the Palm Court or in the main lounge—both are beautifully ornate and luxurious. For C$46 (US$30) (or C$32–C$43/US$21–US$28 Nov–Mar), The Fairmont Empress will pamper and spoil you shamelessly: fresh berries and cream; sandwiches of smoked salmon, cucumber, and carrot and ginger; scones, strawberry preserves, and thick Jersey cream. Even the tea is a special house blend. When you leave you receive a package to brew at home. There are four seatings a day: 12:30, 2, 2:30, and 5pm; reservations are recommended in the summer.

More affordable and just as historic is tea on the lawn of **Point Ellice House,** 2616 Pleasant St. (© 250/380-6506), where the creme of Victoria society used to gather on pleasant afternoons in the early 1900s. On the Gorge waterway, Point Ellice is just a 5-minute trip by ferry from the Inner Harbour, or take bus no. 14 to Pleasant Street. Afternoon tea costs C$17 (US$11) and includes a half-hour tour of the mansion and gardens, plus the opportunity to play a game of croquet. Open daily noon to 5pm (tea served until 4pm) April 1 through Labour Day (first Mon of Sept); phone ahead for Christmas hours.

With impeccably maintained and groomed gardens as a backdrop, "Afternoon Tea at the Gardens," at the **Butchart Gardens Dining Room Restaurant,** 800 Benvenuto Ave. (© 250/652-4422; bus no. 75), is a memorable experience. Looking out over the flowers, you can sit back and savor this fine tradition at C$20 (US$13) per person. Tea is served daily noon to 5pm April 1 through Labour Day. Call ahead for winter hours.

Herald Street Caffe ✪ PASTA/WEST COAST An old warehouse on the far side of Chinatown, this cafe sizzles from midweek onward with the sound of diners young and old. The room is large, its walls painted a warm red and covered with an ever-changing display of local art. This is a fun place to dine and drink. The menu comes with a list of more than 20 martinis, and for oenophiles, the wine list offers French and Canadian labels, along with a good selection of B.C. reds and whites. The cuisine is sophisticated without going too far over the top. Appetizers may include barbecued duck in phyllo pastry with apple-currant chutney or oysters in cornmeal crust on a nest of new potatoes. The entrees include many clever seafood dishes, as well as free-range chicken, duck, and lamb dishes, and a whole page of pastas. Portions are generous and the service is knowledgeable and helpful, particularly when it comes to wine pairings. For dessert, don't miss the Boca Negra, a chocolate cake with rich chocolate bourbon sauce and fresh raspberries.

546 Herald St. ☎ **250/381-1441.** Reservations required. Main courses C$17–C$28 (US$11–US$18). AE, DC, MC, V. Wed–Sat 11:30am–2:30pm; Sun brunch 11am–3pm; daily 5:30–10pm. Bus: 5.

Millos ★★ *(Kids)* GREEK Millos isn't hard to find—look for the blue-and-white windmill behind The Fairmont Empress or listen for the hand clapping and plate breaking as diners get into the swing of things. Flaming *saganaki* (a sharp cheese sautéed in olive oil and flambéed with Greek brandy), grilled halibut souvlaki, baby back ribs, and succulent grilled salmon are a few of the menu items at this lively five-level restaurant. Kids get their own menu. Folk dancers and belly dancers highlight the entertainment on Friday and Saturday nights, and the wait staff is remarkably warm and entertaining at all times.

716 Burdett Ave. ☎ **250/382-4422.** Reservations recommended. Main courses C$10–C$28 (US$6.50–US$18), with most dishes costing around C$15 (US$9.75). AE, DC, MC, V. Mon–Sat 11am–11pm; Sun 4–11pm. Bus: 5.

Pagliacci's ★★ ITALIAN Victoria's night owls used to come here when Pagliacci's was one of the few places to offer late night dining. Though the evening scene has improved since expatriate New Yorker Howie Siegal opened the restaurant in 1979, Pagliacci's can still boast an un-Victorian kind of big city buzz and energy. Tables jostle against one another as guests ogle each other's food and eavesdrop on conversations, while Howie works the room, dispensing a word or two to long-lost friends, many of whom he's just met. The menu is southern Italian—veal parmigiana, tortellini, and 19 or 20 other a la carte pastas, all fresh and made by hand, many quite inventive. The service isn't fast, but when you're having this much fun, who cares? Grab some wine, munch some focaccia, and enjoy the atmosphere. Sunday through Wednesday there's live jazz, swing, blues, or Celtic starting at 8:30pm. On Sunday, Howie hosts a very good brunch.

1011 Broad St. ☎ **250/386-1662.** Reservations not accepted. Main courses C$11–C$19 (US$7.15–US$12). AE, MC, V. Sun–Thurs 11:30am–10pm; Fri–Sat 11:30am–midnight; between 3–5:30pm light lunches and desserts only.

Süze Lounge and Restaurant ★★ BISTRO This fun and happening little lounge is in the heart of the Old Town. The owner's intent was to create the perfect spot for a first date—little tables on their own but not so isolated that escape is impossible, and lots of background noise and eye candy in case you get bored with the one that brung ya. The crowd is young, moneyed, and generally good looking. The menu—covering a huge swath of territory, from dim sum and sushi bento boxes to herb-crusted salmon and pizza and pasta and fusion-y Thai noodle dishes—has made great strides since Süze fired its last chef and brought in Toronto-trained Gordon O'Neil. The quality is now consistently high. Süze is also one of the few—and possibly the most fun—spots for late-night dining in Victoria.

515 Yates St. ℂ **250/383-2829.** Main courses C$9–C$17 (US$5.85–US$11). AE, DC, MC, V. Sun–Wed 5pm–midnight; Thurs–Sat 5pm–1am.

Zambri's ★★★ *(Finds)* ITALIAN   A friend of ours recently threatened to have a full-blown hissy fit if even one more person raved to her about Zambri's. (If she sees this book, hide). Open for a little over a year now, this little deli in a strip mall off Yates Street has earned this and other accolades for its honest and fresh Italian cuisine served in an unpretentious, no-nonsense style. The lunch menu, served cafeteria style, includes five daily pasta specials and a handful of entrees such as fresh rockfish or salmon. In the evenings, the atmosphere is slightly more formal with table service and a regularly changing a la carte menu. Menu items veer from the stereotypical fettuccine Alfredo to include pasta with chicken liver paté or peas and Gorgonzola. The piece de resistance, however is the Saturday night five-course dinner (C$50/US$32) served to those who were lucky enough to snag a reservation.

110–911 Yates St. ℂ **250/360-1171.** www.zambris.com. Reservations not accepted Mon–Fri; Sat dinner by reservation only. Lunch C$9–C$13 (US$5.85–8.45); dinner C$10–C$18 (US$6.45–US$12). MC, V. Mon–Sat 11:30am–4pm and 5–10pm.

 Finding High-Octane Coffee

Good coffee is one of the great joys of life. Fortunately, Victoria's Englishness hasn't stopped it from gleefully throwing itself into the same coffee-craze that's engulfing the rest of the Pacific Northwest. Some to savor:

- **Starbucks** has any number of outposts here. The one at the corner of Fort and Blanshard streets (ℂ **250/383-6208**) is fairly central, open 6am to 11pm Sunday through Thursday and 6am to midnight Friday and Saturday; bus no. 5 to Fort Street.

- Better for taste, and with interesting hand-painted mugs is **Torrefazione,** 1234 Government St. (ℂ **250/920-7203**), open Monday through Friday 6:30am to 9pm, Saturday 7:30am to 10pm, and Sunday 8:30am to 7pm; bus no. 5 to View Street.

- Out in Cook Street Village, the **Moka House,** 345 Cook St. (ℂ **250/ 388-7377**), open daily 6am to midnight, also offers great desserts and snacks; bus no. 5 to Cook and Mary streets.

- For a more bohemian crowd, go to the **Demitasse Coffee Bar** ⭐, 1320 Blanshard St. (ℂ **250/386-4442**). Lattes, mochas, dark rich java, and more elaborate concoctions all come in big mugs, allowing plenty of sipping time to peruse the avant-garde art on the walls. Open Monday through Friday 7am to 4pm, Saturday and Sunday 9am to 5pm; bus no. 5 to Douglas Road and Johnson Street.

- On a sunny day head for coffee on the patio at **Willy's,** 537 Johnson St. (ℂ **250/381-8414**). Order your brew of choice from the counter and head outside where there is usually plenty of space. This bakery also serves up excellent sweets and great hot breakfasts for those who need more than caffeine to jumpstart their system. It's open daily 7am to 5:30pm, later in the summer; bus no. 25.

INEXPENSIVE

Don Mee Restaurant ✷ CHINESE   Since the 1920s, elegant Don Mee's has been serving Victoria's best dim sum, chop suey, and chow mein, along with piquant Szechwan seafood dishes and delectable Cantonese sizzling platters. You can't miss this second-story restaurant—a huge neon Chinese lantern looms above the small doorway. A 4-foot-tall gold-leaf laughing Buddha greets you at the foot of the stairs leading up to the huge dining room, where, if it's lunchtime, you'll find many Chinese-Canadian businesspeople munching away. The dinner specials are particularly good deals if you want to sample lots of everything on the menu.

538 Fisgard St. ✆ **250/383-1032.** Reservations accepted. Main courses C$9–C$14 (US$5.85–US$9.10); 4-course dinner from C$14 (US$9.10). AE, DC, MC, V. Mon–Fri 11am–10pm; Sat–Sun 10am–10pm. Bus: 5.

Green Cuisine *Value* VEGETARIAN   In addition to being undeniably healthy, Victoria's only fully vegan enclave is remarkably tasty, with a self-serve salad bar, hot buffet, dessert bar, and full bakery. Available dishes range from Moroccan chickpea and vegetable soup to pasta primavera salad to pumpkin tofu cheesecake, not to mention a wide selection of freshly baked breads (made with natural sweeteners and fresh-ground organic flour). Green cuisine also has a large selection of freshly squeezed organic juices, smoothies, and shakes, and organic coffees and teas. If you like the food, check out the website, which features monthly recipes from the restaurant.

560 Johnson St., in Market Sq. ✆ **250/385-1809.** www.greencuisine.com. Main courses C$3.95–C$10 (US$2.60–US$6.50). AE, MC, V. Daily 10am–8pm.

J&J Wonton Noodle House ✷✷ *Finds* CHINESE   Real Chinese noodle houses are rare in North America, which is a shame, because they're so much fun. The kitchen here is glassed in so you can watch the chefs spinning out noodles and expertly whisking soups through woks into bowls. Lunch specials—which feature different fresh seafood every day—are good and cheap, so expect a line of locals at the door. If you miss the specials, noodle soups, chow mein, chow fun (wide noodles), and other dishes are also quick, delicious, and inexpensive.

1012 Fort St. ✆ **250/383-0680.** Main courses C$7–C$17 (US$4.50–US$11); lunch specials C$6–C$7 (US$3.90–US$4.55). MC, V. Tues–Sat 11am–2pm and 4:30–8:30pm. Bus: 5.

Q V Bakery & Café BAKERY   The main attraction of the cuisine on offer at this spot on the edge of downtown isn't so much its quality—though the coffee, muffins, cookies, and light meals like lasagnas, quiches, and salads are all quite good—but its availability. Q V is open 24 hours, which in Victoria is enough to make it very special indeed.

1701 Government St. ✆ **250/384-8831.** Main courses C$3.95–C$10 (US$2.60–US$6.50). MC, V. Daily 24 hr.

Re-bar ✷✷ *Kids* VEGETARIAN   Even if you're not hungry, it's worth dropping in for a juice blend—say grapefruit, banana, melon, and pear with bee pollen or blue-green algae for added oomph. If you're hungry, then rejoice: Re-bar is the city's premier dispenser of vegetarian comfort food. Disturbingly wholesome as that may sound, Re-bar is not only tasty, but fun, and a great spot to take the kids for brunch or breakfast. The room—in the basement of an 1890s heritage building—is pastel-tinted funky, with loads of cake tins glued to the walls. The service is friendly and casual. The food tends to the simple and wholesome, including a vegetable-and-almond patty with red onions, sprouts, and fresh tomato salsa on a multigrain kaiser roll, as well as quesadillas, omelets, and crisp salads. Juices are still the crown jewels, with over 80 blends on the menu.

50 Bastion Sq. ⓒ 250/361-9223. www.rebarmodernfood.com. Main courses C$7–C$14 (US$4.55–US$9.10). AE, MC, V. Mon–Thurs 8:30am–9pm; Fri–Sat 8:30am–10pm; Sun 8:30am–3:30pm. Reduced hr. in the winter. Bus: 5.

Sam's Deli 🏃🏃 DELI   If you don't like lines, avoid the lunch hour, for Sam's is *the* lunchtime Victoria soup-and-sandwich spot. Sandwiches come in all tastes and sizes (mostly large), but the shrimp and avocado is the one to get. Sam's homemade soups are excellent, as is his chili. And Sam's is a hop, skip, and sandwich-laden lurch from the harbor—so unless it's raining, there's no excuse not to order to go.

805 Government St. ⓒ 250/382-8424. www.samsdeli.com. Main courses C$3.95–C$10 (US$2.60–US$6.50). MC, V. Daily 9am–7pm.

Siam Thai Restaurant *(Value* THAI   There aren't many opportunities to satisfy your craving for Thai food in Victoria, but tucked away in a vintage building just half a block or so from the waterfront, this little local favorite offers good-quality Thai cooking done with varying levels of spiciness to suit every palate. Menu items are starred from mild to spicy (one to four stars), so there's no risk of having your tongue inadvertently scorched. The menu includes many Thai signature dishes such as coconut–lemon grass chicken or shrimp soup, Pad Thai noodles, garlic and pepper pork, as well as a variety of curries (red, yellow, and green). Most items can be adapted to accommodate vegetarians. The lunch specials (C$7.95/U$5.20) are a great deal.

512 Fort St. ⓒ 250/383-9911. Main courses C$9–C$17 (US$5.85–US$11). MC, V. Mon–Sat 11:30am–2pm; daily 5–9:30pm. Bus: 5.

4 Outside the Central Area

VERY EXPENSIVE

The Aerie 🏃🏃 FRENCH   The dining room of this red-tile villa boasts panoramic windows overlooking Finlayson Inlet, the Straight of Georgia, and on a clear day even the Olympic Peninsula mountains. The room itself is bright and decorated with a 14-carat gold-leaf ceiling, crystal chandeliers, and a large open-hearth fireplace. Views and luxury aside, however, most people come for chef Christophe Letard's cooking. His creations combine West Coast freshness with unmistakably French accents. We started our culinary event with a seared wild sockeye served with a green asparagus salad. Another fish favorite was the peppercorn-crusted lingcod accompanied by steamed young fennel and garlic shoots in a gooseberry and red currant beurre blanc. Sauces were light, while Letard's treatment of vegetables was a revelation, crisp and bursting with flavor. The fish, plus inventive twists on Sooke rabbit and duck breast, were followed by a plate of local goat cheeses. For dessert, the spiced local raspberries served with star anise and fennel ice cream were outstanding.

600 Ebedora Lane, Malahat. ⓒ 800/518-1933 or 250/743-7115. www.aerie.bc.ca. Reservations required. Main courses C$27–C$35 (US$18–US$23); 7-course set menu C$95 (US$61), C$155 (US$100) with wine pairings. AE, DC, MC, V. Daily noon–1:30pm and 6–9:30pm. Free parking. Take Hwy. 1 to the Spectacle Lake turnoff; take the first right and follow the winding driveway.

Sooke Harbour House 🏃🏃🏃 WEST COAST   In a rambling white house on a bluff on the edge of the Pacific, this small restaurant/hotel (see chapter 11) offers spectacular waterfront views, a relaxed atmosphere, and what could be the best food in all Canada. Chef/proprietor Sinclair Philip is both a talented innovator and a stickler for detail, which results an ever-changing menu in which each of the dishes is prepared with care, imagination, and flair. The ingredients are resolutely local (many come from the inn's own organic herb garden or from the ocean at the Harbour House's doorstep). On any given night, dishes might include seared scallops with sea asparagus or chinook salmon with red wine–gooseberry sauce. The presentation is always interesting, and the staff is knowledgeable and professional. The wine cellar is extensive (one of the best in Canada in fact), and the pairings for Philip's culinary creations are particularly well chosen.

1528 Whiffen Spit Rd., Sooke. ✆ **800/889-9688** or 250/642-3421. www.sookeharbourhouse.com. Reservations required. Main courses C$29–C$36 (US$19–US$23); 4-course tasting menu C$65 (US$42). MC, V. Daily 5–9pm. Take the Island Hwy. to the Sooke/Colwood turnoff (Junction Hwy. 14). Continue on Hwy. 14 to Sooke. About a mile past the town's only traffic light, turn left onto Whiffen Spit Rd.

EXPENSIVE

Deep Cove Chalet ★★ FRENCH   Gorgeous! The prettiest place to eat this side of Shangri-la, the garden patio of the Deep Cove Chalet rests beneath spreading chestnut trees at the top of a broad green lawn that rolls down to a tiny bay where the yachts and powerboats ride at anchor. The atmosphere here is a kind of laid-back formal; while you dine on China and linen, an old English spaniel romps around the lawn with his chew toy, swatted now and again by the (otherwise) ingratiating hostess when he strays too near the tables. You may start with the delicious salad of tomato and fresh greens with balsamic vinaigrette. For dinner, the sea bass comes served with a light curry sauce on a bed of mandarins and avocado. For meat eaters there's rack of lamb Provençal or Quails Normandie with apples and a light cream sauce. The wine list is long enough to merit an index and heavily weighted to France. Don't miss Pierre's cheese plate.

11190 Chalet Rd., near Sidney. ✆ **250/656-3541.** www.deepcovechalet.com. Reservations required. Main courses C$28–C$40 (US$18–US$26); 5-course pre-fixe C$46–C$75 (US$30–US$48). AE, MC, V. Wed–Sun 11am–2pm; Tues–Sun 5–10pm. Free parking.

The Marina Restaurant ★★ CONTINENTAL   Set above the yachts of the fashionable Oak Bay marina, the semicircular dark-wood dining room has two levels of seating and panoramic floor-to-ceiling windows. When this restaurant opened, the cuisine was top quality. But after the initial buzz, the downtown foodies stopped making the trek out, and the management discovered that conservative Oak Bay residents weren't quite up to their flights of culinary fancy. So they pulled back and aimed for something a little more down to earth (most say they overshot). It's been coming back since, however, as the Oak Bay burghers warm to the concept of something else for supper besides a patty and two buns. The Marina is perhaps best known for its Sunday brunch—the all-you-can-eat buffet overflows with oysters, clams, prawns, prime rib, poached salmon, fresh salads, marinated vegetables, fruit salads, breakfast foods, and an array of handmade Belgian chocolate truffles, tall cakes, and puddings. Service is quick and friendly, and on a sunny day, the view does seem to make it all worthwhile.

1327 Beach Dr., Oak Bay. ✆ **250/598-8555.** www.marinarestaurant.com. Reservations recommended. Main courses C$8–C$17 (US$5.20–US$11) at lunch, C$17–C$27 (US$11–US$18) at dinner; Sun brunch C$27 (US$18). AE, DC, MC, V. Mon–Sat 11:30am–2:30pm; Sun brunch 10am–2:30pm; daily 5–10pm. Bus: 2.

INEXPENSIVE

Six Mile Pub ★★ PUB GRUB   In an 1855 building, this pub has a rich history. Originally named the Parson's Bridge Hotel (after the man who built Parson's Bridge, which opened the Sooke area to vehicle traffic), it was filled with sailors when the Esquimalt Naval Base opened nearby in 1864. When Victoria elected to continue Prohibition until 1952, the Six Mile Pub became the hub for provincial bootleggers. Loyal locals still come for the atmosphere and the dinner specials. You can enjoy the warm ambience of the fireside room, or the beautiful scenery from the outdoor patio. Start with one of the 10 house brews on tap, then enjoy a hearty Cornish pasty (stringy mystery meat, peas, potatoes, and carrots in a pastry envelope), steak-and-mushroom pie, or juicy prime rib. If meat isn't part of your diet, try a tasty veggie burger.

494 Island Hwy., View Royal. © **250/478-3121.** www.sixmilepub.com. Main courses C$7–C$10 (US$4.55–US$6.50). MC, V. Mon–Sat 11am–1am; Sun 10am–midnight. Must be over 19 to enter.

13

Exploring Victoria

Victoria's top draws are its waterfront—the beautiful viewscape created by The Fairmont Empress and the Parliament Buildings on the edge of the Inner Harbour—and its historic Old Town. So attractive are these that folks sometimes forget to notice what a beautiful and wild part of the world the city is set in. If you have time, step out of town a little and see some nature: Sail out to see killer whales, beachcomb for crabs, kayak along the ocean shorelines, or hike into the hills for some fabulous views and scenery.

SIGHTSEEING SUGGESTIONS

If You Have 1 Day

Have breakfast on the water at the **Blackfish Cafe,** 950 Wharf St. (© **250/385-9996**), open 8am to 9pm daily in summer (8am–4pm in winter), or grab some croissants and coffee for a wharfside picnic. Stroll along the **Inner Harbour** past The Fairmont Empress hotel to **Thunderbird Park** and watch a totem pole being made. Then head to the **Royal BC Museum,** one of the world's best small museums. Afterward, refresh your brain with a stroll through **The Fairmont Empress Rose Garden** on your way in to have **afternoon tea.** Later, walk around the **Old Town.** Duck through **Trounce Alley** into **Market Square** and see if there's a band playing on the outdoor stage. Stop in at the **Starfish Glassworks** (630 Yates St.) and watch some glass-art being blown or browse for antiques on **Fort Street.** Then head off for some seafood, preferably at a restaurant overlooking the water like the Coast Hotel's **Blue Crab Bar and Grill** or the Ocean Pointe's **Victorian Restaurant.** After sundown, see if there's any jazz playing downtown.

If You Have 2 Days

Take a boat out to **see the orcas**—they gather here like almost nowhere else, and seeing them up close is something special. Back in town, lunch at one of the dockside **brew pubs** like Spinnaker's or the Harbour Canoe Club. Then take a walk through **Chinatown.** In the late afternoon, drive out to **Butchart Gardens.** If you have kids (or even if you don't), stop in at the **Victoria Butterfly Gardens** on the way. Watch as the sun goes down and subtle illumination gives the gardens a whole new character. Back in town, have a late-night supper somewhere like **Pagliacci's.** For a nightcap, go for drinks in The Fairmont Empress's **Bengal Lounge.**

If You Have 3 Days

Rent a bike and cycle along the ocean-side Dallas Road to **Clover Point** and **Ross Bay** cemetery, then head up to **Craigdarroch Castle.** In the afternoon, do some **kayaking** in the sheltered waters around Victoria. Or **cycle (or drive) the Galloping Goose trail** to East Sooke Park and do some beachcombing. In the evening, treat yourself to supper somewhere out of town like the **Deep Cove Chalet** (near Sidney) or the **Sooke Harbour House.**

1 Seeing the Sights

THE TOP ATTRACTIONS

British Columbia Aviation Museum ✈ A must for plane buffs, or for anyone with an interest in the history of flight. Located adjacent to Victoria International Airport, this small hanger is crammed to bursting with a score of original, rebuilt, and replica airplanes. The collection ranges from the first Canadiandesigned craft ever to fly (a bizarre kitelike contraption) to World War I–vintage Nieuports and Tiger Moths, to floatplanes and Spitfires and slightly more modern water bombers and helicopters. Thursdays you can watch the all-volunteer crew in the restoration hangar working to bring these old craft back to life. Allow 1 hour.

1910 Norseman Rd., Sidney. © 250/655-3300. www.bcam.net. Admission C$5 (US$3.20) adults, C$4 (US$2.60) seniors, C$3 (US$1.95) students, children under 12 free. V. Summer daily 10am–4pm; winter daily 11am–3pm. Closed Dec 25. Bus: Airport.

Butchart Gardens ✈✈✈ These internationally acclaimed gardens were born after Robert Butchart exhausted the limestone quarry near his Tod Inlet home. His wife, Jenny, gradually landscaped the deserted eyesore into the resplendent **Sunken Garden,** opening it for public display in 1904. A **Rose Garden, Italian Garden,** and **Japanese Garden** were added. As the fame of the 20-hectare (50-acre) gardens grew, the Butcharts also transformed their house into an attraction. The gardens—still in the family—now display more than a million plants throughout the year. As impressive as the numbers is the sheer perfection of each garden—not a blade out of place, each flower the same height, all blooming at the same time. Gardeners will be amazed.

Evenings in summer, the gardens are beautifully illuminated with a variety of softly colored lights. June through September, musical entertainment is provided free Monday through Saturday evenings. You can even watch fireworks displays on Saturdays in July and August. A very good lunch, dinner, and afternoon tea are offered in the Dining Room Restaurant in the historic residence; afternoon and high teas are also served in the Italian Garden (reservations strongly recommended). Allow 2 to 3 hours.

800 Benvenuto Ave., Brentwood Bay. © 250/652-4422; dining reservations 250/652-8222. www.butchart gardens.com. Admission C$19 (US$12) adults, C$9.50 (US$6.20) youths 13–17, C$2 (US$1.30) children 5–12, free for children under 5. Spring, fall, and winter discounts. Gates open daily 9am–sundown (call for seasonal closing time). Visitors can remain in gardens for 1 hour after gate closes. AE, DISC, MC. Bus: 75 or the Gray Line shuttle from the Victoria Bus Station. C$4 (US$2.60) one-way. Shuttle departure times vary seasonally. Call © 250/388-5248 for exact times. Take Blanshard St. (Hwy. 17) north toward the ferry terminal in Saanich, then turn left on Keating Crossroads, which leads directly to the gardens—about 20 min. from downtown Victoria. It's impossible to miss if you follow the trail of billboards.

Craigdarroch Castle ✈ What do you do when you're the richest man in British Columbia, when you've clawed, scraped, and bullied your way up from indentured servant to coal baron and merchant prince? You build a castle, of course, to show the other buggers what you're worth. Located in the highlands above Oak Bay, Robert Dunsmuir's home, built in the 1880s, is a stunner. The four-story, 39-room Highland-style castle is topped with stone turrets and chimneys and filled with the opulent Victorian splendor you'd expect to read about in a romance novel—detailed woodwork, Persian carpets, stained-glass windows, paintings, and sculptures. The nonprofit society that runs Craigdarroch does an excellent job showcasing the castle. You're provided with a self-tour booklet; on every floor are volunteer docents who are happy to provide further information. The castle also hosts many events throughout the year: theater performances, concerts, and dinner tours. To tour the castle takes an hour or so.

1050 Joan Crescent. ℂ **250/592-5323.** www.craigdarrochcastle.com . Admission C$10 (US$6.50) adults, C$6 (US$3.90) students, C$2.50 (US$1.65) children 6–12, children under 6 free. June 15–Sept 3 daily 9am–7pm; Sept 4–June 14 daily 10am–4:30pm (closed Dec 25,26 and Jan 1. Bus: 11. Take Fort St. out of downtown, just past Cook, and turn right on Joan Crescent.

Fort Rodd Hill & Fisgard Lighthouse National Historic Site
Perched on an outcrop of volcanic rock, the **Fisgard Lighthouse** has guided ships toward Victoria's sheltered harbor since 1873. The light no longer has a keeper (the beacon has long been automated), but the site itself has been restored to its 1873 appearance. Two floors worth of exhibits in the light keepers' house recount stories of the lighthouse, its keepers, and the terrible shipwrecks that gave this coastline its ominous moniker "the graveyard of the Pacific."

Adjoining the lighthouse, **Fort Rodd Hill** is a preserved 1890s coastal artillery fort that—though in more than half a century it never fired a shot in anger—still sports camouflaged searchlights, underground magazines, and its original guns. Audiovisual exhibits bring the fort to life with the voices and faces of the men who served at the outpost. Displays of artifacts, room re-creations, and historic film footage add to the experience. Allow 1 to 2 hours.

603 Fort Rodd Hill Rd. ℂ **250/478-5849.** www.parkscanada.pch.gc.ca . Admission C$3 (US$1.95) adults, C$2.25 (US$1.50) seniors, C$1.50 (US$1]) children 6–16, C$7.50 (US$4.90) families, children under 6 free. Mar–Oct daily 10am–5:30pm; Nov–Feb daily 9am–4:30pm. No public transit.

Maritime Museum of British Columbia
Housed in the former provincial courthouse, this museum is dedicated to recalling B.C.'s rich maritime heritage. The displays do a good job of illustrating maritime history, from the early explorers to the fur trading and whaling era to the days of grand ocean liners and military conflict. There's also an impressive collection of ship models and paraphernalia—uniforms, weapons, gear—along with photographs and journals. The museum also shows films in its Vice Admiralty Theatre. Allow 1 to 2 hours.

28 Bastion Sq. ℂ **250/385-4222.** www.mmbc.bc.ca . Admission C$6 (US$3.85) adults, C$5 (US$3.20) seniors, C$3 (US$1.95) students, C$2 (US$1.30) children 6–11, C$15 (US$9.75) families, children under 6 free. Daily 9:30am–4:30pm. Closed Dec 25. Bus: 5 to View St.

Miniature World *(Kids)*
It sounds cheesy—hundreds of dolls and miniatures and scenes from old fairy tales. And yet Miniature World—inside The Fairmont Empress hotel (the entrance is around the corner)—is actually kinda cool. You walk in and you're plunged into darkness, except for a moon, some planets, and a tiny spaceship flying up to rendezvous with an orbiting mother ship. This is the most up-to-date display. Farther in are re-creations of battle scenes, fancy 18th-century dress balls, a miniature CPR railway running all the way across a miniature Canada, a three-ring circus and midway, and scenes from Mother Goose and Charles Dickens stories. Better yet, most of these displays do something. The train moves at the punch of a button; the circus rides whirl around and light up as simulated darkness falls. Allow 1 hour.

649 Humboldt St. ℂ **250/385-9731.** www.miniatureworld.com . Admission C$9 (US$5.85) adults, C$8 (US$5.20) youths, C$7 (US$4.55) children, children under 4 free. AE, MC, V. Summer daily 8:30am–9pm; winter daily 9am–5pm. Bus: 5, 27, 28, or 30.

Pacific Undersea Gardens *(Kids)*
A gently sloping stairway leads down to this unique marine observatory's glass-enclosed viewing area, where you can observe

Emily Carr House **14**
Craigdarroch Castle **11**
Crystal Garden **10**
The Empress **6**
Helmcken House **9**
Maritime Museum of
  British Columbia **2**
Market Square **1**
Miniature World **5**
Pacific Undersea
  Gardens **4**
Parliament Buildings
  (Provincial Legislature) **7**
Ross Bay Cemetery **12**
Royal British Columbia
  Museum **8**
Royal London Wax
  Museum **3**
Trans-Canada Highway
  Mile 0 **13**

the Inner Harbour's marine life up close. Some 5,000 creatures feed, play, hunt, and court in these protected waters. Sharks, wolf eels, poisonous stonefish, sea anemones, starfish, sturgeon, and salmon are just a few of the organisms that make their homes here. One of the harbor's star attractions is a remarkably photogenic huge octopus (reputedly the largest in captivity). Injured seals and orphaned seal pups are cared for in holding pens alongside the observatory as part of a provincial marine-mammal rescue program. Allow 1 hour.

490 Belleville St. ℭ 250/382-5717. www.pacificunderseagardens.com . Admission C$7.50 (US$4.90) adults, C$6.50 (US$4.25) seniors, C$5 (US$3.20) youths 12–17, C$3.50 (US$2.30) children 5–11, free for children under 5. MC, V. Sept–June daily 10am–5pm; July–Aug daily 10am–7pm; in Jan-Feb closed Tue-Wed . Bus: 5, 27, 28, or 30.

Parliament Buildings (Provincial Legislature) ⚐ Designed by 25-year-old Francis Rattenbury and built between 1893 and 1898 at a cost of nearly C$1 million, the Parliament Buildings (also called the Legislature) are an architectural gem. The 40-minute tour comes across at times like an eighth-grade civics lesson, but it's worth it to see the fine mosaics, marble, woodwork, and stained glass. And if you see a harried-looking man surrounded by a pack of minicam crews, it's likely just another B.C. premier getting hounded out of office by the aggressive and hostile media. Politics is a blood sport in B.C.

501 Belleville St. ℭ **250/387-3046.** www.protocol.gov.bc.ca . Free admission. Late May–Labour Day daily 9am–5pm; Sept–late May 9am–5pm Mon–Fri. Tours offered every 20 min. in summer (up to 23 times a day). In winter hours call ahead for the tour schedules as times vary due to school group bookings. No tours noon–1pm.

Royal British Columbia Museum ★★★ *Kids* One of the world's best regional museums, the Royal BC features natural history dioramas indistinguishable from the real thing (except the grizzly bear won't rip your face off). The museum's mandate is to present the land and the people of coastal British Columbia. The second-floor **Natural History Gallery** shows the coastal flora, fauna, and geography from the Ice Age to the present; it includes dioramas of a temperate rain forest, a seacoast, an underground ecology of giant bugs, and (particularly appealing to kids) a live tidal pool with sea stars and anemones. The third-floor **Modern History Gallery** presents the recent past, including historically faithful re-creations of Victoria's downtown and Chinatown. On the same floor, the **First Peoples Gallery** ⚐ is an incredible showpiece of Native art that also houses many artifacts showing day-to-day Native life, a full-size re-creation of a longhouse, and many smaller village scenes. The museum also has an **IMAX theater** showing an ever-changing variety of large-screen movies. On the way out (or in), be sure to stop by **Thunderbird Park,** beside the museum, where a cedar longhouse (Mungo Martin House, named after a famous Kwakiutl artist) houses a workshop where Native carvers work on new totem poles. To see and experience everything would take 3 to 4 hours.

675 Belleville St. ℭ **888/447-7977** or 250/387-3701. www.royalbcmuseum.bc.ca. Admission C$9 (US$5.85) adults, C$6 (US$3.90) seniors/students/youths, C$24 (US$15) families, children under 6 free. Combination admission passes museum and Imax are C$17 (US$11) for adults and C$15 (US$9.75) for seniors/students/youths. Higher rates sometimes in effect for traveling exhibits. AE, MC, V. Daily 9am–5pm. Closed Dec 25 and Jan 1. Bus: 5, 28, or 30.

Royal London Wax Museum *Overrated* See the same royal family you already get too much of on television. See other, older royals of even less significance. See their family pets. All courtesy of Madame Tussaud's 200-year-old wax technology.

470 Belleville St. ⓒ **250/388-4461.** www.waxworld.com. Admission C$8.75 (US$5.70) adults, C$7.75 (US$5.05) seniors, C$4 (US$2.60) children. AE, MC, V. June–Sept 9am–7:30pm; Oct–May 9:30am–5pm. Bus: 5, 27, 28, or 30.

Victoria Butterfly Gardens ★ *Kids*   This is a great spot for kids, nature buffs, or anyone who just likes butterflies. Hundreds of exotic colorful butterflies flutter freely through this lush tropical greenhouse. You're provided with an ID chart and set free to roam around. Species present range from the tiny Central American Julia (a brilliant orange butterfly about 3 inches across) to the Southeast Asian Giant Atlas Moth (mottled brown and red, with a wingspan approaching a foot). Other butterflies are brilliant blue, yellow, or a mix of colors and patterns. Naturalists are on hand to explain butterfly biology, and there's

On the Lookout: Victoria's Best Views

In town, the best view of The Empress and the Parliament Buildings (the Legislature) comes from walking along the pedestrian path in front of the **Ocean Pointe Resort** off the Johnson Street Bridge. In summer, there's a patio where you can grab a coffee. The sunlight's good early in the day.

When the fishing fleets come in, head over to **Fisherman's Wharf** at St. Lawrence and Erie streets, where you can watch the activity as the fishermen unload their catches. Later on, take in the sunset from the wharf along the eastern edge of the Inner Harbour or from the 18th floor of the **Vista Eighteen Restaurant,** 740 Burdett Ave. (ⓒ **250/382-9258**).

Just south of downtown, you can see across the Strait of Juan de Fuca and the San Juan Islands to the mountains of the Olympic Peninsula from the **Ogden Point** breakwater, from the top of the hill in **Beacon Hill Park,** or from the walking path above the beach along **Dallas Road.** Farther afield, **Fort Rodd Hill** and **Fisgard Lighthouse** offer equally good views of the mountains, as well as a view of the warships in Esquimalt Harbour.

Mount Douglas ★, a 15-minute drive north of the city on Shelbourne Street, offers a panoramic view of the entire Saanich Peninsula, with a parking lot just a 2-minute walk from the summit. To the east, **Mount Work** offers an equally good view, but you have to walk up. It takes about 45 minutes. At the top of Little Saanich Mountain (about 16km/10 miles north of Victoria) stands the **Dominion Astrophysical Observatory,** 5071 W. Saanich Rd. (ⓒ **250/363-0001**), where you can survey all that's around you during the day; April through October. Resident astronomers and volunteers are on-hand Saturday 7 to 11pm (in July and Aug also on Wed and Sun) to give you a view of the starlit skies with the aid of various-sized telescopes. The brand new **Centre of the Universe** interpretive center offers guided tours and activities: C$7 (U$4.55) adults, C$5 (U$3.20) youths 6 to 18, and a family pass is available for C$19 (US$13). The observatory and interpretive centre are open daily 10am to 6pm.

a display where you can see the beautiful creatures emerge from their cocoons. Allow 1 hour.

1461 Benvenuto Ave. (P.O. Box 190), Brentwood Bay. © 877/722-0272 or 250/652-3822. www.butterfly gardens.com . Admission C$8 (US$5.20) adults, C$7 (US$4.55) students/seniors, C$4.50 (US$2.95) children 5–12, children under 5 free. DC, MC, V. Mar 1–May 13 and Oct daily 9:30am–4:30pm; May 14–Sept 30 daily 9am–5:30pm. Closed in winter. Bus: 75.

ARCHITECTURAL HIGHLIGHTS & HISTORIC HOMES

First a trading post, then a gold-rush town, naval base, and sleepy provincial capital, Victoria bears architectural witness to all these eras. The best of its buildings date to the pre–World War I years, when gold poured in from the Fraser and Klondike rivers, fueling a building boom responsible for most of downtown.

Perhaps the most intriguing downtown edifice isn't a building but a work of art. The walls of **Fort Victoria,** which once covered much of downtown, have been demarcated in the sidewalk with bricks bearing the names of original settlers and traders. Look on the sidewalk on Government Street at the corner of Fort Street.

Most of the retail establishments in Victoria's Old Town area are housed in 19th-century shipping warehouses that have been carefully restored as part of a heritage-reclamation program. You can take a **self-guided tour** of the buildings, most of which were erected between the 1870s and 1890s; their history is recounted on easy-to-read outdoor plaques. The majority of the restored buildings are between Douglas and Johnson streets from Wharf Street to Government Street. The most impressive structure once housed a number of shipping offices and warehouses and is now the home of a 45-shop complex known as **Market Square,** 560 Johnson St./255 Market Sq. (© **250/386-2441**).

Some of the British immigrants who settled Vancouver Island during the 19th century built magnificent estates and mansions. In addition to architect Francis Rattenbury's crowning turn-of-the-20th-century achievements—the provincial **Parliament Buildings,** 501 Belleville St. (completed in 1898), and the opulent **Fairmont Empress** hotel, 721 Government St. (completed in 1908)—you'll find a number of other magnificent historic architectural sites.

Emily Carr House 👍, 207 Government St. (© **250/383-5843**), is the birthplace of one of Victoria's most distinguished early residents, painter/writer Emily Carr. Though trained in the classical European tradition, Carr developed her own style in response to the powerful landscapes of the Canadian west coast. Eschewing both marriage and stability, she spent her life traveling the coast, capturing the landscapes and Native peoples in vivid and striking works. The house has been restored to the condition it would have been in when Carr lived there. In addition, many of the rooms have been hung with reproductions of her art or quotations from her writings. From mid-May to mid-October, the house is open daily 10am to 5pm (occasionally for special exhibits the rest of the year; off-season call ahead). Admission is C$5.35 (US$3.50) for adults, C$4.25

Tips **A Handy Reference**

For an excellent guide to many of Victoria's buildings, and short bios of its most significant architects, pick up *Exploring Victoria's Architecture,* by Martin Segger and Douglas Franklin. It's available at **Munro's Books,** 1108 Government St. (© **250/382-2464**).

(US$2.80) for students/seniors, and C$3.25 (US$2.15) for children 6 to 12; free for children under 6.

Helmcken House, 610 Elliot St. Square (② **250/361-0021**), was the residence of a pioneer doctor who settled in the area during the 1850s. The doctor's house still contains the original imported British furnishings and his medicine chest. Admission is the same as for Carr House. May through September, the house is open daily 10am to 5pm; October through April, hours are Thursday through Monday 11am to 4pm.

On a promontory above the Gorge Waterway, the completely restored **Point Ellice House** ✦✦, 2616 Pleasant St. (② **250/380-6506**), was the summer gathering place for much of Victoria's Victorian elite. From mid-May to mid-September, it's open for 30-minute guided tours daily noon to 5pm; admission is the same as for Carr House, above. Point Ellice is also one of the better spots for afternoon tea (p. 207). The easiest way to reach the house is by harbor ferry from in front of The Faimont Empress, costing C$4 (US$2.60) one-way.

Craigdarroch Castle ✦, 1050 Joan Crescent (② **250/592-5323**), was built during the 1880s to serve as Scottish coal-mining magnate Robert Dunsmuir's home (p. 215). Dunsmuir's son, James, built his own palatial home, **Hatley Castle.** The younger Dunsmuir reportedly commissioned architect Samuel Maclure with the words "Money doesn't matter, just build what I want." The bill, in 1908, came to over C$1 million. The grounds of the castle, now home to **Royal Roads University,** 2005 Sooke Rd. (② **250/391-2511**), feature extensive floral gardens and are open to the public free of charge. The volunteer-run **Hatley Park Castle and Museum,** 2005 Sooke Rd. (② **250/391-2600,** ext. 4456), offers tours of the grounds and the castle Monday through Friday 1 to 4pm. Admission is by donation. Call ahead—if no volunteers show up or if school events occupy the grounds, the museum doesn't open. Hatley Castle is off Highway 14 in Colwood.

CEMETERIES

Ross Bay Cemetery, 1495 Fairfield St. at Dallas Rd., has to be one of the finest locations in all creation to spend eternity. Luminaries interred here include the first governor of the island, James Douglas; frontier judge Matthew Begbie; and West Coast painter Emily Carr. *An Historic Guide to Ross Bay Cemetery,* available in Munro's Books as well as other bookstores, gives details on people and directions to grave sites.

Pioneer Square, on the corner of Meares and Quadra streets beside Christ Church, is one of British Columbia's oldest cemeteries. Hudson's Bay Company fur traders, ship captains, sailors, fishermen, and crew members from British Royal Navy vessels lie beneath the worn sandstone markers.

Contact the **Old Cemeteries Society** (② **250/598-8870;** www.oldcem.bc. ca) for more information on tours of both of these graveyards.

NEIGHBORHOODS OF NOTE

From the time the Hudson's Bay Company settled here in the mid-1800s, the historic **Old Town** was the center of the city's bustling business in shipping, fur trading, and legal opium manufacturing. Market Square and the surrounding warehouses once brimmed with exports like tinned salmon, furs, and timber bound for England and the United States. Now part of the downtown core, this is still a terrific place to find British, Scottish, and Irish imports (a surprising number of these shops date back to the early 1900s), souvenirs of all sorts, and even outdoor equipment for modern-day adventurers.

Heading North to a Provincial Park, a Native Village & Some Wineries

A short and stunning drive north from Victoria along the Island Highway takes you to three spots well worth a visit: Goldstream Provincial Park, the Quw'utsun' (Cowichan) Cultural Centre, and the Cowichan Valley wineries. The drive—along the ocean, up over the Malahat mountain, and then through the beautiful Cowichan Valley—is short enough to complete in one fairly leisurely day.

GOLDSTREAM PROVINCIAL PARK   This quiet treed little valley overflowed with prospectors during the 1860s gold-rush days. Trails take you past abandoned mine shafts and tunnels as well as 600-year-old stands of towering Douglas fir, lodgepole pine, red cedar, indigenous yew, and arbutus trees. The **Gold Mine Trail** leads to Niagara Creek and the abandoned mine that was operated by Lt. Peter Leech, a Royal Engineer who discovered gold in the creek in 1858. **The Goldstream Trail** leads to the salmon spawning areas. (You might also catch sight of mink and river otters racing along this path.)

For general information on Goldstream Provincial Park and all other provincial parks on the South Island, contact **BC Parks** at ✆ **250/391-2300** or check www.bcparks.ca. Throughout the year, Goldstream Park's **Freeman King Visitor Centre** (✆ **250/478-9414**) offers guided walks, talks, displays, and programs geared toward kids but interesting for adults, too. Open daily 9am to 4pm. Take Highway 1 about 30 minutes north of Victoria. Note that recent BC government cutbacks have significantly reduced the number of events and services in most provincial parks.

Three species of salmon (chum, chinook, and steelhead) make **annual salmon runs** up the Goldstream River during October, November, December, and February. You can easily observe this natural wonder along the riverbanks. Contact the park's **Visitor Centre** for details.

DUNCAN   The main reason for visiting Duncan is to see the **Quw'utsun' Cultural and Conference Centre** (formerly known as the Cowichan Native Village). Created by the Cowichan Indian Band itself, the center, 200 Cowichan Way, Duncan (✆ **877/746-8119** or **250/746-8119;** www.quwutsun.ca), brings Native culture to visitors in a way that's commercially successful yet still respectful of Native traditions.

The longhouses built along the Cowichan River contain an impressive collection of cultural artifacts and presentations of life among the aboriginal tribes who have lived in the area for thousands of years. There are tours on the hour, every hour, as well as ceremonial dances and daily afternoon salmon barbecues. Master and apprentice carvers create poles, masks, and feasting bowls in workshops open to the public. Two large gift shops in the complex sell some of those works as well as

Just a block north on Fisgard Street is **Chinatown.** Founded in 1863, it's the oldest Chinatown in North America. One of the more interesting structures is a three-story school built by the Chinese Benevolent Society in the early 1900s,

Native-made jewelry, clothing, silk-screened prints, and other items. The center and gift shops are open daily 9am to 6pm; admission is C$10 (US$6.50) for adults, C$8 (US$5.20) for seniors and youth 12 to 18, C$6 (US$3.90) for children 6 to 11, and C$25 (US$16) for families of two adults and two children.

The **Duncan-Cowichan Visitor Info Centre** is at 381A Trans-Canada Hwy. (in the Overwaitea Mall), Duncan, B.C. V9L 3R5 (© **250/746-4636; www.duncancc.bc.ca**). July and August, it's open daily 9am to 6pm; September through June, hours are Monday through Saturday 9am to 5pm.

THE COWICHAN VALLEY A gorgeous agricultural valley a couple hours' drive from Victoria, the Cowichan Valley is a little like the south of England, but with looming great mountains in the background. Both the wineries and the seaside town of Cowichan Bay are worth a stop.

The vintners of the Cowichan Valley have gained a solid reputation for producing fine wines. Several of the wineries have opened their doors and offer 1-hour tours that are a great introduction for novices. They usually include a tasting of the vintner's art as well as a chance to purchase bottles or cases of your favorites.

Cherry Point Vineyards, 840 Cherry Point Rd., Cowichan (© **250/743-1272**), looks like a slice of California's Napa Valley. The wine-tasting room and gift shop is open daily 10am to 6pm. **Blue Grouse Vineyards,** 4365 Blue Grouse Rd., Mill Bay (© **250/743-3834**), is a smaller winery that began as a hobby. April through September, it's open for tastings and on-site purchases Wednesday through Sunday 11am to 5pm (Wed–Sat the rest of the year). **Merridale Cider,** another small winery, located just south of Cowichan Bay at 1230 Merridale Rd., is worth a stop to taste their ciders. Phone ahead to confirm opening hours at © **800/998-9908**; open daily 10:30am to 6pm in July and August, and Monday through Saturday 10:30am to 4pm the rest of the year.

Just southeast of Duncan, **Cowichan Bay** is a pretty little seaside town with a few attractions that make it a worthwhile stop, in addition to the view of the ocean. The **Cowichan Bay Maritime Centre,** 1761 Cowichan Bay Rd., Cowichan Bay (© **250/746-4955**), is a unique museum where the displays sit atop a pier that stretches out into the bay. Or go for a sail on the bay on a 55-foot sailing ketch (© **250/746-1720 or 250/746-5257;** www.great-northwestern.com). For a minimum of six people, the cost is C$70 (US$45) per person; smaller groups upon request.

Cowichan Bay (off Hwy. 1, south of Duncan) is a pleasant half-hour drive from the wine country, so you can take a tour, do some sampling, and be back in Victoria before nightfall.

when non-Canadian Chinese children were banned from public schools. Lined with Chinese restaurants, bakeries, and specialty shops, Chinatown is a wonderful spot to stop for dim sum or for a full Hong Kong–style seafood dinner.

Finds **Strolling the Governor's Gardens**

Government House, the official residence of the lieutenant governor, is at 1401 Rockland Ave., in the Fairfield residential district. Round back, the hillside of Garry oaks is one of the last places to see what the area's natural fauna looked like before European settlers arrived. At the front, the rose garden is sumptuous.

The **James Bay** area on the southern shores of the Inner Harbour is a quiet middle-class residential community. As you walk through its tree-lined streets, you'll find many pristine older private residences that have maintained their original Victorian flavor.

Beautiful residential communities such as **Ross Bay** and **Oak Bay** have a more modern West Coast appearance. Houses perch on hills overlooking the beaches amid luscious landscaped gardens. Private marinas are filled with perfectly maintained sailing craft.

PARKS & GARDENS

In addition to **Butchart Gardens** (p. 215), several city parks attract strollers and picnickers whenever the weather is pleasant. The 61-hectare (154-acre) **Beacon Hill Park** stretches from Southgate Street to Dallas Road between Douglas and Cook streets. In 1882, the Hudson's Bay Company gave this property to the city. Stands of indigenous Garry oaks (found only on Vancouver Island, Hornby Island, and Salt Spring Island) and manicured lawns are interspersed with floral gardens and ponds. Hike up Beacon Hill to get a clear view of the Strait of Georgia, Haro Strait, and Washington's Olympic Mountains. The children's farm (see "Especially for Kids" below), aviary, tennis courts, lawn-bowling green, putting green, cricket pitch, wading pool, playground, and picnic area make this a wonderful place to spend a few hours with the family. The Trans-Canada Highway's "Mile 0" marker stands at the edge of the park on Dallas Road.

Victoria has an indoor garden that first opened as a huge saltwater pool in 1925 and was converted into a big-band dance hall during World War II. The **Crystal Garden,** 713 Douglas St. (© **250/953-8800**), is filled with rare and exotic tropical flora and fauna. The garden is open daily 10am to 4:30pm (until 8pm in July and Aug). Admission is C$8 (US$5.20) for adults, C$7 (US$4.55) for seniors, C$4 (US$2.60) for children 5 to 16, and C$22 (US$14) for families; free for children under 5.

Just outside downtown, **Mount Douglas Park** offers great views of the area, several hiking trails, and—down at the waterline—a picnic/play area with a trail leading to a good walking beach.

About 45 minutes southwest of town, **East Sooke Park** ✦ is a 1,400-hectare (3,458-acre) microcosm of the West Coast wilderness: jagged seacoasts, Native petroglyphs, and hiking trails up to a 270m (886-foot) mountaintop. Access is via the Old Island Highway and East Sooke Road.

2 Especially for Kids

Nature's the thing for kids in Victoria. The city offers unique opportunities for kids to pet, prod, and point out creatures from whales to goats to giant butterflies and flying insects to sea anemones to hermit crabs. The oldest of petting zoos is the **Beacon Hill Children's Farm,** Circle Drive, Beacon Hill Park (© **250/381-2532**), where kids can ride ponies; pet goats, rabbits, and other barnyard animals; and even cool off in the wading pool. From mid-March to mid-October, the farm is open daily 10am to 5pm. Admission is by donation; most visitors are asked to give C$1 (US65¢) toward the park's upkeep.

To touch and prod even smaller creatures, visit the **Victoria Butterfly Gardens** (p. 219). The **Crystal Garden** (© **250/953-8800**), behind The Fairmont Empress hotel, also has butterflies, as well as macaws and pelicans, though the tawdry monkey cages give the place something of the aura of a run-down zoo. Closer to town and a tad on the creepy side is the **Victoria Bug Zoo,** 1107 Wharf St. (© **250/384-BUGS;** www.bugzoo.bc.ca), home to praying mantises, stick insects, and giant African cockroaches. Knowledgeable guides bring the bugs out and let you or your kids handle and touch them. Admission is C$6 (US$3.90) for adults, C$5 (US$3.25) for seniors, and C$4 (US$2.60) for children 3 to 16, free for children under 3; open 9:30am to 5:30pm Monday through Saturday and 11am to 5:30pm Sunday.

The **Pacific Undersea Gardens** (p. 216) is a face-to-face introduction to the sea creatures of the Pacific coast. In the underwater observatory, kids can meet a wolf eel eye-to-eye, view a giant octopus up close, and watch harbor seals cavort underwater with their pups. Better still, take the kids out to explore any of the tide pools on the coast. **Botanical Beach Provincial Park** 🏖, near Port Renfrew, is excellent, though the 60km (37-mile) drive west along Highway 14 may make it a bit far for some. Closer to town, try **French Beach** 🏖 or **China Beach** 🏖 (also along Hwy. 14), or even the beach in **Mount Douglas Park.** The trick is to find a good spot, bend down over a tide pool, and look—or else pick up a rock to see crabs scuttle away. Remember to put the rocks back where you found them.

In **Goldstream Provincial Park,** the Visitor Centre (© **250/478-9414**) has nature programs and activities geared especially for children. The **Swan Lake Christmas Hill Nature Sanctuary,** 3873 Swan Lake Rd. (© **250/479-0211;** www.swanlake.bc.ca), offers a number of nature-themed drop-in programs over the summer, including Insectmania and Reptile Day.

Back in the city, the **Royal British Columbia Museum** (p. 218) has many displays geared toward kids, including one simulating a dive to the bottom of the Pacific. Others illustrate the intriguing life and culture of the West Coast Native tribes, who've inhabited the province for more than 10,000 years, and show the majestic beauty of the province's temperate rainforests and coastlines.

Miniature World (p. 216), with its huge collection of dolls and dollhouses, model trains, and diminutive circus displays, is a favorite with kids of all ages.

Located in Elk and Beaver Lake Regional Park (see "Outdoor Activities," below), **Beaver Lake** is a great freshwater spot where kids can enjoy a day of water sports and swimming in safe, lifeguard-attended waters.

On truly hot days, head for the mile-long water slide at the **All Fun Recreation Park,** 2207 Millstream Rd. (© **250/474-3184;** www.allfun.bc.ca). From mid-June to Labour Day (early Sept), it's open daily 11am to 7pm. The cost is C$20 (US$13) for sliders 11 years and older and C$15 (US$9.75) for those 4 to 10 years old; free for children under 4. Cost for observers (which includes use of the hot tub, mini-golf, and beach volleyball courts) is C$6 (US$3.90). The park also has go-carts and batting cages.

3 Organized Tours

BUS TOURS

Gray Line of Victoria, 700 Douglas St. (© **250/388-5248;** www.grayline. ca/victoria), conducts a number of tours of Victoria and Butchart Gardens. The 1½-hour "Grand City Tour" costs C$18 (US$12) for adults and C$9 (US$5.85) for children ages 6 to 12. In summer, tours depart every 30 minutes daily 9:30am to 4:30pm; from December to mid-March, there are daily departures at 10am, noon, and 2pm. For other tours check the website.

SPECIALTY TOURS

Victoria Harbour Ferries , 922 Old Esquimalt Rd. (© **250/708-0201**), offers a terrific 45-minute tour of the Inner and Outer harbors for C$12 (US$7.75) for adults and C$6 (US$3.90) for children under 12. Tours depart from any of the harbor ferry docks. A 50-minute tour of the gorge opposite the Johnson Street Bridge, where tidal falls reverse with each change of the tide, costs C$14 (US$9.10) for adults, C$12 (US$7.80) for seniors, and C$7 (US$4.55) for children. The ferries are adorably cartoonish, 12-person, fully enclosed blue boats, and every seat is a window seat. Harbor tours depart from seven stops around the Inner Harbour every 15 minutes daily 10am to 10pm. If you wish to stop for food or a stroll, you can get a token good for reboarding at any time during the same day. June through September, gorge tours depart from the dock in front of The Fairmont Empress every half-hour 10am to 8pm; at other times the tours operate less frequently, depending on the weather.

Heritage Tours and Daimler Limousine Service, 713 Bexhill Rd. (© **250/ 474-4332**), guides you through the city, Butchart Gardens, and Craigdar-roch Castle in a six-passenger British Daimler limousine. Rates start at C$65 (US$42) for the Daimler per hour per vehicle (not per person). Also available are stretch limos that seat 8 to 10 people, starting at C$70 (US$45) per hour per vehicle.

The bicycle-rickshaws operated by **Kabuki Kabs,** 613 Herald St. (© **250/ 385-4243**), can usually be found on the causeway in front of The Fairmont Empress or hailed in the downtown area. Prices for a tour are C$1 (US65¢) per minute for a two-person cab and C$1.50 (US$1) per minute for a four-person cab.

Tallyho Horse-Drawn Tours, 2044 Milton St. (© **250/383-5067**), has con-ducted tours of Victoria in horse-drawn carriages and trolleys since 1903. Excur-sions start at the corner of Belleville and Menzies streets; fares for the trolley are C$14 (US$9.10) for adults, C$8.50 (US$5.55) for students, C$6 (US$3.90) for children 17 and under; a family rate can be negotiated. Tours operate daily every 30 minutes 9am to 10pm during summer (10am–5:30pm in late Mar, Apr, May, and Sept). Tallyho also offers private tours in carriages (maximum six peo-ple) costing C$35 (US$23) for 15 minutes, C$60 (US$39) for 30 minutes, or C$105 (US$68) for an hour.

To get a bird's-eye view of Victoria, take a 30-minute tour with **Harbour Air Seaplanes,** 1234 Wharf St. (© **250/385-9131;** www.harbour-air.com). Rates are C$93 (US$60) per person, C$40 (US$26) children under 12; flights depart whenever there are three or more people ready (usually about every 30–45 min.). For a romantic evening, try the *Fly and Dine* to Butchart Gardens; C$179 (US$115) includes the flight to the gardens, admission, dinner, and a limousine ride back to Victoria.

> ⌐Finds **Victoria's Cemetery Tours**
>
> The **Old Cemetery Society of Victoria** (℃ 250/598-8870; www.oldcem.bc.
> ca) runs regular cemetery tours throughout the year. Particularly popular
> are the slightly eerie **Lantern Tours of the Old Burying Ground** 🌟, which
> begin at the Cherry Bank Hotel, 845 Burdett St., at 9pm nightly in July
> and August. The tour lasts about 1 hour. On Sundays throughout the year
> the Society offers historically focused tours of Ross Bay Cemetery. Tours
> depart at 2pm from Bagga Pasta, in the Fairfield Plaza, 1516 Fairfield Rd.,
> across from the cemetery gate. Both tours are C$5 (US$3.20) per person
> or C$2 (US$1.30) for society members.

WALKING TOURS

For a pleasant and informative stroll, join a guided walking tour through the downtown and Old Town neighborhoods. **First Island Tours Ltd.** (℃ 250/ 658-5367; www.firstislandtours.com) offers a number of specialized tours. Some are multiday packages for birders or gardeners, or for a fun 1-day tour, try the Victoria Ale Trail, visiting four breweries for a chat with the brew masters and plenty of sampling and dinner (C$119/US$77 per person). Transportation with designated driver is included.

The **Victoria Heritage Foundation,** #1 Centennial Square (℃ 250/383-4546; vhf@pinc.com), offers the excellent free pamphlet *James Bay Heritage Walking Tour.* The well-researched pamphlet (available at the Visitor Info Centre or from the Victoria Heritage office) describes a self-guided walking tour through the historic James Bay neighborhood.

Discover the Past (℃ 250/384-6698; www.discoverthepast.com) organizes two year-round walks: Ghostly Walks explores Victoria's haunted Old Town, Chinatown, and historic waterfront, and the Neighbourhood Discovery Walk is a tour through Victoria's many distinct neighborhoods. Both combine interesting local history as well as natural history, architecture, archaeology and urban legends to bring the city's character to life. The cost is C$10 (US$6.50) adults, C$8 (US$5.20) seniors/students, C$6 (US$3.90) children, and C$25 (US$16) for families. Call ahead for times and locations.

4 Outdoor Activities

Mountain biking, ecotouring, in-line skating, Alpine and Nordic skiing, parasailing, sea kayaking, canoeing, tidal-water fishing, fly-fishing, diving, and hiking are popular in and around Victoria.

BEACHES

The most popular beach is Oak Bay's **Willows Beach,** at Beach and Dalhousie roads along the esplanade. The park, playground, and snack bar make it a great place to spend the day building a sand castle. **Gyro Beach Park,** Beach Road on Cadboro Bay, is another good spot for winding down. At the **Ross Bay Beaches,** below Beacon Hill Park, you can stroll or bike along the promenade at the water's edge.

For a taste of the wild and rocky west coast, hike the oceanside trails in beautiful **East Sooke Regional Park** 🌟. Take Hwy. 14 west, turn south on Gillespie Road, and then take East Sooke Road.

> **Tips Suiting Up for the Outdoors**
>
> In the sections below, specialized rental outfitters are listed for each activity. **Sports Rent,** 611 Discovery St. (© **250/385-7368**), is a great general-equipment and watersports rental outlet. Its entire inventory, including rental rates, is online at **www.sportsrentbc.com.**

Two inland lakes give you the option of swimming in fresh water. **Elk and Beaver Lake Regional Park,** on Patricia Bay Road, is 11km (7 miles) north of downtown Victoria; **Thetis Lake,** about 10km (6 miles) west, is where locals shed all their clothes but none of their civility.

BIKING

This is one of the best ways to get around Victoria. You can rent a bike for a few hours or a few days in the downtown area (see "Getting Around," in chapter 10). The 13km (8-mile) **Scenic Marine Drive** bike path begins at Dallas Road and Douglas Street, at the base of Beacon Hill Park. The paved path follows the walkway along the beaches before winding up through the residential district on Beach Drive. It eventually turns left and heads south toward downtown Victoria on Oak Bay Avenue. The **Inner Harbour pedestrian path** has a bike lane for cyclists who want to take a leisurely ride around the entire city seawall. The new **Galloping Goose Trail** (part of the Trans-Canada Trail) runs from Victoria west through Colwood and Sooke all the way up to Leechtown. If you don't want to bike the whole thing, there are numerous places to park along the way, as well as several places where the trail intersects with public transit. Call **BC Transit** at © **250/382-6161** to find out which bus routes take bikes. Bikes and child trailers are available by the hour or day at **Cycle BC rentals,** 747 Douglas St. (year-round) or 950 Wharf St. (May–Oct) (© **250/885-2453**). Rentals run C$6 (US$3.90) per hour and C$20 (US$13) per day, helmets and locks included.

BIRDING

For those wanting to hook up with the local birding subculture, the **Victoria Natural History Society** runs regular weekend birding excursions. Their **event line** at © **250/479-2054** lists upcoming outings and gives contact numbers. For the self-propelled, **Goldstream Provincial Park** (see "Parks & Gardens," earlier in this chapter) and the village of **Malahat**—both off Highway 1 about 40 minutes north of Victoria—are filled with dozens of varieties of migratory and local birds. Ninety-seven eagles were spotted at Goldstream Provincial Park one January day in 1995. **Elk and Beaver Lake Regional Park,** off Highway 17, has some rare species such as the rose-breasted grosbeak and Hutton's vireo. Ospreys also nest there. **Cowichan Bay,** off Highway 1, is the perfect place to observe ospreys, bald eagles, great egrets, and purple martins.

BOATING

Kayaks, canoes, rowboats and powerboats are available from **Great Pacific Adventures,** 811 Wharf St. (© **877/733-6722** or 250/386-2277; www.greatpacificadventures.com). **BC Yacht Charters,** 1406–450 Simcoe St. (© **800/708-SAIL**), also offers sailing trips and sailboat charters. The **Victoria Marine Adventure Centre,** 950 Wharf St. (© **250/995-2211;** www.marine-adventures.com), on the floatplane docks in the Inner Harbour, can arrange powerboat rentals. Unskippered (bareboat) powerboat rentals start around C$49 (US$32) per hour for a 16-footer, including gas. If you take the wheel yourself, don't forget to check the **marine forecast** by calling ✆ **250/656-7515** before casting off.

CANOEING & KAYAKING

Ocean River Sports, 1437 Store St., Victoria, B.C. V8W 3J6 (✆ **800/909-4233** or 250/381-4233; www.oceanriver.com), can equip you with everything from single kayak, double kayak, and canoe rentals to life jackets, tents, and dry-storage camping gear. Rental costs for a single kayak range from C$14 (US$9.10) per hour to C$42 (US$27) per day. Multiday and weekly rates are also available. In addition, the company offers numerous **guided tours** ☆ of the Gulf Islands and the B.C. west coast. For beginners, there's the guided 3-hour Explore Tour of the coast around Victoria or Sooke, costing C$59 (US$38). There's also a guided 3-day/2-night Expedition trip to explore the nearby Gulf Islands costing C$349 (US$225).

　　Blackfish Wilderness Expeditions (✆ **250/216-2389;** www.coastnet.com/~blackfish) operates a number of interesting kayak-based tours such as the kayak/boat/hike combo where you get a head start by boat to the protected waters of the Discovery Islands. After you explore the coves and inlets and eat a picnic lunch, a naturalist takes you on a hike around one of the islands. Whale-watchers can combine a few hours of kayaking with a trip on a motorized boat to get a better look at the pods of resident killer whales that roam the waters around Victoria. Day tours start at C$110 (US$71) per person.

DIVING

The coastline of **Pacific Rim National Park** is known as "the graveyard of the Pacific." Submerged in the water are dozens of 19th- and 20th-century shipwrecks and the marine life that has taken up residence in them. Underwater interpretive trails help you identify what you see in the artificial reefs. If you want to take a look for yourself, contact **Ocean Sports,** 800 Cloverdale St. (✆ **800/414-2202** or 250/475-2202; www.oceansports.ca), or **The Ogden Point Dive Centre,** 199 Dallas Rd. (✆ **250/380-9119;** www.divevictoria.com). Through Ocean Sports, head-to-toe equipment rental is C$50 (US$32) for 2 days, and dive trips start at C$50 (US$32) for two dives plus lunch.

FISHING

Saltwater fishing's the thing out here, and unless you know the area, it's probably best to take a guide. **Adam's Fishing Charters** (✆ **250/370-2326;** www.adamsfishingcharters.com) and the **Marine Adventure Centre,** 950 Wharf St. (✆ **250/995-2211;** www.marine-adventures.com), are good places to start. Both are on the Inner Harbour down below the Visitor Info Centre. (See also "Boating," above.) Chartering a boat and guide starts around C$80 (US$52) per hour per boat, with a minimum of 3 or 4 hours.

　　To fish, you need a nonresident saltwater fishing license. Licenses for saltwater fishing (including the salmon surcharge) cost C$14 (US$9.10) for 1 day for nonresidents and C$12 (US$7.80) for B.C. residents. Tackle shops sell licenses, have details on current restrictions, and often carry copies of the current publications *BC Tidal Waters Sport Fishing Guide* and *BC Sport Fishing Regulations Synopsis for Non-Tidal Waters.* Independent anglers should also pick up a copy of the *BC Fishing Directory and Atlas.* **Robinson's Sporting Goods Ltd.,** 1307 Broad St. (✆ **250/385-3429**), is a reliable source for information, recommendations, lures, licenses, and gear. For the latest fishing hot spots and recommendations on tackle and lures check out **www.sportfishingbc.com.**

GOLFING

Fortunately for golfers, Victoria's Scottish heritage didn't stop at the tartan shops. The greens here are as beautiful as those at St. Andrew's, yet the fees are reasonable. The **Cedar Hill Municipal Golf Course,** 1400 Derby Rd. (© **250/ 595-3103**), is an 18-hole public course 3.3km (2 miles) from downtown Victoria; daytime greens fees are C$34 (US$22) and twilight fees (after 3pm) are C$20 (US$13). Golf clubs can be rented for C$10 (US$6.50). The **Cordova Bay Golf Course,** 5333 Cordova Bay Rd. (© **250/658-4075;** www.cordova baygolf.com), is northeast of the downtown area. Designed by Bill Robinson, the 18-hole course features 66 sand traps and some tight fairways. Greens fees are C$49 (US$32) Monday through Thursday and C$54 (US$35) on Friday, Saturday, Sunday, and holidays. The **Olympic View Golf Club,** 643 Latoria Rd. (© **250/474-3673;** www.olympicview.bc.ca), is one of the top 35 golf courses in Canada. Amid 12 lakes and a pair of waterfalls, this 18-hole, 6,414-yard course is open daily year-round. Day-time greens fees are C$65 (US$42) and twilight fees are C$32 (US$21), off-season rates are available. Power carts cost an additional C$35 (US$23). You can also call the **Last Minute Golf Hotline** at © **800/684-6344** or, only in Vancouver Island, the **Island Links Hotline** at © **866/266-GOLF,** for substantial discounts and short-notice tee times at courses around the area.

HIKING

Goldstream Provincial Park (30 min. west of downtown along Hwy. 1) is a tranquil site for a short hike through towering cedars and clear, rushing waters. The hour-long hike up **Mount Work** provides excellent views of the Saanich Peninsula and a good view of Finlayson Arm. The trail head is a 30- to 45-minute drive. Take Highway 17 north to Saanich, then take Highway 17a (the West Saanich Rd.) to Wallace Drive, turn right on Willis Point Drive and right again on the Ross-Durrance Road, looking for the parking lot on the right. There are signs along the way. Equally good, though more of a scramble, is the hour-plus climb up **Mount Finlayson** in Gowland-Tod Provincial Park (take Hwy. 1 west, get off at the Millstream Rd. exit, and follow Millstream Rd. north to the very end). The very popular **Sooke Potholes** trail wanders up beside a river to an abandoned mountain lodge. Take Highway 1A west to Colwood, then Highway 14 (the Sooke Rd.). When you reach Sooke, turn north on the Sooke River Road, and follow it to the park.

For a taste of the wild and rocky west coast, hike the oceanside trails in beautiful **East Sooke Regional Park.** Take Hwy. 14 west, turn south on Gillespie Road, and then take East Sooke Road.

For a serious backpacking run, go 104km (65 miles) west of Victoria on Highway 14 to Port Renfrew and **Pacific Rim National Park.** The challenging **West Coast Trail,** extending 77km (48 miles) from Port Renfrew to Bamfield, was originally established as a lifesaving trail for shipwrecked sailors (see chapter 17). Plan a 7-day trek if you want to cover the entire route; reservations are required, so call © **604/663-6000.** The trail is rugged and often wet, but the scenery changes from old-growth forest to magnificent secluded sand beaches, making it worth every step. You may even spot a few whales along the way. **Robinson's Sporting Goods Ltd.,** 1307 Broad St. (© **250/385-3429**), is a good place to gear up before you go. Ask at Robinson's about the newer, less challenging **Juan de Fuca Marine Trail,** connecting Port Renfrew and the Jordan River, about 48km (30 miles) long.

Island Adventure Tours (© 866/812-7103; www.islandadventuretours. com) offers a number of options for folks wanting to get out into the outdoors. There are half-day guided **Rainforest Walks** for C$39 (US$25) or C$95 (US$61) for a full-day hike including transportation and lunch, **Garden Tours** for C$45 (US$29), or **Aboriginal Cultural Tours** for C$75 (US$48) (Native guide and salmon barbecue included), as well as 3-day fully catered **camping trips** to Pacific Rim National Park for C$499 (US$322).

For groups of 10 or more who want to learn more about the surrounding flora and fauna, book a naturalist-guided tour of the island's rainforests and seashore with **Coastal Connections Interpretive Nature Hikes,** 1027 Roslyn Rd. (© 250/480-9560). A 6-hour rain-forest hike, including a gourmet picnic lunch, provides a wonderful introduction to this unique ecosystem. The hike costs C$79 (US$51) per person. For something less strenuous but still scenic, try the **Swan Lake Christmas Hill Nature Sanctuary,** 3873 Swan Lake Rd. (© 250/479-0211; www.swanlake.bc.ca). A floating boardwalk wends its way through this 40-hectare (100-acre) wetland past resident swans that love to be fed; the adjacent Nature House supplies feeding grain on request.

SKIING

Mount Washington Ski Resort, P.O. Box 3069, Courtenay, B.C. V9N 5N3 (© 888/231-1499 or 250/338-1380; 250/338-1515 snow report; www.mt washington.bc.ca), in the Comox Valley, is British Columbia's third-largest ski area, a 5-hour drive from Victoria and open year-round (for hiking or skiing, depending on the season). A 480m (1,600-ft.) vertical drop and 50 groomed runs are serviced by four chairlifts and a beginners' tow. The terrain is very popular among snowboarders and well suited to intermediate skiers. For cross-country skiers, 31km (19 miles) of track-set Nordic trails connect to Strathcona Provincial Park. Full-day rates are C$45 (US$29) for adults, C$37 (US$24) for seniors and students, and C$24 (US$15) for kids 7 to 12; free for kids under 7. Equipment rentals are available at the resort. Take Highway 19 to Courtenay and then the Strathcona Parkway. It's 37km (23 miles) to Mount Washington.

WATERSPORTS

The **Crystal Pool & Fitness Centre,** 2275 Quadra St. (© 250/361-0732), is Victoria's main aquatic facility. The 50m lap pool; children's pool; diving pool; sauna; whirlpool; and steam, weight, and aerobics rooms are open Monday through Friday 5:30am to 10:30pm, Saturday 6am to 4pm, and Sunday 9am to 4pm. Drop-in admission is C$4.50 (US$2.95) for adults, C$3.50 (US$2.30) for seniors and students, and C$2.50 (US$1.65) for children 6 to 12; free for children under 6. **Beaver Lake** in Elk and Beaver Lake Regional Park (see "Birding," above) has lifeguards on duty as well as picnicking facilities along the shore.

Surfing has recently taken off on the island. The best surf is along the west coast at **China, French,** and **Mystic beaches** ⊛ (see "Beaches," above). You can rent boards and wet suits—along with almost any kind of watersport gear—at **Ocean Sports,** 800 Cloverdale St. (© 800/414-2202; www.oceansports.ca).

Windsurfers skim along outside the Inner Harbour and on Elk Lake when the breezes are right. Though there are no specific facilities, French Beach, off Sooke Road on the way to Sooke Harbour, is a popular local windsurfing spot.

WHALE-WATCHING

The waters surrounding the southern tip of Vancouver Island teem with orcas (killer whales), as well as harbor seals, sea lions, bald eagles, and harbor and Dall porpoises. The main difference between whale-watching companies the type of boats they use—a 12-person Zodiac, where the jolting ride is almost as exciting as seeing the whales, and tours that take larger, more leisurely craft. Both offer excellent platforms for seeing whales. In high season (June–Labour Day) most companies offer several trips a day.

The **Victoria Marine Adventure Centre,** 950 Wharf St. (© **250/995-2211;** www.marine-adventures.com), is just one of many outfits offering whale-watching tours in Zodiacs and/or covered boats. Adults and kids will learn a lot from the naturalist guides, who explain the behavior and nature of the orcas, gray whales, sea lions, porpoises, cormorants, eagles, and harbor seals encountered along the way. Fares are C$79 (US$51) for adults and C$49 (US$32) for children.

Oak Bay Beach Hotel and Marine Resort, Oak Bay Beach Hotel, 1175 Beach Dr. (© **800/668-7758** or 250/598-4556; www.oakbaybeachhotel.com), offers 3½-hour whale-watching charters daily on either a 45-foot catamaran or a 28-foot converted pleasure cruiser. Both have restroom facilities and bar service. A picnic lunch is served on the cruise. Fares are C$79 (US$51) for adults and C$49 (US$32) for children 4 to 12; free for children under 4. Lunch is an additional C$8 (US$5.20) per person. There's a complimentary shuttle from downtown.

Other reputable companies are **Prince of Whales,** 812 Wharf St. (© **800/ 383-4884** or 250/383-4884; www.princeofwhales.com), just below the Visitor Info Centre, and **Orca Spirit Adventures** (© **888/672-ORCA** or 250/383-8411; www.orcaspirit.com), which departs from the Coast Harbourside Hotel dock.

14

Victoria Strolls

Victoria has always been a transient's town, from miners and mariners to loggers and lounge-lizards, from hard-core hippies to retired but involved investment counselors. On three occasions I've packed up and moved from Victoria myself.

—folk singer Valdy

Victoria's ambience is made for the wanderer, its pavements picture-perfect for perambulation—Victoria, in short, is a great place to walk. In-line skating's good, too. Scooters and skateboards are also gaining ground. The tours below work whatever your favored form of transportation.

WALKING TOUR 1   THE INNER HARBOUR

Start	The Tourist Info Centre (812 Wharf St.) on the Inner Harbour.
Finish	The Tourist Info Centre.
Time	2 hours, not including shopping, museum, and pub breaks.
Best Times	Late afternoon, when the golden summer sunlight shines on The Fairmont Empress.
Worst Times	Late in the evening, when the shops close and the streets empty.

Victoria was born on the Inner Harbour. When the Hudson's Bay Company's West Coast head of operations, James Douglas, happened across this sheltered inlet in 1843 while searching for a new corporate HQ, it was love at first sight. "The place appears a perfect Eden," he wrote to a friend. High praise indeed, although as Douglas was pretty deep into local real estate, his words should be taken with a wee bit of salt. His confidence in the location certainly paid off, however, for less than 20 years after Douglas set foot onshore, the native stands of Garry oak had been supplanted by small farms, the town was choked with miners and mariners, and the harbor was full of ships, many of which had circumnavigated the globe. This trip doesn't go nearly as far, but it does circumnavigate the Inner Harbour, showing some of its lesser-known nooks and crannies, while providing an opportunity to enjoy the view as a Victorian sailor would have, quaffing a locally brewed pint from the deck of a stout Victoria pub.

We begin our tour at the:

① Victoria Tourist Info Centre
At 812 Wharf St., this is without a doubt the finest-looking tourist center in the world—a masterful Art Deco pavilion topped with a shining white obelisk rising high above the Inner Harbour. It would be a tribute to the taste and vision of city tourism officials, except that it started out life as a gas station.

From the Info Centre, thread your way south through the jugglers and musicians on the causeway until you're opposite 721 Government St., where stands:

❷ The Fairmont Empress

"There is a view, when the morning mists peel off the harbor, where the steamers tie up, of the Houses of Parliament on one hand, and a huge hotel on the other, which is an example of cunningly fitted-in waterfronts and facades worth a very long journey." Thus spoke Rudyard Kipling during a visit to the city in 1908. If he'd come only 5 years earlier he would've been looking at a swamp, and a nasty garbage-choked one at that. The causeway was then a narrow bridge over the tidal inlet, and as Victorians made a habit of pitching their refuse over the rail, the bay was, not surprisingly, a stinking cesspit of garbage and slime. In 1900, the ever-shrewd Canadian Pacific Railway made an offer to the city—we'll build a causeway and fill in the stinky bay if you let us keep the land. The city jumped at the offer. Little was expected—the land was swamp after all. But taking their cue from the good folk in Amsterdam, the CPR drove long pilings down through the muck to provide a solid foundation. And on top of that, they built The Fairmont Empress. The architect was Francis Rattenbury, and his design was masterful, complementing his own Legislature Buildings to create the viewscape that has defined the city ever since.

Round the south side of The Fairmont Empress is a formal rose garden—well worth poking your nose in for a sniff. Cut through the garden and cross over Belleville Street and continue another half block west to the corner of Douglas Street, where you'll find:

❸ Thunderbird Park

The park is instantly recognizable by its forest of totem poles. Even if you've overdosed on the ubiquitous 6-inch souvenir totem, take a second look at these. The original poles on this site had been collected in the early 1900s from various villages up and down the coast. Some decades later, when officials decided the severely weathered

poles needed restoring, they discovered the art of Native carving had eroded, even more than their collection of poles. From all the thousands of carvers on the coast, only one man still carried on the craft. In 1952, Kwakiutl artist Mungo Martin set up a carving shed on the park grounds and began the work of restoration. Martin replaced or repaired all the existing poles. At the same time, he taught his son and step-grandson-in-law to carve. Seeing them at work renewed public interest in the form. Other young artists came to learn and train. Eventually, this modest training ground led to a revival of totem carving and Native artistry among coastal Natives.

All poles have a purpose; most tell a story. The stories associated with the poles in Thunderbird Park have unfortunately been lost, but many of the figures are easily recognized, including Thunderbird (look for the outstretched wings and curly horns on the head), Raven, Bear, and Killer Whale.

On the edge of the park is the shed where Martin carved many of the poles. Feel free to poke your head in to take a look and ask the carvers what they're up to. The Native artists generally welcome questions and enjoy sharing their stories.

Walk west along Belleville past the modern-looking Carillon Tower (a gift from the Dutch people who settled in B.C.) and the not-to-be-missed-in-a-million-years-or-you're-wasting-your-time-in-Victoria Royal British Columbia Museum (see "The Top Attractions" in chapter 13) and cross Government Street. You're now standing in front of 501 Belleville St. at the:

❹ Parliament Buildings

In 1892, a 25-year-old Yorkshireman arrived on the West Coast just as an architectural competition for a new Legislature Building in Victoria was announced. Francis Mawson Rattenbury had no professional credentials but was blessed with both talent and vaulting ambition. He submitted a set of drawings and, to the surprise of all,

1 Victoria Tourist Info
   Centre
2 The Empress
3 Thunderbird Park
4 Provincial Legislature
5 Coast Hotel Docks
5a Fisherman's Wharf
6 West Bay
7 Songhees Point
8 Johnson Street Bridge
9 Bastion Square
10 Floatplane Docks

beat out 65 other entries from around the continent. It made his career. For the next 30 years, nearly all official buildings in Victoria, and many around the province, would be Rattenbury creations.

The Parliament Buildings are open for tours 9am to 5pm. In summer, the 40-minute tours start every 20 minutes (see "The Top Attractions" in chapter 13).

Across the street, the Greek temple–style **Royal London Wax Museum** (see "The Top Attractions" in chapter 13) is another Rattenbury creation, built originally as the CPR's Steamship ticket office. From here, ocean liners once departed for San Francisco, Sydney, and Canton.

From the Legislature lawn, dodge past the horse-drawn calèches parked on Menzies Street and walk west on

Belleville Street for 2 blocks to Pendray Street. The road takes a sharp right, but follow the path leading down to a waterfront walkway as it curves around Laurel Point. This headland was long the site of a stinking, fuming paint factory, so Victorians were delighted when it finally shut down and the luxurious **Laurel Point Inn** was erected in its place. Round the back of the Laurel is a pleasant Japanese garden if you're in a restrained and contemplative mood, and a patio restaurant if you're not.

Continuing around the pathway past the first few jetties takes you to the:

⑤ Coast Hotel Docks

Here is one of several ports of call of the Victoria Harbour Ferry Company (℡ **250/708-0201**). From here, the official Frommer's route is to take the ferry all the way across the harbor to

West Bay (stop 6). Along the way, there'll be views of the Olympic Mountains to the south and possibly a seal or bald eagle for company. Alternatively, you can take a short hop out to Fisherman's Wharf, where there are fresh-fish sales in season. Or you can go directly across to Spinnaker's Brew Pub on the far shore. Or you can go across to Songhees Point (stop 7) or even directly to the Harbour Canoe Club docks (See "Take a Break" after stop 8). You can even give up on your feet entirely and take the full Harbour Ferries tour.

Presuming you stick with the program, however, the next stop is:

6 West Bay

A pleasant little residential neighborhood with a picturesque marina, West Bay isn't anything much to write home about. What is worthwhile is the waterfront walkway that wends its way from here back east toward the city. The trail twists and curves through several parks, and there are views south through the harbor out to the Strait of Juan de Fuca and the Olympic Mountains beyond. After about 20 minutes of walking, if you feel yourself tiring, it may be time to:

TAKE A BREAK
Excellent beer brewed on the premises, combined with an above-average patio, make **Spinnaker's Brew Pub**, 308 Catherine St. (📞 250/386-BREW), open daily 11am to 11pm, a dangerously time-consuming port of call. For those looking for more substantial fare, the pub grub's very good and the entrees are above average. The on-site bakery makes inspired beer bread, as well as a range of more delicate goods.

From the pub, continue along the shoreline until you see the totem pole that stands at:

7 Songhees Point

The point is named after the Native band that once lived on the site. The Songhees had originally set up their village close to Fort Victoria, near the current site of Bastion Square, but relations with the Hudson's Bay Company were always a bit awkward. In 1844, a dispute over a pair of company oxen slaughtered by the Songhees was settled only after Commander Roderick Finlayson blew up the chief's house. A few years later, after a fire, started in the Native village, spread and nearly burned down the fort, Finlayson told the Songhees to relocate across the Inner Harbour. They refused at first, pointing out quite rightly that as it was their land, they could live wherever they liked. They assented to the move only after Finlayson agreed to help dismantle and transport the Songhees' longhouses.

The totem pole here is called the **Spirit of Lakwammen,** presented to the city to commemorate the 1994 Commonwealth Games. Continue on the pathway around the corner. The patio of the **Ocean Point Resort,** on your right, provides a great view of The Fairmont Empress. In summer, they show silent movies after sunset.

A little farther on is the:

8 Johnson Street Bridge

Trivia question: Who designed San Francisco's Golden Gate Bridge? Answer: The same guy who designed Victoria's Johnson Street Bridge. Alas, while the soaring Golden Gate span is justly famous for its elegance, this misshapen lump of steel and concrete is something designer Joseph Strauss would likely wish forgotten. Fortunately for him, word of this effort seems not to have reached San Fran.

Cross the bridge and walk past the Esquimalt and Nanaimo (E&N) Railway station (the daily sightseeing train to/from Nanaimo leaves and departs from here—see chapter 10) and turn left onto Store Street.

Walk 1 block north to Swift Street, turn left, walk downhill to the end of the street, and:

TAKE A BREAK
Having a drink at the **Harbour Canoe Club,** 450 Swift St. (✆ **250/361-1940**), it's hard to know who to admire more: the 19th-century engineers who built everything with brick and beam and always twice as thick as it had to be; the restorers who took this old building (once the site of the City Light Company) and turned it into a sunlit cathedral of a room; the owner, who had the vision to pay the restorers; the chef, who made the delicious plate of appetizers now quickly disappearing from the huge wooden bench; or the brew master, whose copper cauldrons produce such a superior brew. Try the taster option—six small glasses of different brews for about the price of a pint—and toast them all. The Club is open Sunday through Thursday 11:30am to 11pm and Friday and Saturday 11:30am to 1am.

Salutations complete, wander back up Swift Street, turn right, and continue south down Store Street for 2 blocks, where Store Street becomes Wharf Street. Walk another 3 blocks until you reach:

⑨ Bastion Square
As the name implies, this pleasant public space stands on the site of the Hudson's Bay Company's original Fort Victoria. The fort was demolished in 1863 and the land sold off for development. When the B.C. government bought and renovated the Rithet Building on the southwest corner of the square, workers uncovered Fort Victoria's original water well, complete with mechanical pump. It's now in the building's lobby.

Continue south on Wharf Street another 2 blocks until you come to the pinkish **Dominion Customs House.** Built in 1876, it was one of the first tangible signs of British Columbia's new status as a Canadian province. The Second Empire style was meant to impart a touch of Eastern civilization in the midst of this raw Western town.

Take the walkway by the Customs house down to the waterline and walk out on the:

⑩ Floatplane Docks
Early in the morning these docks buzz with activity as floatplanes fly in and out on their way to and from Seattle, Vancouver, and points north. The **Blackfish Cafe,** 950 Wharf St. (✆ **250/385-9996**), open 8am to 4pm, is a good spot to tuck into a big greasy-spoon breakfast and eavesdrop on some pilot gossip. The docks are also the place to come to arrange for diving and whale-watching tours. Back up on Wharf Street, you're just a hop, skip, and a jump from the Visitor Info tower, where the tour began.

WALKING TOUR 2   THE OLD TOWN & CHINATOWN

Start	The Fairmont Empress hotel, 321 Government St.
Finish	The Fairmont Empress hotel.
Time	2 hours, not including shopping, sightseeing, and eating stops.
Best Times	Any day before 6pm.
Worst Times	Any day after 6pm, when the shops close.

This tour also begins at one of Victoria's most impressive landmarks. In front of you is:

① The Fairmont Empress
At 321 Government St., this architectural delight was designed by Francis Rattenbury (see "Architectural Highlights & Historic Homes" in chapter 13).

Walking north up Government Street, you'll find a number of historic buildings. British Columbia's oldest brick structure, at 901 Government St., is the:

② Windsor Hotel building

Built in 1858 as the Victoria Hotel, the building's actually a perfect metaphor for the city. The original structure was a robust yet stylish piece of frontier architecture, with heavy red bricks formed into graceful Romanesque arches. Then, in the 1930s, when the city began pushing the "little bit of England" shtick, the original brick was covered over with stucco and fake Tudor half-timbering. Somewhere under the phony gentility, however, the robust frontier structure survives. (It's been through worse. In 1876, the hotel underwent major unexpected remodeling after the owner searched for a gas leak with a lit candle.)

On the next block, you'll find a brass sidewalk plaque at 1022 Government St., indicating the former site of:

③ Fort Victoria

The fort was constructed in 1843 by the Hudson's Bay Company as the western headquarters of its fur-trading empire. Bound by Broughton and View streets, between Government and Wharf streets, the fort had two octagonal bastions on either side of its tall cedar picket walls. It was torn down during the 1860s gold boom to make room for more businesses. You can get an idea of its size and shape from the line of light-colored bricks— inscribed with the names of early settlers—in the sidewalk that delineates the boundaries of the original walls. The first school in British Columbia was built on this site in 1849. The spot now houses **The Spirit of Christmas** shop.

Continue north 2 more blocks, just past View Street, where a little byway cuts off on the right, running 1 block to Broad Street. It's known as:

④ Trounce Alley

This is where miners and mariners spent their extra cash on the ladies. The alley is still lit by gas lamps, hung with heraldic crests, and ablaze with flower baskets and potted shrubs. You can stroll through shops selling jewelry, fashions, and crafts, or stop for a bite to eat. Trounce Alley ends abruptly at Broad Street.

Turn left on Broad Street, walk north 1 block, turn left on Yates Street, and walk east 1 block until you come to the:

⑤ Starfish Glassworks

At 630 Yates St., the building is closed Tuesday, open Monday and Wednesday through Saturday 10am to 6pm, also Sunday noon to 6pm. This ex-bank building is one of the city's finest examples of the Moderne style, but what makes it worth a visit are the gallery and workshop inside. Set up by a couple of glassblowing artists who couldn't get kiln time in Vancouver, the interior has been cleverly designed with the workshop on the ground floor and the gallery space on an open catwalk above. Step inside and watch the glassblowing, or wander around the gallery and admire the finished products.

From here, go 1 more block west on Yates, turn left on Langley Street, and go 1 block south. Turn right on View Street and you're in:

⑥ Bastion Square

The square was a bustling area with waterfront hotels, saloons, and warehouses during the late 19th century. Earlier, it had been the site of one of Fort Victoria's octagonal gun bastions. In 1963, the area was restored as a heritage square. This is a good place to:

TAKE A BREAK
Even if you're not hungry, it's worth stopping at **"Re-bar,"** 50 Bastion Sq. (© 250/361-9223), for a juice—say a combination of grapefruit, banana, melon, and pear, with bee pollen to keep your energy up. If you're hungry then rejoice: Re-bar has the city's best vegetarian comfort food. Disturbingly wholesome as that may sound, it's not only tasty—it's also fun, and a great spot to go with kids. It's open Monday through Thursday 8:30am to 8pm, Friday and Saturday 8:30am to 10pm, and Sunday 8:30am to 3:30pm.

Walking Tour 2: The Old Town & Chinatown

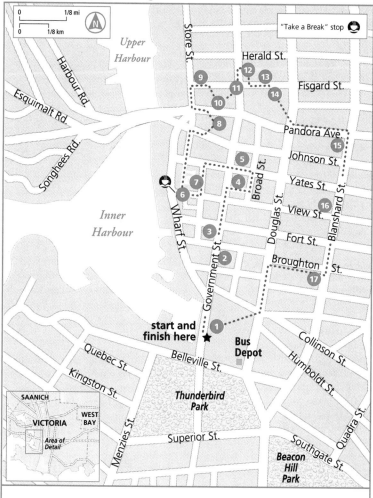

1 The Empress
2 Windsor Hotel building
3 Fort Victoria
4 Trounce Alley
5 Starfish Glassworks
6 Bastion Square
7 Maritime Museum
8 Market Square
9 Chinatown
10 Fan Tan Alley

11 Gate of Harmonious Interest
12 Chinese Settlement House
13 Chinese Imperial School
14 McPherson Playhouse
15 Congregation Emanu-El
   Synagogue
16 St. Andrew's Roman Catholic
   Cathedral
17 Greater Victoria Public
   Library

The provincial courthouse and hangman's square were once located on this restored pedestrian mall, but now you'll find the:

⑦ Maritime Museum

At 28 Bastion Sq. you can get a glimpse into Victoria's naval and shipping history (see "The Top Attractions" in chapter 13). It's housed in Victoria's original courthouse and jail.

More than a century ago, Victoria's business was transacted in this area of winding alleys and walkways. Warehouses, mariner's hotels, and shipping offices have been carefully restored into shops, restaurants, and galleries. You'll occasionally find historic plaques explaining the function of each building before it was renovated.

Turn north up Commercial Alley. Cross Yates Street, and a few steps farther west, turn north again up Waddington Alley. On the other side of Johnson Street is:

⑧ Market Square

This restored historic site was once a two-story complex of shipping offices and supply stores. It now contains more than 40 shops that sell everything from sports equipment and crafts to books and toys. There are also seven restaurants in the square; some have outdoor seating in the large open-air court where musicians often perform in summer.

Go north 1 block on Store Street and turn right (away from the harbor) onto Fisgard Street. You're now in North America's oldest:

⑨ Chinatown

Established in 1858 when the first Chinese arrived as gold seekers and railroad workers, this 6-block district fell into decline after World War I (as did many West Coast Asian communities when the U.S. and Canadian governments restricted Asian immigration). What remains is a fascinating peek into a well-hidden and exotic heritage.

On your right, halfway up the block, you'll find:

⑩ Fan Tan Alley

The world's narrowest street, it's no more than 4 feet wide at either end and expands to a little over 6 feet in the center. Through the maze of doorways (which still have their old Chinese signage), there are entries to small courtyards leading to more doorways.

During the late 1800s, this was the main entrance to "Little Canton," where the scent of legally manufactured opium wafted from the courtyards. Opium dens, gambling parlors, and brothels sprang up between the factories and bachelor rooms where male immigrants shared cramped quarters to save money.

Today, you won't find any sin for sale here—just a few little shops dealing in crafts and souvenirs. You can enter the **Chinatown Trading Company,** 551 Fisgard St., from Fisgard Street or via a back door facing onto Fan Tan Alley. Hidden in its back room are a couple of minimuseums cleverly displaying artifacts from old Chinatown, including the original equipment from a 19th-century Chinese gambling house. When you're finished exploring the alley, return to Fisgard Street and continue heading east.

At the corner of Government and Fisgard streets is the:

⑪ Gate of Harmonious Interest

This lavishly detailed dragon-headed, red-and-gold archway was built in 1981 to commemorate the completion—after years of deterioration—of Chinatown's revitalization by the city and the Chinese Consolidated Benevolent Association. The gate is guarded by a pair of hand-carved stone lions imported from Suzhou, China.

One-half block up at 1715 Government St. is the former location of the:

⑫ Chinese Settlement House

Newly arrived Chinese families once lived upstairs in this balconied building and made use of social services here until they were able to secure work and living quarters. The original Chinese Buddhist temple has been moved from the storefront to the second floor, but it's still open to visitors. Although admission is free, hours vary. You will have to check with temple staff to see if you may enter.

A half block up from the Gate of Harmonious Interest at 36 Fisgard St. is the:

⑬ Chinese Imperial School (Zhongua Xuetang)

This red-and-gold, pagoda-style building with a baked-tile roof and recessed balconies was built by the Chinese Benevolent Society. In 1907, the Victoria School Board banned non-Canadian Chinese children from attending public school, and in response, the society started its own community elementary school the following year. The school is open to the public during the week and still provides children and adults with instruction in Chinese reading and writing on weekends.

Just east of the school at 3 Centennial Sq. is the:

⑭ McPherson Playhouse

Formerly a vaudeville theater, it was the first of the vast Pantages Theatres chain (Alex Pantages went into showbiz after striking it rich in the Klondike gold fields). The building was restored in the 1960s and is now Victoria's main performing arts center (℡ **250/386-6121**). The baroque interior is stunning—well worth a peek. City Hall and the police department are located in the office plaza surrounding the playhouse.

When you get to the southeast corner of Centennial Square, walk up 1 more block on Pandora Avenue to Blanshard Street. At 1461 Blanshard St. (at Pandora Ave.), you'll find:

⑮ Congregation Emanu-El Synagogue

This is the oldest surviving Jewish temple on North America's west coast. Built in 1863, it has been proclaimed a national heritage site.

Turn south on Blanshard Street and walk 3 blocks to 740 View St., where you'll see the impressive:

⑯ St. Andrew's Roman Catholic Cathedral

Built during the 1890s, this is glorious Victorian High Gothic at its best. The facade is 23m (75 ft.) across, the spire 53m (175 ft.) tall, and no frill or flounce or architectural embellishment was forgone in the design. Renovations in the 1980s incorporated the works of First Nations artists into the interior. The altar is by Coast Salish carver Charles Elliot.

One block south at Fort Street is the beginning of Antique Row, which stretches 3 blocks east to Cook Street. Ignore that for the moment (or go explore and then come back) and continue 1 more block south on Blanshard. Walk across the plaza to 735 Broughton St., where you'll find the:

⑰ Greater Victoria Public Library

The attraction here is the huge skylit atrium, complete with George Norris's massive hanging artwork, *Dynamic Mobile Steel Sculpture.* Built in 1979, the library complex takes up most of the block. Library hours are Monday, Wednesday, Friday, and Saturday 9am to 6pm and Tuesday and Thursday 9am to 9pm. The Library is closed on Sunday.

Duck out through the portal on Broughton Street and walk west to Douglas Street, then turn left and walk a block and a half south on Douglas until you see the entrance to the Victoria Convention Centre. Walk in and admire the indoor fountain and aviary. The Centre connects to The Fairmont Empress, which was our starting place.

BIKING TOUR	DALLAS ROAD

Start	The Fairmont Empress, 321 Government St.
Finish	The Fairmont Empress.
Time	2 hours, not including picnic stops, sightseeing, shopping, or food breaks.
Best Times	Clear days with the sun shining, when the Olympic Mountains are out in all their glory.
Worst Times	Gray, rainy days.

Victoria cries out to be biked. The hills are modest, the traffic light and very polite, and the views incredible. When touring around by bike, you rarely have time to stop and pull out a point-by-point guide, so the descriptions offered here are shorter than for walking tours. The route is designed to take you a bit beyond what would be possible on foot, without getting into an expedition-length tour.

Start at **Cycle BC Bike Rental,** 747 Douglas St. (© **250/380-2453**), behind **The Fairmont Empress** hotel. Ride south down Douglas Street to **Thunderbird Park** and have a look at the totem poles. Continue east along Belleville Street past the **Legislature** and the **Coho ferry terminal;** then go round the corner onto Kingston Street, and go left through the small park to **Fisherman's Wharf.** From here, go south along **Dallas Road,** past the helijet pad and the car-ferry docks, and stop at the entrance to the breakwater at **Ogden Point.** By this time, you should have a fabulous view of the Olympic Mountains. Park your bike and wander out along the breakwater or stop in at the **Ogden Point Cafe,** 204 Dallas Rd., for the same view without the wind.

Continue east along the seaside bike path or on Dallas Road. Stop here and there as the urge strikes and do some beachcombing. A little ways on, past Douglas Street, cross Dallas and cut north into **Beacon Hill Park.** Stop at the petting zoo, look at the 127-foot-tall totem pole, or just enjoy Victoria's favorite park. Exit the park

by the northeast corner on Cook Street and cycle a few blocks north into **Cook Street Village.** This is a good spot to grab a coffee and dessert or to shop for picnic supplies at the local deli or supermarket. Head back south on Cook Street to Dallas Road; turn left and continue east a kilometer or so to **Clover Point,** a short peninsula sticking out into the Strait of Juan de Fuca. It makes a fine picnic spot. From here, head east to **Ross Bay Cemetery,** Victoria's second oldest, where many local notables are buried, including former governor James Douglas and painter Emily Carr. From the north side of the cemetery, ride up the hill on **Stannard Street,** skirting the eastern edge of **Government House,** the official residence of the lieutenant governor.

When you reach **Rockland Avenue,** turn right and ride a few hundred meters past the many fine homes of this elite enclave to the main entrance to Government House. Though the residence itself is closed to the public, the formal gardens are open and well worth a wander. Round back, the hillside of Garry oaks is one of the last places to see what the area's natural fauna looked like before European settlers arrived. At the front, the rose garden is sumptuous. Just west of the gate on Rockland Avenue, turn right onto **Joan Crescent** and ride up the small hill to opulent **Craigdarroch Castle,** built by coal magnate Robert Dunsmuir for his wife, Joan. The castle is open for self-guided tours. From here, continue up Joan

Crescent to Fort Street, turn right and go a very short way east to Yates Street, turn left and go 1 block to Fernwood Street, turn right and go 1 block north to **Pandora Street,** then turn left again and ride west down the hill. Keep an eye out for the **Christian Science church** at 1205 Pandora (where the street widens to include a boulevard in its center). Another 6 blocks west and you're at **Pandora and Government streets,** with **Chinatown** to your right and **Market Square** to your left, and The Fairmont Empress and the bike-rental spot just a few blocks south.

15

Victoria Shopping

Victoria has dozens of little specialty shops that appeal to every taste and whim, and because the city is built on such a pedestrian scale, you can wander from place to place seeking out whatever treasure you're after. Nearly all of the areas listed below are within a short walk of The Fairmont Empress, and given Victoria's parking "situation," it's probably best to hoof it. For those shops located more than 6 blocks from The Fairmont Empress hotel, bus information is provided. Stores are generally open Monday through Saturday 10am to 6pm; some, but not many, are open on Sunday during summer.

1 The Shopping Scene

Explorers beware: The brick-paved **Government Street promenade,** from the Inner Harbour 5 blocks north to Yates Street, is a jungle of cheap souvenir shops. There are gems in here, certainly—Irish linen, fine bone china, quality Native art, and Cowichan Indian sweaters thick enough to bivouac in—but to find these riches you'll have to hack your way through tangled creepers of Taiwanese-made knickknacks and forbidding groves of maple-syrup bottles.

Farther north, the **Old Town district** and **Market Square** feature a fascinating blend of heritage buildings and up-to-date shops. Victoria's **Chinatown** is tiny; since most of the city's Chinese population has moved elsewhere, it lacks some of the authenticity of Chinatowns in Vancouver or San Francisco. The area has been charmingly preserved, however, and there are a number of gallery-quality art and ceramic shops, quirky back alleys (including Canada's thinnest commercial street), and at least one tourist trap that knows not to take itself too seriously.

On the eastern edge of downtown, **Antique Row** is justifiably renowned for its high-quality British collectibles. And if you're at all interested in the Native art of the Pacific Northwest, Victoria is a great place to add to your collection. If you're unacquainted with its bold and stylized figures drawn from a mythology as rich as that of ancient Greece, Victoria's a great place to buy a piece or two.

2 Shopping A to Z

ANTIQUES

Victoria has long had a deserved reputation for antiques—particularly those of British origin. That so much Georgian pewter should end up on the Canadian West Coast is largely due to the city's reputation as a retirement home for aging Brits. It's slightly morbid, but so long as they keep coming and time keeps marching forward, estate sales will keep "new" antique stock rolling in. Many of the best stores are in **Antique Row,** a 3-block stretch on Fort Street between Blanshard and Cook streets. In addition to those listed below, check out **Jeffries**

and Co. Silversmiths, 1026 Fort St. (✆ **250/383-8315**); **Romanoff & Company Antiques,** 837 Fort St. (✆ **250/480-1543**); and for furniture fans, **Charles Baird Antiques,** 1044A Fort St. (✆ **250/384-8809**).

David Robinson Antiques   Here you'll find oriental rugs, silver, oil paintings, brass, porcelain, and period furniture. Though it's not as large as Faith Grant's shop, Robinson's pieces—especially his furniture—are particularly well chosen. 1023 Fort St. ✆ 250/384-6425. Bus: 10 to Blanshard or Cook St.

Faith Grant's Connoisseur Shop Ltd. *Finds*   The farthest from downtown, this shop is also the best. The 16 rooms of this 1862 heritage building contain everything from Georgian writing desks to English flatware, not to mention fine ceramics, prints, and paintings. Furniture is an especially strong suit. 1156 Fort St. ✆ 250/383-0121. Bus: 10 to Fort and Cook St.

Vanity Fair Antique Mall *Value*   This large shop is fun to browse, with crystal, glassware, furniture, and lots more. If you're feeling flush, it's certainly possible to spend here, but there are also many items you can easily pick up without taking out a bank loan. 1044 Fort St. ✆ 250/380-7274. Bus: 10 to Blanshard or Cook St.

ART
CONTEMPORARY

Fran Willis Gallery   Soaring white walls and huge arched windows make this one of Victoria's most beautiful display spaces. The collection is strong on contemporary oils, mixed media, and bronzes, almost all by B.C. and Alberta artists. 1619 Store St. ✆ 250/381-3422. www.franwillis.com. Bus: 5 to Douglas and Fisgard.

Open Space   When does self-confidence start edging into pretension? This artist-run gallery and self-declared flag-bearer of the avant-garde has trod one side or the other of that line since 1971. Mostly, they get it right, so the gallery's usually worth a visit. Exhibits run the full gamut, from paintings and sculpture to literary and dance performances. 510 Fort St. ✆ 250/383-8833. www.openspace.ca.

Winchester Galleries   This slightly daring gallery features mostly contemporary oil paintings. Unlike elsewhere in town, very few wildlife paintings ever make it onto the walls. 1010 Broad St. ✆ 250/386-2773. www.winchestergalleriesltd.com.

NATIVE

Alcheringa Gallery   What began as a shop handling imports from the Antipodes has evolved into one of Victoria's truly great stores for aboriginal art connoisseurs. All the coastal tribes are represented in Alcheringa's collection, along with pieces from Papua New Guinea. The presentation is museum quality, with prices to match. 665 Fort St. ✆ 250/383-8224. www.alcheringa-gallery.com.

Hill's Native Art   Exquisite traditional Native art includes wooden masks and carvings, Haida argillite and silver jewelry, bentwood boxes, button blankets, drums and talking sticks, and carved wooden paddles. Hill's is the store for established artists from up and down the B.C. coast, which means the quality is high, and so are the prices. Of course, you don't stay in business for 50 years without pleasing all comers, so Hill's has its share of dream catchers and other knickknacks. 1008 Government St. ✆ 250/385-3911.

Sa Nuu Kwa Gallery   Here you'll find Native art freed from the knickknack shop and placed in the gallery where it belongs—beautiful masks, carvings, prints, and jewelry. 606 Johnson St. ✆ 250/480-5515.

BOOKS

Avalon Metaphysical Centre   It's not the West Coast unless you've had a spiritual experience or brushed auras with someone who has. Avalon specializes in New Age books, angels, crystals, rune stones, body oils, and videotapes of gurus who've already trodden the path to enlightenment. Sales are timed to coincide with the vernal equinox and summer solstice. 62–560 Johnson St. (in Market Sq.). © 250/380-1721.

Crown Publications Inc.   In addition to dry, but informative, government publications, this store stocks an excellent selection of books covering the history, nature, and culture of the Victoria area. Keeping up with the times, digital maps are now available on CD-ROM. 521 Fort St. © 250/386-4636. www.crown pub.bc.ca.

Munro's Books *(Finds)*   All bookstores should look so good: a mile-high ceiling in a 1909 heritage building, complete with heavy brass lamps and murals on the walls (never mind that the building was originally a bank). The store stocks many well-chosen books—over 35,000 titles, including an excellent selection of books about Victoria and books by local authors. The staff is friendly and very good at unearthing obscure titles. The remainder tables have some incredible deals. 1108 Government St. © 1-888/ 243-2464 or 250/382-2464. www.munrobooks.com.

Russell Books *(Value)*   This shop offers two floors of used (and some new, remaindered) books for browsing. 734 Fort St. © 250/361-4447.

CAMERAS

Lens and Shutter   Come here for all your camera needs—film, filters, lenses, cameras, or just advice. 615 Fort St. © 250/383-7443.

CHINA, CRYSTAL & LINENS

Irish Linen Stores   Everything Irish since 1910: handkerchiefs, scarves, doilies, napkins, lace, and more. 1019 Government St. © 250/383-6812.

Sydney Reynolds   This building opened as a saloon in 1908, became a bank in 1909, was converted into a shop in 1929, and now houses a wide array of fine porcelains, including tea sets and Victorian dolls. 801 Government St. © 250/ 383-3931.

CHINESE ARTS & CRAFTS

Chinatown Trading Company *(Finds)*   This unobtrusive storefront on Fisgard opens onto a veritable bazaar—three connected shops stocked with Chinese goods either useful or endearingly corny or both. Who wouldn't want kung fu shoes or a tin pecking chicken? There are also bamboo flutes, origami kits, useful and inexpensive Chinese kitchenware, and a few small museum displays of artifacts from Chinatown's past. Look for the sneaky back entrance off Fan Tan Alley. 551 Fisgard St. © 250/381-5503. Bus: 5 to Douglas and Fisgard St.

Magpie Gift Studio   Small Chinese decorative items like jade- and brass-inlay rosewood boxes are the stock-in-trade here. There are also larger Asian antiques and elegant jewelry. Open daily 11am to 5pm. 556 Fisgard St. © 1-888/ 388-8898 or 250/383-1880. Bus: 5 to Douglas and Fisgard St.

CHRISTMAS ORNAMENTS

The Spirit of Christmas *(Finds)*   The thought of a shop selling Christmas ornaments year-round may send you reaching for lost bits of Dickensian invective, but before you start hurling "Bah humbugs," step inside and have a look. The store has everything from C$300 woven vine wreaths to cotton nightshirts with caroling cows. 1022 Government St. ✆ **250/385-2501.**

CIGARS & TOBACCO

E.A. Morris Tobacconist Ltd. A century-old tradition of custom-blended pipe tobacco is maintained in this small shop. You'll also find an impressive selection of cigars, including Cubans. Cuban cigars can't be brought into the United States, but a few brands like Horvath Bances duck the blockade by importing the tobacco into Canada and rolling the cigars here. You miss out on the special flavor imparted by child labor, but you also miss the year or so in a federal pen. 1116 Government St. ✆ **250/382-4811.**

DEPARTMENT STORES & A SHOPPING MALL

The Bay (Hudson's Bay Company) Here you'll find camping and sports equipment, Hudson's Bay woolen point blankets, and fashions by Tommy Hilfiger, Polo, DKNY, and Liz Claiborne, all under one roof. 1701 Douglas St. ✆ **250/385-1311.**

Victoria Eaton Centre This is actually a full modern shopping mall disguised as a block of heritage buildings. Inside, centered around a glass atrium, are three floors of shops and boutiques that offer both classic and outrageous fashions, china and crystal, housewares, gourmet foods, and books. Between Government and Douglas sts., off Fort and View sts. ✆ **250/389-2228.**

FASHIONS

FOR WOMEN

Breeze This high-energy fashion outlet carries a number of affordable and trendy lines such as Mexx, Powerline, and Mac+Jac. Shoes by 9 West and Steve Madden and other stylish accessories such as purses and jewelry complete the look. 1150 Government St. ✆ **250/383-8871.**

Hughes Ltd. This local favorite features designer fashions and trendy casual wear. 564 Yates St. ✆ **250/381-4405.**

The Plum Clothing Co. This local chain features quality dressy casuals designed with the baby-boomer in mind. 1298 Broad St. ✆ **250/381-5005.**

FOR WOMEN & MEN

A Wear This large airy space in a converted heritage building houses large collections of fashionable threads for men and women. 1205 Government St. ✆ **250/382-9327.**

The Edinburgh Tartan Shop Women love a man in a kilt. Go figure. If there's even a drop of Celtic blood in ye, this shop can set you up in a kilt made from your family tartan. It also stocks sweaters, blankets, tartan by the yard, and kilt pins with authentic clan crests. 909 Government St. ✆ **250/953-7788.**

Still Life Originally known for its vintage clothes, Still Life has updated its collection and moved to a new contemporary style. Fun and active street clothes for young and the young at heart, from Diesel, Workwear, and Toronto designer Damzels-in-distress. 551 Johnson St. ✆ **250/386-5655.**

W. & J. Wilson's Clothiers Canada's oldest family-run clothing store, this shop has been owned/managed by the Wilsons since 1862. When you're in it for the long haul, you try not to get too far ahead of the pack. Look for sensible casuals or elegant cashmeres and leathers from British, Scottish, and other European designers. 1221 Government St. ✆ **250/383-7177.**

FOR MEN

British Importers   Victoria may be laid-back, but a man still needs a power suit, and this is the place to get it. Designer labels include Calvin Klein and Hugo Boss. Ties and leather jackets are also on display in this award-winning retail space. 1125 Government St. ℂ **250/386-1496.**

GARDENING

Better Gnomes and Gardens   Looking at Victoria's many picture-perfect gardens may leave you with a serious case of garden lust. A visit to Better Gnomes and Gardens may just be the solution. Get inspired by the many flowers and plants, statues, and large selection of garden accessories and pick up some "inside" tips from the helpful staff. 3200 Quadra St. (at Tolmie). ℂ **250/386-9366.**

Western Canada Wilderness Committee (WCWC)   Committed to protecting Canada's endangered species and environment, the WCWC sells a variety of items to raise funds for the cause. Choose from beautiful gift cards, posters, and souvenir T-shirts or mugs. 651 Johnson St. ℂ **250/388-9292.**

FOOD

Murchie's   It's worth coming here just to suck up the coffee smell or sniff the many specialty tea flavors, including the custom-made Empress blend, served at the hotel's afternoon tea. While you're imbibing the air, browse the collection of fine china, silver, and crystal. 1110 Government St. ℂ **250/383-3112.**

Rogers' Chocolates   "Quite possibly the best chocolates in the world" is how Roger's bills itself. How daring. For a more accurate (but litigation-proof) description, how about "quite possibly the best 98-year-old shrine to all things dark and sweet; still with original Tiffany glass and old-fashioned counters, and free samples, too." Roger's has shops in Oak Bay and Whistler—quite possibly just as good. 913 Government St. ℂ **800/663-2220** or 250/384-7021.

Silk Road Aromatherapy and Tea Company (Value)   Before setting up shop, the two Victoria women who run this store first trained to become tea masters in China and Taiwan. Their Victoria store on the edge of Chinatown sells a wide variety of teas, including premium loose blends and tea paraphernalia such as teapots, mugs, and kettles; as well, they offer a full line of aromatherapy products. The latest addition is the spa, which offers a range of treatment services at very reasonable prices; a 1½ hour full body and foot massage at C$85 (US$55) is a steal. 1624 Government St. ℂ **250/382-0006.** www.silkroadtea.com. Bus: 5 to Douglas and Fisgard St.

GLASS

Starfish Glassworks (Finds)   Who says artists don't have a head for business? The principals of this gallery-cum-workshop moved to Victoria when they couldn't get kiln time in Vancouver. They took over and renovated an ex-bank building, installing the kiln on the ground floor and the gallery on an open catwalk above, so potential customers could watch works in progress while browsing among the finished products. The glasswork is incredible, the view enjoyable, the gallery highly successful. Glass-blowing demonstrations daily noon to 6pm. Wannabe glass blowers can now take one-day workshops; check www.starfishglass.bc.ca for dates. Closed Tuesday, September to May. 630 Yates St. ℂ **250/388-7827.**

JEWELRY

Jade Tree   You'll find jewelry made from British Columbia jade, which is mined in northern Vancouver Island, then crafted in Victoria and in China into necklaces, bracelets, and other items. 606 Humboldt St. ℂ **250/388-4326.**

MacDonald Jewelry Ian MacDonald designs and makes all his own jewelry: diamonds cut in squares and triangles and styles from the traditional to cutting edge. It's a great place to hunt for rings and pearls as well as precious gems like sapphires, rubies, and emeralds. 618 View St. ⓒ **250/382-4113.**

NATIVE CRAFTS

Natives from the nearby Cowichan band are famous for their warm, durable sweaters, knitted with bold motifs from hand-spun raw wool. In addition to these beautiful knits, craftspeople create soft leather moccasins, moose-hide boots, ceremonial masks, sculptures carved from argillite or soapstone, intricate baskets, bearskin rugs, and jewelry.

Cowichan Trading Company A downtown fixture for almost 50 years, Cowichan Trading follows the standard layout for its displays: junky T-shirts and gewgaws in front, Cowichan sweaters, masks, and fine silver jewelry farther in. 1328 Government St. ⓒ **250/383-0321.**

Quw'utsun' Cultural and Conference Centre Though a bit of a drive out of town, this store, owned/operated by the Cowichan, sells beautiful crafts and stocks an excellent selection of books and publications on First Nations history and lore. You can also watch artisans at work. 200 Cowichan Way, Duncan. ⓒ **250/746-8119.** www.quwutsun.ca. No public transit.

OUTDOOR CLOTHES & EQUIPMENT

Ocean River Sports A kayak shop near Bastion Square, this is the place to go to arrange a sea kayak tour—they'll be happy to sell you a boat and all the gear. This is also a good spot for outdoor clothing and camping knickknacks, like that solar-heated shower or espresso machine. 1824 Store St. ⓒ **250/381-4233.**

Pacific Trekking An excellent source of rain and hiking gear; also good for information on local hiking trails. 1305 Government St. ⓒ **250/388-7088.**

A PAWNSHOP

Universal Trading (Value) So it's not where you normally shop. This isn't your usual down-at-heel pawnbroker, either, but rather a quirky little curio shop with a few pieces that wouldn't be out of place in Antique Row. Case in point, the 1940s-era Harley parked out front. 584 Johnson St. ⓒ **250/383-9512.**

A PUBLIC MARKET

Market Square Constructed from the original warehouses and shipping offices built here in the 1800s, this pleasant and innovative heritage reconstruction features small shops and restaurants surrounding a central courtyard, often the site of live performances in summer. 560 Johnson St. ⓒ **250/386-2441.**

WINE

The Wine Barrel This shop sells over 300 B.C. VQA (Vintner Quality Alliance) wines and so much more: everything to do with wine, from wineglasses and corkscrews to books on snacks to serve with wine. It has the largest selection of B.C. ice wines in Victoria. 644 Broughton St. ⓒ **250/388-0606.**

The Wine Shoppe at Ocean Pointe Resort A great selection of Vancouver Island, Okanagan, French, and Australian wines. The staff is knowledgeable and helpful. 45 Songhees Rd. ⓒ **250/360-5804.** Bus 24 to Colville.

16

Victoria After Dark

Victoria is God's waiting room. It's the only cemetery in the entire world with street lighting.

—a visitor from Gotham, as quoted in *Monday* magazine

Ouch. That's a little harsh. More important, it's not exactly accurate. True, with retirees and civil servants making up a sizable segment of the population, Victoria is never going to set the world on fire. But taken together, the U. Vic. students; tourists; and a small, but dedicated, cadre of Victoria revelers form a party-going critical mass large enough to keep a small, but steady, scene alive.

Monday magazine, a weekly tabloid published on Thursdays, is the place to start. Its listings section provides near-comprehensive coverage of what's happening in town and is particularly good for the club scene. If you can't find *Monday* in cafes or record shops, visit it on the Web at **www.mondaymag.com**.

For information on theater, concerts, and arts events, contact the **Tourism Victoria Visitor Info Centre,** 812 Wharf St. (© **800/663-3883** or 250/953-2033; www.tourismvictoria.com). You can also buy tickets for all of Victoria's venues from the Info Centre, but only in person.

Whatever you decide to do with your evening, chances are your destination's close at hand. One of the great virtues of Victoria's size is that nearly all of its attractions—concert halls, pubs, dance clubs, and theaters—are no more than a 10-minute walk from The Fairmont Empress hotel, easily reached by taking bus no. 5 to the Empress Hotel/Convention Centre. For those few nightlife spots a little farther out, bus route information is provided.

1 The Performing Arts

The **Royal Theatre,** 805 Broughton St., and the **McPherson Playhouse,** 3 Centennial Sq., share a common box office (© **888/717-6121** or 250/386-6121; www.rmts.bc.ca). The **Royal**—built in the early 1900s and renovated in the 1970s—hosts concerts by the Victoria Symphony and performances by the Pacific Opera Victoria, as well as touring dance and theater companies. The **McPherson**—built in 1914 as the first Pantages Vaudeville Theatre—is home to smaller stage plays and performances by the Victoria Operatic Society. The box office is open Monday through Saturday 9:30am to 5:30pm and on performance days for the 2 hours before showtime. Bus no. 6 to Pandora and Government.

THEATER

Performing in an intimate playhouse that was once a church, the **Belfry Theatre Society,** 1291 Gladstone St. (© **250/385-6815;** www.belfry.bc.ca; bus no. 22 to Fernwood St.), is a nationally acclaimed theatrical group that stages four productions October through April and a summer show in August. Expect dramatic works by contemporary Canadian playwrights. Tickets are C$15 to C$25 (US$9.75–US$16) for adults; senior and student discounts are available. The box office is open Monday through Friday 9:30am to 5pm, with hours extended to an hour before showtime on performance days.

The **Intrepid Theatre Company,** 301–1205 Broad St. (© **888/FRINGE2** or 250/383-2663; www.intrepidtheatre.com), runs two yearly theater festivals. In spring, it's the **Uno Festival of Solo Performance,** a unique event of strictly one-person performances. Normally there are 10 to 15 acts, with tickets at C$12 (US$7.75). Come summer, Intrepid puts on the **Victoria Fringe Festival;** see **www.victoriafringe.com** for details. Even if you're not a theater fan—*especially* if you're not—don't miss the Fringe. Unlike mainstream theater, fringe festivals are cheap (about C$8/US$5.20) and short (an hour or so), so you're not gambling much by stepping inside one of the six venues—and the rewards are often spectacular. More than 50 performers or small companies come from around the world, and the plays they put on are often amazingly inventive: one-man comedy, sped-up Shakespeare, multimedia dance, comic film noir, anything's possible. The festival runs from late August to mid-September, and performances go on at six downtown venues daily noon to midnight.

The **Theatre Inconnu** (© **250/360-0234**) is mostly known for its annual production of Victoria's **Shakespeare Festival,** held in a restored theater in the historic St. Ann's Academy, 835 Humboldt St. The festival puts on two or three of the Bard's best for several weeks in July and August. The actors are local and often semi-professional, but quality is excellent and tickets are an eminently affordable C$5 to C$14 (US$3.25–US$9.10). The Theatre Inconnu also stages a two-man adaptation of Charles Dickens's *A Christmas Carol* every year.

The **Langham Court Theatre,** 805 Langham Court (© **250/384-2142**), performs works produced by the Victoria Theatre Guild, a local amateur society dedicated to presenting a wide range of dramatic and comedic works. From downtown take bus no. 14 or 11 to Fort and Moss Street.

OPERA

The **Pacific Opera Victoria,** 1316B Government St. (© **250/385-0222;** box office 250/386-6121; www.pov.bc.ca), presents three productions annually during the October-to-April season. Performances are normally at the McPherson Playhouse and Royal Theatre. The repertoire covers the classical bases, from Mozart and Rossini to Verdi and even Wagner. Tickets cost C$20 to C$72 (US$13–US$46) and are available at the McPherson Playhouse box office or at the Opera box office during office hours.

The **Victoria Operatic Society,** 10–744 Fairview Rd. (© **250/381-1021;** www.vos.bc.ca), presents impressive old-time Broadway musicals and other popular fare at the McPherson Playhouse. In 2003, the company plans a spring performance of Gilbert and Sullivan's *Yeoman of the Guard.* Tickets cost C$18 to C$28 (US$12–US$18).

ORCHESTRAL & CHORAL MUSIC

The well-respected **Victoria Symphony Orchestra,** 846 Broughton St. (© **250/385-9771;** www.victoriasymphony.bc.ca), a smaller orchestra, kicks off its season on the first Sunday of August with **Symphony Splash,** a free concert performed on a barge in the Inner Harbour. Regular performances begin in September and last through May, always under the guidance of musical director Kees Bakels. The Symphony Orchestra normally performs at the Royal Theatre or the University Farquhar Auditorium. Repertoire leans to German masters such as Haydn, Mozart, and Beethoven, but the symphony also performs concertos and brings in internationally known performers. Tickets are C$15 to C$28 (US$9.75–US$18) for most concerts; senior, student, and group discounts are available.

DANCE
Dance recitals and full-scale performances by local and international dance troupes such as **Danceworks** and the **Scottish Dance Society** are scheduled throughout the year. Call the **Visitor Info Centre** at ✆ **250/953-2033** to find out who's performing when you're in town.

COMEDY & SPOKEN WORD
Mocambo, 1028 Blanshard (✆ **250/384-4468**), a coffeehouse near the public library, hosts a range of semi-intellectual, spoken-word events through the week (multimedia fusion demos, philosopher's cafes, argument for the joy of it, slam poetry), then lets loose on Saturdays with improv comedy. No cover.

2 Music & Dance Clubs

MUSIC FESTIVALS
Folkfest   A multicultural celebration of song, performances, food, and crafts, Folkfest is sponsored by the International Cultural Association of greater Victoria. It takes place in June on Ship Point (the parking space below Wharf St. on the edge of the Inner Harbour). ✆ **250/388-4728.** www.icafolkfest.

Summer in the Square   From early July to late August, this festival in downtown's Centennial Square is popular because it offers free music outside every day. Each day features a different band and musical style: The Monday noon-hour concerts feature mostly jazz; Tuesdays offer a noon-hour selection of Big-Band golden oldies; Wednesday through Saturday is potluck (show up at noon and take your chances). The festival's showstoppers are the Concerts Under the Stars held each Sunday 7 to 9:30pm; the series features some 15 local bands over the 6-week length of the festival. And if you can't make it down to the square, the concerts are also broadcast live over a local radio station, the Q (FM 100.3). Centennial Square. ✆ **250/361-0388.**

The TerrifVic Jazz Party   What was for many years known as the Dixieland Jazz festival recently changed names and expanded formats after authorities discovered extended exposure to the bright, relentlessly happy tunes of Dixieland was causing large numbers of locals to throw themselves in front of the red double-decker buses. The new lineup for the 5-day late-April festival features swing, honky-tonk, fusion, some blues, and even Dixieland. ✆ **250/953-2011.** www.islandnet.com/~bbs/jazz.html .

Victoria Jazz Society/Jazz Fest International   The Jazz Society is a good place to call any time of year to find out what's happening; it runs a hot line listing jazz events throughout the year. It's raison d'être, however, is the **Jazz Fest International,** held from late June to early July. The more progressive of Victoria's two summer jazz fests, this one offers a range of styles from Cuban and salsa and world beat to fusion and acid jazz. Many free concerts are given in the Market Square courtyard. Other concerts are in live-music venues around the city. This organization also puts on the excellent **Blues Bash** on Labour Day weekend on an outdoor stage in Victoria's Inner Harbour. ✆ **888/671-2112.** www.vicjazz. bc.ca.

LIVE MUSIC

Legends   This live-music venue is in the city within a city that's the Strath-cona Hotel. Below street level, Legends had degenerated into a veritable black pit until the owners pumped in a major cash injection, transforming it into a pop-music palace. Even better, they began booking some hopping international bands, covering the gamut from afro-pop to blues to R&B and zydeco. Legends is now one of the best places to see live music in the city. 919 Douglas St. ✆ 250/383-7137. www.strathconahotel.com. C$4 (US$2.60) cover or more depending on the band Thurs–Sat.

The Lucky Bar   Currently the hottest spot in Victoria, this long, low cavernous space has a pleasantly grungy feel to it, like something in Seattle's Pioneer Square. Owned and operated by the team in charge of next-door Süze, the Lucky Bar features DJs on Wednesdays, rockabilly on Thursdays, and a lot of good bands (and sometimes DJs) on weekends. Sundays it's reggae or brew & view (beer and old movies). 517 Yates St. ✆ 250/382-5825. www.luckynightclub.com. Cover hovers around C$5 (US$3.25), bigger shows up to C$20 (US$13).

Steamers   Once a grubby peeler parlor, Steamers got a totally new interior and was reborn as the city's premium blues bar. "Blues" here isn't taken too literally, of course. Acts often stray into the far-off musical realms of zydeco, Celtic, and world beat. Whatever it is, Steamers has live music 7 nights a week. On Mondays there's an open-stage acoustic jam (no cover). 570 Yates St. ✆ 250/381-4340. Cover free–C$5 (US$3.25).

Thursdays   This new spot out on Cook Street is the spot to hear Victoria's up-and-coming indie bands of all genres, from alt-country to neo-minimalist rock. 1821 Cook St. ✆ 250/360-2711. Cover C$5–C$8 (US$3.25–US$5.20).

DANCE CLUBS

Most places are open Monday through Saturday until 2am and Sunday until midnight. Drinks run from C$3 to C$4.50 (US$1.95–US$2.95).

Bar Victoria   Formerly the Blues House, just on the edge of downtown, Bar Victoria is a popular all-DJ dance spot, featuring everything from house to trip funk to retro-1970s and 1980s nights on Wednesdays. Local college students flock to the popular Top 40 and hip-hop Thursdays when all drinks are C$2 (US$1.30) 1417 Government St. ✆ 250/386-1717. Cover around C$5 (US$3.25). Bus: 5 to Douglas and Fisgard St.

The One Lounge   This Top 40 club spins dance tracks for a late twenties to early thirties crowd. The format (1970s and 1980s retro) depends on the night of the week. 1318 Broad St. ✆ 250/384-3557. C$5 (US$3.25) cover on weekends.

Sugar   To dance the night away under an old-fashioned disco ball there is no better spot than Sugar, the most popular club according to Clubvibes.com.

Gambling

At the **Great Canadian Casino,** 1708 Old Island Highway (✆ 250/391-0311; www.gcgaming.com), there are no floor shows, no alcohol, no dancing girls in glittering bikinis—just a casual and slightly genteel casino. Games include blackjack, roulette, sic bo, red dog (diamond dog), and Caribbean stud poker. It's open daily noon to 3am. Contact the casino for complimentary shuttle service from downtown Victoria.

Open only Thursday through Saturday; line-ups start at 10pm so come early. DJs spin mostly hip hop, house, and Top 40 tunes. 858 Yates St. ℭ **250/920-9950.** C$3–C$6 (US$1.95–US$3.90) cover Fri–Sat.

Sweetwaters Niteclub   This elegant singles spot for a late-twenties-to-early-forties demographic features classic tracks and Top 40 tunes. 27–570 Store St. ℭ **250/ 383-7844.** C$3 (US$1.95) cover Fri–Sat.

3 Lounges, Bars & Pubs

LOUNGES

Bengal Lounge   A truly unique experience. The Bengal is one of the last outposts of the old empire—a Raffles or a Harry's Bar—except the martinis are ice cold and jazz plays in the background (and on weekends, live in the foreground). The couches are huge and covered in leather thick enough to stop an elephant gun, while the cocktail list is extensive. The combination has lately attracted the young and elegant lounge lizard crowd. 721 Government St., in The Fairmont Empress. ℭ **250/384-8111.**

Rick's Lounge   This is, without a doubt, the best place to watch as the last light of day fades from the Inner Harbour and the lights on the fairy-tale Legislature Building switch on. Rick's offers casual elegance, low-volume live music, and a vast selection of single-malt whiskies. 45 Songhees Rd., in the Ocean Pointe Resort. ℭ **250/360-2999.** Bus: 24 to Colville.

BARS & PUBS

Big Bad John's *Finds*   You have to go to John's. Victoria's first, favorite, and only hillbilly bar is a low, dark warren of a place, with wall gak by the gross ton, inches of discarded peanut shells on the plank floor, and a crowd of drunk and happy rowdies. Tradition dictates that the bartender waits until you aren't looking and then . . . ha, like I'm tellin'. (It involves latex and something long and squirmy.) 919 Douglas St., in the Strathcona Hotel. ℭ **250/383-7137.**

The Harbour Canoe Club   At the Harbour Canoe Club, admire the brick and thick beam construction, a sunlit cathedral of a room. The appetizers are delicious, and the brew produced here is superior. Try the taster option—six small glasses of different brews for more or less the price of a pint. Particularly on weekend nights when the house blues band sets up just beside the bar, the Canoe Club is an excellent spot to let "just one" stretch into an entire evening's sojourn. 450 Swift St. ℭ **250/361-1940.**

Spinnaker's Brew Pub   Without a doubt one of the best brew pubs in town, Spinnaker's did it first and did it well, setting standards other pubs had to match. Overlooking Victoria Harbour on the west side of the Songhees Point Development, Spinnaker's view of the harbor and Legislature is fabulous. On sunny days it's worth it for the view alone. At other times (all times in fact) the brewed-on-the-premises ales, lagers, and stouts are uniformly excellent. For those looking for more substantial fare, the pub grub's good, and the entrees are above average. An on-site bakery sells various beer breads. On the weekends there's often a band, or, if that doesn't suit you, there are dart-boards and pool tables. 308 Catherine St. ℭ **250/386-2739.** Bus: 24 to Songhees Rd.

The Sticky Wicket   This is yet another pub in the Strathcona Hotel—but the Wicket is a standout. Originally installed on an ocean liner, the beautiful wood interior—including dividers, glass, and a long teak bar—was later taken to a new home in Dublin. Only very recently—as part of a C$4-million renova-tion—was the whole package packed up and shipped here to Victoria, making it about as original an Irish bar as you're likely to find. Elevators can whip you from deepest Dublin up three floors to the mini-Malibu on the outdoor patio balcony. Faster than you can say Sinn Fein, that Guinness in your paw has been replaced with a fuzzy navel, and you're spiking and diving on the beach volley-ball courts. Rad. 919 Douglas St., in the Strathcona Hotel. ✆ 250/383-7137.

Süze Lounge and Restaurant   This great little lounge is in the heart of the Old Town. It's the perfect spot, in fact, for a first date: little tables on their own but not so isolated that escape is impossible, and lots of background noise and eye candy if you get bored. The crowd is young and moneyed, and the beer selection's good. 515 Yates St. ✆ 250/383-2829.

Swans Brewpub ★★   There are few drinking spots anywhere more intrigu-ing—or more enjoyable—than Swans. The enjoyment comes from the room itself, on the ground floor of a beautifully converted 1913 feed warehouse across from the Johnson Street Bridge. The intrigue comes from the owner's vast art collection, portions of which he regularly rotates through the pub. The beer here is brewed on-site and utterly delicious. On weekends, Swans now sometimes offers bands. 506 Pandora Ave., in Swans Hotel. ✆ 250/361-3310.

4 Gay & Lesbian Bars

Alas, Victoria's entertainment options for the gay and lesbian community are few. A good resource for local contacts can be found on-line at **http://gay-victoria.ca**.

BJ's Lounge   With a full menu, a lounge decor, and regular drag shows, BJ's makes for a pleasant enough place to spend the evening. On non-show nights, the tunes follow the conventional gay canned music format: a little bit of techno and lots of Gloria Gaynor. Heteros take note: BJ's is militant about preserving its homo-only ambience. Straights are often refused admission. 642 Johnson St. (entrance on Broad St.). ✆ 250/388-0505. There's no cover.

Friends of Dorothy's Café   Dorothy's gone but not forgotten. The *Wizard of Oz* used to play continuously at this pleasant kitschy cafe, but the new own-ers found it was driving them over the rainbow. Now they make do with the voluminous Dorothy memorabilia. Dorothy's staff is friendly and just slightly outré, and the crowd is definitely fun-loving. Try the cocktails, or if you're looking for sustenance in solid form, the enchiladas, burgers, pastas, and salads. 615 Johnson St. ✆ 250/381-2277.

Hush   This gay-yet-straight-friendly space (crowd is about 50/50) features top-end touring DJs spinning house, trance and disco house, hosted by Brent Carmichael, the 40-something granddaddy of Victoria DJs. 1325 Government St. ✆ 250/385-0566. C$5 (US$3.25) cover on weekends.

17

Side Trips: The Best of British Columbia

Set on the very edge of a great wilderness, British Columbia offers some experiences that are truly world class—like the skiing in Whistler—and some that are like nothing else on earth.

1 Whistler: One of North America's Premier Ski Resorts ★★★

The premier ski resort in North America, according to *Ski* and *Snow Country* magazines, the **Whistler/Blackcomb complex** boasts more vertical, more lifts, and more varied ski terrain than any other ski resort in North America. And it isn't all just downhill skiing. There's also backcountry, cross-country, snowboarding, snowmobiling, heli-skiing, and sleigh riding. In summer, there's rafting, hiking, golfing, and horseback riding as well.

And then there's **Whistler Village.** Back in the 1970s, the city fathers, having made a conscious decision to build a resort town, looked to their minions in the planning department and ordered them to make it so. The results are impressive—a resort town of 40,000 beds, arranged around a central village street in a compact enough fashion that you can park your car and remain a pedestrian for the duration of your stay.

What was sacrificed in this drive to become the perfectly planned community was space for the odd, the funky, the quaint, and the nonconforming. Whistler has none of the strip malls, cheap motels, and filling stations that mar some resort towns; however, you won't find that quaint little restaurant run by an old Tyrolean couple, tucked away on an out-of-the-way hillside. So it goes.

The towns north of Whistler, **Pemberton** and **Mount Currie,** are refreshment stops for touring cyclists and hikers and the gateway to the icy alpine waters of **Birkenhead Lake Provincial Park** (see "Fishing," below) and the majestic **Cayoosh Valley,** which winds through the glacier-topped mountains to the Cariboo town of Lillooet.

ESSENTIALS

GETTING THERE   **By Car**   Whistler is about a 2-hour drive from Vancouver along Highway 99, also called the **Sea-to-Sky Highway.** The drive is spectacular, winding first along the edge of Howe Sound before climbing through the mountains. Parking at the mountain is free for day skiers. For overnight visitors, most hotels charge about C$7 (US$4.55).

By Bus   The **Whistler Express,** 8695 Barnard St., Vancouver (© **604/266-5386** in Vancouver or 877/317-7788 in Whistler; www.perimeterbus.com), operates bus service from Vancouver International Airport to the Whistler Bus Loop, as well as drop-off service at many of the hotels. In summer, there are

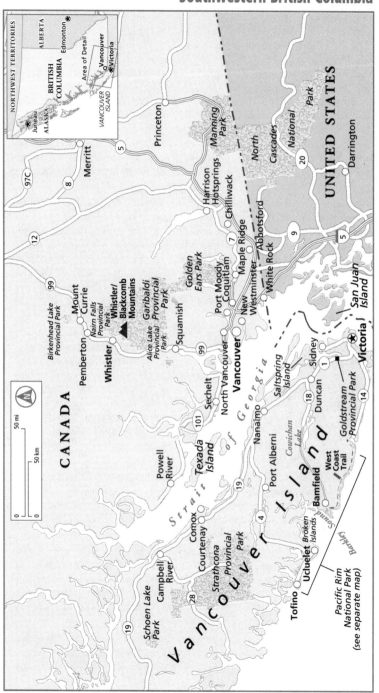

seven daily departures between 9:30am and 9:30pm. In winter, there are eleven departures daily between 9:30am and 11:30pm, with extra buses on weekends. The trip takes about 2½ to 3 hours; round-trip fares are C$106 (US$68) for adults in summer and C$110 (US$71) in winter and C$60 (US$39) for children in summer and C$68 (US$44) in winter; children under 5 ride free. Reservations are required year-round.

Greyhound, Pacific Central Station, 1150 Station St., Vancouver (© **604/ 662-8051** in Vancouver or 604/932-5031 in Whistler), operates bus service from the Vancouver Bus Depot to the Whistler Bus Loop at 8 and 11am and 1, 3, 5, and 7pm daily. Return trips to Whistler leave at 5, 8:30, and 10:30am and 1:30, 4:45, and 7:15pm. The trip takes about 2½ hours; one-way fares are C$20 (US$13) for adults and C$10 (US$6.50) for children 5 to 12; children under 5 ride free.

By Train **BC Rail** (© **604/984-5246**) operates the *Cariboo Prospector* throughout the year. It leaves the North Vancouver train terminal daily at 7am and chugs up the Howe Sound coastline through the scenic Cheakamus River Canyon and Garibaldi Provincial Park until it reaches the Whistler train station on Lake Placid Road, arriving at 9:35am. The same train leaves Whistler at 6:45pm and returns to the North Vancouver train terminal at 9pm. The 2½-hour trip includes breakfast or dinner. A one-way ticket is C$39 (US$25) for adults, C$19 (US$12) for seniors and children 2 to 12, and C$11 (US$7.15) for children under 2.

VISITOR INFORMATION The **Whistler Visitor Info Centre,** 2097 Lake Placid Rd., Whistler, B.C. V0N 1B0 (© **604/932-5528;** www.whistlerchamber ofcommerce.com), is open daily 9am to 5pm. **Information kiosks** on Village Gate Boulevard at the entry to Whistler Village, the main bus stop, and a number of other locations are open from mid-May to early September during the same hours. **Tourism Whistler** is at the Whistler Conference Centre at 4010 Whistler Way, Whistler, B.C. V0N 1B0, open weekdays 9am to 5pm (© **800/ WHISTLER** or 604/932-3928; www.tourismwhistler.com). This office can assist you with event tickets and last-minute accommodations bookings, as well as provide general information.

GETTING AROUND Compact and pedestrian-oriented, Whistler Village has signed trails and pathways linking together all shops and restaurants. If you're staying in the Village, you can park your car and leave it for the duration of your stay. The walk between the Whistler Mountain (Whistler Village) and Blackcomb Mountain (Upper Village) resorts takes about 5 minutes.

By Bus A year-round **public transit service** (© **604/932-4020**) operates frequently from the Tamarisk district and the BC Rail Station to the neighboring districts of Nester's Village, Alpine Meadows, and Emerald Estates. Bus service from the Village to Village North and Upper Village accommodations is free. For other routes, one-way fares are C$1.50 (US$1) for adults and C$1.25 (US85¢) for seniors/students; children under 5 ride free.

By Cab The Village's taxis operate around the clock. Taxi tours, golf course transfers, and airport transport are also offered by **Airport Limousine Service** (© **800/278-8742** or 604/273-1331), **Whistler Taxi** (© **604/938-3333**), and **Sea-to-Sky Taxi** (© **604/932-3333**).

By Car Rental cars are available from **Budget,** at the Holiday Inn Sunspree, 4295 Blackcomb Way (© **604/932-1236;** www.bcbudget.com); and **Thrifty,** in the Listel Whistler Hotel, 4121 Village Green (© **604/938-0302**).

SPECIAL EVENTS   Dozens of downhill **ski competitions** are held December through May. They include the Owens-Corning World Freestyle Competition (Jan), Power Bar Peak to Valley Race (Feb), Kokanee Fantastic Downhill Race (Mar), Air Canada Whistler Cup and World Ski & Snowboard Festival (Apr), and Whistler Snowboard World Cup and World Cup Freestyle (Dec).

Mountain bikers compete in the Power Bar Garibaldi Gruel (Sept) and the Cheakamus Challenge Fall Classic Mountain Bike Race (Sept).

During the third week in July, the Villages host **Whistler's Roots Weekend** (✆ **604/932-2394**). Down in the Villages and up on the mountains, you'll hear the sounds of Celtic, zydeco, bluegrass, Delta blues, Latin, folk, and world-beat music at free and ticketed events.

The **Whistler Summit Concert Series** (✆ **604/932-3434**) is held during August weekends, with the mountains providing a stunning backdrop for the on-mountain concerts. In the past, concert performers have included the Barenaked Ladies, Amanda Marshall, Great Big Sea, the Matthew Good Band, and Blue Rodeo. Call for dates and details.

The **Alpine Wine Festival** (✆ **604/932-3434**) takes place on the mountaintop during the first weekend in September. Featuring wine tastings, a winemaker's dinner, a Sunday brunch, and other events highlighting North America's finest vintages, the festival has become a classic.

And the second weekend in September ushers in the **Whistler Jazz & Blues Festival** (✆ **604/932-2394**), featuring live performances in the village squares and the surrounding clubs. It's a great opportunity to see some Pacific Northwest jazz, gospel, R&B, and blues.

Cornucopia (✆ **604/932-3434**) is Whistler's premier wine-and-food festival. Held the second week in September, the opening gala showcases 50 top wineries from the Pacific region. Other events include a celebrity chef competition, food and wine seminars, and wine tastings.

WHERE TO STAY

The first and biggest decision to make is whether to stay in or out of Whistler Village. Staying in the Village, you can forget your car for the duration of your visit and walk along cobblestone pathways from hotel to ski lift to restaurant to pub. Staying outside the Village, you'll have a short drive to the lifts or restaurants (though many places offer shuttle service), but you'll also have a touch more of that mountain tranquillity. Accommodations within the Village are top quality, while outside the Village, there is a bit more variety, including a fine Austrian-style inn reviewed below.

Whether you decide to stay in or out of town, the best thing to do is simply decide on your price point and call one of the central booking agencies. The studios, condos, town houses, and chalets are available year-round. Prices run from C$90 to C$1,400 (US$58–US$903) per night. **Whistler Central Reservations** (✆ **800/944-7853** or 604/664-5625; fax 604/938-5758; www.mywhistler. com) can book a wide range of accommodations in the Whistler area, from B&Bs to hotel rooms or condos. Furthermore, they can provide a customized package with lift tickets and air or ground transportation to and from Vancouver. Other booking agencies, including **Whistler Chalets and Accommodations Ltd.,** 4360 Lorimer Rd. (✆ **800/663-7711** in Canada, or 604/932-6699; www.whistlerchalets.com), and **Rainbow Retreats Accommodations Ltd.,** 2129 Lake Placid Rd. (✆ **604/932-2343;** www.rainbowretreats.com), have many properties to suit every budget and group size.

Reservations for peak winter periods should be made by September at the latest.

IN THE VILLAGE

The Fairmont Chateau Whistler ★★ The one exception to the everything's-the-same-in-Whistler rule, the Chateau Whistler is outstanding. The Former Canadian Pacific hotel chain, now part of Fairmont, spared little expense in re-creating the look and feel of an old-time country retreat at the foot of Blackcomb Mountain. Massive wooden beams support an airy peaked roof in the lobby, while in the hillside Mallard Bar, double-sided stone fireplaces cast a cozy glow on the couches and leather armchairs. The rooms and suites feature double, queen-, and king-size beds, duvets, and soaker tubs. Gold service guests can have breakfast or relax après-ski in a private lounge with the feel of a Victorian library. All guests can use the heated outdoor pool and Jacuzzis, which look out over the base of the ski hill.

4599 Chateau Blvd., Whistler, B.C. V0N 1B4. © **800/606-8244** in the U.S., 800/606-8244 in Canada, or 604/938-8000. Fax 604/938-2099. www.fairmont.com. 558 units. Winter C$469 (US$303) double; C$570–C$1,200 (US$368–US$774) suite. Summer C$149–C$369 (US$96–US$238) double; C$425–C$1,000 (US$274–US$645) suite. Wheelchair-accessible units available. AE, MC, V. Underground valet parking C$22 (US$14). Pets are welcome. **Amenities:** 2 restaurants; bar; 2 heated outdoor pools; 2 tennis courts (no night play); health club; outstanding spa facility; Jacuzzi; children's programs; concierge; tour desk; business center; shopping arcade; 24-hr. room service; in-room massage; babysitting; coin laundry; laundry service; same-day dry cleaning; nonsmoking rooms; concierge-level rooms. *In room:* A/C, TV w/pay movies, dataport, minibar, coffeemaker, hair dryer, iron, safe.

The Pan Pacific Lodge Whistler ★ The Pan-Pacific's furnishings and appointments are top-notch, and the kitchenettes (in all suites) contain the cutlery and equipment required to cook up a gourmet meal. With sofa beds and fold-down Murphy beds, the studio suites are fine for couples, while the one- and two-bedroom suites allow a bit more space for larger groups or families with kids. Comfortable as the rooms are, however, the true advantage to the Pan Pacific is its location at the foot of the Whistler Mountain gondola. Not only can you ski right to your hotel, but thanks to a large heated outdoor pool and Jacuzzi deck, you can sit at the end of the day sipping a glass of wine, gazing up at the snowy slopes, and marvel at the ameliorative effects of warm water on aching muscles.

4320 Sundial Crescent, Whistler, B.C. V0N 1B4. © **888/905-9995** or 604/905-2999. Fax 604/905-2995. www.panpacific.com. 121 units. High season Nov 22–April 30 C$409–C$599 (US$264–US$386) studio; C$509–C$759 (US$328–US$490) 1-bedroom suite; C$709–C$959 (US$457–US$619) 2-bedroom suite. Low season May–Nov 21 C$309–C$409 (US$199–US$264) studio; C$359–C$509 (US$232–US$328) 1-bedroom suite; C$409–C$709 (US$264–US$457) 2-bedroom suite. Wheelchair-accessible units available. AE, MC, V. Underground valet parking C$15 (US$9.75). **Amenities:** Restaurant; pub; heated outdoor pool; fitness center; Jacuzzi; steam room; concierge; limited room service; laundry. *In room:* A/C, TV, dataport, kitchen, minibar, fridge, coffeemaker, hair dryer, iron, safe.

The Westin Resort & Spa Whistler ★★★ Who says that only the early bird gets the worm? Latecomer to the Whistler hotel scene, the Westin Resort snapped up the best piece of property in town and squeezed itself onto the mountainside at the bottom part of the main ski run into the village. Both the Whistler and Blackcomb gondolas are within a few hundred yards from your doorstep. The hotel is built in the style of a mountain chalet with lots of local stone finishings such as granite and basalt and cedar timbers. All 419 suites in this nonsmoking facility include full kitchens, including the junior suites where a clever bit of design leaves the rest of the room feeling uncramped. The beds,

Westin's signature Heavenly Beds, are indeed divine. Start with a custom-designed brand-name mattress, add a down blanket, then three layers of heavy cotton sheets, and top it off with a down duvet and the best pillows money can buy. To get you going in the morning, little luxuries include a ski valet service and (no more cold toes!) a boot warming service. That is certainly one of the reasons why in the short period since the Westin opened in June 2000, it already grabbed a couple of top awards, including best ski resort hotel in North America by the readers of *Condé Nast Traveler*. In the off-season, the hotel offers fabulous pamper packages with rates starting as low as C$159 (US$103), including a $39 (US$25) dining credit at the Aubergine Grill or towards a spa treatment in the Avello Spa on the Westin's premises.

4090 Whistler Way, Whistler, BC V0N 1B4. © 888/634-5577, 800/WESTIN-1, or 604/905-5000. Fax 604/905-5640. www.westinwhistler.net. 419 units. April 16–Nov 23 C$159–C$469 (US$103–US$303) junior suite; C$249–C$589 (US$161–US$380) 1-bedroom suite; C$409–C$1049 (US$264–US$677) 2-bedroom suite. Nov 24–April 15 C$199–C$569 (US$128–US$380) junior suite; C$319–C$689 (US$206–US$445) 1-bedroom suite; C$519–C$1499 (US$335–US$967) 2-bedroom suite. Children 17 and under stay free in parents' room. AE, DC, DISC, MC, V. Parking C$21 (US$14). **Amenities:** Restaurant; bar; indoor and outdoor pool; nearby golf course; nearby tennis courts; outstanding health club; top-notch spa; indoor and outdoor Jacuzzi; sauna; nearby watersports rental; bike rental; children's program; concierge; business center; shopping arcade; salon; 24-hr. room service; massage; babysitting; laundry; dry cleaning; nonsmoking facility. *In room:* TV w/pay movies, dataport (high-speed Internet), kitchen, fridge, coffeemaker, hair dryer, iron, safe.

OUTSIDE THE VILLAGE

Cedar Springs Bed & Breakfast Lodge   Guests at this charming modern lodge have a choice of king-, queen-, or twin-size beds in comfortably modern yet understated surroundings. The honeymoon suite boasts a fireplace and balcony. The guest sitting room has a TV, VCR, and video library. A sauna and hot tub on the sun deck overlooking the gardens add to the pampering after a day of play. A gourmet breakfast is served by the fireplace in the dining room, and guests are welcome to enjoy afternoon tea. Owners Joann and Jackie Rhode can provide box lunches and special-occasion dinners at this cozy hideaway. A complimentary shuttle service takes you to the ski lifts, and additional public transit is available to and from the Village.

8106 Cedar Springs Rd., Whistler, B.C. V0N 1B8. © 800/727-7547 or 604/938-8007. Fax 604/938-8023. www.whistlerbb.com. 8 units, 6 with private bathroom (5 with shower only). C$85–C$239 (US$55–US$154) double; C$130–C$279 (US$84–US$180) suite. Rates include full breakfast. AE, MC, V. Take Hwy. 99 north toward Pemberton 4km (2½ miles) past Whistler Village. Turn left onto Alpine Way, go a block to Rainbow Dr., and turn left; go a block to Camino St. and turn left. The lodge is a block down at the corner of Camino and Cedar Springs Rd. **Amenities:** Jacuzzi; sauna; game room; bike rental; courtesy car to ski slopes; close to Nicklaus North Golf Course; nonsmoking lodge. *In room:* Hair dryer, no phone.

Durlacher Hof Pension Inn ★★ *Finds*   This lovely inn boasts both an authentic Austrian feel and a sociable atmosphere. Both are the result of the exceptional care and service shown by owners Peter and Erika Durlacher. Guests are greeted by name at the entranceway, provided with slippers, and then given a tour of the two-story chalet-style property. The rooms (on the 2nd floor) vary in size from comfortable to quite spacious and come with goose-down duvets and Ralph Lauren linens on extra long twin- or queen-size beds, private bathrooms (some with jetted tubs) with deluxe toiletries, and incredible mountain views from private balconies. Better still is the downstairs lounge, with a welcoming fireplace and complementary après-ski appetizers baked by Erika (these are delectable enough that guests are drawn from all over the inn to snack, share stories, and strategize on ways to obtain Erika's recipes). For much the same reason, many guests seem to linger over the complimentary (and substantial) hot breakfast.

7055 Nesters Rd. Whistler, B.C. V0N 1B7. ☎ 877/932-1924 or 604/932-1924. Fax 604/938-1980. www.
durlacherhof.com. 8 units. Dec 18–Mar 31 C$150–C$265 (US$97–US$171) double; June 19–Sept 30 C$120–
C$205 (US$77–US$132) double. Extra person C$35 (US$23). Discounts for spring and fall available. Rates
include full breakfast and afternoon tea. 1 wheelchair-accessible unit available. MC, V. Free parking. Take Hwy.
99 about 0.8km (½ mile) north of Whistler Village to Nester's Rd. Turn left and the inn is immediately on the
right. **Amenities:** Jacuzzi; sauna; concierge; tour desk; ski and bike storage; laundry service; dry cleaning;
nonsmoking lodge. *In room:* Hair dryer.

Hostelling International Whistler (Value   One of the few inexpensive spots
in Whistler, the hostel also happens to have one of the nicest locations: on the
south edge of Alta Lake, with a dining room, deck, and lawn looking over the
lake to Whistler Mountain. Inside, the hostel is extremely pleasant; there's a
lounge with a wood-burning stove, a common kitchen, a piano, Ping-Pong
tables, and a sauna, as well as a drying room for ski gear and storage for bikes,
boards, and skis. In the summer, guests have use of a barbecue, canoe, and row-
boat. As with all hostels, most rooms and facilities are shared. Beds at the hostel
book up very early. Book by September at the latest for the winter ski season.

5678 Alta Lake Rd., Whistler, B.C. V0N 1B5. ☎ 604/932-5492. Fax 604/932-4687. www.hihostels.ca. 33 beds
in 4- to 8-bed dorms. C$20 (US$13) IYHA members, C$24 (US$15) nonmembers; annual adult membership
C$35 (US$23). Family and group memberships available. MC, V. Free parking. **Amenities:** Sauna; watersports
equipment; bike rental; nonsmoking facility.

CAMPGROUNDS
South of Whistler on the Sea-to-Sky corridor is the very popular **Alice Lake
Provincial Park.** Free hot showers, flush toilets, and a sani-station are just the
beginning of a long list of available facilities. Hiking trails, picnic areas, sandy
beaches, swimming areas, and fishing spots are on the grounds. You can reserve
spots for Alice Lake at **Discover Camping** (☎ 800/689-9025). Twenty-seven
kilometers (16 miles) north of Whistler, the well-maintained campground at
Nairn Falls on Highway 99 (☎ 604/898-3678) is more adult-oriented, with pit
toilets, pumped well water, fire pits and firewood, but no showers. Its proximity
to the roaring Green River and the town of Pemberton makes it appealing to
many hikers, and the sound of the river is sweeter than any lullaby. Prices for the
88 campsites are C$15 (US$9.75) per night, on a first-come, first-served basis.
The 85 campsites at **Birkenhead Lake Provincial Park,** off Portage Road,
Birken (☎ 604/898-3678), fill up very quickly in summer. To reserve a spot,
call **Discover Camping** (see above). Boat launches, great fishing, and well-maintained tent and RV sites make this an angler's paradise and one of the province's
top 10 camping destinations. Facilities include fire pits, firewood, pumped well
water, and pit toilets. Campsites are C$12 (US$7.80) per night.

WHERE TO DINE
Whistler literally overflows with dining choices. A stroll through the Village will
take you past 25 or 30 restaurants.

A good meal for gourmets on the go can be found at **Chef Bernard's,** 4573
Chateau Blvd., Whistler Village (☎ 604/932-7051), open daily 7am to 7pm. It
serves full breakfasts, soups, salads, and sandwiches, as well as hot entrees for
C$4.95 to C$8 (US$3.22–US$5.20).

Ingrid's Village Cafe (☎ 604/932-7000), open daily 8am to 5pm, is another
local favorite for quality and price. A large bowl of Ingrid's clam chowder costs
just C$4.50 (US$2.93), while a veggie burger comes in at C$5 (US$3.25). **Citta
Bistro,** in Whistler Village Square (☎ 604/932-4177), is a favorite dining and
night spot, open daily 11am to 1am. It serves thin-crust pizzas, gourmet burgers,

and delicious finger foods. Besides having great food and good prices (main courses are C$7–C$11/US$4.50–US$7.15), it has umbrella-covered tables on the terrace, the best people-watching corner in town.

Equally fun indoor dining can be had at the **Dubh Linn Gate Irish Lounge/Pub** (© 604/905-4047) in the Pan Pacific hotel. The Gate offers solid pub grub and the atmosphere of the Emerald Isle. Open Monday through Saturday 7am to 1am, Sundays 7am to midnight. Main courses cost C$11 to C$17 (US$7.15–US$11). New to Whistler but long known in Vancouver for its quality beef is **Hy's Steakhouse,** 4308 Main St. (© **604/905-5555**), open daily 5:30 to 10pm (last reservation at 9pm). Main courses range from C$27 to C$44 (US$17–US$28). Over Blackcomb way, the **Wildflower** (© **604/938-2033**) in the Chateau Whistler does innovative West Coast cuisine in a quiet, civilized room. It's open for dinner daily 6 to 10pm; main courses cost C$18 to C$40 (US$12–US$26).

Araxi Restaurant & Bar ★ ITALIAN/WEST COAST   Frequently awarded
for its wine list, as well as voted "Best Restaurant in Whistler" in 1998 and 1999 by readers of *Vancouver* magazine, this is one of the top places to dine. And thanks to a C$250,000 renovation in the spring of 1999, Araxi now has storage enough for its 12,000-bottle inventory of fine B.C. and foreign wines. Outside, the heated patio seats 80 people amid barrels of flowers, while inside, the artwork, antiques, and terra-cotta tiles give it a subtle Italian ambience. The menu, however, is less Italian and more West Coast, with the emphasis on fresh regional products. The locally caught trout is smoked in the Araxi kitchen. Various soups and salads are made from scratch with fresh ingredients like Pemberton sheep cheese and Okanagan tomatoes. Main courses include seafood such as ahi tuna, salmon filet, and scallops. For meat lovers, the menu offers rack of lamb, tenderloin, and alder-smoked pork loin. And considering the near encyclopedic length of Araxi's famous wine list, don't hesitate to ask sommelier Chris Van Nus for suggestions.

4222 Village Sq. © **604/932-4540**. www.araxi.com. Main courses C$25–C$36 (US$16–US$23). AE, MC, V. Mid-May to Oct daily 11am–10:30pm; during ski season daily 5–10pm.

Caramba! Restaurant MEDITERRANEAN   The room is bright and filled
with the pleasant buzz of nattering diners. The kitchen is open, and the smells wafting out hint tantalizingly of fennel, artichoke, and pasta. Caramba! is casual dining, but its Mediterranean-influenced menu offers fresh ingredients, prepared with a great deal of pizzazz. Try the pasta, free-range chicken, or roasted pork loin. Better still, if you're feeling especially good about your dining companions, order a pizza or two; a plate of grilled calamari; some hot spinach, cheese, and artichoke-and-shallot dip; and a plate of sliced prosciutto and bullfighter's toast (savory toasted Spanish bread with herbs).

12–4314 Main St., Town Plaza. © **604/938-1879**. Main courses C$11–C$17 (US$7.15–US$11). AE, MC, V. Daily 11:30am–10:30pm.

Rimrock Cafe and Oyster Bar ★★ SEAFOOD   Upstairs in a long narrow
room with a high ceiling and a great stone fireplace at one end, Rimrock is very much like a Viking mead hall of old. It's not the atmosphere, however, that causes people to hop in a cab and make the C$5 (US$3.25) journey out from Whistler Village. What draws folks in is the food. The first order of business should be a plate of oysters. Chef Rolf Gunther serves them up half a dozen ways, from raw with champagne to cooked in hell (broiled with fresh chiles). For

my money, though, the signature Rimrock oyster is still the best: broiled with béchamel sauce and smoked salmon. Other appetizers are lightly seared ahi tuna or Québec foie gras with portobello mushrooms. Mains are equally seafood-oriented and inventive. Look for lobster and scallops in light tarragon sauce on a bed of Capellini pasta or swordfish broiled with pecans, almonds, pistachios, and a mild red Thai curry. The accompanying wine list has a number of fine vintages from B.C., California, New Zealand, and Australia.

2117 Whistler Rd. ✆ 877/932-5589 or 604/932-5565. www.rimrockwhistler.com. Main courses C$24–C$40 (US$15–US$26). AE, MC, V. Daily 11:30am–11:30pm.

Uli's Flipside PASTA/ITALIAN   At least one longtime Whistler resident threatened dire, if unspecified, consequences if I told Frommer's readers about this local favorite. It's not that Uli's is the best restaurant in town or even the best pasta place (though for this title it's certainly in the running); it's just that few other spots offer the same combination of excellent pasta, a good wine list, and a pleasant room with vaulted ceiling and intimate window-side booths, all at a very moderate price. Given that Whistler shares the West Coast affliction of early dining (few kitchens are open as late as 10pm), Uli's is also the best bet for late-night dining. Try it for yourself and see—just don't say you heard it from me.

4433 Sundial Place (upstairs). ✆ 604/935-1107. Main courses C$11–C$17 (US$7.15–US$11). AE, DC, MC, V. Mon–Sat 3pm–1am; Sun 3pm–midnight.

Val d'Isère FRENCH   For a different kind of French cuisine, the elegant Val d'Isère offers a taste of Alsace, a hearty regional cuisine that'll warm you even on the coldest days. Try the goat-cheese soufflé to begin, followed by braised duck on a bed of figs, red cabbage, and polenta with port-wine reduction. For lighter fare—perhaps on a summer day on Val d'Isère's great patio—try the seared scallops with candied lemon/ginger sauce. The wine list has a good number of bottles, many hailing from Alsace, but unfortunately doesn't offer many wines by the glass. As in proper French tradition, the desserts are luscious: profiteroles with vanilla ice cream and hot chocolate sauce, a warm chocolate orange gâteau, or a lemon soufflé with chocolate.

4314 Main St., Whistler Town Plaza. ✆ 604/932-4666. www.valdisere-restaurant.com. Main courses C$24–C$40 (US$15–US$26). AE, MC, V. Daily Nov–May 5–10pm; daily June–Oct 11:30am–11pm.

THE OUTDOORS: WHISTLER'S RAISON D'ÈTRE

Whistler/Blackcomb Mountain ★★★   Now that both mountain resorts are jointly operated by Intrawest, your pass gives you access to both ski areas. Locals have their preferences, but the truth is that both offer great skiing. **Whistler Mountain** has 1,502m (4927 ft.) of vertical and over 100 marked runs that are serviced by a high-speed gondola and eight high-speed chairlifts, plus four other lifts and tows. Helicopter service from the top of the mountain makes another 100-plus runs on nearby glaciers accessible. There are cafeterias and gift shops on the peak as well as a fully licensed restaurant. **Blackcomb Mountain** has 1,584m (5,195 ft./1 mile) of vertical and over 100 marked runs that are serviced by nine high-speed chairlifts, plus three other lifts and tows. The cafeteria and gift shop aren't far from the peak, and the fully licensed restaurant is worth the gondola trip even if you're not skiing. The view is spectacular, the food decent. Both mountains also have bowls and glade skiing, with Blackcomb Mountain offering glacier skiing well into August.

4545 Blackcomb Way, Whistler, B.C. V0N 1B4. ✆ 604/932-3434; snow report 604/687-7507 in Vancouver, 604/932-4211 in Whistler. www.whistler-blackcomb.com. Winter lift tickets C$61–C$63 (US$39–US$41) adults, C$52–C$54 (US$34–US$35) youths and seniors, C$31–C$32 (US$20–US$21) children, per day for both mountains. A variety of multiday passes are also available, but rates for the 2002–03 season weren't available at press time. Lifts open daily 8:30am–3:30pm (until 4:30pm mid-Mar until end of season, depending on weather and conditions).

DIFFERENT SLOPES FOR DIFFERENT FOLKS: THE LOWDOWN ON SKIING IN WHISTLER

Whistler/Blackcomb mountain offers **ski lessons and ski guides** for all levels and interests. (For skiers looking to try snowboarding, a rental package and a half-day lesson are particularly attractive options.) Phone **Guest Relations** at ☎ **604/932-3434** for details.

You can **rent ski and snowboard gear** at the base of both Whistler and Blackcomb Villages, just prior to purchasing your lift pass. No appointment is necessary (or accepted) but the system is first-come, first-served. Arrive at 8am and you'll be on the gondola by 8:15. Arrive at 8:30am, and you won't be up until 9:15 at the earliest.

Summit Ski (☎ **604/938-6225** or 604/932-6225), at various locations, including the Delta Whistler Resort and Market Pavilion, rents high performance and regular skis, snowboards, telemark and cross-country skis, and snowshoes.

BACKCOUNTRY SKIING   The **Spearhead Traverse,** which starts at Whistler and finishes at Blackcomb, is a well-marked backcountry route that has become extremely popular in the past few years.

Garibaldi Provincial Park (☎ **604/898-3678**) maintains marked backcountry trails at **Diamond Head, Singing Pass,** and **Cheakamus Lake.** These are ungroomed and unpatrolled rugged trails, and you have to be self-reliant—you should be at least an intermediate skier, bring appropriate clothing and avalanche gear, and know how to use it. There are several access points along Highway 99 between Squamish and Whistler.

CROSS-COUNTRY SKIING   Well-marked, fully groomed cross-country trails run throughout the area. The 30km (18 miles) of easy-to-very-difficult marked trails at **Lost Lake** start a block away from the Blackcomb Mountain parking lot. They're groomed for track skiing and ski-skating. They're also patrolled. Passes are C$8 (US$5.20); a 1-hour cross-country lesson runs about C$35 (US$23) and can be booked at the same station where you buy your trail pass. The **Valley Trail System** in the village becomes a well-marked cross-country ski trail during winter.

HELI-SKIING   For intermediate and advanced skiers who can't get enough fresh powder or vertical on the regular slopes, there's always heli-skiing. A helicopter whisks you and fellow skiers and boarders up to the pristine powder. **Whistler Heli-Skiing** (☎ **888/HELISKI** or 604/932-4105; www.heliskiwhistler.com) is one of the more established operators. A three-run day, with 2,400m to 3,000m (8,000–10,000 ft.) of vertical helicopter lift, costs C$560 (US$361) per person. A four-run day for expert skiers and riders only, with 3,000m to 3,600m (10,000–12,000 ft.) of vertical helicopter lift, costs C$630 (US$406) per person, including a guide and lunch.

OTHER WINTER PURSUITS

SLEIGHING & DOG-SLEDDING   **Whistler Backcountry Adventures** (☎ **604/932-3474;** see below under "Fishing") offers dog sled rides. A musher and his team of Inuit sled dogs will take you for a backcountry ride at C$249 (US$161) per sled, with a maximum of two people or 400 pounds.

The *Whistler Explorer*

If you have only a day to explore the backcountry of Southern B.C., don't miss the *Whistler Explorer* ★★. For centuries, the arid canyons, alpine meadows, and crystal-clear lakes of the area between Whistler and Kelly Lake were inaccessible to all but the most experienced hikers. However, **BC Rail's** (© **800/339-8752** or 604/984-5246) *Whistler Explorer* offers you a leisurely way to see the remote landscape. Departing from the Whistler train station on Lake Placid Road at 8am, the *Explorer* takes an 8½-hour round-trip ramble through the spectacular Pemberton Valley and past Seton Lake and Anderson Lake. After leaving the historic town of Lillooet, the train follows the Fraser River, climbing high above the canyon and offering breathtaking views before arriving at Kelly Lake, which is adjacent to the historic Cariboo Gold Rush Trail.

After a 1-hour stretching-and-strolling break, passengers reboard the train, returning to Whistler at 5:30pm. It's the ideal way to discover the backcountry without braving an overnight camping-and-hiking expedition into this stretch of pristine wilderness. The round-trip fare is C$139 (US$90) for adults/seniors/children over 12 and C$99 (US$64) for children 2 to 12. Lunch is included.

For a different kind of sleigh ride—with horses—contact **Blackcomb Horse-drawn Sleigh Rides,** 103–4338 Main St. (© **604/932-7631;** www.blackcomb sleighrides.com). In winter, tours go out every evening and cost C$45 (US$29) for adults and C$25 (US$16) for children under 12. The tour will take you up past the ski trails and into a wooded trail with a magnificent view of the lights of Whistler Village. A stop at a cabin for a mug of hot chocolate will warm you up for your ride home.

SNOWMOBILING & ATVing The year-round combination ATV and snowmobile tours offered by **Canadian Snowmobile Adventures Ltd.,** Carleton Lodge, 4290 Mountain Sq., Whistler Village (© **604/938-1616;** www. canadiansnowmobile.com), are a unique way to take to the Whistler Mountain trails. All tours are weather and snow conditions permitting. In summer 1999 there was so much snow on top of Whistler Mountain that by early August, the company was still offering full snowmobile tours. Exploring the Fitzsimmons Creek watershed, a 2-hour tour costs C$99 (US$64) for a driver and C$69 (US$45) for a passenger. Drivers on both the snowmobile and ATV must have a valid driver's license. On Blackcomb Mountain, Snowmobile Adventures offers a popular ATV trip, the 2-hour Mountain Explorer, costing C$109 (US$70) for a driver and C$59 (US$38) for a passenger. Conditions permitting, inquire about the combined ATV/snowmobile trip where you ride up to the snowline on the ATV and then switch to a snowmobile for a summertime snow ride.

Blackcomb Snowmobile (© **604/905-7002**) offers 4- to 8-hour guided snowmobile tours on Blackcomb Mountain. The Fresh Tracks tour, including breakfast, costs C$169 (US$109) per person, with two people for a 4-hour tour, or C$259 (US$167) per person with two people for an all-day Braelorne Back Country tour, lunch included.

SNOWSHOEING   Snowshoeing is the world's easiest form of snow locomotion; it requires none of the training and motor skills of skiing or boarding. You can wear your own shoes or boots, provided they're warm and waterproof, strap on your snowshoes, and off you go! Rentals are available at a number of the ski-and-board rental companies. See above.

Outdoor Adventures@Whistler (© **604/932-0647;** www.adventures whistler.com), has guided snowshoe tours for novices at C$39 (US$25) for 1½ hours. A 4-hour tour to a ghost town costs C$69 (US$45), including lunch. If you want to just rent the snowshoes and find your own way around, rentals are C$15 (US$9.70) per day. **Cougar Mountain at Whistler,** 36–4314 Main St. (© **888/297-2222** or 604/932-4086; www.whistlerbackcountry.com), has guided tours to the Cougar Mountain area at C$49 (US$32) for 2 hours, or try a snowshoe/snowmobile combination—a 3-hour trip into the backcountry, C$109 (US$70) per person, with a minimum of two people.

SUMMER PURSUITS

BIKING   Some of the best mountain bike trails in the village are on **Whistler and Blackcomb mountains.** It's not unusual to see bikers loading into the gondolas at both lifts during summer. Some of the backcountry trails at **Lost Lake** are also marked for mountain biking. Lift tickets at both mountains are C$19 to C$30 (US$12–US$19) per day, and discounted season mountain bike passes are available.

You can rent a mountain bike from **Trax & Trails,** Chateau Whistler Hotel, 4599 Chateau Blvd., Upper Village (© **604/938-2017**), and the **Whistler Bike Company,** Delta Whistler Resort, 4050 Whistler Way, Whistler Village (© **604/938-9511**). Prices start at C$10 (US$6.50) per hour and range from C$30 to C$65 (US$19–US$42) per day.

M.X. Mountain Bike Vacations (© **604/905-4914**) offers affordable 6- and 8-day mountain bike camps for C$900 to C$1,200 (US$581–US$774). Packages include accommodations, meals, and daily mountain bike coaching, as well as extracurricular activities such as white-water rafting and rock climbing. Ages 15 and up.

CANOEING & KAYAKING   The 3-hour River of Golden Dreams Kayak & Canoe Tour offered by **Whistler Sailing & Water Sports Center Ltd.** (© **604/ 932-7245**) is a great way for novices, intermediates, and experts to get acquainted with an exhilarating stretch of racing glacial water running between Green Lake and Alta Lake behind the village of Whistler. Packages begin at C$29 (US$19) per person unguided and include all gear and return transportation to the village center. The same company offers lessons and clinics as well as sailboat and windsurfing rentals.

FISHING   Spring runs of steelhead, rainbow trout, and Dolly Varden char; summer runs of cutthroat and salmon; and fall runs of coho salmon attract anglers from around the world to the area's many glacier-fed lakes and rivers and to **Birkenhead Lake Provincial Park,** 67km (41 miles) north of Pemberton. Bring your favorite fly rod and don't forget to buy a fishing license when you arrive at **Whistler Backcountry Adventures,** 36–4314 Main St. (© **604/932-3474**).

Whistler River Adventures (© **888/932-3532** or 604/932-3532; www.whistlerriver.com), and **Sea-to-Sky Reel Adventures** (© **604/894-6928**), offer half-day and full-day catch-and-release fishing trips in the surrounding glacier rivers. Rates are C$125 to C$185 (US$81–US$119) per person, based on two people, which includes all fishing gear, round-trip transport to/from the Whistler Village Bus Loop, and a snack or lunch.

GOLFING   Robert Trent Jones's **Chateau Whistler Golf Club,** at the base of Blackcomb Mountain (© **604/938-2092,** or pro shop 604/938-2095), is an 18-hole, par-72 course. With an elevation gain of more than 120m (400 ft.), this course traverses mountain ledges and crosses cascading creeks. Midcourse, there's a panoramic view of the Coast Mountains. Greens fees are C$130 to C$205 (US$84–US$132), which includes golf-cart rental.

A multiple-award-winning golf course, **Nicklaus North at Whistler** (© **604/ 938-9898**) is a 5-minute drive north of the village on the shores of Green Lake. The par-71 course's mountain views are spectacular. It's only the second Canadian course designed by Nicklaus, and, of all the courses he's designed worldwide, the only one to bear his name. Greens fees are C$125 to C$205 (US$81–US$137).

Whistler Golf Club (© **800/376-1777** or 604/932-4544), designed by Arnold Palmer, features nine lakes, two creeks, and magnificent vistas. Recently having undergone a C$2-million renovation, this 18-hole, par-72 course offers a driving range, putting green, sand bunker, and pitching area. Greens fees are C$69 to 149 (US$45–US$96).

A-1 Last Minute Golf Hotline (© **800/684-6344** or 604/878-1833) can arrange a next-day tee time at Whistler golf courses and elsewhere in B.C. at over 30 courses. Savings can be as much as 40% on next-day, last-minute tee times. No membership is necessary. Call between 3 and 9pm for the next day or before noon for the same day. The hot line also arranges advanced bookings, as much as a year ahead, as well as group bookings.

HIKING   There are numerous easy hiking trails in and around Whistler. Besides taking a lift up to Whistler and Blackcomb mountains' high mountain trails during summer, you have a number of choices.

Lost Lake Trail starts at the northern end of the Day Skier Parking Lot at Blackcomb Mountain. The lake is less than a mile from the entry. The 30km (18 miles) of marked trails that wind around creeks, beaver dams, blueberry patches, and lush cedar groves are ideal for biking, cross-country skiing, or just strolling and picnicking. The **Valley Trail System** is a well-marked paved trail that connects parts of Whistler. The trail starts on the west side of Highway 99 adjacent to the Whistler Golf Course and winds through quiet residential areas as well as golf courses and parks.

Garibaldi Provincial Park's **Singing Pass Trail** is a 4-hour hike of moderate difficulty. The fun way is to take the Whistler Mountain gondola to the top and walk down the well-marked path that ends in the village on an access road. Winding down from above the tree line, the trail takes you through stunted alpine forest into Fitzsimmons Valley. There are several access points into the park along Highway 99 between Squamish and Whistler.

Nairn Falls Provincial Park is about 33km (20 miles) north of Whistler on Highway 99. This provincial park features a mile-long trail that leads you to a stupendous view of the icy-cold Green River as it plunges 59m (196 ft.) over a rocky cliff into a narrow gorge on its way downstream. There's also an incredible view of Mount Currie peeking over the treetops.

On Highway 99 north of Mount Currie, **Joffre Lakes Provincial Park** is an intermediate-level hike that leads past several brilliant blue glacial lakes up to the very foot of a glacier. The **Ancient Cedars** area of Cougar Mountain is an awe-inspiring grove of towering cedars and Douglas firs. (Some of the trees are over 1,000 years old and measure 3m/9 ft. in diameter.) This 4km (2½-mile) hike can be made even more exciting by taking a Land Rover 4×4 up the back-country route. **Off the Beaten Track Wilderness Expeditions** (📞 **604/938-9282**) offers this unique off-road experience and provides a knowledgeable guide and snacks. Three- and 6-hour tours depart from the Whistler Village Bus Loop for C$59 to C$89 (US$38–US$58) per person.

HORSEBACK RIDING   Whistler River Adventures (📞 **888/932-3532** or 604/932-3532) offers 2-hour trail rides along the Green River, through the forest, and across the Pemberton Valley from its 4-hectare (10-acre) riverside facility in nearby Pemberton. You will need your own transportation to get out to Pemberton, a 35-minute drive north of Whistler. The 2-hour ride costs C$49 (US$32); longer rides available on request.

JET BOATING   Whistler River Adventures, Whistler Mountain Village Gondola Base (📞 **888/932-3532** or 604/932-3532; fax 604/932-3559; www.whistlerriver.com), takes guests up the Green River just below Nairn Falls, where moose, deer, and bear sightings are common in the sheer-granite canyon. The Lillooet River tour goes past ancient petroglyphs, fishing sites, and the tiny Native village of Skookumchuck. Tours range from 1-hour-long trips for C$75 (US$48) to 6-hour cruises for C$135 (US$87).

RAFTING   Whistler River Adventures (📞 **604/932-3532**) (see "Jet Boating," above) offers 2-hour and full-day round-trip rafting runs down the Green, Elaho, and Squamish rivers. They include equipment and ground transportation for C$61 to C$135 (US$39–US$87). Children and youths are welcome as long as they're able to hold on by themselves and weigh a minimum of 90 pounds. Novices are taken to the Green River, where small rapids and snowcapped mountain views highlight a half-day trip. Experts are transported to the Elaho River or Squamish River for full-day, Class IV excitement on runs with names like Aitons Alley and Steamroller. May through August, trips depart daily. The full-day trip includes a salmon barbecue lunch. The company also conducts 3-hour round-trip jet-boat tours of the river for C$75 (US$48) per person, including ground transport and wet suit.

For first-timers, **Wedge Rafting,** Carleton Lodge, Whistler Village (📞 **604/932-7171;** www.wedgerafting.com), offers a Green River or a Birkenhead River tour. For the Green River trip, about 2½ hours, the shuttle picks up rafters in Whistler and takes them to the wilderness launch area for briefing and equipping. It's an exciting hour or more on the icy, bubbling rapids. After the run, rafters can relax at the outfitter's log lodge with a snack and soda before being shuttled back into town. Tours cost C$61 (US$39), with up to three daily departures. The Birkenhead River tour takes about 4 hours and costs C$79 (US$51). Discounts are available for youths 10 to 16; however, they must weigh at least 90 pounds.

TENNIS   The Whistler Racquet & Golf Resort, 4500 Northland Blvd. (📞 **604/932-1991;** www.whistlertennis.com), has three covered courts, seven outdoor courts, and a practice cage, all open to drop-in visitors. Indoor courts are C$28 (US$18) per hour and outdoor courts C$14 (US$9) per hour. Adult and junior tennis camps are offered in summer. Camp prices run C$250 to C$365 (US$161–US$235) for a 3-day camp. Kids' camps cost C$40 (US$26) per day drop-in, or C$150 (US$97) for a 5-day camp. Book early, as these camps fill up very quickly.

The **Mountain Spa & Tennis Club,** Delta Whistler Resort, Whistler Village (© 604/938-2044), and the **Chateau Whistler Resort,** Chateau Whistler Hotel, Upper Village (© 604/938-8000), also offer courts to drop-in players. Prices run about C$10 (US$6.45) per hour per court; racquet rentals are available for C$5 (US$3.25) per hour.

There are **free public courts** (© 604/938-PARK) at Myrtle Public School, Alpha Lake Park, Meadow Park, Millar's Pond, Brio, Blackcomb Benchlands, White Gold, and Emerald Park.

URBAN PURSUITS

A MUSEUM   To learn more about Whistler's heritage, flora, and fauna, visit the **Whistler Museum & Archives Society,** 4329 Main St., off Northlands Boulevard (© 604/932-2019). The museum exhibits reveal the life and culture of the Native Indian tribes that have lived in the lush Whistler and Pemberton valleys for thousands of years. There are also re-creations of the village's early settlement by British immigrants during the late 1800s and early 1900s. The museum is open daily 10am to 4pm in summer until Labor Day, and Thursday through Sunday 10am to 4pm until May. Admission is C$2 (US$1.30) for an adult and C$1 (US65¢) for children 6 and over.

SHOPPING   The **Whistler Marketplace** (in the center of Whistler Village) and the area surrounding the **Blackcomb Mountain lift** brim with clothing, jewelry, crafts, specialty, gift, and equipment shops that are generally open daily 10am to 6pm. **Horstman Trading Company** (© 604/938-7725), beside the Chateau Whistler at the base of Blackcomb, carries men's and women's casual wear, from swimwear and footwear to polar-fleece vests and nylon jacket shells. **Escape Route** (© 604/938-3228), at Whistler Marketplace and Crystal Lodge, has a great line of outdoor clothing and equipment. **Whistler Backcountry Adventures,** 4314 Main St. (© 604/932-3474), sells fishing licenses and carries a great selection of fishing rods, tackle, sports gear, and outdoor clothing.

For some of the finer things in life, visit the **Whistler Village Art Gallery** (© 604/938-3001) and **Adele Campbell Gallery** (© 604/938-0887). Their collections include fine art, sculpture, and glass. **Keir Fine Jewelry,** Village Gate House (© 604/932-2944), sells Italian gold, Swiss watches, and Canadian handmade jewelry.

SPAS   That resort lifestyle can be hard on the body, so why not try some relaxation at one of the outstanding spas offered by Whistler? The **Spa at Chateau Whistler Resort** (© 604/938-2086) is the best in town. Open daily 8am to 9pm, the spa offers massage therapy, aromatherapy, skin care, body wraps, steam baths, and makeup, and can put together a package of your choice.

Whistler Body Wrap, 210 St. Andrews House (© 604/932-4710), next to the Keg in the Village, can nurture you with an array of services, such as shiatsu massage, facials, pedicures or manicures, waxings, sunbeds, and aromatherapy. If something didn't quite go right on the slopes or on the trails, **Whistler Physiotherapy** specializes in sports therapy. The therapists at this clinic treat many professional athletes and have a lot of experience with the typical ski, board, and hiking injuries. There are two locations: 339–4370 Lorimer Rd., at Marketplace (© 604/932-4001), and 202–2011 Innsbruck Dr., next to Boston Pizza in Creekside (© 604/938-9001).

ESPECIALLY FOR KIDS

Near the base of the mountains, Whistler Village and the Upper Village sponsor daily activities tailor-made for active kids of all ages. There are mountain bike races; an in-line skating park; trapeze, trampoline, and wall-climbing lessons; summer skiing; snowboarding; and snowshoeing. There's even a first-run multiplex movie theater.

Based at Blackcomb Mountain, the **Dave Murray Summer Ski and Snowboard Camp** (© 604/932-5765; www.skiandsnowboard.com) is North America's longest-running summer ski camp. Junior programs cost about C$1,475 (US$958) per week or C$840 (US$542) for a 5-day package from mid-June to mid-July. The packages include food, lodging, and lift passes, as well as tennis, trapeze, and mountain-biking options. Mornings and early afternoons are spent skiing, boarding, or free-riding on the excellent terrain parks and half-pipes. This ski-and-board camp accommodates a range of abilities from beginners to champion level skiers and riders; the age group is 10 to 18 years. In the afternoons, the campers have a choice from a wide range of other outdoor activities. The comprehensive instruction and adult supervision at this activity-oriented camp are excellent.

WHISTLER AFTER DARK

For a town of just 8,000, Whistler has a more-than-respectable nightlife scene. Bands touring through Vancouver regularly make the trip up the Sea-to-Sky Highway; some even make Whistler their Canadian debut. Concert listings can be found in the *Pique,* a free local paper available at cafes and food stores. Fittingly for such a cosmopolitan place, the night scene divides up not by language or ethnicity but by age.

Tommy Africa's (© 604/932-6090), beneath the Pharmasave at the entrance to the Main Village, and the dark and cavernous **Maxx Fish** (© 604/932-1904) in the Village Square below the Amsterdam Cafe, cater to the 18-to-22-year-old crowd: lots of beat and not much light. The crowd at **Garfinkel's** (© 604/932-2323) at the entrance to Village North, is similar, though the cut-off age can reach as high as 27. The **Boot Pub** (© 604/932-3338), Nancy Green Drive, just off Highway 99, advertises itself as Whistler's living room and more than lives up to its billing: Throngs of young Australian ski-lift operators cram the room, bouncing to the band or DJ and spilling draft beer over the floor. **Buffalo Bills** (© 604/932-6613), across from the Whistler Gondola, and the **Savage Beagle** (© 604/938-3337) in the Village, cater to the 30-something crowd. Bills is bigger, with a pool table and video ski machine, a smallish dance floor, and music straight from the 1980s. The Beagle has a fabulous selection of beer and bar drinks, with a pleasant little pub upstairs and house-oriented dance floor below.

2 Bamfield ⭑

You're alone on the shoreline, where the beach goes on forever. Waves crash in on the rocky outcrops. A seal pops out of the water, stares you in the face for a moment, then drops back beneath the surface. A gull cries. You turn and see the outstretched wings of a bald eagle gliding along the shoreline, passing 6m (20 ft.) over your head. Another follows. And a third. That's **Bamfield.**

There can be few if any towns on earth quite like it. Nestled in a tiny bay between the mountains and a raging ocean, Bamfield's wooden houses are linked by an elevated wooden boardwalk running from house to shop to inn along the rocky shoreline. It gives the place a unique charm. Add to that a beach with sea caves and blowholes, seabird and mammal life galore, and a Native site up for Unesco World Heritage designation, and you're in a memorable location indeed.

Curiously, though thousands hike the **West Coast Trail** every year (see the box below); few make it the extra few kilometers into town.

ESSENTIALS

GETTING THERE   By Car   Bamfield is a 3-hour drive from Victoria. Take Highway 1 to just north of Duncan, then Highway 18 west to Cowichan Lake. When you get to the lake, take the road around the north shore of the lake (through Youbou) and follow the signs to Bamfield. The last 100km (62 miles) are along gravel logging roads. The road surface is kept smooth enough even for a subcompact two-wheel drive, but signage is poor, and the logging trucks can be a little intimidating. (It's best to pull over completely when you see one coming.) Tough it out, wait for weekends or evenings when the trucks aren't running, or—best of all—take the boat.

By Bus   May through September, the daily **West Coast Trail Express** (© 888/ 999-2288 or 250/477-8700; www.trailbus.com) provides Victoria–Bamfield service for C$53 (US$34). Because it partially travels along an unpaved logging road, the ride is usually about 5 hours. This company will also pick you up at the other end of the trail in Port Renfrew and transport you back to Victoria for C$35 (US$23).

By Boat   A 4½-hour ride aboard the **Alberni Marine Transportation** (© **250/723-8313;** www.ladyrosemarine.com), passenger ferry MV *Lady Rose* takes you from Port Alberni through the Alberni Inlet fjord to the boardwalk fishing village of Bamfield. It makes brief stops along the way to deliver mail and packages to solitary cabin dwellers along the coast and to let off or pick up kayakers bound for the Broken Islands Group. The *Lady Rose,* built in Scotland in 1937, departs three times a week (more sailings in summer) to each destination from Alberni Harbour Quay's Angle Street. The one-way fare to Bamfield is C$23 (US$15); the round-trip fare is C$45 (US$29).

VISITOR INFORMATION   Call the **Bamfield Chamber of Commerce** at © **250/728-3006** or visit them online at www.alberni.net/bamcham.

WHERE TO STAY

Bamfield Lodge   A pair of rustic cottages and a lodge/two-bedroom house are the waterfront offerings at this retreat. The twin-bed and double-bed cabins and the guest house have fully equipped kitchens, and all are simply decorated. Bring your own food (freezer space is available) or enjoy the lodge's gourmet meals. The Boardwalk Bistro restaurant is open to the public. Sip an espresso in the resort's cappuccino bar while watching the birds, whales, and boats pass by. Moorage is available for guests and non-guests. The staff specializes in gourmet fishing packages and adventure tours and can also arrange hiking, kayaking, fishing, diving, whale-watching, and intertidal field trips.

275 Boardwalk (P.O. Box 23), Bamfield, B.C. V0R 1B0. © **250/728-3419.** Fax 250/728-3417. www.bamfield lodge.com. 2 cottages, one 2-bedroom house. C$100 (US$65) double; C$250 (US$161) house. Off-season discounts. No refunds July–Aug. V. There are no access roads. The owners pick up guests at the government dock

---

⎛ *Tips*   **A Weather Warning**

They don't call this the rain coast for nothing. Winter storms with lashings of rain and wind gusts up to 100km per hour (62 mph) have their appeal, but it's still an esoteric pleasure. Go between May and September.

Vancouver Island

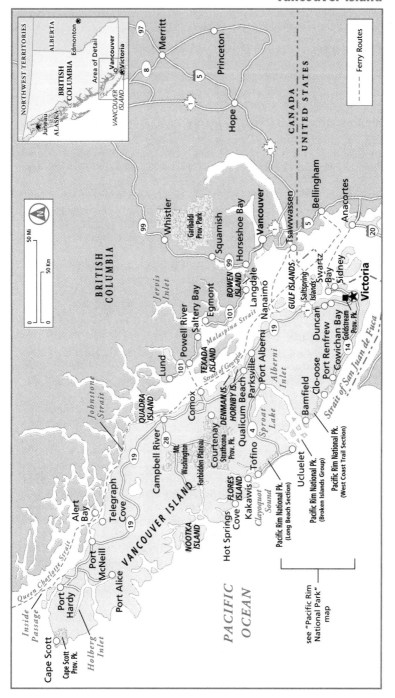

and transport them by boat, just a short ride across the inlet. **Amenities:** Restaurant; moorage; sun deck; access to BBQ grill. *In room:* kitchen, fridge, coffeemaker.

Pacheena Bay Campground   On the Pacheena River estuary and the beach beyond, this is one of the most beautiful campsites in the province. The campground has flush toilets and hot showers. Each site also has a fire pit.

Box 70, Bamfield, B.C. V0R 1B0. ℂ 250/728-1287. 80 units. C$19 (US$12) unit, summer only (May–Sept). No credit cards. Entrance is on the road to Bamfield, about 5km (3 miles) out of town.

Woods End Landing Cottages ⋆   The picturesque timbered cottages on this secluded waterfront wilderness property offer fully equipped kitchens, propane barbecues, and private porches overlooking the 0.8-hectare (2-acre) perennial gardens, with an herb garden available for guest use. The decor features Canadian antiques and collectibles as well as double-size hand-hewn log beds, duvets, large farmhouse tables, exposed timber beams, and skylights. Hiking, fishing, whale-watching, diving, and eagle and sea lion watching; Keeha Beach; part of the West Coast Trail; and the Cape Beale Lighthouse are within walking distance. A private dock, moorage, freezer space, canoe, and fishing tackle are available. Smoking isn't permitted.

Box 108, Bamfield, B.C. V0R 1B0. ℂ 250/728-3383. Fax 250/728-3383. www.woodsend.travel.bc.ca. 6 cottages. C$95–C$205 (US$61–US$132) per cottage for up to 4 people. Off-season discounts available Oct 1–May 31. MC, V. Pets accepted. There are no access roads. The owners pick up guests at the government dock and transport them by boat, just a short ride across the inlet. **Amenities:** Free canoe usage; fishing tackle rental. *In room:* kitchen, fridge, coffeemaker.

WHERE TO DINE

Haute cuisine, alas, hasn't yet reached these far-flung shores. Bamfield, in fact, has only two restaurants. At the **Hawk's Nest Pub,** 48 Grappler Rd. (ℂ **250/ 728-3422**), there's a bar, a pool table, a fireplace, daily specials on the chalkboard, and pub food on the menu. The cuisine is fresh and well prepared and goes great with beer. A sandwich, burger, or dinner special ranges from C$7 to C$11 (US$4.55–US$7.15). May through September open 11am to midnight, October through April open 11:30am to 2:30pm and 4:30 to 11pm, closed Monday and Tuesday. With a reservation, the **McKay Bay Lodge** (ℂ **250/ 728-3323**) will let you sit in on the seafood supper created by their trained chef, for C$20 to C$25 (US$13–US$16) per person. The **Tyee Resort** (ℂ **888/ 493-8933** or 250/728-3296) also accepts nonguests at its supper table, with a previous reservation. Both McKay Lodge and Tyee Resort are accessible by water only. Call ahead for availability, transportation, and hours of operation.

The other option, of course, is to cook your own. Officially, for the usual meddling bureaucratic reasons beloved of interfering governments everywhere, fishers down at the docks aren't allowed to sell their wares directly to the public. On the other hand, were one to inquire of, say, a prawn or shrimp captain whether he had any extra catch on hand, there's a strong possibility fresh spotted prawns might be available.

After dinner, wander down to the boardwalk, where **Judy's Cappuccino** (ℂ **250/728-3419**) serves up a potent brew.

ACTIVITIES

BEACH WALKING   Brady's Beach, a 10-minute walk from the village of Bamfield, is alive with eagles, seals, mink, and other creatures. **Keeha Beach,** a 20-minute drive from town, is one of the most impressive beaches on the West Coast. For those wanting a taste of the West Coast Trail, the trail head is also just a short drive out of town.

The West Coast Trail

After the SS *Valencia* ran aground in 1906 and most of the survivors died of exposure on the beach, the Canadian government built a rescue trail between Bamfield and Port Renfrew. For years, the lifesaving trail was maintained by solitary watchmen who groomed it and checked the telephone line strung along the path.

Upgraded by Parks Canada in the 1970s, the **West Coast Trail** ☆ has gained a reputation as one of the world's greatest extreme hiking/camping adventures. Each year, about 9,000 people hike the entire challenging 73 km (44-mile) route, and thousands more hike the very accessible 11km (7-mile) oceanfront stretch at the northern trail head near Bamfield.

Planning (get a topographic map and tidal table), stamina (besides hiking, you should train for rock climbing), and experience (advanced wilderness survival and minimum-impact camping knowledge) are imperative for the full hike. Veterans recommend you go with at least two companions, pack lightweight weatherproof gear, and bring about 15m (50 ft.) of climbing rope per person. To reduce the impact on the environment, only 52 people per day are allowed to enter the main trail (26 from Port Renfrew, 26 from Bamfield), and registration with the park office is mandatory.

Call **Discover BC** (✆ **800/663-6000** or 604/435-5622) after February 1 to schedule your entry for the coming season (May 1–Sept 30). Make your reservations as early as possible and be prepared for busy signals and long waiting times; you can book only a maximum of 3 months ahead of your travel date. Limited access and increased popularity mean you may not gain admission if you call too late in the season. The C$25 (US$16) per person advance booking fee includes the price of a waterproof trail map, plus there are C$70 (US$45) trail-use fees and C$25 (US$16) ferry fees for various crossings. During summer, you can also contact the parks service at ✆ **250/728-3234** or 250/647-5434.

DIVING   The waters off the **West Coast Trail** are known as "the graveyard of the Pacific." Hundreds of 19th- and 20th-century shipwrecks silently attest to the hazards of sailing without an experienced guide in these unforgiving waters. The Cousteau Society rates this dive area as one of the world's best, second only to the Red Sea. There are even underwater interpretive trails that narrate the area's unique history. **Broken Island Adventures** (✆ **888/728-6200** or 250/728-3500) leads guided diving tours to various locations.

The **Bamfield Marine Station** (✆ **250/728-3301**), a research facility associated with four western Canadian universities, offers free guided tours of its research labs Saturday and Sunday during July and August.

FISHING   The waters off Bamfield teem with fish of all kinds. **Ka-ka-Win Charters** (✆ **250/728-1267**) can show you where. Run by Ed and Pearl Johnson of the nearby Huu-ay-aht Native band, the company has years of experience fishing in Barkley Sound and the open ocean. The **Bamfield Lodge** (✆ **250/728-3419**) offers charters, guided tours, and fishing packages.

KAYAKING   For C$50 (US$32), the **Bamfield Kayak Centre** (© 877/728-3535; www.bamfield-kayak.com) offers a 3-hour marine-biology paddle, exploring the rich intertidal zones, inlets, and surge channels with a local marine biologist. Rentals, instruction, and full-day tours are also available. **Broken Island Adventures** (© **888/728-6200** or 250/728-3500) runs kayak and wildlife adventures to the Broken Islands and the Deer Group. The 6-hour Broken Islands tour is C$90 (US$58) per person.

3 Ucluelet, Tofino & Pacific Rim National Park (Long Beach Section) ⭐⭐⭐

The west coast of Vancouver Island is a magnificent area of old-growth forests, stunning fjords (called "sounds" in local parlance), rocky coasts, and long sandy beaches. And though **Pacific Rim National Park** was established in 1971 as Canada's first marine park, it wasn't until 1993 that it really exploded into the consciousness of people outside the area. That was when thousands of environmentalists from across the province and around the world gathered to protest the clear-cutting of old-growth forests in Clayoquot Sound. Wherever you stand in that debate, one result of the protest was incontrovertible. When news footage of the protests ran on the evening news, people at home who saw the landscape for the first time were moved to come experience it firsthand. Tourism in the area has never looked back.

The three main areas belonging to this section of the West Coast are **Ucluelet, Tofino,** and the **Long Beach section** of Pacific Rim National Park. They lie along the outer edge of a peninsula about halfway up the western shore of Vancouver Island.

The town of Ucluelet (pronounced you-*clue*-let, meaning "safe harbor" in the local Nuu-chah-nulth dialect), sits on the southern end of this peninsula, on the edge of Barkley Sound. Though it has a winter population of only 1,900, thousands of visitors arrive between March and May to see as many as 20,000 Pacific gray whales pass close to the shore as they migrate north to their summer feeding grounds in the Arctic Circle.

About a 15-minute drive north is Long Beach, part of the Pacific Rim National Park group. The beach is more than 30km (19 miles) long, broken here and there by rocky headlands and bordered by tremendous groves of cedar and Sitka spruce. The beach is popular with countless species of birds and marine life and, lately, also with wet-suited surfers.

At the far northern tip of the peninsula, Tofino (pop. 1,300) borders on beautiful Clayoquot Sound. It's the center of the West Coast ecotourism business, though it's still small for all that. Hikers and beachcombers come to Tofino simply for the scenery, while others use Tofino as a base from which to explore Clayoquot Sound.

ESSENTIALS

GETTING THERE   By Bus   Island Coach Lines (© **250/724-1266**) operates regular daily bus service between Victoria and Tofino/Ucluelet. The 7-hour trip, departing Victoria at 7:30am and arriving in Tofino at 2:45pm, costs C$50 (US$32) one-way to Ucluelet and C$52 (US$34) to Tofino. The bus also stops in Nanaimo and can pick up passengers arriving from Vancouver on the ferry.

By Car   The same route takes you to Tofino, Ucluelet, and Long Beach. From Nanaimo, take the Island Highway (Hwy. 19) north for 52km (31 miles). Just

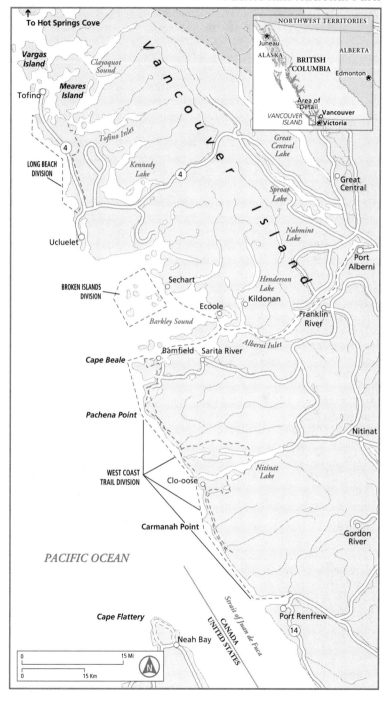

To Hot Springs Cove

Vargas Island

Clayoquot Sound

Meares Island

Tofino

Vancouver Island

Tofino Inlet

4

Kennedy Lake

4

LONG BEACH DIVISION

Great Central Lake

Sproat Lake

Great Central

Nahmint Lake

Ucluelet

Port Alberni

BROKEN ISLANDS DIVISION

Sechart

Henderson Lake

Kildonan

Ecoole

Franklin River

Barkley Sound

Alberni Inlet

Cape Beale

Bamfield   Sarita River

Pachena Point

Nitinat

WEST COAST TRAIL DIVISION

Clo-oose

Nitinat Lake

Carmanah Point

Gordon River

PACIFIC OCEAN

Cape Flattery

Neah Bay

Strait of Juan de Fuca

CANADA
UNITED STATES

Port Renfrew

14

0   15 Mi
0   15 Km

N

NORTHWEST TERRITORIES

Juneau

ALASKA

BRITISH COLUMBIA

ALBERTA

Edmonton

Area of Detail

VANCOUVER ISLAND

Vancouver

Victoria

before the town of Parksville is a turnoff for Highway 4, which leads first to the mid-island town of Port Alberni (about 38km/23 miles west) and then the coastal towns of Tofino (135km/81 miles west of Port Alberni) and Ucluelet (103km/62 miles west). The road is well paved the whole way but gets twisty after Port Alberni.

By Ferry A 4½-hour ride aboard the **Alberni Marine Transportation** (© 250/723-8313; www.ladyrosemarine.com) passenger ferry MV *Lady Rose* takes you from Port Alberni through Alberni Inlet to Ucluelet. It makes brief stops along the way to deliver mail and packages to solitary cabin dwellers along the coast and to let off or pick up kayakers bound for the Broken Islands Group. In summer, the *Lady Rose* departs three times per week to each destination from Alberni Harbour Quay's Angle Street. The fare to Ucluelet is C$23 (US$15) one-way or C$45 (US$29) round-trip.

By Plane **North Vancouver Air** (© 800/228-6608) operates twin-engine, turbo-prop plane service daily between Vancouver or Victoria and Tofino May through September; it runs four times per week October through April. One-way fare, including all taxes and airport fees, is C$175 (US$113); flying time is approximately an hour. **Northwest Seaplanes** (© 800/690-0086) and **Sound Flight** (© 800/825-0722) offer plane service between Seattle and Tofino during the summer (mid-June to late Sept).

VISITOR INFORMATION March through September, the **Tofino Visitor Info Centre** (© 250/725-3414; www.island.net/~tofino), 380 Campbell St., Tofino (P.O. Box 249, Tofino, B.C. V0R 2Z0), is open Monday through Friday 9am to 6pm, and Saturday and Sunday 10am to 6pm in the summer. Call for winter hours. June through September, the **Ucluelet Visitor Info Centre** (© 250/726-4641; www.uclueletinfo.com), at the Junction of Highway 4, Ucluelet (P.O. Box 428, Ucluelet, B.C. V0R 3A0), is open the same hours. The **Long Beach Visitor Information Centre** (© 250/726-4212; http://parkscan. harbour.com/pacrim), about a mile from the Highway 4 junction to Tofino, is open daily 9:30am to 5pm from June until Labour Day.

SPECIAL EVENTS About 20,000 whales migrate here annually. During the third and last week of March, the **Pacific Rim Whale Festival** (© 250/726-4641 or 250/726-7742) is held in Tofino and Ucluelet. Crab races, the Gumboot Golf Tournament, guided whale-watching hikes, and a Native festival are just a few of the events that celebrate the annual Pacific gray whale migration.

UCLUELET

When fishing was the major industry on the coast, **Ucluelet** was the big town. Thanks to its harbor, it was here that most of the ships docked and where the processing and packing plants were located. With the recent boom in eco-tourism, however, the roles have been reversed, and Ucluelet is scrambling to catch up. At the moment it has a beautiful location and a couple of fine B&Bs, but it has yet to develop the same range of restaurants and activities as Tofino. But things are changing fast. And at the moment, Ucluelet is cheaper and just as close to Long Beach. In the high summer when Tofino is packed, Ucluelet will likely still have spots.

WHERE TO STAY

Ocean's Edge B&B This remarkable little B&B sits on its own tiny peninsula jutting out into the Pacific, with only a thicket of interwoven hemlocks sheltering it from the wind and the surf of the ocean, which roars up surge channels on either side. The rooms are pleasant and spotless, without being opulent. The real attractions are the scenery and the wildlife, which abound. Owners Bill and Susan McIntyre installed a skylight in the kitchen so breakfasting guests could keep an eye on the pair of bald eagles and their chicks nesting in a 200-year-old Sitka spruce in the driveway. The former chief naturalist of Pacific Rim National Parks, host Bill McIntyre is a font of information and specializes in storm-watching tours and various hikes around the region (see "Guided Nature Hikes" under "Tofino," below). The brand new Wild Pacific Trail, skirting the spectacularly rugged coast, starts almost from the McIntyre's front door.

855 Barkley Crescent, Box 557, Ucluelet, B.C. V0R 3A0. © 250/726-7099. Fax 250/726-7090. www.oceansedge.bc.ca. 3 units. C$130 (US$84) double. Breakfast included. MC, V. 2-night minimum on long weekends, holidays, and high season. No children permitted. **Amenities:** Nonsmoking facility. *In room:* Binoculars.

A Snug Harbour Inn   A beautiful clifftop B&B overlooking its own little bay, A Snug Harbour Inn makes the most of its location. There are several large viewing decks (one with a hot tub), and guests can make use of a monster-size telescope to watch the sea lions on the reef just offshore. The inn is luxurious—the rooms are spacious, with queen- or king-size beds, opulent bathrooms, and jetted tubs. The heart-shaped tub with a waterfall may be a bit over the top, but who's complaining? Built by a shipwright, its quality craftsmanship shows and the nautical theme is carried out in the decor. The Inn recently added two rooms with private decks, fireplaces, and in-room jetted tubs for your relaxation pleasure.

460 Marine Dr., Box 367, Ucluelet, B.C. V0R 3A0. © 888/936-5222 or 250/726-2686. www.awesomeview.com. 6 units. May–Sept C$230–C$290 (US$148–US$187) double; Oct–Apr C$180–C$200 (US$116–US$129) double. Breakfast included. MC, V. **Amenities:** Jacuzzi; nonsmoking rooms; rooms for disabled travelers and pet-friendly rooms. *In room:* Fridge, coffeemaker, hair dryer.

Tauca Lea By The Sea   If there were ever a sure sign that Ucluelet is a town on the verge of a big tourism boom, it would be the opening of the Whistler-style condos at the Tauca Lea resort in the spring of 2000. The spacious one- and two-bedroom town houses are on a beautiful forested island on the edge of the harbor just off the main area of town. (A causeway connects the resort to the mainland.) All the suites are comfortably furnished and fully equipped with kitchens and all dining- and living-room amenities. You have easy access to whale-watching, kayaking, dining, and day hikes along the beaches and bays of the rugged West Coast.

10 Harbour Rd. Ucluelet, B.C. V0R 3A0 © 800/979-9303 or 250/726-4625. www.taucalearesort.com. 44 units. C$130–C$210 (US$84–US$135) 1-bedroom suite; C$190–C$270 (US$123–US$174) 2-bedroom suite; C$230–C$310 (US$148–US$200) with Jacuzzi on the outside deck. MC, V. **Amenities:** Nearby watersports rental and whale-watching; laundry service; nonsmoking rooms. *In room:* TV, kitchen, hair dryer.

WHERE TO DINE

Fine dining has only just begun in this seacoast town, as urban refugees with a flair for cooking arrive and try to make a go of it. The **Matterson Teahouse and Garden,** 1682 Peninsula Rd. (© 250/726-2200), is on the main street and a great spot for lunch; sandwiches, salads, and a great chowder are served in the cute dining room. On a nice summer day, you have the option of sitting on the shady porch or the sunny back deck, listening to the surfers plan their next ride. The Teahouse also serves dinner, but check for seasonal hours.

Somewhat less ambitious but still good is the **Eagles Nest Marine Pub,** 140 Bay St. (© 250/726-7570).

ACTIVITIES

Fishing, kayaking, and whale-watching are the big attractions in Ucluelet. Of the three, fishing still predominates. Charter companies that can take you out after salmon, halibut, and other fish include **Quest Charters,** in the boat basin (℗ 250/726-7532), and the much larger **Canadian Princess Resort** (℗ 800/663-7090). **Sea Fin Charters,** 1295 Eber Rd. (℗ 250/726-2104) will run charters in the spring. **Subtidal Adventures,** 1950 Peninsula Rd. (℗ 877/444-1134 or 250/726-7336; www.subtidaladventures.com), does nature cruises around the Broken Island group as well as whale-watching trips and rides for kayakers to popular paddle spots. **Jamie's Whaling Station,** 168 Fraser Lane, above the Rusty Anchor restaurant (℗ 877/470-7444 or 250/726-7444; www.jamies.com), has been operating in the Clayoquot Sound area since 1982 and now organizes whale-watching or bear-watching trips out of Ucluelet. Looking for these wild critters is only half the fun—the Barkley Sound area offers spectacular scenery that's best explored from the water. **Majestic Ocean Kayaking,** 1932 Peninsula Rd. (℗ 250/726-2868), runs single- and multiday guided kayak trips. The **Long Beach Nature Tour Company** (℗ 250/726-7099), run by retired Pacific Rim Park chief naturalist Bill McIntyre, does guided beach, rainforest, and storm walks that explain the ecology and wildlife of the area. His walks will take you to the most interesting trails, beaches, and wildlife-viewing spots. The newly completed Wild Pacific Trail skirts along the rugged coast line with fabulous views of the Pacific and the Broken Islands. The trail is easily accessible from the village of Ucluelet; see **www.wild pacifictrail.com** for more information on walks and access points.

TOFINO

The center of the environmental protest against industrial logging—and the center of the ecotourism business ever since—**Tofino** remains a schizophrenic kind of town. Half of the town is composed of ecotourism outfitters, nature lovers, activists, and serious granolas, while the other half is composed of loggers and fishermen. Conflict was common in the early years, but recently the two sides seem to have learned how to get along. For a hilarious take on the culture clash between incoming eco-freaks and long-term rednecks during the summer of discontent, pick up *The Green Shadow* by local eco-freak (and closet redneck) Andrew Stretchers.

WHERE TO STAY

The Clayoquot Wilderness Resort 🐾   The latest in absolute luxury in the area, the Clayoquot Wilderness Resort (CWR) floats alone in splendid isolation on Quoit Bay, about a half-hour boat ride from Tofino. Guests are encouraged to use the lodge as base camp for exploring the natural beauty of the sound. The CWR has set up a number of forest trails nearby and also runs trips out to Hot Springs Cove, as well as horseback-riding excursions and mountain-biking trips. (Most of these activities are charged separately.) There are also spots to fly-fish or simply laze in the sun. Meals, prepared by noted West Coast chef Timothy May, are included and served up with a view of Clayoquot Sound. A luxurious spa and wellness center just opened in June 2001. Surrounded by lush rainforest, the spa offers a range of treatments; weather permitting, massages can be done outside on the cedar deck. For the ultimate pampered outdoor experience try the Outpost camp, located a short boat ride away from the resort on the Bedwell River. Ten luxurious prospector tents, decorated with handmade Adirondack furniture, Persian carpets, and period accessories, welcome guests for an

Rail & Ranch

To experience British Columbia's backcountry—its mountains, alpine lakes, gold-rush towns, and ranch land—combine a scenic rail trip with a stay at a Cariboo guest ranch. **BC Rail** (✆ **800/339-8752;** www.bcrail.com) offers a number of rail-and-ranch packages for every budget and activity.

At an altitude of 1,050m (3,500 ft.), the **Echo Valley Ranch Resort** (✆ **800/253-8831** or 250/459-2386; www.evranch.com) is an oasis in the heart of B.C.'s hard-working ranch land. Norm and his wife, Naan, have built an exquisite ranch resort with all the luxury of a spa. Activities include horseback riding, hiking, gold panning, native studies, and a four × four excursion to the Fraser River Canyon. This section of the river is unbelievably beautiful: steep canyon walls, arid hills, and a rugged inaccessible landscape. Back at Echo Valley, chef Kim Madsen pampers guests with three gourmet meals a day. The Echo Valley Spa, meanwhile, provides the ultimate in relaxation; being a modern cowboy isn't exactly roughing it. A 4-day pamper package, including all meals and activities starts at C$1160 (US$748) per person.

For a more authentic experience and to ride the range on your own, visit the **Flying U Ranch** (✆ **250/456-7717;** www.flyingu.com). The Cariboo Prospector will drop you off at the ranch's own Flying U Station. After you've checked into a cozy log cabin with a wood-burning stove, you'll be given riding gear and outfitted with a horse that suits your riding skill and style. And then you're on your own. The Flying U is one of the few ranches in North America that allows unsupervised riding: no guides, no trail rides. Guests are free to explore the ranch's 40,000 acres of lake, meadow, forest, and rangeland, with only each other and perhaps one of the frisky ranch dogs for company. At the end of the day, relax in the Longhorn Saloon or kick it up with the Flying U band. The meals—served at long tables in the main lodge—are hearty but unsophisticated. The showers and bathrooms are shared. The Flying U is affordable enough to bring along the kids; hay rides, camp fires, a dozen friendly dogs, canoeing, and swimming will keep them busy even after they tire of riding. Four-day Rail-and-Ranch packages, including all meals and activities, start at C$700 (US$452).

adult camping experience. Gourmet food and wine plus a range of activities such as horseback riding, sailing, kayaking, and fishing are included in the Outpost package (2-night minimum stay, May–Sept only).

P.O. Box 130, Tofino, B.C. V0R 2Z0. ✆ 888/333-5405 in North America or 250/725-8235. Fax 250/726-8558. www.wildretreat.com. 16 units in the floating resort. March 15–Nov 30 C$269–C$489 (US$174–US$315) per person in double accommodation. 10 units in luxury outpost camp May 24–Sept 30 C$675 (US$435) per person, includes all activities, meals, transfers to and from Tofino and parking in Tofino. AE, MC, V. **Amenities:** Restaurant; bar; full-service spa; Jacuzzi; sauna; watersports equipment; tour desk; massage; nonsmoking rooms. *In room:* hair dryer, iron.

The Inn at Tough City   This is possibly Tofino's nicest small inn and it certainly is the quirkiest. Built in 1996 from salvaged and recycled material, it's filled with antiques, stained glass, and bric-a-brac. The rooms are spacious, and several feature soaker tubs, fireplaces, or both. Crazy Ron and Johanna are the innkeepers.

350 Main St., P.O. Box 8, Tofino, B.C. V0R 2Z0. ℭ **877/725-2021** or 250/725-2021. Fax 250/725-2088. www.alberni.net/toughcity. 6 units. Mar 1–Feb 28 C$75–C$175 (US$48–US$113) double. MC, V. **Amenities:** Laundry service; nonsmoking rooms. In room: TV.

Long Beach Lodge   The newest kid on the beach, this beautiful lodge offers five-star luxury on the edge of Cox Bay. Using many local materials and crafts, this lodge offers 43 beautifully appointed rooms, furnished with Douglas fir beds and armoires and cedar patio furniture. Guests may choose between ocean views and beachfront rooms but all units come prepped for pampering with gas fireplaces, oversize soaking tubs, and fleece robes. The dining room, which is also open to the public, makes the most of the spectacular scenery with large picture windows overlooking the rugged Pacific. Chef Lisa Ahier focuses on local, fresh ingredients and buys many of the organic products from farmers on Vancouver Island.

P.O. Box 897, Tofino, B.C. V0R 2Z0. ℭ **877/844-7873.** www.longbeachlodgeresort.com. 43 units. June–Sept beachfront C$245–C$290 (US$158–US$187) double; forest room C$190 (US$123) double. Oct–May beachfront C$160–C$220 (US$103–US$142) double; forest room C$125–C$150 (US$81–US$97) double. AE, MC, V. **Amenities:** Restaurant (West Coast); tour desk; laundry service; nonsmoking rooms. In room: TV, fridge, hair dryer, coffeemaker, iron.

Middle Beach Lodge   This beautiful lodge/resort complex is on a headland overlooking the ocean. The rustic look was accomplished by using largely recycled beams, and the result is very pleasant. Accommodations range from simple lodge rooms to cabins with waterside decks, soaker tubs, gas fireplaces, and kitchenettes. All guests have access to a lofty common room overlooking the ocean. It's a good place to pour a coffee or something stronger and look out over the waves crashing in.

P.O. Box 100, Tofino, B.C. V0R 2Z0. ℭ **250/725-2900.** Fax 250/725-2901. www.middlebeach.com. 13 units, 19 cabins. C$110–C$165 (US$71–US$106) double; C$165–C$275 (US$106–US$177) suite; C$175–C$370 (US$113–US$238) single cabin; C$160–C$295 (US$103–US$190) duplex cabin; C$110–C$210 (US$71–US$135) triplex cabin; C$125–C$195 (US$81–US$126) sixplex suite. AE, MC, V. **Amenities:** Exercise room; tour desk; laundry service; nonsmoking facility. In room: TV/VCR, kitchenette, coffeemaker.

The Wickaninnish Inn ★★★   No matter which room you book in this beautiful new cedar, stone, and glass lodge, you'll wake to a magnificent view of the untamed Pacific. The inn is on a rocky promontory, surrounded by an old-growth spruce and cedar rainforest and the sprawling sands of Chesterman Beach. You do have to make some choices: select king- or queen-size beds and decide whether you want a room with an ocean view from the tub. Rustic driftwood, richly printed textiles, and local artwork highlight the rooms, each of which features a fireplace, down duvet, soaker tub, and private balcony. Winter storm-watching packages have become so popular that the inn is as busy in winter as it is in summer. The Pointe Restaurant (see "Where to Dine," below) and On-the-Rocks Bar serve three meals daily and feature an oceanfront view. The staff can arrange whale-watching, golfing, fishing, and diving packages. No-Stress Express packages include air transport and accommodations.

Osprey Lane at Chesterman Beach, P.O. Box 250, Tofino, B.C. V0R 2Z0. ℭ **800/333-4604** in North America, or 250/725-3100. Fax 250/725-3110. www.wickinn.com. 46 units. Mar–Feb C$230–C$420 (US$148–US$271) double. Special packages available year-round. Wheelchair-accessible units available. AE, DC, MC, V. Drive 5km (3 miles) south of Tofino toward Chesterman Beach to Osprey Lane. **Amenities:** Restaurant; bar; spa;

concierge; in-room massage; babysitting; nonsmoking facility. *In room:* TV, dataport, minibar, coffeemaker, hair dryer, iron.

Campgrounds

The 94 campsites on the bluff at **Green Point** are maintained by Pacific Rim National Park (© **250/726-7721**). The grounds are full every day in July and August, and the average wait for a site is 1 to 2 days. Leave your name at the ranger station when you arrive to be placed on the list. In July and August, the cost is C$14 to C$20 (US$9.10–US$13) per night, and in the shoulder season C$12 to C$18 (US$7.80–US$12) per night. You're rewarded for your patience with a magnificent ocean view, pit toilets, fire pits, pumped well water, and free firewood, but no showers or hookups. The campground is closed October through March.

Bella Pacifica Resort & Campground (© **250/725-3400;** www.bella pacifica.com), 3.3km (2 miles) south of Tofino on the Pacific Rim Highway (P.O. Box 413, Tofino, B.C. V0R 2Z0), is privately owned. March through November, it has 165 campsites from which you can walk to Mackenzie Beach or take the resort's private nature trails to Templar Beach. Flush toilets, hot showers, water, laundry, ice, fire pits, firewood, and full and partial hookups are available. Rates are C$18 to C$36 (US$12–US$23) per two-person campsite. Reserve at least a month in advance for a spot on a summer weekend.

WHERE TO DINE

If you're just looking for a cup of java and a snack, it's hard to beat the **Coffee Pod,** 151 Fourth St. (© **250/725-4246**), a laid-back, semi-granola kind of place at the entrance to town. The Pod, open 7am to 6pm (check for seasonal hours), also does an excellent breakfast. Main courses are C$7 to C$10 (US$4.50–US$6.45). The **Common Loaf Bakeshop,** 180 First St. (© **250/725-3915**), open 8am to 9pm, is locally famous as the gathering place for granola lovers, hippies, and other reprobates back when such things mattered in Tofino. At the "far" end of town, the Loaf does baked goods really well and a healthy lunch or dinner can be had for C$6 to C$9 (US$3.90–US$5.85). Liquids include herbal teas, coffee, juices, and wine and beer.

The Pointe Restaurant ★★★ PACIFIC NORTHWEST   This restaurant is perched on the water's edge at Chesterman Beach, where a 280° view of the roaring Pacific is the backdrop to a dining experience that can only be described as pure Pacific Northwest. Top chef Jim Garraway applies his talents to an array of local ingredients, including Dungeness crab, spotted prawns, halibut, salmon, quail, lamb, and rabbit. His signature version of bouillabaisse, Wickaninnish Potlatch, is a chunky, fragrant blend of soft and firm fish, shellfish, and vegetables simmered in a thick seafood broth. Other offerings include delectable appetizers like goat-cheese tarts and shaved fennel salad, and entrees like grilled lamb chops with new potatoes, fresh artichokes, and sea asparagus. Garraway's signature dessert—a double-chocolate mashed-potato brioche—is superb when accompanied by a glass of raspberry wine.

The Wickaninnish Inn, Osprey Lane at Chesterman Beach. © **250/725-3100.** Reservations required. Main courses C$29–C$32 (US$19–US$21). MC, V. Daily 8am–2:30pm, 2–5pm (snacks), 5–9:30pm.

The RainCoast Cafe WEST COAST   This cozy restaurant, just off the main street, has developed a deserved reputation for some of the best—and best value—seafood and vegetarian dishes in town. To start off, try the popular RainCoast salad—smoked salmon, sautéed mushrooms, and chèvre cheese on a bed of greens, with maple balsamic vinaigrette. Fresh fish is a big part of the cuisine, and the menu is supplemented by a catch-of-the-day special. Mainstays include seafood and Asian style noodle dishes, such as the prawns, scallops, and clams served on soba noodles with toasted cashew and miso sauce.

120 Fourth St. ⓒ 250/725-2215. www.raincoastcafe.com. Main courses C$12–C$24 (US$7.80–US$15). AE, MC, V. Daily 11:30am–3pm and 5–10pm; winter dinner only.

WHAT TO SEE & DO

FIRST NATIONS TOURISM   Clayoquot Sound is the traditional home of the Nuu-chah-nulth peoples. Accessed via water taxi, the **Walk the Wild Side Trail** (ⓒ 888/670-9586) runs along the south side of Flores Island to the village of Ahousat. The cost is C$20 (US$13) on your own or C$30 (US$19) with a guide, plus the water taxi to Flores. The above-referenced booking line is supposed to arrange both. Some who have done the trail have reported having incredible experiences: Afterward, they were invited by elders to come to the village to celebrate a potlatch. Others have paid their money only to be foisted off on 12- and 13-year-old Native boys more interested in playing with their two-way radios than looking at nature. So it's a toss-up. If you're interested in native ecotourism, however, it's probably worth giving it a try. Keep an open mind and spirit of adventure and you may be rewarded.

FISHING   Sport fishing for salmon, steelhead, rainbow trout, Dolly Varden char, halibut, cod, and snapper is excellent off the west coast of Vancouver Island. Long Beach is also great for bottom fishing. To fish here, you need a non-resident saltwater or freshwater license. Tackle shops sell licenses, have information on current restrictions, and often carry copies of the current publications *BC Tidal Waters Sport Fishing Guide* and *BC Sport Fishing Regulations Synopsis for Non-tidal Waters.* Independent anglers should also pick up a copy of the *BC Fishing Directory and Atlas.*

Chinook Charters, 450 Campbell St., Tofino (ⓒ 250/725-3431; www.chinookcharters.com), organizes fishing charters throughout the Clayoquot Sound area. Fishing starts in March and goes until December. The company supplies all the gear, a guide, and a boat. Prices start at C$85 (US$57) per hour, with a minimum of 4 hours. A full-day, 10-hour fishing trip for four people, on a 25-foot boat, is C$750 (US$503).

GUIDED NATURE HIKES   Owned and operated by **Bill McIntyre,** former chief naturalist of Pacific Rim National Park, the **Long Beach Nature Tour Co.** ⚘ (ⓒ 250/726-7099; www.oceansedge.bc.ca) offers guided beach walks, storm watching, land-based whale-watching, and rainforest tours, customized to suit your needs. Also excellent are the tours offered by wildlife author Adrienne Mason of **Raincoast Communications** (ⓒ 250/725-2878; amason@port.island.net). A local naturalist and science writer, she can accommodate various group sizes and will greatly enhance your knowledge of the local flora and fauna and the ecology of this unique rainforest.

HIKING   The 11km (7-mile) stretch of rocky headlands, sand, and surf along the **Long Beach Headlands Trail** is the most accessible section of the park system, which incorporates Long Beach, the West Coast Trail, and the Broken Islands Group. No matter where you go in this area, you're bound to meet whale-watchers in spring, surfers and anglers in summer, hearty hikers during the colder months, and kayakers year-round.

In and around **Long Beach,** numerous marked trails 0.8km to 3.3km (½–2 miles) long take you through the thick, temperate rainforest edging the shore.

The 3.3km (2-mile) **Gold Mine Trail** near Florencia Bay still has a few artifacts from the days when a gold-mining operation flourished amid the trees. And the partially boardwalked **South Beach Trail** (less than a mile long) leads through the moss-draped rainforest onto small quiet coves like Lismer Beach and South Beach, where you can see abundant life in the rocky tidal pools.

If you're canoeing or kayaking in Clayoquot Sound, there's another trail to discover. The **Big Cedar Trail** on Meares Island is a 3.3km (2-mile) board-walked path that was built in 1993 to protect the old-growth temperate rain-forest. Maintained by the Tla-o-qui-aht Native Indian band, it has a long staircase leading up to the Hanging Garden Tree, the province's fourth-largest western red cedar. If you aren't paddling yourself, the water taxi (© 250/725-3793) can drop you off and pick you up, C$20 (US$13) round-trip per person.

In town, the **Tofino Botanical Garden,** 1084 Pacific Rim Hwy. (© 250/725-1237), is still very much a work in progress, now in year 4 of a 10-year plan. A number of projects have been completed, such as the frog pond, the old-growth boardwalk, the native plant collection, the iris garden, bird blinds, and the children's garden. This lovely landscaped walking garden with native and exotic plants and gazebos for sitting and contemplating the surroundings is worth a visit. The visitor center and part of the garden are wheelchair accessible.

HOT SPRINGS COVE   A natural hot spring about 67km (40 miles) north of Tofino, the cove is accessible only by water. Take a water taxi, sail, canoe, or kayak up to Clayoquot Sound to enjoy swimming in the steaming pools and bracing waterfalls. A number of kayak outfitters and boat charters offer trips to the springs (see "Whale-Watching & Birding," below).

KAYAKING   Perhaps the quintessential Clayoquot experience, and certainly one of the most fun, is to slip into a kayak and paddle out into the waters of the sound. For beginners, half-day tours to Meares Island (usually with the chance to do a little hiking) are an especially good bet. For rentals, lessons, and tours, try **Pacific Kayak,** 606 Campbell St., at Jamie's Whaling Station (© 250/725-3232; www.tofino-bc.com/pacifickayak); the **Tofino Sea Kayaking Company,** 320 Main St. (© 800/863-4664 or 250/725-4222; www.tofino-kayaking.com); or **Remote Passages Sea Kayaking,** 71 Wharf St. (© 800/666-9833 or 250/725-3330; www.remotepassages.com). Kayaking packages range from 4-hour paddles around Meares Island (from C$52/US$34 per person) to weeklong pad-dling and camping expeditions. Instruction by experienced guides makes even your first kayaking experience a comfortable, safe, and enjoyable one.

STORM WATCHING   Watching the winter storms behind big glass windows has become very popular in Tofino over the past year or so. For a slight twist on this, try the outdoor storm-watching tours offered by the **Long Beach Nature Tour Co.** (© 250/726-7099; www.oceansedge.bc.ca). Owner Bill McIntyre used to be chief naturalist of Pacific Rim National Park. He can explain how storms work and where to stand so you can get close without getting swept away.

SURFING   More and more people make the trip out to Tofino for one reason only: the surfing. The wild Pacific coast is known as one of the best surfing des-tinations in Canada, and most surfers work in the tourism industry around Tofino, spending all their free time in the water. To try this exciting and exhila-rating sport, call **Live to Surf,** 1180 Pacific Rim Hwy. (© 250/725-4464; www. livetosurf.com). Lessons start at C$45 (US$29) for 1½ hours. Live to Surf also rents boards at C$25 (US$16) and wet suits (don't even think about going with-out one) at C$20 (US$13).

WHALE-WATCHING & BIRDING   A number of outfitters conduct tours through this region, which is inhabited by gray whales, bald eagles, porpoises, orcas, seals, and sea lions. **Chinook Charters,** 450 Campbell St. (© **250/725-3431**), offers whale-watching trips in Clayoquot Sound on 25-foot Zodiac boats. The company also conducts trips to Hot Springs Cove on its 32-foot

Moments   **Two Trips of a Lifetime**

These two trips are within striking distance of Vancouver or Victoria and can be done no place else on earth.

SAILING THE GREAT BEAR RAINFOREST ★★   If you look at a map of British Columbia, about halfway up the West Coast you'll see an incredibly convoluted region of mountains, fjords, bays, channels, rivers, and inlets. There are next to no roads in this area—the geography is too intense. The area is only accessible by boat. Thanks to that isolation, this is also one of the last places in the world where grizzly bears are still found in large numbers, not to mention salmon, large trees, killer whales, otters, and porpoises.

Run by an ex-pilot turned naturalist and sailor, **Maple Leaf Adventure,** 2087 Indian Crescent, Duncan (© **888/599-5323** or 250/715-0906; fax 250/715-0912) runs a number of trips to this magic part of the world on a 100-year-old, 92-foot-long, fully rigged sailing schooner. Owner Brian Falconer is extremely knowledgeable and normally brings along a trained naturalist to explain the fauna, especially the whales, dolphins, and grizzlies. Covering territory from the midcoast to the Queen Charlotte Islands (Haida Gwaii) to the coasts of Alaska, the trips vary in duration from 4 days to 2 weeks and in price from C$2,000 to C$4,100 (US$1,290–US$2,645). All include gourmet meals (more than you could ever eat) and comfortable but not luxurious accommodations aboard Brian's beautiful schooner.

HORSE TREKKING THE CHILCOTIN PLATEAU ★★   The high plateau country of the B.C. interior has some of the most impressive scenery around. Soaring peaks rise above deep valleys, and mountain meadows are alive with flowers that bloom for just a few weeks in high summer. The advantages to taking in this territory on horseback are that the horse's feet get sore, not yours; if you come across grizzlies, you've got some height on them; and horses can carry far more and far better food than you can.

In British Columbia, one guide company is granted exclusive rights to run tours through that section of wilderness. The territories are typically 5,000 sq. km (1,930 sq. miles)—5,000 sq. km of high-country wilderness, where you won't meet another horse team except your own. One of the guide-outfitters closest to Vancouver is **Chilcotin Holidays Guest Ranch,** Gun Creek Road, Gold Bridge (© **250/238-2274;** www.chilcotinholidays.com), in the Chilcotin Mountains north of Whistler. Their trips, running from 4 to 7 days and costing C$600 to C$900 (US$387–US$581), involve encounters with wildflowers, bighorn sheep, grizzly bears, and wolves.

Chinook Key. **Jamie's Whaling Station,** 606 Campbell St. (© **800/667-9913** or 250/725-3919), uses a glass-bottomed 65-foot power cruiser as well as a fleet of Zodiacs for tours to watch the gray whales March through October. A combined Hot Springs Cove and whale-watching trip aboard a 32-foot cruiser is offered year-round. Fares for both companies' expeditions generally start at C$75 (US$48) per person for a 3-hour tour; customized trips can run as high as C$200 (US$129) per person for a full day. For an interesting combination, try the Seato-Sky tour, a 5-hour trip with a boat ride, a hike through the rainforest, and a return to Tofino by floatplane, at the cost of C$109 (US$70) for adults.

Remote Passages, Meares Landing, 71 Wharf St. (© **800/666-9833** or 250/725-3330), runs 2½-hour-long whale-watching tours in Clayoquot Sound on Zodiac boats, daily March through November. Fares are C$50 (US$32) for adults and C$35 (US$23) for children under 12. The company also conducts a 7-hour combination whale-watching and hot-springs trip at C$75 (US$48) for adults and C$50 (US$32) for children under 12. Reservations are recommended.

For land-based bird watching, contact local naturalist/science writer Adrienne Mason of **Rainforest Communications** (© **250/725-2878**). Adrienne knows the area and can customize a tour depending on your needs.

4 The Gulf Islands ✦

The several dozen mountainous **Gulf Islands** sprawl across the Strait of Georgia between the B.C. mainland and Vancouver Island. Though only a handful of the islands are served by regular ferry service, this entire area is popular with holidaymakers—and with good reason. In the rain shadow of Washington State's Olympic Mountains, the Gulf Islands have the most temperate climate in all of Canada. Indeed, the climate here is officially listed as semi-Mediterranean.

There have been radical changes to the traditional agricultural culture here. Starting in the 1960s, the Gulf Islands developed a reputation as countercultural hippie enclaves, a reputation the islands still maintain—and still somewhat deserve, for the immigration of artists and back-to-the-landers continues apace. The 1990s witnessed a parallel but different land rush. High-tech moguls, Hollywood stars, and other wealthy refugees from urban centers have been moving here in droves. Land prices have skyrocketed, and so has the quality of island facilities: The islands now boast fine restaurants, elegant small inns, and a multitude of art galleries.

If you're traveling with kids, you'll find the Gulf Islands a fairly inhospitable place to find accommodations. Nearly all B&Bs have minimum ages for guests (usually 12 or 16), and there are only a few standard motels or cottage resorts where families are welcome. It's mandatory to make reservations well in advance, as the ferry system doesn't make it exactly easy to just drive on to the next town to find a place to stay.

ESSENTIALS
GETTING THERE   Getting to the Gulf Islands is half the fun of visiting, but it can be a tad confusing. **BC Ferries** (© **888/223-3779** or 604/444-2890; www.bcferries.bc.ca) operates three ferry routes to the Gulf Islands: from Tsawwassen on the B.C. mainland; and from Swartz Bay and Crofton on Vancouver Island. Be certain to pick up one of the "Southern Gulf Islands" schedules and give yourself plenty of time to analyze it. You can get to any of the major Gulf Islands from Swartz Bay or Tsawwassen, except Saturna Island, which is accessible only from Swartz Bay.

Tips **A Gulf Islands B&B Reservation Service**

Reserve B&Bs, lodges, resorts, and country inns in all price ranges free through a centralized booking agency: The **Canadian Gulf Islands B&B Reservation Service** (© 866/539-3089 or 250/539-3089). It is operated by Galiano Island natives who've inspected over 100 of participating lodgings. They're able to connect you up with exactly what you're looking for, even at the last minute, whether it's a farm vacation, a honeymoon suite, a cozy B&B, or a cottage on the beach.

To ensure that you actually make the ferry you want, arrive at least 30 minutes early; on a summer weekend, allow 45 minutes or more lead time. You can make reservations on the service from Tsawwassen, and these are recommended on summer weekends; however, you can't reserve space on the runs from Swartz Bay.

Here are sample peak-season fares: A car and two passengers from Tsawwassen to Mayne Island costs C$54 (US$35); the same service as a foot passenger is C$9 (US$5.80). From Swartz Bay to Salt Spring Island for a car and two passengers is C$31 (US$20); a single foot passenger is C$6 (US$3.90). Interisland fares are C$13 (US$8.40) for a car plus two passengers or C$3 (US$1.95) for a walk-on. For payment, all Gulf Island ferry terminals take Visa and MasterCard in addition to cash and traveler's checks.

A number of small commuter airlines offer regularly scheduled floatplane service to the Gulf Islands from Vancouver Harbour and Vancouver International Airport's Coal Harbour Terminal. One-way tickets to the islands usually run C$60 to C$70 (US$39–US$45), not a bad fare when you consider the time and hassle of the ferries. For schedules and reservations, contact **Harbour Air** (© **800/665-0212** or 604/688-1277; www.harbour-air.com), **Seair** (© **800/447-3247** or 250/273-8900; www.seairseaplanes.com), or **Pacific Spirit Air** (© **800/665-2359** or 250/537-9359; www.tofinoair.ca).

VISITOR INFORMATION For general information on the Gulf Islands, contact **Tourism Vancouver Island,** Suite 203–335 Wesley St., Nanaimo, BC V9R 2T5 (© **250/754-3500**; www.islands.bc.ca). A comprehensive website is www.gulfislands.com.

GETTING AROUND Most innkeepers are happy to pick up registered guests at either the ferry or the floatplane terminal, if given sufficient notice. There are also taxis on most islands.

Bicycling Winding country roads and bucolic landscapes make the Gulf Islands a favorite destination of cyclists. Although the islands' road networks aren't exactly large, it's great fun to cycle the back roads, jump a ferry, and peddle to an outlying inn for lunch. Several island parks have designated mountain bike trails. Bicycles can be taken onboard BC Ferries for a small surcharge, usually less than C$1.50 (US$1), depending on the route. Bicycle rentals are available on most islands, and it's not unusual for inns and B&Bs to have bikes available for loan for guests.

Kayaking The Gulf Islands' lengthy and rugged coastline, plus their proximity to other more remote island groups, make them a great base for kayaking trips. Low-drawing kayaks are perfect for exploring shallow bays and rocky inlets, centers of marine life. Most of the islands have kayak outfitters; however—depending on their insurance coverage—not all outfitters will offer rentals apart from guided kayak tours. If you're an experienced kayaker and just want to rent a kayak and get out on the water, be sure to call ahead to make sure rentals are available at your destination.

SALT SPRING ISLAND

The largest of the Gulf Islands, **Salt Spring** is a bucolic island getaway filled with artisans, sheep pastures, and cozy B&Bs. It's also a busy cultural crossroads: The super-rich, movie stars, economy-minded retirees, high-tech telecommuters, and hippie farmers all rub shoulders here. The island's hilly terrain and deep forests afford equal privacy for all lifestyles, and that's the way the residents like it.

ESSENTIALS

GETTING THERE   By Plane   Regularly scheduled floatplane service operates between Vancouver International Airport and Vancouver's Inner Harbour seaplane terminal and Ganges Harbour. See above for contact information.

By Ferry   Salt Spring Island is served by three **BC Ferries** routes (© **888/724-5223** in B.C.). From Tsawwassen on the B.C. mainland, ferries depart twice daily for Long Harbour, on the island's northeast coast. If you're on Vancouver Island, you have a choice of the roughly once-per-hour Vesuvius Bay–Crofton run or the approximately every-90-minutes crossing from Swartz Bay to Fulford Harbour.

VISITOR INFORMATION   The Salt Spring Chamber of Commerce operates a **visitor center** at 121 Lower Ganges Rd., Salt Spring Island, B.C. V8K 2T1 (© **250/537-5252**; www.saltspringtoday.com).

GETTING AROUND   There's no public transport on Salt Spring, so if you don't have a car, you'll need to rely on a bicycle or call **Silver Shadow Taxi** (© **250/537-3030**). Another option for interisland transport is **Gulf Islands Water Taxi** (© **250/537-2510**; www.saltspring.com/watertaxi), offering speedboat service among Salt Spring, Mayne, and Galiano islands on Wednesday and Saturday. The taxi leaves from Government Dock in Ganges Harbour.

WHERE TO STAY

Beddis House B&B   Perched above a strand of pebble beach, white clapboard Beddis House was built as a farmhouse in 1900. When the property was purchased for development as a B&B, the owners retained the old farmhouse as the dining room and parlor area and built a new beachfront guest house—the Coach House—in the style of the original home. The spacious rooms have wonderful ocean views, with private patios or balconies, wood-burning stoves, bathrooms with claw-foot tubs, private entrances, and access to multilevel decks, beautifully landscaped gardens, and manicured lawns. Guests are brought an early morning tray of coffee or tea and later a three-course breakfast is served in the farmhouse dining room.

131 Miles Ave., Salt Spring Island, B.C. V8K 2E1. © 250/537-1028. Fax 250/537-9888. www.saltspring. com/beddishouse. 3 units. C$160–C$190 (US$103–US$123) double. Rates include breakfast and tea. MC, V. Closed Dec 15–Feb 1. Children 14 and older only. *In room:* No phone.

The Old Farmhouse B&B ⊛   Strategically located between Ganges (a 5-min. drive) and Vesuvius (a 10-min. drive), the Old Farmhouse is a Victorian-era homestead built in 1894. Beautifully restored and furnished, the house is set on 1.2 hectares (3 acres) of grassy meadows, orchards, and specimen trees—the massive red-barked arbutus tree in the front meadow is one of the largest and oldest in British Columbia. The B&B's four rooms are in a new stylistically harmonious guest house adjoining the restored original farmhouse, two on the ground floor and two on the first floor, each with a balcony or deck. A tray of coffee or tea is brought to your room in the morning, followed by a full breakfast served in the original dining room. Breakfast is supposed to be the most important meal of the day, and Gerti certainly takes it seriously, baking up a storm and serving delicious hot entrees. Doggie bags are provided to take the goodies with you while you explore Salt Spring. Or you may just take them as far as the garden and relax in a hammock or a lawn chair underneath the trees.

1077 North End Rd., Salt Spring Island, B.C. V8K 1L9. ℂ 250/537-4113. Fax 250/537-4969. www.bbcanada.com/oldfarmhouse.com. 4 units. C$170 (US$110) double. Rates include breakfast. No smoking. V. *In room:* No phone.

Seabreeze Inn   An excellent alternative to Salt Spring's expensive B&Bs, the Seabreeze is a well-maintained, attractive motel just south of Ganges. All rooms are very clean and nicely furnished, some with extras like refrigerators and coffeemakers. The 16 kitchen units come with electric cooktops, full-size refrigerators, and microwaves. Just below the motel is a large deck and garden area, with grapevine-covered arbors, picnic tables, and gas barbecues for use by guests. Management also rent mopeds (C$12/US$7.75 per hr., C$60/US$39 per day)—perhaps the perfect way to toodle round the island. The Seabreeze is perfect for families, cyclists, or anyone who doesn't feel the need to be fussed over in a B&B.

101 Bittancourt Rd., Salt Spring Island, B.C. V8K 2K2. ℂ 800/434-4112 or 250/537-4145. Fax 250/537-4323. www.seabreezeinns.com. 29 units. C$85–C$135 (US$55–US$87) double. Extra person C$20 (US$13). Children under 10 stay free in parents' room. Senior discounts and off-season rates available. AE, MC, V. **Amenities:** Bike and moped rental; laundry; nonsmoking rooms. *In room:* TV, coffeemaker, hair dryer.

WHERE TO DINE

If you're heading off on a picnic or traveling on your bicycle or kayak, pick up a pack lunch at the **Tree House Café,** 106 Purvis Lane (ℂ **250/537-5379**), an aptly named little outdoor cafe under an old octopus-limbed plum tree near the waterfront behind Mouat's Hardware Store, 106 Fulford-Ganges Rd. in Ganges. The Café is also a great place to spend a summer evening. Open daily May through September 8am to 10pm; October through April 9am to 3pm. Main courses cost C$8 to C$13 (US$5.20–US$8.45). On a sunny day grab a table on **Calvin's** patio, 133 Lower Ganges Rd. (ℂ **250/538-5551**), overlooking the busy Ganges Marina. Hermann and Rene serve up excellent lunches; the gourmet sandwiches are accompanied by a generous serving of fries and/or salad, or choose from a selection of burgers, pasta, or frittatas. Also open for breakfast and dinner, locals flock here for the affordable seafood dishes. Open daily 8:30am to 9pm; lunch costs under C$10 (US$6.45), dinner C$14 to C$20 (US$9.10–US$13). The deck and glass-fronted dining room at **Vesuvius Inn Neighborhood Pub** (ℂ **250/537-2312**), perched above the ferry dock at the tiny village of Vesuvius Bay, is a great place for a drink or a meal. Main courses cost C$9 to C$15 (US$5.85–US$9.75); it's open daily 11am to 11pm. Check for hours in the winter.

Hastings House PACIFIC NORTHWEST   While the cuisine at Hastings House is top quality, with a daily-changing menu designed to incorporate the best of local fish and produce, the total experience here leaves something to be desired. Dinner begins with a cocktail, served by the fire or in the garden an hour before your dinner seating. The nightly set menu includes an appetizer (perhaps paper-thin wild spring salmon with a lime and pistachio oil) followed by a soup (a sweet pepper and coconut bisque in our case), a small fish course, and a choice of four main dishes. Salt Spring lamb is nearly always featured, as is local salmon or other seasonal fish and Island venison. Though the wine list is good, the Hastings House, somewhat bizarrely for a restaurant with its reputation, has no sommelier on hand to advise on wine pairings. Nor are there any wines by the glass. The serving staff, as a substitute, is obliging, but young and not overly knowledgeable. Male guests are required to wear a suit jacket to enter the formal dining room. The casual dining room is an identical alternative, with the same food, view, and service.

160 Upper Ganges Rd. ℂ **250/537-2362.** Reservations required. Prix-fixe 5-course dinner C$85 (US$55). Summer sitting at 7:30pm, spring and fall sitting at 7pm. AE, MC, V. Closed mid-Nov to mid-Mar.

House Piccolo CONTINENTAL   In a heritage home in Ganges, House Piccolo offers excellent a la carte dining and a good wine list in casually formal surroundings. The northern European accents in the unusual menu reflect the Finnish origins of the chef/owner, particularly the fresh-fish specials that feature the best of the local catch, such as a salmon soup in a creamy dill and white pepper broth, or Salt Spring's finest lamb served with a red wine, shallot, and roasted garlic reduction. However, just for the fun of it, start by ordering the *yrttiriimiharkaa* as an appetizer, an herb crusted beef carpaccio.

108 Hereford Ave., Ganges. ℂ **250/537-1844.** Reservations required. Main courses C$25–C$32 (US$16–US$21). AE, DC, MC, V.

EXPLORING SALT SPRING ISLAND

With a year-round population of 10,000, Salt Spring is served by three ferries, making it by far the easiest Gulf Island to visit. The center of island life is **Ganges,** a little village with gas, grocery stores, banks, and galleries, all overlooking a busy pleasure-boat harbor. You could easily spend most of a day poking around art galleries and boutiques and drinking coffee.

CHECKING OUT THE STUDIOS, GALLERIES & MARKET   In fact, many people head to Salt Spring expressly to visit the galleries; the island is famed across Canada as an artists' colony. At the tourist office, pick up a copy of the *Studio Tour Map,* which locates 35 artists—glassblowers, painters, ceramists, weavers, carvers, and sculptors—around the island. As you're driving, just watch for the STUDIO sign with the blue sheep on it; and if the sign says open, stop in.

Ganges has a number of galleries offering local crafts. The largest gallery, **Artcraft,** 114 Rainbow Rd. in Ganges (ℂ **250/537-0899**), features the works of dozens of Salt Spring artists. **Coastal Currents,** 133 Hereford Ave. (ℂ **250/537-0070**), is an old home converted to a housewares-and-decor gallery. The **Pegasus Gallery,** in Mouat's Mall at 1–104 Fulford Ganges Rd. (ℂ **250/537-2421**), displays contemporary Canadian painting and sculpture as well as a good selection of Northwest Native carving and basketry.

April through October, a not-to-be-missed Salt Spring event is **Market in the Park,** held every Saturday 8am to 4pm on the waterfront's Centennial Park; it brings together an infectious mix of craftspeople, farmers, musicians, bakers, and just about everyone else on the island who might plausibly be able to sell or buy something. It's great fun and a good chance to shop for local products at fair prices. As you might guess, the people-watching possibilities are matchless.

HIKING   On the southeast corner of Salt Spring Island, **Truckle Provincial Park** is the largest park in the Gulf Islands. Eight kilometers (5 miles) of trails wind through forests to rocky headlands where tide-pool exploration is excellent;

some trails are designated for mountain bikes. Truckle Park is also the only public campground on Salt Spring.

BIKING   Although Salt Spring is the largest of the Gulf Islands and has the best network of paved roads, it's not the best island for cycling. Few roads have shoulders, and with 10,000 inhabitants and three ferries unleashing cars throughout the day, there's a lot more traffic here than you'd think. However, these same ferries—plus the summer bikes-and-passengers-only **Gulf Islands Water Taxi** (© 250/537-2510) from Ganges to Mayne and Galiano islands— make Salt Spring a convenient base for cyclists. For bike rentals, contact **Salt Spring Kayaking** (© 250/653-4222) at Fulford Harbour.

KAYAKING   **Island Escapades,** 118 Natalie Lane (© 888/529-2567), offers guided introductory lake trips starting at C$30 (US$19), with guided 3-hour ocean tours at C$50 (US$33). It also offers paddle and mountaineering holidays. **Salt Spring Kayaking** (© 250/653-4222) at Ganges Harbour, also rents kayaks. **Sea Otter Kayaking,** 1168 North End Rd. (© 250/537-5678; www. saltspring.com/kayaking), rents both kayaks and canoes, starting at C$20 (US$13) per hour. Guided tours begin at C$35 (US$23) for a 2-hour harbor exploration; overnight packages are also available.

GALIANO ISLAND

Galiano is a long yet mountainous stringbean of an island stretching along the Gulf Islands' eastern flank. It's the closest Gulf Island to Vancouver, and many of the properties are the second homes of the city's elite. The rural yet genteel feel of the island is perfect for a romantic getaway or a relaxing weeklong break from the urban hassle.

ESSENTIALS

GETTING THERE   BC Ferries (© 888/724-5223 in B.C.) reach Sturdies Bay on Galiano Island from Tsawwassen and Swartz Bay. Floatplanes serve Galiano Island from the docks at Montague Harbour. For contact information, see "Getting There" at the beginning of the Gulf Islands section.

VISITOR INFORMATION   Contact **Galiano Island Tourist/Visitor Info,** 2590 Sturdies Bay Rd., Box 73, Galiano Island, B.C. V0N 1P0 (© 250/539-2233; www.galianoisland.com).

GETTING AROUND   For ferry pickup and other taxi service, contact **Go Galiano** (© 250/539-0202).

WHERE TO STAY

The only public campground on Galiano Island is **Montague Harbour Provincial Marine Park,** with 40 sites for C$10 (US$6.45) per site. The park offers beach access but no showers or flush toilets. Call © 800/689-9025 for reservations or 250/391-2300 for information.

Driftwood Village   This venerable cottage resort is perfect for a laid-back family vacation with the kids and the family pets in tow. Indeed, like a little hamlet, Driftwood Village is a collection of 11 fully equipped cottages of differing vintages and styles scattered around a shady 0.8-hectare (2-acre) garden with ponds, flowers, and fruit trees. Each cottage has a full kitchen, private bathroom, and TV, and most have fireplaces and private decks with views of Sturdies Bay. The one- and two-bedroom cottages are effectively small furnished houses, suitable for two to four people. All are decorated with a sense of artful thrift that will instantly bring back youthful memories of idealized lakeside cabins. The cottages share a large central deck area with a hot tub and a badminton court; barbecues are available to guests. Unlike most places in the Gulf Islands, kids and pets are welcome.

205 Bluff Rd. E., Galiano Island, B.C. V0N 1P0. ⓒ **888/240-1466** or 250/539-5457. www.driftwood cottages.com. 11 cottages. Studio cottages C$65–C$98 (US$42–US$63) double; C$78–C$115 (US$50–US$74) 1-bedroom; C$93–C$143 (US$60–US$92) 2-bedroom. Extra person C$5–C$15 (US$3.25–US$9.70). Complimentary ferry pickup. MC, V. **Amenities:** Jacuzzi; badminton court. *In room:* TV/VCR, kitchen, hair dryer.

Woodstone Country Inn ⭐   The quintessential small country inn, Woodstone sits amid fir trees overlooking a series of meadows serving as a de facto bird sanctuary (in fact, the inn was built as a retreat for birders). The entire two-story inn is beautifully decorated with the owners' personal collection of folk art and sculpture from their world travels, including marvelous carvings from Arctic Canada and southern Africa. The 12 units (a mix of king, queen, and three twin rooms) are large and beautifully furnished. Gleaming white-tiled bathrooms are fitted with soaker or Jacuzzi tubs and luxury soaps and lotions. All rooms have fireplaces, some have sofa beds, and one is fitted for guests with disabilities. All main-floor rooms have small private patios. The inn's restaurant (see below), in a high-ceilinged tiered room off the library, serves Galiano Island's finest cuisine, a mix of classic French savoir faire and Pacific Northwest vitality.

743 Georgeson Bay Rd., RR 1, Galiano Island, B.C. V0N 1P0. ⓒ **888/339-2022** or 250/539-2022. Fax 250/539-5198. www.gulfislands.com/woodstone. 12 units. C$105–C$185 (US$68–US$119) double. Rates include full breakfast and afternoon tea. Packages available. AE, MC, V. **Amenities:** Excellent restaurant; laundry service; nonsmoking facility. *In room:* TV, coffeemaker.

WHERE TO DINE

Galiano has a limited number of fine-dining establishments, though there are a number of informal places to eat. The **Daystar Market Café** (ⓒ **250/539-2800**), just north of Sturdies Bay at the intersection of Georgeson Bay Road and Porlier Pass Road, serves mostly vegetarian light meals and baked goods for lunch and dinner daily. Main courses cost C$6 to C$12 (US$3.90–US$7.80). Summer hours are Monday through Saturday 11:30am to 3pm and 6 to 9pm, Sunday 10:30am to 2:30pm. The **Montague Café** (ⓒ **250/539-5733**), at the Montague Harbour Marina, has sandwiches and light dining right on the water. It's open daily 8am to 9pm daily in summer; check for winter hours. Main courses go for C$7 to C$12 (US$4.55–US$7.80). For a pub meal, go to the pleasant, woodsy **Hummingbird Pub,** 47 Sturdies Bay Rd. (ⓒ **250/539-5472**). Main courses cost C$10 to C$14 (US$6.50–US$9.10). It's open year-round 11am to midnight, although the kitchen closes at 9pm.

Woodstone Country Inn ⭐ INTERNATIONAL   The dining room at Woodhouse Country Inn is easily the best place to eat on Galiano Island and one of the best restaurants in all the Gulf Islands. The daily changing menu is a compelling blend of classic French cuisine enlivened with vivid international flavors. Each day's menu includes three entree choices—meat, fish, or vegetarian—and comes with homemade breads, soup, and a delightful salad course. The Woodstone's specialty dressing (a tart/sweet mix of honey and citrus oils) is wonderful over arugula and slices of pear, and another standout is the pungent salad of grilled tuna, sweet red onion, and balsamica. Desserts like warm bread pudding, white-chocolate/raspberry ice-cream cake, and fresh fruit and berry sorbets end the meal. The wine list is an interesting mix of Okanagan, Californian, and French vintages.

743 Georgeson Bay Rd. (✆ 250/539-2022. Reservations required. 4-course dinner C$22–C$27 (US$14–US$18); minimum menu charge C$22 (US$14) per person. AE, DC, MC, V. Sun–Thurs 5–9pm; Fri–Sat 5–10pm.

EXPLORING GALIANO ISLAND

Galiano is also a center for artists and craftspeople. Check a selection of local and international crafts at **Ixchel,** with locations at both Montague Marina (✆ 250/539-9819) and at 61 Georgeson Bay Rd. (✆ 250/539-3038), or meet many of the local artists at the weekly **Gaia market,** held every Saturday 9:30am to 2:30pm May through September (rain or shine) by the Sturdies Bay ferry terminal.

Galiano is perhaps the most physically striking of the Gulf Islands, particularly the mountainous southern shores. **Mount Sutil, Mount Galiano,** and the exposed cliffs above Georgeson Bay simply called **The Bluffs,** rise above sheep-filled meadows, shadowy forests, and steep fern-lined ravines. **Active Pass,** the narrow strait separating Galiano from Mayne Island, is another scenic high spot: All the pleasure-boat and ferry traffic between Vancouver and Victoria negotiates this turbulent cliff-lined passage (tides churn through this cleft at speeds of 9 knots).

BICYCLING   The farther north you go on Galiano, the more remote the island becomes, making this a favorite of cyclists. While you won't have to worry too much about traffic on the 30km (19-mile) long paved road running up the island's west side, there are enough steep ascents to keep your attention focused. Mountain bikers can follow unmaintained logging roads that skirt the eastern shores. Contact **Galiano Bicycle Rental,** 36 Burrill Rd. (✆ 250/539-9906), for a full range of rental options, including mountain, touring, and tandem bikes.

HIKING   Several short hikes lead to Active Pass overlooks, including the trail to the top of 330m (1,082-ft.) **Mount Galiano** and the cliff-edge path in **Bluffs Park.** Another good hiking destination is **Bodega Ridge,** a park about two-thirds of the way up the island with old-growth forest, wildflower meadows, and extensive views onto the distant Olympic and Cascade mountains.

KAYAKING & BOATING   Home to otters, seals, and bald eagles, the gentle island-shielded waters of Montague Harbour are a perfect kayaking destination. If you haven't kayaked before, **Galiano Island Sea Kayaking** (✆ 888/539-2930) at Sutil Lodge, 637 Southwind Rd., caters to beginners and offers guided 2- and 4-hour trips out onto the bay; a 2-hour wildlife-viewing paddle is C$29 (US$19). If you have more time and want to really get away, consider one of the daylong (C$68/US$44) or multiday kayak camping trips from **Gulf Island Kayaking** (✆ 250/539-2442, www.islandnet.com/tour). Both of the above also offer rental kayaks.

MAYNE ISLAND

Bucolic **Mayne Island** is a beautiful medley of rock-lined bays, forested hills, farm fields, and pastureland. Seemingly distant from the pressures of modern life, Mayne feels like a real island community where most people know and care about one another.

ESSENTIALS

GETTING THERE   **BC Ferries** serves Mayne Island with regularly scheduled runs from Tsawwassen and Swartz Bay. Three commuter airlines offer floatplane service to and from Vancouver. For more information, see "Getting There" at the beginning of the Gulf Islands section.

VISITOR INFORMATION   Contact the **Mayne Island Community Chamber of Commerce,** Box 2, Mayne Island, B.C. V0N 2J0, or visit the website: www.mayneislandchamber.ca.

GETTING AROUND   Midas Taxi (© **250/539-3132**) provides ground transportation and can provide tours.

WHERE TO STAY

Oceanwood Country Inn ⟨★⟩   This large inn has grown from a home-style B&B in a beautiful location to a luxury lodging with an excellent restaurant, a knowledgeable and attentive staff, and extremely spacious rooms with sumptuous furnishings. Each room and suite is decorated according to an understated floral and wildlife theme, and all but one have magnificent views over formal gardens to boat-flecked Navy Channel. The less-expensive rooms, in the original inn, are charming and beautifully fitted with fine furniture and large bathrooms; two have balconies. However, the multitiered rooms in the New Wing are truly large and wonderfully well appointed, all with private water-view decks, large sitting areas with comfy couches and chairs, queen beds, and two-person jetted or soaker tubs facing wood-burning fireplaces.

630 Dinner Bay Rd., Mayne Island, B.C. V0N 2J0. © **250/539-5074.** Fax 250/539-3002. www.ocean wood.com. 12 units. C$149–C$299 (US$96–US$193) double. Extra person C$25 (US$16). Rates include breakfast and afternoon tea. MC, V. Open Mar–Nov. **Amenities:** Jacuzzi; game room; nonsmoking rooms.

WHERE TO DINE

In Miner's Bay's tiny strip mall, the **Manna Bakery Café** (© **250/539-2323**) is the place to go for a cappuccino and freshly baked cinnamon rolls. A soup and sandwich may set you back C$6 (US$3.90); the cafe is open daily 9am to 5pm. **Miner's Bay Café** (© **250/539-9888**), open for breakfast and lunch, features light home-cooked meals and sandwiches (some vegetarian choices) and fresh-baked pies and pastries. Prices are C$4.95 to C$8 (US$3.20–US$5.20); it's open Wednesday through Monday 8am to 4pm, and Friday and Saturday 5 to 8pm for take-out pizza only. Just above the marina and floatplane dock in Miner's Bay, the **Springwater Lodge** (© **250/539-5521**) is a comfortably ramshackle pub/restaurant with great views. Open for lunch and dinner 9am to 9pm; reduced hours in the winter. Main courses cost C$14 to C$20 (US$9.10–US$13). The pub is open until midnight on weekdays and, if busy, later on weekends.

Oceanwood Country Inn ⟨★⟩ PACIFIC NORTHWEST   At the Oceanwood, chef Paul McKinnon brings together the rich bounty of Pacific Northwest fish, meat, game, fruit, and vegetables in a daily-changing tableau of vivid tastes and textures. Dinners include a soup and appetizer course (perhaps roast eggplant soup with chive flowers, followed by rabbit strudel with carrot-and-beet confit) plus a choice of two entrees. The fish selection might be local paupiettes of sole with herb gnocchi and blackberry vinaigrette. Meat selections have included grilled duck breast with cranberry demi-glace served on ravioli stuffed with foie gras. Dinners also include the special dessert, which can be a compote of seasonal fruit or a confection of chocolate, cream, and genoise. To end the evening, dally over coffee or after-dinner drinks (Oceanwood has a good selection of single-malts and ports) in the fireplace-dominated library.

630 Dinner Bay Rd. (℗ 250/539-5074. www.oceanwood.com. Reservations required. Prix-fixe 4-course menu C$44 (US$28). AE, DC, MC, V. Sun–Thurs 5:30–9pm; Fri–Sat 5:30–10pm.

EXPLORING MAYNE ISLAND

Miner's Bay is by default the island's commercial center, though in most locales this somewhat aimless collection of shops, homes, and businesses lolligagging along the Active Pass bayfront wouldn't really qualify as a village. However, it's this understated and soft-focus approach to life that provides Mayne Island its substantial charm. Don't let the rural patina fool you: Some of the lodging and dining is absolutely world class, and even though organized activities are few, few people will be bored on such a lovely island.

There are two beach access paths at **Bennett Bay,** on the island's northeast coast; this is considered the best swimming beach on Mayne. **Campbell Bay,** just northwest, is another favorite pebble beach. Closer to the Village Bay ferry terminal, **Dinner Bay Park** is a lovely site for a picnic. On a sunny day, the grounds of the **Georgina Point Lighthouse** provide dramatic viewpoints; the grounds are now preserved as a national heritage park, with picnic tables and access to the rocky headland.

BIKING   Mayne is one of the best islands for cyclists. The rolling hills provide plenty of uphill challenges, but the terrain is considerably less mountainous than on other islands.

HIKING   The roads on Mayne are usually quiet enough that they can also serve as walkways for hikers and jogging paths for runners. Hikers looking for more solitary forest walks should consider **Mounte Parke Regional Park,** off Fernhill Road in the center of the island. The park's most spectacular views reward hikers who take the hour-long hike to Halliday Viewpoint on the crest of the island.

KAYAKING & BOATING   At Seal Beach in Miner's Bay, **Mayne Island Kayak & Canoe Rentals** (℗ **250/539-2667;** www.mayneisle.com/kayak) rents kayaks and canoes for C$20 (US$13) for 2 hours or C$42 (US$27) for a day. The company will drop off kayaks at any of six launching points on the island and, if you get stranded, will even pick up kayaks (and too-weary kayakers) from other island destinations.

If you'd rather let the wind do the work, see the island on an **Island Charters sailboat** (℗ **250/539-5040**). A half-day excursion at C$135 (US$87) for two explores the coasts of Mayne, Saturna, and the Pender islands (lunch included), or you can arrange for the sailboat to pick up or deliver you to other island destinations (this is the really classy way to get to your country inn). Full-day excursions are C$160 (US$103) per couple, including lunch.

Index

See also Accommodations and Restaurant indexes, below.

FROMMER'S® COMPLETE TRAVEL GUIDES

Alaska
Alaska Cruises & Ports of Call
Amsterdam
Argentina & Chile
Arizona
Atlanta
Australia
Austria
Bahamas
Barcelona, Madrid & Seville
Beijing
Belgium, Holland & Luxembourg
Bermuda
Boston
Brazil
British Columbia & the Canadian
   Rockies
Budapest & the Best of Hungary
California
Canada
Cancún, Cozumel & the Yucatán
Cape Cod, Nantucket & Martha's
   Vineyard
Caribbean
Caribbean Cruises & Ports of Call
Caribbean Ports of Call
Carolinas & Georgia
Chicago
China
Colorado
Costa Rica
Denmark
Denver, Boulder & Colorado
   Springs
England
Europe
European Cruises & Ports of Call
Florida

France
Germany
Great Britain
Greece
Greek Islands
Hawaii
Hong Kong
Honolulu, Waikiki & Oahu
Ireland
Israel
Italy
Jamaica
Japan
Las Vegas
London
Los Angeles
Maryland & Delaware
Maui
Mexico
Montana & Wyoming
Montréal & Québec City
Munich & the Bavarian Alps
Nashville & Memphis
Nepal
New England
New Mexico
New Orleans
New York City
New Zealand
Northern Italy
Nova Scotia, New Brunswick &
   Prince Edward Island
Oregon
Paris
Philadelphia & the Amish Country
Portugal
Prague & the Best of the Czech
   Republic

Provence & the Riviera
Puerto Rico
Rome
San Antonio & Austin
San Diego
San Francisco
Santa Fe, Taos & Albuquerque
Scandinavia
Scotland
Seattle & Portland
Shanghai
Singapore & Malaysia
South Africa
South America
South Florida
South Pacific
Southeast Asia
Spain
Sweden
Switzerland
Texas
Thailand
Tokyo
Toronto
Tuscany & Umbria
USA
Utah
Vancouver & Victoria
Vermont, New Hampshire &
   Maine
Vienna & the Danube Valley
Virgin Islands
Virginia
Walt Disney World® & Orlando
Washington, D.C.
Washington State

FROMMER'S® DOLLAR-A-DAY GUIDES

Australia from $50 a Day
California from $70 a Day
Caribbean from $70 a Day
England from $75 a Day
Europe from $70 a Day

Florida from $70 a Day
Hawaii from $80 a Day
Ireland from $60 a Day
Italy from $70 a Day
London from $85 a Day

New York from $90 a Day
Paris from $80 a Day
San Francisco from $70 a Day
Washington, D.C. from $80 a Day

FROMMER'S® PORTABLE GUIDES

Acapulco, Ixtapa & Zihuatanejo
Amsterdam
Aruba
Australia's Great Barrier Reef
Bahamas
Berlin
Big Island of Hawaii
Boston
California Wine Country
Cancún
Charleston & Savannah
Chicago
Disneyland®
Dublin
Florence

Frankfurt
Hong Kong
Houston
Las Vegas
London
Los Angeles
Los Cabos & Baja
Maine Coast
Maui
Miami
New Orleans
New York City
Paris
Phoenix & Scottsdale

Portland
Puerto Rico
Puerto Vallarta, Manzanillo &
   Guadalajara
Rio de Janeiro
San Diego
San Francisco
Seattle
Sydney
Tampa & St. Petersburg
Vancouver
Venice
Virgin Islands
Washington, D.C.

FROMMER'S® NATIONAL PARK GUIDES

Banff & Jasper
Family Vacations in the National
   Parks
Grand Canyon

National Parks of the American
   West
Rocky Mountain

Yellowstone & Grand Teton
Yosemite & Sequoia/ Kings Canyon
Zion & Bryce Canyon

FROMMER'S® MEMORABLE WALKS

Chicago
London

New York
Paris

San Francisco
Washington, D.C.

FROMMER'S® GREAT OUTDOOR GUIDES

Arizona & New Mexico
New England

Northern California
Southern New England

Vermont & New Hampshire

SUZY GERSHMAN'S BORN TO SHOP GUIDES

Born to Shop: France
Born to Shop: Hong Kong,
  Shanghai & Beijing

Born to Shop: Italy
Born to Shop: London

Born to Shop: New York
Born to Shop: Paris

FROMMER'S® IRREVERENT GUIDES

Amsterdam
Boston
Chicago
Las Vegas
London

Los Angeles
Manhattan
New Orleans
Paris
Rome

San Francisco
Seattle & Portland
Vancouver
Walt Disney World®
Washington, D.C.

FROMMER'S® BEST-LOVED DRIVING TOURS

Britain
California
Florida
France

Germany
Ireland
Italy
New England

Northern Italy
Scotland
Spain
Tuscany & Umbria

HANGING OUT™ GUIDES

Hanging Out in England
Hanging Out in Europe

Hanging Out in France
Hanging Out in Ireland

Hanging Out in Italy
Hanging Out in Spain

THE UNOFFICIAL GUIDES®

Bed & Breakfasts and Country
  Inns in:
  California
  Great Lakes States
  Mid-Atlantic
  New England
  Northwest
  Rockies
  Southeast
  Southwest
Best RV & Tent Campgrounds in:
  California & the West
  Florida & the Southeast
  Great Lakes States
  Mid-Atlantic
  Northeast
  Northwest & Central Plains

  Southwest & South Central
    Plains
    U.S.A.
  Beyond Disney
  Branson, Missouri
  California with Kids
  Chicago
  Cruises
  Disneyland®
  Florida with Kids
  Golf Vacations in the Eastern U.S.
  Great Smoky & Blue Ridge Region
  Inside Disney
  Hawaii
  Las Vegas
  London

Mid-Atlantic with Kids
Mini Las Vegas
Mini-Mickey
New England and New York with
  Kids
New Orleans
New York City
Paris
San Francisco
Skiing in the West
Southeast with Kids
Walt Disney World®
Walt Disney World® for Grown-ups
Walt Disney World® with Kids
Washington, D.C.
World's Best Diving Vacations

SPECIAL-INTEREST TITLES

Frommer's Adventure Guide to Australia &
  New Zealand
Frommer's Adventure Guide to Central America
Frommer's Adventure Guide to India & Pakistan
Frommer's Adventure Guide to South America
Frommer's Adventure Guide to Southeast Asia
Frommer's Adventure Guide to Southern Africa
Frommer's Britain's Best Bed & Breakfasts and
  Country Inns
Frommer's Caribbean Hideaways
Frommer's Exploring America by RV
Frommer's Fly Safe, Fly Smart
Frommer's France's Best Bed & Breakfasts and
  Country Inns
Frommer's Gay & Lesbian Europe

Frommer's Italy's Best Bed & Breakfasts and
  Country Inns
Frommer's New York City with Kids
Frommer's Ottawa with Kids
Frommer's Road Atlas Britain
Frommer's Road Atlas Europe
Frommer's Road Atlas France
Frommer's Toronto with Kids
Frommer's Vancouver with Kids
Frommer's Washington, D.C., with Kids
Israel Past & Present
The New York Times' Guide to Unforgettable
  Weekends
Places Rated Almanac
Retirement Places Rated